THE WHOLE WIDE WORLD

THE
WHOLE
WIDE
WORLD

A Treasury of Great Travel Writings of Our Time

edited by

WILLIAM CLIFFORD

CROWN PUBLISHERS, INC.

NEW YORK

ACKNOWLEDGMENTS

For permission to reprint copyrighted material, the following acknowledgments are gratefully made:

Brandt & Brandt. From EASTER IN SICILY, Simon and Schuster, Inc., copyright 1956 by Herbert Kubly, reprinted by permission of Brandt & Brandt.

* * *

Shirley Collier Agency. From A WORLD OF STRANGERS, copyright © 1958 by Nadine Gordimer, reprinted by permission.

* * *

The Devin-Adair Co. Quoted from A SUMMER IN ITALY by Sean O'Faolain, published 1950 by The Devin-Adair Co., New York, copyright 1950 by Sean O'Faolain.

* * *

The Dial Press. From THE AGE OF HAPPY PROBLEMS by Herbert Gold, copyright © 1962 by Herbert Gold, reprinted by permission of The Dial Press, Inc.

* * *

Dodd, Mead & Co. Reprinted by permission of Dodd, Mead & Company from A TRAVELLER IN ROME by H. V. Morton, copyright © 1957 by Dodd, Mead & Company, Inc. Also Methuen & Co., Ltd. for the same work.

* * *

John Dos Passos. From BRAZIL ON THE MOVE by John Dos Passos, copyright © 1963 by John Dos Passos, published by Doubleday & Co.

* * *

Doubleday & Co. From A FAMILY OF ISLANDS by Alec Waugh, copyright © 1964 by Alec Waugh, reprinted by permission of Doubleday & Company, Inc.

* * *

E. P. Dutton & Co. From the book BALTHAZAR by Lawrence Durrell, copyright © 1958 by Lawrence Durrell, reprinted by permission of E. P. Dutton & Co., Inc. Also Faber and Faber, Ltd. for the same work. From the book SEVEN YEARS IN TIBET by Heinrich Harrer, copyright 1953 by E. P. Dutton & Co., Inc., reprinted by permission of the publishers. Also Rupert Hart-Davis, Ltd. for the same work.

* * *

John Farquharson, Ltd. From THE AUTOBIOGRAPHY OF AN UNKNOWN INDIAN, copyright 1951 by Nirad C. Chaudhuri, published by The Macmillan Co. Also Macmillan & Co., Ltd., for the same work.

* * *

Harcourt, Brace & World. From CITIES, © 1963 by James Morris, reprinted by permission of Harcourt, Brace & World, Inc. Also Faber and Faber, Ltd., for the same work. From WIND, SAND AND STARS, copyright, 1939, by Antoine de Saint Exupéry, reprinted by permission of Harcourt, Brace & World, Inc.

* * *

Harper & Row. From THE SUDDEN VIEW, A Mexican Journey, by Sybille Bedford, copyright 1953 by Sybille Bedford, reprinted by permission of Harper & Row, Publishers, Inc. Also Wm. Collins Sons & Co., Ltd., for the same work, published under the title THE

SUDDEN VIEW (A VISIT TO DON OTAVIO). From STRANGE LANDS AND FRIENDLY PEOPLE by William O. Douglas, copyright 1951 by William O. Douglas, reprinted by permission of Harper & Row, Publishers, Inc. "The Palio at Siena" from ALONG THE ROAD by Aldous Huxley, copyright 1925 by Aldous Huxley, renewed 1953 by Aldous Huxley, reprinted by permission of Harper & Row, Publishers, Inc. Also Chatto and Windus, Ltd. for the same work. From EAST OF HOME by Santha Rama Rau, copyright 1950 by Santha Rama Rau, reprinted by permission of Harper & Row, Publishers, Inc. From HERE IS NEW YORK by E. B. White, copyright 1949 by The Curtis Publishing Co., reprinted by permission of Harper & Row, Publishers, Inc.

*   *   *

Holt, Rinehart and Winston. From SUTTON'S PLACES by Horace Sutton, copyright 1954 by Horace Sutton, reprinted by permission of Holt, Rinehart and Winston, Inc.

*   *   *

Indiana University Press. From BURMESE FAMILY by Mi Mi Khaing, copyright © 1962 by Indiana University Press, reprinted by permission.

*   *   *

Alfred A. Knopf. From ONE MAN'S AMERICA, copyright 1952 by Alistair Cooke, reprinted by permission of Alfred A. Knopf, Inc. Also Rupert Hart-Davis, Ltd. for the same work. From ISLAND OF BALI by Miguel Covarrubias, copyright 1936, 1937 by Alfred A. Knopf, Inc., reprinted by permission of the publisher. From TRAVELS IN THE CONGO by André Gide, translated by Dorothy Bussy, copyright 1929 by Alfred A. Knopf, Inc., reprinted by permission of the publisher. From PERSIA REVISITED, copyright © 1964 by Anne Sinclair Mehdevi, reprinted by permission of Alfred A. Knopf, Inc. From THE LEAF AND THE FLAME, copyright © 1959 by Margaret Parton, reprinted by permission of Alfred A. Knopf, Inc. From THE SPANISH TEMPER, copyright 1954 by V. S. Pritchett, reprinted by permission of Alfred A. Knopf, Inc.

*   *   *

Little, Brown and Co. From MAP OF ANOTHER TOWN by M. F. K. Fisher, copyright © 1964 by M. F. K. Fisher, reprinted by permission of Little, Brown and Co. From TOURIST IN AFRICA by Evelyn Waugh, copyright © 1960 by Evelyn Waugh, reprinted by permission of Little, Brown and Co. Also A. D. Peters & Co. for the same work.

*   *   *

The Macmillan Co. From NO FURTHER WEST by Dan Jacobson, Copyright © 1957, 1958, 1959 by Dan Jacobson, reprinted with permission of The Macmillan Co. Also George Weidenfeld & Nicolson, Ltd., for the same work.

*   *   *

McGraw-Hill Book Co. From ROME FOR OURSELVES by Aubrey Menen, copyright © 1960 by Aubrey Menen, reprinted with permission of McGraw-Hill Book Co., a division of McGraw-Hill, Inc.

*   *   *

New Directions. From THE COLOSSUS OF MAROUSSI by Henry Miller, copyright 1941 by Henry Miller, reprinted by permission of the publishers, New Directions, New York.

*   *   *

Oxford University Press. From CONTEMPORARY CANADA by Miriam Chapin, copyright © 1959 by Oxford University Press, Inc., reprinted by permission. From OROZCO by Alma Reed, copyright © 1956 by Oxford University Press, Inc., reprinted by permission. From BETWEEN OXUS AND JUMNA by Arnold J. Toynbee, copyright © 1961 by Oxford University Press, reprinted by permission. From INDIA CHANGES! by Taya Zinkin, copyright © 1958 by Taya Zinkin, reprinted by permission of Oxford University Press, Inc.

*   *   *

Rand McNally & Co. From KON-TIKI: Across the Pacific by Raft, by Thor Heyerdahl, copyright 1950 by Thor Heyerdahl, published in the U.S.A. by Rand McNally & Company. Also George Allen & Unwin, Ltd., for the same work.

*   *   *

Random House. From "Baptism of Solitude," copyright 1953 by Paul Bowles and "The Rif, to Music," copyright © 1957 by Paul Bowles, both reprinted from THEIR HEADS ARE GREEN AND THEIR HANDS ARE BLUE, by Paul Bowles, by permission of Random House, Inc. From THE MUSES ARE HEARD, by Truman Capote, copyright © 1956 by Truman Capote, reprinted by permission of Random House, Inc. From "New Zealand," copyright 1951 by James A. Michener, reprinted from RETURN TO PARADISE, by James A. Michener, by permission of Random House, Inc. From JAPANESE INN, by Oliver Statler, copyright © 1961 by Oliver Statler, reprinted by permission of Random House, Inc.

*   *   *

Reynal & Co. From VENICE OBSERVED by Mary McCarthy, reprinted by permission of the publisher.

*   *   *

St. Martin's Press. From A PASSAGE TO ENGLAND, copyright © 1959 by Nirad C. Chaudhuri, reprinted by permission of St. Martin's Press. Also Macmillan & Co., Ltd., for the same work.

* * *

Simon and Schuster. From GIVE ME THE WORLD, copyright © 1958 by Leila Hadley, reprinted by permission of Simon and Schuster, Inc. From WESTWARD HA!, copyright 1947, 1948 by S. J. Perelman, reprinted by permission of Simon and Schuster, Inc.

* * *

Mrs. James Thurber. From THURBER COUNTRY, published by Simon and Schuster, copyright © 1953 James Thurber.

* * *

The Viking Press. From THE DONKEY INSIDE by Ludwig Bemelmans, copyright 1937, 1938, 1940, 1941 by Ludwig Bemelmans, reprinted by permission of The Viking Press, Inc. From ANOTHER MEXICO by Graham Greene, copyright 1939 by Graham Greene, all rights reserved, reprinted by permission of The Viking Press, Inc. From MEETING WITH JAPAN by Fosco Maraini, copyright © 1959 by Hutchinson and Co., Ltd., reprinted by permission of The Viking Press, Inc. Also Hutchinson & Co. (Publishers), Ltd., for the same work. From THE LOG FROM THE SEA OF CORTEZ by John Steinbeck, copyright 1951 by John Steinbeck, 1941 by John Steinbeck and Edward F. Ricketts, reprinted by permission of The Viking Press, Inc. From TRAVELS WITH CHARLEY In Search of America by John Steinbeck, copyright © 1961, 1962 by The Curtis Publishing Co., 1962 by John Steinbeck, reprinted by permission of The Viking Press, Inc. From BLACK LAMB AND GREY FALCON by Rebecca West, copyright 1940, 1941 by Rebecca West, reprinted by permission of The Viking Press, Inc.

* * *

The World Publishing Co. From WHERE THE BONG TREE GROWS, copyright © 1963 by James Ramsey Ullman, reprinted by permission of the publisher.

* * *

All color photos courtesy of Pan American Airways.
Black-and-white photos courtesy of Pan American Airways with the following exceptions:
Orozco fresco of Felipe Carillo Puerto, page 84, courtesy New School for Social Research, New York.
Hadassah-Hebrew University Medical Center, Israel, page 294, photo by Hadassah.
Statue of Liberty, Paris, page 433, British European Airways photo.
Photos by William Clifford:
Stone lion and Sun Moon Lake, Taiwan, pages 215 and 220.
Architecture of Kuala Lumpur, page 245.
Taj Mahal, pages 264–65.
House in Deya and olive tree, Majorca, pages 421 and 423.

To Joan and Nicholas,
  with all my love

TABLE OF CONTENTS

AFRICA

EUROPE

EPILOGUE

INTRODUCTION

INTRODUCTION

"ONCE UPON A TIME the world was round and you could go on it around and around," wrote Gertrude Stein in her book for children, *The World Is Round*. As the world whirls on its axis we still go around and around, traveling at about a thousand miles an hour. But we are unaware of this movement, except for the procession of nights and days, and it fails to get us anywhere.

The kind of going around and around that does get us somewhere—across deserts and plains, up mountains, over the seas, into the shimmering heat of the tropics and the brilliant crisp snowbound Arctic —this becomes ever easier to do as the years go by. It becomes ever faster, too, approaching the point where we shall be able to fly against the turning of the earth, fixed as though motionless beneath the sun at high noon. Or fly with the direction of revolution, telescoping twenty-four-hour days into twelve.

Each year more and more people are going around the world, going up and down upon it, too, and back again. Sometimes it seems as though everybody is on tour, particularly in Europe in midsummer. Actually, few of us get to go out and see the world, and if we do make the long-dreamed-of world tour, even of several months' duration, we inevitably leave most of the world out.

A book that simulates a world tour in words and pictures must also inevitably leave something out. But it can (and this one does) offer a generous sampling of the whole world, much more of it than any available tour, for you to enjoy, not in a few crowded months, but over a period of years or a lifetime. Not with the discomforts and tensions of actual travel, but in the comforts of home, warming your toes before the fire, enjoying your familiar bed and board. The cost of this tour is not many thousands of dollars, but pennies for each insight, adventure, or hour of escape. When you have finished, it is yours to enjoy over and over again, gratis.

Insofar as words and pictures can provide it, here is the experience of a world tour in the company of some of the best minds of our time. No combination of professional guides could give you descriptions of life in each country to match the writers assembled here. No selection of your own pictures is likely to match the clarity of these photographs, taken when light and weather were at their best.

In these pages you will see the world mostly as it has developed and changed after the Second World War. Recent changes have been so great that earlier times, perhaps only a generation removed, seem to belong to another era. In Japan, for example, as recently as the 1920's traveling abroad was considered to be such a fearful undertaking that steamship companies gave free railway tickets to departing passengers and their immediate families so that they could pay a short visit for prayer at the Ise shrine. Today a Japanese businessman may vacation in Honolulu as casually as an American.

People everywhere in the world are wonderfully hospitable—but people everywhere hate and fear foreigners. Everyone is the same at heart—but East is East and West is West. If these views seem irreconcilable, at least they bear scrutiny. Nirad Chaudhuri, affirming that Kipling said some of the truest if also the bluntest things about the relations of East and West, disallows his "unconvincing afterthought" that there was neither East nor West when two strong men stood face to face. Convinced of "the irreconcilability of the two modes of human existence, one in the tropics and the other in temperate lands," Chaudhuri says, "The twain shall never meet."

As an interesting aside on a different question, that of writing about a people or place from very brief acquaintance—"Whatever may be thought of the intelligence or even the character of a man who writes a book about a country after seeing it for only five weeks . . ."—Chaudhuri's example proves that with exceptional preparation and precision a man may do it very well. During five weeks in England, plus two weeks in Paris and one in Rome, this extraordinary Indian "saw more paintings, statues, and works of art

1

in general, more plays, fine buildings, gardens, and beautiful landscapes; heard more poetry and music; ate and drank better; and altogether had a more exciting and interesting time than in all the rest of my life. Hardly less important is the fact that among all these things were a great many that I had longed to see since my boyhood." His precision may be judged by his calculation that he was exactly 2,992 weeks old on the day he boarded the airplane for England and had completed a round 3,000 weeks of life by the time he returned to Delhi.

East and West have met in the man who makes these observations. Many others have concluded that human experience is fundamentally the same, whatever its superficial differences. Sometimes even the superficialities have amusing similarities. Few places have remained so remote from the modern Western world as Tibet. Yet Heinrich Harrer reports that the young Dalai Lama had only a limited allowance to use as he pleased, like any American boy—except that in his case it was whatever money happened to be left as an offering at the foot of his throne. And not only in America are the streets figuratively paved with gold. "In Lhasa," writes Harrer, "one can almost pick up money off the street. One only needs a little enterprise."

When Mi Mi Khaing returned to Burma after several years in England, her family asked if she still understood the holy language of the monks "after being so long as it were one human amongst a thousand monkeys." Frequently it comes as a revelation to the traveler to discover that he is one of the monkeys, that people of every nation and every culture consider their own ways of life the most civilized. No stranger or foreigner (no *sale étranger* or foreign devil) is quite human. This chauvinism, provincialism, or familial limitation can be overcome by sufficient exposure to foreigners, but it is a lengthy process.

In spite of this, most peoples have traditions of hospitality to the wayfaring stranger, ranging from guiding an old lady across the street to surrendering one's goods and self, as reported by William O. Douglas. As a rule—granting the generalization that it is unsafe to generalize—Americans find that other peoples tend to be less casual with their hospitality, more lavish when they are committed to give it, but therefore less frequently committed. As another unsafe rule, people in big cities tend to be rude, impatient, inhuman, and alike, while country people remain more human, more traditional, and more diverse.

It is the cities, of course, that receive most of the foreign visitors. There are the lion's share of the tourist attractions and of the people with foreign contacts. If you happen to live in New York (and I suppose Moscow and Mecca), it isn't safe to travel around saying to all the nice people you meet, "Look me up when you get to New York." Many of them will, even from Tahiti, Tasmania, and Timbuktu. When they do, you're surprised and glad to see them. Of course you put yourself out for them. You are hospitable to the point where some of them begin to feel more at home in your home than they ever were in theirs. At that point you begin to withdraw. You have other work to get done, other interests, other visitors. Then your guests are injured by the shallowness of American friendship.

Something like this (and something else too) lies behind Sybille Bedford's not altogether unjust remarks: "Arrival and Departure are the two great pivots of American social intercourse. You arrive. You present your credentials. You are instantly surrounded by some large, unfocused hopefulness. You may be famous; you may be handsome, or witty, or rich; you may even be amiable. What counts is that you are *new*. In Europe where human relations like clothes are supposed to last, one's got to be wearable. In France one has to be interesting, in Italy pleasant, in England one has to fit. Here, where intercourse between man and man is without degrees, *sans lendemain*, where foreign visitors are consumers' goods, it is a matter of turnover. You are taken up, taken out, shown around, introduced, given parties for, and bang, before you can say American Resident, it's farewell parties and steamer baskets. Your cheeks are kissed, your back is slapped, your hand is pressed; you are sent bottles and presents and flowers—you are Sailing. The great empty wheel of hospitality has come full circle."

Despite all these many shortcomings, foreign places are irresistible and travel is habit-forming, narcotic. "With me," wrote Aldous Huxley, "traveling is frankly a vice. The temptation to indulge in it is one which I find almost as hard to resist as the temptation to read promiscuously, omnivorously, and without purpose. From time to time, it is true, I make a desperate resolution to mend my ways. I sketch out programs of useful, serious reading; I try to turn my rambling voyages into systematic tours through the history of art and civilization. But without much success. After a little I relapse into my old bad ways. Deplorable weakness! I try to comfort myself with the hope that even my vices may be of some profit to me. . . . traveling is not a vice of the body (which it mortifies) but of the mind. Your traveler-for-traveling's-sake is like your desultory reader—a man addicted to mental self-indulgence.

"Like all other vicious men, the reader and the traveler have a whole armoury of justifications with which to defend themselves. Reading and traveling, they say, broaden the mind, stimulate imagination, are a liberal education. And so on. These are specious arguments; but nobody is very much impressed by them. For though it may be quite true that, for certain people, desultory reading and aimless traveling are richly educative, it is not for that reason that most true readers and travelers born indulge their tastes. We read and travel, not that we may broaden and enrich our minds, but that we may pleasantly forget they exist. We love reading and traveling because they are the most delightful of all the many substitutes for thought. Sophisticated and somewhat refined substitutes. That is why they are not every man's diversion. The congenital reader or traveler is one of those most fastidious spirits who cannot find the distractions they require in betting, mah-jong, drink, golf or fox-trots.

"There exist a few, a very few, who travel and, for that matter, who read, with purpose and a definite system. This is a morally admirable class. And it is the class to which, in general, the people who achieve something in the world belong."

Whether you achieve something in the world or you're merely dissatisfied with drink, golf, and fox-trots, you are welcome on the present tour. Enjoy your traveling companions, and *bon voyage!*

* * *

Sightseers require something special for the eye as well as for the mind. Blackie Kronfeld, who took most of the color pictures in this book for Pan American Airways, has written a footnote to his work that will amuse any traveling photographer. Resolved to photograph Hirosaki Castle (see pages 178–79), about four hundred miles north of Tokyo, he hurried to the site by plane, car, and train as soon as he learned that cherry-blossom time was near.

Good weather was forecast and the Principal of a dressmaking school was to have two of her most beautiful pupils, who were to be our models, ready at 7:30 A.M., all dressed up in their best kimonos. After a good night's sleep, Japanese fashion with the mattress laid directly on the tatami, we awoke to find a hazy spring day with the sun filtering softly through the scattered clouds. Just the kind of weather to get a good picture. We picked up the girls who were to be our models accompanied by their teacher and much to my surprise they were tall, even by American standards. I was told that tall girls are not unusual for this part of the country. At the castle I chose what I thought was the best location and set up my camera. Everything was perfect; the newly painted red bridge in the foreground, a nice frame of cherry blossoms in full bloom, the angle of the sun, and the models and camera in position—but to me the setting was incomplete without a parasol. We had to send a messenger to find one, which was difficult because this far north parasols are not commonly used. . . . Finally, a parasol arrived and in five minutes I had the pictures finished. While I was shooting, a little Japanese man came out of the crowd and took the same scene and later won first prize with it in a Japanese photo contest.

PROLOGUE

PROLOGUE

Better be imprudent moveables than prudent fixtures.

JOHN KEATS

If there is one thing a traveler doesn't need in a stateroom it is twenty-seven dollars' worth of juicy pears.

HORACE SUTTON

JAMES THURBER

from THURBER COUNTRY

THURBER'S essay "The Pleasure Cruise and How to Survive It" appeared first in Holiday. Because it is gentle, which much of the contemporary world is not, it seems to reflect a bygone era.

IT HAS OCCURRED to me that there may be persons here and there, young and inexperienced in the ways of the world, who might profit from my own personal *Travel Hints*, compiled after looking back on thirty-odd years of knocking about, or being knocked about, the globe. I don't mean the whole globe, of course. I have never been south of Trinidad, north of Quebec, east of Italy, or west of San Francisco, but within these rather roomy limits, I have been knocked about quite a bit.

My first hint—to the gentleman traveler—is a simple one. Never go anywhere without your wife. If your wife won't go, because the concert or canning season is on, or something of the sort, take your sister or your mother or your cousin. The American woman is indispensable in getting the tickets and reservations, packing and unpacking, mixing Bromo-Seltzers, fending off beautiful ladies who are traveling alone, and making herself useful generally. Hers is also the only sex that can successfully close a wardrobe trunk. If a man closes a wardrobe trunk, there is always a sharp snapping sound, caused by the breaking of something that will not bend, such as the handle of a mirror, or the stem of a Dunhill pipe, or the stopper of a perfume bottle. If a woman is deprived of her Chanel No. 5 during, say, a nineteen-day cruise, she will

become irritable, and there is nothing more exasperating on a cruise, or anywhere else, than an irritable female companion.

Now that I have mentioned cruises, let us consider more closely the technique of the sea voyage. After the wife has closed the wardrobe trunk and called a taxi, it is only eight in the morning, and the ship doesn't sail till eleven. The husband will complain that it doesn't take three hours to get to a pier only eight blocks from their hotel. He will point out that they can get to Pier 58 in half an hour, with time to spare. He is right, it turns out, but it also turns out that he doesn't know where Pier 58 is. His wife has unfortunately left this one small detail up to him. He tells the taxi driver to take them to the foot of West 58th Street, but when they get there, it transpires that this is not the point of departure of their ship, the *Santa Maria*. It is the point of departure of the *J. B. Cathcart*, a coastwise fruit steamer bound for French Guiana. The taxi driver suggests that the *Santa Maria* probably sails from Brooklyn or Hoboken The husband figures there is time to try both places, but his wife's sounder judgment prevails. She asks somebody—always an excellent idea—where Pier 58 is, and is told Pier 58 is at the foot of West 16th Street. It is, too.

On the way to the right destination, with time to spare—just as the husband had promised—the taxi driver suddenly has a hunch that the *Santa Maria* sails at 11 P.M., on Tuesdays, and not at 11 A.M., on Thursdays. This throws his male passenger into a panic. The seasoned woman traveler pays no attention to all this unnecessary masculine excitement. She leans back in the cab, closes her eyes and wonders if she forgot to pack her white piqué evening dress. Once aboard the ship, the wife (Ellen) tells her husband (George) that she has to unpack her light things right away or they will crush, and she asks him, for heaven's sake, to get deck chairs on the sunny and windless side of the ship immediately, before they are all gone, and also to make table reservations instantly, so they can have a table for two once in their lives, and not have to sit with a lot of strangers. George wanders away on these important errands and (1) runs into an old classmate from Dartmouth and (2) decides that they ought to find out where the bar is and what time it opens for business. When he returns to his stateroom, an hour later, Ellen is in excellent spirits—she has found the white piqué evening dress—but her amiable mood is not going to last very long. "Did you reserve the chairs and the table?" she asks. "Hm?" says George blankly. I will spare you the scene that follows. Suffice it to say that the Kendalls (their name is Kendall) have to settle for deck chairs on the sunless and windy side of the ship, and are put at a table for eight: two women buyers from Cleveland, an embalmer and his bride, a pair of giggling college girls and Mr. and Mrs. George Kendall. She has the chair with the short right-rear leg.

My private tip here is that the wife should reserve the deck chairs and the table, let the dresses crush where they may, but I have never been able to sell the idea to any woman traveler.

The only woman who doesn't care whether her dresses crush or not is the seasick woman, but I wouldn't recommend seasickness as the way out of anything, not even the way of out sitting next to the embalmer at dinner. Speaking of seasickness, I am unlucky enough to have a stomach of platinum, and I haven't suffered from *mal de mer* since the eastward Atlantic crossing of the U.S.S. *Orizaba*, in November, 1918, but this was a transport that took nine days zigzagging from New York to St. Nazaire in heavy weather, and there was honorable excuse for my condition. I say I am "unlucky" enough to have a stomach of platinum, because the seasick turn to the unseasick on a ship for succor, sanctuary and salvation that are impossible to give. Once, on the Bermuda run—seventeen of us up and around on the second day, out of a passenger list of three hundred—I came upon a lone woman sprawled on a sofa in the library up forward, where rolling and pitching had flung her prostrate and forlorn. She lay on her hat and her right side; one shoe was off; her handbag was open on the floor, its contents scattered; her lipstick was smudged in such a way that she seemed to have bitten her own left cheek. I was appalled—sympathetic, gallant even, but appalled—and when I am appalled, my nervous system becomes an apparatus that, as the French say, *ne fonctionne pas*.

"Do something," she said in a faint, awful voice.

"Madam," I squeaked helplessly. I was unable to say anything, but I did something. I put her things back in her handbag and placed it on a table.

"I put your handbag on the table," I finally managed to croak.

"Do something," she said again, in the same voice. For a moment I considered putting her shoe back on, but like any other Ohio State man, I was restrained by the feeling that the act would be both insensitive and foolish. Then, I suddenly decided to put the shoe on the table with the handbag.

"Do something," she said, in a weaker tone. I staggered out of the library, hunted up a deck steward and told him about the lady and her extremity.

"Do something," I begged him. He just shook his head sadly. I rolled on my way, and came to the elevator that ran from A Deck down to E Deck and back. There was a woman there, frantically pressing the bell button. She was standing, and she had both shoes on, but she looked just as ghastly as the lost lady in the library. She grabbed my arm as I tried to walk by.

"E Deck. Quick!" she gasped.

"The elevator will be up—" I began and caught myself, but not in time. Her face took on a saffron hue.

"I'm sorry," I mumbled. She looked at me with the eyes of a stepped-on spaniel.

"E Deck," she said again. "Please."

I had to do something. I brushed past her and began pushing the bell button wildly. Then I turned and ran. I have often wondered, in my own low and agonized moments, if she made it.

Just what hint to give to the unseasick passenger who may be faced, during an ocean voyage, with crises and suffering similar to my own that terrible day, I frankly do not know. There are certain tortures that we unseasick passengers simply have to endure, I guess. I would appreciate it, though, if you don't go around saying that, in the emergencies I have described, I just "got the hell out." I did what I could. There will, of course, always be two schools of thought about that shoe, the school that contends I should have put it back on, and the school that insists I should have let it lie where I found it. Apparently nobody in the world but me would have put it on the table with the handbag. I can only say that if I had it all to do over again, I would still put the shoe on the table with the handbag.

If you travel much on ships you are bound, sooner or later, to run into Mrs. Abigail Pritchard, as I shall call her. She is not just one woman, but many; I have encountered at least fifteen of her. Mrs. Pritchard may be forty-five, or she may be seventy, but her average age, I should say, is about fifty-seven. She comes from Boston, Hartford, Germantown, Syracuse, Toledo, Chicago, Louisville, St. Louis, Denver, Sacramento, and both Portlands. She is a widow, fairly well off, whose children are happily married and the fathers, or mothers, of the prettiest and brightest youngsters in the world, and she has snapshots and anecdotes to prove it. She takes two Daiquiris before dinner and a highball afterwards, and smokes Players, on the ground that they are made of actual tobacco, whereas American cigarettes, in her opinion, are composed of rum, molasses, shredded cork, and factory sweepings. She prefers domestic Burgundies, however, because the so-called French vintages you find on ships are really only cheap Algerian wine that has been poured into genuine bottles labeled Pommard or Chablis. Mrs. Pritchard is full of interesting little anecdotes about the late Sir Harry Oakes, the late Richard Halliburton ("that dear boy"), a Colonel Grosvenor in Penang, the gifted Courtney girls (whoever they are), John Barrymore ("poor old Jack"), Heifetz, Houdini, Nell Brinkley, Anna Eva Fay, Percy Marmount, Maurice Costello ("the king of them all"), Kip Rhinelander, Mrs. O. H. P. Belmont, Struthers Burt, Ky Laffoon and anybody else whose name you happen to mention. Mrs. Pritchard is certain she saw Judge Crater in the Casino at Cannes in 1937, where he was known as Maltby or Goadby, or some such name. "How do you do, Judge Crater?" she said to him firmly. He started—there could be no doubt of that. "My name is Maltby (or Goadby), madam," the man said, and hurried away.

Mrs. Pritchard can invariably spot, aboard ship, professional gamblers, unmarried couples sharing the same stateroom, fugitives from justice, fingermen formerly in the employ of Al Capone, cocaine sniffers, bay-rum drinkers, professional men of dubious integrity, women who are mortally ill but don't know it, unhappy wives and gentlemen with phony foreign accents. It makes you nervous to talk to, or rather listen to, Mrs. Pritchard. You twist restlessly in your chair, confident that she has you figured for an absconder, a black-marketeer, or a white-slave trader. Mrs. Pritchard spends at least two months of every year on ships, but I often wonder why, since she suspects that there is skulduggery afoot from the chartroom to the hold. If the ship is even half an hour late in shoving off, she whispers that "Uncle Joe is behind this delay." She never clears this up, though, but merely shakes her head wisely, if you ask her what she means. She is sure the ship is going to put to sea with broken pumps, insufficient lifeboats, and a typhoid carrier among the crew. Two days out, she tells you she doesn't like the look of the saxophone player's complexion—he has something contagious, mark her words. The third day out she declares that the chief steward is secreting fifteen thousand pounds of roast beef, which he intends to sell to a syndicate in Port-au-Prince. It costs ten thousand dollars a day to operate a ship, she read in the Reader's Digest, and this ridiculous amount is due to thefts of supplies by the stewards.

Even the captain of the ship is not above her suspicion. She is positive that he forgot to order all those automobiles in the hold lashed down, and she knows they will roll to one side if a storm comes up, causing the ship to list, like the Vestris, and sink. Mrs. Pritchard loves to tell about the time the master of an ocean liner was seized with a heart attack while steering the boat—she still thinks he was an epileptic—and almost ran into an iceberg. But her favorite story is about the time she was on a West Indies cruise, and caught a glimpse of the captain one day. She recognized him instantly as a Major Quantrell (or Chantress, or some such name) wanted in Rangoon for the shooting of a missionary's daughter in a fashionable gambling house. Mrs. Pritchard points out that a captain's cabin is the perfect hide-out for fugitives from justice, since nobody is allowed in the cabin except the officers, and they are probably no better than they ought to be, themselves.

The young traveler will naturally expect old, experienced me to advise him how to avoid, or to deal with, Mrs. Pritchard. Well, you can't avoid her. Just dismiss that from your mind. She pops up from everywhere and out from behind everything. Even if you hid in the engine room, she would search you out. As for dealing with the old girl, I have invented a rather nasty game called Back Her in the Corner, which works wonders.

"You know the Hotel l'Aiglon in Roquebrune, of course?" I say to her, casually.

"To be sure," she replies. "That perfectly gorgeous view of the Bay of Monte Carlo at night!"

We both look dreamy.

"Ah, yes," I sigh, "and those wonderful sardines grilled in triple-sec!"

"Yes, yes," she sighs, "those delicious sardines."

You see, she has to keep up a show of having been every place I have been. And here's where my game gets nasty.

"There isn't any Hotel l'Aiglon in Roquebrune," I say coldly, "and there aren't any sardines grilled in triple-sec."

She is furious. I have tricked her, and hell hath no fury like a woman tricked. She gives me a wide berth after that, not even nodding or smiling when I pass her on deck. I can get away with this little game because I am fifty-six,* but such conduct on the part of the young traveler would seem imprudent, disrespectful and ill-bred. You'll have to devise your own method of dealing with Mrs. Pritchard. You mustn't expect me to solve *all* your travel problems. And please don't write and ask me what to do in the event that you run into the gifted Courtney sisters. I simply do not know.

A few days out of New York (if you sailed from New York), printed copies of the passenger list are usually distributed, containing such names as Jowes, Qmith, Johnsob, Crazier, Aprker, Sommonx and Spider. It takes years of practice to decipher some passenger-list garbles. The letters of my own name have assumed some twenty different permutations, but I am most often listed simply as Jane Phurber, a winsome six-foot Ohio matron who affects men's clothes. My wife, whose name is Helen Thurber, turned up on one ship under the alias of H. Muriel. In some mysterious manner, our false names (I was Joseph Thacher on this occasion) followed us ashore when we debarked at Naples. My wife indignantly showed our true passport names to one Italian official who had insisted we were one J. Thacher and one H. Muriel. He saw his mistake.

"I am all of regret, *signorina*," he said, in excellent English, "and expressing sorrows towards you and Signor Muriel."

"Come on, H.," I said, "let's go."

"O.K., Joe," she said, and we got out of there.

You will most likely have been at sea a week before you get around to reading the literature you picked up at your travel agency, or at the offices of the steamship line itself. This company gets out a pamphlet entitled *General Information*, and you should have read it before you got on the ship. It lists a number of things that should not be carried in a passenger's luggage: "Dangerous articles, such as fireworks, matches, gunpowder, inflammable liquids, cartridges, inflammable motion-picture films." If you have a supply of skyrockets and Roman candles, it would be wise to dump them overboard some night when nobody is watching you. Skyrockets shot from decks

accidentally or out of a misguided burst of patriotic spirit, are certain to be construed as signals of distress by other vessels, and this would vex the commander of your ship, to say the least. So leave your fireworks at home, in a safe, locked place, where the children can't get at them. I don't know why you keep fireworks in your house, anyway, but, of course, that is none of my business.

If you have gone on a cruise to relax, and you don't want to romp, run, race or wrassle, stay away from the sports director, a big, energetic blond young man carrying a medicine ball. The female of this species, the sports directress, is active, alert, athletic, aggressive and capable of throwing your wife, or you, over her shoulder with her left hand. If you are not in training and under twenty-eight, don't monkey around with these two. They will run you ragged. They love squatting exercises, chinning themselves, holding their breath, standing on their hands, and touching the deck two thousand times with their finger tips, without bending their knees. Don't try to keep up with them. Refuse their challenges, ignore their taunts. You can't beat them at anything from squatting to ping-pong, unless you are young Mathias, the decathlon champion, and you probably aren't. The sports directors are supposed to organize group recreational activities. This is both a fact and a warning.

Speaking of ping-pong, I once entered a table-tennis tournament aboard the S. S. *President Garfield*, on a trip from New York through the Canal to Los Angeles. The sports director was determined to get me into the table-tennis tournament, probably because he wanted to see me humiliated in the finals. And he did. I lost two straight games to a pretty, attractive young lady, twenty years * my junior. The table was too short, the net was too high, the rackets were warped, the ship rocked, a small boy among the spectators began riding me and I got something in my eye. I explained to my opponent after the match that, on land and under fair and reasonable conditions, I could have pinned her ears back, the best day she ever saw. She was honest enough to admit this. A very pleasant girl, and the luckiest woman I have ever met on sea or land.

The night before a ship makes home port at the end of a cruise, there is usually a ship's concert, or program of entertainment, in which the Courtney sisters and other gifted passengers are invited to take part. If you are a singer, violinist, bird caller, soft-shoe dancer, whistler, mimic, monologist, contortionist, juggler, hypnotist, ventriloquist, swami, *diseuse* or

---

* Publisher's note: He's fifty-eight if he's a day.

* Publisher's note: Twenty-two years.

zither player, you are likely to be asked to join in the fun and do your act. You may refuse, of course, and you should if you plan to recite all of *Evangeline* or *Hiawatha*. Your fellow passengers will resent any act that lasts longer than five minutes. Once, coming back from the West Indies on the *Conte Grande*, I declined to appear on the concert program, and then suddenly, during a lull at midnight, I grabbed up a lighted megaphone and sang *Who?* and *Bye, Bye, Blackbird* with the orchestra. Well, not *with* it, exactly, since in *Blackbird*, I was singing "*Oh, the hard-luck stories they all hand me*" while the orchestra was playing *No one here can love or understand me*, but we were tied at the finish, I am happy to say. The survivors of that concert will doubtless remember my act, but they will not care to dwell on it any more than I do.

Since my performance that midnight, and possibly because of it, some of the more cautious cruise ships have eliminated passenger participation and turned the program of the final night over to professionals. The last cruise I was on, a few months ago, had no place for amateurs on the Big Night. The entertainment department of WOR provided a soprano, a baritone (to replace me), a prestidigitator, a couple of "dance stylists," an accordionist and several other instrumentalists. Talented passengers who had counted on imitating Tallulah Bankhead or playing Canadian Capers on a makeshift xylophone composed of White Rock bottles were somewhat mollified when they were given funny hats to wear, horns to blow, bells to ring, and rattles to rattle at the Gala Farewell Dinner that preceded the Gala Farewell Revue. In charge of these Galas, and such affairs as the Fancy Headdress Ball and other intellectual goings on, are the cruise director and the cruise directress (not to be confused with the sports director and the sports directress). When, on my recent cruise, I returned to my stateroom after the Gala Farewell Revue, I found a cheerful note from the cruise director. It read: "Rise up in the morning with the will that—smooth or rough—you'll grin!" I decided against this. You never know how a customs man may interpret a grin, especially a fixed grin.

Customs inspection is seldom as trying as you think it's going to be, unless you have a shoeful of diamonds or a trunk full of liqueurs. Just take your place under your proper letter (Q for Smith, E for Perkins, P for Thurber, and so forth) and see that you have assembled all your baggage. You will usually find that your typewriter case is missing and that you have a large gray suitcase that doesn't belong to you. The person who owns the gray suitcase may have your typewriter, and he may not. Don't get excited and rush around ac-

cusing people of stealing your Corona, just relax. You have all day, you know, and if you went to bed instead of to the bar after the Gala Revue, you will find yourself taking this ancient formality in your stride. It is important not to get mad at your inspector because he wants to go through your effects. That is his job. A Virginian I know, a man impatient of red tape and fiddle-faddle, as he describes all activities of the United States Government, once addressed a group of three customs inspectors as follows: "Gentlemen, you are clearly insane." He was the last man off the dock that day.

No travel hints would be complete without some word of caution about shipboard romances, engagements and marriages. The girl or young man you fell in love with on the ship when it was in Southern waters and the orchestra was playing "Night and Day" is going to be subjected to a cruel and rigorous test standing there by a gloomy pile of baggage in a bleak and chilly ship shed. If the swan suddenly becomes a goose, or the knight a clodhopper, it is what is known as "undergoing a land change." If you were married aboard ship, and the bride, or bridegroom, now appeals to you about as much as a piece of cold whole-wheat toast, you are in a rather serious jam. In America you cannot have a marriage annulled on the ground that it was contracted while you were under the influence of the Gulf Stream and Cole Porter. If you are a man, I suggest that you treat your inamorata with a gallantry tempered by caution during the voyage out and back, and refrain from proposing until you have caught her on the dock. If she is going to be met by her mother and father, her Aunt Louise and her Uncle Bert, you will want to get a look at them first too. During the cruise try to engage the girl of your dreams in discussions of books or politics if you find yourself with her on the promenade deck in the moonlight, while the band is playing "I Told Every Little Star." It won't work, but try it. All this, I suppose, is really no more concern of mine than why you keep fireworks in the house, so I will not pursue it further.

I hope that the foregoing helpful hints for a happy holiday will make your future sea voyages a little easier and merrier and safer. You need not, to be sure, take my advice or follow my example, in every situation and contretemps I have described hereinabove. If you want to put the shoe back on the sick lady's foot, or just leave it where you found it, feel free to do so. The reason I put the shoe on the table with the handbag was—but we have been all through that. I am beginning to repeat myself. Bon Voyage!

NORTH AMERICA

NORTH AMERICA

The commuter dies with tremendous mileage to his credit, but he is no rover.

E. B. WHITE

The three most hated peoples in the world—Germans, Americans and British—are the keenest sight-seers.

EVELYN WAUGH

Lindbergh had the right idea. He flew the Atlantic alone.

ART BUCHWALD

E. B. WHITE

from HERE IS NEW YORK

WRITTEN in 1949, this piece is very likely timeless.

THERE ARE ROUGHLY three New Yorks. There is, first, the New York of the man or woman who was born here, who takes the city for granted and accepts its size and its turbulence as natural and inevitable. Second, there is the New York of the commuter—the city that is devoured by locusts each day and spat out each night. Third, there is the New York of the person who was born somewhere else and came to New York in quest of something. Of these three trembling cities the greatest is the last—the city of final destination, the city that is a goal. It is this third city that accounts for New York's high-strung disposition, its poetical deportment, its dedication to the arts, and its incomparable achievements. Commuters give the city its tidal restlessness; natives give it solidity and continuity; but the settlers give it passion. And whether it is a farmer arriving from Italy to set up a small grocery store in a slum or a young girl arriving from a small town in Mississippi to escape the indignity of being observed by her neighbors, or a boy arriving from the Corn Belt with a manuscript in his suitcase and a pain in his heart, it makes no difference: each embraces New York with the intense excitement of first love, each absorbs New York with the fresh eyes of an adventurer, each generates heat and light to dwarf the Consolidated Edison Company.

The commuter is the queerest bird of all. The suburb he inhabits has no essential vitality of its own and is a mere roost where he comes at day's end to go to sleep. Except in rare cases, the man who lives in Mamaroneck or Little Neck or Teaneck, and works in New York, discovers nothing much about the city except the time of arrival and departure of trains and buses, and the path to a quick lunch. He is desk-bound, and has never, idly roaming in the gloaming, stumbled suddenly on Belvedere Tower in the Park, seen the ramparts rise sheer from the water of the pond, and the boys along the shore fishing for minnows, girls stretched out negligently on the shelves of the rocks; he has never come suddenly on anything at all in New York as a loiterer, because he has had no time between trains. He has fished in Manhattan's wallet and dug out coins, but has never listened to Manhattan's breathing, never awakened to its morning, never dropped off to sleep in its night. About 400,000 men and women come charging onto the Island each week-day morning, out of the mouths of tubes and tunnels. Not many among them have ever spent a drowsy afternoon in the great rustling oaken silence of the reading room of the Public

(continued on page 34)

STATUE OF LIBERTY, A TOKEN OF FRANCO-AMERICAN FRIENDSHIP.

(continued from page 12)

Library, with the book elevator (like an old water wheel) spewing out books onto the trays. They tend their furnaces in Westchester and in Jersey, but have never seen the furnaces of the Bowery, the fires that burn in oil drums on zero winter nights. They may work in the financial district downtown and never see the extravagant plantings of Rockefeller Center—the daffodils and grape hyacinths and birches and the flags trimmed to the wind on a fine morning in spring. Or they may work in a midtown office and may let a whole year swing round without sighting Governors Island from the sea wall. The commuter dies with tremendous mileage to his credit, but he is no rover. His entrances and exits are more devious than those in a prairie-dog village; and he calmly plays bridge while buried in the mud at the bottom of the East River. The Long Island Rail Road alone carried forty million commuters last year; but many of them were the same fellow retracing his steps.

The terrain of New York is such that a resident sometimes travels farther, in the end, than a commuter. Irving Berlin's journey from Cherry Street in the lower East Side to an apartment uptown was through an alley and was only three or four miles in length; but it was like going three times around the world.

* * *

A poem compresses much in a small space and adds music, thus heightening its meaning. The city is like poetry: it compresses all life, all races and breeds, into a small island and adds music and the accompaniment of internal engines. The island of Manhattan is without any doubt the greatest human concentrate on earth, the poem whose magic is comprehensible to millions of permanent residents but whose full meaning will always remain illusive. At the feet of the tallest and plushiest offices lie the crummiest slums. The genteel mysteries housed in Riverside Church are only a few blocks from the voodoo charms of Harlem. The merchant princes, riding to Wall Street in their limousines down the East River Drive, pass within a few hundred yards of the gypsy kings; but the princes do not know they are passing kings, and the kings are not up yet anyway —they live a more leisurely life than the princes and get drunk more consistently.

New York is nothing like Paris; it is nothing like London; and it is not Spokane multiplied by sixty, or Detroit multiplied by four. It is by all odds the loftiest of cities. It even managed to reach the highest point in the sky at the lowest moment of the depression. The Empire State Building shot twelve hundred and fifty feet into the air when it was madness to put out as much as six inches of new growth. (The building has a mooring mast that no dirigible has ever tied to; it employs a man to flush toilets in slack times; it has been hit by an airplane in a fog, struck countless times by lightning, and been jumped off of by so many unhappy people that pedestrians instinctively quicken step when passing Fifth Avenue and 34th Street.)

Manhattan has been compelled to expand skyward because of the absence of any other direction in which to grow. This, more than any other thing, is responsible for its physical majesty. It is to the nation what the white church spire is to the village—the visible symbol of aspiration and faith, the white plume saying that the way is up. The summer traveler swings in over Hell Gate Bridge and from the window of his sleeping car as it glides above the pigeon lofts and back yards of Queens looks southwest to where the morning light first strikes the steel peaks of midtown, and he sees its upward thrust unmistakable: the great walls and towers rising, the smoke rising, the heat not yet rising, the hopes and ferments of so many awakening millions rising—this vigorous spear that presses heaven hard.

It is a miracle that New York works at all. The whole thing is implausible. Every time the residents brush their teeth, millions of gallons of water must be drawn from the Catskills and the hills of Westchester. When a young man in Manhattan writes a letter to his girl in Brooklyn, the love message gets blown to her through a pneumatic tube—pfft—just like that. The subterranean system of telephone cables, power lines, steam pipes, gas mains and sewer pipes is reason enough to abandon the island to the gods and the weevils. Every time an incision is made in the pavement, the noisy surgeons expose ganglia that are tangled beyond belief. By rights New York should have destroyed itself long ago, from panic or fire or rioting or failure of some vital supply line in its circulatory system or from some deep labyrinthine short circuit. Long ago the city should have experienced an insoluble traffic snarl at some impossible bottleneck. It should have perished of hunger when food lines failed for a few days. It should have been wiped out by a plague starting in its slums or carried in by ships' rats. It should have been overwhelmed by the sea that licks at it on every side. The workers in its myriad cells should have succumbed to nerves, from the fearful pall of smoke-fog that drifts over every few days from Jersey, blotting out all light at noon and leaving the high offices suspended, men groping and depressed, and the sense of world's end. It should

St. Patrick's Cathedral, New York, with the
Atlas of Rockefeller Center at left.

have been touched in the head by the August heat and gone off its rocker.

Mass hysteria is a terrible force, yet New Yorkers seem always to escape it by some tiny margin: they sit in stalled subways without claustrophobia, they extricate themselves from panic situations by some lucky wisecrack, they meet confusion and congestion with patience and grit—a sort of perpetual muddling through. Every facility is inadequate—the hospitals and schools and playgrounds are overcrowded, the express highways are feverish, the unimproved highways and bridges are bottlenecks; there is not enough air and not enough light, and there is usually either too much heat or too little. But the city makes up for its hazards and its deficiencies by supplying its citizens with massive doses of a supplementary vitamin—the sense of belonging to something unique, cosmopolitan, mighty and unparalleled.

GUGGENHEIM MUSEUM, DESIGNED BY FRANK LLOYD WRIGHT, NEW YORK.

HERBERT GOLD

from THE AGE OF HAPPY PROBLEMS

TO everyone who says "the Village isn't what it used to be," here is the answer, dated 1960.

ON A DUSTY TABLE in the back room of a Greenwich Village antique shop lies an etching that pictures a mighty stand of oak being cleared to make way for the construction of a cabin. A few disconsolate figures, their heads bowed, mourn the vile encroachment of the metropolis. The title on the etching is *The End of Greenwich Village* and the date on it is 1859.

Greenwich Village ended, then, more than a hundred years ago. The crooked lanes of "Grenege," the Green Village, where small landholders grew tobacco and whence large landholders fled to avoid creditors, were being joined to the busy geometrical grid of Manhattan. "This pleasant and salubrious corner," this ancient Dutch settlement of Greenwijk which had appeared on maps as early as 1645, was dying.

It has been "dying" ever since, regularly. Each generation, the Village has had its Cassandras to cry its coming doom, and the present generation is no exception. The truth, of course, is that Greenwich Village is no longer as it was *and never has been*. A living organism, not a fossil, its restless change is the constant proof of its vitality. Today the Village remains an essential element not merely of the New York scene but of America's long love affair with the twin mistresses Freedom and Rebellion.

The importance of the Village as actual place and symbol of change and experiment in America is demonstrated by the pathetic letter sent off by a Village wife, Mrs. Melville, to her mother: "Herman has taken to writing poetry. You need not tell anyone, for you know how such things get around."

The rumor did get around, alas for Herman, whose spouse passionately desired that he spend his time gainfully writing serial stories about whaling; Mrs. Melville bowed her head with oh! the shame of it, that her beloved Herman lay on his couch all morning, deceiving her with a muse; eventually Herman hired himself out as a salaried employee. But there has always been this small throbbing ventricle in the busy heart of New York where the poet might know honor and where the real shame for a wife would come if Herman *stopped* writing poetry. For all these years now, the inventors, composers, painters, poets, playwrights, and the various would-be and might-be geniuses have eventually floated upstream until they came to rest, at least briefly, in Greenwich Village, U.S.A.

They have sometimes been as respectable as Henry James, who later turned into a wooden-nosed Englishman, and sometimes as disreputable as Joe Gould, the shaggy Harvard-graduate hobo, author of the endless and unpublished *Oral History of the World*, a grinning gnome who lived on free cafeteria ketchup and national publicity, both of which are packed with vitamins and minerals. The geniuses have found inspiration in a certain lounging ease of life among an all-American stew of Italians, Irish, Chinese, and Jews who lived in and around the Village simply because it was their neighborhood. As dogs have fleas, so the geniuses also found comfort in the hectoring company of the gaffers, cadgers, sexual experimenters, political evangels, and the doddering remnants of elegance

near Washington Square and Fifth Avenue.

At its earliest beginnings, the Village was a trading post where Canarsie Indians bargained over hides with the Dutch settlers; there were springs of fresh water on Spring Street, and Minetta Brook wound along Minetta Lane, and wolves, panthers, moose, wild turkeys, and heath hens inaugurated a tradition of good hunting which is carried on now only by the Continental-clad wolves who prowl the still-crooked streets of Minetta and Spring and the rest of the drained, lit, built-up and leveled-down Village of today. In those antique times, besides the Dutch and Indians, there came some English, some French Walloons, some Jews (a tiny pre-Revolutionary Portuguese Hebrew cemetery still slices into the barrage of real estate on Eleventh Street near Sixth Avenue); a number of Negro freedmen and escaped slaves took their best hold on liberty in the Village, and according to some authorities, a few Spanish pirates dropped their eye patches into the bounding main and retired to Perry Street. (Do they now model Hathaway Shirts? And is there really any buried treasure? Might be, beneath the pipes and cables and sewers and foundations upon foundations.)

All this began when the Green Village was a tidy little settlement insulated from the Manhattan colony, thanks to swamp, salt marsh, forest, and cripple bush. Gradually the wild berries and nuts disappeared (later to reappear in health stores on Eighth Street, along with queen bee jelly and wheat germ); the English installed tobacco plantations; Sir Peter Warren owned almost the whole caboodle. He died in 1752, "removed by the Almighty from a place of Honour to an eternity of Happiness," and his various heirs began the continuous process of bickering and speculating, dividing and subdividing. On rainy nights bearded duffers warmed their backsides by the fire and grieved over the good old days of the Village.

Soon the skirmishes of 1776 came close; Aaron Burr galloped through the meadow where the Fifth Avenue bus turns around; history advanced. But advance as history must, New York City could never quite digest this winding knot of exception on its favorite island; Manhattan swallowed it down, it swallowed it up, but Greenwich Village would not be dissolved, straightened, tamed, numbed, or numbered. And when it allowed itself partly to be numbered, it produced such examples of arithmetical chaos as an intersection of Fourth and Tenth Streets—a tribute to the old times of Indian trails, when "parallel" and "perpendicular" meant as little as "pension" and "job security" to the true Villager of today. The surveyors who laid out the map of Greenwich Village had irrigated their wits with birchbark wine.

That allegedly parallel streets should meet and cross perhaps helps to explain why Washington Irving, James Fenimore Cooper, and Edgar Allan Poe came to the Village in the early and middle nineteenth century; West Tenth Street and West Fourth Street persisted in meeting and crossing, an assignation which must be a love match since it is the despair of logical minds, and so Ada Clare (author of "the most beautiful poems in the language," according to the *New York Atlas*), also came to smoke (!), drink (!), and talk impertinently with men neither her father, brother, nor husband(!). Artistic types liked dear Ada, who somehow had a child without being married (due to too much smoking, drinking, and conversation), and Henry Clapp, who found in Greenwich Village the gabled houses and the charm of Paris, began to gather the noise of nineteenth-century art about their organizing spirits. Walt Whitman toured the streets with crumbs for the birds on his shoulders ("All the critters come to me," he said); Mark Twain, rescued from bankruptcy by a lecture tour, lived at 14 West Tenth Street and then, perhaps trying to escape that maddening intersection with Fourth Street, moved to 21 Fifth Avenue. Here he took the courage to write blasphemous books which were published only after his death.

There were the famous from all over the world, like John Masefield, or later, like Maxim Gorki, who had a secretary with whom he was not allowed to register in his hotel because he admitted freely that they took dictation together. There were also the generous, like Luke O'Connor, in whose tavern almost anyone could cash a check. Luke's place came to be known as "The Working Girl's Home" because a girl could enjoy a quiet glass under the amiable protection of Luke without being disturbed by the police. When Luke's place closed, the old times were over once again.

Now, of course, time really is moving fast; the 1960 "End of Greenwich Village" tramples down that Greenwich Village which subverts the Greenwich Village which preceded it; and again change destroys its "essential character." New high-rise apartment houses, replacing the handsomely decrepit fretwork tenements, give sign of the alteration in olde New York wrought by cold cash and hot mortgage. The restless spirit of consumership has discovered the charm of nonconformity, along with coffee houses, hi-fi, and girls in tight pants; but the new, prosperous, intelligent, gifted wageslaves who seek to recapture their perhaps never-was youth by moving to the Village want to nonconform in comfort, like everyone else, with built-in air conditioners, speedy silent elevators, and a rent they are not ashamed to murmur aloud.

In the process, some of the old traditional Village landmarks—the old Brevoort Hotel, the gingerbread apartment houses, and the Waldorf Cafeteria, where Maxwell Bodenheim came to make fun of the junkies, and stayed and stayed—have disappeared. Many fine blocks full of wood-burning fireplaces have fallen under the builder's heartless ax, making way for central heating, low ceilings, and high rent. The Village is very much a state of mind, usually centered at such landmarks as Washington Square, Sheridan Square, and a shifting few favorite restaurants, streets, places, and events; unofficially—there can hardly be an official map for a tradition—the outlines of the Village begin to manifest themselves at Fourteenth Street on the north, the Hudson River on the west, Canal Street to the south, and Broadway on the east. But these are not firm outlines, merely hints and histories. Since there are Villagers living on Fifteenth Street, is this not the Village? And what about Sixteenth Street? And Seventeenth? And Eighteenth? No, Eighteenth Street is certainly lost to another style, but still, how many hairs make a beard and what does a neighbor street need in order to join the Village?

Now the traditional locus of the Village is being bulged outward by an American need to build a bigger, better headquarters for nonconformity: There is the chic Fifth Avenue Village, extended up East Eighth Street; there is the clean, new, monumental and boring Washington Square Village development, which replaced an old slum just south of Washington Square with a huge tenement cake of glass and aluminum (abstract expressionist paintings in the lobby); there are the rehabilitated Italian and Irish slums adjoining, and the refurbished dockside tenements, and a general groaning and heaving of the land as real-estate developers rush in to discover "the charm of Village living." Some brilliant mice seem to have discovered a deep truth: Build a better people trap and the world will beat a path to your door. All you have to do is stand in front of a building in a suit with wide lapels and the crusted bricks come slipping down, thinking they recognize a builder.

The Village's first stock-brokerage office has opened on Sixth Avenue, around the corner from the offices of *The Village Voice*, on ground hallowed by the tread of patrolling actors, artists, technocrats, ancient crones, homosexuals; it lies catty-corner across from the Women's House of Detention, a dismal warehouse in which prostitutes, shoplifters, junkies, molls, accessories-after-the-fact are kept in inventory. Occasionally the girls stored in their coolers grow restive, as growing girls will do; they lean against the bars and holler at each other, or bang their eating tools, screaming curses or impractical invitations into the street. Now the stroller below, wild with desire, can shout back up at them the bid and asked price on General Electric or A.T.&T., fresh off the tape.

Today the Village seems, to those for whom it was a part of their youth, like one of those jigsaw puzzles in which you put together the two hundred pieces and are rewarded with a vision of a sylvan glen and a perfect beauty dawdling from a rope swing, dressed only in her smile. Under "B" in the index of a book on the post-World War I Village, we find these entries: Babbittry; Basement tenements; Birth control clinics; Block, the, as a unit; Bodenheim, Maxwell; Bohemianism, pseudo; Bohemians, out-and-out; Book-binding; Bourgeois morality; Bourgeois-romantic family; Bricklayers; Broccoli; Butchers' shops.

The non-"B" pieces of the puzzle, for those now suddenly middle-aged, also include the speakeasies, the old Nick's, Dixieland jazz, the anarchists and Communists and Martha Graham, the Waldorf Cafeteria, rent parties, the *Masses*, Howard Scott (founder of Technocracy), Floyd Dell and Joe Gould (founders of Floyd Dell and Joe Gould), Eugene O'Neill and a few dozen other of the dear departed, and the ageless troglodyte on every block who lived for some harmless madness of dress or manner or erotic preference. Gone, all gone; or if still there, so changed as to be occasion of deep deception to our nostalgia-bound visitor.

And yet, each piece in the eternal jigsaw game has its equivalent today, right now: the White Horse Tavern, the Five Spot for progressive jazz, the co-operative galleries on East Tenth Street which represent the avant-garde of the abstract expressionist habit, the beatniks and the hipsters and the dance students and the Actors Studio gangs, Jim Atkins' glassed-around short-order place on Sheridan Square, the Rienzi and the Figaro coffee houses, a host of vocal painters and sculptors, like Larry Rivers and Ibram Lassaw, and the poets a-reading of the jagged truth in the jazz-and-poetry emporiums like the Bizarre on West Third Street. And so our middle-aged visitor reconstructs the puzzle, every piece falling neatly into place. And yet the vision of a sylvan glen and ardent promise may elude his critical eye, for the crucial elements which give it all its excitement—the eye and hand and moiling heart of the puzzle-fitter—are irrevocably altered. The puzzle needs an organizing principle for its message to be unscrambled, and this principle seems to come from the hot blood within, that first sweet youthful discovery of freedom, passion and rebellion. And thus the word: "The Village isn't what it used to be."

But if those who came to the Village during the Depression utter this mournful complaint, so now do those who traveled toward Charles Street on or off the GI Bill after the war. They too, settled into the second marriage and third child, or into some combination of those elements, having taken on a permanent job and the habit of having habits, must mutter to their wives on their Saturday-night tour: "Ah, the San Remo is spoiled. Ah, what's happened to the old White Horse?"

"Yes, honey, and a bunch of lousy dykes has taken the place of those divine lesbians."

"Yes, darling, and where is *Death* (the magazine which answered *Life*), and where, O where is *Neurotica* (the analysts have their journals, now it's time for the patients to have one)?"

Answer: the Village has always moved fast. A generation lasts only a few seasons. *Death* has died, honey, and the editor of *Neurotica* has moved to St. Louis.

But if these visitors look at the girls down from Sarah Lawrence, searching for the ghost of poor Dylan (whom they could have saved by pure love, of course) or the shadow of Jack Kerouac (who *needs* them, dig?), squired by boys remembering that they were Holden Caulfield in some other, better life, these veterans of old Village campaigns must see familiar faces—their own. The Village jumps tirelessly to its eternal role as the objective expression of an urge to rebel, strike out anew, break the barriers of convention and (very important) have something to shock the old folks about. And in one case out of ten thousand, of course, this "*crise d'originalité juvénile*," as a French psychologist called it, leads to that essential human crisis of discovery and creation. The habit and trapping of rebellion may involve rebellion in fact, and the destruction of worn-out ways of thinking, and the creation of works of mind and art.

For the remaining 9999, they have at least had a fling, some art movies and some pizza late at night, something to be nostalgic about in ten years, when "the Village has really changed, pal—we didn't used to have bomb shelters on Sullivan Street."

Like the mating salmon swarming up the Columbia River, the girls seeking freedom and "self-expression" rush down from the smart women's colleges; they head eastward from the big state institutions, their fins ajiggle and their gill slits pulsing; they forgather for adventure and true love in Manhattan, and a high percentage naturally finds its way to Greenwich Village. The result is a highly abnormal situation in many of the professions: an oversupply of lovely ladies. In the theatre, for example, there are more women than men to begin with; then if you subtract from the pool of available manpower—doing service at dinner and bed—those men who are contentedly married, those who are already engrossed by one girl, and those who prefer non-girls, you have remaining a lovely turmoil of lovely lost ladies, wishing they knew somebody. Because they work hard, they know few people outside the theatre. They spend many an evening walking the dog up and down Tenth Street, dreaming that somewhere in God's Green Village there must be a foot-loose heterosexual. Probably the loneliest girls in the world are theatrical beauties, alien as this idea is to the American fantasy of the wild life of actresses.

In days gone by, men went to the Village to hunt women. Now they go to be hunted; there is a remarkable contemporary tendency of the prey to track down the hunter.

A special example of Village devotion to Thespis is a girl we shall call Norma, a long-legged, creamy-skinned brunette with crisp dramatic gifts and a stubborn crush on Shakespeare and Shaw. Most actors, no matter what their preferences, take the jobs offered them. Norma, who has a degree in theatre from Carnegie Tech, fanatically refuses roles in musicals and contemporary plays because she doesn't want to risk a threat to her classic style. Therefore she makes her living, between productions of *A Midsummer Night's Dream* and *Caesar and Cleopatra*, by working as a skilled, albeit slightly sullen call girl. This she does not consider corruption because only the theatre really matters and the particular act she puts on for certain out-of-town buyers does not affect her diction. Also she plies her trade in the midtown expense-account belt which she holds in contempt; "real life" for her is located on Charles Street, where she remains a svelte young actress, taking her breakfast at lunch time in blue jeans in a drug store while she reads Eric Bentley on the theatre of Bertolt Brecht. She is considering broadening her repertoire.

Norma feels only contempt for the commercial actresses, call them Marge and Jo, who live together in precarious amity. Marge makes a steady living doing all the baby voices for one of the radio networks while she awaits an appropriate Broadway part. Jo, less successful, wrote a book about Marge between jobs and sold it to a paperback publisher. Since it exposed baby-voiced Marge's love life in adult, adulterous, and unadulterated detail, there was a strain between the two roomies which lasted almost a week. They took their meals in separate rooms. Marge calls Jo a fake because she had her nose bobbed *twice*. Once is enough for an honest girl.

"But it wasn't short enough," wails Jo. "And it hung a little to one side."

"So does your bosom, sweets," says her dear friend.

At the traditional street fairs—the big Italian ones and the smaller Spanish one just north of the Village —the aging Village-lover can still find, almost unchanged, the elements which bewitched his youth: fat, savory sausages, fried crustaceans of mysterious varieties, sold cheaply on the street, brilliant colors, gambling and drinking and the penny-toss, Sicilian street singers crying in their broken tenors of lost, lost love, thick-ankled, thick-waisted beauties, with unbobbed noses, leaving streaks of lipstick on bar glasses. On these saints' days, no injection of tourists from uptown can dilute the amiable, loud, distracted calliope pleasure of carnival nights. The parrot tells your fortune for twenty cents, plucking a piece of paper in its horny bill: and what care you if the somber slender gentleman awaiting his future in line behind you is Montgomery Clift, and if the excited lady is Shelley Winters? The Village has room for disconsolate movie actors, too.

The Village, while still a place for the young and the undecided, is inhabited by Villagers—that is, people of all ages and conditions. The contrast between the Village and its recent rival for the hand of Youth—the North Beach area of San Francisco— tells the story clearly. The barefoot beatniks of North Beach make the staid diners at Chumley's on Bedford Street ("Patronized by Writers and Artists") look like elder statesmen. When the North Beach is invaded by middle-aged nostalgists, and the morose beatniks settle down to raising square babies, and there are memories and histories of "the way it was," and novelists, playwrights, poets and painters have fixed the scene in their work, then the North Beach will be on its way toward becoming another Greenwich Village.

In the meantime, the Village still provides the American "capital of hope and paradise of misery." The more the Village changes, settles down, rebuilds, the more it remains the same thing. And perhaps its lack of respect for Village tradition is a sign of its continuing vitality as a reflection of the realities of American life. While the Village changes under pressure, it changes in directions molded not merely by pressure from the outside. The quintessential rebellious Village strikes back, and the rest of the world falters. An example of this lively, restless, spirited Village playfulness can be found in and around *The Village Voice*, a weekly newspaper which is less a newspaper than a cause to its editors and subscribers. Hip, unbeat, irreverent and comical, the newspaper has also sharpened and led a drive against Tammany Hall; with another head it has garrulously and energetically hollered on behalf of off-Broadway theatre; it has led a victorious and well-organized battle against New York City's all-powerful Commissioner of Parks, Robert Moses. This symbolic battle can very well stand for the low-level and personal and heartening struggle of the Village against the rampant force of commercialism.

Stately Washington Square, with its Frenchified Arch and charm, one of the historical landmarks of the Village, had been under attack from several sides. New York University had spread around it, cracking up some fine old Georgian houses in its educational cobra's embrace; the police were shoving away the girls, the digs, the hippies, the hobos, and the babies who played in the grass. Heavy traffic through the little stretch of park was poisoning the green. And then along came Moses. Unlike the Biblical Moses, who wanted to cross the desert, this bureaucratic Moses wanted to produce a desert by widening the roadway through the Square, increasing traffic, renaming and widening a narrow Village street at the opposite end. In order to create "Lower Fifth Avenue," an address which would presumably suggest an increment of verbal prestige, he was willing to destroy the park. Apparently the developers of Washington Square Village, to the south of the Square, had been promised the Fifth Avenue label through some mysterious political process.

Here was a clear issue. It was historical tradition versus real estate speculation, lovers versus automobiles, folk singers versus trucks, green versus asphalt, the people of the Village against the arrogance of New York politicians. With great relish, *The Village Voice* led its tattered battalions into action. Mothers with baby carriages filled with gallant sucklings, united legions of liberal Democrats and progressive Republicans, students and artists and hip kids and off-Broadway geniuses and crones from Washington Mews whose cronish aunts remembered Henry James—all united behind a banner decorated by Jules Feiffer and the impassioned, sometimes grammatical rhetoricians of the *Voice*.

And lo, David slew Goliath. Not only did the Village win its battle to keep the Square undiminished, but then it also attacked and eliminated *all* traffic through Washington Square. The park was preserved for its stoic pursuits—chess on the permanent concrete-and-tile chessboards (where bundled and huffing old men study the board even through the long winter), love, philosophy, the tranquil digestive functioning of dogs, bongo artistry, and all the etceteras of a city park. Robert Moses beat a sullen, screaming retreat; Tammany Hall, responsive to the

pressure of bona fide, licensed, curried and voting voters, even joined *The Village Voice* in its campaign, once victory seemed inevitable.

A small victory? Perhaps. But important as a gesture of defiance against the march of the superhighway and the developer. It gave courage to the Save-the-Village movement a-borning. And on Washington Square the bongos and the guitars, their friends and their fellow travelers, can still idle away a summer evening.

* * *

The Village has set sail for the future, like all of unanchored America, set sail or set adrift, take your choice. A visit to the Village always provokes a crisis of nostalgia in those who have moved on but do not want the Village to move on. The lovely, long-legged blonde girl who used to be seen strolling with Sam Kramer, the bearded jewelry maker—gone. The Waldorf Cafeteria, where the bums and the junkies and Maxwell Bodenheim convened all night over moldy prunes and coffee—gone, replaced by a bank. Romany Marie, who used to feed the wild and the artistic—very quiet. Djuna Barnes and e e cummings—in seclusion. (It is said that a group of beat poets made a pilgrimage one night to cummings' house on Patchin Place. "We're *poets!* We're *poets!*" they shouted, and a ghostly voice issued from a window: "Go away.") And Bodenheim himself, poet of delicate wit and ribald enthusiasm: he went down to drink and died of blows on the head, strokes with a knife, administered by the crazy thug with whom he shared —it seems—both bottle and wife. The Brevoort Hotel, home of elegant artists in moments of triumph—gone, replaced by a boring luxury apartment house. The Rhinelander Gardens—also raped by an apartment house. Joe Gould—dead. Max Eastman—rich. The Group Theatre—disappeared.

And yet . . .

Young Boris, proprietor of the old Borsch Bowl, dispenser of philosophy and black bread, is gone. But long live Boris! Grayer, plumper, presiding over a new Borsch Bowl, Boris lives on, garrulously, offering black bread.

Edna St. Vincent Millay, who once inhabited the narrowest house in New York, at 73 Bedford Street, has finished burning her candle at both ends, but next door another artist works late into the night. This new poet of Bedford Street inhabits a book-lined study; his lovely slim wife stands by with coffee as he works; they can be seen from the street, bending over his desk, he fretting, she peacefully confident, watching with a halfsmile on her face, until she taps him gently on the shoulder: "It's very late, dear." (It turns out, alas, that this nocturnal creator is the author of one of the important comic strips.)

And there is another long-legged blonde who can be seen strolling with Sam Kramer, the still-bearded jewelry maker—the same beard, a similar blonde.

And there are coffee houses which have Sunday-afternoon chamber-music recitals. And some eccentric ones which merely serve coffee.

And Charlie Van Doren, the defrocked quiz star, quietly writing a novel (a play?) which everyone supposes will deal with a simple, true-hearted, slightly greedy young quiz star who, nearly corrupted by the mass media, receives a letter from a little old lady named Checkers, just in time to keep him from perjuring himself before a Congressional committee . . . In Jim Atkins' eatery the odds are against his starring in the movie version.

And the lovely fashion model who transmitted a small crablike infestation to a whole group of poets —"like that's her protest against the whole sex-oriented system, dig," explained one of them, scratching. And the eager virgin who makes a hobby of suggesting that she and her date go back to his place so that she can take a shower—and then she takes a shower. And carries a switch-blade to make sure that her date keeps the peace. And the girls who live by remittances from home while they find their souls, and seem to find them, for they usually disappear into social work after a year or two. And the girls, girls, girls. Italo Calvino, a distinguished Italian novelist, declared that the most monumental, splendid, and architecturally efficient structure he found in America was not a skyscraper but a small flexible device; it was first modeled for him in Greenwich Village: "Change my whole life! the dee-ah-fragum!"

There are no more rent parties, at which you paid a small admission to dance the Charleston, eat cheap spaghetti and drink bathtub gin so that your host could keep body, soul, and furniture off the street, but there are shindigs like the STOMP OUT BOBBY BREEN

JAPANESE TOURISTS IN BROOKLYN BOTANIC GARDENS.

PARTY (at Madame Irma's Dancehall on Second Avenue) to which you are asked to bring your own booze, although the mimeographed invitation assures you that "BEER, MUSIC, ICE CUBES, PAPER CUPS, THE HALL, MOXIE and GENERAL FUNKINESS are provided by the Management." You are also warned: "This party is by private invitation only . . . don't bring your friends . . . don't bring good old Harry who lives in Queens but is a nice guy . . . nor your Aunt Lucy who has always wanted to go to a Real Village Party . . . don't hip the Bronx . . . if your girl is the kind who locks herself in the can at parties to weep, don't bring her . . . if you insist on singing, forget it . . . if your idea of a good time is charades, we don't want you . . . no marrieds except the unhappily . . . don't tell *Life* magazine . . . wear a funny hat if you like, but no costumes!" There are other parties for little companies of off-Broadway players, who offer Gallo wine and corrosive martinis in the hope that you may write a check to help support their production of a symbolic drama by Ionesco, Adamov, Ghelderode, or the omnipresent revival of *Winterset*. The actors now have pads (or live with their hip parents in Forest Hills), and worry about unpaid parking tickets rather than the grocery bill, but the theatre needs a stage, brother, and the union gives us lip. Those uptown bankrollers who used to say "nix" to the avant-garde have now learned to say "Bug-off, Buster." It turns out that many of us need our daily dose of anxiety. If we can't worry about our own landlord, we'll fret about the bourgeois proscenium type who holds the keys to the Circle in the Square.

And so it goes in the eternal Village—that impossible, actual American dream of freedom through bohemia. Amid all the open possibilities of American life, which permits a young man to select any variety of togetherness he chooses, there are many who feel constricted. They ask, Why this? Why not that? And perhaps even, Why not the other thing? Why not try my impulse, try my luck, try my talent, try my skills at loafing and self-generating labor? They are squeezed in the direction of declared rebellion, abstention, disaffiliation.

These patient and impatient yearners after truth, beauty and easy living will always float toward the Village—the artists and the art-lovers, the worshipers of sex, the sick and the spoiled, the young and the special and the adventurous, all making common cause in the pleasure of their differences. In 1960, when the pressure to do like others is high in America, the Village takes a new shape, molded by money. It is becoming an elegant bohemia in which radical politics are replaced by the hip and the beat; the bearded poets are crowded to one side by the bearded advertising men with sports cars sold them by bearded salesmen. Though it changes as it mirrors the times, the Village is still necessary. It is that bottle in which Americans put whatever the suburbs and the colleges and the middle-class family cannot happily contain.

So listen, Herman, tell Mrs. Melville to get in line. Come back to the Village and write poetry if you like. Open the bottle and free the djinn—yourself—into the carrousel whirl of Greenwich Village, where change is everlasting and the permanent never remains the same. There's a fellow over on Cornelia Street who looks like a homesick Canarsie ghost returned to sell wolf pelts and otter meat on his ancient lands. In fact, of course, he is a peaceable poetry-loving Arab weaver, a frequent tea drinker, who grows irate if you call him beat. "I'm a member of the *Post* Beat Generation," he says with quiet dignity, shuckling his hands in his embroidery. "The difference between us and the beats, man, is . . . Well, like we're different. Like we *affirm*, man. I mean, like we protest."

Apparently, affirmative protest is here to stay. Greenwich Village may have ended at twelve o'clock this evening, but it has begun again at midnight.

ALISTAIR COOKE

from ONE MAN'S AMERICA

AN English journalist (American by adoption) looks at the North and the South, vintage 1947.

NOTHING persists more in the fancy of Europeans, and in the superstitious pride of Americans themselves, than the conviction that Americans are tough and rough and ready, scornful of the European niceties and primmer ways of travel. The last thirty years have turned this belief into unmitigated legend.

One of the most precious books to American book

collectors is a copy of Baedeker's *United States* for, I believe, 1906. In the conscientious Baedeker way, it warns the comparatively domesticated European of the coarse pleasures and inconveniences he will have to settle for if he decides to take a holiday in the United States. It is always Baedeker's consolation, however, to the intending tourist that no matter how constant the public spitting, how hard the beds, how ankle-deep the roads and primitive the hotels away from the big cities, the traveler who has any pioneering spirit in him will never regret his courageous visit to the United States because nowhere else will he see the singing color of the New England fall, the blossom of the South in the spring, the grandeur of the Yosemite, the Yellowstone, etc., etc. This guidebook is greatly sought after precisely because today it reads like such a gorgeous joke. If you changed the place-names and made them European, an American could read it with a straight face, since it would record most of his grouches about traveling in Europe today. The application of American technical genius to the mechanics of living has not merely turned the tables on Baedeker, it has turned the American, however reckless or self-reliant his individual character, into the world's most urbanized, most petted traveler.

Mr. Richard Neuberger, who lives in the Far West, in Portland, Oregon, has taken up this theme in a magazine piece. He was in Alaska during the war having, as he puts it, "the sort of experience we had read about eagerly as boys, in the tales of James Fenimore Cooper, Jack London, and Zane Grey." And, he adds, "we hated it . . . we talked nostalgically of percale sheets and fluffy towels, or breakfast in bed and tiled bathrooms." They complained—in Alaska, this is—about "drafty privies and the lack of dry-cleaning facilities." Mr. Neuberger concludes that "with a few bold exceptions, we Americans have come to regard the steam-heated hotel and the internal combustion engine as indispensable to any foray in the open." Nowadays, more millions than ever before (the latest annual count was 15,057,443) visit the American National Parks. But according to the Department of the Interior fewer and fewer people each year attempt the two-day hikes, or even drive up the highest peaks, or, having looked at the Grand Canyon, will undertake the day-long mule journey down to the overnight camp at the bottom. It is very hard to say how Americans would compare with other peoples in this new-found lassitude. Driving around most of the National Parks is pretty strenuous in itself. If you could put Yosemite and Yellowstone together, you would have something about the area of Wales, whose geography is a combination of Switzerland, Persia, and the Day of Judgment. But even so, these parks

were lovingly created two generations ago by men who chopped through thousands of feet of lumber, who rode into them on a horse, who discovered the sublime with an ax, a botanist's kit, a piece of bacon, a tent and a stout heart. Now through all of them, even over the hair-raising pass into Tuolumne Meadows on top of the Yosemite, American engineers have built incomparable cement highways, blasted through prehistoric rock, encircling mountains where no other race would dream of cutting out a dirt road.

This suggests a cheerful contradiction. That even if the traveler *is* a sissy sitting over an internal combustion engine, the heroes who in his behalf comb cement to the smoothness of toothpaste under the desert sun, and build his highways through the Rockies and Sierras: they are Americans too. And this leads us into a famous cliché. I hope I can then lead us out of it. (I have nothing against clichés. Most of them are true, though you have to live through the denial of them to know it.) It is the assumption that Americans have grown soft and unable to fend for themselves, that their enslaving gadgets, through which they flip their way so expertly, are crutches or props to living, essential to a people sinking contentedly into a decadence that out-Romans the Romans.

I'm sorry to report that the Americans' devotion to urban comfort, their ingenuity with gadgets, even their reliance on them, proves no such thing. In my own experience, the Americans who are most devoted to convertible automobiles and glass-enclosed showers made no complaint on this score when they ripped up Japanese jungles for airfields or waded ashore at Okinawa. The women I know who can whip up a delicious meal in ten minutes with the skilled aid of pressure cookers, bean slicers, electric beaters and deep-frozen vegetables are also the ones who can make the best meal the slow way with none of these things. And the most skillful fisherman I know is a man who can charm a trout with his fingernail, but prefers to have a compact tackle-box along, which contains exquisite scales the size of your thumb and a leader cutter which is a little circle of plastic molds that exudes fine wire and cuts it in one motion.

Most Americans, even rich ones, were brought up in a culture that never expected somebody else to do the rough work. Most boys in college who can afford good cars can also take them apart and put them together again. This may all be changing. Still, I doubt that a devotion to gadgets is a reflection in the American character of a terrified dependence on them. They are loved for themselves, for the humorous felicity with which they dispose of elementary labor. A Texan I know, whom I would never like to meet in anger whether the choice of weapons was a jet-propelled torpedo or the back of the raw hand, put it neatly once when he said to me, "I'll ride fifty miles on a horse for the fun of it, but out of necessity I drive." One of the irritating troubles about Americans, in violation of the best advice of the best English divines, is that they just don't believe that whatever is uncomfortable is good for the character.

* * *

Before going into the life of a state that has been called the last economic frontier, and which I should call the Unknown State, it might be as well to picture where it is and what it looks like.

It hangs down from the extreme eastern corner of the United States like a pistol held at the head of the Caribbean. The handle touches Alabama. The chamber forms the coast that faces on the Gulf of Mexico. The long barrel pointing south and west forms the peninsula, four hundred miles long, and it is this that means Florida to Americans. What they *think* of, however, as Florida is the shining rim of the pistol's foresight—the linked strands of beaches where in the past twenty years towering hotels, shops in rainbow colors, yacht harbors, trailer camps, and a whole market-place of pleasure has been built on a

long strip of coastline literally dredged up from the ocean. There was a time only a generation ago when no one probed this ocean except Greek sponge-fishers, who have now settled westward along the Gulf Coast. But today the ocean dashes gently against the most expensive bodies, the best-fed stomachs, and some of the sharpest heads in America. Today the offshore waters flash with dinghies and yachts from which, as Westbrook Pegler says, "fishermen use little fish the size of billygoats as bait for fish the size of cows."

Like many another American institution, then, Florida is the victim of its advertising. Of course, the curse of bad advertising is that it creates a false issue which the wise as well as the stupid come to think is the essential thing to talk about; so that even people who repudiate the advertising don't know anything else to look for. If they don't like salt water or find the beach-life vacuous, then that is all there is to Florida, and it's a miserable thing.

The physical approach to the pleasure domes of Miami and Miami Beach contributes to this deception. For it is not what the travel-folders illustrate. You cross the Georgia border and streak monotonously over bare, cut-over pineland. You may just glimpse a few Negroes chipping the pine trees for gum, which is then distilled into turpentine. But mostly you will

A PART OF MIAMI BEACH, FLORIDA.

see nothing but sandy wastes, decorated at times by piles of lumber. A few cattle, and pigs snuffling in cypress swamps. You race through run-down shrimp ports. Slowly the vegetation, such as there is of it, gets more tropical, but never lush. Cabbage palms blob by, and at the water's edge you see cormorants trundling, like model planes in trouble. The last hundred miles are an assault and battery by advertising. Haphazard battalions of billboards go by, advertising miraculously profitable orange groves, nightclubs, trailer camps, ice cream, real estate ("This is God's country—you'd be at home in Heaven"). Your mileage is calculated for you by roadside signs screaming—"Only ten miles to tupelo honey," or two miles to an alligator farm, or "Twelve miles to Sandy's super-duper jumbo hamburgers." Occasionally there is a crude sign painted by some wandering evangelist and striking a chillier note: "Prepare to Meet Thy God."

You might remember that sign when you come to open the state guidebook and find on an early page this warning: "Caution to Tourists: do not enter bushes at the side of highway; snakes and redbugs usually infest such places." That may be a shock to the tourist, but if he followed it up he might go on to learn something of the state as it is only ten miles inland from Miami's garish suburbs, and there meet a Florida that is much as it was a thousand years ago. In none of the forty-eight states does life leap so suddenly, in an hour's motor drive, from the suburban snooze to the primeval ooze. Only a thin strip of pine and palmetto woods stands guardian between what we laughingly call "civilization as we know it" and the seething cypress swamp known as the Everglades; where four hundred species and sub-species of birds carol and whine over a slimy wilderness dignified by the white plumes of the egret; where orchid trees of a thousand blooms rise out of the pure muck that seems to have inundated the whole visible earth. It is at night that this contrast is most compelling. And you feel it most dramatically going west from Miami. Go by plane and in a minute or two Miami is a scum of bright bubbles on the edge of a stagnant pond. Or drive out at twilight, as the floodlights are switched on to the vertical hotels, and the bartenders begin to rattle their ice, and blondes with coal-black tans appear in their backless finery. Within a half-hour Miami is a memory of a Hollywood musical to a man stranded on the Amazon. An eagle circles against a purple sky. A buzzard flaps away from some dark carrion on the road ahead. You stop your motor and see no living thing. But the loneliness, and the awe of living close to a jungle before it was ever tamed into lumber or tailored into farms or gardens, is intensified by the insane symphony of sound that strikes your ear. Over a bubbling, rumbling percussion of bullfrogs, you will hear the chuck-chuck of tropical woodpeckers, the wheezy sigh of bull-rats, a low slush of alligator. If you are lucky you may see the scarlet glowing wing of a flamingo. The din lets up for a moment, and then you are terrified into alertness again by a thin wailing sound, like that of a lost man gone crazed. It is the everyday song of a water-bird that hobbles as it walks and is known as the limpkin.

Yet inside this dense inland swamp there are living humans who seldom come out. They are the Seminole Indians, who have mingled with the white man possibly less than any other tribe in the United States. They have a long and resentful history of relations with him and there is no certainty that they yet regard themselves as being at peace with the United States Government. A final treaty of peace between the Seminoles and the Government was signed in 1934, and another "final" treaty in 1937. They live entirely by hunting and they hunt well. Because most of the land is under water, they live on encampments built of dried tree-trunks fastened together like the spokes of a wheel. The family pots and pans are anchored nearby on rafts. When it's wet they sleep on platforms made of saplings above the swamp and covered with a roof of palm leaves. Here, one hour from Miami, they worship their god Yo-He-Wah, who is the symbol of all virtue and purity and love, and whose name may never be mentioned except at a religious festival. They disapprove of capital punishment, they rule themselves with a council of medicine men, and they have rather curious beliefs about marriage. Being so near and yet so far from the civilized whites of Miami and Palm Beach, they look on marriage as a sacred and serious undertaking which may only be severed—indeed must be severed—for a single reason. The reason is "incompatibility." There are no other grounds for divorce, because in their primitive way they think it is a crime to stay married to someone you no longer love.

This contrast between the pleasure industry of Miami and the timeless life of the Seminoles, between a façade of civilization and the primitive culture that lies behind it, is not unique in the United States. You might recall the community of Salt Lake City and the almost unexplored Robber's Roost country that lies not far away. The luxury hotels and saloons of Las Vegas, Nevada, lie on the very edge of the fearful Mojave Desert. You might even discover that only ninety miles from New York is the fashionable resort of Southampton and scratching its handsome back is the scrubby reservation of the Shinnecock Indians. But nowhere is the contrast as extreme as it is in Florida. It is so vivid to the tourist that he comes into Florida and goes out of it under the impression that the state has nothing behind the night-clubs, the beaches, and the race-track but a mess of swamp. However, when the tourists depart in the late winter, they leave behind one half the winter population. These are the two million Floridians who live neither on the east coast nor in the swamp. They have a life of their own, and it is time to talk about them, who inhabit the other three-quarters of the Unknown State.

Running down the center of the peninsula and across to its west coast is a lakeland district which is busy harvesting Florida's second money crop—the first being, of course, the tourists. These people, too, sell the climate, in the shape of oranges and grapefruit and, since the war, in the shape of little cans containing their concentrated juices. The Government set up a laboratory early in the war to make citrus concentrate under the Lend-Lease program. It was a brilliant reply to the challenge of the Nazi submarines, which just then were sinking Allied tankers and freighters every night from the Jersey coast to the Florida keys. One shipload of concentrate could be converted when it was safe in port into as much orange-juice as it would otherwise take five ships to carry. The conversion process is very simple. It requires one housewife and running water.[1] Each can of concentrate can be watered down to make whole orange-juice of five times the volume of the original. Like other expedients thought up in wartime, this experiment done in the name of the Allies is now paying off handsomely for the natives. For the Government, in its little laboratory at Dunedin, incidentally disposed of a prejudice that is common not only to you and me but to the Florida orange-growers. It is the idea that oranges are something to get juice out of. The firm that took over and expanded the government laboratory when the war was over is now a very profitable commercial enterprise canning a fortune in concentrated orange-juice and boasting that orange-juice is a by-product. Once the juice is out, they are left with what used to be thrown away: with the pulp, the peel, the seeds. Now they extract from the seeds oleomargarine, vegetable fats for cooking, and a dye that will fix any known color in artificial silk. From the colored layer of the peel they extract terpenes for battleship paint, and carotene, which provides trillions of units a year of vitamin A. From the white pulp they get pectin, a superlative jelling

agent and a medical godsend for the early treatment of deep wounds. That still leaves cellulose and sugar, from which they take ethyl alcohol for gun cotton, the vitamin B complex, and feed yeast for cattle. So the orange grove has turned into a chemical industry.

They joke in Florida about how, at the end of winter, a trainload of millionaires going home will be shunted on to a siding to let a trainload of cabbages go through. If you are a Florida truck-farmer this is no joke. Most of the land of Florida is poor land, and of its thirty-five million acres only five million are in crops. The climate of the central region and the Gulf Coast is not much more genial than the climate of Georgia and South Carolina to the north. So in late winter there's always a race on to ship north the vegetables which in a few weeks will be ready for delivery from Georgia and the Carolinas. They will be harvesting them up there in the early spring, and once they start, that is the end of the Florida crop. Hence when a train of cabbages starts north, the signals go down all the way and there's nobody important enough to slow it, especially if the weather in the Carolinas has taken a turn for the better.

Floridians have always regretted having to wince when anybody mentions beef or praises the cattle bred in Texas and fattened in Kansas and Iowa. Florida has been trying for a hundred years to build up a cattle-bowl to compete with Texas. But scrub pineland is not the best pasture. And Florida was pestered for decades by a tick which other states killed off, through compulsory cattle-dipping laws. The Florida cattlemen would not dip their cattle, and when the state tried to make them they dynamited the vats. They were rebellious because they knew that the Florida tick is a special bug that thrives not only on cattle but on deer and dogs and horses. You can imagine the feelings of the race-track owners when a quarantine was extended to racehorses. But there was no hope for a cattle industry until the cattlemen gave in. Just before the war they did and today you will see forest fires everywhere—the favorite method, and in this poor land the compulsory method, of burning the range for better pasture. The result, I am staggered to confess, is the best beef I have tasted anywhere.

You may have been trying to picture the people of Florida. It is quite a strain. For Florida is in the South but not of it. Two-party politics rears its hydra head again. Most of the native Southerners are in the north of the state; the southern part is ninety per cent Northern, people who came here in the last forty years to retire, to run a small orange farm, to sell real estate, to mock at their families stuck in the Northern winters. But there are two industries run

---

[1] The same hazard of war, and the identical ingenuity, were responsible in the sixteenth century for the invention of brandy.

by what you can be bold enough to call traditional Floridians, by people who are not seen on beaches, who seldom pitch horseshoes and never lunch at tables carrying a vase of camellias.

They are the cigar industry and the turpentine industry. The cigar industry offers an ironic little essay in labor relations. Eighty years ago some Cuban cigar-makers came up to Key West to avoid the import duty on Cuban cigars and to free themselves from the pressure of a growing Cuban labor union. But the cigar-workers promptly started their unions in Key West. Mr. Ybor, the leading manufacturer, who must have heard about the boundless possibilities of self-expression in God's country, decided to move his pitch. He moved his factories once more. But the unions didn't have to move. They just growed wherever the manufacturer moved his tent. Mr. Ybor eventually landed up in Tampa. There were only a few hundred people there in 1880. Today the population includes about twenty thousand Cubans and ten thousand Italians. Every kind of "discipline" was exercised to suppress the growing unions and in the 1920's there was a militant parade of the Ku Klux Klan. But, one cigar-worker recalled, "We just sat on our porches with our guns across our laps and watched the parade. It was sure a quiet parade." The strike that brought on this visitation of the familiar hooded men lasted ten months and the Florida cigar-trade has barely regained what it lost to its competitors. In 1935 the older cigar-workers sent a petition to the Cuban Government asking to be taken back and pensioned off. Nothing came of it. The travel literature tells you of the glow and charm of the Latin life of the cigar-workers. Perhaps they are thinking of a colored witch-doctor, just out of jail for practicing voodoo, who sneaks from shack to wretched shack in Tampa selling charms to wear around the neck, a particular high-priced charm guaranteed "to ward off unemployment."

The turpentine industry, the chipping of pine trees for the resinous gum, which is then distilled to get turpentine and rosin, is an American industry more than three hundred years old. Its enforced wanderings are typical of the American appetite for raping the timber and the soil of one region and then moving on with a smack of the lips to the next virgin territory. It started in northern New England in the seventeenth century, and when the forests of New Hampshire and Massachusetts and Connecticut were tapped dry it moved down to the Carolinas and by the same ruinous process south into Georgia. When the Georgia trees were giving out, down into Florida. "A turpentine nigger" is in Florida a term of contempt.

It is also the name of a mystery not one Floridian in a thousand has even seen.

In the swampy interior the turpentine Negroes live in camps and are supervised by a "rider," a foreman on horseback, employed by the turpentine corporation. They seldom if ever come out of the jungle. They tap away for a few dollars a day, they produce children, often they are married, their women work with them. America to them is a small clearing for work, a fringe of dark pine, a two-room cabin in which they breed and die. Their life on this earth is at the disposal of the rider. He is the law, the good or bad provider, the judge of all their ways. They call him the Captain. Their drabness, their suppressed hopes, their sense of lowliness and sin are thoroughly purged once a week at what they call a jook party or tonk. These parties are the dim and little-known origin of the honky-tonk and the juke box. A Saturday night jook is a simple uninhibited orgy of drinking, dancing, singing, gambling, love-play, and occasionally knife-play, in the pines outside. If you could have got into one of these jungles in the 1930's [2] you would have heard all that is melancholy and desperate in the only indigenous American music—the blues. They cover every topic these people have heard of and all the work they or their kind have done. Blues about the pine tree that flowed gum till Judgment Day; about the lightning that struck the Captain down and freed them from the jungle; about John Henry, who in this version ran away to the Gulf Coast and made a kingly fortune plucking sponges from the ocean bed with his naked hands. And when their special grievances are exhausted, they revert as country Negroes do everywhere in the South to the perpetual themes captured and taunted for all time in one tune, three lines of lyric, twelve bars of music: the song of people to whom life consists of a few riotous or appalling propositions—the need of a woman, the misery of a lover gone, the hope of a train to take you away from unhappiness, a train to bring you back to what is familiar and warm.

When you see me comin', raise your window high,
When you see me comin', raise your window high,
But if you see me goin', hang yo' head and cry.

And far from these jungles, wherever you go in inland Florida, you will hear against the weird sky the songs of Negroes. In the orange fields, pulling a

---

[2] They are now all but abandoned. A new process has transferred the work to large steam distilleries, which produce less folk-song but less misery.

sack from tree to tree, a fat girl shouts up to the bristling sun: "Go down, Ol' Hannah, don't you rise no mo'." By a railroad branch line near enough to the sea to taste a salt breeze, three Negroes squatting near the track hunched their shoulders and slapped their feet and sang:

God rode out the ocean,
Chained the lightnin' to his wheel;
Stepped on land at West Palm Beach,
And the wicked hearts did yield.

If you roam long and far enough you will begin to compose a picture of Florida whose symbol is no girl in an evening gown and a golden tan. You will come away from it with a memory of an old crone, around her neck the diamond necklace of Miami Beach, and for the rest a woman part Indian, part Negro, part Spanish, mostly Southern mountaineer; who grows oranges and smells of turpentine; who practices voodoo and smokes cigars; who counts cheap beads with her hands and keeps a union card in her pocket.

* * *

There are times of the year when anybody with an itch for travel must think of those parts of the earth that God favored above all others when He handed out the seasons. There are two of these that I have enjoyed many times but I still find myself goggling and marveling every time they come around. One is the English spring and the other is New England in the fall.

The best of English poets have celebrated the rich, somber English autumn, but an American fall bears little resemblance to that "season of mists and mellow fruitfulness." Many famous Britons have put on record their astonishment at the youthful, trumpeting quality of the fall, at the hot days and the Mediterranean blue skies encircling a landscape of blinding scarlet and gold. Lord Bryce, not a reticent man about American vices, couldn't trust his English reserve to speak properly about its virtues. Lloyd George confessed after his only trip to America that no matter how inconclusive his political mission had been he would at least go home remembering the overwhelming experience of the fall. A hundred years ago, Mrs. Trollope, who liked very little about these United States, broke down and wrote that at this season of the year "the whole country goes to glory."

The fall ranges throughout the whole hardwood or deciduous region of the country, from the north woods of Maine clear across the Midwest as far as the Dakotas and way down South to the foothills of the Rockies in Texas. Since no American can bear to believe that he or his parents chose a second-rate place to be born in, there is no agreement about where the fall is at its best. The residents of the Great Lakes say that no sumacs flame like their sumacs. And the pride of a man from Arkansas in his blazing hawthorn trees is a wild grab at plucking a virtue out of necessity. A native of another land can simply report that the fall of New England is to all others as a four-alarm fire to a lighted match. There is no way to describe it or talk about it, except in the language of Milton and Shakespeare, who never saw it.

But it is possible to say why it's so. Everybody enthuses about the fall but nobody explains it. It is due to a happy accident of climate, a steady brilliance of October sun going to work on the great variety of American hardwoods and the fairly arid soil they stand in. The superiority of New England's fall—of that in Vermont, New Hampshire, and Massachusetts especially—is due to their latitude. These states are far enough north to get an early cold spell to quicken the sap before the prolonged sunshine of October brings it out as color in the leaves. They are far enough south to escape a continuous and withering frost, which is what nips the Canadian fall before it can come to its prime. Farther south—in Pennsylvania, Maryland, Virginia, and the Carolinas—they get no summer cold, except at high altitudes, and by the time the sap is forced up and ready for showing off, the leaves are crumbling and falling.

In most temperate countries the strong pigments that have been hidden from view in the greens of summer never do come out, because the autumn brings in rain and mists and threatening gray skies. The whole trick of the New England fall is nothing more complicated than that of a photographic negative handled by a superior developer. In the autumn, the countrymen tell us, the sap is blocked from the leaf by a new growth of hard cells at the base of the twig. So the greens fade. Now all you need is an October of brilliant light and warmth to develop out the yellows and the reds. The only other qualification is a lack of rain. On rich and rainy soils like those of England the leaves stay green too late till the frost kills them. New England, on the contrary, has many causes to lament its rather poor soils. But it never regrets them in the fall, for their very lack of nitrogen stimulates a great range of yellows and golds. And the acid in the leaves is what burns them scarlet. The fall, then, is nothing more than the thorough burning out of what is poor in the soil and what is bitter in the leaf. "It is," says Donald Culross Peattie, "essentially death that causes all the brave show." But it is a fierce and productive death.

I once went north from New York City at the very beginning of the fall to meet the peak of it wherever it might be between Maine and southern Connecticut. The first signal of the glory to come is a bare tree, which is never bare until the fall is ready to ripen. It is the butternut tree, and it sheds everything just as the bushes and berries are beginning to trickle out their purple. By the green edge of the parkway on which I was driving, little piles of brown leaves, already dead, lay at the foot of hickory trees. The ferns were dry. The bracken and blueberry bushes were wine dark, the sumac a throbbing vermilion. Everywhere there was the smell of burning wood, letting off violet wisps of smoke to smear the cloudless sky—like trickles of milk on window panes.

At this point I wanted to take off my glasses, which a notation on my driving license forbids. This is another thing about the fall. The sparkling clarity of the light gives to short-sighted people the constant sense that their eyesight has marvelously improved and that they are seeing fences, barns, steeples, and billboards in the sharp outline they probably have for other people all the time.

I drove up and over the hills across from New York State into Connecticut, past roadside stands piled high with jugs of cider and pyramids of pumpkins. And then I started to follow a river whose banks were black with stands of evergreen. By now a green field was just another daub on the crowded palette of the landscape. We were still far from the fall's peak. It was still the small, treeless things that were trying to be splendid. The briar and bushes and vines were sparkling. I do not know them well enough to single out their separate charms, but it is an annual joy to see brush which most of the time is a mesh of old wire suddenly disclose a jewel of a flower. Pokeweed, and pitchpine cone, and unpretentious things like partridge berry and jack-in-the-pulpit. All of them have a special shining berry, a bursting husk, a momentary bloom.

I got out of the car and wallowed in the silence and the singing color and the balmy heat. At the rim of my tire I noticed that the smooth white cement of the highway had cracked under the tension of a cranberry vine. And through this crack, and edging into the highway, wild cranberries grew. I looked ahead at the engineered boulevard of the highway, pouring like two ribbons of toothpaste to the horizon, quite heedless of its defeat by the concentrated violence of a tiny and delicate vine. That just about put industrial know-how in its proper place. And I climbed back and went on, warming to the excitement of what was to come.

And now the trees took over. After another twenty miles, the evergreens came in thick and fast. Even a pine looked like a new invention seen in its inkiness against a flaming maple. Now I was surrounded by two other properties that make the New England fall unique. First and above all the maple, with its bursting sugar, which blazes into scarlet. And then the oaks. An Englishman is surprised to wonder about many slender trees and hear them called oaks. The fat old oak tree of England, with his legs planted solidly on lush damp ground, is a rare sight. But New England has a teeming variety of oaks, and their value as a spectacle is that in the fall they entirely revise your ideas about the infinite fine range of color between gold and lemon. And beside this perpetual shower of scarlet and lemon and gold, the white birches slid by like slivers of mercury. And rising from the foam of every valley, slim as thermometers, were the white spires of Colonial churches, keeping count of the general fever. I had hit the peak, and the state of our language being what it is, in my hands at least, there is no more point in going on about it in prose. Some great composer might convey the majesty of it. Only a child in ecstasy could hit off the youth and hilarity of it. For children are natural impressionists, taking the adjectives of music and knifing them close to the nouns of sight and touch. Every child knows that color sings and trees walk. But puberty is the end. They acquire the logic that is death to the spirit and life to what is called maturity, and like the rest of us repress the wild energy of their instinctive knowledge. And so we can only guess at the form of art in which perhaps some hundreds of years from now the New England fall will come to be represented. I would take a bet that, by our present resources, Cézanne and Handel together might give a fair account of it. For the present I can only tell you that the fall is wonderful in life and awful in painting.

In this setting you can find an American life, proud but not prosperous, that also seems doomed to die in the industrial democracy that surrounds it. Don't imagine that the small village I am taking you into, in the south of Vermont, is typical of New England today. It is typical of nowhere else, but New England is many things besides small memorials to the declining eighteenth century. The New England puritan of English stock has not been the typical New Englander for two generations. Sixty per cent of the people in the six states of New England have at least one parent foreign-born, against only five per cent in the Southern states. Today the Connecticut Yankee has only one chance in three of being, like the first settlers, a Protestant with an English name. It's two to one that he's an Italian or a Pole, and a wise newspaper editor once warned me to take for granted that any stranger I met on the streets of New England was a Catholic. To make certain that what I am going to talk about, though once radical and typical in New England, is now conservative and odd, I should also warn you that the typical Yankee is no longer a farmer. In 1790, ninety-seven New Englanders in every hundred lived on the land, and three in towns. In 1870, it was still only twenty-one townsfolk against seventy-nine countrymen. Today in the United States, fifty-six per cent of the people live in cities. In New England, seventy-seven per cent of the entire population lives in cities, only twenty-three per cent in the country. So New England is the most industrialized of all American regions. If this shocks you, it would shock most Americans more, for they stubbornly think back to New England as the source and replenisher of all their canniest and most down-to-earth virtues.

Bearing in mind, then, that we are looking at a tiny green spot in the upper right-hand corner of the turbulent industrial landscape of the Northeastern states, let's take a look at the sort of place that bred New England. It is a small valley six miles long and two miles wide. You might say that it was bounded by mountains, but to a Westerner this would be low, well-wooded hills, for those that enclose this valley are no higher than fifteen hundred feet. Yet the valley is more fertile than most places in Vermont, with grass for summer pasture and winter hay. It grows corn and perhaps a crop of oats. And the farmer's cash in the bank comes from the one cow a year he sells. To a stranger it would look like good sheep country, and so it would be if there weren't out West the vast hills of Montana and Wyoming and Colorado to make it hardly worth while for a Vermonter to breed them. Then, there's so much rock and boulder in the hills of Vermont that by now the oldest Vermont joke tells how the sheep have their noses sharpened so they can get at the grass. (God anticipated the plight of Vermont by making sheep with cleft lips.)

If you were to motor along this valley, and your car had some sort of trouble, a quiet hard-bitten Vermonter would in time—his time—appear and tinker awhile and in the end put it right. He wouldn't say a word. And you'd have to be an outlander to try and pay him in any way. For Vermonters, settled long ago on a poor soil, and used to winters that hold more snow than the Arctic, don't expect a smiling face from Nature and don't reflect it in themselves. An Englishman coming here and going straight to Vermont and expecting to meet casual, back-slapping people would be in for a ghastly surprise. A man is a stranger there up to the third and fourth generation. And the only reliable way they have of placing a face or a name is to ask who his mother was. (His father simply served his mother's turn.) It's been said that Vermonters look on life as a necessary struggle against evil, a struggle you must make and expect to lose. It's also the only state in the United States where you will hear the word "thrift" used all the time. They never throw anything away. In a little booklet about this valley I am talking about, written by a couple of natives, you will read this sentence: "The people are friendly and always willing to help a neighbor. This means more to us who live here than material wealth, which none of us possess." To walk into the center of this village of Newfane, you would never believe it. It is a handsome common with a couple of shops, an inn, and a quite magnificent courthouse. The town was settled in 1776, but the county courthouse didn't go up until fifty years later, and we can be thankful for that. For in the interval Americans conceived a passion for everything Greek. Believing that they had just successfully established the first genuine democracy since the Greeks and the grandest republic since Rome, they took to naming their towns with classical names. Hence Philadelphia, Annapolis, Laconia, Athens, Sparta, Seneca, Cicero, Troy. Thomas Jefferson built a home with a columned portico. And soon country courts, and inns, and farmhouses were doing the same. It may sound like a dubious fad, but Americans stuck to their preference for wooden houses, and today New England is glorified with hundreds of churches, houses, courthouses, the wood painted white, with pillared porticos and graceful spires. In this small village in Vermont, the county courthouse is an exquisite symbol of what Americans did in wood with Greek forms.

Opposite the courthouse is the inn, which is also the jail. Newfane has kept up its habit of feeding its prisoners from the inn, and since the inn serves the best food around here, it's sometimes hard to get the inmates out of jail. Theodore Roosevelt said he would like to retire here, commit some "mild crime," and eat his way through a cheerful old age.

If you went along the valley you would be walking without knowing it through another town called Brookline, for Brookline is simply the scattered houses of the valley. It has less than a hundred people, mostly farmers, and they are their own rulers. Its first town meeting was held in 1795 and the last

Marina City apartments, Chicago.

one was held last week. The names at the first meeting are still there: Moore and Waters, and Ebenezer Wellman and Cyrus Whitcomb, and Christopher Osgood (there has always been a Christopher on the Osgood farm). Walking along the road you might run into the tractor of a Mr. Hoyt. He is to all intents a farmer. And so he is. He is also the road commissioner of the valley. His wife, Minnie Hoyt, is the town clerk, a justice of the peace, and when she isn't doing the farming chores she's busy signing fishing licenses, or marrying a visiting couple, or telling the comfortable city-people who have made a summer home here that by decision made at the last town meeting their taxes will be twice as much next year. What is striking to an Englishman here is that the few fairly well-to-do people are all what they call "summer folks," people who made a farm over as a summer retreat from New York or Boston. But the summer folks are strangers and underlings. The valley has heard many delicate sounds through the years. But it has never heard the advice of a squire or the accent of *noblesse oblige*. The farmers are ruled and rulers. The wealthy stranger goes cap in hand and pays his rates according to Minnie Hoyt and does what Mr. Hoyt says to keep his part of the highway safe and sound.

Our pilgrimage ends with an odd little building, a round schoolhouse. It was put up in the 1820's and is shaped like a silo, just one room with five windows equally spaced in a circle around it. It was so built, they say, because at that time the valley lived in fear of a highwayman called Thunderbolt, whom no one had ever seen. The schoolmaster, a Scot from Muirkirk, one Dr. Wilson, had his desk facing the door and could see through all the windows the first approach of any robber, or of the dreaded Thunderbolt. Thunderbolt's presence seems to have haunted the valley for a couple of decades, but one gets a reassuring picture of Yankee vigilance in the dour figure of Dr. Wilson, spelling out his lessons to the valley children and in the twilight letting his fingers play on the barrel of his shotgun as his protective eye rolled around the five windows.

I leave you with this comforting image of the rude forefathers of today's New Englanders. Having led you so far into a mystery, though, it occurs to me you may wonder if they ever caught Thunderbolt. Yes, they did.

When the good Dr. Wilson died they took off the high scarf he always wore and on his neck they saw scars and the marks of chains. Sure enough, HE was Thunderbolt.

JOHN STEINBECK

from TRAVELS WITH CHARLEY IN SEARCH OF AMERICA

AMERICA'S latest Nobel laureate here honors two of the glorious fifty, Montana and Texas.

THE NEXT PASSAGE in my journey is a love affair. I am in love with Montana. For other states I have admiration, respect, recognition, even some affection, but with Montana it is love, and it's difficult to analyze love when you're in it. Once, when I raptured in a violet glow given off by the Queen of the World, my father asked me why and I thought he was crazy not to see. Of course I know now she was a mouse-haired, freckle-nosed, scabby-kneed little girl with a voice like a bat and the loving kindness of a gila monster, but then she lighted up the landscape and me. It seems to me that Montana is a great splash of grandeur. The scale is huge but not overpowering. The land is rich with grass and color, and the mountains are the kind I would create if mountains were

ever put on my agenda. Montana seems to me to be what a small boy would think Texas is like from hearing Texans. Here for the first time I heard a definite regional accent unaffected by TV-ese, a slow-paced warm speech. It seemed to me that the frantic bustle of America was not in Montana. Its people did not seem afraid of shadows in a John Birch Society sense. The calm of the mountains and the rolling grasslands had got into the inhabitants. It was hunting season when I drove through the state. The men I talked to seemed to me not moved to a riot of seasonal slaughter but simply to be going out to kill edible meat. Again my attitude may be informed by love, but it seemed to me that the towns were places to live in rather than nervous hives. People had time to pause in their occupations to undertake the passing art of neighborliness.

I found I did not rush through the towns to get them over with. I even found things I had to buy to make myself linger. In Billings I bought a hat, in Livingston a jacket, in Butte a rifle I didn't particularly need, a Remington bolt-action 222, second-hand but in beautiful condition. Then I found a telescope sight I had to have, and waited while it was mounted on the rifle, and in the process got to know everyone in the shop and any customers who entered. With the gun in a vise and the bolt out, we zeroed the new sight on a chimney three blocks away, and later when I got to shooting the little gun I found no reason to change it. I spent a good part of a morning at this, mostly because I wanted to stay. But I see that, as usual, love is inarticulate. Montana has a spell on me. It is grandeur and warmth. If Montana had a seacoast, or if I could live away from the sea, I would instantly move there and petition for admission. Of all the states it is my favorite and my love.

At Custer we made a side trip south to pay our respects to General Custer and Sitting Bull on the battlefield of Little Big Horn. I don't suppose there is an American who doesn't carry Remington's painting of the last defense of the center column of the 7th Cavalry in his head. I removed my hat in memory of brave men, and Charley saluted in his own manner but I thought with great respect.

The whole of eastern Montana and the western Dakotas is memory-marked as Injun country, and the memories are not very old either. Some years ago my neighbor was Charles Erskine Scott Wood, who wrote *Heavenly Discourse*. He was a very old man when I knew him, but as a young lieutenant just out of military academy he had been assigned to General Miles and he served in the Chief Joseph campaign. His memory of it was very clear and very sad. He said it was one of the most gallant retreats in all history. Chief Joseph and the Nez Percés with squaws and children, dogs, and all their possessions, retreated under heavy fire for over a thousand miles, trying to escape to Canada. Wood said they fought every step of the way against odds until finally they were surrounded by the cavalry under General Miles and the large part of them wiped out. It was the saddest duty he had ever performed, Wood said, and he had never lost his respect for the fighting qualities of the Nez Percés. "If they hadn't had their families with them we could never have caught them," he said. "And if we had been evenly matched in men and weapons, we couldn't have beaten them. They were men," he said, "real men."

*   *   *

I do not intend to dwell long on Texas. Since the death of Hollywood the Lone Star State has taken its place at the top for being interviewed, inspected, and discussed. But no account of Texas would be complete without a Texas orgy, showing men of great wealth squandering their millions on tasteless and impassioned exhibitionism. My wife had come from New York to join me, and we were invited to a Texas ranch for Thanksgiving. It is owned by a friend who sometimes comes to New York, where we give him an orgy. I shall not name him, following the tradition of letting the reader guess. I presume that he is rich, although I have never asked him about it. As invited, we arrived at the ranch on the afternoon before the Thanksgiving orgy. It is a beautiful ranch, rich in water and trees and grazing land. Everywhere bulldozers had pushed up earth dams to hold back the water, making a series of life-giving lakes down the center of the ranch. On well-grassed flats the blooded Herefords grazed, only looking up as we drove by in a cloud of dust. I don't know how big the ranch is. I didn't ask my host.

The house, a one-story brick structure, stood in a grove of cottonwoods on a little eminence over a pool made by a dammed-up spring. The dark surface of the water was disturbed by trout that had been planted there. The house was comfortable, had three bedrooms, each room with a bath—both tub and shower. The living room, paneled in stained pine, served as a dining room, with a fireplace at one end and a glass-fronted gun case against the side. Through the open kitchen door the staff could be seen—a large dark lady and a giggleful girl. Our host met us and helped carry our bags in.

The orgy began at once. We had a bath and on emerging were given scotch and soda, which we drank thirstily. After that we inspected the barn across the way, the kennels in which there were three pointers, one of them not feeling so well. Then to the corral, where the daughter of the house was working on the training of a quarter horse, an animal of parts named Specklebottom. After that we inspected two new dams with water building slowly behind them, and at several drinking stations communed with a small herd of recently purchased cattle. This violence exhausted us and we went back to the house for a short nap.

We awakened from this to find neighboring friends arriving; they brought a large pot of chili con carne, made from a family recipe, the best I have ever tasted. Now other rich people began to arrive, concealing their status in blue jeans and riding boots. Drinks were passed and a gay conversation ensued having to do with hunting, riding, and cattle-breeding, with many bursts of laughter. I reclined on a window seat and in the gathering dusk watched the wild turkeys come in to roost in the cottonwood trees. They fly up clumsily and distribute themselves and then suddenly they blend with the tree and disappear. At least thirty of them came in to roost.

As the darkness came the window became a mirror in which I could watch my host and his guests without their knowledge. They sat about the little paneled room, some in rocking chairs and three of the ladies on a couch. And the subtlety of their ostentation drew my attention. One of the ladies was making a sweater while another worked a puzzle, tapping her teeth with the eraser of a yellow pencil. The men talked casually of grass and water, and So-and-So who had bought a new champion bull in England and flown it home. They were dressed in jeans of that light blue, lighter and a little frayed at the seams, that can be achieved only by a hundred washings.

But the studied detail did not stop there. Boots were scuffed on the inside and salted with horse sweat, and the heels run over. The open collars of the men's shirts showed dark red lines of sunburn on their throats, and one guest had gone to the trouble and expense of breaking his forefinger, which was splinted and covered with laced leather cut from a glove. My host went to the extreme of serving his guests from a bar which consisted of a tub of ice, quart bottles of soda, two bottles of whisky and a case of pop.

The smell of money was everywhere. The daughter of the house, for example, sat on the floor cleaning a .22 rifle, telling a sophisticated and ribald story of how Specklebottom, her stallion, had leaped a five-bar corral gate and visited a mare in the next county. She thought she had property rights in the foal, Specklebottom's blood line being what it was. The scene verified what we have all heard about fabulous Texas millionaires.

I was reminded of a time in Pacific Grove when I was painting the inside of a cottage my father had built there before I was born. My hired helper worked beside me, and neither of us being expert we were well splattered. Suddenly we found ourselves out of paint. I said, "Neal, run up to Holman's and get a half-gallon of paint and a quart of thinner."

"I'll have to clean up and change my clothes," he said.

"Nuts! Go as you are."

"I can't do it."

"Why not? I would."

Then he said a wise and memorable thing. "You got to be awful rich to dress as bad as you do," he said.

And this isn't funny. It's true. And it was true at the orgy. How unthinkably rich these Texans must be to live as simply as they were.

I took a walk with my wife, around the trout pool and over against the hill. The air was chill and the wind blowing from the north had winter in it. We listened for frogs, but they had shacked up for the winter. But we heard a coyote howl upwind and we heard a cow bawling for her late weaned bairn. The pointers came to the wire mesh of the kennel, wriggling like happy snakes and sneezing with enthusiasm, and even the sickly one came out of his house and fleered at us. Then we stood in the high entrance of the great barn and smelled at the sweetness of alfalfa and the bready odor of rolled barley. At the corral the stock horses snorted at us and rubbed their heads against the bars, and Specklebottom took a kick at a gelded friend just to keep in practice. Owls were flying this night, shrieking to start their prey, and a nighthawk made soft rhythmic whoops in the distance. I wished that Able Baker Charley Dog could have been with us. He would have admired this night. But he was resting under sedatives in Amarillo curing his prostatitis. The sharp north wind clashed the naked branches of the cottonwoods. It seemed to me that winter, which had been on my tail during the whole trip, had finally caught up with me. Somewhere in our, or at least my, recent zoologic past, hibernation must have been a fact of being. Else why does cold night air make me so sleepy? It does and it did, and we went in to the house where the ghosts had already retired and we went to bed.

I awakened early. I had seen two trout rods leaning against the screen outside our room. I went down the grassed hill, slipping in the frost to the edge of the dark pool. A fly was ready fastened on the line, a black gnat, a little frayed but still hairy enough. As it touched the surface of the pool the water boiled and churned. I brought in a ten-inch rainbow trout and skidded him up on the grass and knocked him on the head. I cast four times and had four trout. I cleaned them and threw the innards to their friends.

In the kitchen the cook gave me coffee and I sat in an alcove while she dipped my fish in corn meal and fried them crisp in bacon fat and served them to me under a coverlet of bacon that crumbled in my mouth. It was a long time since I had eaten trout like that, five minutes from water to pan. You take him in your fingers delicately by head and tail and nibble him from off his backbone, and finally you eat the tail, crisp as a potato chip. Coffee has a special taste for a frosty morning, and the third cup is as good as the first. I would have lingered in the kitchen discussing nothing with the staff, but she cleared me out because she had to stuff two turkeys for the Thanksgiving orgy.

The French Quarter, New Orleans.

In the mid-morning sunshine we went quail-hunting, I with my old and shiny 12-bore with the dented barrel, which I carried in Rocinante. That gun was no great shakes when I bought it second-hand fifteen years ago, and it has never got any better. But I suppose it is as good as I am. If I can hit them the gun will pull them down. But before we started I looked with a certain longing through the glass door at a Luigi Franchi 12-gauge double with a Purdy lock so beautiful that I was filled with covetousness. The carving on the steel had the pearly gleam of a Damascus blade, while the stock flowed into lock and lock into barrels as though they had grown that way from a magic planted seed. I'm sure that if my host had seen my envy he would have loaned me the beauty, but I didn't ask. Suppose I tripped and fell, or dropped it, or knocked its lovely tubes against a rock? No, it would be like carrying the crown jewels through a mine field. My old beat-up gun is no bargain, but at least anything that could happen to it has, and there's no worrying.

For a week our host had noted where the coveys were gathering. We spread out and moved through brush and thicket, down into water, out, and up, while the spring-steel pointers worked ahead of us and a fat old bitch pointer named Duchess with flame in her eyes outworked them all, and us too. We found quail tracks in the dust, quail tracks in the sand and mud of stream beds, bits of quail-feather fluff in the dry tips of the sage. We walked for miles, slowly, guns up and ready to throw shot at a drumming flight. And we never saw a quail. The dogs never saw or smelled a quail. We told stories and some lies about previous quail hunts, but it did no good. The quail had gone, really gone. I am only a reasonable quail shot but the men with me were excellent, the dogs were professional, keen, hard, and hard-working. No quail. But there's one nice thing about hunting. Even with no birds, you'd rather go than not.

My host thought my heart was breaking. He said, "Look. You take that little 222 of yours this afternoon and shoot yourself a wild turkey."

"How many are there?" I asked.

"Well, two years ago I planted thirty. I think there are about eighty now."

"I counted thirty in the band that flew up near the house last night."

"There's two other bands," he said.

I really didn't want a turkey. What would I do with it in Rocinante? I said, "Wait a year. When they top a hundred birds, I'll come down and hunt with you."

We came back to the house and showered and shaved, and because it was Thanksgiving we put on white shirts and jackets and ties. The orgy came off on schedule at two o'clock. I'll skip through the details quickly in order not to shock the readers, and also I see no reason to hold these people up to scorn. After two good drinks of whisky, the two brown and glazed turkeys were brought in, carved by our host and served by us. We said grace and afterward drank a toast all around and ate ourselves into a proper insensibility. Then, like decadent Romans at Petronius's board, we took a walk and retired for the necessary and inevitable nap. And that was my Thanksgiving orgy in Texas.

Of course I don't think they do it every day. They couldn't. And somewhat the same thing happens when they visit us in New York. Of course they want to see shows and go to night clubs. And at the end of a few days of this they say, "We just don't see how you can live like this." To which we reply, "We don't. And when you go home, we won't."

And now I feel better for having exposed to the light of scrutiny the decadent practices of the rich Texans I know. But I don't for one moment think they eat chili con carne or roast turkey every day.

DAN JACOBSON

from No Further West

A WRITER *from South Africa introduces his observations of California, drawn from a year's residence there (circa 1957), with the following apology:*

"If I had not been heartened and exhilarated by what I saw in California, I would not have written

about it—the effort would have been too great and the result would have been too dispiriting. I am aware that the first part of the book—in which I record so many things that distressed me—may appear to have a direct and concrete quality absent from some of the later and perhaps more encouraging chapters.

But I can only say that ideas discussed in the latter half of the book did not come to me as abstractions— they were as much, for me, to be felt and encountered in personal terms as anything else in California, entering fully into the texture and immediacy of the life that was lived around me. If this had not been so, I could not have dealt with these ideas at all, for I can certainly make no claim to specialist knowledge of any aspect of American life or history. My account is throughout that of an interested visitor, and no more."

WHY HADN'T anyone *told* me? That was the question I asked of myself in awe, in fear, in anger, in despair. What I saw was all new, brand-new, and of a size and a populousness and a busyness that I couldn't begin to comprehend. Why hadn't anyone told me about it? Why hadn't I been warned?

And I asked this question though what we saw of Palo Alto by daylight on our first morning there confirmed my first impression that the town was very similar to the small towns I had known in South Africa. There was the same sense of space, newness, and sandiness; there were the same wide tarred streets, empty in the sun; there were the same lawns of grass shrivelling at the edges; the leaves of familiar trees hung down spiritlessly in front of houses that were often of a style I had known in South Africa; there was a main street, with its shop windows and department stores stretching away from the pavements, and few people about.

But the difficulty was that this main street wasn't main at all, and the town wasn't a small one, if it existed at all; and of that I wasn't sure. What I saw in the days following our arrival seemed to be a single sprawl that stretched all the thirty miles between San Francisco and Palo Alto and for another thirty miles beyond; and what it was anywhere along the length was precisely what it was anywhere else along its length. And what *that* was—I had no word for it. It was a sprawl, a mess, a nightmare of repetition and disjunction and incoherence, all grown permanent and powerful.

There were shops, identical houses in tracts, drive-ins, motels, factories, shopping centres, supermarkets, giant billboards, filling-stations, used-car lots all along El Camino Real. There were identical houses in tracts, drive-ins, motels, shopping-centres, supermarkets, giant billboards all along the Bayshore Highway; there were whole towns of identical houses in tracts between the Bayshore Highway and El Camino Real; and further again, and further yet, there were used-car lots and giant billboards and shopping centres and supermarkets . . .

And all the buildings sprawled wide, drunkenly, sharing no style, no size, having no relation to one another but that imposed on them by the single thing they did share: a frontage of the road, a view of the traffic, a gaze across to the other side of the road where there were other motels, drive-ins, gas-stations and other names—The Crown, Crazy Jack's, Ole Olsen's, Top-T Service, and a supermarket spaciously spelling out its name with a single letter in each of its stucco arches. They were all spread away from one another, pushed apart physically. Every car of the thousands that rushed at all times and along all the length of the roads had to have a place for it when it swung off the road and stopped. So, sprawling enough in themselves, the places spread their grounds wider still, in hope that one car or a hundred would stop in this drive-in rather than the fifty others over the last few miles, this supermarket rather than the last. Perhaps the car would stop because in front of this supermarket someone had taken the trouble to advertise—in black letters six inches high against a white illuminated background—*Celery: 10 Cents a Stalk*. How could anyone go to so much trouble to sell stalks of celery, one wondered; but one wondered about nothing very long on that road, because next there was a car mounted on a platform twenty feet high, and slowly the whole platform turned round, bearing the car on its palm. Below it, and stretching away from it was a used-car lot, and another, all decorated with streamers and bunting and strings of plastic whirligigs, as if royalty were soon to pass by, to inspect the acres upon acres of used cars, glittering in their lots on the sand. Then a service-station, or two, or three, a motel with all its Swiss-styled gabled little chalets in a row along the road, a second-hand furniture mart, a liquor store, more used-car lots. It was impossible to tell which of all the cars in rows belonged to one lot and which to another, for there were no fences between them; but there were names on poles, names on billboards, names as high as the little wooden offices that bore them, and each name was different from the last—unless it was a name that had been seen before, fifty times before, in front of other lots, on other hoardings, further back along the road.

The used-car lots covered their spaces, they stretched down the road, and then beyond them there rose the grandeur of a new shopping centre. This one looked something like the Palais de Chaillot in Paris. It was white, it gleamed, it flung its arms open as if to embrace not a terraced garden but a plain of parked cars as wide as that first one we saw in front of the airport. These shopping centres were things that we had never seen before—places that under a single sprawling roof housed enough shops to supply the wants of a town. That one was like the Palais de Chaillot; the next was quaint, rural, timbered, with flagged walks, low buildings with overhanging eaves, at every corner a loudspeaker playing soft music. In this shopping centre there was a shop that sold only electronically-operated garage doors; but otherwise there was nothing in it that was not repeated shabbily or elegantly by some single shop belonging to the sprawl directly and not through the *imperium in imperio* of the shopping centre. They both contributed to the sprawl, and who could say which contribution was the greater—that of the shopping centre, with all its elegant arcades and galleries, or of this shabby drive-in shaped like a Mexican hat, with its brim over the place where cars were parked?

But what did shabby mean here, and what did elegant mean? Here was a shack of shingles and nails all smeared and disfigured with the great letters that give it its name—but within there was wall-to-wall carpeting, marble-topped desks, mobiles hanging from the ceilings, and sheer glass partitions; there was a neon sign blazing away so fiercely that it almost hid the little barn behind it where food was served. And the cars in the used-car lots, were they shabby or are they elegant? And that hospital for dogs, where on the roof a neon dog wagged its long neon tail?

But it was gone too, behind us, in a moment, for one always travelled by car down the roads, one never walked.

Those highways were able along their length to provide you with any material thing you might ever need. There were all the shops of various kinds: there were banks, travel-agencies, money-lenders, real-estate agents who would sell you a house, and furniture stores that would sell you the furniture to fill it with. There were bookstores and shops selling the latest selection of records, and little establishments that offered tropical fish in bowls, and imported Danish cutlery. There were the shops and the facilities for whole cities of prosperous people; but the curious, the frightening thing was that all the shops and facilities belonged only to the highways and to no city.

Nowhere along their length did the highways seem to contract, confine themselves, centre themselves for a community around them. There were no parks along the highways, no statues, no plaques commemorating notable events; there were no vistas, no views, no streets that radiated from this point or that; there was nowhere that one could turn and look back the way one had come. The highways ran with all their businesses and townships from San Francisco to Palo Alto and beyond, simply ploughing across the country; and it was as if some kind of

vital tendon had been severed, so that they could grasp nothing to themselves, could enclose nothing in themselves, could make no order of themselves, but could only lie sprawling, incoherent, centreless, viewless, shapeless, faceless—offering all the products a community might need and yet making the establishment of a community impossible.

For it was by the roads and from the roads that the towns like ours seemed to live. Every morning half of the male inhabitants of the towns seemed to get into their cars and go thundering along the highways to San Francisco or elsewhere, and every evening they thundered back again. The women drove along the highways to do their shopping; the very air of the towns was filled night and day with the whisper of the traffic on the highways. As our town seemed to be, so seemed all the others—flat, indistinguishable appendages to the highways, equal parts of a brand-new nameless sprawl across a country.

* * *

There was nothing in San Francisco that so became it as the ways along which one could approach or leave it. The first half of the Bay Bridge, before it dives through Treasure Island and re-emerges in a less graceful form on the other side—the first half of the Bay Bridge is one of the most superb human structures I have ever seen, or hope to see. It stands so high, it is so huge and grey, with all its steel and concrete and its wide and ever-busy lanes of traffic on two decks, like a whole city; and yet it travels so easily, with arcs suspending it so lightly as they rise to the towers and sink away, only to rise again. Golden Gate Bridge too had the same strength and lightness, the same purposefulness and ease; but it is the Bay Bridge that I most remember, perhaps because I had not been warned about it and it came as such a surprise.

And on the other side of Bay Bridge one came to a place where roads swooped up to the bridge and spiralled down from it, where the roads were woven over and under the bridge and each other—and all in the air!—as if there were nothing to marvel at that so many roads of such sizes should be up in the air. There were places like this on both sides of the bridge and again a little further out of San Francisco. To me they were a wonder every time I saw them; and I still don't understand why no one talks more of these astonishing structures. And structures like them stand outside every big American city.

Or one could leave San Francisco on the far side of the Golden Gate, and fall among bare hills of grass, the city behind one assuming some dignity and order the further one got from it, each of the thousand tall

SAN FRANCISCO'S GOLDEN GATE BRIDGE.

shoulders of concrete cut clean against the air. Or one could sail under the Bay Bridge, seeing from below how it hung in the air; as the boat moved the glittering towers of the city seemed to move too, crowding closer and closer together, until in the distance they seemed all to have been struck from a single rock.

And southwards one could drive along the saddle of the Santa Cruz mountains, with reservoirs for the city in the valleys below, and green forests of pine and firs and coast redwoods standing upright against the slopes from which they grew, and glimpses of brown-grassed hills further off. Coming down on the east there was the brown plain of the Bay Area laid out flat below, with the dots and cubes of houses shining in glints against the paleness of the earth and the grey haze of the Bay Area smog. Westwards the mountains dropped down to the Pacific, the hills undulating towards the sea; every hill broken only by the sallow flattened humps of the liveoak trees.

On the foothills of the mountains were the houses of the rich, within easy reach of the suburban towns and the highways, yet set comfortably back from them. They were modern enough, these houses, many of them of bold and elaborate architecture, with split-levels and patios and carports and light timber beams exposed and flagged verandas outside glass doors that remained open through all the summer days and evenings. Yet somehow they did not seem attractive to live in, and I am still a little puzzled to know why; I think I would have preferred a house in one of the suburban towns, if I had to live in California permanently, rather than those houses perched on the hill-tops or set against the flanks of the mountains.

In the towns, I suppose, one was able pretty much to forget about the seasons, about natural California altogether. This forgetfulness was helped by the fact that the seasons in California were not really noticeable: the sun shone most of the year, and while it was true that we had rain in the winter and none in the summer, there was no snow, no really bitter cold; when spring came the grass turned green and some of the trees put on a few more leaves, and that was all; in summer the grass turned brown. These movements were all small; there was none of the slow profound turning of the year that one has in other climates, and that penetrates the consciousness of even the most boxed-in city dweller in the blackest of cities. And then one's indifference to what lay beyond the highways and the drive-ins and the little wooden houses was encouraged too by the fact that so very often one could not see beyond them, anyway: hills and mountains and horizons were hidden often by the smog that came creeping down the Bay Area, walling

it in, concentrating the light upon what glittered and flickered near to hand. So sunk in the jumble, one was not reminded of the failure of the Californians to come to terms with the country that surrounded them. When the fog lifted, or when one was visiting one of these houses in the foothills, the reminder was always there.

It is difficult enough to talk about the relation of any people to the country that surrounds them; but in California the relationship which one felt seems even more difficult to describe than is usually the case. In South Africa, for instance, there is also a failure on the part of the country's inhabitants to come to terms with the country in which they live. The cities are dwarfed by the spaces and silences that surround them; in Cape Town, in Kimberley, even in Johannesburg, one has just to lift one's head to become aware so often of the thinness and tenuousness of the relationship that the bold buildings and the telegraph poles have to the naked and indifferent veld around them. South Africans have just scratched the surface of their country, which remains always beyond them, unassailable, uninterpretable, always bigger and dryer and more imposing than they are or what they do to it. There is pathos in the relationship, a sense of loss and powerlessness.

And England again, is quite different. The people seem to fit the country (what is left of the country, outside the cities) and the country the people, so that one can hardly tell what is natural and what man-made. Each at its best over the centuries has become the other, in a congruence, a harmony of field and house, road and hedge, wood and village, moor and harbour, that is a continual surprise and reassurance to the spirit.

But in both South Africa and England there is this relationship, to be perceived and described. In California, however, there seemed to be no congruence, as in England; nor was there defeat and powerlessness, as in South Africa; powerlessness is the last thing one would ascribe to the Californians. Their towns and their houses are simply thrust down, ignoring, making null and unnoticeable the country on which they are built; and the country, for its part, seems to have nothing to do with the towns and the houses that have been placed on it. There is an abruptness in the change from what is man-made and what is natural, an equality of powers that has produced merely a disjuncture and an indifference.

And this too is new: that men should have been powerful enough to do this, to seem to ignore in this way the land they settle in.

We left Palo Alto on one Sunday morning, and

turned the car southwards on the Bayshore High-way. The road was crowded with Sunday traffic: all the weekday trucks were there, and all the private cars carrying their families to visit other families, and cars towing speedboats behind them, and cars with leather-jacketed boys towing motor bikes in trailers behind them, and stripped and numbered hot-rod cars, all pelting along the main road between San Francisco and Los Angeles, as if all week no one had been able to move and everyone was now moving as fast and as far as he possibly could in the one day given to him. We followed Highway 101 some way be-yond San Jose, suburban town after town passing to the left and right; and then turned off into a side-road that was emptier, and that took us through the Pacheco Pass. On the other side of the Pass the hills were all green and silver, falling and rising in curves, covered only with the unstirring, silver-tipped grass that threw no shadow but lay in equal light every-where, under the sun—the softest light and the least harsh country we saw anywhere in California.

In the San Joaquin Valley the light was dulled by dust, and the earth neither lifted nor dropped, and the road ran straight into the east like an arm pointing: only the silver water-tanks of each dusty and be-draggled and shapeless little township of wooden houses rose above the level of the plain. The tanks gleamed in the confused light: but all other colours were yellow and whitish. The flat fields had been cut, and only a stubble was left. The miles passed without distinction, like the townships lost behind us, and all the fields and wire fences running to the horizon at right angles from the road.

Then sluggish and black ahead of us we saw a main highway, with the traffic moving ant-like on it, and we came to the highway, and turned among the traffic, which once we were close to it was a continual roar and an intermittent thud and a flashing of the sun-light against metal and glass. Sadder and dirtier and more haphazard than on the roads near Palo Alto were all the drive-ins and filling-stations and motels, and shadeless too, no trees anywhere near the wide expanse of the highway or the jumbled occasional buildings alongside it or the fields that stretched away from it. Like a cataract moving in both direc-tions the road poured through a place called Madera, but we stopped there for petrol, and as we stretched our legs we were able to feel the continual nerve-like shudder of the earth beneath our feet, as the traffic passed on the road.

And Madera has remained in the mind as the type of all those inland towns we passed through on our way to Yosemite and our way back again: a place without shade, laid down square in a grid that loses its shape on either side, where hot little cool-drink and hamburger stands and the motels string themselves out along the highway. Its central shopping area was a muck of buildings, of neon signs thrust close against one another and flickering against the fierce daylight —neither paint nor neon hiding anything of the clap-board shabbiness of the place, but only showing it up more crudely still. The sun blistered everything it touched, and there was nothing that it did not touch; there was nowhere to hide from it in Madera, or from the highway which drove wide through the town, with a noise like thunder and shaking of the earth, and swept on again, with all its width of tar and traffic. The forlornness of this place had nothing in common with the South African forlornness which I had known before: there was too much movement; too many people; too much metal, too much power to be forlorn in the South African way. Almost one might say that Madera was forlorn with an excess of power, were it not for the poverty and shabbiness of its frame buildings, and the harshness of the country around it.

And as Madera was, so was Modesto, and Los Banos and so too were many of the places whose names we never learned but saw briefly from a car or train in the United States—places of a barrenness and a harsh-ness and an ugliness that was like an act of violence, an explosion of anger, a blow with a clenched fist, a pistol shot. The sense of violence done was inescap-able: each place looked as though it had been flung down so hard that it cracked, and what was spattered furthest lay in the fragments of orange-juice stands and motel signs on the outskirts. Brutally, these places had nothing that was not for use: all that they were was exposed at a glance; they were without seclusion, without secrecy.

And indeed, one cannot come to the United States and travel about within it without developing a sense of violence having been done, and still being done, and even more dangerously impending. It is there in the dark, busy cities, with all their tall buildings and streets between; it is there on the roads that are built to carry the cars that rush like things gone amok; it is there in the raw and distant towns flung down like Madera for the selling of petrol, the canning of peas, the milling of lucerne, the housing of those who transact this business. Always, there is this sense of violence when one looks at the places that the people have put their hands to; towns so harsh and neon-lit and unpitied, so new, so restless with traffic and people who have the air always of having come from elsewhere. And one expects these people to be as harsh and unpitying as their cities and roads and towns; and there is, indeed, more violence in the United States than in a country like England; there are more murders, rapes, riots, lynchings, more sudden, savage and unpredictable outbreaks of rage and fear and frustration.

But when one sees a place like Modesto or Madera, the wonder is only that there is not more yet; and when one considers that most of these people do in fact come from elsewhere, and are new to their country, and that their loudest guides to conduct seem to be the advertisers and the radio and the television and the tabloid press, the wonder is that they aren't all continuously and desperately at war with one another, that there is so little frenzy, so few stabbings and acts of arson and bombing, that over a continent of towns like Modesto and even worse cities, there should be so much peace, so much gentleness.

We left the highway at Madera, and turned again into a side-road, that ran level for some time, and then started lifting, always lifting, to the mountains whose white peaks we could see far ahead of us. The grass gave way to wood, and liveoaks and cottonwood gave way to conifers, and soon we were driving through pine forests, every tree upright, straight-trunked, like a jet thrown up. And so the mountains went on, still higher, and now among all the darkness of tree trunks and the bristling of the pine needles, there lay white patches of snow disregarded on the ground. The peaks we had seen earlier no longer seemed to hang disconnected; but we could see the pine-covered slopes sweeping up towards each one and tumbling down from it, rock and pine and snow, each at rest where it stood, and all part of the wild upward surge.

We stopped at a place where there were two motels and a store and a creek that the road passed over on a bridge. The buildings were set on levels cut out of the slopes, where the trees had been felled, one slope ascending in shadow, the other in sunlight. But the shadow came soon enough on them both. We were the only guests at the motel, which was very new and clean; I walked down later to the other motel, which was also new and clean and empty, and had a drink at the bar there. The proprietors of this motel were a pair of brothers—extraordinary-looking young men, so tall that they had to bend their heads when they entered their own doors, with long thin faces and large eyes and small twisted mouths and dark skins. They looked like something remote—Abyssinians, Khazaks, something like that—but one played the juke-box and imitated Elvis Presley; the other stood behind the bar and admired his brother's display of talent; and a fat little man in blue overalls—the only customer—said that he couldn't stand Elvis Presley's singing but he sure admired the —— —— —— for making so much money.

The next morning we entered the Yosemite National Park. We were right out of season, and most of the park was closed; but what was open to us was as big as several English counties, and we gladly exchanged the area we couldn't visit for the advantage of having the park so much to ourselves. We stayed at one of the lodges in the Yosemite Valley, and I remember that when I came out of our cabin the first morning, I looked up at the granite wall nearest to me—and I looked up, and up, and up, involuntarily, unconsciously, looking for the end, and not finding it until my head was strained far back. And then only did I see the rim of the cliff, thousands of feet above me. The valley was narrower than seemed possible to support the weight and height of the walls that towered up so closely on both sides. And it seemed too small also to take the flow of water that all day and all night, from twenty different points, fell from the cliffs in slender streams with such lightness and speed that it was almost frightening to see them, as if one feared the water could be hurt in its fall.

Beyond the granite walls were the Sierra Nevadas, white with snow, fanged with rock, slashed and cut by gorges and ravines and river-beds, crowned by peaks and the bold trees bristling. Spur and crest and ridge stood up across a waste of spurs and crests and ridges, with the high hidden valleys between; and what was not white was black—the trees, and the clefts in the rock, and the tiny birds that were the only things to be seen moving. Then we would go down to the valley again, away from the fierceness and desolation of the mountains to the archaic, impregnable shelter of granite, with its floor of grass.

But the shelter was not impregnable. A tribe of Indians had once lived in the Valley: the Yosemites they had called themselves, and they had been found by prospectors whose other finds had been marked with lying names like Coarsegold and El Dorado and Chinaman's Luck, on our way to Yosemite. As I remember the story, the Yosemite Indians had clashed with the prospectors, then with a team of Government surveyors, and then, and finally, with a detachment of the United States Army. That had been the end of the Yosemite Indians, who had been carted away to a reservation. Of them nothing remained but some photographs in the little museum near the lodge where we stayed, and a place called the Indian Camp, on the floor of the valley. Indian Camp was a few tumbled boulders and a few fissures in the granite wall, where a man could have hidden; the boulders were as big as rooms, and on the top of the flattest one of them a few holes had been scooped out of the rock. They were mortar holes, for grinding corn, pathetic little semi-artefacts filled now with dust and cigarette stubs.

The cars pulled up, their occupants climbed out, walked about among the boulders, peered doubtfully into the caves, had themselves photographed in front of the rock with the mortar-holes, and drove away again. Who would celebrate the dispossessed Yosemite Indians? What was there to celebrate? But who could celebrate the cars and the neat signposts pointing to the Indian Camp and the cameras that recorded the visit of each party? It was impossible not to feel guilt before the mortar-holes of these Yosemite Indians—guilt for their defeat, their failure, the smallness of all

they had managed to leave behind them. Amid towering scenery in the shelter of their valley these people had lived for who knew how long until they had been driven out: and what a small ruin they had left. No Athens, no Rome, no Jerusalem, not even a Zimbabwe had they managed to build; and it was their powerlessness and simplicity that made the guilt stronger, not less so.

Yet between those gigantic glacial walls, those who came in their cars to be photographed with their children in front of the boulders and then drive on again—they had their deep pathos too. And this made it harder to patronize the Yosemite Indians, who had tried their best, as these people were doing. There is no way out of the struggle, for any of us.

MIRIAM CHAPIN

from CONTEMPORARY CANADA

AN AMERICAN journalist surveys the vast land where she lived for more than thirty years.

THE CANADIAN SHIELD, the pre-cambrian rock that makes up two-thirds of the land surface, stretches down to Lake Superior and to the St. Lawrence River east of Lake Ontario. Together with the Rocky Mountains that separate the Prairies from the West Coast (far harder to cross than the American Rockies) and the Appalachian Highland that sets the Maritimes apart

LOOKOUT ON THE PACIFIC, NEAR LOS ANGELES.

from Quebec, these extensions of the Shield divide the narrow band of peopled Canada into five regions. They are the Atlantic Coast, the St. Lawrence Valley, the land north of Lake Ontario and Lake Erie, the Prairies, and the Far West. A thousand-mile block of rock and forests cuts off Ontario's tillable land from the Prairies; a five-hundred-mile wilderness of peaks and valleys encloses the Prairies to the West. Canada could easily have been—indeed, came close to being—four or five distinct colonies which never united.

In the past million years every inch of this surface, except a patch in the Yukon Valley, has four times been loaded down with ice, scraped, chewed by the moving masses, littered with debris when these ice fields slunk back, dripping boulders. Because of the glaciers Canada has more lakes than all the rest of the world together, many with no outlets. They freeze, melt, evaporate, and are replenished by rain and snow. Before the ice ages, dinosaurs floundered in the swamps of the West; in the long intervals between glacial times the little animals of the woods crept north, only to retreat again. Some time, no one is sure when, giant ferns grew inside the Arctic Circle, for there is coal in Ellesmere Land. We may now be coming out of a glacial period into a warm interlude, when the northern fields will produce and the long nights be mild the year round. But in our time five-sixths of Canada is harsh country, bare and unkind.

*   *   *

The Shield lies like a gigantic O around Hudson Bay, with a break for Hudson Straits. It encloses not only the Bay but wide stretches of swamp of a later vintage, left as the Bay shrunk. Most of it is a plateau a few hundred feet above sea level, rising into mountains in Labrador. The band varies in width from two hundred to a thousand miles. It reaches from the Mackenzie River Valley to the Atlantic Ocean, from the Arctic to Lake Superior, jutting into Minnesota and New York. On most of it only trees, bushes, and woods plants will grow, and in the north nothing but lichen; south of James Bay old lakes left clay belts that can be farmed. In nothern Ontario and Manitoba, and in middle Quebec, the Shield is lovely country of white birch and dark firs, of lakes, brooks and flowers, birds and ferns and deer, a land of innocence and freedom. It is one of the last reservoirs of out-door living, a re-creation place for weary folk; lonely, cleansing, wild.

*   *   *

Inhabited Canada stretches from St. John's in Newfoundland to Victoria on big Vancouver Island. Settlement began along the Atlantic Coast, where the sinking of the land makes every river mouth a harbor. The Gulf of St. Lawrence splits the seaboard in two, isolating Newfoundland. The Bay of Chaleurs separates Quebec's Gaspé Peninsula from New Brunswick, the Bay of Fundy lies between New Brunswick and Nova Scotia, and Prince Edward Island is cut off from the mainland of New Brunswick by nine-mile-wide Northumberland Strait. These small communities grew up apart, never joining to deal with their common problems. Even in the air age, the habit of rivalry persists. Yet they are not rivals, and they need to unite.

Newfoundland is ancient rock, with a few wisps of soil in river valleys and great forests in the north. Nova Scotia and New Brunswick form a rough basin, of which Fundy is the submerged bottom. On the outer edges the pre-cambrian rock sticks up in rugged hills. In Prince Edward Island and the Annapolis Valley the rotted old red sandstone grows fruit and potatoes bountifully. Gaspé is mountainous; since it is part of Quebec, its political and linguistic differences reinforce its separation from its neighbors. All this region resembles New England—with the same kind of safe harbors, rough land with pockets of good soil, and the disadvantages of distance from markets and lack of capital. Its troubles are aggravated by greater distances, poorer markets, less capital and colder weather.

North of the Gulf lies desolate Labrador, never fully explored. Quebec shares it with Newfoundland by the decree of a Privy Council in London on whose appointment Canada had no say. The boundary line runs through the iron deposits; in some places they are so close to the surface that a man can shovel up ore. The new towns plumped down by the big companies make tiny specks on the landscape; claims are haggled over and provincial governments bargain for royalties.

Four or five thousand Indians, Eskimos and white 'liveyeres' along the Labrador coast depend on the seal hunting and the cod fishing. The Grenfell Mission has saved many from death or crippling. The airport at Goose Bay, where Americans and Canadians live comfortably, with only air communication for eight months of the year, is a twentieth century world by itself. North of the inlet where it stands are vast forests of spruce and balsam, as yet untroubled by the insect parasites that devastate Quebec's and New Brunswick's woods. All this region looks to the harnessing of the tremendous Grand Falls on the Hamilton River, which the Rothschilds have undertaken to develop under contract with Newfoundland. With the light, heat and power such a plant can bring, Labrador may some day be a peopled land.

Newfoundland is cut off from the mainland by twelve miles of swift water, the chasm of Belle Isle

Straits. It probably was there before the ice ages, for the island's animal life differs oddly from the continent. It has no skunks, squirrels, woodchucks or wolves. Moose had to be imported from New Brunswick so they could be hunted. Nobody has yet imported skunks. Engineers talk of a causeway to dam the strait and keep icebergs out of the Gulf. The cost of a dam, and of a canal to let the liners pass, would be billions. Even so, the Gulf would still be cold, for far upstream a thick layer of ice-cold water lies two hundred feet down, where the sunlight never penetrates. As the wind drives surface water toward the Atlantic, the depths well up, so that the north shore is always chilled.

For three hundred years Newfoundland was little more than a fishing depot. What brought men there was the enormous plateau beneath the waves, a five-hundred-mile triangle pointing toward Morocco, built up in layers from glacial drift and ooze from the animal and vegetable life of the sea. The shallow water above it is full of plankton, the one-celled creatures that are the food of all sea beings. Squid and herring and mackerel live in the surface waters, haddock and flounder lower down, and the fat silvery codfish by the million swim below.

* * *

Of the four Atlantic provinces, only on Prince Edward Island does farming pay enough to keep the youth at home. Sheltered from fogs and the worst cold, it has neither mountains nor waste land. It overflows with pigs and fruit, lobsters and butter, cheese, beef, and, most of all, potatoes. Surpluses pile up, government payments roll in. Without minerals or water power, the Island's destiny may turn out to be the provisioning of the mining towns coming to life on the barren lands of Quebec and Labrador. Its greatest desire is for a causeway to hitch it to the mainland, over which trucks can carry its products to market.

* * *

All the main cities of these provinces are seaports— St. John's in Newfoundland, Halifax in Nova Scotia, Saint John in New Brunswick, and Charlottetown, the capital of Prince Edward Island and the place where the Dominion of Canada was born. All are beautiful in the way that old ports are, high above the blue water, with winding streets and old houses and the smell of the sea. Halifax and Saint John are Canada's winter ports and its railway terminals. Grain goes out, oil and rubber come in. When the Seaway is fully operating and the time comes, as it must, that the Seaway is kept open all winter, the Maritime cities are likely to be only local shipping points. When

European trade goes through to Toronto and Chicago the year round, Halifax and Saint John will have to develop their own industry or fade away.

In spite of the struggle its people have had to endure to live, Nova Scotia and, to a lesser extent, its neighbors have managed to foster the most interesting regional culture of English Canda. Theirs is a rather rigid class society, in which only those whose families have long been acquainted feel loyalty to each other and where kinship is as important as it is in Quebec. These clans look with some perplexity and no admiration at the social problems brought by coal and steel. To them poverty is an inconvenience but no disgrace. Men are expected to stay in the state and condition of their fathers. The members of this upper-class group are far from feeling any lack of appreciation for money and the ease it brings, but they prefer to have it by inheritance, not immediately from trade. However, a few generations could purify the bullion of Morgan the Pirate. This is a delightful and beloved society for those born in its upper reaches, but its bonds and standards give way under pressures from the farmers and wage-earners, who refuse to consider themselves doomed to poverty, and from the middle-class, who want more industry and more change.

In spite of the dependence on American trade and American tourists, and the close communication with New England, the Atlantic Provinces are to all appearance less affected by American influence than any other part of Canada. They stay British, they are loyally Canadian—except Newfoundland, which sometimes wonders why it ever joined—and they like their own way of life: quiet, unhurried, with time to enjoy the beauties of the sea and the wild back country.

* * *

The river system which made colonial Canada is still the thread on which eastern Canada is strung, from the Straits of Belle Isle to the cities on Lake Superior. The wide gullet on the St. Lawrence, the only open way into the mid-continent from the Atlantic, gave the French the chance to maintain their fur trade and their settlements, and so made certain the double nation Canada has become. The French made little use of the Great Lakes, for the hazards of storms and the long stretches of rapids above Montreal were discouraging. The St. Lawrence and Ottawa rivers were the main highway by which the *voyageurs* brought down their furs. Missions and fur-trading were not enough to hold and develop the French inland empire; the core of their domain was the valley below Montreal. The English were in full control of the interior long before the Lachine and Welland Canals opened it to the sternwheelers in the 1830's. In winter, Canadian trade went by way of Boston and New York, so the American ports grew and soon surpassed Montreal.

Though other continents have their great rivers, none leads to such inland seas as does the St. Lawrence; none offers inland cities such access to the oceans as Toronto and Chicago are now to have. The Amazon is a slowly moving flood, unsubdued to use of man. The Yangtse gives difficult access to the interior of China, but not to any great lake. Africa remained unknown for long partly because the Congo cataracts are so near the coast. The St. Lawrence greeted Europe's ships, led them a thousand miles in, and made it inevitable that Canada should be an extension of the Old World.

Quebec is Canada's largest province, the only one that possesses its own northland all the way to the Arctic. Because its rivers fall from the Shield on four sides, it has almost half Canada's potential water power. It is second only to Ontario in industrial production; it contains the largest city in Canada, one of the most interesting in North America. Its good farming land, mostly south of the river, 'old Quebec,' is the bed of the ancient Champlain Sea. After the glaciers, the land rose and tipped out the water, leaving a strip less than a hundred miles wide. No irrigation was needed, and therefore there was no compulsion to establish a central authority to control the river and the community. The family was the unit, the parish the community, the parish priest the local ruler. The traffic of the river slid by without affecting the villages; it was the concern of Montreal and Quebec.

Now, however, only about a fifth of the people of Quebec are on farms. People tire of the subsistence farm, of subsisting by tenacity, miserliness, and greed. The land goes back to brush. The number of farms dropped from 154,000 in 1941 to 122,000 in 1956. The Quebec farmhouse was customarily part of the village, since the system of land tenure divides the land into long strips, running back from some river and including tillable land, pasture and woodlot. Houses are strung along the main road, which is often one continuous village. Thus the farm is not isolated. Today, though the village is still conservative, deeply pious, distrustful of urban ways, it is no longer a self-sufficient unit, no longer fully convinced of its own righteousness, and no longer decisive in Quebec life. The automobile, television, the efforts of government agronomes to teach scientific farming, and the departure of youth to shops and factories have broken the old pattern.

The net of industry has been pulled tight over this society, ruled by the clergy and professional politicians. The dynamo was invented in 1870. It settled the future of Quebec. One by one the rivers are conquered: first the Saguenay, the St. Maurice, and the St. Lawrence above Montreal; now the Bersimis and the Outarde, great foaming streams far to the northeast. Others which flow to Hudson Bay, whose high falls have been seen by only two or three white men, are measured and held waiting.

* * *

Montreal never grew from its hinterland and has never depended on it, except for the hands which it draws from the farms to work in its shops. It is not like Toronto, solidly based on its countryside. It is rootless, or rather its roots are outstretched far to the West and North, spanning the lands nearby. It began as a trading post, which it still is, and as a fort against English and Iroquois. It was a location for churches, convents, schools, and at times government. The Sieur de la Salle built his stone house with three-foot-thick walls and tiny dormers close to the head of the Lachine Rapids so the canoes could bring their furs to his door. Ever since then Montreal has been a storage place for all the products of Canada, waiting to be loaded on ships. The railroads set their depots on its harbor; the money to build them had been accumulated there. Sugar from the West Indies comes to its dock for its refineries. Flour from the prairie wheat, beer from the prairie barley, shoes from the western cattle hides, tobacco from the Ontario fields, all are processed there. Railway cars, trucks, clothing, electrical gadgets, a thousand things are made in Montreal factories. On that foundation rest the department stores, the hospitals, the churches, the banks, the priests and lawyers and doctors, the French publishers, the transport men, and the mothers with their children. The city holds nearly half Quebec's population, 60 per cent of its manufacturing. Without it Quebec would be another Maritime Province—rural, grumbling, helpless.

Montreal is flung around the volcanic core, named Mont Royal, which thrusts up from the island base. The old business and residence sections are jammed between mountain and river. Streets climb steeply toward the mountain park, with the older wealthy houses abutting on the mountain—a lovely place for coolness in summer and for skiing in winter. One by one, these old mansions decline into roominghouses, college fraternity houses, private schools, and monasteries. The center of the city loses population by the decay of slum properties, though the old stone buildings stand until they are torn down, and by the growth of office buildings and hotels whose employees must find homes elsewhere. All the eastern end of the city is French, its streets lined with three- and four-story houses whose fronts are cluttered by the winding outside stairways seen nowhere else in North America. (Since at Montreal the river runs north, east is really north, and so on around the compass. The south end of the big bridge across the St. Lawrence is farther north than the north end. Streets are divided between east and west at St. Lawrence Main, though actually they run north and south. Typical of Montreal is the fact that nobody cares.)

French and English sprawl into the mass suburbs. The new shopping centers cater to both. Both cross the river to fill the bulging 'south' shore towns, where a twin city of Montreal will stand if the Seaway brings the industry expected of it.

The suburbs alleviate the language bar somewhat, but in the apartment houses it accentuates the lack of contact between neighbors. Montreal calls its apartments self-contained, and they are. The city is indifferent. It is also tolerant. It enjoys its scandals, being a very gossipy place, but it visits few social penalties on trangressors unless they run afoul of the law. If they have money they can avoid that.

The island that was so convenient for a trading post is not so convenient for a metropolis. The city chokes with only two direct outlets toward the south, both toll bridges. At each end the cars wait in long rows. The Seaway will eventually bring another bridge, but Montreal is powerless to ransom itself from the tolls, because the bridges are under federal control—one under the Ministry of Transport, the other the property of the Canadian National. The Federal Government penetrates Montreal's affairs through its control of the river and harbor. The city holds its charter from the Province and so is subject to provincial control of its finances, transportation, schools, housing, and liquor. It is extraordinarily badly governed, being a battleground of federal, provincial, and municipal authority.

*   *   *

Montreal probably enfolds as much sullen ill-will as do the more explosive Jerusalem and Singapore. There is seldom gaiety in its streets or public places, however wild the synthetic revelry of the night clubs. French Canadians laugh at wit, but they have little humor. French resent English and Jews, English resent French and Jews. Winter wears nerves thin, what with the waiting for jammed buses and streetcars on open corners in storm and cold, the wading through slush and slipping on icy sidewalks. From December to March pavements are a pudding of snow, salt, and sand. In some seasons a hundred inches of snow falls; streets are cleaned but sidewalks are trampled before they can be swept.

Yet, with all its discomforts, Montreal is an exciting place in which to live. Like New Orleans and San Francisco, it has character. The lilt of French everywhere marks it as foreign to North American custom. Every old city has its secret life, its own reality, its own smell. Every American city smells of burned gasoline, but Montreal also smells of dead leaves burning in the fall, of breweries and the river and cheap perfume and horses, for it has kept the use of horse-drawn vehicles longer than any other big city on the continent. The differences between rich and poor are more noticeable here than elsewhere in Canada. They are marked in dress and in the kind of housing that people can afford.

Quebec, the provincial capital, a hundred and seventy miles down the river from Montreal, is almost completely a French city. The few thousand *Anglais* are rather subdued. They have little influence on the life of the town and keep themselves in dignified segregation. During the winters government officials take the limelight with formal entertaining. The ancient city, high on its cliff above the river in one of the most spectacular locations in the world, is a tourist goal. Laval University has moved to the outskirts, but the beautiful old seminary buildings remain. The harbor is busy, some industries have come in, but essentially Quebec is the capital of French Canada, not a business center.

*   *   *

Ontario is a miniature Canada, itself larger than many nations. The tremendous extent of Canada impresses even the careless traveler, and Ontario alone, the part of the country which most tourists see, is enough to impress. With five million people, and more arriving every day by birth and immigration, with a small Quebec spilled over into its eastern counties, with a wilderness to west and north, booming industry and flourishing farms in its south, it is fully sufficient unto itself if need be, and able to impose its control on much of the country's activity. The Shield arches around the good land, stretching down claws on east and west. Ontario has six hundred miles of shore line on salt water, open to the Atlantic through Hudson Bay. So far nobody has made much use of it, but there are plans for a port with docks for ocean shipping. The Ontario Northland Railway, owned by the Provincial Government and linked with the Canadian National, crosses the height of land far to the north and trundles down to James Bay at Moosonee. Three times a week it dumps a few missionaries, Indians, lumbermen, prospectors, and nurses for the government hospital at that remote spot, and carries out furs and lumber. A little trade begins.

The essence of the Province is concentrated in the triangle of fertile land between the lakes. This section is becoming one long city as Toronto reaches out to join Oshawa on one side and Hamilton on the other; as Windsor overflows to Chatham and London swallows the countryside near it. Town planners no longer dream of green belts around cities, for the cities have burst their girdles. They talk now of ribbon developments and metropolitan areas, of how life can be made endurable in the confusion of main traffic arteries and shopping centers and lights that flash off and on all night long. Over 60 per cent of Canada lives in cities now, and thinks of farms and forests as vacation spots only.

The growth of this horseshoe around the end of Lake Ontario began with the easy trade across it to Buffalo and Rochester, helped by the canals and power of Niagara. The railways and ships to the west carried the manufactured goods out and brought back the grain and meat. It is a solid growth from lake and land. Ontario is still a great agricultural province. It raises wheat and makes flour, finishes off in its lush fields the rawboned steers from the western ranches, grows thousands of tons of vegetables and fruit for canning, and makes wine from its vineyards. Its dairy herds are among the finest, though its cities consume the margarine for which it imports oils. The new immigrants drain its marshes and pluck fresh lettuce and tomatoes for its city markets.

*   *   *

Ottawa is a very Canadian city in its deficiencies and its beauties. Ramshackle temporary buildings lie close by fine ones, and the loveliness of nature surrounds the work of man. In obvious ways the product of Canadian discords, it manages to rise above them to a sort of tentative tranquillity.

The Federal District Commission is hard at work. It moves the railway station to the edge of town, away from the center, where it squats almost in front of Parliament Hill. It tries to cure the plague of mosquitoes by dumping trash in the marshes and planting flowers on top. It plans to lay out green belts and scenic drives, and to exile factories to the outskirts. The National Library, the National Gallery, and the National Museum are to fit into the Plan some day. The frantic expansion of the war days left Ottawa cluttered with frame construction; departments roost where space can be rented, and wait for permanent quarters to hatch.

Ottawa is a hard place in which to foster civic pride, because it is full of large groups of temporary inhabitants—civil servants who usually came from elsewhere and expect to retire elsewhere someday, politicians who are also quite often temporary, service employees, and diplomats. Many have no stake in the community, for they think of home as being some-

where else. Local merchants say they cannot afford to stock the best goods, because women go to Montreal, only a hundred and twenty-five miles away, to shop. Audiences are too small to attract the best performers in music and theater. Social life naturally revolves around official circles, and so is formal.

Ottawa is also a poor city in which to look for work, because civil service employees whose salaries are lagging behind the rising cost of living grab part-time jobs. They 'moonlight,' driving taxis, clerking in rush hours, waiting in restaurants, doing home typing. The Cabinet disapproves of their taking selling jobs, where they might put pressure on subordinates to buy, but it does not raise their pay to the level where they will not need to turn to outside expedients. The civil servant stays in his job because he is lured by the pension for his old age. Meanwhile he may not engage in any partisan work or deal with party funds; he is officially cautioned not to let partisan activities or relatives be construed as receiving his support. Thus the majority of Ottawa's population is politically sterilized, though not deprived of the franchise.

In the old countries, capitals grew into their functions by being centers of national life, homes of kings or chieftains, like Paris, London, Moscow, and Peking. The new nations set up special cities whose main occupation is government—Washington, Ottawa, Canberra. They lack the closeness to national life and to ordinary people which the old capitals conserve. They generate a hushed atmosphere, a tremendous respect for rank and protocol which is not always entirely wholesome, and they cannot avoid the disadvantage of being artificial constructions. Since Canada had no national center, Ottawa was chosen and has served well.

*   *   *

Because the prairies were so hard to reach, for a long time they were traversed but not inhabited, left to the gopher and the buffalo. Men accustomed to clearing land for settlement wanted to be in sight of wood for fuel and timber. They disliked the sod house of the prairie and the lack of running water. The fringe of settlement extended slowly. The American border was vague, turbulent, and disregarded as late as the 1870's.

It is a mistake to think of this Middle West as all fertile grain land. Only a strip grows wheat, but what a strip it is! More than half of Manitoba is within the Shield, all rock and lake. Lake Winnipeg covers more ground with its shallow waters than does Lake Ontario, and Manitoba has other big lakes and marshes full of wild fowl. The northern half of Saskatchewan is a watery waste. These sections are rich only in fish and lumber, and in the new metals which are coming to light.

But the wide band that runs from Winnipeg across the southwest corner of Manitoba, southern Saskatchewan, and up to the Alberta foothills, is dark brown or black soil three to ten feet deep, left by the lakes that once drained to Hudson Bay, slowly built up by the grasses that grew, were fertilized by the buffalo, died and rotted. The central ribbon of short grasses is usually too dry for the kind of farming the early settlers understood; the southern belt is almost desert and can be depended on for crops every year only if it is put under irrigation. But Saskatchewan alone has thirty million acres that will grow wheat, two-thirds of Canada's wheat, the best in North America, perhaps the best in the world. The low rainfall, averaging less than thirteen inches a year, drives the roots deep in search of moisture. The cold winters and hot summers, combined with the good earth, make Number One Northern the standard, hard, protein-full bread grain.

* * *

Winnipeg is the capital of Manitoba, the site of the provincial university, the center of everything in the Province, including the Ukrainian minority. Its newspapers and politicians have influenced Canadian policy in times past. Now they squabble over local issues. Its Ukrainian mayor, himself a teetotaler, wants sensible drinking laws. He wants to build a new City Hall, not because the old one is so spectacularly hideous, but because he is afraid it will fall down. His administration stands up to the local power company, threatening to install municipal gas works if the rates do not come down. This is the everlasting battle of city against province for more autonomy.

Regina and Saskatoon are the rival twin cities of Saskatchewan. Regina has the Government, Saskatoon the University. First of all, they are railroad towns, as are all prairie communities. Regina is an artificial capital, rising from the bare plain and determined to be beautiful. It succeeds by main strength, damming a tiny creek to make a lake, building parks and art galleries and hotels and museums. Saskatoon has the finest location on the prairies, high above a Saskatchewan River gorge. These communities believe truly in progress, in making a good life for their people; and their faith is touching and inspiring.

* * *

Calgary has a magnificent location, high above the plains, in distant view of the Rockies. Its clear air, its wide clean streets, the sense of space all about it, make it a city of remarkable beauty. Less hurried by the oil boom than Edmonton, Alberta's

provincial capital and Calgary's fierce rival, it has planned its growth, leaving room for parks and zoos and giving no feeling of bulging into straggly suburbs. At Calgary one first encounters an innovation for which the pedestrian is grateful, the 'scramble corner.' All traffic at busy corners is stopped for a moment between red and green lights, to let people walk as they please. The nearness to the mountains, the ease of access to outdoor life, and Calgary's own self-reliant, nonchalant air make it one of the most attractive of Canadian cities.

* * *

Nobody knows the Rockies, for the only way to learn them truly is on foot, and one lifetime is not enough. The paths of the Selkirks and the Kootenay, the Liard River and the Peel, the Stikine and the Yukon, the Mackenzie Mountains and the Coast Range remain formidable, treacherous, and secret. A plane that crashes against a peak sixty miles from Vancouver may lie undiscovered for months. Clouds back up in the valleys and rise in the twisting winds; turbulence seizes the plane; ice forms on the wings; and the pilot who loses his way in the gorges may never be seen again. Trans-Canada sends fourteen flights a day over Route Green One, just north of the American border, and treats the trip as routine, but the little plane that gets off course is in real trouble. The bush pilots take chances and come through terrible dangers. The men who know the mountains best, the trappers who spend their winters in some cabin on an unnamed stream, fear them while they defy them. Mapping from the air tells the sources of the rivers and their direction, but it cannot tell when they will swell in sudden flood, or when the avalanche will loosen from the cliffs.

The Rockies are young mountains, heaved up in convulsions, not yet ground down by weather and glaciers, like the Laurentians. On the eastern slope are the great national parks at Jasper and Banff, where the high peaks tower over the blue, much-pictured lakes. This is the scenic Canada familiar in every magazine. These parks, magnificent as they are, are footholds men have carved out on the margin of a harsh world. They are a little tarnished, since they offer access by rail and road, luxurious hotels and golf courses. But just beyond them are the valleys where men can die of hunger and cold and exhaustion with little hope of rescue. The Rockies are imminent over Canada. In the West no one can escape being conscious of their vastness and their invulnerability.

* * *

On this Pacific Coast everything is different, everything is a trifle exaggerated. This country does not look like Canada, the spongy turf underfoot does not feel like Canada, the voices in the street do not sound like Canada. It is damp and chilly the year round, but seldom cold. Its people are brash and imaginative, a little self-conscious, with gaze turned to an unpredictable future. The caution of English Canada is cast aside.

The settlements cling to the foot of the mountains that rise so steeply from the sea, or nest on big Vancouver Island. The colony began there, not on the hostile coast, drenched with rain, tangled on every hillside with that most persistent of small shrubs, the evergreen salal with its unbreakable stems. Victoria, on Vancouver Island, gets only half as much rain as Vancouver on the mainland. Vancouver dwells in beauty against a superb backdrop of inlets from the ocean and sharp-ridged mountains streaked with snow. Flowers are brilliant on every street. It is all like a striking poster, with a kind of thinness, a rawness about it, an unsureness pointed up by the demands the inhabitants make on the visitor to admire the magnificence of their city, to praise its loveliness, to envy those who live in this paradise. Like Texans, they itch to be told that they are the blessed of the earth. And surely they are justified, for some are rich and many are handsome, and they abide in surroundings of unrivaled splendor. The wonder is that they need reassurance.

* * *

These people think of themselves as loyal Canadians, but their economy is as tightly bound to the American as Ontario's. They resemble Californians more than they do other Canadians. The Federal Government in Ottawa interests them little unless it is considering some legislation which directly affects them, such as on pipelines or salmon fishing or trade with China. French Canada scarcely exists for them, except as a troublesome little sect in their own midst. British Columbians are the most insular, the gayest, the most carelessly generous, the most exasperating people in Canada.

* * *

Victoria, the capital of British Columbia, is a city of the past, or so the rest of Canada considers it. People repeat the myths about the teas at the Empress, the turreted old Canadian Pacific hotel; about the retired colonels, the snobbish old ladies, the knickerbockered inhabitants of some nearby towns, who bring their English accents and customs to this distant land. They are old now, these English army officers and pensioned Indian civil servants. English people no longer come here to retire, since the pound has lost value, the Canadian cost of living has risen

high, and the British Health Service makes the old country more attractive. The retired couples who come in these days are from the prairies, people who are not rich enough for the Bahamas but whose old age pensions and savings enable them to buy a cottage, plant a garden, and live comfortably in the mild climate. They are socially and politically conservative, a contrast to the occasionally eccentric dwellers on the islands between Victoria and the mainland, where the warm weather, the pleasure of small-boat travel, and the tolerance of unconventional dress and manners welcome more genially than other Canadian regions the impecunious lover of casual living.

Victoria becomes more Canadian, indeed more American, every day. Bobbies turn into cops, scones become biscuits, and biscuits crackers. A man holding his fork in his right hand has been observed in the Empress Hotel dining room. Still, Victoria manages a happy blending and remains a delightful place to live. It keeps to the old ways, while it smiles at them. The informed visitor signs the book at Government House, as a matter of course, as in no other provincial capital. He or she attends the Lieutenant-governor's garden party, complete with top hat and cutaway or flowered chiffon gown, to take refreshment under a real marquee. Downtown one can still buy an excellent cup of tea for a nickel, served with a smile. May Victoria long flourish, and its changes come slowly!

* * *

The North makes Canada a frontier country. The American frontier, aside from Alaska, closed before 1890; the Canadian bids fair to be open in 1990. The Sub-Arctic extends from the southern limit of permanently frozen ground, hard to fix precisely, to the limit of tree growth. The Arctic is above the tree line, which runs diagonally from Churchill on Hudson Bay northwest into the Yukon and northeast to Ungava Bay. Neither of these rough divisions is homogeneous in contour, climate, vegetation, animal life, or population. Each can be divided into a dozen regions with distinct characteristics. All slopes to the north; three-quarters of Canada drains to the Arctic Ocean.

Toward Alaska are the high mountains of the Yukon, where the glaciers flow, where the mountain sheep and the grizzly bear are at home. The Yukon Rush is on again—this time for oil, not gold. Crews contend with the cold and darkness of winter, because in summer they cannot drag their machinery through the bottomless swamps fed by the permafrost below. No one doubts that the oil is there, perhaps enough to supply the world in the future, but neither does anyone know when world prices will rise enough to make it worth while to carry it out.

LATIN AMERICA

LATIN AMERICA

Four hours upright on a seat are a bore; eight damned long, twelve frightful.
                                                        SYBILLE BEDFORD

Grimly devout, complaining but undaunted, they make their way over the mountains . . . gasping in the high altitudes, vomiting and terrified in planes, rattled like dice in buses, dragged out of bed before dawn to race along precipice roads, poisoned with strange foods, tricked by shopkeepers, appalled by toilets.
                                                        CHRISTOPHER ISHERWOOD

ALEC WAUGH

from A FAMILY OF ISLANDS

FOR Americans some of the most remote and exotic places are the closest to home. Haiti and Mexico are two of them.

THERE was a sneer on his [Pétion's] lips as he listened to the tales of Christophe that his spies brought to him. So Christophe was making a great man of himself up there! He had a splendid court and many palaces and counts and dukes and barons. He had a gold currency. And English admirals called on him. Professors came out from England to establish schools. The country was rich and that meant that the people of the country were enslaved. He smiled when they told him of the palace of Sans Souci. The Negro's love of vanity, he called it. They told him of the citadel above Milhot, of how the people of the plains struggled to carry bronze cannon up the slope. How when the slaves paused, panting at their load, Christophe would line them up and shoot every tenth man, with the remark, "You were too many. No doubt now you are fewer you will find it easier." Of how to prove his authority· he would give his troops on the citadel the order to advance and watch file after file crash over the wall to death.

Pétion sneered at Christophe. What else could you expect from an illiterate nigger? How long did they imagine it would last? Tyranny had its own medicine.

He sneered, too, at the citadel. What was it, he asked, but an expression, as was all else that Christophe staged up there, of the Negro's inordinate self-pride? What was the use of it, after all? It would be the easiest thing in the world to surround it, to starve it out. And as for all that gold stored there in its recesses, of what use would that be there? What could it buy but ransoms? Bullion was not wealth. One day he would take his troops up there to show what it was worth.

He never did.

Pétion was never to see the citadel, never to see the sun strike yellow on its curved prow from the road to Milhot. But with the mind's clearer eye, the poet's eye, he saw it, and seeing it foresaw how that proud ship would outlive the purpose it was built for, the imperial idea that it enthroned; how it would stand, derelict through the decades, to outlive ultimately even the quarrel, so eternal-seeming, of brown and black.

*   *   *

Today those pages of John Vandercook's in *Black Majesty* that describe all that Christophe achieved within his brief fourteen years of power read like a fairy tale. You cannot believe that the book is history, that one man, and at that a Negro, could in so short a time have done so much. You have to go to the Cap itself to realize that.

Milhot, from Cap Haitien, is a half hour's drive. It is a bad road through a green and lovely wilderness. You can scarcely believe that this bumpy track was once an even carriage drive, that these untended fields were orderly with care, that the crumbling stone gateways, half buried in the hedge, opened on carefully kept lawns, on verandaed houses, on aqueducts and sugar mills. Along the road passes an unending stream of women carrying, some of them on their heads, some of them on donkeys, bags of charcoal and sticks of sugarcane to market. They move slowly. The sun is hot. There is no hurry.

Milhot was once a pretty suburb of Cap Français. It is now a collection of squat, white-plastered houses, the majority of them with cone-shaped corrugated iron roofs; looking down on them from the hills they seem like the bell tents of a military encampment. Nothing remains of the old Milhot except the ruins of Christophe's palace, and of that only the facade and the terraces are left. Goats and lizards drowse under the trees where the King delivered judgment. The underground passage to La Ferrière is blocked. The outhouse walls are creeper-covered.

Christophe's carriage drive to the citadel is little more than a mountain path. It is a hard two and a half hours' climb by mule or pony. You pass little along the way: a thatch-roofed hut or two from whose doors natives will run out in the hope of selling you bananas, a gendarme returning from the citadel to duty, a Negro collecting coconuts. For a hundred years that road had been abandoned. The natives were frightened of the citadel. It was a symbol of tyranny. They could not be prevailed upon to go there. As the road mounts you have a feeling of nature returned into possession of its own. The lizards are larger and greener that dart across the road, the butterflies brighter and more numerous, the birds that dip into a richer foliage are wider-winged. For ninety minutes you climb in silence. Then, suddenly, at a bend of the road, you see high above you the citadel's red-rusted prow.

Words cannot describe the citadel. In photographs it would look like any other ruin. A cinematograph, worked from a circling airplane, would give no more than an impression of it. To appreciate its meaning you have to come to it as they that built it did, with the hot sun upon you, with your back damp against your shirt, with the fatigue of riding in your knees, with the infinitely varied landscape before your eyes, with the innumerable jungle sounds in your ears, and in your nostrils the innumerable jungle scents. Then you can walk along the grass-grown courtyards, the galleries with their guns that will never fire, the battlements through whose windows trees are sprouting; then you can realize the prodigious effort that the citadel's building cost; you realize that nothing that has been said of it has been an exaggeration, that it is the most remarkable monument in the modern world.

SYBILLE BEDFORD

from THE SUDDEN VIEW

"I HAD spent some years in the United States and was about to return to England for good," Mrs. Bedford writes. *"I had a great longing to move, to hear another language, eat new food; to be in a country with a long nasty history in the past and as little present history as possible. I longed in short to travel."*

THERE ARE THREE CLIMATIC ZONES in Mexico, one hot, one cold, one temperate. The *Tierras Calientes, Fría* and *Templada*. The Hot Zone is very hot, the Cold not as cold as it sounds; the Temperate is celestial perfection.

It is also the most inhabited portion of the Republic —the best part of the *Mesa Central* lies in *Tierra Templada*. Yet this plateau is not a temperate place at all: the mildness is luxuriant and dynamic, the temperance the product of the clash between two intemperances. It is a tropical region anomalously cool, combining the geographical extremes of Switzerland and Central Africa, as high as Mont-Blanc and as equatorial as the Sahara. At sea-level the Mexican latitudes would be desert and jungle; in the north the Mexican heights would be Alpine wastes. Joined, these excesses of parallel and altitude created a perennial Simla better than Simla. As a matter of recorded fact, the annual mean temperatures of the *Tierra Templada* vary between 66° and 73° Fahrenheit. The average rainfall is some 80 inches a year and concentrated within four months, June to October. In terms of human experience this means: it is always warm; it is never hot; it is never cold. It only rains in season and when it does it pours at fixed and regular hours, and afterwards the air is again dry and light, leaves and fields shine, there is no damp, no mud, no dripping, only a great new freshness. Grey days are unknown. Except for a few minutes of dramatic preparation for the actual burst, the sky is always clear. There is little difference in the weather between July and February; it may get rather warm in the late Spring and there are chilly evenings when the wind is blowing from the Coast, yet a person with a change of clothes suitable for an exceptionally fine English June, a blanket and a hut made of bamboo canes and waterproof leaves, would be comfortable day and night from one end of the year to the other. The possession of a mud cottage, and some pine cones for a fire around Christmas, would assure a sybaritic existence. This opens, and closes, economic vistas. A promoter from Germany, one is told by Gruening in his wonderfully detailed *History of Mexico*, arrived some time in the nineteenth century full of business projects, and departed so disgusted that he wrote a long and angry volume on the natives' cursed lack of wants, their *verdammte Beduerfnigslosigkeit*. He should see them now, poor man, sipping their Coca-Colas.

The second climatic zone is at sea-level and frankly tropical. Hundreds of miles of jungle, beach and silted port on the Pacific. The Gulf, with Vera Cruz, the oil trade, coffee fincas and a certain commercial bustle. The flat country of the deep South: Chiapas, Tabasco, Campeche, Yucatán—swamps, forests, sugar cane and pre-Columbian ruins. The third, the Cold Zone, is not a region but a number of separate points of especial altitude on the temperate plateau. It is a matter of exposure, though on the whole every place above seven thousand feet is considered to be *Terra Fría*.

Thus Mexico City belongs to the cold land. It is, however, a rule unto itself. It has four distinct climates, one for the night—which is bitter—and three for every day. Of these none is cold. The City also changes seasons every few hours. In the morning we are on the coast of New England. It is Autumn. A golden late September; the air is brisk but informed with warmth, luminous with sun. The kind of morning when one cannot bear to be in bed, when numbed insects stir to a new lease and one picks up one's tea-

cup and walks out into the garden. Here the unexpected gift comes every day. Breakfast is laid in the patio: there is fruit, the absurd goldfish are swishing in the fountain and everything smells of geranium; warmth lies gently across one's shoulders; E. has ceased to talk politics, the housekeeper stops to chat, the boy comes running with hot rolls and butter. . . . It is good to be alive.

At eleven, the climate becomes continental. It is the height of summer on the top of a mountain. The sun is burning, brilliant, not to be fooled with; the *fond de l'air* cool and flowing like fine water. One feels tremendously exhilarated, charged with energy. This is the time of day when I like to pick my way through the streets, to stand and stare, to walk slowly across the Cathedral Square under the shade of the brim of my hat. This full noon lasts for several hours. Then comes the cloud-burst and through the early evening, rain falls with the sound of rain falling in the hot countries all over the world, in Egypt, in Burma. . . . Later, it is a spring evening in a large city: mild, tenuous, nostalgic, laid out to be long. It is not long. Darkness descends with a sudden extinguishing sweep like the cover on the canary's cage. Energy ebbs, the heart contracts with fear. This is no time to be out in the streets, this is the hour of return, of the house, the hearth, the familiar ritual. *Alors, il s'est retiré dans son intérieur.*

The hotel room is desolate, the lamp dim. There is nothing then but the panicked dash for the clean, well-lighted places.

There are none. The current is wretched all over the city. The story goes that the last President's brother is still selling power across the border. There are no cafés, no pubs, only bars for men, and huge pastry-shops. You do not dine before ten, unless you are willing to eat waffles in a pharmacy got up like a mosque at Sanborn's astonishing emporium; the cinemas waste no money on illumination; there is going to be a concert on Friday week. . . . Some of the hotel bars are open to women. They are full of tourists and Mexicans emphatically without wives. Besides, this is not a good country to drink in: in daytime one does not want it at all, and at night one wants it too much.

We decide to have dinner at Henri's, a French restaurant that enjoys a reputation in the hemisphere. We push through the doors. One night in the early nineteen-thirties, a friend was good enough to take me to a restaurant in London which in its day had been a very famous restaurant indeed. The list of its patrons was literary and glamorous, the wine and cooking admirable; it had a speakeasy cachet. Our elders and betters had talked and drunk there through the nights of the First War when they were young and notorious; they had dined there in the 'twenties when they were well-known and middle-aged. It had had the honours of at least five contemporary novels. Let us call it Spisa's. I had never been there, and I believe it was my twentieth birthday, or the eve of my twentieth birthday. When we got to Spisa's the shutters were down, the dining-room dark and the owner dying. I mean literally dying. Mr. S. was on his death-bed and the priest had just been. My friend was a face from the better days, so they were much touched to see her at this hour. She was also a Catholic. They took her in to Mr. S.'s where she stayed in prayer for some time. I was put into a parlour where an Austrian waiter and an Italian waiter were saying their rosaries. I had no rosary, but the Italian waiter went and found me one. Later they would not let us go but insisted that we have our dinner. They sent out for some chops and lager from the pub in Charlotte Street and made us eat it in the dining-room. There was just one lamp lit above our table, otherwise it was quite dark. As we ate people came to us and whispered to my friend in Italian. I could see she had been weeping. Presently we walked home and later became quite unreasonably gay.

As E. and I pushed through Henri's swing doors, there was just one lamp lit above one table. The waiters stood huddled in gloom. I sank into self-pity. I know it is futile to indulge in my regret that I came too late upon this earth to enjoy the pleasures of the table at Edwardian house parties, but to think what I missed in my own time—I never have been to the Chapon Fin at Bordeaux, I was too late for Voisin's at Paris, too late for Spisa's, and now too late for Henri of Mexico City. Then I pulled myself together: a fellow creature was dying; I still had no rosary but I was ready to pay such respects as I could.

A second lamp was lit with small effect above a second table, chairs were pushed back and one of those French menus, large as a poster, was laid before us decorously like a floral tribute. No one in extremis? Service as usual? But no, the place was too preposterous: the hush, the darkness, the gloom; no funeral parlour in the U.S.A. could stay in business for a week with such an atmosphere. We had yet to learn that this was merely the regular nightly aspect of public eating places all over the Republic.

I must try some Mexican wine. I order a bottle of something called Santo Tomás. When poured out, it looks quite black. I sniff before tasting, so the shock when it comes is not as devastating as it might have been. I yell into the darkness to have the bottle removed.

The head waiter shuffles up gracefully. "Anything wrong, Señora?"

"Taste it."

He does. His face stays serene. Sheer self-control.

"There is something very wrong with this bottle. Taste it again."

"? ? ? es regulár."

Regular? Cheap ink dosed with prune juice and industrial alcohol, as harsh on the tongue as a carrot-grater? Regular! What a country, what palates, what digestions. They refuse to change the Santo Tomás for another bottle of Mexican wine—rather disobliging of them I thought then—but insist that we take an imported wine instead. I choose a Spanish claret, one of the Marqués de Riscal's honest *riojas*. It is good, but it costs ten shillings a bottle, which is too much to pay for one's glass or two at dinner in a wine country. Perhaps, it begins to dawn on me, Mexico is not a wine country. It was by nature and in God knows what fashion before the Conquest; but then the Spanish dug up the vines, the idea being to import wine from Spain and charge duty. For the same reason they cut down the olive trees and forbade the culture of silk-worms. Oil, silk and wine were to New Spain what rum and tea were to Massachusetts and Maryland. After Independence, everybody was too busy murdering each other to plant vineyards and olive groves, and what is being produced now is only a new incentive to murder. Santo Tomás comes from some infernal valley in Baja California where the climate is so unsalubrious that the very grapes breed acid antidotes inside their skins. And what the Indios do not do to those grapes . . . Santo Tomás is the best wine in the Republic. For one thing it contains only a limited amount of syrup, and the vats are always rinsed after their scrubbing with turkey excrement. I have learned to swallow my Santo Tomás, with a liberal admixture of water, like a man.

The food at Henri's is excellent; French in cooking and Mexican in lavishness. The service is as regular as the lighting and the wine. To sit in the penumbra with nothing but death and Santo Tomás to occupy one's mind is like an Irish wake without whisky, unnerving. Again my cries rend the shadows for something to eat.

"Where is that *Terrine* we ordered? It must be ready."

"It is ready. But the Prawns-and-Rice are not."

"But we are having the *Terrine* first."

"Yes, the *Terrine* comes first, but the Prawns are not ready."

"We are not going to have them at the same time. Please bring us the *Terrine* now."

"Señora: we must wait for the Prawns. Then you

will have the *Terrine* first."

"I mean first now, not first then."

"Yes, Señora, first. First in a little while."

"*Will you please bring the* Terrine *at once.*"

"At your taste, Señora. I shall run to tell the chef to hurry up the Prawns."

We wait. Then the *Terrine* is brought over from the sideboard in the Stygian corner where it had been reposing, and here on its heels are the Prawns, sizzling. They should not wait. So much is clear now, everything is allowed to take its time but once your dinner is on its breathless way, there must be no pause. The custom must have ruined better digestions than mine. It is unfathomable, and it is bedrock.

*   *   *

"Not more *streets?*" said E., and refuses to come for another stroll in the crumbling quarters behind the Plaza Mayor. We agree that I shall meet her at three o'clock in the Ritz Bar. I did not really want to come back to the centre. I love wandering about

the markets and those worn pink facades between the University and the Monte di Pietà, and to eat *enchiladas* off a stall.

The city has many open squares in which markets are continuously held and the general buying and selling proceeds. . . . There are barber-shops where you may have your hair washed and cut. There are other shops where you may obtain food and drink. There are street porters such as there are in Spain to carry packages. There is a great quantity of wood, charcoal, braziers made of clay, mats of all sorts, some for beds and others more finely woven for seats, still others for furnishing halls and private apartments. All kinds of vegetables may be found there, in particular onions, leeks, garlic, cresses, watercress, borage, sorrel, artichokes, and golden thistles. There are many different sorts of fruit, including cherries and plums. They sell honey obtained from bees. . . . All kinds of cotton threads in various colours may be bought in skeins. . . . A great deal of chinaware is sold, including earthenware jars of all sizes for holding liquids,

MEXICAN TRIO SERENADING AMERICAN TRIO, ACAPULCO.

pitchers, pots, tiles and an infinite variety of earthenware all made of very special clay and almost all decorated and painted in some way. Maize is sold both as grain and in the form of bread. . . . Pasties are made from game and fish pies may be seen on sale and there are large quantities of fresh and salt fish both in their natural states and cooked ready for eating. Eggs from fowls, geese, and all others may be had, and likewise omelets ready made.

The last paragraph was written in 1520. It is part of a letter by Cortez to the Emperor Charles V. on the Aztec capital as he found it on his first entry as a guest of Montezuma's. The description still serves.

*   *   *

I had been rather curious about Acapulco, that Saint Moritz of the Tropics where Americans fast and rich are supposed to go for big game fishing as well as dancing. I could not see anything being run on quite those lines here. Acapulco was once a port; and when Magellan discovered the Philippines, it became linked with the China Trade, and the Viceroys were able to get their silks and porcelain directly from the East. The climate was always felt to be a trial, and Philip III. had Negroes imported to do the pearl-diving and thrash the sugar cane as the Indios turned out to be too frail. Acapulco is ruined now, quite monstrous, many said. But others—ah, it is still very lovely; and if one wants to see that coast at all, there is nowhere else in the nine hundred miles between there and Mazatlàn where one could lay one's head. Two things I was not prepared for, that the impact of the—very great—natural beauty of the South-Sea setting would be weakened by photography, impoverished by previous reels and albums of other Lagoons and Bays (the very opposite would have happened had one seen Tuscany or the Seine Valley for the first time after the Impressionists and the Florentines); and that the man-made part of the place was a gipsy slum squeezed between the jungle and the ocean. Oh, the hotels were there, two unequal clumps of them on either side of the unpaved town. Above the mosquito belt, on a breezy cliff, stand the luxury hotels, so called because they are built of stone and provide the conveniences appropriate to the climate—air-cooling, shower-baths, electric fans—as well as such advertised attractions as nocturnal tennis courts, a sea lift and a subterranean bar. The family establishments, executed in match-board, straggle in a line along the beach. The season is very short —enrichissez-vous—December to mid-January really, though the hardier native petty-rich keep on coming until Holy Week, and the rest of the year the town bakes in its own mud. Indeed, it does little else in mid-season: the cliff hotels with their hairdressers and gift shops are self-contained and their guests lead the life of liners, while the families by the water-front rarely heave themselves beyond beach and dining-room. Imagine a major resort, imagine Cannes, consisting solely of the Carlton, the Majestic and the Martinez, some acres of churned mud and fly-blown stands, and a strip of boarding houses.

We were rather early in the year for comfort, though the prices were already high, and stayed at Los Pinguinos, a place—front on the beach, back open to leaf-hut and camp fire—managed by a discouraged, young, lean and single German of a type that might have gone in with more success for a civil service career in the Silesian forestry, who kept mum about his possible political antecedents and appeared to have been unable to maintain in these parts the reputed energy of his compatriots. He was always lying down. He did have a police dog, Flora, but she seemed to be affected by the heat as much as was her master. Our fellow guests were a Mexican family and four jolly middle-aged Saxonians from Saxony, who sat in the dining-room in their underwear, drinking whisky and eating plum-cake through the siesta hours. They were in business in Mexico City and had not been out of the country these twenty years and thus had no political past to hide, which must have been a thorn to them for if anybody ever had occasion to use Dorothy Parker's hallucinating sentence from the book of etiquette, "We regret that we have come too late to accompany you upon your harp," it was they.

The Mexican mother upset E. by wearing the kind of old-fashioned stays that brought her to the verge of public apoplexy at the end of every meal. "Ought I not to tell the poor lady to unlace herself? How can I put it?" she said. "One doesn't want to offend her."

I told her that my grandmother always boasted of having worn stays throughout the hot weather in India.

"Very bad for her," said E., un-detracted. She never told the Mexican lady, and we had the same conversation every day.

We discovered what one knew but had not realized, that at daytime in the tropics, unless one has to earn a living, there is nothing for one to do, and even if one braced oneself to be about there is little that can be described as doing. One could be rowed by Mulattos looking like Chinese under an awning of mats across an even bay, bathe with a straw hat in waters of topaz and pellucid green, alas warm; sit in a sweltering grove drinking the milk of freshly opened coconuts wishing that it were water and that it were cold. One could be drawn across the town by mules, and up the cliff, sit in a transparent frigidaire above the sea, order from a list of forty-six rum cocktails, watch boys dive off a ninety-foot crag for coins, listen to Riviera voices dropping names. Three Starlit Swizzles, please . . . *Un quinto por caridàd* . . . Willy, Wally . . .

One could bathe, from our beach, only before sunrise and at brief dusk, that exquisite ten minutes when the waves stand almost black and fifty pelicans swoop plumply by one's side teaching their young to fish.

The bulk of the day one lay on one's bed, between showers, and read. The book was heavy, the paper stuck, the light through close-drawn blinds was never right. Soon one dozed. For meals, one pulled oneself up, bathed, dressed, felt bucked by the change. There was ice but it was not comestible, so the manager kept a bottle of gin on it for us, of which we drank a tumblerful diluted with a little lime-juice before lunch and dinner, enjoying a moment, but a moment only, of refreshment. Then we ate a little dull food. Every scrap of clothes began to stick—the dining-room was always 95°—the jolly Saxonians sang, the Mexican mother puffed, the manager went about the tables moaning, quite truthfully, about the bad quality of everything, the soap, the plaster, the fish. So often before the pudding, one went upstairs again. Another shower, a book . . .

In this limbo we stayed rather longer than we need have stayed. Until one day we performed the necessary actions, and got away.

GRAHAM GREENE

from ANOTHER MEXICO

WHATEVER else he may experience of Mexico's infinite variety, nearly every visitor sees what Graham Greene saw in and around Mexico City.

How to describe a city? Even for an old inhabitant it is impossible; one can present only a simplified plan, taking a house here, a park there as symbols of the whole. If I were trying to describe London to a foreigner, I might take Trafalgar Square and Piccadilly Circus, the Strand and Fleet Street, the grim wastes of Queen Victoria Street and Tottenham Court Road, villages like Chelsea and Clapham and Highgate struggling for individual existence, Great Portland Street because of the second-hand cars and the faded genial men with old school ties, Paddington for the vicious hotels . . . and how much would remain left out, the Bloomsbury Square with its inexpensive vice and its homesick Indians and its sense of rainy nostalgia, the docks . . . ?

The shape of most cities can be simplified as a cross; not so Mexico City, elongated and lopsided on its mountain plateau. It emerges like a railway-track from a tunnel—the obscure narrow streets lying to the west of the Zocalo, the great square in which the cathedral sails like an old rambling Spanish galleon close to the National Palace. Behind, in the tunnel, the university quarter—high dark stony streets like those of the Left Bank in Paris—fades among the tramways and dingy shops into red-light districts and street markets. In the tunnel you become aware that Mexico City is older and less Central European than it appears at first—a baby alligator tied to a pail of water; a whole family of Indians eating their lunch on the sidewalk edge; railed off among the drugstores and the tramlines, near the cathedral, a portion of the Aztec temple Cortés destroyed. And always, everywhere, stuck between the shops, hidden behind the new American hotels, are the old baroque churches and convents, some of them still open, some converted to the oddest uses—the Cine Mundial, once the Convent of Jesús María; the Government Library, once the Betlemite's church; a warehouse which was a Catholic college; a shop, a garage, a newspaper office still bearing the old baroque façades. Between November 11, 1931, and April 28, 1936, four hundred and eighty Catholic churches, schools, orphanages, hospitals were closed by the Government or converted to other uses. The National Preparatory School itself was formerly a Jesuit college, built in the eighteenth century.

Out of the Zocalo our imaginary train emerges into sunlight. The Cinco de Mayo and the Francisco Madero, fashionable shopping streets, run like twin tracks, containing smart Mayfair stations—the best antique shops, American teashops, Sanborn's—towards the Palace of Arts and the Alameda. Tucked behind

PALACE OF FINE ARTS, MEXICO CITY.

them is the goods track—Tacuba—where you can buy your clothes cheap if you don't care much for appearances. After the Palace of Arts the parallel tracks are given different names as they run along beside the trees and fountains of Montezuma's park—the Avenida Juárez full of tourist shops and milk bars and little stalls of confectionery, and the Avenida Hidalgo, where hideous funeral wreaths are made—ten feet high and six across—of mauve and white flowers. Then Hidalgo wanders off where no one troubles to go and Juárez is closed by the great Arch of the Republic, which frames a sky-sign of Moctezuma Beer, and the Hotel Regis, where the American Rotarians go and the place where they draw the lottery. We turn south-west into the Paseo de la Reforma, the great avenue Maximilian made, running right out of the city to the gates of Chapultepec, past Columbus and Guatemoc and the glassy Colon Café, like the Crystal Palace, where President Huerta, the man who shot Madero and fled from Carranza, used to get drunk (when he became helpless, they turned out the

lights and people passing said: "The President's going to bed"; it wouldn't have been a good thing to see the President of Mexico carried to his car), on past the Hotel Reforma and the Statue of Independence, all vague aspiration and expensive golden wings, to the lions at the gates. And on either side branch off the new smart streets, pink and blue wash and trailing flowers, where the diplomats live, and the smell of sweets blows heavily along from Juárez.

*   *   *

I went and saw Orozco's and Rivera's frescoes at the National Preparatory School and the Ministry of Education in the university quarter. The frescoes in the Preparatory School are mainly by Orozco. Rivera contributes only one mural with typical grandiloquence—all outstretched arms and noble faces, white robes and haloes. It is called "Creation"; it is full of literary symbols—the Tree of Life, Dionysus, Man, Woman, Music, Comedy, Dance, Tragedy, Science, Temperance, Fortitude. It adapts Christian emblems to a vague political idea, and they become unbearably sentimental in the new setting, far more sentimental than repository art. That pale blue madonna with the seven swords does, however inadequately, represent an exact idea; but the Son in Rivera's "Creation"— what is he but Progress, Human Dignity, great empty Victorian conceptions that life denies at every turn? This is always Rivera's way—to try to get the best of both worlds. He is the Leighton or the Watts of the Revolution.

Orozco—however invalid one may believe his ideology to be—knows his own mind and his own world; it is very seldom that the great abstractions—"Maternity"—billow their sentimental draperies across *his* walls. His subjects are "The Trench," "Soldaderas," "The Indian," "The Missionary," "St. Francis," "The Eternal Father"—guyed with white woolly beard and little birdlike beak, lightning, and grumpy eyes. The Franciscan monk clasping with huge arms the starving Indian in a strangling embrace, the patient hopeless women trailing after their soldiers into the umber future—these represent emotions of pity and hate that one can respect.

In the Ministry of Education Rivera has it all his own way. Occasionally—very occasionally—his moral is where it should be, implicit: "The Rural Teacher" —the little group of Indians sitting in a circle on the baked ground, while the woman speaks to them out of a book and the trooper sits his horse, his rifle ready, and the men plough a tiny field under the mountains; "Inspection on Leaving the Mine"—the white-clothed worker standing on a plank across the abyss, head bowed and arms outstretched, while the officials search him for stolen silver. But even here we are aware of the stolen symbol—the cross, the agony.

Perhaps we have no right to criticize—Christianity itself adapted the feast days and the holy places of the older faiths. In Mexico City the cathedral is built on the site of the great Aztec temple, and perhaps we are only experiencing the uneasiness of the old Aztec priests when we turn impatiently away from these murals of rural teachers dressed in white with pious apostolic faces and fingers raised in blessing—"Suffer little children to come unto me." Perhaps they are only making things gentle for us, so that we shan't miss our faith in the new drilled totalitarian day.

*   *   *

The Alameda on a Sunday is like a scene from a René Clair film: the bourgeois families under the great trees, and the photographers, with odd Edwardian painted backgrounds, all pale blue and pink, roses and châteaux and lakes and swans and absurd flying machines, dating back to the Wright brothers, lumbering overhead. Everywhere churches lift up their

MARIACHI BAND ADRIFT IN THE FLOATING
GARDENS OF XOCHIMILCO, MEXICO.

bruised and antique heads above the walls and trees. A Holy Child stands in a Libera Religiosa with lottery tickets spread over his outstretched arms. On the ceiling of San Fernando potentates are tossed lightly up into the cerulean, jackboots buoyed up by the enormous torrent of air, clouds thrown about like tennis balls by winged figures, an effect of freedom and jubilation (all crippling gravity cut off) as we mount to the Son of Man radiant on a blue globe.

All the world that doesn't go to the bull-fight goes to Chapultepec, and the streets of the city are empty. Chapultepec Park, as well as the Alameda, is said to date back to Montezuma: huge old trees—one of them is two hundred feet tall and forty-five feet round—draped with Spanish moss, lakes with little boats, sham caves and cold rocky tunnels out of the sun, and, on the precipitous rock above, the unoccupied castle guarded by small careless soldiers, who go wandering off into shrubberies after a girl, or sit on the parapet by the guardroom reading a cheap novel; the palace of Maximilian with a glass front like the Crystal Palace tacked onto the staid eighteenth-century stonework, and down below a monument to useless heroism—to the Cadets who fell, at the time of the American invasion, guarding the Castle. The last Cadet to survive wrapped the Mexican flag around his body and leapt from the rock—the same old flag people wear on shirts and paint on gourds for tourists, the eagle eating the snake. All the monuments in Mexico are to violent deaths.

In the paper there were two assassinations—of senators. One was shot in Juárez on the American border, and the other last night three minutes' walk from my hotel, at the other end of the Cinco de Mayo, in the Opera Bar. He was plugged full of bullets after a discussion and the assassin walked away to his car and escaped from the city. These deaths are distinguished from all the other deaths that happen every day only by the senatorial rank. "Riddled with bullets" is the stock phrase.

Perhaps it is the atmosphere of violence—perhaps only the altitude, seven thousand-odd feet—but after a few days no one can escape the depression of Mexico City.

A little party of peons came down the hill from Chapultepec Castle wearing big hats; they carried bread in the brims. Oh, it's comic too sometimes—in a way—like the cock-fight.

*   *   *

One day I went on a Cook's tour to the Monastery of San Agustín Acolman and the pyramids of Teotihuacán. The monastery lies below the level of what was once all lake; it had to be abandoned more than a hundred years ago. It was founded by twelve sur-vivors of twenty Augustinian friars who landed in Mexico at the beginning of the sixteenth century, before the city of Mexico had fallen to Cortés. The monastery was built first and the little balcony still remains where Mass was said in view of the Indians on the plain outside. Then after twenty years, in 1539, the great tall church was completed, and one wonders how it was that twelve friars, picked at random by Providence to survive, were able to plan a building of such beauty. They planned, I suppose, on the lines of what they knew, but what an exact—and loving—memory they must have had of the Spanish monasteries. We think of these churches now as Mexican, or Colonial; but in those first decades in a continent which had been discovered less than fifty years before, in the appalling strangeness of a land which should have been over the world's edge, they must have seemed not a style of architecture but an acre of home. In the cloisters are the remains of the oldest wall paintings in Mexico—the faint line still visible of some representation of Hell and Judgment whitewashed over when that lesson had been learned by the Indians, the crude and elementary idea of punishment in terms of flame and cauldron and pincers. What remains today is the last and most difficult lesson of all—the lesson of love and the mysterious death of the Creator on the cross, and the little quiet European countryside, copied by Indians, still going quietly and securely on as the Universe ends: with both a sun and a moon in the sky.

In the great grey courtyard of Teotihuacán, surrounded by the platforms of small pyramidal temples, you do get the sense of a continent over the world's edge—a flatness, a vacancy, through which peer plumed serpents and faces like gas-masks over orifices that might be the mouths of Lewis guns or flamethrowers. Archæologists maintain theories of what happened here from the number of steps in each pyramid—mathematical computations that lead to a human sacrifice or a struggle between rival cults, rather in the same way as the British Israelites foretell the future from the comparative measurements of the Egyptian pyramids. It is fantastic—and credible. The mathematical sense seems to have run riot—everything is symmetrical; it is important that the Pyramid of the Sun should be sixty-six metres high and have five terraces and the Pyramid of the Moon be forty-four metres high and have—I forget how many terraces. Heresy here was not an aberration of human feeling—like the Manichæan—but a mathematical error. Death was important only as solving an equation. In the museum you see the little black glassy knives with which the breast of the sacrifice was opened—they look as hygienic as surgeons' instruments. Only the Temple of Quetzalcoatl is decorated —with horrors, serpents, and gas-masks—and he was the white Toltec god of culture, the mildest god of the lot, and was defeated by this stony mathematical discipline. One expects to see Q.E.D. written on the paving of the great court—the pyramids adding up correctly, the number of terraces multiplied by the number of steps, and divided by the square metres of the surface area, proving—something, something as inhuman as a problem in algebra.

ALMA REED

from OROZCO

AND the greatest of the great Mexican muralists was Orozco. Alma Reed, "La Peregrina," is the American who knew him best.

A DISCERNING psychologist might have discovered, of course, that Orozco's façade of average "regularity" shielded a complex personality. There was the firm, square-set jaw countering the delicately modeled mouth. On closer acquaintance, one might have sensed certain departures from the accepted norm— for example, the painter's "impractical" attitude, if a total rejection of mediocre values and cheaply won success may be so classified. But the real potentialities of the man and the artist, the sage and the seer, were securely locked within the secret dynamo of his unique genius. If any clue to Orozco's vast creative range existed in his facial complex, it was to be found in the questioning glance of his large brown eyes, their flash of authority from behind thick bifocals. Orozco's eyes also held the clue to his superb humor, long a recognized force in Mexico's political life. Like his feeling for the tragic, the artist's sense of humor was rooted in clarity of perception. One observed even at first meeting an idiosyncrasy that strongly denoted his passion for personal verification of truth or falsehood. When studying a person or an object he would draw his head back a little and tilt it to one side in a gesture of appraisal. At these moments, the keen intensity of his gaze seemed to bore through to the essential worth of situations or human beings. Rarely did he commu-

OROZCO FRESCO OF FELIPE CARILLO PUERTO, MARTYRED
GOVERNOR OF YUCATÁN, AT THE NEW SCHOOL
FOR SOCIAL RESEARCH, NEW YORK.

nicate censure or approval; his conclusions would be registered later, on some wall or canvas. Meanwhile he appeared to be satisfied with having, in the interests of realism, punctured sham or uncovered hidden merit.

It was well known that Orozco's fame with his own people rested for the most part on the satirical acumen he had projected through the Mexican press during the entire Revolutionary decade. Day after day, in the years of turmoil and treachery, he had aimed his powerful knife-edged caricatures at offending *políticos* both to the right and to the left. The nerve-racked capital eagerly awaited his graphic contributions, never knowing just where the *enfant terrible* of *El Ahuizote* (1911), *La Vanguardia* (1917), *El Machete* (1922), *El Malora* (1923-4), and *L'A.B.C* (1926-7) would strike next. Newsboys on busy corners capitalized on public suspense. To whip up sales they would open their paper at the page that carried the Orozco drawing. It was common belief that the formidable incisiveness of the artist's pen could "make or unmake presidents" as effectively as the intrigue or violence that customarily accomplished the purpose.

* * *

In his *Autobiography* Orozco outlines with characteristic brevity the theme of the New School murals: "In the center," he writes, "the table of universal brotherhood; men of all races presided over by a Negro. On the side walls allegories of world revolution. Gandhi. Carrillo Puerto and Lenin. A group of slaves; another group of workers entering their home after the labor of the day. On a wall outside the dining room an allegory of the sciences and arts."

* * *

On the lower end of the east wall, Orozco painted the dawn over Asia, the awakening of the enslaved native races. The naked backs of the chained slaves await the lash of the oppressor. The profile figure of an old man, his hands raised in piteous but futile appeal to his callous masters, highlights the misery of the slaves. Four bald-headed, "white collar" men, chains drawn tightly about their necks, suggest that slavery is not confined to the "underprivileged" areas of the earth.

On the west wall Orozco interpreted the struggle in the Occident. As he had promised on our trip from San Francisco, he painted the apotheosis of Felipe Carrillo Puerto. The martyred Governor of Yucatán, often called the Abraham Lincoln of Mexico, is seen emerging above the horizon, beside the Maya pyramids of the highest ancient American culture, as though to link the remote past and the unborn future in his great dream of a happy, liberated humanity.

Around his radiant image are grouped his devoted people, the women carrying the red banners of the feminist leagues which he organized as the first official advocate in the New World of women's political emancipation. On the right, the diffused glow of the setting sun joins the Mexican panel to the one which represents the Communist experiment.

The different races of the Soviet Union are depicted as marching workers, each holding a conventional tool to symbolize a mobilized industry. The workers are supported by an army of the Soviet military, bayonets bristling above their red-starred helmets. The pale gray tones that envelop the military suggest a withdrawal into the past, while the vivid coloring of the workers indicates their active role in the present and future. In the background, on the Kremlin wall, appears an image of the dead Lenin painted in the somber mood of a Russian ikon. Above the wall rises the familiar red banner of the October revolution.

I recall that after submitting to Dr. Johnson the sketch for the Soviet panel, I had several conversations with the educator on its significance, and I carried his questions and Orozco's replies back and forth. Dr. Johnson finally agreed with the painter that the Marxist idea and its leader could hardly be omitted from any realistic appraisal of political trends. He was of the opinion that Orozco could not be accused of propaganda since his murals gave equal space and impartial treatment to all three political philosophies. He conceded that Orozco had the same right as the historian to evaluate the events of the past and to forecast from their impact "the shape of things to come."

On the south wall, facing the guest entering the dining room, Orozco painted the *Table of Brotherhood*. The massive yellow table, drawn in striking false perspective, serves not only as the traditional symbol for a refectory but also to bind into a single unit the murals of the entire room. At three sides of the table are seated the representatives of all the races of the earth. The places of honor at the head of the universal board are reserved for what the painter called the "despised races"—a Mexican peon and a Jew, flanking an American Negro in the role of presiding officer. On the left are seated five figures—a Chinese Mandarin, a blond Anglo-Saxon, a European Nordic, a fur-capped Iranian Kurd, and a turbaned Indian. On the right are seated three solid, block-like forms—a thick-lipped African Negro, a bearded Frenchman with classic features, and another Chinese, with the broad nose and high cheek bones of the Cantonese "coolie," to symbolize the Chinese masses, one-fourth of the world's population. China's dual representation at the *Table of Brotherhood* is

(continued on page 108)

KRONFELD © PAA

(continued from page 85)

another prophetic note which time has materialized for Orozco into the existing situation between the Peiping Government and the Chiang Kai-shek regime on Formosa. On the table rests a single opened book with a vivid red cover.

On the north wall, facing the *Table of Brotherhood*, is a panel entitled the *Family Table*, in which Orozco registers his personal hopes for an evolved humanity as the ultimate outcome of the world struggle. This table is laden with food and drink to symbolize abundance and stacked with books to indicate cultural progress. A mother and her children are seated at the table, while a happy worker returning from his labor advances to join them. A radiant girl rises to greet a younger worker. In the distance through an open door is seen the factory, guarantee of employment and source of the family's security and well-being.

On the afternoon of 19 January 1931, I went with Orozco for a final inspection of his work before the official preview and reception. "You are always going to feel very much at home here, Almita," the artist said with his happiest smile as we entered the dining room. "You will be among your friends; it is just another Ashram."

Certainly Orozco's analogy was accurately applied to the *Table of Brotherhood*, where several of the seated figures were portraits of my most revered friends, courageous forerunners of an enlightened order, whose lives were dedicated to the realization of lofty dreams. But dominating the scene so far as my personal emotions were concerned was the luminous portrait of Felipe Carrillo Puerto. In keeping with his respect for simple ritual rooted in depth of feeling, Orozco led me to the west wall, where we stood silently before his stirring tribute to the gallant Yucatecan leader. "Well, Almita, here it is," he said. "I hope it pleases you. At any rate it is the first monument in your country to Felipe's memory. Someday there will be others—and on a grander scale."

*   *   *

A later mural work that gave Orozco an opportunity to indulge his flair for caustic humor was provided by an art-loving friend who owned the Turf Club, a fashionable establishment on the outskirts of Mexico City. On the spacious wall of the main dining room and on another in the patio, Orozco registered his estimation of French culinary art and French art in general. In a mood of hilarious *ironía* he combined on the dining-room wall, like so many ingredients in a huge bouillabaisse, a French chef, a demimondaine, a Parisian boulevardier, and a Montmartre painter in smock and beret. They are shown, "all for one and one for all" and the lot for *viva la France*, creating and catering to the false taste of the postwar public.

Another example of Orozco's humor was related to me by Siqueiros. In 1948 when Rivera's fresco, *Dream of a Sunday Afternoon in the Alameda*—which had just been unveiled in the main dining room of the Hotel del Prado—was defaced and covered in a tumultuous riot, Diego and Siqueiros rushed to Orozco's Calle Mariscal studio. Although his visitors were bitter political enemies and leaders of opposing Marxist factions, they had joined in common cause in the defense of aesthetic freedom. Siqueiros had stoutly defended Rivera's right to include in his work the quotation of the educator, Ignacio Ramirez: *"Dios no existe"*—God does not exist, the words that provoked the riot. When Orozco greeted them at his door he exclaimed: "To what do I owe the signal honor that Trotsky and Stalin should call on me—and together? Am I to assume a United Front?"

JOHN STEINBECK

from The Log from the Sea of Cortez

*T*HE *"La Paz" here is a small Mexican port near the Tropic of Cancer, at the end of Lower California.*

LA PAZ GREW in fascination as we approached. The square, iron-shuttered colonial houses stood up right in back of the beach with rows of beautiful trees in front of them. It is a lovely place. There is a broad promenade along the water lined with benches, named for dead residents of the city, where one may rest oneself.

Soon after we had anchored, the port captain, customs man, and agent came aboard. The captain read our papers, which complimented us rather highly, and was so impressed that he immediately assigned us an armed guard—or, rather, three shifts of armed guards—to protect us from theft. At first we did not like this, since we had to pay these men, but we soon found the wisdom of it. For we swarmed with visitors from morning to night; little boys clustered on us like flies, in the rigging and on the deck. And although we were infested and crawling with very poor people and children, we lost nothing; and this in spite of the fact that there were little gadgets lying about that any one of us would have stolen if we had had the chance. The guards simply kept our visitors out of the galley and out of the cabin. But we do not think they prevented theft, for in other ports where we had no guard nothing was stolen.

The guards, big pleasant men armed with heavy automatics, wore uniforms that were starched and clean, and they were helpful and sociable. They ate with us and drank coffee with us and told us many valuable things about the town. And in the end we gave each of them a carton of cigarettes, which seemed valuable to them. But they were the reverse of what is usually thought and written of Mexican soldiers— they were clean, efficient, and friendly.

With the port captain came the agent, probably the finest invention of all. He did everything for us, provisioned us, escorted us, took us to dinner, argued prices for us in local stores, warned us about some places and recommended others. His fee was so small that we doubled it out of pure gratitude.

As soon as we were cleared, Sparky and Tiny and Tex went ashore and disappeared, and we did not see them until late that night, when they came back with the usual presents: shawls and carved cowhorns and colored handkerchiefs. They were so delighted with the exchange (which was then six pesos for a dollar) that we were very soon deeply laden with curios. There were five huge stuffed sea-turtles in one bunk alone, and Japanese toys, combs from New England, Spanish shawls from New Jersey, machetes from Sheffield and New York; but all of them, from having merely lived a while in La Paz, had taken on a definite Mexican flavor. Tony, who does not trust foreigners, stayed aboard, but later even he went ashore for a while.

The tide was running out and the low shore east of the town was beginning to show through the shallow water. We gathered our paraphernalia and started for the beach, expecting and finding a fauna new to us. Here on the flats the water is warm, very warm, and there is no wave-shock. It would be strange indeed if, with few exceptions of ubiquitous animals, there should not be a definite change. The base of this flat was of rubble in which many knobs and limbs of old coral were imbedded, making an easy hiding place for burrowing animals. In rubber boots we moved over the flat uncovered by the dropping tide; a silty sand made the water obscure when a rock or a piece of coral was turned over. And as always when one is collecting, we were soon joined by a number of small boys. The very posture of search, the slow movement with the head down, seems to draw people. "What did you lose?" they ask.

"Nothing."

"Then what do you search for?" And this is an embarrassing question. We search for something that will seem like truth to us; we search for understanding; we search for that principle which keys us deeply into the pattern of all life; we search for the relations of things, one to another, as this young man searches for a warm light in his wife's eyes and that one for the hot warmth of fighting. These little boys and young men on the tide flat do not even know that they search for such things too. We say to them, "We are looking for curios, for certain small animals."

Then the little boys help us to search. They are ragged and dark and each one carries a small iron harpoon. It is the toy of La Paz, owned and treasured as tops or marbles are in America. They poke about the rocks with their little harpoons, and now and then a lazing fish which blunders too close feels the bite of the iron.

There is a small ghost shrimp which lives on these flats, an efficient little fellow who lives in a burrow. He moves very rapidly, and is armed with claws which can pinch painfully. He retires backward into his hole, so that to come at him from above is to invite his weapons. The little boys solved the problem for us. We offered ten centavos for each one they took. They dug into the rubble and old coral until they got behind the ghost shrimp in his burrow, then, prodding, they drove him outraged from his hole. Then they banged him good to reduce his pinching power. We refused to buy the banged-up ones—they had to get us lively ones. Small boys are the best collectors in the world. Soon they worked out a technique for catching the shrimps with only an occasionally pinched finger, and then the ten-centavo pieces began running out, and an increasing cloud of little boys brought us specimens. Small boys have such sharp eyes, and they are quick to notice deviation. Once they know you are generally curious, they bring amazing things. Perhaps we only practice an extension of their urge. It is easy to remember when we were small and lay on our stomachs beside a tide pool and our minds and eyes went so deeply into it that size and identity were lost, and the creeping hermit crab was our size and the tiny octopus a monster. Then the waving algae covered us and we hid under a rock at the bottom and leaped out at fish. It is very possible that we, and even those who probe space with equations, simply extend this wonder.

Among small-boy groups there is usually a stupid one who understands nothing, who brings dull things, rocks and pieces of weed, and pretends that he knows what he does. When we think of La Paz, it is always of the small boys that we think first, for we had many dealings with them on many levels.

The profile of this flat was easy to get. The ghost shrimps, called "*langusta*," were quite common; our enemy the stinging worm was about, to make us careful of our fingers; the big brittle-stars were there under the old coral, but not in such great masses as at Espíritu Santo. A number of sponges clung to the stones, and small decorated crabs skulked in the interstices. Beautiful purple polyclad worms crawled over lawns of purple tunicates; the giant oyster-like hacha was not often found, but we took a few specimens. There were several growth forms of the common corals; the larger and handsomer of the two slim asteroids; anemones of at least three types; some club urchins and snails and many hydroids.

Some of the exposed snails were so masked with forests of algae and hydroids that they were invisible to us. We found a worm-like fixed gastropod, many bivalves, including the long peanut-shaped boring clam; large brilliant-orange nudibranchs; hermit crabs; mantids; flatworms which seemed to flow over the rocks like living gelatin; sipunculids; and many limpets. There were a few sun-stars, but not so many or so large as they had been at Cape San Lucas.

The little boys ran to and fro with full hands, and our buckets and tubes were soon filled. The ten-centavo pieces had long run out, and ten little boys often had to join a club whose center and interest was a silver peso, to be changed and divided later. They seemed to trust one another for the division. And certainly they felt there was no chance of their being robbed. Perhaps they are not civilized and do not know how valuable money is. The poor little savages seem not to have learned the great principle of cheating one another.

The population of small boys at La Paz is tremendous, and we had business dealings with a good part of it. Hardly had we returned to the *Western Flyer* and begun to lay out our specimens when we were invaded. Word had spread that there were crazy people in port who gave money for things a boy could pick up on the rocks. We were more than invaded—we were deluged with small boys bearing specimens. They came out in canoes, in flatboats, some even swam out, and all of them carried specimens. Some of the things they brought we wanted and some we did not want. There were hurt feelings about this, but no bitterness. Battalions of boys swarmed back to the flats and returned again. The second day little boys came even from the hills, and they brought every conceivable living thing. If we had not sailed the second night they would have swamped the boat.

Meanwhile, in our dealings on shore, more small boys were involved. They carried packages, ran errands, directed us (mostly wrongly), tried to anticipate our wishes; but one boy soon emerged. He was not like the others. His shoulders were not slender, but broad, and there was a hint about his face and expression that seemed Germanic or perhaps Anglo-Saxon. Whereas the other little boys lived for the job and the payment, this boy created jobs and looked ahead. He did errands that were not necessary, he made himself indispensable. Late at night he waited, and the first dawn saw him on our deck. Further, the other small boys seemed a little afraid of him, and gradually they faded into the background and left him in charge.

Some day this boy will be very rich and La Paz will be proud of him, for he will own the things other people must buy or rent. He has the look and the method of success. Even the first day success went to his head, and he began to cheat us a little. We did not mind, for it is a good thing to be cheated a little; it causes a geniality and can be limited fairly easily. His method was simple. He performed a task, and then, getting each of us alone, he collected for the job so that he was paid several times. We decided we would not use him any more, but the other little boys decided even better than we. He disappeared, and later we saw him in the town, his nose and lips heavily bandaged. We had the story from another little boy. Our financial wizard told the others that he was our sole servant and that we had said that they weren't to come around any more. But they discovered the lie and waylaid him and beat him very badly. He wasn't a very brave little boy, but he will be a rich one because he wants to. The others wanted only sweets or a new handkerchief, but the aggressive little boy wishes to be rich, and they will not be able to compete with him.

On the evening of our sailing we had rather a sad experience with another small boy. We had come ashore for a stroll, leaving our boat tied to a log on the beach. We walked up the curiously familiar streets and ended, oddly enough, in a bar to have a glass of beer. It was a large bar with high ceilings, and nearly deserted. As we sat sipping our beer we saw a ferocious face scowling at us. It was a very small, very black Indian boy, and the look in his eyes was one of hatred. He stared at us so long and so fiercely that we finished our glasses and got up to go. But outside he fell into step with us, saying nothing. We walked back through the softly lighted streets, and he kept pace. But near the beach he began to pant deeply. Finally we got to the beach and as we were about to untie the skiff he shouted in panic, "*Cinco centavos!*" and stepped back as from a blow. And then it seemed that we could see almost how it was. We have been the same way trying to get a job. Perhaps the father of this little boy said, "Stupid one, there are strangers in the town and they are throwing money away. Here sits your father with a sore leg and you do nothing. Other boys are becoming rich, but you, because of your sloth, are not taking advantage of this miracle. Señor Ruiz had a cigar this afternoon and a glass of beer at the *cantina* because his fine son is not like you. When have you known me, your father, to have a cigar? Never. Now go and bring back some little piece of money."

Then that little boy, hating to do it, was burdened with it nevertheless. He hated us, just as we have hated the men we have had to ask for jobs. And he was afraid, too, for we were foreigners. He put it off as long as he could, but when we were about to go he had to ask and he made it very humble. Five centavos. It did seem that we knew how hard it had been. We gave him a peso, and then he smiled broadly and he looked about for something he could do for us. The boat was tied up, and he attacked the water-soaked knot like a terrier, even working at it with his teeth. But he was too little and he could not do it. He nearly cried then. We cast off and pushed the boat away, and he waded out to guide us as far as he could. We felt both good and bad about it; we hope his father bought a cigar and an *aguardiente*, and be-

came mellow and said to a group of men in that little boy's hearing, "Now you take Juanito. You have rarely seen such a good son. This very cigar is a gift to his father who has hurt his leg. It is a matter of pride, my friends, to have a son like Juanito." And we hope he gave Juanito, if that was his name, five centavos to buy an ice and a paper bull with a firecracker inside.

No doubt we were badly cheated in La Paz. Perhaps the boatmen cheated us and maybe we paid too much for supplies—it is very hard to know. And besides, we were so incredibly rich that we couldn't tell, and we had no instinct for knowing when we were cheated. Here we were rich, but in our own country it was not so. The very rich develop an instinct which tells them when they are cheated. We knew a rich man who owned several large office buildings. Once in reading his reports he found that two electric-light bulbs had been stolen from one of the toilets in one of his office buildings. It hurt him; he brooded for weeks about it. "Civilization is dying," he said. "Whom can you trust any more? This little theft is an indication that the whole people is morally rotten."

But we were so newly rich that we didn't know, and besides we were a little flattered. The boatmen raised their price as soon as they saw the Sea-Cow wouldn't work, but as they said, times are very hard and there is no money.

LUDWIG BEMELMANS

from THE DONKEY INSIDE

THE proprietor of Hotel Bemelmans carried his (European) background along when he went to Ecuador. What traveler doesn't do likewise?

QUITO, THE OLDEST CITY in the New World, is seemingly built over a sunken roller coaster. Up and down in wide curves and sudden drops go its streets and white houses; the base of one monument is above the spray of the fountain in the next plaza. It is at once like Tunis and like Bruges, and its near-by backdrop of mountains reminds one of Innsbruck.

I have often expected, at night, that out on the roof of the cathedral, under a foolish golden cockerel that turns in the silent wind, would come Rimsky-Korsakov's star-hatted magician and sing the prologue to the *Coq d'Or.*

It has been said of Quito that it had one hundred churches and one bathtub. There are more bathtubs now, but the churches are still ahead—and they make themselves heard. Their bells are high and insistent; they start ringing for early mass with the crowing of the roosters—clank-clank-clank, bim-bim-bim-bim-bim-bim, bang-bang-bang-bang, and ping-ping-ping-ping. They sound more like large alarm clocks than church bells. The deepest gives off a sound like that of a bathtub hit with a sledgehammer; the others are nervous and quick, and none of them has much music—one right next to the hotel goes: "Beany bunk, beany bunk, beany bunk."

In the early Sunday morning hours, when you ride above Quito to the foot of the volcano Pichincha and look down, the city appears as if made of marzipan crawling with numberless black flies. The flies are

OUTSKIRTS
OF QUITO,
ECUADOR.

priests and little women in black shawls running to and from the churches, and in this respect it is like Bruges; but in Bruges the little women walk in twos, and here they walk alone.

The churches are crammed from floor to dome with gold and statuary; their walls are like pages from the Tickhill psalter. The dogs go to church here, they wander in and out, and during the midday heat they lie on the cool floors and sleep in the confessionals. The Indians unpack their children here, sit close to-gether, and everyone prays half audibly—the church seems filled with the flights of bumblebees; fleas hop from one Indian to another. Santa María, Santa María, Santa María, they love the Virgin most and to her they sing and pray, and they believe that a child nursed in church is particularly blessed. They slide on their knees to their saints and light candles and hold their hands aloft in rigid poses of adoration and prayer.

The sacristies are elaborate apartments, filled with statuary, gilded again and behung with paintings and rows of closets that hold magnificent robes.

The sacristans, complicated bent old men, acting their parts like grand pensionaries of the Comédie Française, creep around in faded soutanes, carting silver candelabra, hanging up brocade curtains, ar-ranging plants, and lighting or snuffing out candles —always followed by the large dark eyes of the Indians. Altar boys run around and chase one another except in front of the altar—they are Indian boys with black hair and brown, round faces over pink cassocks and white surplices. They finally line up at the door of the sacristy—one has an old and heavy silver censer which he begins to swing, another holds a set of small bells, and the one in the middle carries a tall, thin silver and gold cross. He has discovered that a ring of gold at the height of his nose, when touched with his tongue at the same time as the silver, gives out a tingling sour taste, and so he licks that part like a small dog during the procession and the mass.

Bim-bim bim-bim, the bell up above begins. Vamos —let's go—and they march into the church. The Protestant religion, they told me, never made much progress here, because the pastors lack the power to forgive sins; but the Catholic Church is busy all day long. One mass ends, another begins—there are lit-anies, sermons, adorations, vespers, benedictions, novenas, forty-hour devotions, rosaries, all day long. Bim-bim-bim. Bang-bang-bang.

Even the poorest sections of Quito have music and design. From the most decayed hovel leaning against its neighbor comes the sound of a guitar, and the building is made interesting by several coats of white-wash, each a different shade, as if three large bedsheets

of varying degrees of use, one above another, were draped over it. Other houses insist on a character of their own by being painted with the left-over colors of some better abode, coming out red, blue, green, and mauve. People here are brave with colors, and magnificent names are written over the doors of the humblest houses.

The roofs are universally nice, bent, of tile so old that it is green and gray, with small fields of light and blind, smoky sides with the edges worn. The tiles are curved, two rows with the concave side uppermost and between them a third row, reversed, covering the joint. The evidence of the hand and of play is everywhere; exactly the point where someone grew tired of painting his house is visible in a final upward stroke of the brush. There are peculiar designs above windows and doors; benches are built into walls; chimneys lean and balconies sag.

The houses, good and poor, all have patios. In some of them are chickens and workbenches and in the others pools of water or a fountain, an arrangement of palms, cacti, and tangerine trees. You find floors done in colored tiles, inlaid with the vertebrae of oxen, walked on until the bone has taken on the feeling of old ivory, and so arranged that the inlay forms a design or spells the family name, the date of the house, the name of a favorite saint, or a motto.

Some of the patios are also painted with landscapes or naïve, bright designs done with great individuality, sometimes by the owner of the house. There are majolica vases with a thousand small cracks in them and banisters, doorways, columns, and cornucopias which show restraint, good judgment of space, and a quiet humor. It is all old, worn, bleached, and made by hand.

With these ancient, fine, and practical examples in front of you, it is doubly saddening to go into the modern quarter, into what is the elegant suburb, and see what they have done there. A pastrycook of an architect who has become fashionable has been let loose here and built a street in which he has carefully assembled everything that is bad and awful.

The first house is a Moroccan château, pink and green, with a memory of the Taj Mahal injected somewhere among its doors and windows. Next to it he has given shape to the nostalgia of a German émigré and perpetrated a Black Forest chalet that lacks only snow, Christmas music, pine trees, and a wolf with a basket in its mouth. The third exercise of his unhappy initiative is modern, a pastel-colored bath-room turned inside out, a shiny small box with over-sized round windows, oval doors, and a chromium ship's rail on its roof. This row of houses, each one a few feet from the other, ends in a stone sentinel, a midget Lohengrin castle. Every one of these villas has been indulged with a wall or fence, lanterns, door-knobs, bells, and landscaping to match its character —the fixtures seem all personally selected by the architect.

Happy to be out of this street, you run into another architectural disaster a few blocks to the north—one that is even more depressing because you cannot laugh. In a superb landscape that is difficult to equal, an ambitious builder has set down two rows of houses facing each other—about twenty of them, alike as foxterriers, built of stone, painted red, with carefully drawn white lines dividing the red surface into bricks. Each little house has the same number of windows, the same door, and the same mat of grass to the left and right of the entrance. They accomplish the heartlessness of a company street in the Pennsylvania coal districts.

The owners of all these properties are extremely proud of them, and one can console oneself by thinking of their happiness and by riding away in any direction. In one short hour from Quito, to the south, is a replica of the road from Nice to Monte Carlo; to the west, Africa with bananas, Negroes, monkeys, and malaria; to the north, the badlands of the Dakotas; to the east, Capuchin and Dominican monks in sandals, walking over soft carpets of green grass like those along the Danube between Stift, Melk, and Linz.

JOHN DOS PASSOS

from BRAZIL ON THE MOVE

DOS PASSOS visits the 16th parallel latitude south.

YOU DRIVE OUT to the airport in the steaming dark over the rackety cobbles of Manaus: you step into a jet plane and in four hours and a half you are in Brasília. It is the greatest contrast imaginable. Manaus is as redolent of the nineteenth century as a story by Jules Verne. The air is dense with green exhalations of the rainforest. Brasília is an arid red. The sun is hot but the air has a cool upland tang. The glimpses, as the plane banks for a landing, of glass and concrete constructions spread like an unfinished world's fair along the red ridge, between the two arms of the lake, are desperately contemporary. You are reminded of the story that's going the rounds about how a visiting Russian astronaut cried out on landing in Brasília: "I hadn't expected to reach Mars so soon."

In New York Brazilians told us: You mustn't go to the hotel that was new four years ago. You must go to the new hotel. We found the new new hotel, though of course many floors were still unfinished, to be remarkably pleasant, with its big kidneyshaped swimming pool in the sunny central court, which was flanked by a firstrate restaurant. Under the same management as the Jaraguá in São Paulo it is probably one of the best in South America.

The Nacional stands on a rise overlooking the central bus station where the arterial roads that form the city's backbone—the fuselage of Lucio Costa's jet plane—converge through cloverleaves into the roads that serve the wings. From the front door you look out across a rubbly hillside which will someday be Lucio Costa's modern Montmartre, past large Park Avenue type office buildings occupied by banks and insurance companies, down what corresponds to the mall in Washington, D.C. towards the shining tile-shaped twin skyscrapers of the congressional offices. The confusing pile of masonry beyond the bus station will eventually become the white marble pyramid which will house Niemeyer's interlocking theaters.

To get from the hotel to the bus station on foot is a scramble. If paths for pedestrians were included in the plans, they haven't been built yet. There are of course no traffic lights. You have to wait for a lull and lope across the broad curving roadways as best you can. Many a pedestrian, so people tell us, has already lost his life on his way to the bus station.

When you finally reach the platform you can walk around in safety. Shining new Mercedes-Benz buses, produced in São Paulo, come in from all directions: Belo Horizonte, Anápolis, Ceres, Goiânia. Escalators take you to the upper levels. There are small stores, newsstands, snackbars, and coffee bars. The place has a cheerful practical look, except that the smooth-finished white concrete of the underpasses is already stained by the pervasive red dust.

There's no way to see the town without a car. In Brasília a man without a car is a secondclass citizen. The poorer inhabitants will have to grow wheels instead of feet.

The two buildings that flank the Congress Square, the Palacio do Planalto for the executive departments, and the Supreme Court building, are oblongs of transparent glass, each shaded by a broad slab of concrete supported by delicate white buttresscolumns. To my way of thinking they are among Niemeyer's best. Suited to the climate and the landscape. Fine examples of his paper cutout style. So are the odd little presidential chapel (which according to some irreverent people looks more like a urinal than a house of worship) and the charmingly simple Church of Our Lady of Fátima.

The congress building itself seems to me to be a conspicuous failure. The interior is cramped and illplanned for its purpose. There is a frivolous ugliness about the exterior hard to explain in a designer with such great talent for sculptural effects. Jefferson used to call architecture the most important of the arts "because it showed so much." Possibly the design of the congress hall expresses the faithful Communist's scorn for representative democracy.

Niemeyer's cathedral, an enormous coronet of stressed concrete, remains unfinished. The design calls for glass to fill in the spaces between the soaring piers. It is impressive as it is. One wonders whether it should ever be finished.

Though the long horizontals of the apartment buildings suit the city plan better than the occasional outbreak of New York style skyscrapers, the routine monotony of their design becomes depressing. The apartments themselves, seen from the inside, show little interest on the part of the designers for the needs of the people who have to live in them. The rows of identical concrete hutches for lower income renters express, even more perfectly than some federal housing in the United States, the twentieth century bureaucrat's disdain of the faceless multitudes to whose interests he is supposed to be devoted and whose exploitation furnishes his keep. The worst shack in the adjacent shantytowns of Cidade Livre or Taguatinga would be a better place to live.

Still, even after canvassing all the objections, you have to admit that the designers of Brasília have created a magnificent frame for a future city. The long straight thoroughfares, the vast open spaces between low white buildings are exhilarating. It's a city for the automotive age, for the age of jets and helicopters. Its vast spaces match the vast smooth arid ridges of the landscape of the planalto.

The lake greatly enhances the effect of the city and of the landscape. It is blue. I was afraid it would turn out muddy. It reflects the desert clouds and the gaudy sunsets and the bright firmament of the upland nights. There's a yachtclub and sailboats. We saw people fishing in it. Competent engineers after my last visit had told me so much about the possibility of seepage through the earth dam, that I had ceased to believe in the lake, but there it is, and protected from pollution by what looks to a layman like a thoroughly adequate sewage disposal plant.

Already signs are appearing of a post-Niemeyer architecture. The University of Brasília, which was only started some eight months back, is already conducting classes amid the hammering of carpenters and the dust of construction. Students on their way to lectures step over candongos laying tiled floors. The one building that's almost finished, named Os Dois Candongos for two bricklayers who were killed in its construction, offers a series of well-proportioned whitewalled halls, some lit from above and some from the side, which open on patios landscaped with specimens of the native vegetation of the planalto. It's all in human scale. A skilled balance—important under that glary sky—seems to have been struck between too little and too much light in the classrooms.

Courses in law, administration, humanities, Portuguese literature are already functioning. There is a school of architecture headed by Alcides da Rocha Miranda who designed the buildings we walked through. The curriculum so we were told is modeled on that of North American universities, and there is considerable emphasis, unusual in Brazil, on night school and extension courses for boys and girls who have to work to support themselves. The homey dormitory in frame and plaster with Japanese style woodwork balconies is a pleasure to look at after so much glass and concrete.

In the cafeteria there some of the teachers fed us one of the best feijoadas I ever ate. Feijoada is the Boston baked beans of Brazil and oddly enough also tends to appear on Saturdays. If the instruction proves as good as the cookery the University of Brasília should go far.

The Japanese, by the way, have added greatly to the variety of the architecture of Brasília by the daintily proportioned chancellery they have put up on their embassy lot. Our State Department, too, has done well with its chancellery. The courtyard is unusually attractive. There, and, in some of the suburban houses across the lake, you can see some intimation of the appearance of a Brasília style, suited to the light and to the climate and to the needs of the human beings who are going to inhabit the city.

When Oscar Niemeyer put up a residence to live in himself, way out of town near the country club, he built himself an oblong house with a tile roof and tall windows in the simple Brazilian colonial style which, in the first giddy enthusiasm for Le Corbusier's glass and steel, used to be considered hopelessly outmoded. People tell you he only built it to please his wife, but there it is.

JAMES MORRIS

from CITIES

WHO has seen so much of the contemporary world, and written about it so clearly, as the Manchester Guardian's James Morris?

WHEN I WAS once hanging around an airfield in Patagonia, hoping to thumb a lift to the north, I noticed a small group of people, dressed apparently for *après-ski*, who seemed to dominate the waiting-room with a kind of steely radiance. They looked very rich, and very brassy, and very thrusting. Their children were ill-mannered but intensely vivacious, their women were gimlet-eyed but seductive, their men had a feline Italian elegance to them: and unexpectedly, when I offered a smile in their glittering direction, one and all suddenly, brilliantly, delightfully smiled back. I asked where these magical creatures were making for, and was answered in one short tingling word: "Rio!"

Angels they are not, the people of Rio, but instantly I felt like an old Pope in a slave market, for to me there seemed something remote and romantic about their manner of effervescent, if not reckless, audacity. It is this spirit of excitement, this animal crackling of the spirits, that sets their city apart from its South American peers, and makes it such a shot in the arm, such a haunting tune in the head. Rio is not, as legend has her, one perpetual Mardi Gras, thumping and blaring in false noses all night long. She is a place of deep and humane variety, full of fun indeed, but tinged also with a high-strung melancholy. Here you may well be deafened by the sambas blazing down Copacabana Beach, but you may also stumble across some elderly grey Negro, in dungarees paled by many a scrub, plucking upon his guitar melodies of a very different kind, half African, half Portuguese, part New World, part Old, sad as an east wind, soft as any courtier's lyric, and played with such grave and sophisticated intellectualism that you may feel yourself, down there by the harbour-front, in the presence of some remarkable inheritance, some old and unassailable attitude of mind.

For Rio is a manner of thought: not just a spectacle, not just a song and dance, but a particular approach to the problems of human progress. In this city you suck your milk out of the coconut with an impeccably hygienic straw: and whether you are discussing economic philosophy with some whiskered academic, or holding hands with a mulatto courtesan in the dim of a night-club dawn—whether you are twanging your guitar in the Dorian or the Lydian mode, you will find that here, by some happy freak of the time mechanism, the clock always stops at midnight.

Everything they say about her, all the same, is factually true. Never did a city better live up to her reputation, or more handsomely justify the picture-postcard flattery. In her splendour of situation, encouched among bays and humped hills, she has only half a dozen rivals on earth—Hong Kong perhaps, Venice, Wellington, San Francisco, Naples, Sydney if you happen to be Australian, possibly Beirut, Cape Town at a pinch. Her brilliant beaches, lined with parades of skyscraper hotels and patrolled by gaudy bird-shaped kites, have become the very emblem of sunshine hedonism—to my own taste ineffably boring, but to those who enjoy the salacious torpor of a rich sandy foreshore, incomparable in their kind. Her climate, sometimes desperately hot but often softened by sea mist, gives her a sensual, heavy-lidded, perfumed temperament. Her old culture, inherited equally from Portuguese gentlemen and Muslim slaves out of Africa, makes her much more than just a pleasure-drome. The miserable hovels of her slums, perched in sad incongruity above the waterside highways, or crouched hang-dog among the apartment blocks, remind us that she is a city in the round, where every kind of man lives and makes love, and women in rags can look across a pavement to see the ripple of Balenciaga. The squalid indigence of her countryside, only twenty miles from Copacabana, rams home the truth that she is only the beautiful pinnacle of a vast, half-ignorant, disease-ridden, mostly empty, partly unexplored hinterland. Rio is all things to everyone. She fulfils every preconception.

She is an urgent, overcrowded city, invested in the rear by the Brazilian jungle, still creeping gloomily down her hillsides, and giving to some imaginative visitors a spectral impression of impending doom. Her topography is cramped and awkward. She is sprawled about the big bay of Guanabara, big enough to shelter half the navies of the world, and all around her stand mountains, some in massive forested ridges, some in sudden bumps and protrusions at the water's edge. If you stand beneath the gigantic hilltop figure of Christ, where the tourists buy their pictorial crockery or their cases of pickled Brazilian beetles—if you stand up there on the peak called Corcovado beneath the outstretched arms of the statue, you may see how sinuously Rio weaves her purlieus among the contours, sometimes slinking behind a mountain, sometimes huddling beneath a ridge, sometimes charging clean through a hillside in a pair of masterly tunnels. The water-front of Rio is all curves, all unexpected coves, lined with trees and tall white buildings, cut off one part from another by high ground or inlets. The roads of Rio are a congested clamour. The waters of Rio stream with shipping, from the chugging Niterói ferry-boats to the big Brazilian carrier lying like a grandee beyond Flamengo. Even the skies of Rio are full of animation, for never did a city plunge so enthusiastically into the air age, so that the municipal airport lies slap in the middle of town, beside the water, and there are four hundred services a week to São Paulo alone.

But if she is sometimes frantic, she is also handsome, in a curled and burnished taste. São Paulo to the south is genially plebeian, a haven, a labour market and a gold mine. Brasília across the mountains is doggedly futuristic, airily above class or controversy. But in Rio it is easy to accept the unlikely fact that Brazil was once an Empire of her own, and that up the road in Petropolis a pretender to the imperial throne still sits hopefully in a florid palace. We call her Rio indeed, but her proper name is São Sebastião do Rio de Janeiro, and her origins are nothing if not high-flown. She does not feel an old city, though in fact she was founded in 1560. Her impatient gusto has torn down most of the old structures, and long ago discarded the old design, leaving only an occasional gilded church among the office blocks, or a splendid theatre high and dry among the traffic jams. Her manner, though, is seldom blatant, and more than most cities she feels organic to her setting. This is a place naturally clothed, as the Scottish wanderer John Robertson said in the early eighteen-hundreds, "with richness and beauty altogether marvellous." The modern architecture of Rio is not often ugly, and is sometimes magnificent. Her elderly suburbs do not feel unwanted or humiliated, but are allowed to age there quietly among their palms, like rather cantankerous, but still affectionately regarded relatives. The famous mosaic pavements of the city blend as happily with glass and concrete as they did with sculptured stone and whirligigs. Almost nothing feels intrusive, from the incomprehensibly abstract war memorial on the water-front to the famous cable car swinging hungrily across the bay to the restaurant on top of the Sugar Loaf.

For the spirit of this city is tolerant and sanguine to a fault, and makes you feel that nothing is unwelcome,

and nothing altogether impossible. In Chicago you are regarded as Negro if you have a drop of black blood in your veins: in Rio you are accepted as European if you have a speckle of white. Here you can be, by and large, what you want to be, behave how you like, wear a frock-coat to dinner or a Jamaica shirt, a mink stole or a bikini. Rio takes you as you are, impelled by the conviction that in a community of such endless and pulsating variety, every little helps. Of course this magnanimity has its seamier concomitants—greed, exploitation, corruption, extravagance, materialism, ostentation. Even the transient visitor to Copacabana, searching desperately for a hotel room, will soon detect the advantages of greasing a Rio palm. Somehow, though, one is not affronted by these weaknesses, for all the fiddlings and coarser ambitions of the place are blunted, softened and made innocent by the warm tropical air of Brazil, which brings to this city's affairs a faint languorous suggestion of *dolce far niente* —not enervating enough to prevent the making of fortunes or the beating of drums, but sufficiently soothing to make you feel that here, more than in places of more rigid principle, humanity still lingers on. For Rio is, as a hard-boiled oil-man once observed to me, a very benediction among cities, like a morning of English summer among days of the year, or an apple pie among puddings.

The sceptics will scoff, and of course this is the romantic's view of Rio. It is true that there is to this city a certain never-never feeling, just as there is to Brazil as a whole a certain naïveté or childish enthusiasm. It is not exactly power that you feel in Rio, immense though the resources of this city are, but a sense of heady appetite—a looking-glass appetite, where you may shrink or grow by a nibble or a sip, sing wild songs or consort with strange knights. Brazil has been the Country of the Future for several centuries now, and Rio is her mirror. The overwhelming impact of the place is one of always impending euphoria, as though things are just about to be all for the best in practically the best of all possible worlds. Some people liken her to a supremely talented dilettante, perpetually about to fulfil the promise of youth, mincing down the years with a novel always at the back of his mind.

But Rio cares not what they say. She is never put out, never discouraged, always hopeful, always sure. She has far more faults than I have cared to enumerate, but I loved her from the start, and I think her carping critics, sniffing at her over-drafts and deploring her excesses, cannot see the oaks for the nettles. Perhaps, like Brazil itself, she lacks some niggling virtues of common sense, but she glories in that grandest of historical qualities, style. Whatever she does is big, whatever she thinks is generous. Great God! I will swap you a dozen prim and thrifty boroughs for one such lovely greatheart!

ANTOINE DE SAINT EXUPÉRY

from WIND, SAND AND STARS

PUNTA ARENAS, in Chile's Tierra del Fuego, is as far south as Goose Bay, Labrador, is north. It has changed far less in the generation since Saint Exupéry wrote of it than the means of getting there. Air travel, or the experience of flight, has entered a new era, not yet recorded by any writer with the sensitivity this man brought to it in his time.

THE AIRPLANE has unveiled for us the true face of the earth. For centuries, highways had been deceiving us. We were like that queen who determined to move among her subjects so that she might learn for herself whether or not they rejoiced in her reign. Her courtiers took advantage of her innocence to garland the road she traveled and set dancers in her path. Led forward on their halter, she saw nothing of her kingdom and could not know that over the countryside the famished were cursing her.

Even so have we been making our way along the winding roads. Roads avoid the barren lands, the rocks, the sands. They shape themselves to man's needs and run from stream to stream. They lead the farmer from his barns to his wheatfields, receive at the thresholds of stables the sleepy cattle and pour them forth at dawn into meadows of alfalfa. They join village to village, for between villages marriages are made.

And even when a road hazards its way over the desert, you will see it make a thousand détours to take its pleasure at the oases. Thus, led astray by the divagations of roads, as by other indulgent fictions, having in the course of our travels skirted so many well-watered lands, so many orchards, so many meadows, we have from the beginning of time embellished the picture of our prison. We have elected to believe that our planet was merciful and fruitful.

But a cruel light has blazed, and our sight has been sharpened. The plane has taught us to travel as the crow flies. Scarcely have we taken off when we abandon these winding highways that slope down to watering troughs and stables or run away to towns dreaming in the shade of their trees. Freed henceforth from this happy servitude, delivered from the need of fountains, we set our course for distant destinations. And then, only, from the height of our rectilinear trajectories, do we discover the essential foundation, the fundament of rock and sand and salt in which here and there and from time to time life like a little moss in the crevices of ruins has risked its precarious existence.

We to whom humble journeyings were once permitted have now been transformed into physicists, biologists, students of the civilizations that beautify the depths of valleys and now and again, by some miracle, bloom like gardens where the climate allows. We are able to judge man in cosmic terms, scrutinize him through our portholes as through instruments of the laboratory. I remember a few of these scenes.

* * *

The pilot flying towards the Straits of Magellan sees below him, a little to the south of the Gallegos River, an ancient lava flow, an erupted waste of a thickness of sixty feet that crushes down the plain on which it has congealed. Farther south he meets a second flow, then a third; and thereafter every hump on the globe, every mound a few hundred feet high, carries a crater in its flank. No Vesuvius rises up to reign in the clouds; merely, flat on the plain, a succession of gaping howitzer mouths.

This day, as I fly, the lava world is calm. There is something surprising in the tranquillity of this deserted landscape where once a thousand volcanoes boomed to each other in their great subterranean organs and spat forth their fire. I fly over a world mute and abandoned, strewn with black glaciers.

South of these glaciers there are yet older volcanoes veiled with the passing of time in a golden sward. Here and there a tree rises out of a crevice like a plant out of a cracked pot. In the soft and yellow light the plain appears as luxuriant as a garden; the short grass seems to civilize it, and round its giant throats there is scarcely a swelling to be seen. A hare scampers off; a bird wheels in the air; life has taken possession of a new planet where the decent loam of our earth has at last spread over the surface of the star.

Finally, crossing the line into Chile, a little north

of Punta Arenas, you come to the last of the craters, and here the mouths have been stopped with earth. A silky turf lies snug over the curves of the volcanoes, and all is suavity in the scene. Each fissure in the crust is sutured up by this tender flax. The earth is smooth, the slopes are gentle; one forgets the travail that gave them birth. This turf effaces from the flanks of the hillocks the sombre sign of their origin.

We have reached the most southerly habitation of the world, a town born of the chance presence of a little mud between the timeless lava and the austral ice. So near the black scoria, how thrilling it is to feel the miraculous nature of man! What a strange encounter! Who knows how, or why, man visits these gardens ready to hand, habitable for so short a time —a geologic age—for a single day blessed among days?

I landed in the peace of evening. Punta Arenas! I leaned against a fountain and looked at the girls in the square. Standing there within a couple of feet of their grace, I felt more poignantly than ever the human mystery.

In a world in which life so perfectly responds to life, where flowers mingle with flowers in the wind's eye, where the swan is the familiar of all swans, man alone builds his isolation. What a space between men their spiritual natures create! A girl's reverie isolates her from me, and how shall I enter into it? What can one know of a girl who passes, walking with slow steps homeward, eyes lowered, smiling to herself, filled with adorable inventions and with fables? Out of the thoughts, the voice, the silences of a lover, she can form an empire, and thereafter she sees in all the world but him a people of barbarians. More surely than if she were on another planet, I feel her to be locked up in her language, in her secret, in her habits, in the singing echoes of her memory. Born yesterday of the volcanoes, of green-swards, of brine of the sea, she walks here already half divine.

Punta Arenas! I lean against a fountain. Old women come up to draw water: of their drama I shall know nothing but these gestures of farm servants. A child, his head against a wall, weeps in silence: there will remain of him in my memory only a beautiful child forever inconsolable. I am a stranger. I know nothing. I do not enter into their empires. Man in the presence of man is as solitary as in the face of a wide winter sky in which there sweeps, never to be tamed, a flight of trumpeting geese.

How shallow is the stage on which this vast drama of human hates and joys and friendships is played! Whence do men draw this passion for eternity, flung by chance as they are upon a scarcely cooled bed of lava, threatened from the beginning by the deserts that are to be, and under the constant menace of the snows? Their civilizations are but fragile gildings: a volcano can blot them out, a new sea, a sand-storm.

This town seemed to be built upon a true humus, a soil one might imagine to be as rich as the wheatlands of the Beauce. These men live heedless of the fact that, here as elsewhere, life is a luxury; and that nowhere on the globe is the soil really rich beneath the feet of men.

Yet, ten miles from Punta Arenas there is a lake that ought to be reminding them of this. Surrounded by stunted trees and squat huts, as modest as a pool in a farm-yard, this lake is subject to the preternatural pull of the tides. Night and day, among the peaceful realities of swaying reeds and playing children, it performs its low respiration, obedient to unearthly laws. Beneath the glassy surface, beneath the motionless ice, beneath the keel of the single dilapidated bark on the waters, the energy of the moon is at work. Ocean eddies stir in the depths of this black mass. Strange digestions take their peristaltic course there and down as far as the Straits of Magellan, under the thin layer of grasses and flowers. This lake that is a hundred yards wide, that laps the threshold of a town which seems to be built on man's own earth and where men believe themselves secure, beats with the pulse of the sea.

OCEANIA

OCEANIA

The vagabond, when rich, is called a tourist.

PAUL RICHARD

They [Hawaiians] seem to me the very sweetest of people, even if they did eat Captain Cook.

JAMES MORRIS

THOR HEYERDAHL

from KON-TIKI

THE best way to see Polynesia, unspoiled, is by private yacht. If you don't have a private yacht, the next best way is wading ashore with Thor Heyerdahl.

I SHALL NEVER FORGET that wade across the reef toward the heavenly palm island that grew larger as it came to meet us. When I reached the sunny sand beach, I slipped off my shoes and thrust my bare toes down into the warm, bone-dry sand. It was as though I enjoyed the sight of every footprint which dug itself into the virgin sand beach that led up to the palm trunks. Soon the palm tops closed over my head, and I went on, right in toward the center of the tiny island. Green coconuts hung under the palm tufts, and some luxuriant bushes were thickly covered with snow-white blossoms, which smelled so sweet and seductive that I felt quite faint. In the interior of the island two quite tame terns flew about my shoulders. They were as white and light as wisps of cloud. Small lizards shot away from my feet, and the most important inhabitants of the island were large blood-red hermit crabs which lumbered along in every direction with stolen snail shells as large as eggs adhering to their soft hinder parts.

I was completely overwhelmed. I sank down on my knees and thrust my fingers deep down into the dry warm sand.

The voyage was over. We were all alive. We had run ashore on a small uninhabited South Sea island. And what an island! Torstein came in, flung away a sack, threw himself flat on his back and looked up at the palm tops and the white birds, light as down, which circled noiselessly just above us. Soon we were all six lying there. Herman, always energetic, climbed up a small palm and pulled down a cluster of large green coconuts. We cut off their soft tops with our machete knives, as if they were eggs, and poured down our throats the most delicious refreshing drink in the world—sweet, cold milk from young and seedless palm fruit. On the reef outside resounded the monotonous drum beats from the guard at the gates of paradise.

"Purgatory was a bit damp," said Bengt, "but heaven is more or less as I'd imagined it."

We stretched ourselves luxuriously on the ground and smiled up at the white trade-wind clouds drifting by westward up above the palm tops. Now we were no longer following them helplessly; now we lay on a fixed, motionless island, in Polynesia.

And as we lay and stretched ourselves, the breakers outside us rumbled like a train, to and fro, to and fro, all along the horizon.

Bengt was right; this was heaven.

*   *   *

Our little island was uninhabited. We soon got to know every palm clump and every beach, for the island was barely two hundred yards across. The highest point was less than six feet above the lagoon.

Over our heads, in the palm tops, there hung great clusters of green coconut husks, which insulated their contents of cold coconut milk from the tropical sun, so we should not be thirsty in the first weeks. There were also ripe coconuts, a swarm of hermit crabs, and all sorts of fish in the lagoon; we should be well off.

On the north side of the island we found the remnants of an old, unpainted wooden cross, half buried in the coral sand. Here there was the view northward along the reef to the stripped wreck, which we had first seen closer in as we drifted by on the way to our stranding. Still farther northward we saw in a bluish haze the palm tufts of another small island. The island to southward, on which the trees grew thickly, was much closer. We saw no sign of life there, either, but for the time we had other matters to think about.

Robinson Crusoe Hesselberg came limping up in his big straw hat with his arms full of crawling hermit crabs. Knut set fire to some dry wood, and soon we had crab and coconut milk with coffee for dessert.

"Feels all right being ashore, doesn't it, boys?" Knut asked delightedly.

He had himself enjoyed this feeling once before on the voyage, at Angatau. As he spoke, he stumbled and poured half a kettle of boiling water over Bengt's bare feet. We were all of us a bit unsteady the first day ashore, after 101 days on board the raft, and would suddenly begin reeling about among the palm trunks because we had put out a foot to counter a sea that did not come.

When Bengt handed over to us our respective mess utensils, Erik grinned broadly. I remember that, after the last meal on board, I had leaned over the side of the raft and washed up as usual, while Erik looked in across the reef, saying: "I don't think I shall bother to wash up today." When he found his things in the kitchen box, they were as clean as mine.

After the meal and a good stretch on the ground we set about putting together the soaked radio apparatus; we must do it quickly so that Torstein and Knut might get on the air before the man on Rarotonga sent out a report of our sad end.

Most of the radio equipment had already been brought ashore, and among the things which lay drifting on the reef Bengt found a box, on which he laid his hands. He jumped high into the air from electric shock; there was no doubt that the contents belonged to the radio section. While the operators unscrewed, coupled, and put together, we others set about pitching camp.

Out on the wreck we found the heavy waterlogged sail and dragged it ashore. We stretched it between two big palms in a little opening, looking on to the lagoon, and supported two other corners with bamboo sticks which came drifting in from the wreck. A thick hedge of wild flowering bushes forced the sail together so that we had a roof and three walls and, moreover, a clear view of the shining lagoon, while our nostrils were filled with an insinuating scent of blossoms. It was good to be here. We all laughed quietly and enjoyed our ease; we each made our beds of fresh palm leaves, pulling up loose branches of coral which stuck up inconveniently out of the sand. Before night fell we had a very pleasant rest, and over our heads we saw the big bearded face of good old Kon-Tiki. No longer did he swell out his breast with the east wind behind him. He now lay motionless on his back looking up at the stars which came twinkling out over Polynesia.

On the bushes round us hung wet flags and sleeping bags, and soaked articles lay on the sand to dry. Another day on this island of sunshine and everything would be nicely dry. Even the radio boys had to give it up until the sun had a chance of drying the inside of their apparatus next day. We took the sleeping bags down from the trees and turned in, disputing boastfully as to who had the driest bag. Bengt won, for his did not squelch when he turned over. Heavens, how good it was to be able to sleep!

When we woke next morning at sunrise, the sail was bent down and full of rain water as pure as crystal. Bengt took charge of this asset and then ambled down to the lagoon and jerked ashore some curious breakfast fish which he decoyed into channels in the sand.

That night Herman had had pains in the neck and back where he had injured himself before the start from Lima, and Erik had a return of his vanished lumbago. Otherwise we had come out of the trip over the reef astonishingly lightly, with scratches and small wounds, except for Bengt who had had a blow on the forehead when the mast fell and had a slight concussion. I myself looked most peculiar, with my arms and legs bruised blue black all over by the pressure against the rope.

But none of us was in such a bad state that the sparkling clear lagoon did not entice him to a brisk swim before breakfast. It was an immense lagoon. Far out it was blue and rippled by the trade wind, and it was so wide that we could only just see the tops of a row of misty, blue palm islands which marked the curve of the atoll on the other side. But here, in the lee of the islands, the trade wind rustled peacefully in the fringed palm tops, making them stir and sway, while the lagoon lay like a motionless mirror below and reflected all their beauty. The bitter salt water was so pure and clear that gaily colored corals in nine feet of water seemed so near the surface that we thought we should cut our toes on them in swimming. And the water abounded in beautiful varieties of colorful fish. It was a marvelous world in which to disport oneself. The water was just cold enough to be refreshing, and the air was pleasantly warm and dry from the sun. But we must get ashore again quickly today; Rarotonga would broadcast alarming news if nothing had been heard from the raft at the end of the day.

Coils and radio parts lay drying in the tropical sun on slabs of coral, and Torstein and Knut coupled and screwed. The whole day passed, and the atmosphere grew more and more hectic. The rest of us abandoned all other jobs and crowded round the radio in hope of being able to give assistance. We must be on the air before 10 P.M. Then the thirty-six hours' time limit would be up, and the radio amateur on Rarotonga would send out appeals for airplane and relief expeditions.

Noon came, afternoon came, and the sun set. If only the man on Rarotonga would contain himself! Seven o'clock, eight, nine. The tension was at breaking point. Not a sign of life in the transmitter, but the receiver, an NC-173, began to liven up somewhere at the bottom of the scale and we heard faint music. But not on the amateur wave length. It was eating its way up, however; perhaps it was a wet coil which was drying inward from one end. The transmitter was still stone-dead—short circuits and sparks everywhere.

There was less than an hour left. This would never do. The regular transmitter was given up, and a little sabotage transmitter from wartime was tried again. We had tested it several times before in the course of the day, but without result. Now perhaps it had become a little drier. All the batteries were completely ruined, and we got power by cranking a tiny hand generator. It was heavy, and we four who were laymen in radio matters took turns all day long sitting and turning the infernal thing.

The thirty-six hours would soon be up. I remember someone whispering "Seven minutes more," "Five minutes more," and then no one would look at his watch again. The transmitter was as dumb as ever, but the receiver was sputtering upward toward the right wave length. Suddenly it crackled on the Rarotonga man's frequency, and we gathered that he was in full contact with the telegraph station in Tahiti. Soon afterward we picked up the following fragment of a message sent out from Rarotonga:

"- - - no plane this side of Samoa. I am quite sure - - -."

Then it died away again. The tension was unbearable. What was brewing out there? Had they already begun to send out plane and rescue expeditions? Now, no doubt, messages concerning us were going over the air in every direction.

The two operators worked feverishly. The sweat trickled from their faces as freely as it did from ours who sat turning the handle. Power began slowly to come into the transmitter's aerial, and Torstein pointed ecstatically to an arrow which swung slowly up over a scale when he held the Morse key down. Now it was coming!

We turned the handle madly while Torstein called Rarotonga. No one heard us. Once more. Now the receiver was working again, but Rarotonga did not hear us. We called Hal and Frank at Los Angeles and the Naval School at Lima, but no one heard us.

Then Torstein sent out a CQ message: that is to say, he called all the stations in the world which could hear us on our special amateur wave length.

That was of some use. Now a faint voice out in the ether began to call us slowly. We called again and said that we heard him. Then the slow voice out in the ether said:

"My name is Paul—I live in Colorado. What is your name and where do you live?"

This was a radio amateur. Torstein seized the key, while we turned the handle, and replied:

"This is the Kon-Tiki. We are stranded on a desert island in the Pacific."

Paul did not believe the message. He thought it was a radio amateur in the next street pulling his leg, and he did not come on the air again. We tore our hair in desperation. Here were we, sitting under the palm tops on a starry night on a desert island, and no one even believed what we said.

Torstein did not give up; he was at the key again sending "All well, all well, all well," unceasingly. We must at all costs stop all this rescue machinery from starting out across the Pacific.

Then we heard, rather faintly, in the receiver:

"If all's well, why worry?"

Then all was quiet in the ether. That was all.

We could have leaped into the air and shaken down all the coconuts for sheer desperation, and heaven knows what we should have done if both Rarotonga and good old Hal had not suddenly heard us. Hal wept for delight, he said, at hearing LI 2 B again. All the tension stopped immediately; we were once more alone and undisturbed on our South Sea island and turned in, worn out, on our beds of palm leaves.

Next day we took it easy and enjoyed life to the full. Some bathed, others fished or went out exploring on the reef in search of curious marine creatures, while the most energetic cleared up in camp and made our surroundings pleasant. Out on the point which looked toward the Kon-Tiki we dug a hole on the edge of the trees, lined it with leaves, and planted in it the sprouting coconut from Peru. A cairn of corals was erected beside it, opposite the place where the Kon-Tiki had run ashore.

The Kon-Tiki had been washed still farther in

during the night and lay almost dry in a few pools of water, squeezed in among a group of big coral blocks a long way through the reef.

After a thorough baking in the warm sand Erik and Herman were in fine fettle again and were anxious to go southward along the reef in the hope of getting over to the large island which lay down there. I warned them more against eels than against sharks, and each of them stuck his long machete knife into his belt. I knew the coral reef was the habitat of a frightful eel with long poisonous teeth which could easily tear off a man's leg. They wriggle to the attack with lightning rapidity and are the terror of the natives, who are not afraid to swim round a shark.

The two men were able to wade over long stretches of the reef to southward, but there were occasional channels of deeper water running this way and that where they had to jump in and swim. They reached the big island safely and waded ashore. The island, long and narrow and covered with palm forest, ran farther south between sunny beaches under the shelter of the reef. The two continued along the island till they came to the southern point. From here the reef, covered with white foam, ran on southward to other distant islands. They found the wreck of a big ship down there; she had four masts and lay on the shore cut in two. She was an old Spanish sailing vessel which had been loaded with rails, and rusty rails lay scattered all along the reef. They returned along the other side of the island but did not find so much as a track in the sand.

On the way back across the reef they were continually coming upon curious fish and were trying to catch some of them when they were suddenly attacked by no fewer than eight large eels. They saw them coming in the clear water and jumped up on to a large coral block, round and under which the eels writhed. The slimy brutes were as thick as a man's calf and speckled green and black like poisonous snakes, with small heads, malignant snake eyes, and teeth an inch long and as sharp as an awl. The men hacked with their machete knives at the little swaying heads which came writhing toward them; they cut the head off one and another was injured. The blood in the sea attracted a whole flock of young blue sharks which attacked the dead and injured eels, while Erik and Herman were able to jump over to another block of coral and get away.

On the same day I was wading in toward the island when something, with a lightning movement, caught hold of my ankle on both sides and held on tight. It was a cuttlefish. It was not large, but it was a horrible feeling to have the cold gripping arms about one's limb and to exchange looks with the evil little eyes

in the bluish-red, beaked sack which constituted the body. I jerked in my foot as hard as I could, and the squid, which was barely three feet long, followed it without letting go. It must have been the bandage on my foot which attracted it. I dragged myself in jerks toward the beach with the disgusting carcass hanging on to my foot. Only when I reached the edge of the dry sand did it let go and retreat slowly through the shallow water, with arms outstretched and eyes directed shoreward, as though ready for a new attack if I wanted one. When I threw a few lumps of coral at it, it darted away.

Our various experiences out on the reef only added a spice to our heavenly existence on the island within. But we could not spend all our lives here, and we must begin to think about how we should get back to the outer world. After a week the *Kon-Tiki* had bumped her way in to the middle of the reef, where she lay stuck fast on dry land. The great logs had pushed away and broken off large slabs of coral in the effort to force their way forward to the lagoon, but now the wooden raft lay immovable, and all our pulling and all our pushing were equally unavailing. If we could only get the wreck into the lagoon, we could always splice the mast and rig her sufficiently to be able to sail with the wind across the friendly lagoon and see what we found on the other side. If any of the islands were inhabited, it must be some of those which lay along the horizon away in the east, where the atoll turned its façade toward the lee side.

The days passed.

Then one morning some of the fellows came tearing up and said they had seen a white sail on the lagoon. From up among the palm trunks we could see a tiny speck which was curiously white against the opal-blue lagoon. It was evidently a sail close to land on the other side. We could see that it was tacking. Soon another appeared.

They grew in size, as the morning went on, and came nearer. They came straight toward us. We hoisted the French flag on a palm tree and waved our own Norwegian flag on a pole. One of the sails was now so near that we could see that it belongs to a Polynesian outrigger canoe. The rig was of more recent type. Two brown figures stood on board gazing at us. We waved. They waved back and sailed straight in on to the shallows.

"Ia-ora-na," we greeted them in Polynesian.

"Ia-ora-na," they shouted back in chorus, and one jumped out and dragged his canoe after him as he came wading over the sandy shallows straight toward us.

The two men had white men's clothes but brown men's bodies. They were barelegged, well built, and wore home-made straw hats to protect them from the sun. They landed and approached us rather uncertainly, but, when we smiled and shook hands with them in turn, they beamed on us with rows of pearly teeth which said more than words.

Our Polynesian greeting had astonished and encouraged the two canoers in exactly the same way as we ourselves had been deceived when their kinsman off Angatau had called out "Good night," and they reeled off a long rhapsody in Polynesian before they realized that their outpourings were going wide of the mark. Then they had nothing more to say but giggled amiably and pointed to the other canoe which was approaching.

There were three men in this, and, when they waded ashore and greeted us, it appeared that one of them could talk a little French. We learned that there was a native village on one of the islands across the lagoon, and from it the Polynesians had seen our fire several nights earlier. Now there was only one passage leading in through the Raroia reef to the circle of islands around the lagoon, and, as this passage ran right past the village, no one could approach these islands inside the reef without being seen by the inhabitants of the village. The old people in the village, therefore, had come to the conclusion that the light they saw on the reef to eastward could not be the work of men but must be something supernatural. This had quenched in them all desire to go across and see for themselves. But then part of a box had come drifting across the lagoon, and on it some signs were painted. Two of the natives, who had been on Tahiti and learned the alphabet, had deciphered the inscription and read TIKI in big black letters on the slab of wood. Then there was no longer any doubt that there were ghosts on the reef, for Tiki was the long-dead founder of their own race—they all knew that. But then tinned bread, cigarettes, cocoa, and a box with an old shoe in it came drifting across the lagoon. Now they all realized that there had been a shipwreck on the eastern side of the reef, and the chief sent out two canoes to search for the survivors whose fire they had seen on the island.

Urged on by the others, the brown man who spoke French asked why the slab of wood that drifted across the lagoon had "Tiki" on it. We explained that "Kon-Tiki" was on all our equipment and that it was the name of the vessel in which we had come.

Our new friends were loud in their astonishment when they heard that all on board had been saved, when the vessel stranded, and that the flattened wreck out on the reef was actually the craft in which we had come. They wanted to put us all into the canoes at once and take us across to the village. We thanked them and refused, as we wanted to stay till we had got the Kon-Tiki off the reef. They looked aghast at the flat contraption out on the reef; surely we could not dream of getting that collapsed hull afloat again! Finally the spokesman said emphatically that we must go with them; the chief had given them strict orders not to return without us.

We then decided that one of us should go with the natives as envoy to the chief and should then come back and report to us on the conditions on the other island. We would not let the raft remain on the reef and could not abandon all the equipment on our little island. Bengt went with the natives. The two canoes were pushed off from the sand and soon disappeared westward with a fair wind.

Next day the horizon swarmed with white sails. Now, it seemed, the natives were coming to fetch us with all the craft they had.

The whole convoy tacked across toward us, and, when they came near, we saw our good friend Bengt waving his hat in the first canoe, surrounded by brown figures. He shouted to us that the chief himself was with him, and the five of us formed up respectfully down on the beach where they were wading ashore.

Bengt presented us to the chief with great ceremony. The chief's name, Bengt said, was Tepiuraiarii Teriifaatau, but he would understand whom we meant if we called him Teka. We called him Teka.

Teka was a tall, slender Polynesian with uncommonly intelligent eyes. He was an important person, a descendant of the old royal line in Tahiti, and was chief of both the Raroia and the Takume islands. He had been to school in Tahiti, so that he spoke French and could both read and write. He told me that the capital of Norway was called Christiania and asked if I knew Bing Crosby. He also told us that only three foreign vessels had called at Raroia in the last ten years, but that the village was visited several times a year by the native copra schooner from Tahiti, which brought merchandise and took away coconut kernels in exchange. They had been expecting the schooner for some weeks now, so she might come at any time.

Bengt's report, summarized, was that there was no school, radio, or any white men on Raroia, but that the 127 Polynesians in the village had done all they could to make us comfortable there and had prepared a great reception for us when we came over.

The chief's first request was to see the boat which had brought us ashore on the reef alive. We waded out toward the Kon-Tiki with a string of natives after us. When we drew near, the natives suddenly stopped and uttered loud exclamations, all talking at once.

We could now see the logs of the *Kon-Tiki* plainly, and one of the natives burst out:

"That's not a boat, it's a *pae-pae!*"

"*Pae-pae!*" they all repeated in chorus.

They splashed out across the reef at a gallop and clambered up on to the *Kon-Tiki*. They scrambled about everywhere like excited children, feeling the logs, the bamboo plaiting, and the ropes. The chief was in as high spirits as the others; he came back and repeated with an inquiring expression:

"The *Tiki* isn't a boat, she's a *pae-pae.*"

Pae-pae is the Polynesian word for "raft" and "plat-form," and on Easter Island it is also the word used for the natives' canoes. The chief told us that such *pae-pae* no longer existed, but that the oldest men in the village could relate old traditions of them. The natives all outshouted one another in admiration for the great balsa logs, but they turned up their noses at the ropes. Ropes like that did not last many months in salt water and sun. They showed us with pride the lashings on their own outriggers; they had plaited them themselves of coconut hemp, and such ropes remained as good as new for five years at sea.

POLYNESIAN VILLAGE, SAMOA.

When we waded back to our little island, it was named Fenua Kon-Tiki, or Kon-Tiki Island. This was a name we could all pronounce, but our brown friends had a hard job trying to pronounce our short Nordic Christian names. They were delighted when I said they could call me Terai Mateata, for the great chief in Tahiti had given me that name when adopting me as his "son" the first time I was in those parts.

The natives brought out fowls and eggs and breadfruit from the canoes, while others speared big fish in the lagoon with three-pronged spears, and we had a feast round the campfire. We had to narrate all our experiences with the *pae-pae* at sea, and they wanted to hear about the whale shark again and again. And every time we came to the point at which Erik rammed the harpoon into its skull, they uttered the same cries of excitement. They recognized at once every single fish of which we showed them sketches and promptly gave us the names in Polynesian. But they had never seen or heard of the whale shark or the *Gempylus*.

When the evening came, we turned on the radio, to the great delight of the whole assemblage. Church music was most to their taste until, to our own astonishment, we picked up real hula music from America. Then the liveliest of them began to wriggle with their arms curved over their heads, and soon the whole company sprang up on their haunches and danced the hula-hula in time with the music. When night came, all camped round a fire on the beach. It was as much of an adventure to the natives as it was to us.

When we awoke next morning, they were already up and frying newly caught fish, while six freshly opened coconut shells stood ready for us to quench our morning thirst.

The reef was thundering more than usual that day; the wind had increased in strength, and the surf was whipping high into the air out there behind the wreck.

"The *Tiki* will come in today," said the chief, pointing to the wreck. "There'll be a high tide."

About eleven o'clock the water began to flow past us into the lagoon. The lagoon began to fill like a big basin, and the water rose all round the island. Later in the day the real inflow from the sea came. The water came rolling in, terrace after terrace, and more and more of the reef sank below the surface of the sea. The masses of water rolled forward along both sides of the island. They tore away large coral blocks and dug up great sandbanks which disappeared like flour before the wind, while others were built up. Loose bamboos from the wreck came sailing past us, and the Kon-Tiki began to move. Everything that was lying along the beach had to be carried up into the interior of the island so that it might not be caught by the tide. Soon only the highest stones on the reef were visible, and all the beaches round our island had gone, while the water flowed up toward the herbage of the pancake island. This was eerie. It looked as if the whole sea was invading us. The *Kon-Tiki* swung right round and drifted until she was caught by some other coral blocks.

The natives flung themselves into the water and swam and waded through the eddies till, moving from bank to bank, they reached the raft. Knut and Erik followed. Ropes lay ready on board the raft, and, when she rolled over the last coral blocks and broke loose from the reef, the natives jumped overboard and tried to hold her. They did not know the *Kon-Tiki* and her ungovernable urge to push on westward; so they were towed along helplessly with her. She was soon moving at a good speed right across the reef and into the lagoon. She became slightly at a loss when she reached quieter water and seemed to be looking round as though to obtain a survey of further possibilities. Before she began to move again and discovered the exit across the lagoon, the natives had already succeeded in getting the end of the rope around a palm on land. And there the *Kon-Tiki* hung, tied up fast in the lagoon. The craft that went over land and water had made her way across the barricade and into the lagoon in the interior of Raroia.

With inspiring war cries, to which "*ke-ke-te-huru-huru*" formed an animating refrain, we hauled the *Kon-Tiki* by our combined efforts in to the shore of the island of her own name. The tide had reached a point four feet above normal high water. We had thought the whole island was going to disappear before our eyes.

The wind-whipped waves were breaking all over the lagoon, and we could not get much of our equipment into the narrow, wet canoes. The natives had to get back to the village in a hurry, and Bengt and Herman went with them to see a small boy who lay dying in a hut in the village. The boy had an abscess on his head, and we had penicillin.

Next day we four were alone on Kon-Tiki Island. The east wind was now so strong that the natives could not come across the lagoon, which was studded with sharp coral formations and shoals. The tide, which had somewhat receded, flowed in again fiercely, in long, rushing step formations.

Next day it was quieter again. We were now able to dive under the *Kon-Tiki* and ascertain that the nine logs were intact, even if the reef had planed an inch or two off the bottom. The cordage lay so deep in its grooves that only four of the numerous ropes had been cut by the corals. We set about clearing up on board. Our proud vessel looked better when the mess had been removed from the deck, the cabin pulled out again like a concertina, and the mast spliced and set upright.

In the course of the day the sails appeared on the horizon again; the natives were coming to fetch us and the rest of the cargo. Herman and Bengt were with them, and they told us that the natives had prepared great festivities in the village. When we got over to the other island, we must not leave the canoes till the chief himself had indicated that we might do so.

We ran across the lagoon, which here was seven miles wide, before a fresh breeze. It was with real sorrow that we saw the familiar palms on Kon-Tiki Island waving us goodby as they changed into a clump and shrank into one small indefinable island like all the others along the eastern reef.

JAMES RAMSEY ULLMAN

from WHERE THE BONG TREE GROWS

NOT every traveler likes places completely unspoiled. They are too unfamiliar and uncomfortable. Tahiti is certainly spoiled, and delightful.

ONLY IN AMERICA, according to Harry Golden, can certain things happen. And only in Tahiti, it may be added, can certain others.

I began making this discovery at precisely the moment that fellow passengers and I stepped out of the now silently wallowing Solent into the launch that would take us ashore, and there in the lagoon before us rode a French destroyer named, belligerently, *La Capricieuse*. A little farther in sported a group of French-shouting Chinese water skiers. Along the *quai*, as we neared it, sped a motor scooter carrying a man, woman, baby, and live pig. And on nearby curb sat a classically ragged bum clasping a gold-capped bottle of Pol Roger.

Then came my first evening, and dinner at the roof-top restaurant of Papeete's Grand Hotel. Behind me, gastronomically, were months of taro-breadfruit-coconut, varied by hash-hamburger-pisupo, and the bounties that now appeared were enough to make eyes pop and stomach gurgle. In a gourmand's trance I dined on *pâté* Strasbourg, *langouste* (*avec Chablis*), *château-briant et artichaut* (*avec Pommard*), *camembert et café* (*avec cognac*). And the trance was made no less euphoric by the fact that I was served by a Tahitian vahine with golden skin, waist-length black hair, and a yellow hibiscus behind each ear. As I sipped my cognac she sat down beside me, introduced herself as Louise, and inquired if I had enjoyed my meal. It had been the climax of my life, I assured her. . . . And now that it was over, what were my plans for the evening? Well—er—they were a bit vague. In fact I had no plans. . . . "So we go dancing at Quinn's," said Louise. And we went dancing at Quinn's.

Some dreams are private, one's very own. Others are in the public domain. Over the past few centuries in our Western world, none had beguiled the minds of men more potently than the Dream of the South Seas; and, within the larger dream, the heart, the essence has been the island to which I now had come. I am well aware that I am neither the first nor the tenth nor the ten thousandth traveler to say, "Only in Tahiti—"

Almost two centuries ago its first European visitors—the men who sailed with Wallis, Bougainville, and Cook—came and landed and looked about them, and were never again quite the same for the experience. Its charms, feminine and otherwise, were the direct cause (with a slight assist from Captain Bligh) of the mutiny on the *Bounty*. And through all the years since it has had a magical lure for generations of bemused pilgrims. In early days it was the haven de luxe for ship-jumping sailors and whalers—and, on the other face of the coin, the toughest challenge a missionary could meet this side of the Day of Judgment.* Even Charles Darwin—scarcely a romantic escapist—who came to Tahiti as a young scientist on the world-circling *Beagle*, conceded that it "must ever remain classical to the voyager in the South Seas." And here, of course, my retinue of writing ghosts swarmed thicker than anywhere else in the Pacific. There have been painters by the dozen and hundred: among them,

---

* Ironically, it has been the missionary—in theory at least, a spiritual man—who has been least motivated by the South Seas Dream. Far from seeking paradise in the islands, he has, on the contrary, been under the impression that he is bringing it with him.

toweringly, Gauguin. There have been tycoons with their yachts, playboys with their neuroses, film stars with their mistresses, rebel youngsters and sated sybarites, would-be saints and *de facto* con men, rich and poor, plain and fancy, from every corner of the earth—to the point where the very name Tahiti has become globally synonymous with Romance and Escape.

So much so, indeed, that the governing French have in late years imposed firm controls. The length of an outsider's stay is now strictly limited, and to be admitted at all he must either possess an outbound ticket or have posted a bond covering its cost. Only in special circumstances (usually involving marriage into a local family) can he buy property, take employment, or go into business. Without such restrictions, Tahitians and French alike would by now have been all but obliterated by a tide of immigrants: half retired millionaires, half dead-beat beachcombers.

Romance—Escape—Tahiti. . . . And one is tempted to add, *On the lagoon, 'neath the moon, with my sweetie . . .* for the island's fame has ballooned, over the years, into the ultimate tin-pan alley cliché. What makes the cliché especially hard to exorcise, even for the most relentless realist, is that it is roughly ninety-nine per cent true. There *is* a lagoon girdling its shores, of almost breath-taking beauty. When the moon shines it puts a tunesmith's daydream to shame. And as for "sweeties" (i.e., vahines) let us face the fact: Tahiti teems with them. And, as anyone from Captain Cook to the latest package-toured tripper off

Dancing girls in grass skirts, Tahiti.

the *Mariposa* will testify, there is nothing else like them on land or sea or foam.

"Ah, but it's not what it used to be," one hears from the old-timers (as one does from old-timers about everything, everywhere). And the answer is, of course it's not. It wasn't the same on the day after the first white man landed as it was on the day before. And ever since—sometimes avidly, sometimes reluctantly—it has been making its terms and compromises with the encroaching outer world. As to the end, or at least present, result, there is some difference of opinion. There are those who think that Tahiti, even today, is God's chosen spot on earth. There are others who call it "Tobacco Road with palms." On only one point, I believe, will everyone have to agree: that it is, for better or worse, unique.

The land mass of Tahiti consists of two rugged, long-extinct volcanic cones, joined by a narrow isthmus to form a figure eight. The larger loop is Tahiti proper, the smaller the peninsula of Taiarapu, or Little Tahiti, and together they comprise an area of 402 square miles. The total population is in the upper thirty thousands, of which about half lives in the capital—and only—town of Papeete, on the northwest shore of Big Tahiti, with the rest scattered along the belt of level coastal land that encircles the island. The interior is deserted: an almost trackless wilderness of peaks and valleys, crags and gorges and plunging waterfalls, all deeply festooned by lush tropical growth. And a trip across it is rugged going. The highest point, Mount Orohéna (7,339 feet), was not climbed until 1953—the same year as Everest. And few visitors to Tahiti catch even a glimpse of it: for even while the coasts are flooded with sunlight, the uplands remain almost always shrouded in great tiers of cloud.

It is not upward and inward that Tahiti looks, but outward to the sea. And its seascapes are dazzling in their loveliness. Only the beaches—as on so many Pacific islands—are apt to be disappointing to the visitor; for they are neither numerous nor well cared for, and on most the sand is dark brown or black. But all the rest is a prismatic dream: the gleaming emerald of the shore line; the lighter green of the lagoon, darkening, turning to azure and then sapphire blue as it deepens seaward; the white frieze of breakers on the girdling reef; and beyond the reef, nine miles across the shining water from the northwest coast, the neighbor island of Mooréa thrusting its incredible silhouette of dome and spire—now green, now purple, now black, now sunset red—into the ocean sky.

As with the sea, so with the land itself. A circuit of the island, along its ninety miles of twisting coastal road, is a journey through a tropical Land of Oz. On either side, always, are the immensities of mountain and ocean; but here on the narrow strip between them everything is small, soft, gentle, intimate. Palm trees, of course, are everywhere, their plumes nodding gently seaward. And among them mango and bread-fruit, avocado and pandanus, banana and bamboo and causarina, in prodigal profusion. In the low damp places are taro patches; on firmer ground rows of coffee and vanilla bushes. For a while, as you move on, the scent of vanilla fills the air. Then the scent of copra. Then—more enduringly—the scent of flowers. And always in your eyes there is the brilliance of the flowers: hibiscus, bougainvillaea, frangipani, gardenia, and the island's own fabled *tiare Tahiti*.

For the conscientious, there is also, of course, a generous spate of "sights-to-see": from the ruins of ancient temples, through the landing places of explorers, to the bridge where the hell-raising black-velvet painter, Edgar Leeteg, crashed to his death on a motor bike. But *l'ambiance Tahitienne* is notoriously hostile to conscientiousness, and the average wayfarer will find himself considerably more involved in the here-and-now life about him. For almost every Pacific island is lavish in history, as it is in beauty; but the life, the *ambiance*,* of Tahiti is its very own. You feel it even in the country, in the villages of bamboo and thatch (or plant and tin), where the roosters can hardly be heard over the thump of guitars and the click of billiard balls. In the Toonerville buses, jam-packed to—and on—the roofs with brown bodies, smiling faces, squealing pigs, and flapping fowls. In the girls in shorts and halters, on motor bikes and scooters, whizzing past (to Leeteg's fate?) with long hair streaming behind them. In the multiplication of bikes and scooters—plus buses and trucks and sports cars and jalopies—until, as you approach Papeete, you are in a traffic snarl worthy of the Place de la Concorde.

It has often been said that Papeete† is not the "real Tahiti." And echo answers: New York is not the "real U.S.A." . . . To both charges I should like to reply, "Then what is? Siltbottom, Arkansas? A grass shack in a taro patch?" . . . Tahiti—let thanks resound—is not yet a Waikiki or Miami Beach; but, as of the seventh decade of the twentieth century, it is no more the primitive South Sea Island of song and story than America is a domain of cowboys and Indians. And Papeete is its heart and center; the focus of its present, the key to its future. One may like or dislike it, approve or disapprove. But it is as "real" as you can get.

* *Ambiance* has become more or less an English word, as well as a French one. But spelled without italics and pronounced as English, it would bear no remotest relationship to the atmosphere of Tahiti.

† I have rarely heard anyone who has not been to Tahiti say *Papeete* correctly. It is pronounced "Pap-ay-ay-tay," or if you prefer the French, "Papé-été."

And as alive. For Papeete hums and throbs, and often positively jerks, with animation. Certainly its waterfront is one of the sights of the world: the only harbor I know of in which liners and freighters—not to mention schooners and yachts, ferries and fishing boats—tie up directly along the main street of the town. On the inland side of the *quais* are the mercantile houses, the major stores, shipping and tourist offices, cafés and restaurants, all of them seeming to be crowded all the time. And behind them the smaller shops, almost a hundred per cent Chinese, fan out in confused array along the labyrinthine back streets. Everywhere there are buyers, sellers, sight-seers, loungers, forests of parked motor bikes, and hordes of unparked ones plunging around corners. Except for the seafront, it is an ugly town. A nondescript, ramshackle, decrepit town. But you will not find a livelier one between Montmartre and the Golden Gate.

Other South Pacific centers fold up completely at nightfall: but here Papeete is even more the exception than by day. The lights go on. The music starts. The swarm of bikes grows even thicker. While I was there, Les Tropiques, then the island's leading hotel, had dancing on an average of four evenings a week; and in what might be called the "downtown joints"—Bar Léa, Au Col Bleu, and the famous Quinn's—every night was Saturday night, with all the stops out. Fashions change quickly in such matters, but, at the time, Quinn's (minus its long-time maestro, Eddie Lund, who was in exile in Fiji) was looked on by the *cognoscenti* as "for the tourists"; Au Col Bleu was French Army and Navy headquarters; leaving Bar Léa as the haven of the hipsters. And it must be conceded that its music and dancing (of which more anon) were something to hear and behold. The one concession to respectability required by law of all three was a firm 11:30 closing. But for the die-hards—and there were plenty—there was always the Lafayette, a few miles out of town, where the curfew matched the endurance of the die-hardest.

Of all the world's people, I think, the Tahitian is the prime apostle of The Good Time, and his dedication to its pursuit is something awesome to see. When he sits down to a feast it is with a gusto and capacity that would put a Roman Emperor to shame. When he drinks it's bottoms up, and not just for the glass but for the bottle. Give him (or her) a guitar, and he will strum and sing until its strings break; or set him dancing, and he may or may not stop for a late breakfast. Perhaps the favorite of all activities are picnics and round-the-island tours. And such junkets, awash in beer, flowered garlands, music, and laughter, can assume epic proportions.

"Ah, but you're here at the wrong season," I was

PREPARATION FOR FIRE WALKING, FIJI.

told on several occasions. "The time the Tahitian really goes to town is during the *fête*, around July Fourteenth". . . . And the word *around*, I soon learned, was not loosely used. . . . In France they may celebrate Bastille Day, but in Tahiti it's Bastille Month, at the minimum. And I should think that the only non-Tahitian who could weather it would be one who had preconditioned himself with, say, New Year's Eve in New York, Carnival in Rio, and Independence Day in a new African republic.

In the interests of accuracy it must be admitted that not all Tahitians are on a spree *all* the time. The very young and very old are the most notable exceptions, and even those in between will occasionally be found at other pursuits. Within reason, that is. Work of the slogging day-in-day-out variety is left almost wholly to the Chinese, who, like the Indians in Fiji, were brought in a century ago as plantation laborers, and have—at a handsome profit—kept the wheels turning ever since. The Tahitian is not interested in profit. When he works, it is at something that not only needs doing but that he enjoys doing: at fishing, for instance, at building a house or canoe, at sailing a ship or driving a nice big noisy truck. And his capacity for enjoyment —here as in his revels—is unique. On boat day at Papeete's docks the handling of baggage and freight resembles nothing so much as a lively basketball game. In a restaurant, my *amie* Louise and her sister waitresses were as likely as not to be practicing a dance step as they toted your tray in from the kitchen. One day, while I was in my seaside bungalow, a sharp squall blew up, and from the shrouded wind-lashed water I heard what I took to be shouts for help. But when, a few minutes later, a group of fishermen stumbled ashore dragging their capsized canoe, I found they were still shouting—with sheer delight at the excitement.

How does the Tahitian get this way? . . . It is on the record, plain and grim, that for some two hundred years he has been plundered, corrupted, and victimized by the white man; and there are those who contend that, beneath the surface, he is sad and lost, awash in a world he never made or asked for, and knowing himself doomed to racial extinction. If this contention is true, however—and it is at least debatable—he is assuredly the world's Pagliacci par excellence. Whatever his past and future, he gives, today, an impeccable performance as the happiest of men.

For this happiness, real or apparent, I would say there are three principal reasons, of which the first is the Tahitians themselves; for even in the days of the first Western explorers they were the most easygoing and pleasure-loving of the Pacific peoples. Second is the fact—not unrelated to the first—that the missions have never succeeded in dominating their lives, as they have those of other Polynesians, and that the white man's faiths, whether Protestant or Catholic, rest lightly on both their souls and habits. And third is the happenstance of history that gave their island to France.

Not that the French, over the years, have been a shining light of colonialism. Nor that the *fonctionnaire* in his government office or the *commerçant* in his countinghouse are the best beloved of men. But few—

and they should have their heads examined—would argue that things would be better with British or American counterparts. The French are concerned with making money. They are concerned with international prestige and holding together their shreds of empire. But they are *not* concerned with private lives; with who drinks what, who sleeps with whom, and what time you go to bed at night, or in the morning. And these—not the ploys and gambits of world politics—are what matter on the island.

Most important of all, there is no color line. True, "color" in golden-tan Tahiti is not the same thing as in black Melanesia or Africa, and there has been so much interbreeding—between native and French, native and Chinese, native or part native and almost every nationality in the almanac—that it is hard today to determine just what *is* a Tahitian and what isn't. But under British or Americans there would still, inevitably, be some form of racial distinction, whereas under the French there is none. Financial and professional status varies, as anywhere—including Russia and China. But social equality is absolute. During my term as escapist-in-residence, the lounge, dock, and terrace of the Hotel Les Tropiques belonged as much to passing fishermen and stray children (not to mention stray cats) as they did to the paying guests. My taxi driver of one day could very well, on the next, be my host at a party. Six nights a week Louise waited on table at the Grand Hotel; but on the seventh, as likely as not, she was right back there *sitting* at table, while her escort (who shall be nameless) ordered her *tournedos* with sauce Béarnaise.

Of such things is the island's *ambiance* compounded: a blend of old ways and new ways, Tahitian and French, the languorously easygoing and the feverishly frenetic. And they add up to a world of marvelous charm and fascination—but not quite to paradise. For Tahiti, however remote, however "special," is still part of a world in which a price must be paid for everything.

Strictly nonparadisaical, for instance, are its sloppiness and decrepitude; its rats and roaches and streets carpeted with squashed mangoes. And anyone under the unfortunate necessity of "getting something done" will feel himself a lot farther from heaven than from its antipode. The management of Les Tropiques was not singing the charms of Tahiti on the night of one of its "galas" (150 reservations) when two of its fourteen waitresses showed up—the others having taken off on a beach picnic. Nor was I, on a certain golden morning when I spent four traumatic hours making two phone calls, sending a cable, and cashing a check at the bank. The moment you left the lagoon or put down

(continued on page 145)

KRONFELD © PAA

FIJI CHIEF WITH GARLAND OF FLOWERS.

TRAFFIC POLICEMAN IN SERRATED-EDGE SKIRT, FIJI.

(continued from page 133)

the guitar, the frustrations could mount to the ulcer point with horrid rapidity.

These, to be sure, are hazards only for the popaa*—the white man. For the Tahitian there are other, and more serious problems: pre-eminently disease. The old island curse of filariasis/elephantiasis has by now been brought pretty well under control. But tuberculosis is rampant. As is venereal disease. And with the sale of liquor virtually uncontrolled, there is widespread drunkenness. The right-minded popaa is apt to have a bad conscience about all this, for he is well aware that it was he—or his forebears—who inflicted it on the island. But it is typical of the Tahitian that he wastes little time in self-sympathy. "Aué," says he (aué—pronounced "Ah-way"—being his all-purpose expletive for anything from "gee whiz" to "#*@#%&#!")—"Aué, we would rather have the *maladies d'amour* than no *amour*, and rather the drunkenness than no drinks."

A monument to his philosophy, no less than to deceased royalty, is the tomb of the island's last king, Pomare V, in the countryside near Papeete. Pomare drank himself to death. His favorite drink was Benedictine. So what more fitting—in Tahiti—than that atop the tomb there should be a king-sized replica of a Benedictine bottle, lovingly carved in coral stone?

God's chosen spot? Tobacco Road with palms? . . . Tahiti is both, I should say; and opinion depends on what one seeks, and on what one brings along as spiritual baggage. Old—and not so old—lady tourists (perhaps accustomed to associating dancing with church socials) have been known to bolt from Quinn's or Bar Léa murmuring, "My God, get me off this awful island!" And assuredly the plumbing, kitchen fixtures, sidewalk hygiene, and insect life do not appeal to those accustomed only to the Pasteurized Polynesia of Waikiki Beach. At the other extreme, there are some who find Tahiti too civilized, too Westernized; who yearn for thatched shacks, taro patches, lonely beaches, and spuming reefs. And these—unlike category A—can rectify matters without total retreat.

For Tahiti itself, though the hub and center, is still only part of the domain known by the resounding name of *Les Établissements français de l'Océanie*. And in the other parts, spread over a million and a half square miles of Pacific Ocean, are some of the loveliest and least spoiled islands that nature could fashion or man imagine. Even Moorea, a mere nine miles from Papeete, has a life wholly different in texture and tempo. And the farther one gets—to *Les Iles Sous le Vent* (Raiatéa, Bora Bora), the Australs, the Tuamotus, the remote Marquesas and Gambiers—the more one is back in the old domain of storybook Polynesia. Some of these are now accessible from Tahiti by plane; others can still be reached only by trading boats at long and irregular intervals. But even in the ultimate outposts there is apt to be—besides the inevitable French gendarme—an outsider or two: the true hard-core loners and escapists who have chosen to make their home there.

For most long-termers, however, as for most come-and-go visitors, it is Tahiti itself that has called, and there that they have settled. Among the popaa, the French are of course in the majority, but almost all are there in the call of government or business. Those who have come, and stayed, simply because they wanted to are of every conceivable nationality, with Americans—numbering about two hundred—now predominating. The old-style classic beachcomber is—thanks to the French dragnet—now obsolete; but his place has been more or less taken by the new-style "nature man," who somehow avoids becoming a public charge; and from this subsistence level the scale ascends to well-heeled luxury. Many Westerners have married locally and raised part-Tahitian families, of which those of the late Charles Nordhoff and James Norman Hall are distinguished examples. A few lead as active lives as they would in America or Europe, with a keen eye on the golden fallout from the coming "tourist explosion." A few bestir themselves only to munch languidly on a lotus and then roll over for the next siesta. In only one matter is there complete conformity, and that is in the conviction that anyone who could live in Tahiti but chooses to live elsewhere is hopelessly out of his mind.

I myself was, in status, somewhere between the long-termer and the come-and-goer, for my stay was of several months; and I was there theoretically, to work: i.e., to write. . . . "But of course. *Mais oui. Aué!*" said the long-termers indulgently, when I announced my intention, smiling that special long-termer's smile that I was soon to understand all too well. . . . For while closing oneself in one's room is not technically illegal in Tahiti, it is considered, by popaas no less than Tahitians, a most peculiar way of spending one's time;* and everyone I knew—or didn't know—banded together to protect me from such folly. Elsewhere in the Pacific my "writing block" had been largely a subjective affair. Here it was a community project.

—As, for instance, on a certain morning in my

---

* Popaa, of course, is cognate with the Samoan *papalagi*. In the various Polynesian languages some words are similar, even identical, and others are wholly unrelated. Roughly, the language relationship is about that of French-Spanish-Italian or German-Dutch-Scandinavian.

* "What about Nordhoff and Hall?" I would ask. "Well, they were peculiar," I was told. "But *bien gentils*."

bungalow at Les Tropiques, with the sun bright, the lagoon agleam, and myself trying hard not to look at them, but at the blank sheet of paper in my typewriter. The phone rings. "Tennis? Well—er—no, thanks a lot, but—" The phone rings. "How's for lunch? Just a few of us—about twenty. Rum punch, *vin rouge*, and— Oh. Oh, I see. *Admirable*. Well, to-morrow then—" And back to the typewriter. Click, click; perhaps ten clicks. Then from the hotel lounge, a hundred yards distant, a blast of Tahitian drums comes over the radio. And after ten minutes I walk over. There is no one around but Marie, the receptionist, behind the desk, and Marie is practicing the *Tamure*, the Tahitian hula. I point to the loud-speaker, hold my ears, and she considerately turns down the volume. Then she grabs hold of me, and for another ten minutes, to more dulcet drumming, we practice the *Tamure* together.

Whew, that's over. Back to the bungalow. And on the porch is another girl—a girl I've never seen before—a very pretty girl, tiny and chic, half Tahitian and half Chinese. "Allo, I am Yvette," she says. And I say, "Allo, Yvette." Then she asks, do I have an *amie*? Yes, I do, I confess. And her face falls, but quickly brightens. Then I should have a second *amie*, she suggests. The first one is not here. She is. It is very simple. . . . No, not so simple, I explain. She, Yvette, is very small. My *amie*, Louise, is not small. She is, however, possessive. If she found Yvette with me, she would eat her—and probably me too—for *petit déjeuner*. . . . Yvette, I gather, does not wholly understand the syllogism; but at least, after a few more efforts, she tosses her head and departs. By the time Louise arrives—unexpectedly—a half-hour later, to announce that we're going on a picnic, I have typed three words. They are:

Only in Tahiti—

So much has been written, for so long, about the Tahitian vahine that I hesitate to add the two cents of a Johnny-come-lately. But a portrait of the island that failed to take note of her would be like one of, say, Detroit that omitted the automobile. Louise, Marie, Yvette, and their sisterhood are not mere incidentals in this never-never land. They are its *force majeure*, the very incarnation of the *ambiance* of Tahiti.*

Physically they vary greatly; for the pure Polynesian

---

* In the interests of sober reporting, it should be noted that there *are* male inhabitants. But historically and literarily they have been given short shrift, and unless otherwise stated, it is generally assumed that all indigenes are women—just as all visitors are men. An interesting and poignant anthropological thesis could, I think, be written on the subject of those "forgotten ones"—the Tahitian male and the visiting female.

is today a rare bird on the island, and, as likely as not, the so-called Tahitienne will have inherited a different racial strain from each of her four grandparents. Those of preponderantly native blood are apt to run to heft and girth, to a degree rather forbidding to Western tastes. But those of mixed ancestry—called *demis*—are usually far more delicate of frame and feature; and the half Tahitian half Chinese, in particular, are often (and I make the statement categorically) as beautiful as a woman can get. Fat or thin, however, beautiful or only middling, all—if they are short of the old-crone stage—have a quality of style. Whether in a Dior replica, a pareu with garlands, or blue jeans and their boy friend's sport shirt, I never once saw a vahine whom I would call a frump.

As for their well-known "availability," the answer is that it's as advertised. But while the newcomer may be prepared for this, he is apt to be surprised by the sweetness and gentility that go with it. There are exceptions, of course. At Quinn's and along the wharfs on boat days there are girls as brassily professional as any tramp in San Francisco or Marseille. But these are a minority. Most are not brassy. And they are not tramps. By their own lights they are thoroughly decent and self-respecting vahines. And it is their lights, not ours, that make the rule of the road in Tahiti.

Reams of analysis, learned and leering, have been written about Tahitian sex morality, but it seems to me that the old Ethel Merman song gets to the point quickest and best. It's a matter of "doing what comes naturally." In our Western world, society and church, economics and romance, have combined to make the mating of male and female a fearsomely complex affair; but to the Polynesian it is no more complex than breathing, eating, sleeping, or any of the other normal functions of life. In the pre-white world, in which their customs evolved, venereal disease did not exist. And even today, no opprobrium—or problem—is attached to an illegitimate child. Indeed, the very word "illegitimate" is meaningless; for whose laws are we talking about? Surely none that the Tahitian would ever have dreamed up for himself.

This is not to say that there is no code of sexual conduct, or that animal license reigns supreme. Incest is considered the blackest of offenses, the ban on intra-family relations being extended even to distant cousins. Postmarital infidelity is probably no worse, if no better, than elsewhere; and faithfulness, whether to spouse or *ami*, is highly esteemed. As in all human societies, everywhere, poaching on another's preserve is generally taboo—and can be (as I pointed out to Yvette) positively dangerous. For the venerable emotion of jealousy is as indigenous to mid-Pacific as to either shore of the Atlantic, and a vahine scorned is as formidable in reprisal as her Western sister. Like her, too, she reserves the right to pick and choose. And it is this, I think, more than anything else, that makes her—despite what we would call her promiscuity—fundamentally a lady. True, she will probably not think the worse of her *ami* (what woman does?) if he should come through with an occasional gift. But, except in the case of the few waterfront tramps, he will not be her *ami* in the first place unless she thinks he is *bien gentil*.

Aué, aué te vahine Tahiti, goes the first line of the island's best-known song. And an echoing "*Aué!*" is about as coherent as the visiting fireman, from Cook to Cook's Tourist, has been able to get. Her frontal assault (if she finds you *bien gentil*) will probably stagger you. Her giggle, when she is with others of her kind, will drive you crazy. But when she stops giggling and looks up at you, her eyes and smile will light up the Pacific night. One thing that is understood from the outset is that she is a woman, you are a man (*vide* earlier footnote), and there is no nonsense about "let's just be friends." Her dancing—whether the classic otea, the wild tamure, or a pseudo-Western importation—will be, unabashedly, the best facsimile she can provide, perpendicular and clothed, of the act of love. When she plunks her guitar and sings, it will be of love. When she talks, it will be of love; and not romantically and vaguely, but in specific detail, as if she were discussing a new dress or recipe.

In conclusion, it must be added that one hears few complaints along the line of Mark Twain's: that everyone talks about the weather but no one does anything about it. . . . In Tahiti—aué—it is otherwise.

Apart from vahines and such, the one topic of universal interest on the island is that of Tahiti's future. It is, to be sure, a well-worn subject. For years, the arrival of virtually every ship, plane, car, refrigerator, or tourist has been greeted with the lament, "This is the end of the old Tahiti." But, in all sobriety, it would seem that *the* big change is now under way.

When I was there, back in remote 1959–60, it was still a fairly hard place to get to, its attainment involving either a long sea voyage or the roundabout (for Americans) approach by TEAL via Fiji and Samoa. But now there is jet air service not only from Hawaii but direct from California, and the once beyond-the-blue Eden can be reached in a few hours. By the simplest ABC of cause and effect, this means that the tide of visitors is swelling enormously; the Smiths and the Joneses—not to mention the Marlon Brandos—are coming; and the island's age-old remoteness has become a thing of the past.

Traditionally, the governing French resisted the pressure of invasion, catering not at all to the tourist and strewing his path with procedural difficulties.

Indeed, the standard joke had them telling the prospective visitor, "Why don't you just send us your money and stay at home?" But the pressures have now become too strong. Realistically, if reluctantly, Tahiti has had to concede that it, too, is part of the twentieth-century world. And it is now not dikes, but facilities, that are being built against the deluge. Already, during my visit, new bungalow-type hotels were mushrooming along the shore line. Many more were in the planning stage, and the air was thick with talk of package tours, stall showers, and dry martinis. All day and most of the night, a procession of trucks, laden with rock and gravel, rumbled along the coast road under the palms and breadfruit trees. And its destination was the then half-finished airport that now accommodates the largest of jet planes.

Inexorably, along with all this, Tahiti's cost of living —or at least of touring—has increased, until it is now the highest in the Pacific, excepting Hawaii's. And the prospect, and intention, is that it will become more so, for what both government and businessmen want is strictly the "luxury trade." Most of it will, inevitably, be American. Tahiti will become part of the new $outh $eas. Prosperity will spread and boom. In the eyes of most of the world prosperity is an unqualifiedly fine thing, but in the fabled isle a huge question mark hangs on the horizon. The question is: can Tahiti absorb the impact of what is to come, and still remain —Tahiti?

Sitting late one afternoon on my seaside veranda, I had the sharp sudden feeling that it was all there right before me. From behind the hibiscus bushes, toward the hotel, came the sound of a strumming guitar and a woman softly singing. Straight ahead was the lagoon, the sea—a miracle of green and blue—and beyond them, aglow in soft sunlight, the fairy-tale castle of the hills of Mooréa. In the middle distance, on the lagoon, an outrigger canoe lay transfixed in stillness, and two tiny brown figures in prow and stern were motionless, too. Only in one place was there movement: off to the west, along the shore. For here too, as on Mooréa, were spires and ramparts—but of a different sort. The spires were of steel, the arms of great cranes tilted skyward; the ramparts of concrete and crushed rubble. And the cranes dipped and swung, gravel poured, trucks jolted, jackhammers clattered, as hour by hour, foot by foot, the new jet airstrip pushed out into the lagoon.

Jet and lagoon; jackhammer and guitar; package tour and unpackaged vahine. . . . Aué, Tahiti has its problems ahead, as it struggles to hold its *ambiance* against the onslaught of the outer world. It will have its prosperity. It will have its dislocations and miseries and bitter lessons in the ways of that world. But it has, I think, more to teach than to learn.

JAMES MICHENER

from RETURN TO PARADISE

JAMES MICHENER staked an early claim on the whole South Pacific and has mined the area well.

NEW ZEALAND is probably the most beautiful country on earth. The official school history says that when Richard John Seddon, the great Prime Minister, died, "he passed on to a better place even than God's Own Country."

The New Zealander finds it difficult to believe that there could be a better land than his, either on earth or in heaven. He is always ready to boast of four national distinctions. "We have a land of unmatched beauty. (True) We have demonstrated that two races of different color can inhabit one land in peace and honor. (True) We showed the world how to pass social legislation for the good of all. (True) And today we enjoy the highest standard of living known by any nation. (False)"

As regards the first claim, the natural beauty of New Zealand is difficult to believe. Its two islands, no larger than Colorado, combine all types of alluring scenery, all kinds of climates. Consider what you could see in one day's travel.

At the northern tip of North Island you find a dazzling tropical beach sixty miles long. (New Zealanders call it Ninety Mile Beach.) It ends in a cluster of handsome islands around which sport immense marlin and swordfish. Farther south are prehistoric sub-tropical forests with towering kauri pines that took 1500 years to mature. In the center of North Island is a brooding desert surmounted by three majestic volcanoes, one or the other of which seems always to be active, spouting lava ash by day and beacon fires at night. At Rotorua the wonders of Yellowstone Park are challenged, for here geysers play, mud pools bubble and hot waters tumble down over colored terraces.

On the west coast you will see Mount Egmont, rising in beauty, the perfect snow-capped cone of a dead volcano, cloud wreathed and pointed like Fujiyama. But in New Zealand you always say, "Fujiyama looks a lot like Mount Egmont."

Now you leave the North Island and fly south across Cook Strait, where vast mountains sank into the sea until only their tips remained aloft. Here earth and ocean mingle in astonishing beauty, varied, twisted, glowing in the sunlight.

Ahead lies South Island, where the real beauty of New Zealand is found. Here Mount Cook rises more than 12,000 feet, perpetually glaciated, with huge fingers of ice reaching almost into the sea. Nearby are the Southern Alps, immense rows of jagged peaks beneath which nestle dozens of wonderful lakes, each serving as a mirror for some great range of mountains.

On the coast, near the glaciers, you find dramatic evidence of New Zealand's turbulent geological history. During millions of years this land rose and fell repeatedly. When it lay under the sea, sand covered it. When it was thrust upward, limestone deposits collected. Finally the resulting rocks were forced high into the air, where howling winds eroded the sandstone layers and left tall rounded pillars of limestone wafers piled one upon the other, appropriately called The Pancakes. And then, since New Zealand scenery is completely prodigal in its wonders, the hungry Tasman Sea ate huge caverns beneath The Pancakes into which tides roar, bursting upward through crevices and shooting thin strands of spray high into the air.

Farther south lies Milford Sound, first and finest of the fjords. Cutting deep inland, it is enclosed by brooding and majestic peaks. High waterfalls plunge from mountain plateaus directly into its waters, and jagged bays probe into dark forests. At the head of one such indentation Sutherland Falls leaps nearly 2,000 feet down into a solemn glen, one of the superb waterfalls of the world. Almost inaccessible, it is reached by means of a difficult trail labeled on maps "The World's Finest Walk." Along ten casual miles I counted forty sheer granite cliffs, each at least 800 feet high, three of them dropping precipitously for more than a thousand feet. I also saw at least 200 waterfalls, some of them hundreds of feet high. One unnamed one—there are so many wonders in this part of New Zealand that they are not even recorded—fell 300 feet and then leaped backward, borne aloft on surging currents of air. Another zigzagged eight times to get down a cliff face. A third fell some hundred feet, then dashed upon a huge projecting boulder which split the fall and threw each half high into the air, so that the falling plumes looked like two Grecian horses plunging into battle. At no point in the ten miles did I fail to see at least three waterfalls. Frequently more than ten were visible. And this was in the dry season!

In the same ten miles there were other spectacular phenomena so far unnamed: a cataract that had gnawed its way sixty feet through solid rock, leaving at the land's surface a gorge only 36 inches across; a tiny lake of perfect ultramarine; a balanced boulder bigger than a cathedral; a walled valley hidden in circles of granite cliff. And often above me flamed that most brilliant tree, the pohutukawa, at the end of whose branches grow massive clusters of scarlet flowers, so that sometimes the forest seemed to be on fire.

On even the best maps the land south of Milford Sound is marked UNEXPLORED. New Zealand has dozens of fjords still to be opened to travel. It has hundreds of natural wonders still to be discovered. One who knows the region said, "For the rest of this century my country could open up each year some new spectacle that would astonish the eye."

Proof of this came dramatically in 1949. New Zealand is geologically a recent land and has few animals that resemble those found elsewhere. It does, however, have some that are unique. Among those still living is the kiwi, a long-billed, flightless bird that has become the national symbol. (New Zealand fighting men are Kiwis.) Now almost extinct, the kiwi is famous for two qualities: it feeds by stomping its feet over worm holes to imitate rain, thus luring the hors d'oeuvre into position; and it lays an egg of ridiculous size. If a hen were to do comparatively as well, chicken eggs would be 14 inches long and would weigh three pounds each!

The most famous of New Zealand's extinct creatures was the moa, a gigantic bird that towered above the heads of men who liked its rich meat so much they exterminated it about 150 years ago. (There's a great fight on about this, some scholars maintaining that moas were never seen after 1350.) Another of the extinct birds was the notornis, a beautiful turkey-like creature with blue-green feathers and a brilliant red toucan-like bill. The last one was seen in 1898, a previous specimen having been eaten by shipwrecked sailors some years before.

Then in 1949 some explorers in the wild southern valleys came upon a family of notornis that had miraculously survived. Cautious investigators probed the area and discovered perhaps fifty of the handsome fowl. A surge of excitement swept across the scientific world and other expeditions were hastily outfitted. Warned the Government: "It is ridiculous to call these excursions moa hunts. No moa could possibly be alive in New Zealand." But the scientists point out that there used to be a dwarf moa and in most bars you can get even money that sooner or later a moa is going to turn up in those southern valleys

marked UNEXPLORED.

The first human beings to see this compact wonderland of New Zealand were a mysterious unidentified people who left carvings on the walls of caves. Scientists are divided as to whether these rude artists were ancestors of the famous Morioris who were found here later and whose history is terrible to contemplate. Profoundly peaceful, they outlawed war and settled arguments by play-duels, the mock battle ending whenever a contestant cried, "Behold! I bleed!" For centuries they lived in quiet peace. Then the warlike Maoris fell upon them, killed the men, carried off the women. In 1930 there was only one Moriori left alive. He was a grotesque fellow, Tommy Solomon, weighing 588 pounds. He liked to ride horses and always carried with him a small ladder by which to mount. In 1933 Tommy Solomon died, completely wiping out a distinct human race of which it was said, "They were gentle, therefore they perished."

The Maoris, who took their place, were certainly not gentle and they are not even close to perishing. They won New Zealand by some of the bravest exploits in maritime history. About the year 900 an intrepid Polynesian named Kupe drifted down to New Zealand from Tahiti and on his return established in Polynesian memory a description of a favored land called The Long White Cloud. In 1350 a great fleet of canoes migrated from Polynesia and brought permanent settlers to New Zealand.

Regarding this hegira more specific information is recorded than is known about Columbus' voyage some 150 years later. Today each Maori tribe traces its ancestry back to one of the original canoes and takes its name therefrom. For example, the Tainui tribe can relate proudly that the canoe Tainui was 70 feet long, captained by Hoturoa, that it sailed on the fourth night of December in 1350, and that "Taikehu was in charge of the great paddle Huahuaterangi." The name of each paddler is remembered, plus the fact that the canoe's priest turned out to be a thieving rascal who ran off with Hoturoa's daughter. Even the chant that kept hope alive is recited: "Seek ye the way! Though the distance be great, though the way be long, keep thy course, O son! Across the waters is thy path."

The Maoris were wonderfully capable settlers, and are today the best off of all Polynesian peoples. They are darker, perhaps because of intermarriage with native tribes. They are more healthy, for their climate is better. And they are more gifted in self-government, because they stood boldly toe-to-toe with English invaders and slugged it out to a standstill. The Maoris were never totally defeated, so a sagacious treaty was devised whereby two vastly different civilizations

Maori (Polynesian) carving, New Zealand.

could live together in mutual respect. The spirit of this Treaty of Waitongi still animates relations between Maori and Pakeha, as the white man is known. At the time of signing a native chief exclaimed, "The shadow of our land goes to Queen Victoria, but the substance remains with us." Surely one day the Maoris will merge into the white stream that engulfs them, but for the present they cling boldly to their Maorihood, slowly acquiring the skills and tricks necessary for survival in a white man's world.

In the meantime they have a good life. They elect their own members of Parliament, who vote the straight Labor line because it was Labor that passed the law which gives parents $1.50 a week for each child. (Maoris call this the Stallion Fee.) Maoris can marry whites, live where they wish, enter whatever professions they prefer. As proof of their citizenship they fought with renowned bravery in both world wars, marching to battle singing their "Maori Battalion Song."

But you don't live long in New Zealand without discovering that the Maori-Pakeha relationship is not all pleasant. A good deal of hypocrisy obscures realities. Many Maori villages are in fact slums. Sensitive Maoris confide that they never really feel at ease among whites, who shout public acceptance but practice private ostracism. As one complete realist said, "White men don't marry our girls much any more, because Maori brides no longer inherit huge landed estates." Even so, the relationship between brown and white in New Zealand is far superior to that between black and white in America.

And the Maoris have a good time! At elections they often vote six or seven times if they particularly favor a candidate. They are great practical jokers, a favorite jest being to pick one's teeth in the face of an enemy, thus signifying, "The flesh of your ancestors is caught in my teeth." As a learned judge of Maori land disputes reported, "If Maori A claims land that once belonged to B's family, there is one bit of evidence that supersedes all others. Can A prove that some ancestor of his killed and ate B's ancestor? If so, the land clearly belongs to A."

Maoris have only vague concepts of private property. "The first Maori up in the morning is the best dressed." It is not uncommon for a man who has bought a fine hat to give it ungrudgingly to the first friend who admires it. Says the white man: "The New Zealand Maori is the finest man on earth. But don't lend him anything!"

There is one aspect of Maori culture that is a sheer delight, one of those perfect art forms that haunts the memory with true loveliness. Young Maori girls, dressed in knotted cord blouses and skirts made of flax stems, become adept in swinging poi balls, made of compressed rushes tied to strings. (Short poi, six-inch string; long poi, eighteen inches.) In delicate rhythms, sometimes brushing their skirts so as to yield an extra beat, teams of girls execute prolonged and intricate drills.

On festive days they do the canoe poi. Then, with each girl whirling two short poi, they seat themselves upon the ground so as to represent their tribal canoe. In back of them a chief rushes up and down flourishing a greenstone club and urging them on. Somewhere in the shadows an old woman stands, chanting through blue-tattooed lips some wild Polynesian account of the great migration.

Now, in their canoe, the girls make the poi balls fly. At first it seems nothing, merely another dance. Then slowly the poi take on the rhythms of the sea. Shoulders begin to weave as if hands carried great paddles. The chief rants and cries. Always the mournful woman chants in her husky voice.

Now the poi balls whirr in the air, striking beaded skirts, tapping against the body. The entire audience is sailing in that ancestral canoe and the night is tense with the sound of the poi balls. Suddenly the woman moans. In silence the girls fall backwards, as their ancestors had once collapsed from near starvation. There is now no sound but that of the mysterious poi balls, echoing the tiny slap of waves against the historic canoe. Then the chief shouts. The old woman screams the last measures of the chant. The girls revive, and the trembling poi balls leap to a beat of joy. And there is no one in the room who cannot see that early vision of The Long White Cloud!

The white men who share New Zealand with the Maoris are all of British stock—English as far south as Christchurch, Scots the rest of the way—and no matter for how many generations a family has lived in New Zealand, everyone still speaks of going Home, and they proudly insist, "We are more English than the English." Perhaps New Zealand's position at the very antipodes from England has led them to cling tenaciously to every fragment of their English ancestry. This has both good and bad results. New Zealand has a more homogeneous population than any other major country, and in the last war only four illiterate New Zealanders were found. On the other hand, gifted young people tend to run away from their own land, back to the security of England. Katherine Mansfield, the gifted storyteller, David Low, the cartoonist, and Lord Rutherford, the atomic trail blazer, are only three of thousands who fled their homeland.

Every outstanding prime minister has been born outside New Zealand, and it is interesting to read the boast carved into the beautiful memorial church at Cave: "1928. It is noteworthy that all the men engaged in the building of this Church were British-born." This yearning for the womb of England combined with life in a vivid new land has resulted in a nation which is most conservative in social life yet completely radical in social legislation.

*   *   *

Few Americans appreciate the tremendous sacrifices made by New Zealand in the last two wars. Among the Allies she had the highest percentage of men in arms—much higher than the United States—the greatest percentage overseas, and the largest percentage killed. She rushed the cream of her manhood into Africa and Crete and Narvik and Singapore. Then she watched helplessly as the Japs crept down the islands until only the miracle at Coral Sea prevented actual invasion. So many New Zealanders were overseas that even women were conscripted into labor corps and told where they must work. Many American families learned how terrible it was to have men overseas for three years. New Zealand men were gone five years, or more.

Bernard Freyberg was born in England of undistinguished parents and soon emigrated to New Zealand, where he became a dentist. He was not too successful and quit to serve as a mercenary soldier under Pancho Villa. While in the Mexican desert he heard that England had gone to war. Rushing across the Atlantic he joined the New Zealand forces in London in time to serve at Gallipoli, where under intense Turkish fire he swam the Hellespont towing a barge full of flares which lighted the way for invasion. Later, in France, while suffering from four bullet wounds, he led three forlorn charges and in a fourth took a fortified village. Later he performed other wild feats and won all the medals a soldier could win. He was hailed by Sir James Barrie, a specialist in these matters, as "the bravest soldier in the war." Now he has returned to New Zealand as the personal representative of the King, a post previously held by titled nobodies. Even the conservative press applauded the appointment, observing, "Sir Bernard is a happy choice, even if somewhat revolutionary."

Today when Freyberg stands stiffly at attention during public functions he is often attended by a stumpy, square-jawed chap who is generally conceded to have been the bravest soldier in World War II. Charles Upham was a schoolteacher, but his behavior under fire seems incredible. Once he rose from a raging attack of dysentery to lead his men against insuperable odds, "thus becoming the first skeleton ever to win the Victoria Cross." In fact, he is the only fighting man ever to win two Victoria Crosses in a row, and he was even recommended for a third! But the generals said halt: "Three would be too many, even for a New Zealander." When he returned home his nation offered him a gift of $30,000, but he refused saying, "Set up a scholarship for the children of the blokes who didn't get back." Now he tends cows on his small farm, a quiet, sawed-off chap who might serve as the model for the typical New Zealander we've been talking about.

The nation lives by trading agricultural products to Great Britain. The first Merino sheep were landed by Captain Cook in 1773, and within a hundred years the wool industry supported the country. Smart scientists discovered that New Zealand's grass could be the world's best except for a lack of cobalt in the soil. Now the blue mineral is added each year, sometimes by airplane, and the pasturage is spectacularly rich.

Great sheep ranches, called stations, run Merinos on the sides of mountains ranges. Lilybank is typical, a station of 70,000 acres and 6,000 sheep nestled between 10,000-foot peaks at the head of a superb lake. In the fall (April–June) the Merinos are mustered out of the mountains for eye clipping—so they can see—and belly stripping—so their shaggy wool won't freeze into the snow. To do the rounding up teams of three comb the mountains. Top man walks along the slopes at the 7,000-foot line, tossing stones at the sheep to keep them moving downhill. He signals his two companions by setting fires on mountain peaks, and upon him depends the thoroughness of the muster.

During winter (July–September) the men of Lilybank do the hard work of a sheep station. Sometimes on foot, often on snowshoes, they snow-rake, or scuff tracks through blizzards so that sheep can follow them to caches of feed. Fortunately, the Merino has learned to live through snow that would kill other sheep and has the good habit, if totally stranded, of eating wool off the backs of other sheep to stay alive. Even so, during a winter of bad snow Lilybank may lose up to 25 per cent of its flock and in 1895 lost every one.

In spring (October–December) Lilybank becomes a flowering wonderland, and since Merinos lamb best when left alone, the men rebuild fences, cull out bad stock and clean up the station.

In summer (January–March) the shearing takes place. Since the climate is rugged, all shearing is done by hand so as to leave about an inch of wool to warm the sheep. This is slow work, for a stripping machine could handle 160 sheep while hand clippers take care of 100. But since few Merinos are ever sold for meat, careful clipping is the most important part of the year's work.

The profit would be greater if it were not for the kea, a magnificent native parrot with a two-inch scimitar beak and a passion for sheep fat. In teams the keas hunt down ewes. A big bird will dart down, fix his talons in the wool and then slash his beak deep into the ewe's back muscles. The terrified animal starts to dash about, whereupon the rest of the team screams with infuriating joy. Again and again the cruel rider shifts position and slashes at the back until the agonized sheep falls prostrate, when the keas strip off the kidney fat and leave the animal to die. It is understandable why station hands will track a kea crew for days.

Today the dairy industry of North Island has passed wool in national importance, and many New Zealanders predict that soon huge refrigerator ships will run between Auckland and San Francisco carrying "our beautiful butter north."

But no matter how important dairying becomes, the sheep industry will always be remembered as the one which gave New Zealand its character. The lore of the top man, tramping the lonely peaks, is strong in New Zealand blood. For example, touching Lilybank on the east, high among mountain passes, is the most famous of stations, Mesopotamia. Here in 1860 appeared a scrawny Englishman with $12,000 of his father's money. He had many wild and moving experiences, including a hundred-mile dash through a snowstorm to the land office where he defended his station against a fraudulent claim, after which "he astonished everyone by working off his excitement playing Bach's Fugues for two hours." He was obsessed by the mountains that fringed Mesopotamia, and from his speculation concerning what might lie beyond them grew *Erewhon*, by Samuel Butler. The young social dreamer was successful as a station owner and in three years doubled his investment, yet locally he is remembered for the fact that when he built his thatched hut he stupidly placed the thatches upside down so that all the rain ran inside, "an extraordinary thing for so clever a man to do."

New Zealand's legendary hero also came from the sheep country and gave his name to vast reaches of magnificent upland moors. In 1845 Queen Victoria visited Aberdeen in Scotland, and the city fathers, wishing to provide an unforgettable feast, advertised for some prime cattle, whereupon an enterprising young Scot named John Mackenzie went from one farm to another and stole the prize steers, delivering them boldly for the Queen's table. Then he hopped the next boat for Australia.

He wound up in New Zealand and disappeared into the unexplored wastelands where sheep were beginning to graze. He became a poetic figure, moving among the great mountains with a mournful bullock and a mute dog. At rivers he would hold fast to the bullock's tail and ferry across. At night he pitched his camp where no men had been before.

Soon rich station owners began to miss their sheep, and it was deduced that John Mackenzie was driving them off in thousand-lot hauls. Rewards were offered, but sly John and his dog were too cautious. Then they were caught with more than a thousand marked sheep. The crafty Scot escaped but was captured at the coast as he tried to board a ship. He knocked his jailer out with a length of leg chain and was recaptured only after having a bullet pumped through him. Twice thereafter he broke loose and once he was dragged back to prison trussed up like a pig. Finally the Government decided it would be cheaper to pardon him than to have him wrecking the jail each month, so John Mackenzie was banished from New Zealand, but it is rumored that he sneaked back to his wild upland moors where his ghost may still be seen at times, tramping the barren Mackenzie Country with his silent dog and mournful bullock.

The modern New Zealander is apt to be impatient with the sheep men. Now the emphasis is all upon manufacturing, with the nation trying vainly to make all sorts of items which common sense would tell her to import from either England or Australia. (Any importation from America is inconceivable at present.) The result is close to economic stagnation and has resulted in a marked decline from what was once "the highest standard of living yet attained by all the people of any nation."

The competition for labor is ridiculous. Employers must bribe help to work and are lucky if beginners stay long enough to learn a trade. Consider one advertisement of thirty-nine lines, begging girls to come to work. Twenty-five lines relate to the bonus system, the newly decorated tea room, provisions for time off, assurance of constant radio music during working hours plus the plea, "Bring your parents with you if you would like their opinion of the working conditions." The ad ends: "What Girl Could Ask For More?"

Apparently many do, because another shop offers, in addition to the above: free permanent waves, daily carfare, taxis home on late nights, tickets to the movies twice a week, and—illegally—an extra two weeks' pay above vacation pay if the girls will consent to report to work on Monday after the annual holiday!

A totally inadequate labor force plus a rigid 40-hour week means that New Zealand is underproduced in everything except mutton, butter and wool. For example, the country has immense deposits of coal, yet coal is often imported from Australia or even the

United States. There is abundance of wool, but carpeting is simply not available. There are fine forests, but no lumber; great wealth, but not enough homes.

At Foxdown Farm near Timaru I watched Bob Ford work 1200 acres, run 3200 Romney sheep for mutton and 100 Aberdeen-Angus cattle for beef. He had no hired help. Could get none. Bob and his wife worked fourteen hours a day, seven days a week. They made a pile of money, but they were burning themselves out.

The result is that New Zealand's once-high standard of living has drooped pitifully. In ten homes where husbands earned what would be $8,000 a year in America, only one wife had both a refrigerator and a washing machine. In three of the homes there was neither, yet both husband and wife desperately wanted both. None available.

Until recently New Zealanders refused to believe that their living standards had slipped. Then, in 1950, they played host to the Empire Games, which brought newsmen from all parts of the Commonwealth. The result was some of the most shocking criticism a country has ever had to absorb, and all of it delivered by members of the family. An Australian: "I get an over-all impression of gloom and depression. All public services are shockingly out of date." A Londoner: "Even our English cities, with austerity and restrictions, are immeasurably more cheerful, better equipped and better serviced for out-of-town visitors." Another Australian: "The transport system is painfully obsolete." A Canadian: "New Zealand does not have a single public restaurant that would be classed as anything better than third-rate in Vancouver." Another Canadian: "Service in stores and shops is poor. Goods are shoddy . . . If this is a vicious indictment of Auckland as a tourist town, it is vicious only because it is the only honest impression one can take away." An American: "In five days I visited five cities and could not find a single hotel room. I slept in dingy rooms or in none at all. What was disturbing was that hotel clerks were outraged that any sensible human being should simply step up to a hotel desk and expect a room!"

New Zealand was shocked by the reports of its friends. In the discussions that followed this seemed to be the common explanation: "Everyone's got it too easy. We've all got minimum wages, social security. Nobody gives a hang."

Actually, many thoughtful New Zealanders have known for a long time that their socialistic paradise wouldn't stand up under careful scrutiny. There is much that is truly wonderful in New Zealand, much that is third class. Only very hard work will eliminate the latter.

The question then arises: "Who will do the work?" New Zealand is dangerously underpopulated. (World average 41 per square mile. United States 48. Japan 532. New Zealand 16.) Steps are being taken to increase immigration, but the fact that New Zealand is exclusively British means that only British immigrants are welcome. In Dunedin a committee facing this problem seriously passed the three following resolutions: (1) Our population lack is critical. Something must be done. (2) But since we are of British stock, only British immigrants should be sought. (3) And since Australia is so much worse off than we (less than three to the square mile) let's wait until they get all they need!

Tragically, of every hundred Englishmen who do arrive as immigrants, as many as forty go right back home. Their reasons: no houses to live in; the beer is too weak; we can't stand those dreadful New Zealand week-ends.

These latter are an astonishing phenomenon. Because of the forty-hour week, no stores of any kind—except fruit, candy, hot food—may open on Saturday. You cannot buy groceries, meat, milk, or bread. No haircuts, no doctor visits, no dentist, no shoes repaired. You can buy gasoline only in proved emergencies and then from only one station in each city. You also need an emergency to warrant sending a telegram after 12 noon. Telephone and train services are curtailed. Few restaurants are open. Life comes to a deathly standstill. The best description came from a workingman: "We have two Sundays a week, except that on Saturday we have horse racing." The result of knocking two full days out of every week, plus working only about thirty-three hours out of the forty-hour week, is that economic production has inevitably deteriorated. It is quite possible that the social legislation of Seddon and Savage has reached the point of diminishing returns.

Yet I myself cannot wholly subscribe to the harsh criticism of the British visitors. Life in New Zealand is wonderfully pleasant. Each home has a garden of glorious flowers. Evergreen trees abound and make the landscape lovely. The sea is always available and no home can be far from mountains and clear lakes. New Zealand food is superb, even if the cooking is apt to be pretty dreadful. There are, however, five unique delicacies: soup made from sautéed toheroa clams, pronounced by the Prince of Wales to be "the finest soup ever made," an understatement; grilled mutton bird, a baby sea fowl whose parents cram its rubber belly with so many fresh fish that it cannot move, so that when it is cooked it tastes like chicken with a streak of trout; Colonial Goose, which is strong mutton sliced wafer thin and served with onion stuffing and an almost black gravy; the best little tea cakes in the world; and whitebait. Gourmets can go into trances over a mess of fresh whitebait, pitched into a batter of whipped eggs with a touch of onion and fried into a thick, brown fritter.

The relaxation of life in New Zealand is appealing. In addition to the two Sundays there are frequent stops for tea, a willingness to yarn at any time, plus an unbounded hospitality. New Zealand children are kept in school uniforms till they are seventeen or eighteen on the theory that if a boy is in knee pants till that age he won't be in a hurry to mature into a criminal. The plan works, for the crime rate is low.

The care of children has always been a special New Zealand concern. In the late nineteenth century, Truby King, a childless doctor at a mental institution, became fascinated by his hobby of feeding pigs, on whom he developed scientific nutrition tables. After adopting a waif he found that his pig principles worked equally well on humans, and within a few years he had pioneered child-care centers under the direction of the Plunket Society, so named after the wife of a Governor-General. Later, young girls were encouraged to study child care and today Karitanes—named after the hill where Truby King worked—study for sixteen months the problem of "Helping the mother and saving the child." When a Karitane reports, and they are in great demand, she assumes sole charge of the child and soon she has it gurgling and fat. Karitanes are neither nurses nor servants. They usually marry young and make wonderful mothers. To them is given much credit for the fact that New Zealand babies are unusually healthy.

Actually, all young things seem to grow fabulously in this country. Animals have been brought here from all over the world, and because New Zealand had no natural predatory creatures, introduced animals have multiplied enormously. American deer increased so freely that now the Government must hire cullers

SYDNEY, AUSTRALIA, ONE OF THE WORLD'S
MOST BEAUTIFUL HARBORS.

who roam the valleys shooting does, whose carcasses are not even gathered. The rabbit is a national pest, having made deserts out of much of the South Island. Goats, pigs, opossums, sparrows, hawks and even wallabies (midget kangaroos) have all found New Zealand a bonanza and are now pests. Even plants run wild in this fertile land. Gorse was brought in to decorate gardens, and in a few years the magnificent yellow shrub was a national menace, engulfing whole fields like a sweeping golden flame.

But there was one introduction which has made New Zealand famous wherever sportsmen gather. The rainbow trout was brought down from Canada and the United States. Instantly it took to the cold, dashing rivers where no predators fed upon its young. Soon the famous game fish grew to gigantic size and New Zealand became known, quite properly, as the Sportsman's Paradise. To see this wonderland at its best you must stop a while at Alan Pye's Huka Lodge, at the northern end of Lake Taupo.

Here, beside the swift-flowing Waikato River near a gorge where waters roar between rocks, Pye has built a fisherman's retreat that can have few equals anywhere. In a homey lodge he serves remarkable meals: fresh chicken, trout for breakfast, all the eggs you can eat, steak, always two immense desserts with four pitchers of cream that has to be ladled out. Nearby a thermal spring pumps mildly sulphurous hot water into a deep pool walled off by evergreens so that fishermen and their wives can go bathing nude.

But food and hot baths are not the attraction at Huka Lodge, for in the river and in Lake Taupo abound monstrous rainbows. The average fish caught at Pye's weighs about seven pounds, and each will feed four people. Above the fire are two mounted beauties that tipped the scales at more than 12, but Pye himself, a red-faced, weather-bitten Irishman—all famous New Zealanders were born somewhere else —says, "Those fish are not to be regarded. The champion picked out of this river was 26 pounds. And mark you, the flesh was firm. They aren't lazy, the New Zealand trout."

For years Pye has conducted a running feud with the Tongariro crowd upstream. They fish the legendary Tongariro River, termed "the most perfect reach of trout water ever known," where each pool bears a famous name: Vera's, Swirl, Nursing, Stump, Log and Mud. Pye used to insist that Tongariro trout were overrated, but in recent years he has said little, for evil luck has fallen upon the Tongariro pools.

To the west three great volcanoes have been throwing torrents of volcanic ash into the air, and prevailing winds have carried it across the river. Its effect upon the superlative Tongariro trout is unpredictable; for the present the fish have grown sluggish. The water near Pye's lodge is so far unaffected, but he does not gloat. For if the volcanoes continue to erupt, the ash could well destroy all the trout.

In the meantime, Pye provides near perfect fishing for $5 a day, all expenses covered. He also has a remarkable cottage which costs more and which provides the finest accommodation in New Zealand. He will not tell you how he happens to have such quarters, for he has not yet got over the shock of acquiring them.

It happened this way. About fifteen years ago a handsome United States naval officer became fascinated by the fishing at Pye's and prevailed upon Alan to lease a corner of land by the river. Here a super fishing lodge was built and decorated at princely expense. Year after year the young officer, now a full commander, came vacationing to try the trout. When the war broke out he served with distinction as liaison with New Zealand forces.

Then peace came and with it the shocking news from New York! The handsome naval officer, this favored man, had been proved beyond doubt to be involved in a worldwide narcotics ring, to which he was himself a slave. By God's grace he died shortly after the story broke, and now his fishing lodge, more beautiful than ever, stands by the trout-filled Waikato, waiting for other fishermen.

I have known New Zealand in many weathers and I have served with its quiet men in most corners of the Pacific. I have never met people more deeply convinced that theirs is the one good land. But whenever I think I understand even slightly what makes this radical-conservative country tick, I am brought up sharp by some new experience. When I started to write this essay I went for one last look at a city I have grown to love: placid Christchurch with its English cathedral and terribly stuffy manner. Here on the broad plains of Canterbury I felt that I had come at last to the true meaning of New Zealand: English forever, reluctant to move ahead, confirmed in the defense of human dignity. Then I turned one more corner and stumbled upon the fastest-growing religion in conservative Christchurch. There it was! A store-front chapel with the pastor's Model T Ford parked outside and on the walls the mystical words: PEACE! PEACE! PEACE! FATHER DIVINE!

"FOR MOST SYDNEY CITIZENS THE
PURPOSE OF LIFE MAY PERHAPS BE
SUMMARIZED IN THE PARADE OF THE
LIFESAVERS ON MANLY BEACH, ALL
BRONZED OPEN-AIR FUN ON SATURDAY
AFTERNOONS."—JAMES MORRIS.

BOWLING ON THE GREEN, SYDNEY, WITH
HARBOR BRIDGE IN THE BACKGROUND.

ASIA

ASIA

Adventures do occur, but not punctually.

E. M. FORSTER

Any man can travel hot and dusty Asia by car with safety and comfort—provided he has an urge for adventure and a wife who is a good mechanic.

WILLIAM O. DOUGLAS

FOSCO MARAINI

from MEETING WITH JAPAN

AN ITALIAN who lived many years in Japan makes some international comparisons.

JAPAN AND BRITAIN have many things in common. Both are islands on the edge of huge oceans, both have civilizations with a strong individual imprint resulting from the integration of originally diverse elements (German-Latin, Yamato-Chinese); both have been strongly centralized for centuries, and historically both have had a decidedly aristocratic social structure. The British-Japanese encounter has consequently been characterized by mutual esteem rather than warmth. Each of the two people like form, ceremony, self-control; these characteristics lead to respect for the individuality of the other rather than to close contact. The Anglo-Japanese alliance (1902–21), the longest of modern times, was more than a mere political agreement, though in Japan its influence was restricted to the nobility and the upper bourgeoisie. It is still possible from time to time to meet aristocratic old Japanese gentlemen who were educated at Oxford, dress like country gentlemen, play golf, and tell dry, humorous stories about the hunting field over a whisky-and-soda in front of the fire after dinner.

The Anglo-Japanese encounter yielded lasting results, however, in the field of scholarship. Our deep and thorough knowledge of Japanese is in great part due to the British.

*   *   *

If Anglo-Japanese accord seems possible only at a high social and intellectual level, I should say that German-Japanese accord is easier at all levels; I have the impression that the only mixed marriages that have any chance of success are Japanese-German. In Japan *Doitsu* (Germany) always has a serious connotation. *Igirisu* (England) evokes in the mind of a well-disposed Japanese the picture of a nice, elderly, sporting uncle who climbs the highest mountains in the world, invites you to tea and cakes and raspberries and cream, is not a genius, but is so honest and reliable; *Doitsu*, on the other hand, suggests a cousin whom you do not know whether or not to admire, but with whom you are linked by certain nocturnal adventures and a taste for certain forbidden things. When your German cousin is about, you know that something is going to happen.

The most satisfactory, the happiest, the most natural of these encounters is the Franco-Japanese. Here too contact has always been at a high level, a high intellectual level in particular. The France concerned is not the narrow world of the French provinces, of the petty bourgeoisie, but that of the *littérateurs*, the artists, and the servants. At this level France and Japan are two exquisitely pagan and sophisticated countries, made to understand each other. The Japanese like French taste, its caprice, its fashions, its deep, unpedantic humanism, the tinge of frivolity which serves the better to conceal the flame within. The French like the aesthetic sense which pervades the whole of Japanese life; as soon as they set foot in a Japanese house, fall in love with a Japanese woman, read a Japanese poem or piece of good prose, they discover a new, real, and entirely unexpected France among a thousand possible and conceivable Frances. I should say, in fact, that French and Japanese approach each other with the fewest mental reservations, the most open mutual humanity; that is why they achieve understanding.

*   *   *

Finally, there is the encounter which from many points of view is the most important of all, the Japanese-American. This is the only one which has taken place on a mass scale. It is estimated that since the end of the war at least a million Americans have spent at any rate some time in Japan. As we have mentioned, the occupation began under rosy auspices; but relations deteriorated, and ended by being bad. That is a chapter of contemporary history; here I propose to confine myself to a more humble plane.

Apart from the fact that Japanese-American relations were those between victor and vanquished, which always makes understanding difficult, there are many reasons why even in the most favourable circumstances the Japanese-American encounter would tend to be only moderately successful. On the one hand we have America, a country of Puritan traditions, of straightforward, practical men without a true and constant interest in the arts and the things of the mind, always ready to cut the Gordian knot; on the other we have Japan, whose people are as pagan as ancient Mediterranean man, always tending to argue in terms of *kimochi* (states of mind), dominated by what may be called *baai, yōsu, arisama, jōkyō, jijō, moyō, jōtai, jōsei, jitai,* and a hundred other things, but merely mean circumstances; an extremely complicated people, full of ancient fears and new ambitions, extremely sensitive to all forms of beauty, intellectual values, emotional claims, always ready, when confronted with a Gordian knot, not to cut it, but to tie another, bigger one all round it and thus put it out of sight. We are, in fact, confronted with two attitudes of life, two interior universes, which differ so profoundly that it is hard to think that a greater contrast could be possible.

*   *   *

The Japanese certainly know little about Italy, and what they know tends to come to them through writers of other countries—at best Goethe, Stendhal, or Aldous Huxley. I recall the celebrated remark of the member of the Japanese Diet who, on seeing the Claudian aqueduct in Rome, said that post-war reconstruction did not seem to have got very far yet.

In conclusion, I should like to mention a recent investigation by Unesco into what young people in Japan think of other countries. The results were interesting, and demonstrated a knowledge that was far from superficial. The United States came first for science and industrial technique, followed by Germany and the Soviet Union; France came first in the category of intellectual values, followed by Britain; Switzerland came first for political development, while Denmark reigned supreme and almost unchallenged for economic development. For spiritual values the palm went to Britain. Italy was mentioned (last but one, after China) only by a few under the heading: Which country would you most like to visit? In other words, the interest was purely touristic.

*   *   *

A comparison between Kyoto and Florence is almost impossible to avoid. Not only do they have similar connotations in their respective civilizations; there is also a physical resemblance. True, the valley of the Arno between San Domenico and San Miniato is narrower than that of the Kamogawa, but Florence seen from the Viale dei Colli and Kyoto from the Higashi-yama are essentially two seas of houses filling flat valleys between mountains and hills; and, just as Florence has Fiesole, the Poggio Imperiale, Settignano, so Kyoto has Higashi-yama, Saga, and Ohara. Moreover, the economic basis of the two places is similar. In both it is agriculture, for the most part in the hands of old families, and in both a class of artisans is gradually being industrialized. However, the view that lay below me was far less beautiful than that of Florence seen, say, from the Piazzale Michelangelo. In this sea of grey roofs you would search in vain for the counterpoint of lines, spaces, and volumes that springs to life from the bridges across the Arno, from the towers, domes, and *campanili*; for the sense of completeness and unity of which the supreme examples are San Gimignano among the cities of the Old World, and New York, the modern San Gimignano, among the cities of the New.

Moreover, going down into Kyoto and walking about the central streets between the Shi-jo and San-jo bridges and the avenues of Imadegawa, it is easy to feel a great sense of disappointment. In contrast to the cities of Europe, which offer new perspectives at every turn, Kyoto, like every other Japanese town, consists of broad, anonymous streets intersecting at right-angles and flanked by neat, often attractive-looking, houses, all similar except when they are interrupted by ugly modern buildings of no style at all. True, at Kyoto everything is better cared-for, less brazenly utilitarian, than in other Japanese towns, and near some of the temples (Higashi and Nishi Hongan-ji), in certain streets (Teramachi, Ponto-cho), and in the parks surrounding the Imperial Palaces, there are views which are sometimes impressive, sometimes pleasing and full of fascination, and sometimes truly magnificent; nevertheless a superficial drive through the city rouses no particular enthusiasm.

In spite of that Kyoto has a wealth of beauty which is not surpassed anywhere in the world. Once more we touch on one of the fundamental differences between Europe and the Far East. Florence is western beauty displayed for all to see; Kyoto is eastern; its beauty is concealed, a secret to be wrested from it little by little. True, you can spend a month at Florence, visiting churches, galleries, villas, *palazzi*; but you can also claim to be able to see it in a single afternoon, from the surrounding hills, the tops of its towers, from its streets, squares, bridges. It is characteristic that the Higashi-yama ("Eastern Mount"), the Fiesole of Kyoto, has no street or viewpoint from which the city can be seen as a whole; the point to which I climbed was a woodman's path, full of slippery slopes and covered with pine-needles. The idea of a view is entirely western and entirely un-Japanese. What bad taste, what barbarism, what childishness, to want to see everything all at once! Hence the things that matter at Kyoto are tucked away in little valleys, in green alcoves between the folds of the hills. Its beauties do not present themselves, but have to be sought out.

Kyoto, at the time of its foundation in 794, was called Heian ("Peace and Tranquillity"). The Emperor Kwammu built it as his capital after deciding to abandon Nara, where the power and intrigues of the Buddhist monks had got out of hand. Heian, like Nara, was built to an ambitious chequer-board pattern, about three miles square, modelled on the capital of the Chinese emperors at Ch'ang-an. The court and government buildings, according to the chroniclers, were exceedingly handsome; the most magnificent of them, the Taikyoku-den, contained a great state room nearly two hundred feet long and fifty feet wide and was built on a platform surrounded by a red lacquer balustrade; the whole building was painted scarlet, and the roof was covered with emerald-blue tiles. Not far away was the Pavilion of Sumptuous Pleasures (Hōgaku-den), used for official banquets, the Pavilion of Martial Virtues (Butoku-den), with a courtyard for equestrian games and archery competitions, the Imperial Celestial Pavilion (Shishin-den), used for ceremonial purposes, and the Pavilion of Sweet Coolness (Seiryō-den), which contained the Emperor's quarters. The Empress, the imperial concubines, and the ladies of the palace lived in the "Prohibited Precinct" in quarters distinguished by the names of the neighbouring trees—the Pear Hall, the Wistaria Hall, the Plum Hall. There were also many houses for noble families, to say nothing of a number of Shinto shrines and a big university with three principal faculties: Chinese letters, mathematics, and law. Heian at the time seems to have had about half a million inhabitants. There is no doubt that it was one of the biggest and most splendid cities in the world.

Nothing, however, could be more alien to the Japanese spirit than the formalism dear to their neighbours of the Celestial Empire. Just as in the case of the Taikwa reform of 645, when they adopted the Chinese bureaucratic system in its outward form only, neglecting its great secret, that of a democratic government of sages and men of letters selected by an extremely severe examination system from every section of the population, so did they now reproduce an impressive, Chinese-style, chequer-board town plan, with wide straight roads which did not lead up to any of the impressive culminating points—arches, gateways, palaces, towers, or monuments—which in the same circumstances other civilizations would certainly have demanded. The outline remains. The roads still cross each other at right angles and convey the atmosphere of a capital of mathematicians and ritualists, but the Japanese love of the devious and unexpected, their aversion to the obvious, to anything that can be grasped at first sight, has ended by concealing the true spiritual centres of the city, its most beautiful and precious things, removing them from the geometrical pattern, hiding them away from the streets behind walls and clumps of trees.

The city falls naturally into two parts. There is the town centre, equipped with every modern urban characteristic—crowded streets, smart women, theatres, restaurants, cinemas, shops; and in addition there are the famous geisha districts. This part of the city can be called that of the terrestrial pleasures. The other, that of the ascetic pleasures, lies outside this, in an area of wooded hills, in which lakes, temples, gardens, hermitages, monasteries are scattered about. There is no hard-and-fast dividing line, of course; there are temples, museums, to say nothing of fourteen universities, in the central area, and in the outskirts there are places dedicated to the pleasures of *samsara* (the vortex of becoming) rather than to the peace of *nirvana*. Nevertheless the distinction is broadly true.

The peculiar spirit of this city is the result of the harmonious coexistence of the most diverse elements: monastic asceticism, the cultivation of the arts, the ephemeral pleasures of *uki-yo*, the "floating world," devoted scholarship, a patient artisan class, keen tradesmen, and an ancient, impoverished nobility.

But let us return to the domain of ascetic pleasures. The names of the places are a delight in themselves. At the foot of the Mount of Knowledge (Hiei-zan), not far from the imperial villa of the Ascetic Doctrine (Shugaku-in), among the maples which were assuming their autumn red, there is the Temple of the Calm Light, that is to say, of Nirvana (Ohara no Jakkō-in).

On the other side of the valley is the Temple of the Absolute (Ohara no Sanzen-in). Nearer the city is a temple dedicated to Manjusri, Enchanting Knowledge, the Buddhist Apollo (Manju-in), as well as the Poet's Pavilion (Shisen-do) and the Silver Pavilion (Ginkaku-ji). In this direction, where the first slopes of the Eastern Mount (Higashi-yama) bring Kyoto to a sudden stop, every little valley, every sylvan recess, every shady thicket along the side of the streams, has been adorned by monkish piety. The Temple of Enlightenment (Nanzen-ji) and that of Gratitude (Chion-in) are near the Temple of Pure Fountains (Kiyomizu-dera), that of the Blue Lotus (Shōren-in), that of Serene Quietude (Seikan-ji), and that of the Marvellous Law (Myōhō-in).

To the south the Eastern Mount descends in little hills towards the plain of the Uji river, and the distances are a little greater. Beyond Peach Mount (Momo-yama) and the Palace of Noble Fragrance (Goko-no-Miya) there is the Temple of the Three Treasures, *i.e.*, the Buddha, the Law, and the community of monks (the Sambō-in), near a huge park which conceals the pavilions and pagodas of the big temple dedicated to the Quintessence of Enlightenment (the Daigo-ji).

To the west the mountains are steeper and wilder, the woods darker and more solemn; a big expanse of rice-fields lies between the city and the first slopes. Here too, particularly near the Stormy Mountain (Arashi-yama), where the Hozu river plunges down into the valley, there are some delightful places. As soon as you leave the city there is the Golden Pavilion (Kinkaku-ji), destroyed by fire, alas! in our own life-time, the Temple of the Dragon's Repose (Ryoan-ji) with its famous abstract garden, the Temple of Benevolent Harmony (Ninna-ji), the Temple of the Great Science (Daikaku-ji). Finally, hidden in the outskirts of the mountain forest, there is the Temple of the Celestial Dragon (Tenryu-ji), near an enchanting lake, and the Temple of the Western Fragrance (Saihō-ji), where twenty-four different kinds of moss display their humble beauty.

JAPANESE DEPARTMENT STORES HAVE WONDERFUL
FOOD DEPARTMENTS IN THE BASEMENT.

The great Torii at Miya-jima, Japan.

OLIVER STATLER

from Japanese Inn

THE EMPEROR visits a Japanese inn. His exquisite experience is available in kind, if not quite in degree, to every traveler in Japan.

RUMORS WERE heard in July, consultations began in August, and official notification came on the sixteenth of September. The Minaguchi-ya had been chosen to play host to the Emperor and Empress of Japan when they came to Shizuoka City for the National Athletic Meet of 1957. It was an event which would bring young athletes from every section of the country. Their Majesties would open the games. They would arrive at the Minaguchi-ya on the twenty-fifth of October for two days.

No greater honor, no greater responsibility, can come to any Japanese inn. From the day of notification, there was little rest for the staff of the Minaguchi-ya or for the Mochizukis themselves.

They divided the work. Mr. Mochizuki, Hanjuro IV, took charge of preparing the rooms. His wife, Isako, arranged for the day-to-day requirements of service.

Their Majesties' apartment would be the Minaguchi-ya's finest, the suite called *Akebono*, Dawn. It lies at the base of the wide flat U of the inn. Though the wings of the Minaguchi-ya rise to two stories, *Akebono*, in the middle, is on ground level, commanding a view of the whole garden as it sweeps towards the sea. Behind its two spacious living rooms are a dressing room, a tiled lavatory, an airy bath, a compartmented toilet, a big foyer, and a large waiting room facing a pleasant inner garden. *Akebono* adds up to quiet luxury.

On the first of October, *Akebono* was taken out of use. Workmen moved in.

The inner doors, which set off the rooms from their enclosed terraces, were lifted from their grooves and carried away to a workroom. The paper was stripped off, the wood was cleansed, and new paper, soft, strong, but white, was meticulously pasted on the frames.

The straw *tatami* mats of the floor were taken up. They would come back with new covers, made, like the paper of the doors, in remote villages famed for centuries because their craftsmanship has been the finest in all Japan.

Men mounted ladders to wash the ceiling, the wide boards of natural pine that stretch, without knot or flaw, from one end of the room to the other. They scrubbed with soap, and they scrubbed with disinfectant, and they gave the same treatment to the woodwork of the walls.

Every square inch of plaster was ripped off, from the foyer straight through to the terraces. Every wall was newly plastered, and surfaced in the Japanese way with the warm texture of fine brown sand.

In the bath, the sunken tub of tile was ripped out and replaced by a new tub of satiny white cypress. A tub of tile is coolly handsome modernity; a tub of cypress is warm and timeless indulgence.

All this renovation was Mochizuki's responsibility.

Isako was busy too. She kept a watchful eye on the seamstresses as they made new bedding, three thick pads for each Imperial bed, two light quilts for covers. They fluffed the softest cotton, and sheathed it in rich white silk figured in felicitous designs.

They made new uniforms for all the staff: kimonos for the maids in the deep purple of ripe eggplant, with obi sashes of golden yellow; starched whites for the chef, his four cooks, and his kitchen helpers; and navy-blue jackets for the other men, with the inn's name on the lapels, and its crest, given by the Lord of Satsuma, on the back.

They made an extra jacket for Yoshi. His years of service had earned him the right to be on hand for these triumphant days, and so he was called back from retirement. He came quickly, glad to be back at work, proud to be wanted.

Isako summoned the suppliers and ordered new dishes. The soup bowls would be the house's old and treasured lacquer, but all the china had to be new.

The menus were planned. This was the chef's responsibility and he rose to it nobly, but there were long and earnest consultations between him and Mochizuki. What local specialties should be included? What seasonal delicacies would be at their peak? And since the Emperor is a teetotaler, what subtle adjustments to create dinners at which no saké would be poured?

"We appreciated that the Emperor prefers Western foods," Mochizuki said later, "but the Minaguchi-ya is a Japanese inn, and it would have been quite out of character for us to serve Western dishes, even if we could have prepared them properly. What we tried to do was to create Japanese menus which would appeal to a Western palate."

It is not only in the matter of food that the Emperor's tastes have been trained away from things Japanese: the whole style of life at the palace is Western. Nor in this new, secular age would it seem proper to accommodate the Emperor, as his forebears were accommodated, in temples; indeed, the temples, having lost their government subsidies, are scarcely in a position to dispense lavish hospitality. For years, whenever the present Emperor traveled, he was housed in the temples of our times—prefectural office buildings, schoolhouses, or public halls, temporarily fitted out with beds and other furniture. It can be assumed that the Emperor was made reasonably comfortable, but there were never enough beds for his chamberlains, and those travel-weary attendants finally tried the daring experiment of an inn, which could offer Japanese-style comfort to the whole party. The Emperor, who had not stayed in an inn since his boyhood, was so pleased to rediscover their allure that thereafter inns were prescribed for all Imperial jaunts.

There have been other changes as well. Before the war, ordinary people were afraid to gaze on the Emperor's countenance. He could scarcely appear before his own people. Since the war, millions have seen and cheered him as a symbol of national unity.

On October 9, palace officials came to the Minaguchi-ya to check the menus, and pronounced themselves pleased. They made one change: they added fresh milk. With this they succeeded in startling the chef, for most Japanese still do not consider milk a food for adults. They might also have succeeded in prostrating the local health department, had not Mochizuki speedily called on prefectural officials for help; they made arrangements to have milk rushed twice daily from their model research dairy, an hour away.

Even without the milk problem, local health authorities were almost overcome by their sense of responsibility. To Mochizuki, there seemed to be an inspector behind every door. They tested the water and found it clean and pure, but they insisted that the well be newly concreted anyway. They poked into the kitchen and were unable to make a suggestion of any kind: the chef snorted with satisfaction.

The police, too, were everywhere. They scanned blueprints, went over the grounds, checked the neighborhood, working out their plans to guard His Majesty.

In the flutter from morning till night, only Junzo and Chikue, the youngest children and still living at home, remained cool. Teen-aged, modern, and emancipated, they chided their parents for becoming so excited, and when they came home from school to find that no one had remembered to prepare their supper, they were indignant; their protests went unheeded as arrival day grew closer.

Obaasan, their grandmother, was as busy as anyone, and she worked the same long hours, but she found time to unearth an old book with a record of other visits by members of the Imperial family since the revolution—not the Emperor, of course, but at least his sisters and his cousins and his aunts, and his male kin as well. When visitors came, on business or merely because they were curious about the great preparations, she would sometimes seize the chance to rest a few moments. She would bring out the old book, turn its pages, and read the great names. "No one else thinks this book is important," she would murmur, not quite accurately, "but I've kept it all these years. See, Princess Arisugawa used to spend a month here every spring. . . ."

Red carpet arrived and was cut and fitted to cover the polished floor and *tatami* mats of the entrance. There had to be carpet because, like no other guests the inn had ever received, the Emperor and Empress would wear their shoes into the foyer, where a chair and a bootjack would be provided.

The workmen in *Akebono* suite finished and moved out, leaving it fresh and glistening. Furniture was moved in, new tables, chairs, and mirrors for the dressing room, new stools and buckets for the bath, and in the living room, a radio, a television receiver, sofa and chairs (all new, of course): there would be that much concession to the Western living habits of Japan's sovereign.

Into the other room, which at night would become bedroom, went the Minaguchi-ya's treasured old gold screens, to be placed around the Imperial beds. The Imperial bedding was laid in the closets.

In the garden, curried and combed, the autumn-softened green was brightened with a clump of huge yellow chrysanthemums, a gift from one of the inn's long-time patrons.

More chrysanthemums were delivered for the inn's entrance hall, prize plants from members of the Okitsu Flower Club, big blooms standing proudly erect, miniatures cascading from their pots.

On the twenty-third of October the inn was closed to the public. Every room gleamed. The first of the palace chamberlains arrived, vanguard of the staff that would bulge the inn. Once more everything was checked.

On the twenty-fourth the four oldest children left their work or their college classes and came home from Tokyo. The family was together. Morning coats and trousers were pressed, kimonos were laid out, and the chamberlains gave their final drill in the demanding etiquette of the occasion. They emphasized that none of the inn's family or servants would be permitted to speak directly to Their Majesties, not even a word of greeting or farewell. Preferably there would be no circumstances requiring words, but if something had to be said it was to be said through a member of the palace staff.

Mochizuki wrestled a problem. It was he, the host, who would, wordlessly, welcome the Emperor and escort him from his car to his rooms. A critical moment, the chamberlains pointed out, would come in the entry, for there Mochizuki was to shed his shoes but the Emperor was not to remove his. There were any number of dire possibilities, said the chamberlains, none of which must be allowed to happen. Mochizuki must not let the Emperor get the idea that this was the spot to remove the Imperial shoes. Mochizuki must not fumble with his shoes and keep the Emperor waiting. And the chamberlains didn't even have to say what any Japanese gentleman would know, that it would be a nasty bungle if Mochizuki were not to get out of his shoes neatly and gracefully, if a shoe were to fall over, or, heaven forbid, land across the other.

Mochizuki's problem was that his shoes were tight, and it is not easy to step smoothly out of tight shoes. Of his son's shoes, he could wear only Yasuo's, but they seemed loose, so loose, in fact, that it occurred to Mochizuki that he might walk right out of them while guiding the Emperor in from the street. On the night of the twenty-fourth, Hanjuro IV was still pondering this problem when he went to bed.

The twenty-fifth was warm but overcast. Early in the morning every house along the highway put out the national flag and a paper lantern likewise blazoned with the Rising Sun, though there were sprinkles of rain which sometimes made shopkeepers scurry to bring these emblems briefly under cover. The gate of the Minaguchi-ya was bracketed by flags and lanterns.

At 11:25 a special train thundered through Okitsu bound for Shizuoka City, flags streaming from the locomotive. There were coaches for railway officials, for palace officials, and the press. Then came a car marked with the Imperial insignia, the sixteen-petaled gold chrysanthemum. Railwaymen who worked this car have their fingernails specially clipped so they will not mar its delicate lacquer-work.

The train crew, had they been asked, could have furnished insight into the tension that had been building up behind the gray wall of the Minaguchi-ya. "Supervising this train is hard on the nerves," the man in charge had said. "Once we tightened the springs too much, and the result was most embarrassing. The Empress became train-sick and had to move to another coach."

The engineer has confided: "At departure time my throat is dry, my voice is hoarse, my heart beats fast. My nerves are taut until we are safely at our destination."

In *Akebono* suite health officials had decreed a last minute chore. The door fittings, the faucets, the light-switch covers were being wiped with alcohol. There was grim determination that the Emperor pick up no bug in Okitsu.

Since the athletic meet would not open until the following day, Their Majesties were scheduled to spend the afternoon visiting a hospital endowed by the Emperor's mother, and a factory considered a model of its kind. The factory was in Kambara, and so they motored back along the Tokaido and through Okitsu before they stopped for the night. The Emperor passed the house of his old ally, Saionji. He passed below Seikenji, the gray old temple flag-bedecked but silent and withdrawn as if remembering earlier days when sovereigns rested within its gates. The Emperor passed the Minaguchi-ya, moved down the flag-lined highway.

The crowds were sparse for this unheralded passage, and jovial policemen urged those on hand to step up to the curb so they could get a good look. The old folks shook their heads. This was a far cry from prewar days when it was almost an act of treason to look at all.

After the motorcade passed by, onlookers were rewarded with another pageant. More than two weeks earlier, the flag of the national athletic meet had been borne from Kobe, scene of the previous year's games, and, in a ritual based on that surrounding the Olympic torch, runners had since been carrying it towards this year's site. Their route had been a tortuous one, designed to take the flag through almost every town in Shizuoka Prefecture, so that they had doubled around Shizuoka City and now were approaching it from the direction opposite to Kobe.

It had been carried by relays, a new team taking over at every town and village. By this means, according to officials, 12,325 men had been involved during the 875-mile course. There had been such a scramble for the honor that it had been necessary to break the short trip from Yui to Okitsu by setting up two intermediate stations so that extra teams could go into action. This decision also had its humane overtones, in view of the number of elderly athletes who insisted on doing their bit.

Now the flag passed through Okitsu to applause from the small crowd. Tomorrow it would be trotted into the stadium, with the Emperor in attendance, and the games would begin.

It was still two hours before the Emperor would return, but slowly the sidewalks began to fill. Schools let out, and children lined the curb, each youngster clutching a small flag. Grownups began to jockey for good positions but, despite the obvious advantage, no one appeared at second-story windows. An old taboo against looking down on the Emperor remains strong.

The reserved spaces close to the Minaguchi-ya's gate began to fill, each section distinguished by the color of ribbon worn in the lapel or on the breast. Red denoted officers of the town, stiff and proper in their cutaways. Purple marked families of war dead. Pink designated club officials, those who headed the time-honored fraternities of fishermen, of farmers, and of youths, and the new but formidable association of women. There were yellow ribbons for men and women over seventy, and an especially good spot for them, for age is a certain passport to respect; many of them arrived on the arms of children or grandchildren, but once they were suitably installed with old friends, the younger generation slipped away to unreserved space down the line.

At frequent intervals the police loudspeaker boomed a report on the Imperial progress and the latest estimate of arrival time in Okitsu. Police jeeps rolled slowly down the street, each one causing an abortive flutter of flags. All regular traffic had been halted outside the town.

The police were at their station in front and back of the inn, linked by walkie-talkie radios. In addition to the entire Okitsu force, there were seventy prefectural policemen among the crowd, plus an undisclosed number of roving plainclothesmen.

Now, between the patrolmen who flanked the Minaguchi-ya's gate, Mochizuki appeared, backed by some of the palace staff. The original plan had been that the Emperor's car would be driven through the gate to the inn's entrance, but town officials had pleaded for a more intimate encounter, and it was finally agreed that the car would be halted in the street, giving at least a few people a chance to see the Imperial couple as they crossed the sidewalk. A loudspeaker truck moved past: "The Emperor has entered Okitsu." There were ominous drops of rain but no one left.

The crowd strained to see down the street, its steady murmur growing louder, every flag in motion. A police jeep, and then another, went by very slowly. Two motorcycle policemen appeared, moving just fast enough to keep their machines erect.

And then it came, the big Mercedes-Benz, a regal automobile with a regal disdain for fashion. Its angular black top loomed a foot higher than the submissively curved sedans that crawled behind, its maroon body was big and boxy. It bore the gold chrysanthemum.

It glided to a stop at the Minaguchi-ya's gate and a footman opened a door. A motherly woman and a little man in gray flannel climbed out.

Mochizuki bowed low, the town dignitaries bowed low, and their Emperor bowed in return. They straightened, and there was a moment's paralysis as the leaders of Okitsu shifted mental gears to meet the still alien requirements of the new age. Then their cheer went up, self-conscious but sincere, and over their heads the crowd saw a gray felt hat raised in acknowledgment, a gesture equally self-conscious and equally sincere.

Mochizuki, bowing again, caught the Emperor's attention, guided him through the gate. The entire family and staff of the inn, lining the drive, bowed their greeting. In the entrance hall, Mochizuki stepped nimbly out of his shoes and kept the Emperor in motion.

"The chamberlains complimented me on that moment," he reminisced later. "I had finally worn my own shoes, tight as they were, but I laced them very loosely. And, fortunately, I wasn't nervous. I have nerves of steel."

He smiled, remembering that small triumph, and then continued. "I showed the Emperor to the chair and bootjack, expecting he would sit down, but he only stood against the back of the chair and pulled his shoes off in the jack. I caught my breath. Instead of landing neatly, they rolled half across the room. For one ghastly moment my impulse was to retrieve them, but I restrained myself and showed him down the corridor to his suite. I bowed him into the rooms—I never did see his face that first day, I was so busy bowing—and then I retreated."

Until the Emperor and Empress left, two days later, no member of the family or of the staff of the inn entered those rooms, for Their Majesties, as is the custom, were served solely by their own servants from the palace. Food was delivered to the door by Isako and the two senior maids. By decree of the health authorities, the trays were draped in white cloth and the women carrying them wore surgical masks.

Isako made the first trip almost at once, bearing the welcoming tea and sweets. The cakes were the first of the local products to which the Emperor was treated. Said Mochizuki, "The easy thing would have been to order sweets from one of Tokyo's famous shops, but I knew that the Emperor gets those all the time, and I wanted to give him something different. That first day we served miniature cakes originated in Okitsu and called *miyasama manju*. About fifty years ago they were served to an Imperial prince when he stopped at Seikenji, and that's how they got their name, *miyasama* for prince and *manju* meaning sweet beancake. The prince liked them and I'm happy to say that the Emperor did, too."

As dusk settled over the town, Rising Sun lanterns were lighted in front of every shop. As far as the eye could see, from the river, past Minaguchi-ya's guarded gate, and down around Seikenji's curve, the highway was lined with friendly, festive pods of light.

Inside the inn, there was bustle and intentness. Every room was filled with palace functionaries. Even the old Ivy suite, still comfortable but now almost lost behind newer buildings and relegated to being a sewing room and maid's bedroom, was brushed up and once again held guests, the palace chauffeurs.

At six-thirty a little masked procession delivered the first course of dinner to *Akebono* suite. The Emperor and Empress, dining alone, praised the food, and, like Ieyasu, three and a half centuries before, they particularly liked the *Okitsu-tai*, sea bream partially sun-dried, broiled over charcoal.

After dinner the town proclaimed its welcome with fireworks, rockets over the beach and a set-piece mounted on a boat offshore. Unfortunately, the Emperor, having briefly retired from the living room, missed the whole display, but the Empress watched it and expressed her pleasure.

The Imperial couple, early to bed, were up at six, but the inn's staff was bustling long before that. There was, for instance, the matter of the newspapers. All the Tokyo and Shizuoka dailies were rushed to the Minaguchi-ya, but the health authorities, doggedly alert, had ordered that before being delivered to the Emperor they must be sterilized with steam or disinfectant solution. Either method resulted in very soggy journals, and it took several of the maids, using all the electric irons in the laundry room, to press them dry and smooth again.

After breakfast, the Emperor went out the garden gate to check first-hand this bit of ocean. A marine biologist by inclination, the Emperor of Japan by fate, he was now in his element, and he moved nimbly across a rocky beach, his chamberlains scrambling unsteadily behind. At ocean's edge he was a scientist, and none of his entourage intruded with poetic remarks about the pines of Miho, or pointed out, down the beach in front of Seikenji and Saionji's house, the cluster of offshore rocks where a stele proclaims that his father often swam. When he had used up the little time that was his own, the Emperor returned to the inn, and minutes later, when the big Mercedes-Benz swung out of the gate, he was back in frozen-faced character as the Emperor of Japan, waving stiffly to his people as he rode with the Empress at his side to open the games.

They returned in the afternoon for another night's rest at the Minaguchi-ya. That evening the Grand Chamberlain met with Mochizuki to present gifts from the Emperor in return for the hospitality which had been shown him. There was a ceremonial saké cup, in brilliant red lacquer with a gold chrysanthemum heavily embossed in the shallow bowl: it would become one of the Minaguchi-ya's cherished possessions. There was a box of cigarettes, cardboard-tipped and bearing the Imperial emblem but filled with notably cheap tobacco (a little economy the Imperial household can indulge since the Emperor does not smoke): these would be smoked by Mochizuki and favored friends. And, carefully wrapped in the finest vellum-like paper, there was money—not much, it is true (a sum "about the size of a sparrow's tears"), but Mochizuki had not entertained his Emperor with thoughts of remuneration.

When Mochizuki returned to his office with the Emperor's gifts, the family and staff pressed in to see them. They were pleased with themselves, for everything had gone beautifully. They had another, more intimate, reason for elation: there was a letter from Yoshi's son saying that he had come to understand his father's desire to continue working at the Minaguchi-ya; there would be no more objections; he could stay as long as he wished.

Next morning all the people of the inn lined up before the entrance, and when the Emperor emerged he spoke to them there. For the Empress and himself, he expressed appreciation for their stay, and for all the kindly labor that had made it possible. *Obaasan* wept with gratitude.

Their Majesties climbed into their limousine and rolled away. Once again, most of the population of Okitsu had gathered in the street. They cheered their Emperor and Empress off that morning as they had welcomed them two days before, but now they did not disperse. Only a few went back to tending shops or to household chores. Most of them turned through the gate of the Minaguchi-ya.

They came by the hundreds. They filed through the entrance, across the red carpet, past the chair and bootjack, down the gleaming corridor, into the Emperor's suite. They gazed at the bedding on which he had slept, the bath in which he had bathed, the rooms in which he had lived.

The name of those rooms was changed now. It was no longer *Akebono*, but *Miyuki*. The new name proclaims one more chapter in the fabled history of the Minaguchi-ya. In the pageant of the Tokaido, sometimes turbulent, sometimes peaceful, the inn had sheltered many travelers and now it had sheltered their Emperor. *Miyuki* is a name that breathes good fortune and high honor. It means Imperial Visit.

(continued on page 210)

KRONFELD © PAA

KRONFELD © PAA

KRONFELD © PAA

KRONFELD © PAA

KRONFELD © PAA

(continued from page 169)

As the curious continued to press through the doors, the inn's staff settled down to work. Hanjuro IV retired to his office. Yasuo left by the family entrance to board a train which would take him back to the marble and chrome hotel in Tokyo. Isako waved goodbye to her son, and then began to check the linen.

But an inn is truly an inn only when it has guests.

Half an hour after the big maroon and black limousine had disappeared down the highway, a saucy little taxi thrust through the gate. Horn blasting, it pushed aside the crowd, achieved the entrance, deposited its passenger. A maid dropped to her knees to welcome him. Yoshi rushed out to take possession of his bags. The Minaguchi-ya was in business again.

S. J. PERELMAN

from WESTWARD HA!

CHINA IN 1947, with the Bamboo Curtain beginning to fall, was hardly able to stop two case-hardened New Yorkers determined to see the world.

AN EARLY morning mist, periodically illuminated by the feeble rays of a wintry sun, shrouded the harbor of Chinwangtao as I thrust my head through our porthole on the *Marine Flier* and stared drowsily about me. All I could discern of fabled Cathay was a sullen range of hills disturbingly similar to those we had left behind in Southern California. Into a mind befogged with sleep there gradually crept a dark, hobgoblin suspicion. Suppose that through some error of navigation, some ghastly official blunder, we had overshot Asia and for the past three weeks had been floundering in a vast, idiotic circle around the Pacific. After all, stranger things had happened in the annals of the sea—the celebrated riddle of the *Mary Celeste*, the mysterious disappearance of the Danish training-ship *Kobenhavn*, the enigma of the *Waratah*. I sank down on the edge of the bunk and, head in hands, weighed the evidence. Yes, there was no doubt of it: the captain had made a serious miscalculation in his charts. Instead of pocketing his pride and availing himself of my superior seamanship to get him out of his pickle, he had manifestly preferred to brazen it out. His manner the past few days, now that I reconsidered it, had been extremely evasive; he had slunk past me deliberately avoiding my eye, fearful lest an unguarded word or gesture betray him. If this were indeed Southern California, the captain's intent became only too clear: he was planning to steam straight for Hollywood and drop anchor at Grauman's Chinese, hoping to fob it off on us as the Temple of the Thousand Sleeping Buddhas. There was not a moment to be lost; unless the man's duplicity was unmasked within the hour, our global junket stood in danger of being knocked

into a cocked hat. Crossing with a bound to Hirschfeld, my *fidus Achates*, who lay snoring bestially in his bunk, I shook him into consciousness.

"What is it? What's the matter?" the poor fellow cried out, leaping up with his usual faulty co-ordination and inflicting a small gash on his noggin as it struck the upper bunk. I explained our predicament, but his ignorance of matters maritime was abysmal and I could see he only half understood. Wearying of his dramatic groans and fumbling attempts to stanch the blood with a towel (the injury was petty and ceased bleeding long before nightfall), I went forward to reconnoiter and evolve a plan of action.

My fears, luckily, were unfounded; the first thing I beheld was a couple of junks leisurely standing into the harbor and a pilot tug flying the Chinese flag. Just ahead of us was the silvery line of a breakwater and beyond it the cluster of buildings which marked the Kai Lan Mining Administration, the British coal concession controlling the port. By midmorning, our customs and quarantine inspection completed, the ship edged cautiously into her berth beside a dingy, soot-blackened pier striped with railroad tracks. The coolies awaiting us on the dock were decked out in what was unquestionably the most fantastic collection of rags ever assembled anywhere to ward off the weather. A good half possessed no single garment worthy of the name (that is, worthy of the name of garment); the rest wore mangy fur-lined hats or beanies and long, shapeless coats that trailed handfuls of cotton wadding, looped about with odds and ends of canvas and burlap. Their faces were markedly Mongol, and our first impression of them, *en masse* under a gray, lowering sky, was hardly reassuring. I for one would not have been excessively surprised to see Genghis Khan himself appear, flourishing a yataghan, and begin carving a new empire out of the

Marine Flier. This judgment, however, shortly proved premature. The stevedores were amicable, even jolly; they greeted us warmly, indulged in a good deal of lighthearted banter, and altogether behaved with much more gusto and spirit than hungry people have any right to display. They were particularly awed by Hirschfeld's beard, and expressed their belief to our Jesuit fellow-passenger, who spoke Chinese, that he must be a renowned sage. It would have been shattering to the illusions of these simple folk, not to say disloyal to my friend, to reveal that he could barely read or write, and I prudently kept silence. Hirschfeld, of course, made the most of their homage; he strutted about, stroked his beard portentously, puckered his brow into a frown, moved his lips as though framing some momentous apothegm, and generally managed to create a pitiable travesty of a man deep in thought.

The only Occidental visible in the shifting crowd was a vinegary, tight-lipped Englishman in flannels and elegant brown suède shoes, who eyed the ship and everyone aboard her with ill-concealed disfavor. It was obvious that to our British cousin the arrival of the *Marine Flier* was no signal to fling his beret into the air. The junior mate, leaning beside us on the docking bridge, watched him with foreboding. "Trouble," he predicted gloomily. It appeared that we had called at Chinwangtao, a port rarely included in the freight schedule, to discharge twenty-five hundred tons of girdles (at least, it sounded like that; the engine-room bell was clanging and he may have said girders). Whatever they were, they lay well down in the hatches, and piled on top of them were quantities of miscellaneous cargo destined for Shanghai. This overstow would have to be removed, stored in godowns, or warehouses, while the girdles were being unloaded, and subsequently replaced. It was an expensive and tedious process, and if, he observed darkly, the port had no godown facilities, we would be in a pretty fix.

"What would we do then?"

"Search me, lover," he shrugged. "The inside of this here vessel is just one big grab-bag." I left him staring balefully at the wharf, and rounding up Hirschfeld, the Jesuit father, and the Philadelphia cotton converter, I proposed a stroll into the town. At the foot of the gangplank, the Englishman accosted us.

"I shouldn't go up there if I were you."

"We were just going to stretch our legs."

"You may get your necks stretched." He uttered a short, mirthless laugh. "There's the very devil to pay. The whole town's under martial law. The Communists are only five miles away. They've been blowing up the tracks between here and Tientsin every other night." Assuming a formidable Russian accent, Hirschfeld informed him that we were American Communist agents sent to bolster the morale of our Red comrades and that we would stick at nothing to help drive the parasites out of China, leaving no question in his voice whom he meant. The Englishman's lip curled. Our political sympathies were our own affair, he said, but he could tell us that if we ventured into Chinwangtao, he could not personally be responsible for our safety. We exchanged smiles tipped with the most malignant hatred and set off.

Our route into town lay across a tangle of railroad tracks skirting the bay; the wind was bitter and the scenery reminiscent of the less attractive suburbs of Carteret, New Jersey. Presently we came out upon a cement highway bordered by dusty, leafless saplings, along which hurried hordes of rather tense Chinese. Dispersed along the road at intervals were brick pillboxes manned by fifteen-year-old soldiers in heavily padded blue uniforms, exhibiting fixed bayonets with some ostentation. Before very long, a party of rickshaw men waylaid us. One of them, not to be put off by our repeated plea that we wanted to walk, scampered beside me. He offered to lead me to a house of tolerance, where, he implied, delights never imagined by Havelock Ellis and Krafft-Ebing might be viewed at moderate cost. I regretfully declined. He pondered a second, then withdrew from his singlet a packet of photographs which I gathered to be sporting scenes. I rarely hunt or fish, and I told him so. Undeterred, he inquired whether I wished to dally with his sister. I assured him I had every regard for her, but I had sworn to remain celibate until Ireland assumes its rightful place in the comity of nations. I was sorry when he finally fell astern and vanished up an alley. He was an engaging rogue, and though he would have cheerfully slit my windpipe for a shiny red apple, it had been fun knowing him.

A veritable fusillade of smells, compounded of the pungent odors of deep fat, shark's fin, sandalwood, and open drains, now bombarded our nostrils and we found ourselves in the thriving hamlet of Chinwangtao. Every sort of object imaginable was being offered by street hawkers—basketwork, noodles, poodles, hardware, leeches, breeches, peaches, watermelon seeds, roots, boots, flutes, coats, shoats, stoats, even early vintage phonograph records. In a pile of the latter, I discovered a fairly well-preserved copy of that classical minstrelsy, "Cohen on the Telephone," but the moment the merchant sensed he was dealing with an American, the price shot up to three cents and I thought better of it. A band of ten or fifteen urchins trooped at our heels constantly, wiping their noses freely on our sleeves and demanding cumshaw. Children, I may as well confess it, are my weakness; I distributed a few worn gold pieces which were of no further use to me and earned their undying gratitude. It is pathetic that trinkets like these, utterly without value in the States, should be sought after so eagerly throughout the rest of the world. The prospective traveler who seeks an advantageous rate of exchange will do far better to fill his trunks with gold pieces than the oft-heralded nylons, chewing gum, and cigarettes.*

It was almost lunchtime when we started back toward the ship, each in his individual rickshaw. I experienced what I am told is the customary sense of embarrassment at having a fellow-creature act as one's beast of burden, but mine was such a wiry specimen, weighing as he did well over eighty pounds and amazingly fleet for a man of sixty with tuberculosis, that I quickly overcame my compunctions. Besides, as your old China hand loves to observe, if everybody stopped riding in rickshaws through humanitarian scruples, their pullers would soon starve. It was, therefore, with the fairly cocky feeling I had done my bit to avert a possible famine that I dismounted and gave my boy his eleven cents. He must have appreciated my altruistic motives, for the instant he ceased coughing and sponged the perspiration from his face, he was profuse in his thanks.

We were treading gingerly through the maze of the freight yards when the faint blast of a steamer whistle echoed from the direction of the port. We stood momentarily rooted to the spot, and then, like a cork blown out of a bottle, the Jesuit father took off. I will stake my wig that, paced by Father Houlihan, the four of us broke every hurdle record in the last fifty years. It was a gallant try but foredoomed to failure. By the time we reached the pierhead, tongues lolling out of our mouths, the *Marine Flier* was beyond the breakwater and fading fast. The sole person in sight was our English milord, teetering on his heels and richly enjoying our dismay. "I warned you," he chuckled. Slowly, and savoring each word, he revealed that since there was no storage space for the overstow, our ship had left for Shanghai without unloading. It was a bleak prospect: all our passports, luggage, and funds slipped over the horizon, a civil war five miles away, and no American consul this side of Peiping. Ultimately, the Englishman finished draining his cup of triumph and relented. A tug was summoned and we were taken aboard ingloriously, in a heaving sea, amid the jeers and catcalls of the other passengers. One of them was so unsporting as to snap a photograph of me creeping on my hands and knees across the gang-

plank, which he later showed around to much raucous laughter. To tell the truth, I found the levity a trifle mechanical, but I joined in good-naturedly, ever ready to guffaw over the discomfiture of another human being.

Two mornings later, we steamed slowly up the muddy mouth of the Yangtze past the Woosung Forts and began threading our way through the sixteen miles of river traffic that separated us from our anchorage. How the pilot ever managed to maneuver the ship to her berth without running down a single sampan I do not profess to know; a dozen times it looked like Judgment Day for entire families of Chinese, but grandmother and three-year-old alike would throw themselves on the sweep and pump hysterically until the craft veered out of our path. Freighters from every conceivable port in the world—Oslo, Honduras, Liverpool, Veracruz, Amsterdam—were being lightered in midstream, further adding to the hazard. At last, around a bend of the Whangpoo, Shanghai came into sight and we slid along the Bund, fronted by hotels and office buildings, up to the Dollar docks on the Pootung side.

A charming bit of intelligence greeted us. The bowlines were scarcely secured before word arrived that in three days we were to head back to Chinwangtao and discharge the girdles after all. A pall descended on the ship; Hirschfeld and I sat drearily in the deserted smoking room, wondering whether to transfer to another ship, or stay ashore until the *Flier* returned, or just hang ourselves from the nearest yardarm. We probably would have done the last had not the captain anticipated us and hid it in a locker. Eventually we decided to spend a night or two in Shanghai and see what diversions it offered. All the way across the Pacific there had been rumors of exquisitely complaisant White Russian countesses and unimaginable sins. Neither of us smoked opium, but we had no objection to learning. We thought we might even pick up a priceless bit of jade. We were in a mood for adventure. We got it.

We received the first installment before we even set foot on the levee. The tender which bore us to the Bund had no allotted slip or jetty; it merely tied up in slapdash fashion against five other boats, each moored to the one adjoining it, and the passengers swarmed over the lot like ants over a sugar bowl. In effect, what you had was a Bronx subway rush with water jumps. One moment I was braced against a stanchion gaping at the skyline; the next, I was caught up in a swirl of coolies and shot forward down into a barge full of stones. I clawed my way across it, sprang down a dark companionway, stumbled over three

---

* This was written in the early spring of 1947. The situation may have altered since, of course.—*Author's note.*

citizens stuffing themselves with bean curd, and landed in a perilously tossing sampan. As I straightened up to catch my breath, the second wave hit me. I saw Hirschfeld go past, flailing and kicking, his beard high in the air. "Hirschfeld!" I screamed piteously, "*Tovarisch!*" He paid me no attention; he had other fish to fry. I lowered my head like a bull and, with two Cantonese encircling me, did a line plunge. I reached terra firma a broken man, my collar in shreds, eyeglasses twisted, streaming with perspiration. Hirschfeld was nursing a wrenched knee, having slipped and fallen between two boats in the melee. He had a bloody nose and had lost a shoe, but otherwise he was as fit as a fiddle.

To regain some measure of poise, we proceeded to the Cathay Hotel, reputedly Shanghai's finest, and had a drink apiece. The bill came to $39,000 Chinese National Currency—about $3.36—and we left a tip of $5000, or 41 cents. The exchange rate at the moment was twelve thousand Chinese dollars to the American one, and prices had more or less kept abreast. Our room, for instance, was $120,000 a day—slightly over ten dollars—and our breakfast $14,000. The real drawback, though, was the complete lack of any form of heat. A ton of coal cost three hundred U. S. dollars— in any case, a purely academic consideration at the Cathay, as the Japanese had stripped it of radiators and boilers. That night will linger in my memory as one of the most agonizing I have ever endured. Our teeth chattered so loudly that several Americans resident there phoned the Embassy to report gunfire. Just to indicate how cold it was, I left a tumbler of water at my bedside and when I woke up, it was gone. Hirschfeld had drunk it and also had eaten the glass. That was one cold night.

The following day we embarked on a shopping tour of the antique bazaars in the Kwantung Road, charmed at every turn by the indescribable wealth of imagination the Chinese lavish on their art. Surrounded by so much beauty, it was difficult to determine what to choose; Hirschfeld finally settled on an imitation cloisonné cigarette stand complete with match receptacle and ashtrays, and I bought three ivory backscratchers you could not duplicate in San Francisco for less than a quarter. About midafternoon we traced our steps to the American Club, a pleasant establishment in Foochow Road made doubly delightful by the circumstance that it had the only heated bar in town. Five whisky sours drove the chill from our bones, and we decided to have a drink. There then ensued a hazy interval during which I seem to recall the sound of a cupful of poker dice being thrown repeatedly against a board and a playful attempt on my part to comb Hirschfeld's beard with a back-scratcher. From time to time strange faces swam into my field of vision; I remember a laborious, protracted recital by an UNRRA official of his difficulties in persuading the Chinese to eat canned peaches, but part of it was being given in Russian and some men were accompanying him on balalaikas. It suddenly grew much colder and I found myself in a very dim night club, teaching an exophthalmic Hungarian girl the Cubanola glide. The next morning I felt remarkably listless and there was an outbreak of beef Stroganoff on my tie as though I were coming down with a fever, but these symptoms soon passed, and by noon I was able to keep down a little clear broth made of Angostura, lemon peel, and bourbon.

What with the penetrating cold and the cost of living in Shanghai, it seemed on the whole inadvisable to tarry, and folding our hands submissively we journeyed north once more to Chinwangtao on the *Flier*. It took four interminable days to get rid of our cargo; my companion mooned in the cabin buffing his nails and I made a short excursion to Shanhaikwan to see the Great Wall. The Great Wall can also be seen facing page 556 of the Encyclopaedia Britannica by simply stretching your hand toward the bookcase, though the chances of picking up a flea are very much smaller. Shanhaikwan, it is interesting to note, has the smallest fleas in China; they are much prized by collectors, but I was fortunate enough to secure three or four fine specimens. As the Chinese government strictly forbids their export, I had to smuggle them out in my clothing, but I managed to get them through to Singapore safe and sound.

Shanghai once more, and this time it was the twenty-eighth of March, the end of the first week of spring. All through it we had lain alongside the wharf, the Plimsoll line rising hourly higher as ton after ton of goods went over the side. Across the river, in the barren fields, the trees had begun to show a cloudy green nimbus; the sun was hot, and in the sampans drifting downstream groups of children were playing jacks. I lounged on the boat deck and thought of the Pennsylvania countryside, of the forsythia primrose-yellow against the barn, the Judas tree bursting into bloom, the swollen creek tumbling through the pasture. I asked myself what I was doing ten thousand miles from home, on what obscure quest I had come, and I could find no answer. Perhaps Thoreau knew; he knew everything. I went into my cabin and got out *Walden*. There it was, in that always concise and astringent prose, the *vade mecum* for every wanderer.

"It is not worth the while to go round the world to count the cats in Zanzibar. Yet do this even till you can do better, and you may perhaps find some

'Symmes' Hole' by which to get at the inside at last. England and France, Spain and Portugal, Gold Coast and Slave Coast, all front on this private sea; but no bark from them has ventured out of sight of land, though it is without doubt the direct way to India. If you would learn to speak all tongues and conform to the customs of all nations, if you would travel farther than all travellers, be naturalized in all climes, and cause the Sphinx to dash her head against a stone, even obey the precept of the old philosopher, and Explore thyself. Herein are demanded the eye and the nerve. Only the defeated and deserters go to the wars, cowards that run away and enlist. Start now on that farthest western way, which does not pause at the Mississippi or the Pacific, nor conduct toward a worn-out China or Japan, but leads on direct, a tangent to this sphere, summer and winter, day and night, sun down, moon down, and at last earth down too."

SANTHA RAMA RAU

from EAST OF HOME

I N 1948, *Santha Rama Rau set out from Japan, where her father was India's ambassador, on a visit to China and Southeast Asia. Her companions were two Americans, one of whom, Faubion Bowers, later became her husband.*

WE LEFT Lanchow on the twenty-sixth of November, a clear, sunny day, cold, but with little wind. We hadn't even discussed the purchase of furs or bedding, partly because we couldn't afford it, and partly because we naively believed it would be only a four-day trip. There was one free place beside the driver, and Clare and I took it in turns. We started in the morning, cheerful and rather excited by our little adventure.

Faubion and Michael were by now used to the technique of traveling on the tops of trucks. They showed me that the best place is near the front so that you don't get the dust, and with one row of yellow fish between you and the edge so that you are sheltered by them from the wind. If it is possible to persuade someone to sit on your feet, then you are really fortunate because the slow freezing of your hands and feet is the hardest to bear. The truck was carrying large barrels of oil south from Sinkiang. We climbed on top of the barrels, and realized for the first time the intelligence of carrying a bedding roll. The other yellow fish sat on theirs, and it didn't take me long to learn that, once the truck is moving, the cold and draught can attack you from the most extraordinary angles. A Mongolian climbed on at the village where we stopped for lunch, and Faubion immediately christened him the Mongolian idiot, partly for his looks, and partly because he had placed a large dead goat in Faubion's place while we had been eating. The ethics of yellow-fishing dictate that you cannot take someone else's place if you are a late-comer but nothing prevents you from putting your luggage there, as the other yellow fish can always sit on it.

"It isn't that it is uncomfortable," Faubion said, "It is simply that I have become Chinese enough to feel that one should respect the dead." However, the other yellow fish patted the goat and congratulated Faubion on having such a warm, resilient seat.

A pleasant camaraderie springs up among the yellow fish on such a journey. Since they suffer from no inhibitions about asking what they want to know their questions are direct and to the point. Only Michael was embarrassed by what he called "personal questions." Faubion, of course, was delighted because, being of a very inquisitive turn of mind, it gave him the perfect excuse to ask dozens of questions back. The opening questions are always, "Where do you come from? Where are you going? What are you doing in China?"

When Faubion answered, "Just traveling about and seeing your country," they were entirely satisfied. They had an easy conviction that China was certainly the greatest country in the world. The character of the word "China," which also means center, or the Middle Kingdom, seemed to them a literal statement of the truth. *Of course* China was the center of the universe, so of course foreigners would come there if they could.

The Mongolian idiot turned out to be a most engaging young man. Huddled in his furs, jolting along a road which was growing progressively worse, he asked more questions than anyone. "Which of the two men is she married to?" he asked nodding at me.

"Neither."

"Then where is her husband? In India? Why does he let her travel with foreigners?"

"She is not married."

The Mongolian and several of the other yellow fish turned at once and comforted me, "There is still a little time. But do not waste it. You must marry as soon as you return to your country. Certainly you cannot marry a foreigner." The women smiled cozily at me.

"The American sitting with the driver," pursued the Mongolian, "she is married to the Englishman?"

When Faubion translated this, Michael turned scarlet and stared with passionate interest at the receding hills. "No," he said.

"Ah? Not yet? But she will later on?"

"I shouldn't think so for a moment," Michael said in a strangled voice.

Most of the yellow fish were soldiers and their families. One of the soldiers, whose padded khaki uniform made him look like a Teddy bear, lifted the ear flaps from his cap to hear the conversation better. When he heard Faubion was an American he was very excited, and his round peasant face puckered into a smile. His skin was taut and shining from the cold, and his teeth were green and badly rotted. "Roosevelt," he said with delight, "Tru-man!"

"Wonderful. Where did you learn that?"

"In our army we are taught those names because your country helps us. *Mei-guo ren ding hao!*" he said, laughing and turning his thumb up. He introduced us to his wife, a shy little girl who was carrying a baby. He asked why we didn't fly to Chungking,

Stone lion guarding approach to Grand Hotel, Taipei, Taiwan.

"Foreigners are rich."

"We aren't," Faubion said, "we can't afford it."

The soldier was at once full of sympathy. "Then you must come with me when we reach Ting-hsi. I will arrange for you to stay in the soldiers' inn. It is cheaper."

Ting-hsi, which was scarcely even a village, looked in the light of the setting sun as though it were quite deserted. As soon as the truck stopped there, however, children, dogs, and adults dashed into the street and surrounded the truck. Heated conversations and questionings began at once. We waited patiently while our soldier friend explained who we were and what we were doing, and then were conducted to the soldier inn. It was built around a square courtyard, clean and bare, and groups of soldiers squatted on the ground chatting and singing. We ate dinner with the Mongolian and some of the other yellow fish, and returned to the inn to find that the soldier had hired quilts for us, arranged two rooms, and was haggling with a man about the price of a small basket of charcoal so that we could have a fire.

I woke very early the next morning feeling stiff from the board bed, and with all kinds of unsuspected aches from the truck ride. I hobbled to the door of our room and found the courtyard a sheet of white. It had snowed heavily during the night, and the moon paling behind the last of the snow clouds gave the snow a weird luminous look, as though it were lit from underneath.

At first when we got up and drank our tea we were still warm from sleep and didn't realize that the winter had arrived, and from now on would grip the northwest until the spring loosened the ground, brought the rain, and allowed the lives of the people to thaw into an easier pattern that was not built entirely around escaping the cold.

It was my turn to ride inside the truck, but after we felt the wind and the dense cold outside, Clare and I decided to divide the days rather than take alternate days in the cab. "Only another three days," we kept telling each other, "and Chungking should be much warmer."

At the lunch stop, Clare climbed painfully off the truck, scarcely able to straighten her frozen joints. Tears were streaming down her face and for the first few minutes inside the restaurant she couldn't hold a tea cup. I had wondered how Faubion would survive, because he had returned the sheepskin he had borrowed from the university student in Lanchow, and had only a raincoat over his army uniform. The Mongolian, appalled at his stupidity, had lent him his own sheepskin, and had pulled out the covers from his bedding roll for himself.

In the afternoon I began to understand Clare's state. I was wearing three sweaters and a pair of flannel slacks underneath Clare's ski suit. The suit itself was wool, with a windproofed jacket, but the blizzard across those deserted hills swept through as though I had been wearing muslin. Clare and I rubbed cream all over our faces, but nothing seemed to prevent our skin from cracking and flaking. The only thing that redeemed the situation was that under snow the country looked beautiful. The flat surfaces of the villages—roofs, the tops of walls, window ledges—caught the snow and gave an architectural effect to scenes that were normally monotone and two-dimensional.

That night at Chingan, where there was no soldier inn, we followed the other yellow fish, and learned the importance of the k'ang method of sleeping. The slight warmth of the other people does reach you through furs and quilts and bedding, and keeps you alive through a night that you couldn't otherwise survive.

Overnight the cold had intensified so greatly that further snow was unlikely, but the remains of the blizzard on the roads had frozen solid, leaving a wildly slippery surface to the narrow uncertain road with a sheer rise of mountain on one side and a precipice on the other. The truck, of course, had no chains. I shut my eyes and buried my face in the Mongolian's dead goat. Faubion with all the curiosity frozen out of him didn't say a word until we were nearly in Tienshui, our next stop.

I was wondering, in a lightheaded and rather detached way, whether I would live through this trip. It was hard to explain why, since my whole body was numb, it should ache so violently. I had never realized that cold could be painful. Faubion said in a strange cracked voice, "Look."

I brought my face out of the goat's flank and saw a row of men in a sort of uniform, straggling along in the snow and ice of the road outside the town walls of Tienshui. They were roped together, wrist to wrist, guarded at both ends of the column by armed Nationalist soldiers. The men were barefoot.

"Those must be the first prisoners of war we have seen," Faubion said. He asked our soldier friend what battle the Communists might have been captured in. The soldier laughed with all his rotten teeth showing, and said, "Those are not Communist prisoners, those are new recruits to the army."

Faubion turned to me and said very bitterly, "It's the usual thing apparently. To recruit new soldiers they send a few men with guns into the villages; they pick the men off the streets, rope them together, and march them into a military camp."

"Their shoes—" I said, horrified.

"The shoes are taken away. It makes desertion harder. As soon as possible they are sent away from their home provinces. That makes it harder still."

* * *

Tienshui turned out to be a fair-sized town. Our soldier and his wife, who were immediately involved in conversation when we arrived, told us that the town was full of troops at that time and that all the inn space had been requisitioned. We went with them to an inn entirely filled by soldiers, where after much argument and gesticulating the innkeeper said he could give us one room (normally his own room) for the four of us. We walked through the very dark and dirty restaurant to the room at the back. It was tiny, dark and extremely cold. It had one narrow plank bed in it and a table. The soldier smiled, waved his hand and vanished. We all sat in a row on the bed too depressed to speak.

"Well," Michael said at last, "it's only for one night. Faubion and I don't mind sleeping on the floor." We stared at the earth floor which showed clearly the places where people had spat and thrown tea dregs, as they do in all Chinese restaurants. The smell of mildew was strong from the sweating walls. Somehow the room managed to combine stuffiness with bitter cold. There was no window.

"We could always," said Clare with an unsuccessful attempt at lightness, "phone the Waldorf." A large rat strolled casually across the floor. Clare suddenly started to cry. "Oh *damn* it!" she said. "It would have been worth every penny of five hundred dollars!"

Two small children came and stood in the doorway. The soldier had sent them to us with a couple of handsful of nuts as a present. Their parents were sharing a room with our soldier and his wife and all three children. They stayed and talked to us for a while. The little girl, about six years old, was the older and by far the more intelligent of the two, but when they were showing us how many characters they could write and what big figures they could add, she always deferred to him. Already she knew the place of a girl in the family.

Faubion asked her the price of the little felt shoes she was wearing.

"Fifteen gold yuan," she said.

"Isn't that very expensive?"

"No," she was most emphatic, and recited off the prices in other villages she had been through on the journey south.

"But we bought some like that for only eight."

"Then you must have bought them more than a month ago, because since then money is not worth so much."

"Yes, that's true."

Our soldier came in to tell us that he had been talking to the truck driver and had heard that we wouldn't be leaving Tienshui for two or three days. The roads were impassable.

Michael stood up with sudden decision, "We'll have to do something. We can't stay in this room for three days. Ask the man if there are any foreigners in this town."

"Yes," said the soldier, rather surprised that after a whole hour in Tienshui we shouldn't know all about the town. "There are some Christians."

The Catholic fathers in the Tienshui Mission, when we eventually found it, were most cordial and seemed delighted to see new faces. Most of them were German, a couple of Spaniards and one American, Father Rudolf. They gave us a couple of rooms in their little hospital, which are normally kept free for the Fathers themselves, served us mission-made wine and biscuits in front of the old-fashioned stove in their refectory, and then sent us off to collect our luggage.

At the inn our soldier was waiting for us. Rather shame-facedly we told him that we would stay at the Mission while we were in Tienshui. He seemed to think it a good idea, "You like to be with your own people sometimes," and suggested that we tell the innkeeper that one of us was ill, and that was why we were moving. It would save his face, and in any case he would find out where we were staying.

Meals at the Mission were extraordinary. Fifteen bearded old men sat around the refectory table eating solidly German food—sausages, meatballs, sauerkraut—made by the nuns who helped in the hospital. The cabbages had to be specially grown in their own garden—Chinese cabbage somehow isn't quite right for sauerkraut.

Tienshui, which means Heavenly Water, was at one time a well-known cultural center of China; since then, the increasing poverty of the soil has scattered some of the population. It still has many schools and some beautiful old buildings and temples which the Chinese rather casually use to keep their cattle in. Gazing at one of the temples, Faubion remarked, "The Chinese must be the only people in the world who have evolved a code of ethics—or manners if you want to call it that—without a 'fear of God.' They can lead a good life, when they do, without the need for a religion in the accepted sense." Then feeling that this was not precisely the remark to make to a missionary, he went on by asking whether the Mission would be disbanded since the Communists were so near to Tienshui.

"No, no. This is our home. Some of us have been here for thirty and forty years. Why should we leave now? One of our fathers went back to his village in Europe for the first time in thirty-eight years. He saw his first movie and heard the radio for the first time on the ship going over. Most of us don't even take our home leave."

We were shown around the hospital, a series of cottages built in the Chinese way, but dazzlingly clean, whitewashed and well cared for compared with most Chinese interiors. The haggard men rotting away with syphilis, the children with brilliant cheeks and tuberculosis, the wasted mothers waiting for children to be born who would live no longer than their previous ones. It was easy to understand why movies and radios were unimportant.

*   *   *

Three days later the truck left Tienshui. The days were still overcast and rigidly cold. We were all grimly depressed at the thought of facing more of those agonized days of truck travel, particularly since we had learned that only the most ignorant amateur at travel in China could have hoped to reach Chungking from Lanchow in four days. It takes at least ten in the very best weather.

The roads were still frozen and we skidded recklessly along over the treacherous passes south of Tienshui. We got to the top of one long hill which was entirely iced over. At the top of it there were three trucks and several ox carts and horse carts waiting to go on and afraid to try the downgrade. The animals were too precious to lose by broken legs, and the truck drivers didn't feel up to risking their necks.

Our driver decided to be brave and told us all to get off the truck while he took it down the hill. He started off with a crowd of enthralled yellow fish watching him. We all stood well out of the way on top of the hill. The engine roared, a cloud of smoke from the exhaust hung in the frozen air, and a few yards down the truck skidded so violently on a road that was too narrow even for overtaking that it whirled around in its tracks and teetered madly on the edge of the precipice. Horrified gasps from us, and gales of laughter from the yellow fish and the other drivers. Our man got it back under control when the truck was facing up the hill again. We looked down the cliff to see another truck caught halfway down where it had fallen the evening before after rashly attempting the same descent.

Slowly the driver got the truck back up the hill, and then all the drivers got together and had a conference. Faubion, naturally, was listening avidly, but I didn't even bother to try to understand what was going on because I was feeling immensely happy and exhilarated. The sun had come out for the first time since we had left Lanchow. During the previous few days we

had all developed large, painful chilblains, and a passionate worship of the sun. Every few minutes we had gazed at the sky, looking for a break in the clouds. I hadn't thought it possible that one's life could come to revolve with such fervor around the appearance of the sun.

We were on the wrong side of the hill so the sunlight, pale and without much warmth, reached us only for about an hour, but during that time I couldn't seem to take seriously the fact that we would probably have to spend the rest of the day and all night on that hill without food or bedding. Michael, in his matter-of-fact way, said, "Look, we've only got about three hours of daylight left. I think we should abandon the truck and walk to the next village and get accommodations for the night. We're bound to freeze to death if we stay here."

"What about the luggage?" Clare asked.

"We'll just have to leave it."

Clare checked through the things in her handbag—bobby-pins—lipstick—toothbrush—comb—and finally said, "Okay. Let's go."

Faubion explained our plans to our soldier friend and told him that in case the truck had to go back or cracked up completely, he could have whatever he wanted of our luggage.

The next village was about seven kilometers away, but when we got there we could find no restaurant. There were about twenty huts in the village, and we asked at each one, but they all said that food was too scarce, and that there was no room to sleep. We walked on until after dark to another similar village to receive the same replies.

We were sitting dejectedly at the edge of the road, too tired and cold to talk. Two brilliant beams of light came swinging around the corner, and our friend shouted to us from the top of the truck. They had managed to get it down the hill, the soldier said, by digging into the hillside and getting out cans of earth. They all sprinkled this on the road and finally made a surface that the truck could manage to grip. I had never ridden on top of a truck after dark before, and I found that the cold of the first days of the trip was like a pleasant summer breeze compared to the icy winds of the night.

Several hours later, when we did get to a small town (of which I never discovered the name), my limbs were entirely dead. I tried to climb off the truck but I couldn't grip with my hands, and slipped and fell rather heavily on my right wrist. In the panic of the moment I was certain I had broken it. People from the village and the yellow fish from the truck stood around laughing as though they had never seen anything so amusing.

Clare, in a fury of worry, yelled, "For Christ's sake get a doctor! Don't just stand there grinning!" They laughed again at her anger, and stood where they were. She turned on Faubion, "Aren't you going to do something? Or do you think it's funny too?"

Faubion said to someone in the crowd, "Is there a doctor in this town?" They smiled and chatted with him while Clare and Michael led me off to the inn. We walked through the usual sort of restaurant with people sitting about playing the finger game and gobbling their food. Little cups of oil, each with a wick in it, flickered on the tables. The room at the back opened onto a small, filthy courtyard with two enormous pigs in one corner, and chickens walking disdainfully around in the refuse. A pervasive stink came from the latrine in the courtyard—both doors had gone from it, and there were just the two little mud-walled cubicles. Across the walls the frozen fields stretched in the starlight. At least tomorrow would be a clear day.

I lay on the k'ang in the back room and listened to the rats, feeling too sick to eat. I could just hear Clare and Michael in the restaurant, just outside the door, whispering. After some time Faubion came back with a man in a blue gown. The doctor was obviously terrified at the idea of dealing with foreigners. He looked at the wrist. It was beginning to swell. Faubion wrote out the characters of "Is it broken?"

The doctor asked me to clench my fist, which I could do, but it was painful. He wouldn't touch it except to paint it with some dark-brown liquid on a dirty bit of cotton.

Michael said, "He's scared that if it gets worse he'll have to take the responsibility. In Shanghai foreign doctors get a written guarantee from a patient before an operation that they won't be taken to court by the family if the patient doesn't recover. Under Chinese law they can be sued for manslaughter."

"Isn't there someone that knows about American medicine?" Clare asked.

The doctor caught the word "American," apparently, for he produced a box of pills which he said were American medicine.

"Sulfa?" Clare asked. The doctor nodded agreement.

"Aspirin?" Michael said. The doctor nodded again, smiling.

"Oh, hell," said Clare, "better let it go. It probably isn't broken if you can move it. Does one put hot things on a sprain or cold things?"

None of us knew, so we did nothing. The doctor left the name of a Chinese ointment with us, and said, expecting an argument, that his fee was five golden yuan (about thirteen cents at the time). Clare said, "And cheap at the price—the education, not the treatment." We found out much later that the ointment he had suggested was something like Iodex, and perfectly good for a sprain.

All night, since I couldn't sleep, I lay and listened to the sounds of a Chinese village. I tried to keep still so that I wouldn't disturb the others, but nothing seems to disturb a Chinese when he is sleeping. He may wake at a particularly loud noise, but he sleeps at once right afterward. Equally, he has no hesitation in making a noise himself when others are sleeping. In the early part of the night a few people talked and laughed in loud voices, heavy steps trudged across the courtyard to the latrine. There was the clatter of bowls and chopsticks being put away, or tea cups still clinking against the pot—none of it subdued at all. A child cried, somebody shouted to somebody across the street, then there was the sudden dead silence as the day ended for good.

In the night a rat ran across Clare's leg, and she sat up and screamed. Only Michael woke up and said, "What's the matter?" Somebody else on the k'ang grunted and muttered something. Then there was silence again until the animals started waking up in the courtyard and the sound of donkeys being led down the road began.

JAMES MORRIS

from CITIES

EVERYONE agrees that Hong Kong is a good place to go shopping.

MORE PEOPLE live in Hong Kong than in all the rest of the world put together, and they make more noise than a million electric drills, and they work like automation: and their babies are beyond computation, and their machinery chitter-chatters away for twenty-five hours every day: and in their markets they sell every fish that was ever caught, and every shrimp that ever wriggled, and every crab that ever pinched: and their excellent shirts cost fourpence-ha'penny

Sun Moon Lake, Taiwan.

apiece: and there are five million Chinese for every European in the city, each one of them more energetic than a power station: and all these unbelievable paradoxes of prolixity and profusion are a lesson in the impermanence of power and the mutability of history.

Just over a hundred years ago the British seized Hong Kong from an addled China, and were conceded sovereignty over it "in perpetuity." The island was almost uninhabited, but they made of it a tremendous port and a gunboat station supreme, where British merchants could command the China trade beneath the guns of the Royal Navy. Hong Kong became one of the greatest of free ports and entrepôts, and a brilliant symbol of European superiority. Here the techniques of the Western world were applied to the corrupt and ramshackle structure of China. The merchant princes lived in splendour on the eminence of the Peak, while across the hills in China the impotent Asians squabbled and cheated each other and carved the ivory ornaments that would one day look so pretty upon the mantelpiece in Epsom.

Today the British are still in Hong Kong, and the rich merchants roll down from the Peak each morning in their big black ponderous limousines. The great banks and merchant houses are still magnificently bustling, the company flags fly bravely beside the Union Jack. But you cannot spend a day in Hong Kong without realizing that she lives by the courtesy, and at the mercy, of the new China. Times have changed with an imperial vengeance. The long grey warships that still lie in the harbour (successors to *Aphis* and *Mantis* and the elegant old river gunboats) no longer fool anybody, least of all the hard-headed British. Hong Kong is indefensible, militarily and economically, and she lives half on trust and half on cynicism.

Consider her geographical situation. If you stand on a high place on Hong Kong Island you can see virtually the whole of the Colony. Below you is Hong Kong herself, for ever England, and beyond it is the glorious sweep of the harbour, crammed with the steamers and junks and ferryboats and launches of free enterprise, never silent, never motionless, one of the great mercantile waterways of the world. But in the middle distance are the mountains of China proper, and most of the land in between—the essential hinterland of Hong Kong—does not belong to Britain, but is only held on a lease that expires towards the end of this century (if international leases have any meaning by then). Not only is China ominously close. In her own back yard British Hong Kong has only the precarious rights of tenancy.

Or move, for another view, to an economic vantage point. At West Point on Hong Kong Island there is a wharf where the junks arrive from Pearl River and Canton, in Communist China. It makes no bones about its affiliations. In the tumbledown eating-house, where the labourers stoically consume their rice and villainous fish, a huge poster proclaims the industrial potential of Communist China, and the tugboat outside carries on its superstructure a series of slogans about people's rights and imperialist aggression and that kind of thing. Somewhere in an attic above your head a lonely but determined flautist plays a Communist propaganda melody, and the ducks that are off-loaded in their thousands from the rickety junks, crammed in huge wicker baskets and carried by relays of cheerful and courteous coolies—even the ducks are brainwashed Khaki Campbells. Without this traffic from China, without its ducks and hens and vegetables, Hong Kong probably could not long survive. The Communists know that when the lease of that hinterland expires in 1998, Hong Kong will be theirs for the plucking: but they also know that if need be they could squeeze her into submission long before then. All the cards are theirs. They can take the place by force, if they are willing to risk a world war. They can starve it out. Or they can simply wait for another few decades, a mere flicker of time among the Chinese centuries.

With so plump and once cocky a mouse between its claws, it is perhaps understandable that the Chinese cat enjoys playing with its victim with that strange mixture of the purr and the snarl that usually accompanies such kitchen-corner exercises. There is an element of sadism to the attitude of Peking to Hong Kong. The Communist propagandists are blatantly active in the city, flaunting their huge posters and their red flags, selling their books and their magazines and their newspapers, infiltrating the schools and threatening the unions. But if the Hong Kong Government allows itself a mild riposte, closing a school, expelling a subversive educationist, or tearing down a flag or two, swift and menacing is the protest from Peking. "I once brought a message to the Governor from Peking," a strikingly slimy Communist told me in Hong Kong, "after some riots in Kowloon. It was simply this: 'Don't let it happen again, Your Excellency.'"

Because of all this, because of the overwhelming strength of the new China, people sometimes say cleverly that Hong Kong is in effect Chinese already. This is no more than a quarter truth. Hong Kong is, of course, a Chinese city in the racial sense, and it is obviously humiliating to the British to endure these political degradations. But the Britishness of the place, for all its insecurity, is still staunch and admirable. Everywhere there are great new public projects—huge housing schemes, hospitals, airport runways, roads, dams, land reclamations—some of the biggest of them in the New Territories themselves. The administration is still by all accounts excellent, and since Hong Kong remains pre-eminently a place of business there is not much pressure for legislative reform, and almost none at all for self-government. What is more the British are still, to this awkward day, reaping rewards from Hong Kong. Practically the whole cost of the administration comes from local revenues, and Hong Kong earns a lot of dollars, offers a flourishing market for British goods, and sustains a number of great British merchant houses. She is a valuable intelligence outpost on the edge of Asia, and she provides a lavish example—too lavish, many Englishmen might think—of the capitalist system with all its thrusting, barging, shoving, no-holds-barred stimulation.

She is also a haven. Hong Kong is jammed full of refugees and deportees and émigrés from Communist China. Some of them have come here because it is a fine place to make money, with its low taxes, its splendid port, its cheap labour and its stable government. Many others have come, as Chinese have through all Hong Kong's history, to escape the hardships or the dangers of life in China. The Hong Kong Government has done its best to help and assimilate these people, and to my mind this is a duty that is satisfying beyond political pin-pricks, and not to be abandoned without dishonour. Greed, self-interest, pride and morality all contribute to the flavour of the British presence in Hong Kong: and Heaven knows they have met each other before.

But though the British are not doing badly in Hong Kong, and are performing some good for the world, too, nevertheless the moral of the Colony's situation is a daunting one. The Communist Chinese tolerate its independence partly because they have bigger things to think about, and partly because they don't want to arouse new issues needlessly; partly

because they need bargaining counters, and partly because they themselves find the economic services of Hong Kong useful (the tallest building on the Hong Kong waterfront is the Bank of China, an invaluable clearing house of foreign exchange for Peking). The capitalists of Hong Kong thrive because they do not believe the Communists will move before 1998, at the earliest, thus leaving them time to make a quick new fortune or embellish an old one. The simple people get what benefit they can from good government and economic opportunity, and try not to think about the future. But above all these several attitudes, the place is haunted by a sense of the hugeness and fertility and brute strength of Asia. Not so long ago a writer could observe that England had cut a notch in China as a woodsman cuts a tree—"to mark it for felling at a convenient opportunity." In Hong Kong today, with Asia already flooding through Queen Victoria Street and Waterloo Road, and with six hundred million more Chinese over there across the hills, and with the whole place a tumult of Asian energy and noise, and constantly threatened by Asian power, and riddled with Asian ideologies—here in Hong Kong you cannot help wondering how ambitious a woodsman China will be when she reaches the summit of her power, and how many of us old elms she is going to notch for firewood.

*   *   *

In the central market of Hong Kong the edible frogs are tied together in bundles while they are still alive, a string of straw binding them around their stomachs. They thus present a multi-limbed symmetrical appearance, and one pair of little legs is constantly jumping to the left, and another pair kicking out to the right, in a very erratic and unpredictable conflict of impulses. This, though clearly uncomfortable for the poor frogs, is not altogether unfunny to watch: and when I saw it for the first time, my goodness, said I to myself, how are we to compete with this extraordinary people, when even their frogs have twelve legs apiece, and lunge about with such comic and irresistible vigour?

MIGUEL COVARRUBIAS

from THE ISLAND OF BALI

A MEXICAN artist appreciates Bali, especially for its art.

THE CAPITALS of the princes' districts, the seats of regencies, are commercialized half-European, half-

Chinese towns like Den Pasar and Buleleng; but the true life of Bali is concentrated in thousands of villages and hamlets. With their thatched roofs they lie buried under awnings of tropical vegetation, the groves and gardens that provide for the needs of the villagers. Out of the chartreuse sea of ricefields they surge like dark green islands of tall palms, breadfruit, mango, papaya, and banana trees.

Underneath the cool darkness, pierced only by the shafts of sunlight that sift through the mesh of leaves, are the houses hidden from view by interminable mud walls that are broken at regular intervals by long narrow gates. All the gates are alike: two mud pillars supporting a small roof of thick thatch, giving access to each household by a raised doorstep of rough stones. In front of every gate is a stone bridge, or, simpler still, a section of coconut tree trunk to ford the deep irrigation ditch that runs invariably along both sides of the road.

A simple village consists of family compounds, each completely surrounded by walls, lined on each side of a wide well-built avenue that runs in the direction of the cardinal points; from the mountain to the sea, the Balinese equivalent to our "north" and "south." The villages grew as they spread in these directions, and the Dutch had only to pave the main streets and extend them through the ricefields to obtain the five-hundred-mile net of automobile roads that covers this small island.

The Balinese, being still essentially pedestrians, took good care to shade the roads with large trees, and every morning and every evening one sees the people in the streets, men going to work nonchalantly beating rhythms on their agricultural implements, or returning from the fields overloaded with sheaves of rice heavy with grain. Poised women come and go with great loads of shiny black clay pots on their heads. If it happens to be market day in the village, at dawn the roads are crowded with husky people from the near-by villages who come to sell their produce—piles of coconuts, bananas, or vegetables, pottery, mats, baskets, and so forth—carrying on their heads even the table that serves as a stand. If there is a feast in the village temple, the people parade in yellow, green, and magenta silks with fantastic pyramids of fruit and flowers, offerings to the gods, in a pageant that would have made Diaghilev turn green with envy.

Naked children play at the gates by the bell-shaped baskets where the fighting cocks are kept. Each morning the baskets are lined out on the street so that the roosters may enjoy the spectacle of people passing by. Small boys wearing only oversize sun-hats drive the enormous water-buffaloes, which in Bali appear in two colours, a dark muddy grey, and a pale, almost transparent pink, an albino variety. A water-buffalo will not hesitate to attack a tiger; their ponderous calm and their gigantic horns are awe-inspiring to Europeans, who have been told that their odour infuriates the buffaloes. They have often charged

white people for no apparent reason, although the smallest Balinese boy can manhandle the great beasts. They love to lie in the water and be scrubbed by their little guardians, who climb all over them and hang from their horns when they take them for their evening bath. The buffalo tolerates the children perhaps as a rhinoceros tolerates the birds that eat the ticks on its back.

The Balinese raise a fine breed of cattle, a beautiful variety of cow, with delicate legs and a long neck, that resembles overgrown deer more than ordinary cows. Ducks are driven in flocks to the ricefields, where they feed on all sorts of small water animals. Their guardian is a boy or an old man who leads them with a little banner of white cloth on the end of a bamboo pole topped by a bunch of white feathers. This he plants on the ground and he can then go away for the rest of the day, sure that his ducks will not wander away. At sundown the trained ducks gather around the flag waiting to be taken home. When the duck-guardian arrives, the flock is all together, and at a signal from the flag, they march home, straight as penguins and in perfect military formation.

All Balinese domestic animals are rather extraordinary; chickens are killed constantly by rushing automobiles, but their owners make no provision to keep them from the road except the low bamboo fence that bars the house gate, and that is intended, perhaps, more for the pigs, which in Bali belong to a monstrous variety that surely exists nowhere else. The Balinese pig, an untamed descendant of the wild hog, has an absurd sagging back and a fat stomach that drags on the ground like a heavy bag suspended loosely from its bony hips and shoulders.

The roads are particularly infested with miserable dogs, the scavengers of the island. Most dogs are attached to the house they protect and keep clean of garbage, but they reproduce unchecked and there are thousands of homeless living skeletons, covered with ulcers and mange, that bark and wail all night in great choruses. The Balinese are not disturbed by them and sleep peacefully through the hideous noise. The curs are supposed to frighten away witches and evil spirits, but I could never discover how our neighbours knew when it was an ordinary mortal and not a devil that the dogs barked at; they always awoke when a stranger came into the house at night. Such dogs were undoubtedly provided by the gods to keep Bali from perfection.

The Balinese make a clear distinction between the dwelling-grounds and the "unlived" parts of the village, those for public use such as the temples, assembly halls, market, cemeteries, public baths. The village is a unified organism in which every individual is a corpuscle and every institution an organ. The heart of the village is the central square, invariably located in the "centre" of the village, the intersection of the two main avenues: the big road that runs from the Balinese "North-South" and a street that cuts it at right angles from "East-West." Consequently the crossroads are the centre of a Rose of the Winds formed by the entire village; the cardinal directions mean a great deal to the Balinese and the crossroads are a magic spot of great importance.

All around and in the square are the important public places of the village; the town temple (*pura desa*), with its hall of assembly (*balé agung*), the palace of the local feudal prince, the market, the large shed for cockfights (*wantilan*), and the tall and often elaborate tower where hang the alarm tomtoms (*kulkul*) to call to meetings, announce events, or warn of dangers. Also important to the village life is the ever present *waringin*, a giant banyan, the sacred tree of the Hindus planted in the square. Under its shadow take place the shows and dances given in connection with the frequent festivals; market is also held there in villages that do not have a special market enclosure. In ancient villages the *waringin* grows to a giant size, shading the entire square and dripping aerial roots that, unless clipped before they reached the ground, would grow into trunks that unchecked might swallow up a village. A beautiful village *waringin* is an enormous rounded dome of shiny leaves supported by a mossy, gnarled single trunk hung with a curtain of tentacles that are cut evenly at the height of a man; but in the *waringins* that have grown freely outside the village, the tree spreads in every direction in fantastic shapes. The aerial filaments dig into the earth and grow into whitish trunks and branches emerging at illogical angles and filled with parasite ferns, a dreamlike forest that is in reality a single tree.

Somewhere in the outskirts of the village are the public baths and the cemetery, a neglected field overgrown with weeds and decaying bamboo altars, with its temple of the Dead and its mournful *kepuh* tree, a sad and eerie place. The bathing-place is generally a cool spot shaded by clusters of bamboo in the river that runs near the village, where all day long men and women bathe in the brown water in separate modest groups. Some villages have special bathing-places with fancy water-spouts and low walls of carved stone, with separate compartments for men and women. Tedjakula in North Bali is famous for its horse bath, a special compartment that is larger and even more elaborate than the baths for the people.

*   *   *

Everybody in Bali seems to be an artist. Coolies and princes, priests and peasants, men and women alike, can dance, play musical instruments, paint, or carve in wood and stone. It was often surprising to discover that an otherwise poor and dilapidated village harboured an elaborate temple, a great orchestra, or a group of actors of repute.

One of the most famous orchestras in Bali is to be found in the remote mountain village of Selat, and the finest dancers of *legong* were in Saba, an unimportant little village hidden among the ricefields. Villages such as Mas, Batuan, Gelgel, are made up of families of painters, sculptors, and actors, and Sanur produces, besides priests and witch-doctors, fine story-tellers and dancers. In Sebatu, another isolated mountain village, even the children can carve little statues from odd bits of wood, some to be used as bottle-stoppers, perches for birds, handles, but most often simply absurd little human figures in comic attitudes, strange animals, birds of their own invention, frogs, snakes, larvæ of insects, figures without reason or purpose, simply as an outlet for their creative urge. In contrast to the devil-may-care primitive works of Sebatu are the super-refined, masterful carvings from Badung, Ubud, Pliatan, and especially those by the family of young Brahmanas from Mas who turn out intricate statues of hard wood or with equal ability paint a picture, design a temple gate, or act and dance.

Painting, sculpture, and playing on musical instruments are arts by tradition reserved to the men, but almost any woman can weave beautiful stuffs and it is curious that the most intriguing textiles, those in which the dyeing and weaving process is so complicated that years of labour are required to complete a scarf, are made by the women of Tenganan, an ancient village of six hundred souls who are so conservative that they will not maintain connections with the rest of Bali and who punish with exile whoever dares to marry outside the village.

The main artistic activity of the women goes into the making of beautiful offerings for the gods. These are intricate structures of cut-out palm-leaf, or great pyramids of fruit, flowers, cakes, and even roast chickens, arranged with splendid taste, masterpieces of composition in which the relative form of the elements employed, their texture and colour are taken into consideration. I have seen monuments, seven feet in height, made entirely of roasted pig's meat on skewers, decorated into shapes cut out of the waxy fat of the pig and surmounted with banners and little umbrellas of the lacy stomach tissues, the whole relieved by the vivid vermilion of chili-peppers. Although women of all ages have always taken part in the ritual offering dances, in olden times only little girls became dancers and actresses; but today beautiful girls take part in theatrical performances, playing the parts of princesses formerly performed exclusively by female impersonators.

The effervescence of artistic activity and the highly developed æsthetic sense of the population can perhaps be explained by a natural urge to express themselves, combined with the important factor of leisure resulting from well-organized agricultural cooperatism. However, the most important element for the development of a popular culture, with primitive as well as refined characteristics, was perhaps the fact that the Balinese did not permit the centralization of the artistic knowledge in a special intellectual class. In old Balinese books on ethics, like the *Niti Sastra*, it is stated that a man who is ignorant of the writings is like a man who has lost his speech, because he shall have to remain silent during the conversation of other men. Furthermore, it was a requirement for the education of every prince that he should know mythology, history, and poetry well enough; should learn painting, woodcarving, music, and the making of musical instruments; should be able to dance and to sing in Kawi, the classic language of literature. There is hardly a prince who does not possess a good number of these attributes, and those deprived of talent themselves support artists, musicians, and actors as part of their retinue. Ordinary people look upon their feudal lords as models of conduct and do not hesitate to imitate them, learning their poetry, dancing, painting, and carving in order to be like them.

Thus, not only the aristocracy can create informal beauty, but a commoner may be as finished an artist as the educated nobleman, although he may be an agriculturist, a tradesman, or even a coolie. Our host in Bali was a prince and a musician, but there were others of the common class who were among the finest musicians of the neighbourhood. Of the leaders of the famous orchestras of our district, one was a coolie, another a goldsmith, and a third a chauffeur.

Until a few years ago the Balinese did not paint pictures or make statues without some definite purpose. It has often been stated that there are no words in the Balinese language for "art" and "artist." This is true and logical; making a beautiful offering, and carving a stone temple gate, and making a set of masks are tasks of equal æsthetic importance, and although the artist is regarded as a preferred member of the community, there is no separate class of artists, and a sculptor is simply a "carver" or a figure-maker, and the painter is a picture-maker. A dancer is a *legong*, a *djanger*, and so forth—the names of the dances they perform.

The artist is in Bali essentially a craftsman and at the same time an amateur, casual and anonymous, who uses his talent knowing that no one will care to record his name for posterity. His only aim is to serve his community, seeing that the work is well done when he is called to embellish the temple of the village, or when he carves his neighbour's gate in exchange for a new roof or some other similar service. Actors and musicians play for the feasts of the village without pay, and when they perform for private festivals they are lavishly entertained and banqueted instead. Foreigners have to pay a good amount for a performance: from five to thirty guilders according to the quality of the show and the pretensions of the actors; but a Balinese who calls the village's orchestra or a troupe of actors for a home festival provides special food, refreshments, *sirih*, and cigarettes for them. If he pays a small amount besides, from a guilder to five, it is not considered as remuneration, but rather as a present to help the finances of the musical or theatrical club. Whatever money they receive goes to the funds of the association to cover the expenses of the feasts given by the club or to buy new costumes or instruments.

Nothing in Bali is made for posterity; the only available stone is a soft sandstone that crumbles away after a few years, and the temples and reliefs have to be renewed constantly; white ants devour the wooden sculptures, and the humidity rots away all paper and cloth, so their arts have never suffered from fossilization. The Balinese are extremely proud of their traditions, but they are also progressive and unconservative, and when a foreign idea strikes their fancy, they adopt it with great enthusiasm as their own. All sorts of influences from the outside, Indian, Chinese, Javanese, have left their mark on Balinese art, but they are always translated into their own manner and they become strongly Balinese in the process.

Thus the lively Balinese art is in constant flux. What becomes the rage for a while may be suddenly abandoned and forgotten when a new fashion is invented, new styles in music or in the theatre, or new ways of making sculpture and paintings. But the traditional art also remains, and when the artists tire of a new idea, they go back to the classic forms until a new style is again invented. They are great copyists and it is not surprising to find in a temple, as part of the decoration, a fat Chinese god or a scene representing a highway hold-up, or a crashing plane, events unknown in Bali, that can only be explained as having been copied from some Western magazine. Once a young Balinese painter saw my friend Walter Spies painting yellow high-lights on the tips of the leaves of a jungle scene. He went home and made a painting that was thoroughly Balinese, but with modelling and high-lights until then unknown in Balinese painting. Artistic property cannot exist in the communal Balinese culture; if an artist invents or copies something that is an interesting novelty, soon all the others are reproducing the new find. Once a sculptor made a little statue representing the larvæ of an insect standing upright on its tail; a few weeks later everybody was making them and soon the statue market was flooded with Brancusi-like little erect worms on square bases.

SANTHA RAMA RAU

from EAST OF HOME

THE LONGEST and most rewarding stop on Santha Rama Rau's 1948–1949 trip through Southeast Asia was in Bali.

IN THE FOUR MONTHS that Clare, Faubion and I spent in Indonesia, we all changed a good deal. To all of us the changes were important. Indonesia meant to Clare the reorganization of ideas which were so deep a part of her nature that she wasn't conscious of ever having learned them. To Faubion it meant not only the climax of his book on Asian dance and drama, but also a deeper concern in something he calls "abstract esthetics."

For me Indonesia was my first experience of what I think is a healthy society. In all the months of travel through Asia—superficial as my observations had been —I had retained an impression of the growing consciousness of being Asian that was accompanying the death of colonialism in Asia. In Bali, for the first time, I felt myself a part of that Asian identity, and acquired a greater confidence in our way of life.

The resistance movement against the Dutch was in one of its more violent phases, and when we arrived in Batavia (Jakarta,) we found that it was virtually impossible to travel in Java or Sumatra. Faubion had been in Indonesia before the war and had learned Malay at that time. He suggested that we go to Bali for a few weeks until the Republican leaders were released from jail and we could get some idea of whether it would be possible to travel more extensively after that.

"The only thing," Faubion said, "is that I refuse to stay in the Dutch Hotel in Den Pasar." It was his usual refrain, "We must get out of the town at once."

Fortunately a friend of ours in Batavia gave us a letter of introduction to a Balinese chokorda (a title denoting both caste and social status—the chokordas are the layer of aristocracy immediately under the rajas). Chokorda Agung, we learned, occasionally took paying guests. We decided to take advantage of this letter and left for Bali immediately.

I had heard so much about Bali that I was not too surprised to find it a beautiful country, in a tropical way, with narrow roads winding between coconut groves, a brilliant sparkle from the sea on one side, and the neat rice fields stretching away on the other to where the hills began. The people, however, did come as something of a shock. I have never seen a race as universally graceful and lovely to look at.

Faubion said, "It's something to do with the light. The Balinese skin acquires a glow and a color that diminishes all imperfections of feature or complexion."

Clare said, "More likely something to do with the diet."

But I think it is due to the extraordinary charm of the Balinese, a charm that you feel even if you don't speak to them. There is a security in their way of walking, an ease and directness in their conversation, great tolerance and humor in their general approach. It is one of the few countries of Asia where a foreigner cannot make the popular mistake of assuming that Oriental manners and politeness are due to obsequiousness or subservience.

We made arrangements as soon as possible to leave Den Pasar, Bali's capital, for the small village of Ubud where we were to stay with Chokorda Agung.

*   *   *

The *puri* of Chokorda Agung in Ubud was a series of interconnected courtyards. The big entry gate from the road opened into the first courtyard which was given to Faubion. It had a living pavilion on one side, built of stone with big decorative panels in the walls sculptured from the soft local sandstone. It had a little veranda and a porch, and inside, a living room, bedroom and bath. The rest of the courtyard was empty, kept as a place for dance performances. Three open pavilions in the other three corners were for spectators.

It opened on both sides into more courtyards. In one of them Chokorda Agung's uncle, the old Chokorda Ngura, lived, and that courtyard in turn, opened on to the courtyard which Clare and I shared with one of Chokorda Agung's wives, who acted as our chaperon. It was a particularly beautiful part of the *puri*, with two living pavilions in it. On one side was the tooth-filing pavilion, which was used at other times as a dining room, a rehearsal room, art gallery or anything else one wanted to make it. In the middle of the courtyard was an open pavilion, higher than the others, from which orchestras played during formal dinners. All the buildings were of whitewashed adobe, with thatched roofs and magnificent wooden pillars carved by the Chokorda's craftsmen, and decorated with gold and paint. In every room were a few samples of his fantastic collection of Balinese paintings.

The first morning Clare and I woke at about five o'clock to the most extraordinary racket in the court-yard behind ours. After daylight, when we got up, we looked out and saw that the old Chokorda kept his fighting cocks behind our pavilion, and as soon as one started crowing, all the others started, too. Within a few days we scarcely noticed the noise, and in any case our hours had changed completely. There was, of course, no electricity so we fell into the Balinese way of rising at daybreak and sleeping immediately after dinner. Oil lamps are not precisely the thing to read by in bed.

There was no hot water either, but in that delightful climate it was no hardship. Our bathroom was across the courtyard, and the first night we were there Clare fussed about trying to find a dressing gown. In the morning we noticed that most of the people who trotted across the courtyard were so scantily clad that our modesty couldn't hold out very long. The bath itself was Indian in style. You pour water from one of the huge urns over yourself, soap yourself, and wash off the soap with more water. At first Clare used to come out rather miserably with damp curls and a feeling that she wasn't really having a bath, but soon she, too, like the Balinese, began to find the idea of a tub dirty. Fancy sitting in your own dirty water! Aren't Westerners dirty in their habits!

Clare and I had, as a servant, Agung G'dé, a high-caste boy who was serving a sort of apprenticeship in Chokorda Agung's *puri*. He was a most graceful young man, light-skinned, and with shaved eyebrows which he kept very carefully trimmed. His manners were perfect. He brought coffee to us on our veranda. We sat there feeling too peaceful even to talk, and watched the morning sunlight blaze on the cannas and hibiscus in our courtyard. The gold paint on the pillars glittered, and under the thatched eaves were deep-blue shadows.

Chokorda Agung came to visit with us for a few moments. "I wish you to be happy guests," he said.

"And you," he said to me, "are the first Indian to stay here. As we are all Hindus we should have much in common. Yours and mine are the only two Hindu countries left in the world." He then produced an extraordinary and beautiful carving of two men with a fish, with their arms up and their knees bent. He asked us to put it in our room as an amulet against thieves. Finally he said, "May I ask what caste are you?"

"I am a Brahmin."

"Ah a Brachman! Then I will call you Daiyu from now on. That is what we call an unmarried Brachman girl among us."

Eventually we wandered through the flowers and the many decorated gates to Faubion's courtyard. We found him sitting with Gusti Agung Ngura, the cook. They were talking earnestly. Gusti Agung Ngura was very elegant indeed, and high caste. Because his language was so beautiful, Chokorda Agung had suggested that he help Faubion to recapture his Malay, much of which he had forgotten during the war.

That first day we were not used to the magical air of Bali, and the extraordinary way that it slows you down to an easy, gentle pace of living. We wondered why we were content simply to sit and watch people walk through the *puri* or, perhaps, stroll along the one road of the tiny village, smile at the people or stare at the sky reflected in the flooded rice fields.

Ubud has about two hundred people living in the immediate village area, in the little compounds enclosed by mud walls opening off the road. The population would be about five hundred if you include all the Ubud area. Always in the village there is a faint smell of coconut oil and perfume from the hair of people who have just passed you, and when that vanishes you can smell the freshly ground coffee and the spices in the cooking from the various houses. That first day we thought of Ubud as the perfect place for a quiet couple of weeks' holiday. Later we realized how wrong we were. By then we were mixed up in all the village activities and saw that, far from being restful, it was the busiest and most time-consuming life imaginable. But we didn't leave Ubud until months later when we finally left Bali altogether, because we entirely lost interest in a quiet holiday when we found that we had stumbled on the most complete and satisfying life that any of us had ever known.

*   *   *

Within a couple of days Chokorda Agung decided that we should start meeting the village and learning about its various activities. He was a plumpish, jolly man, of enormous kindness, and with the most devoted

love of his village. Hearing that Faubion was a musician, he took us first to see where the rehearsals of the music society were held—the courtyard of Gusti Agung Ngura's house. There we found Chokorda Agung's nephew, Chokorda Mas, sitting by himself, tinkling on one of the instruments. He immediately played for us some of the old music, the special music that accompanies the *Ramayana* stories, and after that some modern music and some of his own compositions. He was famous as a musician in all the neighboring villages, and loved to compose.

Walking back to the *puri*, Chokorda Agung said to Faubion, "Tell me, what is American music like?"

Faubion said, "It is hard to describe like this, in words, but I can tell you this—I don't think it is as vibrant or magical as Balinese music."

"No, I agree. I have never heard American music, but I have a *feeling* that Balinese music is better."

In the afternoon he walked with us to a place about a mile from the *puri* where a waterfall had been channeled to make a small swimming pool. "We bathe in the river when we want to wash. This pool is for pleasure, not for washing."

That evening Chokorda Agung's uncle, old Chokorda Ngura, came from his courtyard to where we were sitting on Faubion's veranda. He felt that we were sufficiently settled, and had come to call on us. He was a tall, severe man, most fastidious in dress and formal in manners. He wore a brown and white printed *kain* (as opposed to the commoner and cheaper sarongs which are tubular pieces of material) wrapped round his waist and falling in flawless pleats to his ankles. His headband was elaborately folded and decorated with a scarlet hibiscus. His nephew, Chokorda Agung, sat with us, too. His manner in front of the old man was entirely different. Deferential, quiet but, as always, exceedingly polite, he recounted everything he knew about us, so that Chokorda Ngura should know exactly what guests were under his roof. He called Faubion's servant, Kunter, and ordered *brum*, Bali's sweet, rather heavy rice wine, and served it to all of us.

After a while, the old man said, "Perhaps these young people would like to go and watch the dance rehearsal." That was our dismissal. We all bowed, wished him good night and went to the music society's pavilion. There in the half-light of Gusti Agung Ngura's compound, I saw my first Balinese dancing, and it was a remarkable experience. In the flickering lights and shadows of the little oil wicks, eight girls were dancing a *gabor*, the dance of the attendants of Kali, the goddess of death. I had ex-

AT THE CROSSROADS IN UBUD, BALI.

pected something rather languorous and South-Sea-Islandish, instead of which the dance held more vitality than any I have seen. It was brilliant, angular, and infinitely powerful. It had the grace of great discipline and perfect technique, and none of the soft prettiness of less developed dancing. The music, too, was almost electric in its strength, with an extraordinary combination of precision and emotion. We walked home in the starlight to the receding sound of the flutes and bells. The deep note of the gongs reached us even after we were inside the *puri*.

Within a week our days began to take on a more regular pattern. Faubion, with constant practice, was already speaking Malay fluently again, and Clare and I found that we had to learn it, too, as nobody in Ubud, with the exception of Chokorda Agung, spoke English. Even Clare's firm prejudice against foreign languages began to break down, because Malay is simple to learn, and there seemed so much to talk to the Balinese about. Neither of us ever spoke it really well, but we learned enough to be able to conduct simple conversations and to get through the everyday

Rice terraces, Bali.

shrine at the top, especially for offerings to the good spirits who live above. In the evenings the little girls would come again with more offerings, and this time they would be placed on the ground and in odd places about the *puri*. Those were to appease the bad spirits who live below, and were immediately eaten by stray dogs, or the *puri* hens if they happened to reach them first. Usually the girls would stay and talk for a few moments in the morning; they were the children of various retainers or relations who lived in the *puri*. Then they would hurry off saying they had to get ready for school.

A little later we would see the old Chokorda's two daughters, very neat and clean in their blue jackets and tightly wrapped *kains*, with flowers in their hair, walk through our courtyard on their way to school. They were the teachers.

Then the boys would come to clean the rooms and wash our clothes, and the clatter and the fragrance of the cooking would begin. When Gusti Agung Ngura had the food for lunch organized, cleaned and ready to cook, he would come and talk to us in Malay for a while in the morning. Clare and I were interested only in the conversation, so after we had finished Faubion would continue with the reading and writing. Meanwhile, since in Bali one always takes the shortest and most sensible path from place to place, flocks of geese would be driven through the *puri*, odd cows, pigs or hens would stray about—sometimes with a small boy watching them, and sometimes not. The fighting cocks would be brought out into the sunlight and be groomed, massaged and fed. Everybody, as they walked through, would stop to exchange a few words, relay a piece of gossip or ask some questions.

By eleven o'clock everyone was busy either in the fields, or with their animals, with work in the *puri*, or on errands to neighboring villages. The children were in school and the women did their household jobs. Faubion was studying, and Clare and I went for walks and explored the country around Ubud.

Light in Bali is like no other light that I have ever seen. It changes colors to curious Balinese versions of themselves, it gives a special radiance to skins, it washes over the land with a strange and beautiful distinctness. The landscape around Ubud is hilly, intensely cultivated, and with many trees. In any one view one sees very little of the sky. The curved, terraced *sawahs* (rice fields when they are filled with water) form great brilliant steps down the hillsides, so that much of the light is reflected from them, shining upward on trees and faces, instead of from more familiar angles. We used to spend hours walking along the ridges dividing the fields, and found new streams, different ravines and bathing places, little

details of life without appealing constantly to Faubion for help.

Mornings were busy times. While we were dressing and having breakfast, the little girls of the *puri* would come through carrying baskets on their heads. The baskets were filled with small dishes made of strips of banana leaves woven together. Each dish held a few grains of rice, some flowers and sometimes a chili. They would place them on the steps of the various pavilions or in the gateways. In each courtyard there are special pillars, about five feet high with a tiny

BALINESE WOMEN POUNDING RICE.

TRANSPORTING RICE PADDY, BALI.

villages and temples, and never got tired of the *sawahs* themselves at all times of day and in any light.

Lunch, which Clare, Faubion and I ate in whichever courtyard happened to please us that day, was at about one o'clock. The food in the *puri* was Balinese, with slight concessions to Clare's and Faubion's foreign taste. With the usual chilies and spices we would have plenty of rice, of course; vegetables that we had never tasted before; and a great variety of meats, steamed in banana leaves or made as a sort of shashlik; eels, roast suckling pig, and many other things. Agung G'dé had caught an enormous bat, which he exhibited proudly to us one morning. Clare recoiled, and said, "Do take it away quickly."

We thought no more about it till that evening when Clare had an argument with Faubion about its size. She asked Agung G'dé if he still had it to show Faubion. He looked most surprised and said, "But you ate it for lunch. Didn't you recognize the taste?"

The early afternoon was one's time for privacy. You could take a siesta if you felt like it, type notes or read, or merely sit in the courtyard and meditate. About half-past three or four, Ubud came to life again with a renewed burst of energy. The children came back from school and played in the courtyards or in the road. The men came back from the fields. The football society started its daily game on the village green. The girls went to their dance rehearsals. The women, with the day's chores behind them, visited each other, sat on their steps and talked with passersby. The young men bought their jars of *tuak*, the local palm beer, and laughed together or gambled. Everyone

was friendly, eager to discuss the day's events, full of plans for the next day, with the prospect of an amusing evening ahead.

Almost every evening there was some sort of entertainment, dances or a concert, or a play. In a social unit as small as Ubud, the people must contribute to the entertainment of the village, just as it is essential that they help each other with their work in the fields. Occasionally there was the excitement of dancers from another village coming to give a performance or a traveling group of players who would act all night in Ubud.

Faubion christened that time before sunset the "violent hour" because all of Ubud was so energetically engaged in one activity or another. As soon as it was dark, however, it was time for the quiet gossip, the timeless conversation, and the casual exchange of information. We had evolved our own cocktail from *arak*, which is distilled from rice wine, smells dreadful but tastes divine and is very strong, mixed with *brum* which made it sweet and milder. *Tuak* cost the equivalent of one American cent a bottle, and *arak* and *brum* were about twenty cents a bottle each. All transactions had to be in silver because in the villages of Bali they didn't trust paper money.

We ate dinner by oil light whenever we wanted it, depending on what time the dancing started afterward. The day ended either immediately after dinner or as soon as the entertainment was over. Then we would walk back to our courtyards shouting to friends, "Safety in sleeping!" or "Safety in going home!" if they lived far from the *puri*.

MI MI KHAING

from BURMESE FAMILY

NOT included on today's world tours, Burma remains distinctive and rewarding to those fortunate enough to know her.

THEY [the people of Burma] had been a people easily governed by an uncompromising paternalist rule: now they would hold rallies and make long speeches to reiterate that there should be no reservation of opportunity of privilege for any small group of people. A spirit of upheaval, of celebration and disorganization, and, naturally, of many disappointed ideals, replaces the old unruffled background. There is little security of life or prosperity guaranteed in such stirring times.

These are indeed great changes from the placid background against which *Burmese Family* was sketched. Yet I have heard visitors comment in surprise that so much written in the book is still true! It is a different Burma, with the same people.

In order to make this observation credible, I should, perhaps, try to explain why such big and rapid changes in the background of national life leave family and social life in Burma so little altered.

There are two respects in which traditional Burmese society has affinities with the spirit of modern times.

One is the position of Burmese women, who, having from early on in our history enjoyed equal civic and property rights with men, took modern equalities of

Balinese legong dancers, girls about twelve, on temple steps.

opportunity as a matter of course. This meant that there was no great change in their position in the family or in society. The other point is that there has always been a near-equality in the living conditions of our "rich" and "poor," in that housing, style of meals, dress, and household effects vary as little as could possibly be expected with differences in the financial conditions of families.

Where tradition is to this extent in tune with current ideas, it is not likely to be thrown overboard. As modern life brought little that could make the Burmese women's lot more active than it had always been, for example, it was natural to retain their deference to the higher spiritual status of men, and the modesty expected of them in public. The national dress is a case in point. As it was already simple enough to allow easy movement, and followed the natural lines of the body sufficiently to suit modern taste, it has been retained, with extremely small concessions to international standards of fashion.

Though it is this stable position of Burmese women which has helped to keep society much the same, the other factor has contributed also. That near-equality in living conditions saved wealthier men's resources for a religio-social activity in which all classes could join with positive enjoyment. The feasting of monks and community which is described in the book is the prime expression of this. There has been no temptation to displace such a satisfactory system with imported and ready-made amusements. In fact, independence brought with it a livelier exercise of traditional activities, more and bigger feasts being given in the old style, or collections being taken to enable poorer men to give a communal one in their turn, because people felt they were now masters in their own house, led by a government which, from the Prime Minister downward, would be finding joy in these specially Burmese pursuits. And as this social life has elements of religion as its base, values such as the high place of monks and the attitude of reverence toward elders persist. The status goal continues to be identified with the spiritually satisfying goals of the son's novitiation and the monastery endowments, no less in present-day Burma than twenty years ago.

One strong feature of this book is the picture it gave of government officials' families. That surely should have disappeared, as a hated reminder of British rule. Certainly, the nomenclature has been deliberately changed, the idea of a privileged class has gone, the sacrosanct atmosphere altogether dispelled. Yet the essential feature of that life, the benefactor-dependent relationship, is still here. Our people, when deprived of cherished reverential submissions toward their exiled monarchy, gave tacit submissiveness and deference to the government set up by Britain; when that hand was withdrawn, with a great release of spirit as it were, they transferred deference elaborated and vociferated manifold, to ministers, new office-holders, or any citizens of importance who would carry on the traditional role of kind patron under a different name.

What has really vanished is the unquestioned sense of security and of the abiding nature of conditions under which we grew up. This is partly in line with changes over most of the world, but more because our country is particularly unsettled at the present time. Yet even in this respect, as we are volatile rather than deeply intense in our attitude toward life, any area of lull from dacoity and insurgent raids finds the untouched families still free from preoccupation with national cares, and still happy enough to enjoy their country-garden pleasures, while preparing in accustomed ways for a better and easier niche in the next existence.

*   *   *

All Burmese social gatherings center round either religious observances or eating. We are still unsophisticated enough to have the same way of enjoying ourselves whether in city or country, and for that reason these district towns formed such a perfect background for happy days. In the towns that I remember, a river ran through, with sandbanks at edges or in midstream; this, with the monasteries and pagoda precincts a little way out of the busy quarters, private garden orchards and the houses of friends, provided the background for all the social life which my parents had, and is the reason why Burmese people never form social clubs. Most of the officials went to play tennis at the Gymkhana club with European members, but it had no real part in their lives.

When we went on *pyaw-pwè-sas*, happy-eating-gatherings, at pagodas, with two or three other families, the grown-ups, including aunts and dependents of the families, made elaborate food arrangements because the joy of the occasion was to cook on a large scale in the open air. They took pots, dishes, food and washing apparatus for about twenty people. We started with silent recitation of prayers before the golden spire in the cool morning air, holding silver lilies between folded hands and being so careful not to breathe in the fragrance of the flowers, because my mother taught us that we should not first enjoy the beauty of flowers which are to be offered. When our short prayers were through, we stuck the flowers in a vase or niche at the pagoda base, lighted a row of candles along a ledge or parapet, and walked quietly round the pagoda with the paved stones so cool be-

(continued on page 242)

Barong dance, Bali.

ELABORATE TEMPLE COMPOUND IN BALI.

APPROACHING THE BUDDHIST AND HINDU RUINS OF ANGKOR, CAMBODIA.

GUARDIANS OF A PATH AT ANGKOR.

GIANT HEADS AT LE BAYON, ANGKOR.

A FOREST OF HEADS RISING
FROM THE ANGKOR JUNGLE.

(continued from page 236)

neath our bare feet, while the grown-ups still prayed silently. As soon as they finished and got up, it was the signal to release our spirits and bound away to the far corner, where the servants were already beginning to unpack the pots and arrange three stones around for each fire. We were allowed to cut up onions or chillies until we got bored, and spent the rest of the morning playing games or exploring the country around, coming back to find a meal miraculously cooked, with curries in lacquer dishes and rice in banana leaves. After the meal, mats were spread in the breeziest spot, and we lay down beside the grown-ups, who told beads and talked by turns.

Garden orchards were another source of deep long whole-day joy. The Burmese u-yin is usually translated as orchard, but after seeing English apple and cherry orchards I must translate it more fully. A u-yin is more arboreal and leafy; also one must enjoy it positively, that is, there must be in it a bamboo or light wooden house. In a hot climate an u-yin raises visions of shade; cool dark shade, leaves, only a few flowers unless they are of flowering trees, eating of the fruits and vegetables while there, and lying on a mat in the afternoon breeze. None of the a-so-ya mins could possess u-yins or gardens like this where they were posted, because their stay was so transitory. But the education officer, that is, the D.I.S. (District Inspector of Schools), whether active or retired, was usually more permanent and could dig his toes in more happily. The social relationship was also ideal. Earning less than the other officials, he could yet offer them this rich hospitality of natural pleasures.

*   *   *

My aunt's clothes were also aggressively her own. This was noticeable especially with her going-out clothes, for which she would never have any imported materials. She declared that imported silks, crêpe-de-chine and the like, could not be washed and beaten clean like the Burmese silks and cottons. Neither did they produce suitable colors and designs for elderly spinster ladies like her—they were either gay and skittish, or of a soberness that depressed without pleasing one. What she loved most were the ya-khaing longyis, silks and cottons woven in Arakan, in small check patterns, but so stout that you soaked them and beat them hard before the first wearing, and then washed them again and again until you had a pliant closely-woven fabric whose color and freshness lasted a lifetime. One of my sisters, whom my aunt pressed to wear a ya-khaing longyi in preference to a crêpe-de-chine piece whose bright butterflies had appealed to her sixteen-year-old fancy, stated that no doubt if she slept in the ya-khaing longyi every night for seven years, it would just be at its best for her to wear when

she reached the age of twenty-five. For more dressy occasions, my aunt wore zin-mè silks, the design of which was reputed to come from Chiengmai in Siam, and in imitation of which Burmese weavers now produce zin-mè longyis in dull red and green geometrical designs, like old lacquer colors. Kyi-Kyi sometimes wore Bangauk longyis also, said to come truly from Bangkok, but more often woven in Burma in imitation of the characteristic twist in the weave. These were produced in smoky blues, ambers and dull greens so beloved of elderly Burmese ladies.

Silk weaving is one of the old industries of Burma, but the yarn is mostly imported, for the rearing of silkworms, like fishing, is a form of taking life. Fortunately, around Prome on the central Irrawaddy, there live a tribe of hill people called Yabeins who are animists and may safely cultivate the po-sa, worm food mulberry tree. The silk from here is coarse, but is used for the weaving of the most elaborately patterned silks called cheik. These valuable pieces are used for wedding skirts and ceremonial wear. Few people possess more than one cheik skirt; the great number of spools—a hundred or more—necessary to produce the intricate patterns in minute waves of blended colors makes the price vary from Rs. 40/- to Rs. 400/- per piece, a high price compared to the present imported silks. All the weaving is done by hand looms, rectangular frames about five feet long, holding the warp threads of four yards in length and 40 to 45 inches in width, operated by girls sitting on high stools, raising the alternate threads by a foot-pedal, and banging the pushboard against the woven threads each time they throw the spool across by pulling on a cord, producing eventually an ok, a book, a piece for two skirts folded flat and stiff like a book.

With imported yarns dyed with native vegetable dyes, the weavers at Mandalay, Amarapura, Prome and Shwedaung, Kyangin, Tavoy, Kindat and the Yaw valley produced silks of exquisite pinks, blue-greys, gold and amber, strong reds and purples, dull dirty greens, all from the sunset skies, water-vegetation, birds and trees, never fading: pan-nu, kho, mi-go, hpet-hpu, may-yan, pasun-hsi, payin, kyet-thway, yay-hnyi, a-sein-bok: tender flowers, dove, smoke, leaf-bud, marian seed, prawn oil, amber, cock's blood, slime-moss, rotten vegetation. Plain colors, checks, stripes and geometrical designs all cost only Rs. 3/- or Rs. 5/- or, perhaps, Rs. 10/- per piece and could be washed forever. No wonder Kyi-Kyi did not understand why we bought imported silks. She did not understand the desire for novelty, for frivolity of birds, giant flowers or sprouting fruit such as are never seen on land or sea.

*   *   *

Since I had left Burma, my mother and brother and sisters had settled themselves in Rangoon and I wondered how the city would seem after the big cities of the West. Rangoon is not one of the ancient cities of Burma. Its present position in the life of the country and people is a complete turnabout from its traditional place, for in days gone by it had attracted inhabitants through spiritual rather than material renown. While Pagan, Ava, Toungoo and Mandalay rose and fell in political and commercial importance, Rangoon—Dagon as it was called—continued unchangingly a seat of pilgrimage, connected with fable and divinity, forming an actual link with another world cycle that existed in the universe before this present arrangement of Mount Myinmo, with its surrounding heavenly, earthly, and hellish regions, was formed.

For it was on the hill called Theinguttara, which now casts its shadow on the city of Rangoon with its crown of the Shwe Dagon Pagoda, that the omens for the spiritual life of this world cycle were manifested, before the last world was dissolved in chaos. On this hill five lotus buds sprang out of the earth; they opened into blossom, and from each flew a sacred bird which bore a sacred yellow robe towards the heavens. These five robes presaged the coming of five Buddhas who would guide the future world along the noble path to Nirvana. After this sign, that former world was destroyed; the present world followed, and the Buddhas appeared as foretold: Kaukathan, Gaunagong, Kathapa and Gautama, who successively attained enlightenment in this world, and whose statues now sit, each fifty feet tall and twenty feet broad, back to back in a great quadrate at the Kyaikpun Pagoda, calm and majestic as the grass grows about them and the rain washes down on their faces, awaiting the arrival of the fifth and last Buddha, after which this world cycle will be destroyed in a universal chaos. As each Buddha saw his enlightenment in this world he left a relic at the Theinguttara Hill, which had foretold his coming and which would now mark his attainment of wisdom—Kaukathan his staff, Gaunagong his water filter, Kathapa a portion of his robe, and Gautama his eight hairs which were enshrined in the first Shwe Dagon Pagoda after many perilous journeys.

But now the importance of Rangoon banishes all that into the realm of our dreams. The beginnings of trade date from about 1760 after King Alaungpaya had won a battle here and called the place *Yangon:* end of strife; but the big foreign port sprang up suddenly after 1852 when the British gained possession of it; the ships coming into its harbor from the oceans grew larger and larger, buildings followed the expanding commerce, roads and railways were built to all parts of Burma, foreigners crowded in and stamped its character, and by 1941 Rangoon had become a cosmopolitan city of over 500,000 inhabitants, more than three times larger than the next largest city in Burma and controlling over 80 per cent of its export trade.

If the Burmese Empire of former days had been a sea-power, the development of Rangoon would not have been left to this late day, for its position makes it the obvious port for the whole country, and it had many natural beauties which would have made it a fair metropolis. Twenty-one miles up from the open sea, the Rangoon River gives a broad sweep to the left and allows a frontage of over two miles for ocean shipping to anchor. The river is a continuation of the Hlaing River flowing southwards from about fifty miles north of Rangoon and this, with the Pegu River and the Pazundaung Creek, which joins its waters opposite Rangoon from the right, made inland water transport also easy. The land giving on to the Rangoon River was open and flat for the layout of a fine city, with, further in, lakes and wooded hillocks, but just north of Rangoon the range of hills known as the Pegu Yomas stretched northwards for about 300 miles, dividing the valley of the Irrawaddy from that of the Sittang, both rich alluvial valleys, so that Rangoon could stretch out its arms uninterruptedly, by road and rail and water, far up these valleys, and draw down their teak, oil and other products for export.

The actual development had taken advantage of these natural points. Along the river front were several wharves which, dredged and drained carefully, could take vessels up to 8,000 tons. Back from the Strand the city was laid out in three parallel rows, roughly two miles from east to west. Cutting down across these rows to the biggest wharf area was the broad Sule Pagoda Road with the hill of the pagoda forming the natural central circus of the city. In this area of neatly laid-out streets were the shops, offices, congested city dwellings, bazaars, narrow shut-in buildings and all the appurtenances of a city; and just where the innermost parallel ended, the railway looped through, flinging one arm up to join Prome on the central Irrawaddy, the other to Mandalay 386 miles away, and from this arm, a line down to the Tenasserim coast. Beyond the city area the residential areas and suburbs stretched—fringing the Royal Lakes just outside with big houses of rich people; nestling among the wooded hilly Golden Valley round the slopes of the Shwe Dagon Hill, the smallness of this hilly area being drawn out with the meandering of the roads, so that the Burmese named part of it *Wingaba*, a maze, which hid cool retreats like the *Nga Dat Gyi:* Five Levels Pagoda, and a tank of sacred turtles; extending miles in a pleasant garden city of newer rich bungalows till it reached the

Victoria Lakes, the University Estate and the airport beyond; taking on a village character in small wooden houses of a Burmese quarter at Kemmendine, along which the Rangoon River flowed as a country river; and straggling out in less pleasant poor suburbs to the east along the Pazundaung Creek.

Over all this area, the Shwe Dagon Pagoda shone like a golden light. Theinguttara Hill, besides being an echo of the last world, is also the last spur of the Pegu Yomas chain, which gradually peters out north of Rangoon. It has been built up to about 150 feet above the surrounding area, and from this platform the Shwe Dagon Pagoda rises, from an octagonal plinth moulded into a lotus bloom turned downwards, tapering into soft encircling rings from which is moulded again a gently swelling plantain bud, the clay merging into more soft undulations which rise to the very summit in the tightest bud of all—the *seinbu*, diamond bud—forming, by a re-echoing of the lotus buds which once sprang up here, a shapely slender spire, tapering to the point of a bud and yet composed of curves and gentle fullness. The whole pagoda was covered with pure gold leaf and its summit was crowned with a delicate *hti*, an umbrella of gold on whose rings were hung gold and silver jewelled bells which tinkled with every passing breeze. The Shwe Dagon Pagoda was a beautiful and sacred thing. In the early mornings it gave a radiance to the clear air and the blue sky; in the daylight it shone forth like a blaze of gold, burning and pure; in the evenings it glowed softly as the breeze tinkled its bells, and filled the heart with a gentle sadness which is not grief but a sweet perception of unearthly things; and at night the lights flooded it to stand high and illumined above the dark wooded slopes of the hill. At all times and from all parts of Rangoon it could be seen, calm and sublime, with the same smiling look as is seen on the face of the Buddha, not smiling in the eyes or mouth but in the serene expression of inward calm.

As we landed in Rangoon we saw a great gathering of people waiting to meet us. Going abroad for years of study is still a rare enough event to be of interest to all relatives and neighbors, so that the people were assembled not only for an affectionate reunion, but also to observe in what way the stay in England might have corrupted Burmese habits. In the case of a man it is always feared that he may bring back an English wife, and it sometimes happens that a loved child who has been away for five and six years may be greeted with tears and mourning rather than expressions of joy, if he has married an English girl. The tears of mother and sisters are very heartfelt; they express shame at what the neighbors will think, sorrow at the alienation of the man and his children which must inevitably occur, and chagrin at the loss of the rich dowry which might have been procured in the marriage market.

LEILA HADLEY

from GIVE ME THE WORLD

DIVORCED, bored with New York, Leila Hadley set out with her six-year-old son Kippy to see the world. Like Santha Rama Rau, she subsequently married a traveling companion, Yvor, who was one of four American men she met sailing their ship, the California, across the seven seas.

THE SCHOONER'S LIBRARY yielded little information about the Nicobars. *Sailing Directions* mentioned that this group of nineteen islands, located in the Andaman Sea off the northwestern tip of Sumatra, had been used by the Japanese during World War II as an out-of-the-way submarine base; warned all craft to be on the lookout for uncharted wreckage in the area; and said nothing else about the islands except that they came under the control of the Indian Government, that the climate was unhealthy for Europeans and that the fresh-water supply was bad.

Professor Lips, in *The Savage Hits Back*, referred to the Nicobarese natives as an animistic tribe of Malay origin and made note of the curious fact that they often used drawings and carved wooden figures of white men to frighten away thieves, ghosts and evil spirits.

From Yvor's ornithology text, I learned that the Nicobar Islands were a habitat of *Collocalia nidifica*, the species of swift famed for its edible nests, which were esteemed in Hong Kong as the choicest of delicacies.

This was all I could find about the Nicobars, and in a way I was glad, strangely pleased to be coming to a place so little contained in any frame of reference.

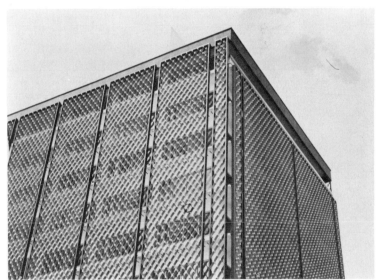

FROM ARABIAN NIGHTS TO VENETIAN GOTHIC TO TUDOR HALF-TIMBERED
TO INTERNATIONAL MODERN, ALL IN AN HOUR'S WALK
THROUGH KUALA LUMPUR, MALAYSIA.

Vic and Yvor hovered over a dog-eared chart and laid out a course to Nancowry Harbor. The harbor, a deep lagoon embraced by the islands of Nancowry and Camorta, was only accessible through a shallow sliver of a pass on the east and by a slightly deeper sliver of a pass on the west. *Sailing Directions* warned that both entrances were hazardous.

"Huh," Vic scoffed. "We've been through worse than that." With a stubby pencil, he drew a firm line marking our course through the western pass.

At dawn, when I was on watch, I looked over the quiescent stretch of the Andaman Sea and saw on the horizon the filmy, unsubstantial image of landfall. Settled over with the peace that comes from gliding forward into a meditating world of waveless calm, I watched the tiny thickening of the horizon grow into a violet smudge. Later in the day sounds would fuse, but now each sound was distinct: the sibilance of the sea; the schooner's creaking; the clicking of Scupper's toenails as he made his way purposefully toward the bow to perform his morning functions to the right of the anchor chain; and the alarm clock on the wheelhouse ledge that defied conventional onomatopoeia and went brink-brunk, brink-brunk.

The level space of water between us and the violet shadow of Nancowry and Camorta shook with the gold of the sun. Space all about, and the islands now coming closer, darkening, expanding to a long, low mound of jungly vegetation, with the palms so closely crushed together that no one tree was outlined, the whole a solid palisade of dark, quivering foliage. Finally, unexpectedly, the pass appeared between the islands. We sailed cautiously through the narrow breach, the jungly headlands seeming to slide back together behind us, cutting off all sight of the sea. On either side, the islands' massive palm forests sloped down to a beach of lime-white sand dotted with beehive huts hunched beneath the clotted plumage of silvery thatch. The lagoon curved out and round again, the water turquoise where it lapped over coral reefs and sapphire where the coral ended.

"It's beautiful," I said.

"Beautiful, hell," Art retorted. "That's coral and it's a bastard to anchor in."

We sailed toward a sheltered cove rimmed by Champin Village, the main settlement on Nancowry Island. Crowned with the arching plumes of areca and coconut palms, the village took on shape, the sun catching and blazing on a shed roofed with galvanized iron, the shaggy huts set high on stilts clustering all about.

I leaned against the wheelhouse and stared at the village, my consciousness flowing out to the alien huts and the palms beyond. It was a moment which filled me with a kind of ecstasy, and I find I return to it time and time again in memory.

We anchored. The sails were dropped, the boom lifts were pushed into place, and the anchor chain was clankingly paid out through the hawsepipe. While I was helping to fold the stiff canvas sails, I saw that a crowd of natives had lined up on the beach, all of them solemnly shading their eyes to look at us. A group of coppery-colored men in scarlet-tailed loin cloths detached themselves from the crowd, shoved a high-prowed outrigger into the water and paddled out to us. Standing up in the outrigger's tapering prow, which was painted with a black telesmatic eye, they caught hold of our gunwale cap to steady themselves as they came alongside.

"Gooks," Hal muttered, as the natives stared at us and began to babble excitedly.

"Boy, they sound just like you, Hadley," Art said. "Why don't you try talking to them?"

Trying what little Malay I knew, I had already done just that, with no response other than wide grins exposing blackened teeth and gums stained crimson from betel-chewing.

"Save your breath, Hadley, and watch the expert," Yvor said, flourishing a box of stick tobacco left over from Polynesian trading days. "I'm going to have a go at cornering the coconut market."

When he had finished bartering, there was a hill of green coconuts on the deck. With a long-bladed knife Yvor whacked off the top of one of them and gave it to me to drink. It was the first coconut I had ever drunk. The sweet-tasting liquid reached coolingly inside me and I sat on deck drinking it slowly. My eyes ambled over the shore where my feet wanted to, exploring the cluster of thatched huts with the jagged frieze of villagers standing in front and the little chickens and thin pigs darting around them. The natives in the outrigger cast off, and almost at once another outrigger pulled alongside bearing a barefooted, khaki-clad, portly Indian civil servant with gray hair and features oddly similar to those of Ezio Pinza. A stethoscope hung around his neck and he carried a furled black umbrella as though it were a scepter.

"I am the government doctor and port official," he said in hesitant English as he climbed aboard. "Are any of you diseased?"

He plugged the stethoscope tubes into his ears and gravely listened to the sound of our hearts, inspected our health certificates, shuffled and reshuffled the ship's papers, and finally, sitting down on one of the barrel seats in the lounge, inquired if we had a drop of whisky on board. The heat, he said, had given him a tickling thirst. His manner was glazed with a Victorian punctilio which was strangely accented by the singsong diphthongs of his speech. He tossed down two neat jiggerfuls of whisky, rewarded us with a dazzling smile and suggested that we go ashore and pay our respects to the Queen. Yes, yes, there was a Queen, the Ranee Islon, and it was customary for all strangers upon their arrival to have an audience with her. He hinted delicately that the Ranee Islon, like himself, was not above a wee nip now and then, and that she might appreciate an offering of this sort.

"We're low on liquor," Art said pointedly. It was decided that a tin of Spam and a canister of cocoa would be acceptable as gifts to royalty.

The doctor cleared his throat and turned upon me an uncertain, appeasing regard from large brown eyes with yellowish whites. "You have the honor to be the first European lady to set foot on the shores of Nancowry," he said. "I believe," he continued, glancing at my halter and shorts and then glancing away again, "I believe that it would perhaps be fitting to change to more formal attire before honoring the Queen with your presence."

I changed to a skirt and blouse, the crew put on their pandanus hats banded with Tahitian shells, and Kippy put on shoes and a clean shirt. The doctor summoned his outrigger by raising his umbrella and waving it in the air; and we set out for our royal visit.

The doctor pointed to five poles festooned with tufts of palm leaves which stood in the water a little way from the beach. "Those are scare-devils to frighten away the twin fiends of the monsoon," he said. "I do not believe in such things. I am Hindu myself," he pronounced loftily.

When we landed on the beach, the soft murmur of the villagers' voices hushed. Every eye turned to stare at us. "Do not be timid," the doctor said. "The people are friendly here. They are just curious about you. Many have never seen a white face before."

As we walked up the beach and along the edge of the jungle, the natives remained at a respectful distance. Chickens, dogs and pigs fled at our approach, squawking, yapping and squealing. From the stilt-raised huts on either side, faces peered down, watching us go by.

"Please to wait here," the doctor said, stopping before a round hut bigger than the rest and roofed with a woven dome of thatch. He mounted a ladder and disappeared inside. The wooden lintel of the doorway was impressed with a red-stained hand print, a talisman to guard the dwelling against the evil eye. A few minutes later the doctor's head reappeared. "Now you may enter," he said.

Up the ladder we all went, Kippy and I leading the way, and the doctor ushered us into the royal sitting room, which hardly seemed large enough to hold us all. The room was circular, and equipped with a window, a table, two wooden chairs and a bench. The woven wall matting was plastered and painted blue around the lower half and separated from the white-painted upper half by a broad orange stripe. The Queen entered from another chamber in the back. Correctly imperturbable, she greeted us with the calm dignity of her station and motioned us to be seated. She then sat down on one of the wooden chairs, smoothed her flower-printed sarong over her knees, adjusted the safety pins fastening her red blouse and smilingly surveyed us over the tops of spectacles from which both lenses were missing.

She was a plump and pleasant-looking woman. Age had narrowed her mouth and eyes and somewhat spread her nose, and her cinnamon-colored skin, like the jacket of a baked apple, wrinkled loosely over flesh that was no longer firm. Since she spoke only Tamil and Nicobarese, the doctor acted as interpreter. At the Queen's suggestion, he produced a gilt-clasped, leather-bound guest register, discolored and peeling with age. The entries dated back to 1870, and most of them had been made by captains of sailing whalers and trading schooners who had been driven by typhoons to seek refuge in the landlocked shelter of Nancowry Harbor. We signed the register and, having neatly blotted our signatures, presented the Queen with the Spam, the cocoa and a silk scarf saying "I Love You" in six languages which I had thought to bring along. I don't think the doctor thought much of the scarf, but Ranee Islon seemed pleased. Then Princess Laxshmi, the Queen's daughter, and Laxshmi's daughter, Mochan, glided in.

Princess Laxshmi was a handsome woman with an air of distinction. Her gray-black hair was pulled back smoothly into a knot at the nape of her neck, and her features were arresting in their delicacy. Mochan, shy and round with adolescence and a little awkward in a mauve crepe-de-Chine sari, handed us each coconuts to drink and carefully decanted mine into a cloudy jelly glass.

Since Easterners are not obsessed with the notion of keeping up a sustained conversation, little was said, but for our entertainment photographs were passed around showing Laxshmi and Mochan at the amusement park in Madras, where they had gone for a vacation several years before. When our smiles began to stiffen and Kippy began to fidget, Mochan brought out a wind-up gramophone, and after she had played several scratched and warping Indian records, the doctor said that it was in order for us to leave.

Laxshmi filled Art's pandanus hat to its brim with bantam-sized hen's eggs. She and Mochan smiled good-by, and the Queen cheerfully exposed two rows of blackened and stumpy teeth.

We spent what was left of the afternoon visiting the trading store. The store, stocked with such necessities as salt, matches, yard-long bars of soap and bolts of cloth, was a branch of a Madrasi firm that annually sent out a dozen or so clerks to run the establishment and to handle the export of copra and betel nuts which an itinerant trading schooner collected every month.

Since the trading schooner was due the next morning, villagers were already at work stacking sacks of copra and betel in the clearing in front of the trading store, while the clerks from Madras stood in the shade of the veranda directing them. The clerks offered us weak, heavily sugared tea which made my stomach feel hot and sleepy. To a man, they said that they found the islands dull and monotonous and couldn't wait until the time came for them to be returned to India. "There is nothing here to do but work," they said, sighing wearily as they lighted the Coleman lanterns in their quarters and closed up the store for the night.

Early the next morning the *Mahmoodia*, the monthly trading schooner, two-masted, square-sailed and disheveled, anchored close to the *California*. For the rest of the day, natives, with their long-ended loincloths wagging behind them like scarlet tails, transferred the sacks of copra stacked inside the stockaded clearing of the trading store to the schooner's hold.

After watching the proceedings for some time, I paddled the *California*'s outrigger over to the white, starfish-dotted beach, where I found all sorts of shells as I wandered along—ruffled white tridacnas, some the size of a small ashtray, others as large as a giant bird bath; creamy spider shells with splayed white fingers; dark and speckled cowries with a golden sheen; white shells, pink shells, gray shells. The clerks at the trading store gave me a wooden box, and I walked along the beach, picking up shells and putting them into it. I was followed by a flock of native children who would scatter whenever I glanced behind me and scamper like sandpipers to hide behind the talipot palms by the trampled path that edged the jungle.

Beneath the sun's nearly vertical rays, the sand was parched and bleached with heat, the clear water along the curving littoral a brilliant blue-green. Farther along, there were the rusted remains of a Japanese landing craft and a submarine. A pig squealed as it rooted in the palms, and from the jungle came the monotonous piping of parakeets. Behind me the voices of the copra carriers were muted with distance.

I waited for the children to come closer. They bunched together and watched me with brow-dark eyes. I smiled and waved and they looked at each other uncertainly. Presently, a girl, whose adolescent breasts threatened to burst from the prison of her safety-pinned chemise, edged forward. When she was within a few yards of me, she stopped and held out a cowry shell. It was the gesture of Psyche offering a sop to Cerberus. I placed the cowry on top of my other shells and gave her the only thing I had with me that I thought she might like—a blue hair ribbon, which she immediately tied around her waist. From then on, she followed me about like a solicitous shadow. A transient missionary had baptized her Sophia and had taught her the meaning of "yes," "what" and "no," and this knowledge equipped her to become my interpreter. She combed the beach for shells to add to my collection—none but the perfect ones would do, the ones with the sharpest steeples, the ones fresh from the cove, with their lustrous patina unimpaired—and she brought me black-beaked nautiluses and the white-gold cowries which were so hard to find.

She led me from one thatched hut to another until we had made the rounds of all thirty-one, a guided tour that took several days, for each stop required a formal ritual of greeting and an exchange of cigarettes for drinking coconuts. The villagers were a gentle, friendly lot, and if they weren't a particularly handsome people, they were obviously healthy and cheerfully disposed to spinning out their lives in an isolated state of grace.

Their arrangements for living were of the simplest. Few huts were furnished with more than sleeping mats, coconut calabashes and earthenware pots, a tin trunk and a lamp. Each family owned an outrigger, a dog and a small flock of chickens and pigs that roamed the village in a noisy foraging company during the day and dutifully assembled at nightfall beneath their respective huts.

Sophia took me to the village carpenter, who carved for me one of the demonifuges which I had read about, a top-hatted wooden figure with nautilus-shell eyes and one arm raised in a gesture of power. Sitting on the ladder of a hut with a pet parakeet swinging on its perch beside me, I watched the carpenter whittling. Beneath me, at the foot of the ladder, a rusted gasoline drum left over from the days of the Japanese occupation and a bird-bath-sized tridacna shell served as rain-catchers. The sun's rays slanting through the canopy of palms dappled the settlement with light, and under this chiaroscuro everything was washed in a soft haze. Parakeets piped and chittered in the jungle; the water whispered over the white beach. In the great quietness of the afternoon the air seemed weighted with a stillness which human voices never quite penetrated—it was as though the voices were an illusion. Sometimes the whole village seemed to be an illusion. It was the first time since my childhood that I had been able to sit for hours doing nothing and not feel guilty about it.

For once I felt I had enough time between the rising of the sun and the setting of it to do as I pleased, enough time to sit mindlessly gazing at the pattern made by the smooth, burnished leaves of the talipot palms against the sky, enough time to wander along the beach picking up shells and feeling the hot, sugary sands scrunching between my toes, enough time with Kippy to search for starfish and make stones skip across the water until our wrists ached, and to hunt lizards and lungfish. Then, having found them, we would watch until they were hidden from sight in a crevice, when, according to the rules of our game, we could go on until we found another one and start all over. And when the shore was explored, there was time enough to explore the bay in the *California's* outrigger, which the crew had picked up in Samoa.

The water was as clear as glass, and in the deep places trout-sized trigger fish looked like minnows as they swam up and over the knobbly, branching arms of red-purple coral. In the shallow places the coral lightened to creamy white, carpeting the bay with a lobed and lacelike web which rose higher and higher as I skimmed toward the far shore until it massed before me in a long, jagged reef, beyond which the water rippled onto a shell-strewn beach.

The afternoon of our last day in the Nicobars I invited Ranee Islon, Laxshmi, Mochan and Sophia to a farewell get-together on the *California.* They filed into the lounge and, encouraged by gestures and smiles from me, seated themselves in a row on the couch. Sophia, evidently intimidated by the presence of royalty, bowed her glossy black head and could hardly be persuaded to raise her eyes. The party began to flag before it had even started.

I passed around tea and slices of a chocolate cake Art had baked, and brought out the schooner's photograph album. From time to time the crew sauntered in, looked over the situation and left. Time wore on, and at last the Queen rose with dignity, adjusted her spectacles and, in her wake, the entourage trooped on deck. The royal outrigger was summoned from the shore, and when it came alongside, the oarsman handed up two baskets, which Ranee Islon presented to me. One was filled with taros and papayas, the other with clumps of pink and lavender coral, sea-wet and glowing. In the center, half-hidden, were two tortoise-shell combs which Sophia indicated with shy pride were a special gift from her.

We hoisted sail early the next morning, the doctor, the clerks and the villagers lining up along the beach to wave good-by. The Queen, wearing a crimson sarong, was prominent in the foreground and one of the most vigorous of the wavers. Our sails were sheeted out, and soon Nancowry faded and blurred on the horizon. The last swift which was keeping us company wheeled in the sky and disappeared. The sun blazed down on the crates of shells that I had lashed to the shrouds, and the coral smelled as it died and began to lose its color.

NIRAD C. CHAUDHURI

from THE AUTOBIOGRAPHY OF AN UNKNOWN INDIAN

"ACCORDING to the Greek saying, the first requisite to happiness is that a man should be born in a famous city. The natives of Calcutta did not appear to stand in need of a second." In the fifteen or more years since Nirad Chaudhuri wrote these words and those that follow, Calcutta has grown tremendously. Once the brightest jewel in the imperial crown, it may now well be the fourth largest city on earth.

CALCUTTA grew enormously during the thirty-two years I lived in it, and became amorphous. Since 1942 it has received hundreds of thousands of additional immigrants and, according to old residents, is no longer recognizable as its familiar self. I have not seen Calcutta after this recent adulteration, but even in 1910 it was not one city. In certain of its quarters a man could easily fancy that he was in China. Other parts looked like *mohallas* torn out of the cities of upper India, and, in fact, till recently Calcutta had the largest Hindi-speaking population of any city in India. Along the Chowringhee and south of Park Street the city had an appearance which probably was not materially different from that of the European adjuncts of Chinese, Malay, or Egyptian ports, but even here it did not exhale mere commerce, club life, sport, and turf. Those who were historically conscious could sense these parts of Calcutta to be very perceptibly breathing the spirit of the builders of the British Empire in India. The rest of the city was purely Bengali.

Between the European and the Bengali parts, however, there always was a Eurasian and Muhammadan belt, very characteristic in appearance and still more so in smell. One of the typical sights of these quarters were the butcher's shops with beef hanging from iron hooks in huge carcasses, very much bigger than the goat carcasses to whose size we the Bengali Hindus were more used. These wayside stalls were redolent of lard, and were frequented by pariah or mongrel dogs of far stronger build and fiercer looks than the dogs of the Hindu parts of the city. These animals always reminded me of the dogs in the butcher's shops of the *Arabian Nights*. All the components of Calcutta had personality and character, but the foreign elements seemed to be even more particularly assertive. In spite of the numerical preponderance of Bengalis the city was, and perhaps still is, an international concession, once flourishing but now moribund, on the mud-flats of deltaic Bengal.

Even when we first came to it Calcutta was vast. At the same time it was very close-knit and compact. It was not broken in relief like Rome with its Seven Hills, not scattered in space like Delhi with its seven historic sites. That did not mean, however, that from a height the city had a smooth appearance. Looked at from the top of the Ochterlony Monument, or even from the roof of a high private house, the house-tops of Calcutta seemed in their crowded and untidy rows to bid the most solid and the ugliest imaginable defiance to the sky. They made a deep impression on me when I contemplated them with the newly acquired sense of being a citizen, immediately after our arrival in 1910. Our house, which was in the Bowbazar quarter, was a four-storied building, and as we went up to its roof an amazing confusion met our eyes. There was an immense expanse of house-tops fading away on all sides into the smoky horizon, but no two house-tops were alike in shape, height, colour or arrangement. If one had a parapet, another had a wooden or iron railing, and a third nothing. The levels were nowhere uniform, nor even rising or falling

in any discernible pattern of tiers, banks, or terraces. Another extraordinary thing we noticed was that the roofs seemed to be the favourite dumping ground for lumber and waste of all kinds, from broken furniture to smashed earthenware and pieces of torn canvas or sack. The irregular upper surface of Calcutta was made more jagged still by the edges and points of this junk.

The only place where the skyline appeared to suggest architecture was the extreme west. There we could see in one ample curve the tops of the well-known public buildings of the Esplanade and Dalhousie Square. The line began with the cupolas, small and big, of the new building of Whiteaways and ran through the tower of the High Court, the flat dome of the Government House, the square tower of the old Central Telegraph Office, the high dome of the General Post Office, the leads of Writers' Buildings and the statues on its cornices, to the steeple of the Church of St. Andrew. The scene gave the impression of an ugly sea of tossing brickwork contained along a clearly marked line by an architectural breakwater. If the view of Calcutta from above was ever softened it was only by its own appalling domestic smoke and the not very much more pleasant mist rising from the river to the west and the marshes to the east.

But three special features of the top face of Calcutta must also be mentioned, not only because they somewhat redeemed the squalid general effect, but also because they could not have been missed by anybody looking at Calcutta from an elevated point in the years following 1910. They were, first, chimneys and church spires. Two of each could be very prominently seen from the roof of our house. To the south-east rose the very tall chimney of the sewage pumping station at the Entally end of Dhurrumtollah Street, and the other was the ornamental chimney of the municipal waterworks on Wellington Square. Both the chimneys have now disappeared. The church spire nearest to us was that of the Roman Catholic church at Bowbazar-Sealdah corner, but we could see the taller spire of the church on Wellesley Square almost equally distinctly. In Calcutta of those days no temple or mosque rose into the air. If any bells rang they were church bells. The people of Calcutta were so used to church spires that they gave the distinctive name of Bald Church to a steepleless church in our locality. In my time the church had disappeared, but it had bequeathed its name to the quarter.

The second landmark in the Calcutta sky was the group of five cranes on the site of the Victoria Memorial, then in the course of construction. These impressive architectural ancillaries were not less decorative and monumental than architecture itself, and for many years these magnificently arranged objects, imprinted as they were on the southern sky of Calcutta, created the illusion of a vast Brangwyn etching overhanging the city or some colossal ghost ship working its derricks in the upper air. When with the completion of the building the cranes disappeared, with them also disappeared one of the most vivid and poetic associations of my first years in Calcutta.

The third feature we noticed has also become rare, if it has not disappeared altogether. Every thousand yards square or so of the top face of Calcutta had a bamboo mast bearing on its head a bird-table, consisting only of a trellised frame, for pigeons to sit on. At the foot of the mast crouched a watchful man with an upturned face; he held a long and thin stick in his hand and from time to time prodded the birds with it. The birds at first tried to avoid the stick by changing places; then one or two began unwillingly and lazily to ascend with laboriously flapping wings; but as soon as three or four had gone up the whole flock rose with a whirr and began to fly to and fro over an orbit of about a quarter of a mile, keeping the trellis at the centre. They flew in one direction to begin with, and then took a complete right-about turn towards the other direction. At the turning points they wholly melted away in the atmosphere, but as soon as they had taken their turn flashed back into vision like silvery scales on the blue-grey sky. After about half-a-dozen turns in this fashion they came back to their frame and began to drop by twos and threes on it, and with a little jostling and elbowing settled down for the time being, to be prodded up again after a while by their keeper. Eight, ten, or even a dozen flocks were seen flying at the same time, and they gave a feathery and shot effect to the Calcutta sky. This sky was never gorgeous, but it had at times a pearly tenderness, and to this softness the flying birds added not only a suggestion of the pastel shades of the pigeon's throat, but also a turtledove sensibility. The contrast of such a sky with what lay spread out below was very marked. It seemed as if a crowd of misbehaved and naughty children were showing their tongues and behinds to a mother with the face of Michelangelo's Night.

Within a few days of my coming to Calcutta I learned with astonishment from my new schoolfellows that the pigeons, and, even more so, their keepers were held in the worst possible disrepute by the human beings of the city. I casually mentioned to some of my school-fellows that I used to keep pigeons at Kishorganj. They looked with scandalized incredulity at me, because I had already given proof in the class that I was clever at books, and in my general behaviour, too, there was nothing to suggest a keeper of pigeons to these Calcutta boys: I showed no obvious signs of the moral degeneration which pigeons were supposed in Calcutta to bring on mankind. Fortunately, the boys took my former pigeon-keeping as the oddity of an East Bengal boy and did not report to the teachers. In the case of a Calcutta boy a cry would have arisen: "Sir, this boy flies pigeons," and at that cry the cane would have descended mercilessly on my back.

On the ground Calcutta presented a very impressive façade. But it was a façade which looked inwards, like the amphitheatre on the arena. The arena was formed by the famous Maidan or, as it is called in Bengali, the Field of the Fort, and the city stood in a rough arc round it like the inner face of the Coliseum. The parallel is not as correct for the two wings of the façade of Calcutta as it is for the eastern or Chowringhee section, for both the wings—the first from Hastings to St. Paul's Cathedral and the second from Esplanade corner to Outram Ghat—were leafy. To the north, the Government House was all but hidden by the trees which stood trunk to trunk along the low white balustrade which formed its outer boundary wall, and towards the river the long line of the beautiful *polyalthia longifolia* of the Eden Gardens hid the High Court and the Town Hall even more effectively. Only through the funnel-like opening of the road called Government Place West could a glimpse of the Treasury Buildings be caught. At this entrance a formidable group of statuary stood on guard. Queen Victoria, Lawrence, Hardinge, Canning in greenish bronze reminded everybody in 1910, even if the unobtrusive Government House modelled on Kedleston Hall did not, that he was very near the heart of the British Empire in India. To the south of the Maidan there was a similar line of trees along Lower Circular Road, and although there was not in that quarter the same reminder of British power in India as there was to the north, there was at least a reminder of British sickness, both civil and military. For one set of the buildings which could be seen through the trees constituted the British Military Hospital and the other the Presidency General Hospital. The first was reserved for British soldiers and the second for British civilians.

Although the wings of the façade of Calcutta were leafy, the brickwork on the eastern side was long, high, and solid enough to obliterate all sylvan atmosphere. This front would not have stood the scrutiny, building by building, of an architectural designer, but, seen from the distance and as a whole, it was not unimpressive. The skyline, though not absolutely uniform, was not unbalanced by any pronounced irregularity. I once saw the Chowringhee from the River Hooghly when going to the Botanical Gardens at Sibpur in one of the Port Commissioners' ferry service steamers, and the familiar line of buildings beginning with the Army and Navy Stores and ending in Whiteaways was estranged to my eyes by the beauty shed on it by the distance.

The central point in this façade of Calcutta was certainly the high pile of the Indian Museum, rather dull-looking from the outside but always enlivened by the thought of what it contained within. There was no place in Calcutta, unless it was the zoological gardens of Alipur, of which I was more fond. The huge galleries, each at least one hundred feet long, forty feet wide, and as many high, were always reeking of the sweating upcountry men who visited the museum as a matter of duty and trudged through the galleries as solemnly and steadily as my Kishorganj peasants marching to the field of Id prayers. They never stopped before anything unless they saw some visitor taking particular interest in one or other of the exhibits or comparing something in a book with the objects. Then they crowded round that visitor and asphyxiated him with their body odour. It was, however, impossible to get angry with them. They were as natural and primitive as the exhibits, though not as monumental. In the entrance hall were the bull and lion capitals of the pillars of Asoka, in the hall to the right were the highly ornamental red sandstone railings of the Bharhut Stupa, and in the hall to the left the Siwalik fossils together with the skeletons of the huge Hasti Ganesa or *Elephas Antiquus Namadicus Falc.* of the Nerbudda valley. It could be said that in these galleries of the Indian Museum were represented all the previous empires in India from that of the gigantic prehistoric elephants to that of Asoka the Buddist and Samudragupta the Vishnuite.

Facing the Indian Museum across the Maidan stood Fort William, equally silent from the outside but busy and humming like a beehive within with sun-helmeted British soldiers. It was impossible for any person endowed with the consciousness of history to overlook the correlation of the museum with the fort. It was as if those who were living for the time being in Fort William were saying to those who had been housed for all time in the Indian Museum—"Hail, dead emperors, emperors about to die salute ye!" In 1911, unknown to all of us, the shadow of death had already fallen. I still remember my father reading with his friends the news of the transfer of the capital to Delhi. *The Statesman* of Calcutta was furious, but

was thinking more of the past than of the future and was not inspired to prophecies like Cassandra. We, the Bengalis, were, but not in the spirit of Cassandra. We were flippant. One of my father's friends dryly said, "They are going to Delhi, the graveyard of empires, to be buried there." Everybody present laughed, but none of us on that day imagined that although the burial was the object of our most fervent hopes it was only thirty-six years away.

Only one section of the façade of Calcutta had depth, and that was the section between Park Street and Lower Circular Road. The interior here was like the front, only quieter and more spacious. To walk down Middleton Street, Harrington Street, and Theatre Road was to walk into an area of large, still houses standing in their own grounds planted with *lagerstroemia indica*, canna, and ixora, and of wide silent streets shaded by *gul mohurs*, and cassias, and an occasional *lagerstroemia flos-reginae*. All these flowering trees and shrubs blossomed from April to September, making a gorgeous blaze of colours—scarlet, vermilion, pink, purple, lilac, blue, white, and golden yellow—in the midst of which the houses looked dull and ordinary. They did not, however, jar with any obtrusive ugliness. The majority were impressive by reason of their size and solidity, although not by their architecture. But a few had style. They were old buildings in the modified Georgian manner of the East India Company. Here too, as in the façade, it was the effect as a whole and not the details which constituted the attraction, and in this attraction space and silence were the principal elements. The whole area was very much like the old cemetery at its centre, where Landor's Rose Aylmer lies buried.

> Ah, what avails the sceptred race!
>   Ah, what the form divine!
> What every virtue, every grace!
>   Rose Alymer, all were thine.
>
> Rose Aylmer, whom these wakeful eyes
>   May weep, but never see,
> A night of memories and sighs
>   I consecrate to thee.

The inhabitants of the locality prized the silence greatly, and they wrote angry letters to the newspapers against the tooting of horns by taxis prowling for fares at night.

For us Bengalis one street of the area came to acquire a dreaded notoriety. It was Elysium Row. This was an inviting name, to which the great Bengali barrister, Sir S. P. Sinha, the first Indian member of the Viceroy's Executive Council, and later to become

Under-Secretary of State in India and the first Indian peer and Governor of an Indian province, who lived in the street, added greater lure. But the pleasantness of the name and the pride evoked by the association with Sinha were wholly smothered for us by the fear inspired by Number Fourteen, the headquarters of the Special Branch or the political police. There were few Bengali young men with any stuff in them who did not have dossiers in Number Fourteen, and many had to go there in person, to be questioned, or to be tortured, or to be sent off to a detention camp. After the passing of the Defence of India Act of 1915 we began to think of Elysium Row more in connexion with the police than with Sinha. To have been in Elysium Row came to be regarded as equivalent to being branded on the forehead or having a ribbon on the chest, according to the standpoint or courage of the dragooned visitor. My younger brother as a young man of eighteen was taken there, questioned by third-degree methods, and then photographed in full face and in profile for future identification. That did not, however, prevent his identity being mixed up in the mind of the police with quite a different person's, and this confusion caused no small amount of harassment to my brother. I did not have to go there at any time of my life, but at a late stage I had a dossier. In my school and college days I did not come in the way of the political police nor did they come in my way, and I never walked through Elysium Row. Therefore the spaciousness, the silence, and the flowers remained my only impressions of this part of Calcutta.

The rest of the Chowringhee façade was only skindeep, and the hinterland was a strange world whose strangeness was not felt by us only because everybody took it for granted. Russa Road at the southern end of Chowringhee led into the old and respectable Bengali quarter of Bhowanipore, best known for its lawyers, and through Bhowanipore to the less wealthy but more religious quarter of Kalighat; Bentinck Street at the opposite end was famous for its Chinese shoemakers; Dhurrumtollah, which was at the same end, was itself a street of shops, bazaars and Eurasians, but it was also the ingress to the main Bengali parts of the city. An observer could stand at the Chowringhee ends of Dhurrumtollah and Russa Road and watch men coming out between nine and ten in the morning and going in between five and six in the afternoon like ants out of and into their holes. The Bengali parts of Calcutta, both north and south, sent them out in the morning for office work and sucked them back in the evening. These were the men to whom Calcutta belonged by birthright. They loved Calcutta as nobody else did. They lived in it like deepsea fauna in the depths of the sea. Most of them would have preferred death to being removed from Calcutta.

Their Calcutta, which was also my Calcutta for thirty-two years, was an immense maze of brickwork cut up by streets and lanes. It was not labyrinthine like the Indian quarters of the cities of northern India, and it did not bring on that claustrophobia which impels newcomers to those cities to rush out into open spaces in order to breathe easily. Nor did it have that putrid squalor which makes the inhabitants of the same upper-Indian cities feel like living in the intestines of the Leviathan. Also, there was not that accumulated dust, to try to remove which was equivalent to raising only more dust. All these unlovely features of urban life in upper India, our part of Calcutta did not possess, but there was no limit to its architectural meanness. Walking along the ever-lengthening streets and lanes of these quarters one expected at every turn and step to come upon some spot of handsomeness and repose, for instance, a fine building, a spacious square, a wide vista, or at least a colourful bazaar. These expectations were never fulfilled. The more one trudged, the more one felt like swallowing an endless tape of shabbiness.

On account of this all-pervasive inelegance even the wider streets gave no impression of being straight, although they were straight in layout. The awry fronts on either side, taken with the erratic skyline and the unfinished surfaces, checked the growth of any impression of symmetry and harmony. Three or four times every hundred yards the skyline would be falling down abruptly from sixty to ten feet and changing its outline from that of a straight parapet of a flat-roofed brick house to that of the sloping roof of a mud-walled and tiled *bustee*. For the same distance the street front would be presenting three or four incongruous patches: a gaping shed, a solidly built wall pierced by small windows, an unglazed shop window or, rather, a mere opening, and a house with venetian blinds. There was not a single inviting front-door anywhere. The Bengalis of Calcutta seemed to have a particular aversion to attractive entrances. One of the two entrances to a particular house I knew had a new door. But it had its attractiveness, which in truth was no more than that of newness, reduced if not wholly suppressed by an unfelicitous attempt on the part of the owner at being helpful to his visitors. What welcome the door offered was rendered unwelcome for persons with a sensitive verbal taste by a signboard bearing in English the inscription: "Female Entrance." Even where the interiors were luxurious the front door was made to disguise the fact as completely as possible. This particular aspect of the architectural dowdiness had its counterpart in the insensitiveness often displayed in

Calcutta in the naming of persons. "Demon," "Goblin," "Owl," "Idiot," "Tuppence," "Snub-nosed," were quite common names for men and women there. In fact, through a whimsical affectation of Calcutta ways my eldest son came to acquire, to the great disgust and indignation of my father, the nickname of "Imbecile." Of course, these names never bore any relation to the appearance or abilities of the persons so named. When upon the announcement of such names you would expect the emergence of a corresponding physiognomy, a very handsome man indeed might step into your room. In regard to names the trick was meant to avert the Evil Eye or befool evil spirits, but I am unable to account for its extension to the design of front-doors, unless it happens to be a legacy from the days of Muslim rule when rich people did not care to give any outward expression to their affluence for fear of attracting the attentions of the tax-farmer.

To this morphological dinginess the Bengali parts of Calcutta added the ebbs and flows of a functional dinginess: the first daily, the second seasonal, and the third yearly. The Bengalis wash (i.e., rinse in plain unsoaped water) their cotton *dhotis* and *saris* at home every day, and the Bengalis of Calcutta are even more fond of this daily washing than other Bengalis. Actually, the afternoon toilet of Calcutta women passes under the name of "washing" in thoroughbred circles. Thus, at least twice a day, and sometimes more often, an immense amount of washing has to be hung up to dry. The front veranda, if there is any, or the roof is the place reserved for this purpose. In some houses there are a number of clothes-lines, in others the *dhotis* and *saris* are simply let down from the parapet or railing with the top ends tied to a pillar or rail. When wet they hang heavy and straight, dripping water on the footpath below, and when dry they flutter and twirl in the wind. As each piece is at least fifteen feet in length and forty-four inches in width, the houses when the washing is drying have the appearance of being draped in dirty linen. In addition, there always are subsidiary lines carrying the children's shirts, frocks, vests and drawers, and the napkins and sheets of the very large number of babies that there always are in these houses, and on most occasions the exhibition of cotton garments is reinforced by bedclothes—mattresses and quilts, large and small, wetted by the children and the babies.

The gathering up of these articles in the afternoon is almost a ritual, like the hauling down of flags on warships in the evening. Except in the houses of the rich this is in the hands of the girls of the family. In the afternoon two or three comely persons appear on the veranda or roof, as the case may be, advance to the railing or parapet, and, leaning on the one or the other, carry out a composed survey of what is going on below. If anything particularly interests them they rest their chins on the rail or wall and contemplate it with wide open, round, solemn eyes. There never is any mobility or change in their expression, but suddenly a face is tossed up and an electric glance flashed towards the window across the street, where the presence of a lurking admirer is suspected. But this ripple passes away as soon as it makes its appearance. The face relapses into the usual immobile placidity, and the girls go on gathering up or pulling down the *dhotis* and *saris*, normally in a very unconcerned manner, but sometimes screwing a puckered mouth in undoing the knots. They move up and down, piling up the clothes on one of their shoulders or arms, and when at last they walk away they look like huge washerwomen.

Another source of untidiness in our parts of Calcutta was the inexplicable but at the same time the most complete non-co-operation between the domestic servants and the municipal sweepers. In Calcutta of olden days the municipal sanitary service was not haphazard as it has grown recently. The streets were regularly watered, swept, and even scrubbed. But while the street-cleaning ended by about six o'clock in the morning and three in the afternoon, the kitchen-maids would begin to deposit the offscourings exactly at quarter-past six and quarter-past three. Nothing seemed capable of making either party modify its hours. So little piles of waste food, ashes, and vegetable scraps and peelings lay in individualistic autonomy near the kerb from one sweeping-time to another sweeping-time. During this interval, however, the refuse deposit was respected like an archaeological deposit, and was never trampled on or kicked about. All Bengali Hindus are very particular about left-over food, which they consider to be very unclean; therefore they never go anywhere near it. A small boy I knew used to take the most intelligent conceivable advantage of this prejudice in order to escape punishment for his naughtiness. He would make straight for the garbage heap before his house and stand on it. Then there was nothing else to be done but for his elder sister to throw away all her clothing, go up to him, retrieve him, and, dragging him inside, give him a scrubbing under the tap and have an untimely bath herself. The prejudice did not, however, extend to fruit rinds. They were thrown indiscriminately on the footpaths to be trampled on by all and sundry. To slip on a mango or banana skin and have a sprained ankle was a very common mishap in Calcutta.

The contribution of the seasons has now to be considered. It was in Calcutta that I learned for the first time that the seasons could uglify no less than beautify. At Kishorganj, Banagram, and Kalikutch every season added something to the attraction of the world around us. The summer sun, hot as it was, shed more happiness than discomfort, for besides being white and clear it had a life-giving quality. This, we used to say, is the sun to ripen the mango, the jack-fruit, and the melon, and it did ripen not only the fruits but also the earth, which became seasoned and mellow like an old violin. To this heat there was an extraordinarily harmonious accompaniment of sound, a sound so intense and energetic and yet so mild and musical, that one could imagine its having been produced by the revolving top that our earth is. It was the crickets which converted the earth into a humming top. They began at about ten o'clock in the morning, just as the earth and the trees also began to feel warm to the touch. They constituted the Grass-hopper's Green Herbarian Band. We hardly ever saw the brown little creatures, but we could call up before our eyes an immense string orchestra madly scraping, bowing and fingering, swaying and stretching. The *Yatra* parties had made us quite familiar with the movements of violinists. This rilloby-rilloby rilloby-rill went on till about five in the afternoon and then suddenly ceased. As dusk fell, there began the gorgeous outings of the fireflies in clustered nebulae of phosphorescent light in the midst of the darkened foliage.

These were my summer associations in the country, but on coming to Calcutta I saw that the summer heat could only produce stench more quickly, and make the streets even more messy than they normally were. They would now be strewn with empty coconut shells, whose milk is the favourite summer drink. The only thing which in our parts of Calcutta redeemed the summer was the cool evening breeze from the south and the sea. Without this breeze, I believe, the *embonpoint* of all denizens of Calcutta, who in their inordinate fondness for *ghee*, sweets and starchy foods take immense quantities of them daily, would have rotted away in sleep and the bodies begun to emit stench like the tight carcasses of dead bullocks. It may have been some instinctive fear of this kind which made all weathly citizens of Calcutta keep the electric fan on all through the night.

The winter was not pleasanter. The temperature never went down low enough to make the cold bracing, but it became just cold enough to make people catch cold. There was grime everywhere, and, in addition, an accumulation of dust which, if it was not as overwhelming in quantity as the dust of upper-Indian cities, was worse in quality, for it was a dis-

honest half-breed between honest coal and honest earth. The winter mornings in the city were never refreshed for me by the dew I was accustomed to in the country, where to walk through the grass at dawn was to crush a mass of diamonds. The only evidence of dew that I saw in Calcutta was the damp surface of the footpaths. But the worst thing was the smoke and the combination of smoke and mist in the evenings. At Kishorganj the mist hung over the land-scape exactly like a veil of fine muslin. In Calcutta both the smoke and the mist spited each other. The mist would not allow the smoke to go up, and the smoke would mix itself up with the mist as it came down. We could never determine how much of the dark mixture we saw all around us was mist and how much smoke, but it was so thick that we could fancy beating it up with a stick. In any case, we were suffocated, and the gas-lamps in the streets looked reddish yellow. It was only on those rare evenings when a strong cold wind blew from the north that the atmosphere was swept clean of this dirt and the street lamps in their long lines took on the appear-ance of an endless and wavy festoon of soft greenish light. But in these evenings no true son of Calcutta came out willingly into the streets. He stood in mortal fear of catching pneumonia. He preferred to die of consumption in his dovecote.

But drab as the summer and winter were in Calcutta, in order to measure the full power of uglification of the seasons it was necessary to live through the rains. I have already described the rainy season at Kishorganj, but I might recall one or two impressions to bring home the contrast which Calcutta presented. The sheet-like downpour at Kishorganj had the quality of crystal, drizzle was opaline, and both were set off by a shining green. The clouds varied from the deepest collyrium blue to soft pearly shades, and apart from this infinite graduation from dark to white, they burnt in piled-up masses of gold, orange and red, or blushed in equally immense masses of pink, at sun-rise and sunset. On moonlight nights, if the sky was lightly clouded, a ring with rainbow colours appeared round the moon; if there were those beautifully dia-pered cirro-cumulus clouds, their rippling outlines would be edged with amber. I never saw any of these things in Calcutta. The buildings hid the lower sky, and all the finer shades of the portions overhead were blotted out by the smoke and the lights of the city. For most of the time we could see only an unbroken shroud of grey.

The grey on the ground was worse. In Calcutta of those days tar-macadam was reserved for the so-called European quarters, and we, the Bengalis, had only rubble and earth on our streets. This mass decomposed during the rains, became thin and watery enough to be capable of being splashed head-high, but even in that diluted state lost none of its stickiness. This mud, as it lay on the flagstones of the footpaths, converted them into grindstones for our shoes. Thus it happened that those of us who could not go about in carriages were always down at heel and bespattered on the back during this season. Those who went about in carriages spared themselves but made the lot of the pedestrians harder. Fortunately, nobody minded anybody else's appearance, since it was taken to be the normal aspect of mankind during the rains. As for the houses, they looked worse. There were very few of them which did not wear a thoroughly bedraggled and miserable air. The trees, though washed of the dust which normally lay thick on them, did not look bright or refreshed. At Kishorganj, even after a violent gale, they looked as if they had had only a bit of wild horseplay, but in Calcutta they appeared as if they had undergone a ducking.

Sometimes the rains were so heavy that instead of the usual mud we had floods in the streets. The sewers of Calcutta were never equal to coping with the rains. The difference between their highest capacity and the demand made on them during the rains could be stated only in astronomical figures of cu.-sec.-s. I had once to go into the subject, but have forgotten all about it except the esoteric abbreviation I have used. The tangible fact was that after even a moderate shower certain streets and crossings were inevitably flooded, and heavy showers converted them literally into canals and ponds. I have seen collapsible boats brought out in the streets. People who piqued themselves on their wit used to say that such and such a street in Calcutta was flooded if a dog raised its hind leg. The water was of the dirtiest shade of brown, with all the floatable elements in the garbage afloat, and all the soluble elements in solution. It was knee-deep at certain places, at others even deeper. Some carriages and motor cars would be ploughing their way through it, leaving swirling wakes and backwashes behind, but the trams would be completely held up. The anxious inspectors would be wading about, with their trousers tucked half-way up the thigh, taking soundings with their own lower limbs. The sweepers stood at attention at regular intervals like statues, each at his manhole, after having opened it to let the water pass down into the sewers quickly. Even then the water did not subside for three or four hours. Sometimes even a whole day or night was required. It was being Venice with a vengeance.

Tagore began a famous political speech of his with a reference in his characteristic style to these immemorial floods. "No sooner has the smallest pluvious wind blown," he declared, "than the floods rage from our lane to our main street, the wayfarer's pair of footgear is borne aloft over the head like his umbrella, and at least the denizens of this lane are seen to be no better adapted to life than the amphibians—these are the things I have been observing from our veranda year after year from my childhood till my hair has grown grey." Tagore attributed it half to foreign rule and half to the fatalistic resignation to evil and authority of his countrymen. His countrymen attributed it wholly to foreign rule. The Calcutta Corporation attributed it to a number of causes which it was difficult to understand without a considerable knowledge of irrigation and sanitary engineering combined. But whosoever's the fault, the fact indeed was that those of us who cared for our shoes did wade through the streets with the precious pair in hand. I did so on a few occasions, but the universal spectacle of men going about shoes-in-hand sometimes drove me to attempts at originality. I tried to walk in my shoes. It was worse still. There was more unpleasantness in having them on, for the water was clammy enough by itself, and to have equally clammy leather round the feet, and to feel and hear the water in the shoes squirting in and out noisily at every step were sensations even more unbearable. So our wading shoes-in-hand was not wholly parsimony, it had in it an aesthetic impulse as well.

Last of all I must refer to the yearly accumulation of shabbiness. The house-owners in Calcutta had no notion of maintenance, and even though the preservation of their own property was involved in it considered expenditure on such things as annual repairs and painting utter waste. It would be only after a sustained campaign of complaints and dunning on the part of the tenants that they would send a workman or two to give the house a coat of dirty whitewash inside and a dirty coat of paint outside. Thus the general run of houses in Calcutta, even at their best, looked as if the sharp edge of their cleanly appearance had been rubbed off. This dinginess accumulated from year to year till the general effect became one of mottled grey.

To go out of the city into the suburbs or the countryside did not offer better prospects or aspects. The immediate outskirts of the city were squalid and congested beyond description. They were full of mean and insanitary sheds and *bustees*, built wall to wall, and separated only by dusty roads when not by narrow and evil-smelling lanes. All the bigger roads had open drains on both sides, running with coal-black sewage, and this drain had to be crossed and recrossed every time when one wanted to go into or come out of a house or a shop. None but the inhabitants of these localities could go about in them without handkerchiefs to the nose.

Little relief awaited me even when I broke my way through the suburbs, for the countryside just around Calcutta, though open, seemed to have been poisoned to death. It lay like a mangy bandicoot bitten by a snake. The trees did not thrive there, the grass had a burnt-up look, the cottages were exact replicas of the suburban *bustees*. These parts brought desolation into one's heart.

The next ring was chlorosis-stricken. Here too the trees did not flourish. They were pallid. The houses, both brick-built and thatched, wore a deserted appearance. It was not till one had moved twenty-five miles away that the earth seemed to be its old self. I noticed these concentric rings of different atmospheres and effects whenever I had to come to Calcutta by train.

So, ultimately, one had to work one's way back towards the Chowringhee front in search of repose and order. As long as I lived in Calcutta, I kept up the habit of walking down to the Maidan as far as the Victoria Memorial, or to the Eden Gardens and the riverside between Outram and Prinsep's Ghat. But my yearning for fine architecture was never destined to be satisfied. Domestic architecture was, of course, inconceivable, but even the public buildings I scrutinized in vain. Some of them were presentable, some even imposing and handsome to my unformed taste in architecture. But I soon learned that they were all imitations. The High Court was a copy of the Cloth Hall of Ypres, the Government House of Kedleston Hall; Writers' Buildings and the Revenue Office were passable imitations of the style of the French Renaissance; certain other buildings were pseudo-Greek—Doric, Ionic, or Corinthian. The Cathedral, which had a western window of stained glass after designs by Burne-Jones, was in very pinchbeck Gothic. The Military Secretariat built for Kitchener, although ambitious, was so devoid of true character that in the medallions on its façade the heads of Venus could hardly be distinguished from those of Mars. Nowhere was there anything authentic or original. Only in 1921 did Calcutta get a genuine specimen of architecture in the Victoria Memorial. It has faults of design, but still it is the only thing to redeem the City of Palaces architecturally. Yet it is extraordinary to relate that the Bengali citizens of Calcutta, who are totally unconscious how many of their pre-existent public buildings are imitations, regard the Victoria Memorial as such. They think that it is an unsuccessful imitation of the Taj Mahal. Let alone Emerson, the designer of the memorial, even if Brunelleschi, Bramante, Michelangelo and Wren had appeared in person and sworn otherwise, they would not have convinced these scoffers.

JAMES MORRIS

from CITIES

AT LEAST eight capitals have flourished and died on the site that is now Delhi. The prediction made in 1911, when King George V announced the removal of the imperial capital from Calcutta, that New Delhi would be but one more to meet the same fate, now seems in doubt.

SOME CITIES give an instant impression of provinciality, however urbane they are, however cultivated: such are Stockholm, San Francisco, Brussels, Karachi. Some, though, strike you the moment you arrive with the pulse and posture of history: and such a one is Delhi. Before your aircraft even lands you know you are moving into the big time, for few capitals await you with an air of such solemn distinction, sprawling vast, brown and mottled among its desiccated plains, the sand lapping at its suburbs and curling around its ruined redoubts. Such a setting is this, so infinitely far from the sea, so invested by all the immensities of Asia, so lost in everything big, and crowded, and old, and gnarled with legend, and scarred with tragedy, and hazed with uncertainty, and tinged with nostalgia—such a setting is this, where everything is larger and more intense than life, that when you land in Delhi you feel you are setting foot in some ultimate headquarters, far behind the lines, where the marshals meet to deploy their armies. Only Moscow offers quite the same sensation of inner power; and it is no coincidence that only Russia and India, among the big nations of the earth, are known to their peoples as Mother.

Delhi has been a metropolis for longer than history remembers, and eminence comes easily to her. Here, before the Muslim conquerors stormed across India, the blurred monarchs of Hindu tradition built the city of Indraprastha. Here the Slave Kings erected the stupendous tower of victory called the Kutb Minar, still standing talismanic in the southern outskirts. The successive capitals of Siri, Tughlakabad, Jahanapahan and Firozabad, the fifth, sixth, seventh and eighth cities of Delhi, were all built on this tremendous site; the Tughlak dynasty flourished and waned here, and the Sayyid, and the Lodi; and when the Moguls established their empire in Hindustan, it was in Delhi that Shah Jehan built the Red Fort, home of the Peacock Throne, one of the great fortresses of the earth, and one of the most perpetually haunting. The centuries have never left Delhi alone. Nadir Shah the Persian captured her in 1739, Ahmed Shah Durrani the Afghan in 1757, Mahdo Rao Scindia the Mahratta in 1771, General Lake of His Majesty's Army in 1803, the blood-crazed sepoys of the Indian Mutiny in 1857; and when in the nineteen-hundreds the regnant British cast around for a new Imperial capital, it was to the plains of Delhi that they sent Lutyens and Baker, commissioned to erect the greatest of all monuments to that diligent, blazing but ephemeral Raj. Seventy kings, two queens and a president have all ruled in Delhi. Empires one after the other have tumbled through her chronicles. Cultures have fused here, styles have succeeded one another, the pride of one era has given way to the pretensions of the next. As Murray's *Handbook* put it a century ago, this is the Rome of Asia.

Every stone of Delhi is thus soaked in the essence of history, but it is not really the past that fosters her sense of towering significance. Delhi is awe-inspiring today because she is the scene of a supreme experiment. Like almost every country on earth, the Republic of India has recognized that the way to national self-esteem, if not actually to survival, is industrialization. Like England two centuries ago, like the United States in the nineteenth century, like Soviet Russia since the revolution, like China today, like Egypt with one thing in mind, and Siam with another—like all the rest of the world, India has launched her industrial revolution, destined to transform her from an agricultural, subsistence economy into the kind of society that lives by buying and selling, by making things and putting things together. In the past such fundamental social convulsions have seldom been achieved without compulsion, overt or implicit. In Huddersfield and Halifax the English achieved it by the brutal exploitation of ignorant peasants—cruelly long hours in the mills, child labour underground, methods so ruthless that you may still recognize their legacies in the bandy legs and wizened frames of elderly North Countrymen. The Americans achieved it, scarcely less insensitively, by harnessing those millions of poor immigrants who would endure almost any hardship, work almost any hours for a chance of eventual dignity and security. The Russians

have achieved it by brute force—sometimes, indeed, by nothing less than mass murder. The Chinese are achieving it by absolute despotism, at the cost of individual self-respect.

But Delhi is trying to do it without coercion, threat or exploitation. She is mounting an industrial revolution within a free society on a scale staggering to conceive, among a community of peoples traditionally and endemically centrifugal, disputatious, caste-ridden, proud and superstitious. Such a portentous adventure has never been risked before. It is this that makes Delhi a city of such daunting import, and fosters her paradoxical affinities to Moscow, on the other side of the Asian divide. She is not just the capital of the largest of all democracies, 432 million strong and not a gauleiter among them. She is also a champion and a pioneer. In Moscow they are proving, year by year, that a people can be whipped into greatness. In Delhi they are trying to show that greatness can be voted into office, if applied for in triplicate, through the proper channels.

The first impact of democracy, in such a climate, at such a moment of history, is exceedingly slovenly. Delhi is two cities, the old walled part, the monumental new: and the shabby confusion of the older districts is anything but lovely. Up the road in Rawalpindi the Pakistanis, standing at a similar historical staging-post, have used the instruments of benevolent autocracy to fashion a capital very spanking, trim and orderly. Here, where Government is only by will of the people, things look much messier. The boulevards of Old Delhi are cracked, crumbled and rubbish-strewn. The thirteen-gated city walls look villainous and neglected. The tired tongas have lost their varnish, their bright paint and their nodding horse-plumes. The scrambled bazaars have little sense of craftsmanship or dedication, and the street bands always wandering through the Chandni Chauk, with their faded drooping epaulettes, their grubby white breeches and their tarnished tubas, look demoralized by the discordant monotony of their own art. The traffic of Delhi is dented and ill organized, and the policemen, in uniforms slightly frayed, boots slightly worn, and belts that often need a polish, are sometimes to be seen, to the horror of visiting Englishmen, smoking drooping cigarettes on point duty.

Even in New Delhi, the grandiose geometrical capital of the Republic, wherever the people are, there is muddle. It is rather as though a million gipsies have been let loose within the purlieus of Capitol Hill. The shops of Connaught Place, the Place Vendôme of Delhi, have little elegance or panache, but are mostly frumpish and down-at-heel, forlornly preserving some

KUTUB MINAR, A VICTORY TOWER NEAR DELHI SEVEN CENTURIES OLD.

dying sense of horse-leather and English tweed, or frankly subsiding into lassitude—dusty books in heedless tumble, fabrics in bilious disharmony, comical signs in misspelt English or scratched toys that nobody can find the key to. Into the crevices among the palaces of State all the welter of India has penetrated, like brambles overgrowing a gazebo: wherever there is a space there is a crooked ill-printed notice, a tangle of barbed wire, a ramshackle hut or a covey of old men cooking something on a fire. Behind each grand façade, there is a hint of disorder. It may be a ping-pong table in a lofty courtyard, or a dirty cup on a counter. It may be the rusty squeak of an ornamental gate, or the incipient beard of an official, or the dead-beat, dog-eared procrastination of Indian bureaucracy. It may be the general emanation of imprecision and

THE GREAT MOSQUE AT DELHI.

unpunctuality. It may be the atrophy of inefficiency. Whatever it is, it feels raggety and flaccid. Any dictator would dislike Delhi. Any posturing two-penny despot would feel impelled to take her in hand, clean up her litter, put her clocks right and dust down her venerable pants.

But people of a gentler vision will see more than just the muddle, as a perceptive schoolmaster can detect, beneath the incurable untidiness of a gifted boy, other and more essential talents. The infatuated visitor, indeed, may find the moral of Delhi in her very dishevelment: for without tolerance, without a blind eye, without profusion and variety this would be quite a different kind of city, occupying an altogether different niche in history. Delhi is a cemetery of petty tyrants, and stands above the primping and window displays of autocracy. Everywhere in this city you feel the easy benediction of *noblesse oblige*—just as you do, come to think of it, in the best Romany encampments. It is true that often, out of the halls of Government, you may hear a waspish buzz or the rattling of vulgar sabres—when the armies of non-violence march upon a Goa, for example, or the spokesmen of Gandhian love hiss an imprecation towards some distant antagonist. But the spirit of the city itself is seldom resentful. Delhi does not harbour recriminations, and takes the transient world as it comes. She is, for all her unkempt illiterate veneer, a cultivated city, a sophisticated city in the oldest sense. She is full of cultured men, scholarly or avid to understand. She is rich with immemorial experience. She pushes nothing down your throat, and seldom says, "I told you so." She accepts each facet of her history, heroic or humiliating, and blends it carefully and sadly into the fabric of her presence. Her environs are littered with the relics of a dozen kingdoms, crumbled mosques or broken pavilions, stumps of columns and dust-heaps of forts. Her slums are pierced by the noble mosques of the Muslims, calm and commanding still in this Hindu capital. The queer Iron Pillar of the Guptas still stands venerated in its enclosure, as it has for nearly a millennium. Beside the Kashmir Gate the white Church of St. James is as gleaming today as it was when Colonel James Skinner, drawing ten thousand pounds from his bank account, erected it in thanksgiving for his own survival in battle.

Most of all will you feel this bigness, this sense of generosity, inside the Red Fort, sprawling in red sandstone above the city walls. This has been many things in its time, Imperial court to British Army barracks, but today it stands to the Republic of India precisely as the Kremlin stands to the Union of Soviet Socialist Republics. It is more than just a tourist sight. It has a savour almost religious, so ark-like does it embody all the convictions of national independence. Physically it has not much changed since the days of the Raj. The little shops of the covered bazaar, the entrance to the fort, are still spiced and dim-lit. The sentries still stand with fixed bayonet at the gate. The Diwan-i-Khas still faintly reflects the opulence of the Peacock Throne, embellished once with a thousand sapphires, pearls and rubies, guarded by two dazzlingly jewelled peacocks and a parrot carved from a single emerald. Beneath the walls the lumbering Himalayan bears still enact their clumsy boxing matches, staggering and cuffing one another in the dust, while their masters beat time on muffled drums or scurry to catch the tourists' tossed rupees. The guides still quote, with a lyrical quiver, the famous Persian distich carved above an archway—"If Paradise there be on earth, it is here, it is here, it is here!" Physically nothing much has altered: but in the feeling of the crowds that wander through this old fortress you will sense something altogether new, something unique to the world in our time, and inspiriting to contemplate.

What incomparable crowds they are! What variety of face, costume, gesture, language, tone of voice! What proliferation of styles and costumes, dazzling yellow toga beside pin-stripe reach-me-down, slinky sari after bouffant skirt! Here is a man from the northern frontiers, squat and Mongoloid, swarthy and slant-eyed, wearing an amulet around his neck and smelling of sweat and musk. Here, in the shadow of the Lion Tower, two Muslim women stand breathing heavily, shrouded from head to foot in suffocating cloth, and peering out at the world through a tight-meshed grille about the eyes. Here are dark-skinned people from the south, from Madras and the Coromandel Coast, and here are gigantic Sikhs, whiskered and turbaned, and here are stunted shrivelled folk from the central flatlands. Here are pilgrims from Assam and Kerala, Mysore and West Bengal, from the buffer States of Nepal and Bhutan, from the distant island dependencies of Minicoy and Nicobar. A group of young soldiers clatters laughing by, their shirts emblazoned with military symbolisms, their ammunition boots striking sparks on the steps of the Pearl Mosque. An Indian patrician of the old school consults his guide-book beside the Royal Baths, wearing a jacket of impeccable cut and leaning gently on a shooting-stick. Perhaps a Buddhist priest stalks by, rake-thin in flowing saffron, or perhaps you hear behind your back a barked succession of irritable commands, and down the pathway a young man chivvies, like a shepherd with his silly sheep, a flock of Rajasthani women, chattering squeakily among themselves, hastening with a jerky barefoot motion, aflutter with orange cotton, and so hung about with ivory bracelets, silver bangles, necklaces, anklets, belts, charms and ear-pendants that they overtake you like a jiggling, tinkling orchestra, fading away towards the Delhi Gate in a long exotic diminuendo.

For this is an imperial city indeed, ruling a dizzy variety of peoples and provinces—Kutch to the Naga Hills, Arabian Sea to Chinese frontier. The sight-seers at the Red Fort are responding, like the Kremlin crowds, to all the pride of common ownership, to the slow swell of patriotism in a nation of a million diverse loyalties. But the distinction of Delhi is this: that these people are masters of their own contemplations. They have not come to the Red Fort in tagged and regimented groups, hectored by a State-trained educator. Nobody is going to brainwash them, or send them away for reorientation, or even tell them which mosaic to examine. To any autocracy, even the grandest, there is a second-rate, next-best, parochial right-hand side of the road, are the much-revered feeling, whether you are sensing it among the squabbling military juntas of today or the endless gossiping soirées of the Tolstoyan yesterday. This sensation will never nag you in Delhi. She is the capital of one of the poorest, most backward, most problem-ridden of all nations: but she is free, and she has style.

Lastly you must look at New Delhi, for there in the seat of Government you will glimpse the grandeur of the Indian experiment—not its intimacy, nor even its pathos, but its sweep, scale, risk and possibility. The British built New Delhi, and it remains the greatest memorial to an Empire that was mostly metaphysical —the only British relic, outside London, that has the tremor of power to it, like Baalbek in Lebanon, the pyramids of the Egyptians, the fearful jungle cities of the Aztecs and the Incas, or the Roman aqueducts lording it across Provence. New Delhi has the strut of inherited confidence, just beginning to sour, perhaps, into the flatulence of doubt. Here the British dismissed, for once, their rooted instinct for the rolling way, the crooked way, and abandoned themselves almost sensually to symmetry, size and splendour. There is undeniable glory to New Delhi: the very wealth, pride and energy that could build such a place has majesty. There is beauty to it, for of all the planned capitals, from Washington to Brasília, this is perhaps the most successful. There is nostalgia: gone, gone are the plumed English satraps of this city, the Viceroy among his attendant Indian gentlemen, the Etonian cavalry colonels at the garden parties, and today only King George V is left, all

alone and slightly elongated, beneath the tall cupola of his memorial. And there is a tinge of gentle irony to the place: "Liberty will not descend to a people," says an aphorism above one gate of Government, "a people must raise themselves to liberty."

But today the British shades of New Delhi, quietly retreating into the past, are only incidental to the fascination of the city. Today, if you stand on Raisina Hill, you will feel only a native grandeur, for in two short decades of independence this has become one of the pilot-capitals of the world. Look to the west, and you will see the enclaves of the foreign ambassadors, brilliant evidence of this Republic's sudden importance—the American Embassy resplendent in its moat, the British High Commission a huge compound of offices, villas and apartment blocks. Look to the east, and there arise the big new offices of Government, four-square and functional, filling in the gaps of Lutyens's grand design—for already this vast State has outgrown the imperial capital, as it leaps from one phase of history into another. Look behind you, and there stand the splendid lancers of the Presidential guard, languid but commanding, lofty but alert. Look in front, and there rolls away into the sandy distance the immense ceremonial mall, along which, on occasions of State festivity, the splendid troops of India march, horsemen gorgeously caparisoned, infantry lithe out of the northern hills.

And look to your left, and you will see the laboratory that is the real heart of Delhi—more vital than any desert reactor, nobler than any rocket workshop. There, in its pillared rotunda, half a mile round, sits the Parliament of India. It is the only properly democratic assembly between Athens and Tokyo, and one of the earth's political poles. It is a body often testy, often childish, sometimes arrogant, occasionally hypocritical. Sometimes its disputations make the Jeffersonians squirm and the eager sceptics scoff. But it is the very point and purpose of Delhi, and makes her a far greater capital today than she has ever been before, in all her incarnations. If her immense experiment succeeds—social revolution within a free but half-stunted society—then the whole democratic world can breathe more proudly and more confidently. If it fails, the grimmer philosophy of Communism, sweeping down from Russia and China like an energy of Tartars, will eventually master all Asia, and possibly all the world.

No wonder Delhi leaves you solemn, respectful and a little scared. She carries a millstone of history on her back, and she bears herself like a statesman of terrible responsibility, or an Atlas groaning beneath the hemispheres.

TAYA ZINKIN

from INDIA CHANGES!

IT HAS BEEN SAID that to know and understand India, you must go to the villages, here described by a sympathetic journalist.

THERE IS NO SUCH THING as a typical Indian village. In India there are over 558,000 villages, and they vary astonishingly from area to area. There are the smoky, filthy pigsties on stilts in which the Naga headhunters of Assam live; the prow-shaped, thatched Toda villages of Madras; the mud-walled fortresses of the Punjab; the rural cities of Gujerat, with their hundred-thousand-dollar, three-story mansions; the Ladakhi hill-cut houses, strangely akin to the creations of Frank Lloyd Wright; the houseboats of Kashmir with their floating vegetable gardens; the palm-matted bashas of Bengal; the neat little wooden houses of Travancore-Cochin; the scattered huts of the coast of Malabar; and the painted villages of Rajasthan, where charging elephants trample over sleeping lions and the blue smoke of prehistoric railway engines coats the mud walls.

In some villages, the houses have straw roofs; in others, the roofs are corrugated iron sheets; elsewhere again they are made of cool Mangalore tiles, raw mud bricks, or bamboo tubes. Some houses are huts with only one room; others are a maze of structures, with courtyard following courtyard and roof overlapping roof in unending succession. In Saurashtra, animals get pride of place in the inner courtyard, in front of the living room, next to the kitchen. Elsewhere, animals are housed on the ground floor, below their owners, or even are kept on rafters overhead. In some villages, the hearth is in the one room where people sit, eat, sleep, and keep stores; in many others, the hearth is outside, in the open, by the stack of cow-dung cakes.

By and large, Indian villages fall into two categories: Northern villages and Southern villages. The majority are nucleated villages, with the houses gathered close together, but dispersed villages are an exception dear to the hearts of individualistic aboriginals and the Indians of the coconut country in the far Southwest. Southern villages are, on the whole, clean and pleasant. Northern villages, which the hasty tourist sees because they are around Delhi and the Taj Mahal, are nearly always dirty and rarely pleasant, though some are prosperous. Yet, North or South, Telugu or Punjabi, Mahratta or Assamese, Hindu or Moslem, all Indian villages have certain features in common.

Indian villages have no shape; they are not picturesque like French villages, which cluster around a château or a church. India has had little feudalism in the Western sense and, since Hinduism has no real congregational worship, there is no great need for temples. Many villages do have temples, but few of them are well kept and some are mere shacks. There are of course a few magnificent and elaborate temples. These were built by kings as an expression of their faith or, as in Malabar, by the landed rich who wanted temples of their own to avoid hobnobbing with all and sundry in the house of the Lord. Even where there are temples in India, villages do not cluster around them, in the way they do around churches in the West.

As a rule, an Indian village presents no center of worship to the foreigner's eye. This is an illusion. An Indian village really swarms with temples of all kinds —important temples, small temples, old temples, new temples. To discover them, the foreigner must have the diviner's gift for detecting the hidden. How could he guess that the two bricks, smeared with cow dung, against the stump of the tree behind the hut on the right-hand side of the road, are the much-revered temple of a local godling who makes women bear sons and protects the village—all its castes, from top to bottom—from smallpox? Or that the stone at the entrance of the village is worshiped by the people in the neighboring houses? The stone looks like any old stone, greasy on top, with a few withered marigold petals scattered on the dust around it. The Westerner, accustomed to churches with a recognizable structure, has no way of guessing what every Indian infant knows: God is everywhere—in the stone, in the peepul tree, in the dung of the cow. It does not matter how, where, or under what name He is worshiped as long as His existence is remembered.

An Indian friend of mine in the Forest Department once complained bitterly that in his subdivision he had great difficulty shifting a boundary mark. The mark was a stone painted red, to which the villagers of the surrounding hills were in the habit of offering flowers and food. It did no good to tell them that the stone was only a landmark of the Forest Department. Each time the officer's men moved the boundary mark they ran grave risks from protesting villagers.

Indian villages are not planned. They spread jaggedly into their own fields as the population grows. That is why their houses straggle down a long main street in-

TAJ MAHAL, A WHITE MARBLE MAUSOLEUM BUILT BY SHAH JEHAN FOR HIS WIFE MUMTAZ, BESIDE THE JUMNA RIVER AT AGRA. IT WAS TO HAVE BEEN DUPLICATED IN BLACK MARBLE, FOR THE SHAH, ON THE OPPOSITE BANK, THE TWO JOINED BY A SILVER BRIDGE. BUT SHAH JEHAN WAS DEPOSED AND IMPRISONED BY HIS SON, AURANGZEB, WHO HAD OTHER USES FOR THE STATE REVENUES.

stead of circling around the well, which is the heart of the village. Indeed, though it may be half a mile or more from the newest house, the well is to an Indian village what the village green is to an English village.

Indian villages are not beautiful, except for those on the West Coast and in Rajasthan. They have no shaded alleys. The houses encroach messily on each other and on the gutters which serve as streets. There are neither flowers nor public gardens; at best, the lone blob of green of a papaya tree, sticking up in a corner next to a rubbish heap, relieves the monotony. There is no sewage system, not even a trench latrine, and refuse is often dumped on the path, right in front of the house. In Rajasthan, flayed carcasses sometimes rot in the village itself; nobody seems to mind. In Northern India, even the sewage pits of individual houses may overflow into the street, vomiting their stench and germs to the delight of flies, pie dogs, and rats.

Many villages are in urgent need of repair. They are as messy and dirty as backward Savoy villages, but lack their solidity, because in India durable construction materials such as brick, stone, or hard wood have, in most areas, been reserved for temples and palaces. That is why the Indian village is not old; its decrepitude is not because of its years but the junkiness of its building materials, the rigor of the climate, and the lack of skill of its masons. There are exceptions, of course, such as the houses of peasant landlords in Gujerat and Malabar, but on the whole, village houses are built of junk.

Indeed, the only thing an Indian village has in common with an American village or town is its comparative newness. The oldest house in a Gujerat village, where they often build in stone, will be perhaps one hundred and fifty years old and an object of great local pride because of its age.

Many of the houses beyond repair have been abandoned haphazardly in mid-village, to the delight of children who use them for games of hide-and-seek and slide-down-my-bottom. They also serve the men, who have in them facilities of an almost French ubiquity but with more privacy. Such conveniences are necessary, for the Indian village has no toilet facilities—a situation that the Community Projects are only beginning to change.

As a rule, there are no roads, drains, or lavatories (public or private); also there is normally no running water. No matter how prosperous it is, every household has to get its water from a well—which is often between twenty and seventy feet deep—in buckets or jars. This means an endless trek for the women, to and fro through mud and dirt between their house and the well—unless they have a well in their courtyard.

Even carrying three copper pots at a time on her head, a woman may make many trips to provide the day's water for her household.

The Indian village has none of the community life that centers around the castle, the church, or the bakery in Europe, or around the drug store in America. Nor does an outsider immediately see any signs of trade. Small villages have no shop at all, and only big villages have a store. Often the only place for trade is a few stalls or a local weekly market. There is no Main Street, no shopping center. Most villagers trade at market places or with itinerant vendors who amble along with their wares—glass bangles, plastic toys or combs, colored lithographs, glass beads, bright ribbons, and pocket mirrors—dangling from trays precariously suspended around their waists. In the dingy stall of the merchant the villager may buy rusty nails, indigenous cigarettes rolled in tree leaves, stale cigarettes in packets of ten, grains, pulses, and spices in little mounds of color, betel nuts and pan leaves (India's pungent chewing gum), coarse salt, cheap mill-made cloth, kerosene and cooking oil in dirty bottles, soap, and matches—but little else. For the rest, either the villager is self-sufficient or he goes to market once a month in the nearest big village, which is perhaps a mile away across plowed fields. However, the mud track, which is the main "road," may well snake along two or three miles before reaching it.

The things the villager does regularly in the village —such as getting a shave, having his plow repaired, or buying a pot—are most likely paid for in kind after the harvest. If he needs money he has no bank to approach about a loan; he borrows from his better-off neighbor or from a moneylender, who is a merchant or a rich peasant.

The village has no movie house, no hotel, no restaurant, and no railroad station. It has no amenities in the Western sense, and a foreigner in an Indian village is entirely at the mercy of local hospitality for even a drop of water or a place to sit down. Nowadays the Indian village has a school. Bigger villages have a post office, and many smaller ones have a letter box. If a village is really big, it will have a radio set and it may have a dispensary or a weekly fair or a whole street of shops.

The villager is not wholly cut off from the world. He makes an occasional visit to the local *tetsil* (county) town to sell his crops, and while there he listens to a newspaper being read aloud or goes to a movie. Perhaps he enjoys the movies so much because he goes only once in three months. At home he must rely on wandering minstrels, beggars, neighbors' disputes, and family ceremonies to keep him amused.

It is easy to see why outsiders who do not know

them might consider Indian villages squalid beyond words, poor beyond despair. Yet, for those who know, it is a good place to live. It has beauty, friendliness and fun, an organization of its own and a place for everybody.

The village may be dirty, but the people are clean and the houses are swept. The average Indian bathes every day or every other day, and, in the South, almost everyone washes his clothes every day or, at the very least, twice a week. There are exceptions, of course. In Rajasthan and Saurashtra, people bathe only once a week or once a fortnight, while the Ladakhis are bathed only twice in a lifetime: when they are born and before they are cremated. Because soap is new and not yet fully accepted, many people bathe with plain water, gram flour, pumice stone, mud, or soap nut; they save soap for ceremonial occasions.

As for the houses, they are swept at least once a day with a broom made of sticks. This is a less efficient tool than a vacuum cleaner, for it only displaces dust, but it leaves few cobwebs. Every day the kitchen floor is smeared with a mixture of mud, water, and cow dung, whose very real antiseptic properties are appreciated in India as they are not in the West. The cooking vessels, too, are spotless, although they are cleaned with ashes or mud. The Pasteurian revolution has not yet reached India.

To an outsider the village looks formless—not so to the initiated. The street—that dawdling foot path which zigzags haphazardly from one rubbish heap to the next—has a rigorous organization. In one street live only the potters of the village. They may not all make pots, but they all belong to the potter caste. The Brahmins have their streets; the peasants, theirs. A bit of field separates the touchable village from the Harijan, or untouchable. The Harijans have the same rigid organization: the sweepers' street, the leatherworkers' street, and, far removed, the carrion-eating basketweavers' street—the lowest of the low.

The village is organized in accordance with the implicit but formidable tradition of caste. A Brahmin cannot eat with a lower caste; a barber will not take water from a leatherworker; and a barber will feel free of pollution, whether he is polluting or being polluted, only in the company of another barber. It is, therefore, sensible to put likes together—not only to make eating and drinking easy, but also to reduce the snubs of a rigidly stratified world for a growing child.

This is not the only organization in the village. There is also organization within each house, camouflaged in a maze of inner and outer courtyards and sheds. The houses may follow a wavering building line and their walls may have cracks, but inside all is busy order. In one corner of the courtyard, the youngest child swings in a hammock in time with the rhythmic pounding of the grain. "Hong ho" go the tall, polished wooden poles, which fall in perfect rhythm from the hands of the two women. The husk is tossed up from a deep hole as the bouncing beam is thrust down. "Grum, grum" go the heavy stone wheels as, turned by the twist of an expert hand, they grind their rough surfaces together, spilling the nourishing dust of the flour around this homemade mill, ancient as civilization itself. In another corner, above the stacks of wooden implements—the hoe, the plow, the pitchfork—a patch of bright red peppers drying in the heat makes, with a lonely sunflower or a yellowy white cluster of frangipane, a cheerful dash of color.

Inside, the walls are decorated with tinsel, a peacock-feather fan, a beaded fringe, a gaudy one-cent colored lithograph of Mahatma Gandhi or Hanuman (the monkey god) or Krishna playing his flute. In the alcove, a shabby photograph of an ancestor, garlanded with dead marigolds, is safely locked in a hollow behind glass. And in the farthest corner of all, away from the light, there are jars of baked clay, dried mud, or matted bamboos, large enough to hide not only Ali Baba but also his forty thieves. The family savings are the grain and seed stored in these giant jars from year to year. The only other source of savings is the gold and silver ornaments which the women wear. Silver in crude but artistic designs drips from the necks, ankles, toes, arms, waists, ears, and even the noses and the hair of the younger women. Babies have silver belts around their naked bellies. The whole household jingles and tinkles to the song of its savings.

The house or hut is not comfortable. There is no furniture. There are, at most, the few nuptial trunks in which the dowry came and which are now kept under a string cot. Most people sleep on the ground or on matting; the string cot is for the sick or to sit on in the shade during the day. Vegetables that are drying for storage, or anything that must be kept safe from ants and mud, may be on the cot.

The individuality of each home comes from the earth-colored frescoes so frequently painted on its mud walls. An airplane, childish in outline, outmoded in design, perilously tilts its nose next to a window; or a bird on a twig cheers up the main wall. At times the patterns are geometric, if only the repetition of tapering fingers, fanwise around the walls, at eye level. The ingenuity of the women is never exhausted. They spend hours, indeed days, decorating the hut with their imaginative art.

Even the well, such a wearying distance from the hut, is a center of beauty when the women gather to gossip. There you can see the unerring beauty of the

Indian color sense. Only a village lass would dare mix in her clothes the colors of Rouault, of Matisse, and of Marie Laurencin: a bright deep violet skirt; a lemon green scarf, fuschia dotted, with a hint of absinthe on maroon; gold or silver tinsel on the hem; and somewhere a shy, tender pink. The close-fitting brassiere is more daring still—black and burnt sienna, with a splash of azure, just on the tip. And below this Impressionist's rainbow is the lovely golden brown of a body that has never run to fat. Silver bells jingle around slim ankles, the sun glistens on the copper pots high on her head giving the appearance of a triple-tiered crown. Her hips sway, her head is erect, her body is straight with the straightness of a sugar cane; she treads barefoot with the bearing of a queen.

Beauty in an Indian village does not end with the women. There are the children, dark imps with huge, velvety eyes. And there is the damp muzzle of the new-born water-buffalo calf, licking a fly away with his pale blue tongue. In the distance are the creaking music of the bullock cart's wheels, the hunter's call of its driver, the colorful turbans of the men.

Life in the village is so warm and comfortable that the villager leaves it only when he is pushed by hunger or ambition. But, even if he becomes a big man in the city, he retains a deep loyalty for his village, for no success, however great, can re-create for him the warmth of belonging that he has left behind.

MARGARET PARTON

from The Leaf and the Flame

ANOTHER sympathetic journalist, perhaps the best that America has sent to India, sees and records non-village India.

LAST YEAR, when my ever-eager mother and her friend Lucile visited us in India, they too stayed in Jaipur, but under somewhat different circumstances. For weeks they had sought and sometimes found spiritual values among our Indian friends, but they had seen little of the blazing color of India, the old feudal splendor which still exists. Eric and I decided that Jaipur would be just the place for them, and mentioned the matter to an official in the State's Ministry. Since there was no hotel in Jaipur, it would be necessary, we knew, for them to stay at the State Guest House, where a minor functionary and a few servants would probably be assigned to look after their comfort and entertainment.

In due time an invitation arrived from His Highness Lieutenant-General Saramd-i-Rajahai Hindustan Raj Rajendra Sri Maharajah Dhiraj Sir Sawai Man Singhji Bahadur, thirty-ninth Ruler of Jaipur, inviting the two ladies to come and stay not at the guest house, but at his palace! Knowing that there had been some misunderstanding about the importance (or possibly ages) of the two ladies, we packed them off by train and awaited their report with only mild trepidation.

"Well, it was very interesting, but not quite what we expected," Mother said when she returned to the Cecil. "We were met at the station by a palace official and a chauffeur who drove us to the palace. We had adjoining rooms about the size of a basketball court, with marble floors and chandeliers and huge four-poster beds. They told us that cocktails would be served on the terrace at eight o'clock and Please Dress. I'm certainly glad I took your advice and brought along that nice Macy evening dress, although it's years since I wore one. Well, we went down a great flight of marble steps to the terrace, and there was the Maharajah and a lot of elegant-looking young people in saris and tuxedos, and some very good martinis, too.

"Well, the Maharajah is an Indian, so naturally I began asking him about the Bhagavad-Gita, and telling him of my own deep spiritual interest in Hindu philosophy. He was very polite, but he looked a little bewildered, and after awhile he began talking about his polo ponies and some kind of automobile in which he seemed interested. I believe he called them sports cars. Dinner was at ten o'clock, and the champagne was lovely, but everyone talked about horses. It all seemed very odd, considering that we were in India, where everyone is supposed to be so spiritual.

"The next morning, just after I had finished dressing, I saw a mouse in my bedroom. Well, you know how terrified I am of mice, so I screamed and jumped on the bed. After awhile a servant came in, but he couldn't understand me, and just looked at me as if I were simply another silly foreigner doing morning exercises. I kept squeaking and imitating a mouse, and finally he grinned and went away. A long time passed, and then another servant came with a great big cage about the size of a bird cage, and put it on the floor.

"We went sight-seeing all day with one of the palace officials and didn't get back until evening. Sure

JAIPUR, INDIA.

enough, there was a mouse in the cage! Then I called a servant, but he only shook his head and went away. Then another one came and explained to me that the job of taking away mice belonged to one particular caste. Maybe it was the untouchables, but I can't remember. Anyway, it was Sunday, he said, and those men were all off duty. Nobody else would do it, so I would have to wait until the next day for the mouse to be removed from my room.

"That night we weren't invited downstairs. But cocktails and a delicious dinner were served on the balcony outside our rooms. It was very luxurious, and very peaceful.

"I knew, though, that I couldn't sleep with that

DETAIL OF WALL AT JAIPUR.

mouse in the room, squeaking and running around in the cage. So I waited until long after midnight, when the palace was finally quiet. Then I pushed the cage with my toe over to the door. I opened the door and peered out along the corridor. There was nobody around, just moonlight and shadows. So I pushed the cage down the corridor to the top of the long flight of marble steps which lead down to the terrace where the Maharajah drinks his martinis. Then I gave the cage a big boot out into the moonlight. And that was the last I saw of it. I slept beautifully, and the next day we left. All in all, it was a very interesting time, as I said."

We, too, are having an interesting if not quite so exotic a time in Jaipur, which we are seeing for the first time. "A rose-red city, half as old as time" . . . No, that was Petra. Yet the line seems appropriate here, where houses and palaces are painted a lovely rosy pink, decorated with white scrolls and geometric designs and flowers. And where the feudal traditions of pageantry, opulence, fighting, luxurious mustaches, glorious turbans, and turned-up toes of golden slippers go back several thousand years. Now the Congress government has very properly taken over, and the writing is on the wall for all the princes of the Rajasthan desert. Yet the glamour lingers.

We saw the mingling of the old and the new on our first day here, when His Highness held a durbar (a formal reception) in his marble-pillared throne room. Around the great room, open on one side to a magnificent garden, stood tall guards in cream-colored uniforms, with blue-and-gold sashes and turbans with a cockade of silver plumes. The Maharajah, who presided from his crimson-and-gold throne, wore tight black trousers with a red stripe, a white jacket festooned with gold, and a glittering turban of red and gold, with a gold cockade. The old Rajput nobles appeared in flowing brocades and brilliant turbans of scarlet and orange, lime and pink. Each dignified, curly-mustached old gentleman carried a long curved sword symbolic of the ancient fighting traditions of Rajput nobility.

Then arrived the Indian Congressmen, representing the people of free India; the politicians and bureaucrats who actually govern Jaipur today. They straggled in late, a procession of fat, unshaven, graceless men in wrinkled and often dirty white shirts and flapping dhotis, bare feet in dusty sandals, and crumpled Gandhi caps.

That night His Highness gave a reception for two thousand guests in the gardens of his City Palace. On a bluff high above the city, the old, deserted Tiger Palace was festooned with lights and seemed to float in the darkness among the stars. Down in the gardens where we were, fountains played, many of them illuminated in yellow, red, and green. All the trees were hung with strings of blue and green Christmas lights. At the far end of the garden a little orchestra played soft Indian music, and at a distance peacocks mourned among clipped cypresses. Drinks flowed for several hours, and at eleven o'clock a buffet supper of English and Indian food was served from long tables. Then a carpet was spread at one end of the lawn, chairs were re-arranged, and for an hour we listened to nautch girls, sedate in silver saris, sing plaintive songs of ancient Rajput love. After the first ten minutes I thought them a deadly bore, for they danced only by waving a languid arm now and then, and to Western ears their songs all sounded the same. However, now I can say I've seen dancing girls at a prince's palace.

Perhaps because they disapprove of lavish hospitality in times of austerity, perhaps because alcohol was served, the Congressmen who had been invited did not appear. And I must admit that I was glad that for this one enchanted evening the good, colorless men of India's future had left the field to the possibly wicked but definitely colorful men of India's past. The Congressmen, one hopes, will give the peasants bread; the princes gave them only circuses. Inevitably, the princes and all their glory must vanish. But how the recalcitrant heart mourns for the disappearance of pageantry!

We have been staying for four days at the Maharajah's State Guest House, where white peacocks wander over the green lawns, and food and drinks are free. A lovely arrangement. And we have done so many things I'm dizzy. We watched His Highness play polo. We wandered through the city and talked to people. We looked at jewels in a famous shop patronized by princes; sat cross-legged on cushions on the floor and let streams of pearls and rubies trickle through our fingers. We didn't buy any, but we dreamed a little over the sixteenth-century enameled necklaces.

One morning we went up the steep hill to the old Palace of Amber, once the capital of Jaipur, but now uninhabited. It is still kept in a perfect state of preservation, and we wandered for hours under marble archways and among elegant, airy rooms where walls inlaid with tiny mirrors could reflect the light of a single candle a thousand million times. Before we left, we took off our shoes and socks, watches and belts—anything associated with leather—and visited the white marble temple of Shila Mata, the presiding deity of the House of Jaipur, where grave young priests in scarlet robes rang golden bells.

This afternoon we watched an elephant-keeper painting complicated floral designs on the trunk, head, and legs of one of his charges in preparation for the great religious procession which was held this evening. And just at sunset we climbed a winding staircase to an assigned place high on the City Palace battlements, and watched the procession.

Blazing with color and light, led by three of His Highness's elephants in golden trappings, it wound through the city and finally passed below the royal box on the palace walls.

Following the elephants came twenty camels, twenty white horses, and finally one hundred men of the palace staff, all in red tunics and pink turbans. Behind them they pulled a chariot lighted by pink flares of phosphorescence. It bore the golden image of Gangor, the goddess of plenty, in whose honor the procession is held. At the end came one hundred more men, each carrying an enormous black shield and a gleaming silver sword.

Lights blazed, dust tinged by sunset and pink phosphorescence swirled above the marching men, the watching crowd shouted, the drums throbbed. With a final triumphant blast of conch horns the goddess and her attendants disappeared beyond a gate in the rosy palace walls.

There will be a few more processions in years to come, a few more garden parties. But not forever, and always with diminishing grandeur. The Maharajah, whose privy purse has been sharply cut, will sell off his elephants, for at the moment he owns fifteen, and each one costs a thousand dollars a month to maintain. The polo ponies, the court musicians, the mace-bearers, the dancing girls, and the sword-polishers will go.

With their disappearance will come democracy and a better way of life for the notoriously oppressed peasants of Rajasthan. It is all very good, very right. But also rather sad.

*   *   *

A strange sort of revelation came to me tonight.

We went to a small party given by an Indian journalist in a Connaught Circle restaurant, and afterwards, a few of us went up to his hotel room to talk and drink a little longer. We all knew each other very well, so it was easy to relax, to sit on the floor, to kick off the high-heeled sandals. One of the boys began singing Indian folk songs, while the rest of us clapped a soft accompaniment. In a corner Eric was teasing his best Indian friend about "Indian spirituality" and "moral superiority." Eric is the only Westerner I know who feels perfectly free to slap an Indian colleague on the back and say: "Oh, come off it old boy!" And they love it and laughingly admit that they were being a bit stuffy. Like most people, Indians enjoy being teased, if it is done with amiability and affection.

The room was filled with a warm yellow light and people. Most of the faces were brown, for Eric, another American, and I were the only Westerners. As we sang, my eyes ranged at first unconsciously, and then with deliberation, over the brown faces: wheat, honey, café-au-lait, rich cream, earthen, sun-ripened.

"Why, brown is the proper shade for a skin to be," I thought suddenly. I contemplated the American. He looked sick—unfinished. I looked at the Indians again. They looked healthy and absolutely right, as if Nature had finally found herself when she at last came to use the brown pigment.

On the way home I told the American that I had decided brown skins were more beautiful than white. He looked at me strangely. "So you've discovered that too," he said. "I've known it for a long time."

ARNOLD TOYNBEE

from BETWEEN OXUS AND JUMNA

THE DISTINGUISHED historian on tour in Rajasthan and Kashmir.

"YOUR LECTURE tonight at Udaipur is at 7:30 P.M." were the professor's first words as he greeted us at Udaipur airport. No lecture had been on my programme, so I had come unprovided with notes, and indeed with a subject. And it was not helpful when the professor went on to say that the Commissioner would be delighted to hear me lecture on any subject in the world that I might choose. Well, 7:30 was still

nine hours away, and Udaipur airport is 15 miles out of Udaipur on the Chittor road. It was now or never for Chittor; and we headed the professor's car in that direction. The distance was 68 miles each way. So there would be just time to snatch some lunch at Chittor railway-station, mount the citadel, climb the Tower of Victory, make the round of the walls, and have half an hour to spare at Udaipur for rest, bath, and lucubration before the lecture-hour overtook me.

This dash to Chittor and back would have been worth while just for the sight of the intervening country, even if Chittor fort had sunk below the ground while we were on our way. The southern fringe of Rajasthan is the moistest and greenest strip of this semi-desert country. Here there are running streams and continuous fields of wheat and millet. It gives a foretaste of Rajasthan's southern neighbour Gujerat, of which I had had a glimpse thirty-one years ago. In this southern clime the harvest had already been reaped, and, everywhere, men and women were winnowing the grain from the chaff. The purples and yellows of the women's saris outshone the colours worn in the other parts of Rajasthan that I had visited. Gaily piebald sheep and goats were feasting on the stubble-fields. Altogether, it was a cheerful scene.

Rajasthan is a low tableland ruckled into ridges or twisted up into clumps of mountains here and there. Wherever the surface has been tilted and tormented in these ways, there is water. And, wherever there is water, there is an outburst of life: a fortress, a palace, a city, a shrine, or a cluster of shops in which beautiful things are not merely sold but are made. Forty or fifty miles out from Udaipur airport, the ground began to undulate and break into a spray of jagged rocks, and then foot-hills and mountains began to appear on the horizon. After a time, through a gap in the hills, a long, flat-topped mountain rose into view. Could this, by chance, be the fort of Chittor? I knew that it was huge, but I had not been prepared for a fortress on this scale. Yet, sure enough, this great ridge was the goal of our present journey; and, before we reached the railway, we could see the massive man-made walls crowning the top of the long mountain's precipitous flank. The length of this Rajput acropolis is two and a half miles, and its breadth, at its broadest, must be half a mile at least. So, on the wall-girt summit, there is room not only for palaces, temples, towers, and tanks, but also for fields. In fact, the summit could yield enough bread and water to sustain a frugal Rajput garrison for years. A river, flowing round the foot of the great rock, provides a natural moat for about half the perimeter. When the local Rajput ruler defied the Mughal emperor Akbar, he believed that Chittor fort was impregnable. But this mediaeval-minded Rajput strategist had not reckoned with the Mughal invader's Turkish art of gunnery. Akbar raised mounds high enough to allow his artillery to play upon the walls, and it played havoc. The walls were breached; the fort was stormed; for the Rajputs it was an undreamed-of catastrophe.

It was a catastrophe, but not a crushing one. Forbidden to re-fortify Chittor, the Rajput rulers of Mewar did better. In a remoter corner of their territory, they conjured up, out of nothing, a new capital city that foiled the Mughals at the next trial of strength. Udai-

pur, like Chittor, depends on natural defenses supplemented by human art; but here Nature has been enlisted to serve quite a different strategic plan. Instead of being planted, like Chittor fort, on the top of a mountain, Udaipur city nestles in a basin surrounded by a continuous mountain-wall. The approach to Udaipur from the airport is like the approach to Alice Springs. The road seems to be running, full tilt, at this mountain rampart. What will happen to our radiator —and to ourselves—when we ram the rock? And then, at the last moment, a cleft opens and we drive through it. At Udaipur the cleft is bridged by a fortified gate, and, on either side, battlemented curtain-walls climb the mountain-flanks up to a level where these become too precipitous to give a would-be invader any foothold. Here Akbar's victory at Chittor was avenged upon Akbar's great-grandson Aurangzeb. From this gate, Aurangzeb's invading army was flung back. Our car, however, was not being denied entry; so we shot through the gate, whizzed past a flurry of grey monkeys, and found ourselves inside the mountain-girt basin, with the first of Udaipur's local man-made lakes soon making its appearance on our left as we drove towards the city.

This lake-ringed Rajput capital has been painted, photographed, and described so many times in the course of the last 150 years that a repetition would be boring. Of course I have carried away with me an unforgettable mental vision of sound and colour: the women beating the clothes that they have washed; the bathers splashing in the water; the water-level view from the water-palaces, and the kite-level view from the city-palace roof. But what impressed me most was not the beauty of the scene or the massiveness and sumptuousness of the buildings. It was the indomitableness of the people. Like ants whose nest has been destroyed, they turned to, without pausing, to build another. The fall of Chittor was the signal for Udaipur to rise. The Rajput princes who gave the word of command were figures from the ancient world, and, with the rest of the ancient world, they are being swept out of the swiftly changing India of our day. But the people who translated those formidable commands into living realities are still on the map. These twentieth-century descendants of the sixteenth-century builders of Udaipur will surely make their mark on our new "One World" that is now in the act of arising.

*   *   *

When you have crossed the Gilgit suspension-bridge and have turned up the Hunza Valley, you are heading for the Pamirs and for Sinkiang. But, even today, a jeep will not take you the whole way. Evenutally the jeep-road will turn into a pony-road, the pony-road

Life on the river in Srinagar, Kashmir.

A MOUNTAIN MEADOW IN THE HIMALAYAS, KASHMIR.

into a yak-road, and the yak-road into a foot-road. I took no more than a taste of even the jeep-road. We followed it, out of Gilgit, for about 40 miles, till it brought Rakaposhi into view. Rakaposhi stands 25,550 feet high, and it has a lovely shape—as individual as that of a living body. After sighting Rakaposhi, we turned back. But those first 40 miles have given me a notion of what the rest of the way must be like.

The Hunza River behaves as most rivers do in a gorge. It flings itself against one precipice and, rebounding from it, hits the opposite precipice; and it repeats this alternating movement any number of times. At each place where the river lashes round a precipice's foot, there is no room for a road at river-level. The only way of making a road here is to scoop it out of the precipice's face. And no limit is set to the height at which the road-cutter is to apply his chisel. He studies the whole face of the cliff from top to bottom,

and he will choose the least unfavourable altitude, however high this may carry the road above the valley-bottom.

This road is designed for jeeps, and for nothing even just one size bigger. The overarching rocks have been cut away just high enough to clear a travelling jeep's roof. The roadway has been built out just wide enough to make room, between the upper and the lower precipice, for a jeep's two pairs of wheels. The road's outer edge is carried on dry-stone walling. The lowest courses are laid, Heaven knows how, on the merest vestige of a ledge. Where even this is lacking, a beam is laid between one slightly projecting rock and another, and the dry-stone courses are founded on that. Where there is no foot-hold for beam-ends, a wooden bridge is thrown across the abyss, to join one stretch of dry-stone with the next. One cannot see the structure of the road immediately below one's advancing wheels,

YOU HAVE A FRIEND UP IN KATHMANDU, NEPAL.

Pagodas of Kathmandu.

and ignorance is bliss. Unfortunately the road twists and turns round the cliff's gnarled face; and, at some points, this gives one a broadside pre-view of what is coming to one within the next few seconds. When it does come, and the bridge-boards clatter and sing as the jeep trundles over them, one's heart is in one's mouth. It is a relief to find onself borne up again by a dry-stone wall, even if its foundations are exiguous.

When jeep meets donkey, they must feel their way past each other at one of those rare points at which the road has a foot or two's surplus width. The most dangerous donkeys are those that are coming down to Gilgit with a great beam of wood slung on either side of the pack-saddle. When they turn sidewise in a fit of nerves at the jeep's approach, the beams swing ponderously across the road. They are ponderous enough to sweep a jeep over the edge if they were to give it a slap on the cheek.

What happens when jeep meets jeep on this single-track jeep-way? Well, we had the experience. Just, but only just, after we had surmounted the highest and most hair-raising hump of all, we sighted, ahead of us, some way down below, another jeep travelling in the opposite direction. At that sight, our driver did the right thing: he accelerated. We dashed across a shingle-ledge over which a waterfall was gushing out of the foot of a miniature glacier, and so managed, just in time, to draw in at a point where we could leave room for the approaching jeep to pass us.

What would have happened if our two jeeps had met half a mile farther back? I can think of only one solution. We should have had to draw lots, heave the losing jeep over the brink, and let its crew crawl through between the winning jeep's wheels (jeeps have a high clearance). They could then have continued their journey alive, though on foot.

It is difficult to describe the Hunza Valley jeep-road without making it appear to be more dangerous than it really is. But no description could do justice to the dangerousness of the pony-road which the jeep-road has recently replaced. When, at the turning-point of our journey, I had taken my fill of gazing at Rakaposhi, my eye was caught by a set of scars up aloft on the flank of the precipice on the opposite side of the river. "What is that?" "Oh, that is the old pony-road, now fallen out of use." Try to imagine it: the fifty days' journey along that cornice from Srinagar to Kashghar. The pioneer explorer of those ledges ranks with the pioneer navigator of the seas. He, too, must have been built of *robur et aes triplex*.

HEINRICH HARRER

from SEVEN YEARS IN TIBET

ESCAPED from a British prisoner-of-war camp in northern India, Heinrich Harrer stayed in Tibet until forced to flee from the Chinese Communists, in 1950.

I HAD ALWAYS wanted to get to know the life of a monastery from the inside. Up to now, like any other pilgrim, I had enjoyed only fleeting glances at the temples and gardens. My friends took me to one of the numerous standard-pattern stone houses, where I was given Spartan lodgings. Pema, a monk who was soon to take his final examinations and already had pupils of his own, acted as my guide to the monastic city and explained to me the layout and organization. No comparison can be drawn between this and any of our religious institutions. Behind these cloister walls the hands of Time's clock seem to have been put back a thousand years; there is nothing to show that one is living in the twentieth century. The thick gray walls of the buildings have an age-old appearance, and the overpowering smell of rancid butter and unwashed monks has sunk deep into the stonework.

Every house has from fifty to sixty inhabitants and is divided into tiny cells. There is a kitchen on every floor and plenty of food to eat. The average monk has no other mundane satisfaction, but the more intelligent ones buoy themselves up with the prospect of reaching high positions to reward their zealous studies. They have no private property except for their butter lamps and an icon, or maybe an amulet box. A simple bed is the only concession to comfort. Absolute obedience is the rule. The students enter the monastery as children and immediately don the red cowl, which they are to wear for the rest of their lives. During the first five years they have to perform the most menial services for their teachers. The intelligent ones learn how to read and write and are admitted to examinations. Only a few succeed in passing out from one grade into another, and most of them remain all their lives in the servant class. The elect are those who after studying the teaching of Buddha for thirty or forty years are able to pass the final tests. They are then qualified for appointment to the highest offices in the

Church. The monasteries are the high schools for religious education, and the staff of all purely religious institutions is chosen from their graduates. The monastic officials of the government received their education in the Tsedrung School.

The final examinations of the monastic schools are held once a year in public in the cathedral. From the whole of Tibet only twenty-two candidates are admitted to the examination. After a severe oral test held under the auspices of the Dalai Lama's own teachers, the five best candidates are promoted to the highest monastic grade. The student who passes first may become a hermit and devote himself to religious exercises, or he may enter public life with the possibility of one day becoming regent. This happens rarely, because that high post is usually reserved for Incarnations, but cases have occurred in which a man of the people—neither a noble nor a Living Buddha—has been appointed to this great office. The last time this happened was in 1910 when the thirteenth Dalai Lama fled to India before the invading Chinese, and a delegate had to be appointed to represent him.

The ten thousand monks of Drebung are divided into groups, each of which has its own temple and garden. Here they spend the morning hours in communal religious exercises, after which they get their butter tea and soup, only returning to their houses for study in the afternoon. However, they have enough free time to take walks and play simple games. They are also allowed to cook any supplementary food they may receive from their own communities. The groups are organized as far as possible according to their places of origin. In some houses you will find only Mongolians or Nepalese, or students from a particular town such as Shigatse.

Within the monastery, of course, no living creature may be killed, but the cold climate makes it necessary to eat some meat: so the communities send supplies of dried yak meat, and it must be said, fresh meat is often to be had in one of the neighboring villages.

In addition to free food and lodging the monks receive a little pocket money derived from government grants and the gifts of pilgrims. However, when a monk possesses outstanding gifts, he generally finds a patron among the nobles or the wealthy tradespeople. The Church in Tibet is very rich, owning, as it does, most of the land, and the revenues of enormous estates are enjoyed by the monasteries. Every monastery has its own dealer, who procures provisions and other necessities. One would hardly believe what enormous sums are spent on the upkeep of the monasteries and their inmates. I once helped a monk with his accounts and noted that during the first month of the year, which all the monks spend in Lhasa, the government supplied them with three tons of tea and fifty tons of butter, in addition to pocket money to the value of something over £40,000.

The red-cowled forms are not all gentle and learned brothers. Most of them are rough, tough fellows for whom the whip is not discipline enough. The worst of them belong to the unauthorized but tolerated organization of the Dob-Dobs, or monkish soldiery. They wear a red arm band and blacken their faces with soot. In their belts they stick a huge key which they can use as a cosh or a missile and they often have a sharp cobbler's knife in their pockets. Many of them are well-known bullies. Their gait is provocative and they are quick to strike. Sensible people give them a wide berth. In the war against the Chinese Communists they formed a battalion which gained a reputation for courage. In peacetime, too, they have opportunities for getting rid of their superfluous energy, as the Dob-Dobs of the different monasteries are always at war with one another. It is fair to add that their differences are not always settled by violence, and that some of their pugnacity is expended in athletic contests between rival monasteries. Drebung is usually the victor, having a larger choice of athletes than its competitors. As a former sports instructor I used often to go to Drebung, and the monks were always glad to have me taking part in their training. This was the only place in Tibet where I found men with athletic figures and trained muscles.

The great cloisters of Drebung, Sera, and Ganden—the three Pillars of the State—play a decisive role in the political life of Tibet. Their abbots, together with eight government officials, preside over the National Assembly. No decision is taken without the assent of these clerics, who naturally are interested, first and foremost, in the supremacy of the monasteries. Their intervention has prevented the realization of many progressive ideas. At one time they looked on Aufschnaiter and me as thorns in their flesh, but when they saw we had no political ambitions and that we fitted ourselves into the customs of the land and carried out undertakings from which they, too, profited, they withdrew their opposition to us.

The cloisters are, as I have said, the high schools of the Church. For that reason every lama—and there are more than a thousand of them in Tibet—must be educated in a monastery. These Incarnations are a constant attraction for pilgrims, who come in thousands to visit them and receive their blessing.

Even during the Dalai Lama's visit to Drebung these Incarnations attended all the ceremonies and sat in the front seats—a regular concourse of the gods! Meanwhile, a religious discussion was held every day in the shady cloister gardens between the ruler and one of the abbots. This is one of the most intimate acts in the religious life of Lamaism, and I never had the slightest hope of being allowed to witness it.

However, one day as I was breakfasting with Lobsang, he asked me if I would like to come with him. I owe it to this unexpected gesture on his part that I was privileged to witness a drama which no other person of another faith has certainly ever witnessed. As I was in the company of the Dalai Lama's brother no one thought of preventing me from entering the sequestered garden. A strange scene unfolded itself. In front of a dark grove of trees a great multitude of red-cowled monks, perhaps two thousand of them, squatted on the gravel, while from a high place the Dalai Lama preached from Holy Writ. For the first time I heard his clear boyish voice. He spoke without any embarrassment and with the assurance of a grown man. This was his first public appearance. The fourteen-year-old boy had been studying for many years and now his knowledge was being tested before a critical audience. This first appearance might have fateful consequences. It is true that he would never be allowed to renounce his prescribed career, but his performance that day would show whether he was destined to be the instrument of the monks or their ruler. Not all of his predecessors had been as able as the fifth and the thirteenth Dalai Lamas. Many of them remained throughout their lives puppets in the hands of the men who had trained them, and the destiny of the country was controlled by the regents. People spoke of the intelligence of this boy as miraculous. It was said that he had only to read a book to know it by heart; and it was known that he had long taken an interest in all that happened in his country and used to criticize or commend the decisions of the National Assembly.

Now that it came to debating, I saw that his powers had not been exaggerated. The Dalai Lama sat down on the gravel, so as not to emphasize the superiority of his birth, while the abbot in whose monastery the discussion was taking place stood before him and punctuated his questions with the conventional gestures. The Dalai Lama answered all the questions which were put to him, even the "teasers," with readiness and good humor and was never for a moment disconcerted.

After a while the antagonists changed places and it was the Dalai Lama who put questions to the seated abbot. One could see that this was not an act prepared to show off the intelligence of the young Buddha; it was a genuine contest of wits in which the abbot was hard put to it to hold his own.

When the debate was over the young God-King mounted once more on to his golden throne and his mother, the only woman present, handed him tea in a golden cup. He stole a friendly glance at me as if to assure himself of my approval of his performance. For my part I was deeply impressed by what I had seen and heard, and felt genuine admiration for the presence of mind of this God-Boy from a humble family. He almost persuaded me to believe in reincarnation.

At the end of the religious debate everyone prayed in chorus. It sounded like a litany and lasted a long time. After that the Dalai Lama, supported by his abbots, returned to the palace. I had always wondered at the senile gait of the Dalai Lama, and now learned that it is part of the ritual and that all these different movements are prescribed. It is supposed to be an imitation of the gait of the Buddha, and at the same time is designed to enhance the dignity of the Dalai Lama.

* * *

After filming the scenes in the Norbulingka I was riding slowly home when, a little way out of Lhasa, I was overhauled by an excited soldier of the bodyguard, who told me that they had been looking for me everywhere and that I must at once ride back to the Summer Garden. My first thought was that the motion-picture apparatus was out of order, as I could hardly imagine that the young ruler, still a minor, would override all conventions and summon me directly to see him. I immediately turned around and was soon back at the Norbulingka, where everything was now peaceful and still. At the door of the yellow gate a couple of monks were waiting. As soon as they saw me they signaled to me to hurry up and when I reached them they ushered me into the Inner Garden. There Lobsang Samten awaited me. He whispered something to me and put a white scarf in my hand. There was no doubt about it. His brother was going to receive me.

I at once went toward the motion-picture theater, but before I could enter the door opened from the inside and I was standing before the Living Buddha. Conquering my surprise I bowed deeply and handed him the scarf. He took it in his left hand and with an impulsive gesture blessed me with his right. It seemed less like the ceremonial laying on of hands than an impetuous expression of feeling on the part of a boy who had at last got his way. In the theater three abbots were waiting with bowed heads—the guardians of His Holiness. I knew them all well and did not fail to observe how coldly they returned my greeting. They certainly did not approve of this intrusion into their domain, but they had not dared openly to oppose the will of the Dalai Lama.

The young ruler was all the more cordial. He beamed all over his face and poured out a flood of questions. He seemed to me like a person who had for years brooded in solitude over different problems, and now that he had at last someone to talk to, wanted to know all the answers at once. He gave me no time to think over my answers, but pressed me to go to the projector and put on a film which he had long been wanting to see. It was a documentary film of the capitulation of Japan. He came with me to the apparatus and sent the abbots into the theater to act as spectators.

I must have seemed slow and clumsy in handling the projector as he impatiently pushed me on one side and, taking hold of the film, showed me that he was a much more practiced operator than I was. He told me that he had been busy the whole winter learning how to work the apparatus and that he had even taken a projector to pieces and put it together again. I observed then, for the first time, that he liked to get to the bottom of things instead of taking them for granted. And so, later on, like many a good father who wishes to earn the respect of his son, I often spent the evening reviving my knowledge of half-forgotten things or studying new ones. I took the utmost trouble to treat every question seriously and scientifically, as it was clear to me that my answers would form the basis of his knowledge of the Western world.

His obvious talent for technical things astonished me at our first meeting. It was a masterly performance for a boy of fourteen years to take a projector to pieces and then to reassemble it without any help, for he could not read the English prospectus. Now that the film was running well, he was delighted with the arrangements and could not praise my work too highly. We sat together in the projecting room and looked at the picture through the peep holes in the wall and he took the greatest pleasure in what he saw and heard, often clasping my hands excitedly with the vivacity of youth. Although it was the first time in his life that he had been alone with a white man he was in no way embarrassed or shy. While he was putting the next film on the reel, he pressed the microphone into my hands and insisted on my speaking into it. At the same time he looked through the peep holes into the electrically lit theater in which his tutors sat on carpets. I could see how keen he was to observe the wondering faces of the worthy abbots when a voice should suddenly come out of the loudspeaker. I did not want to disappoint him so I invited the nonexistent public to remain in their seats as the next film would present sensational scenes from Tibet. He laughed enthusiastically at the surprised and shocked faces of the monks when they heard my cheerful, disrespectful tones. Such light, unceremonious language had never

been used in the presence of the Divine Ruler, whose gleaming eyes showed how he enjoyed the situation.

He made me turn the film which I had made in Lhasa while he looked after the switches. I was as curious as he was to see the results, as this was my first full-length picture. An expert could have picked out faults in it, but it seemed quite satisfactory to us. It contained my shots of the "little" New Year Festival. Even the formal abbots forgot their dignity when they recognized themselves on the flickering screen. There was a burst of laughter when a full-length picture appeared of a minister who had gone to sleep during the ceremonies. There was no malice in their laughter, for each of the abbots had sometimes to struggle to keep awake during these endless festivities. All the same the upper classes must have got to know that the Dalai Lama had witnessed his minister's weakness, for afterwards whenever I appeared with my camera, everyone sat up and posed.

The Dalai Lama himself took more pleasure than anyone in the pictures. His usually slow movements became youthful and lively and he commented enthusiastically on every picture. After a while I asked him to turn a film which he had made himself. He very modestly said that he would not dare to show his apprentice efforts after the pictures we had already seen. But I was anxious to see what subjects he had chosen for filming and persuaded him to put his roll onto the screen. He had not, of course, had a large choice of subjects. He had done a big sweeping landscape of the valley of Lhasa, which he turned much too fast. Then came a few underlighted long-distance pictures of mounted noblemen and caravans passing through Shö. A close-up of his cook showed that he would have liked to take film portraits. The film he had shown me was absolutely his first attempt and had been made without instructions or help. When it was over he got me to announce through the microphone that the performance was over. He then opened the door leading into the theater, told the abbots that he did not need them any more and dismissed them with a wave of the hand. It was again clear to me that here was no animated puppet, but a clear-cut individual will capable of imposing itself on others.

When we were alone we cleared away the films and put the yellow covers on the machines. Then we sat down on a magnificent carpet in the theater with the sun streaming through the open windows. It was fortunate that I had long acquired the habit of sitting cross-legged, as chairs and cushions are not included in the Dalai Lama's household furniture. At the start I had wished to decline his invitation to sit down, knowing that even ministers were not supposed to sit in his presence, but he just took me by the sleeve and pulled me down, which put an end to my misgiving.

He told me that he had long been planning this meeting as he had not been able to think of any other way of becoming acquainted with the outside world. He expected the regent to raise objections but he was determined to have his own way and had already thought up a rejoinder in case of opposition. He was resolved to extend his knowledge beyond purely religious subjects, and it seemed to him that I was the only person who could help him to do so. He had no idea that I was a qualified teacher, and had he known this it would probably not have influenced him. He asked my age and was surprised to learn that I was only thirty-seven. Like many Tibetans he thought that my "yellow" hair was a sign of age. He studied my features with childish curiosity and teased me about my long nose, which, though of normal size as we reckon noses, had often attracted the attention of the snub-nosed Mongolians. At last he noticed that I had hair growing on the back of my hands and said with a broad grin: "Henrig, you have hair like a monkey." I had an answer ready, as I was familiar with the legend that the Tibetans derive their descent from the union of their god Chenrezi with a female demon. Before coupling with his demon lover Chenrezi had assumed the shape of a monkey, and since the Dalai Lama is one of the Incarnations of this god, I found that in comparing me with an ape he had really flattered me.

With remarks such as this our conversation soon became unconstrained and we both lost our shyness. I now felt the attraction of his personality, which at our earlier fleeting contacts I had only guessed at. His complexion was much lighter than that of the average Tibetan. His eyes, hardly narrower than those of most Europeans, were full of expression, charm, and vivacity. His cheeks glowed with excitement, and as he sat he kept sliding from side to side. His ears stood out a little from his head. This was a characteristic of the Buddha and, as I learned later, was one of the signs by which as a child he had been recognized as an incarnation. His hair was longer than is customary. He probably wore it so as a protection against the cold of the Potala. He was tall for his age and looked as though he would reach the stature of his parents, both of whom had striking figures. Unfortunately, as a result of much study in a seated posture with his body bent forward, he held himself badly. He had beautiful aristocratic hands with long fingers which were generally folded in an attitude of peace. I noticed that he often looked at my hands with astonishment when I emphasized what I was saying with a gesture. Gesticulation is entirely foreign to the Tibetans, who in their reposeful attitudes express the calm of Asia. He always wore the red robe of a monk, once prescribed by

Buddha, and his costume differed in no way from that of the monastic officials.

Time passed swiftly. It seemed as if a dam had burst, so urgent and continuous was the flood of questions which he put to me. I was astounded to see how much disconnected knowledge he had acquired out of books and newspapers. He possessed an English work on the Second World War in seven volumes, which he had had translated into Tibetan. He knew how to distinguish between different types of airplanes, automobiles, and tanks. The names of personages like Churchill, Eisenhower, and Molotov were familiar to him, but as he had nobody to put questions to, he often did not know how persons and events were connected with each other. Now he was happy, because he had found someone to whom he could bring all the questions about which he had been puzzling for years.

It must have been about three o'clock when Sopön Khenpo came in to say that it was time to eat. This was the abbot whose duty it was to look after the physical welfare of the Dalai Lama. When he gave his message, I immediately rose to my feet meaning to take my leave, but the God-King drew me down again and told the abbot to come again later. He then, very modestly, took out an exercise book with all sorts of drawings on the cover and asked me to look at his work. To my surprise I saw that he had been transcribing the capital letters of the Latin alphabet. What versatility and what initiative! Strenuous religious studies, tinkering with complicated mechanical appliances, and now modern languages! He insisted that I should immediately begin to teach him English, transcribing the pronunciation in elegant Tibetan characters. Another hour must have passed, when Sopön Khenpo came in again and this time insisted that his master should take his dinner. He had a dish of cakes, white bread, and sheep's cheese in his hand which he pressed on me. As I wanted to refuse it, he rolled the food up in a white cloth for me to take home with me.

But the Dalai Lama still did not want to end our conversation. In wheedling tones he begged his cupbearer to wait a little longer. With a loving look at his charge the abbot agreed and left us. I had the feeling that he was as fond of the boy and as devoted as if he had been his father. This white-haired ancient had served the thirteenth Dalai Lama in the same capacity and had remained in the service. This was a great tribute to his trustworthiness and loyalty, for in Tibet when there is a change of masters, there is a change of servants. The Dalai Lama proposed that I should visit his family who lived in the Norbulingka during the summer. He told me to wait in their house till he should send for me. When I left him he shook my hand warmly—a new gesture for him.

As I walked through the empty garden and pushed back the gate bolts, I could hardly realize that I had just spent five hours with the God-King of Lama Land. A gardener shut the gate behind me and the guard, which had been changed more than once since I came in, presented arms in some surprise. I rode slowly back to Lhasa and, but for the bundle of cakes which I was carrying, I would have thought it was all a dream. Which of my friends would have believed me if I had told him that I had just spent several hours alone in conversation with the Dalai Lama?

ANNE SINCLAIR MEHDEVI

from Persia Revisited

"THE family will provide" is as true in Persia today as it always has been from the beginning of civilization.

SHEMIRAN MIGHT HAVE been a thousand miles from Teheran, it was so unlike the city. I discovered there a concentrate of Persia in a few square miles—its beauty and squalor side by side, its poor and its rich, and something else, something that was missing in the city, its tenderness and melancholy.

Shemiran nestles at the foot of the Alborz Mountains, which rise behind it and hover over it, so sheer that I couldn't see the sky without looking directly overhead. Most of the richest families in Persia live there, for Shemiran has something priceless—water.

I had lived long enough in Iran to share with Persians their love of water, to delight in the sound of it, to feel an almost physical pleasure at the sight of it. From the heights above Shemiran, water cascades down the mountain sides in streaks of silver and rushes in little unbanked streams down either side of every street. Water brings green, the most achingly beautiful of colors to desert dwellers. The mountains above Shemiran are barren and brown; the desert plain which separates it from the city is treeless and empty. Between these two lies the violently, shockingly green townlet, a tangle of exuberant trees and vines and flowers—like a fulfillment of hope.

In the center of Shemiran is the square, or *meidan*, like any small town *meidan* anywhere in Iran. None of the rich residents ever goes there, only their servants. But Mohamed and I went there every time we drove by to see Villa No. 1.

In the midst of luxury, the Shemiran *meidan* is a market and meeting place for the humble. Itinerant barbers set up their stools near the bus stop and shave and tonsure customers on the crowded sidewalk. Fruit sellers wander nearby, and candy sellers with their poisonously colored wares balanced on their heads on wooden plaques. Dervishes squat in the sun, holding out polished begging bowls. Little white donkeys, loaded with faggots, thread daintily through the litter, their necks hung with turquoise-colored beads to ward off the evil eye. Here and there I used to see porters waiting for hire—men whose profession was to carry things on their backs. They had bulky triangular blocks in the shape of prisms yoked over their shoulders and covered with beautiful carpeting.

Sometimes a shepherd brought his flock in from the desert plain. They were the fat-tailed sheep called Baluchis. Growing from their rear ends and hanging down behind was a sac of fat, so bulky that it often dragged the ground and occasionally weighed as much as one fifth the weight of the sheep. Poking out from this wool-covered sac was the real tail, pert and tiny, like an afterthought pasted on for a joke.

On the northern side of the square are the ice-cream shops, where the middle-class youth of Teheran come for their outings—to be fashionably near the rich perhaps, or just to get out of the city. Carloads of adolescent boys with pointed shoes and greased hair park their jalopies outside these white-tiled shops, which are too small to contain tables or booths. The boys buy ice-cream sticks and Pepsis at the counter and then lean against their cars and suck their food, ogling maidservants and making sly comments about the passers-by.

Fanning out from the teeming square of Shemiran are the drowsy lanes and streets where the rich of Teheran live behind sunburnt walls. These streets are like tunnels, flanked by head-high walls and heaped over with arching lime trees. It was early November when I first saw these side streets—buried under the fallen lime-tree leaves. The odor of fall permeated the air; the peaks of the mountains were tinged with snow, as white as paper against a sky without end, a clear, ice-blue sky.

While my husband dropped in at Mitrah's, I used to walk the lonely byways—the only place I found in Iran where an unveiled and unaccompanied woman could stroll at ease without fear of being molested. Sometimes in the distance I would see a servant girl wrapped in her veil, hurrying along with a basket of groceries on her shoulder. Not a voice was to be heard, just the sound of the rushing streamlets and the soft rustle of autumn leaves under my feet.

The lanes of Shemiran bcame a haven to me, the only place I could feel unwatched and unjudged, where I no longer felt foreign. I would draw in deep the stinging air—almost too pure, too crisp, too crackling-dry. A wild, almost passionate sense of freedom would quicken my steps as I wandered away the afternoon, ankle-deep in big papery leaves, until with the approach of dusk a car would draw up alongside. It was Mitrah's chauffeur, come to take me back.

In mid-January the garden gate of Villa No. 1 finally opened to us. We were welcomed by the gardener Jaffar, who came with the place and lived with his wife and a passel of somber-eyed children at the bottom of the garden. The wife would act as part-time servant if we required her.

The villa did not look in the least like a palace. It was a squarish, two-story house of the inevitable dun-colored brick. One wall was hung with bright creepers; the roof was grey slate and the only hint of splendor was a fan-shaped incrustation glittering over the doorway, a kind of triumphal transom made of bits of looking glass inlaid into the brick in swirling designs. To the right of the house was the swimming pool, its surface floating with sodden plane-tree leaves. The gardener's wife squatted beside the pool, lathering shirts.

The Shah's palace, the real palace, was nowhere visible. I had imagined it rising in gorgeous tiers outside my window. But, as I later learned, it was tucked in deep privacy within the Sa'adabad grounds, which, separated by a dirt road, abutted the east side of our garden. I was, however—as I instantly learned—the immediate neighbor of the palace servants, two three-story apartment houses full of them next door. They lived in delightfully unbuttoned abandon, with laundry hanging from the windows and hawkers calling their wares at the doors.

South of this busy hive of apartments was a parade ground. The Imperial Guard, I was told. Some two hundred smartly uniformed soldiers were marching there to the music of a brass band the day we entered. The music sounded familiar. I listened and recognized "Old Black Joe" quickened into march time:

"Gone are the days when my heart was young and gay,
Gone are my friends from the cotton fields away . . ."

Though Villa No. 1 did not conform to my idea of a palace, it did not look like any house I had lived in, either. Once inside, I discovered why. It wasn't two stories—just a towering one-story house. The ceilings were so high that winter mist had gathered in the upper corners. There were only four enormous rooms, each measuring around thirty by forty-five feet, yet they gave me an uncanny boxed-in feeling because they were higher than they were wide, as if they had been put down on their sides by mistake. I felt like a midget. Everything in Villa No. 1 was king-sized except me.

There was no furniture. As we walked from room to room, our footsteps echoed and thundered within the stone walls and our voices seemed to get lost in the vastness. A kitchen and a bathroom had been made from the former entrance hall, now partitioned down the middle. The bathroom was fitted out with pale yellow fixtures, but the kitchen was bare except for a water heater and a faucet.

"What are we going to do about furniture?" I said to Mohamed. We had bought a few odd tables and chairs in anticipation—suitable for a small apartment. Villa No 1 cried out for baronial furnishings—huge oaken chests, thronelike chairs, and a carved dining table to seat forty guests. Along the southern wall twelve gargantuan windows looked out over the tree-tops. I calculated roughly that some hundred and fifty yards of material would be required to cover them. And what about the walls? I had never before been faced with furnishing a house vertically as well as horizontally. The walls called for tapestries and silken hangings and crossed lances.

"Oh, don't worry," said Mohamed. Then came the same insouciant answer: "The family will give us a few things till we can get our own."

And the family did. My husband and I continued to live at his mother's, but every day I drove out to Villa No. 1 to inspect the chairs and tables, the beds and linens and curtains which began to pile up in the rooms. A four-burner gas range with infrared oven appeared and, with it, a twelve-foot refrigerator; they came from Mitrah. Khanoum-june sent eiderdowns and a silver tea set. Chinaware, lamps, a samovar, settees were soon placed in their appointed spots—all loans from Hamid and Bachtar and Asad and others.

One day Mohamed gave me a few pieces of paper

The Apadana, Persepolis, Iran.

Lion attacking horse, Persepolis.

STONES OF PERSEPOLIS.

that looked like bank receipts. "Here are your rugs," he said. "Take your pick. You know, in Farsi we don't say 'to furnish' a house, we say 'to rug' a house. After you've made your selection, our house will be 'rugged' and we can move in."

I looked at the pieces of paper, mystified.

He explained. Persians invest in rugs as people in other countries invest in blue-chip stocks or real estate. When not in use, the rugs are deposited at the Bank Melli, the government bank, which has hermetically sealed labyrinthine underground vaults set aside for rug storage. Rugs are negotiable; money can be borrowed on them. They can be given in payment, in lieu of cash, and they are always acceptable security. The pieces of paper in his hand were bank receipts for half a dozen rugs.

"But I hate to use them," I said. "It's sort of like using someone's money."

Not at all, he assured me. Persians regard their rugs as indestructible. The older they are, the better they are. I now recalled driving through the rug district and seeing the street spread here and there with rugs. Traffic passed over them, donkeys trod on them, and the smiling shopkeeper stood by and watched without turning a hair. "They're being tempered. New rugs give off a little fluff," Mohamed had said. "The best way to get rid of it is through rough usage."

"But they'll get dirty."

"Dirt won't hurt rugs. When they're sufficiently tamped down by the trucks and traffic, the merchant sends them to Reh to be washed in the river. Then they're ready for sale."

At the bank we selected three large Kashan rugs and one from Meshed. Their owners had reason to be grateful three months later, when the rug vault at the bank caught fire. This was equivalent to news of a stock-market panic in other countries. Everyone raced downtown, but the streets around the bank had been chained off. Smoke billowed from the basement and hundreds of people began to count themselves bankrupt. The fire raged for twenty-four hours and losses ran into the hundreds of thousands. But the four rugs which Mohamed and I had borrowed were safe, and their owners thanked me as if I had done them a favor. I began to understand how family members, even accidentally, could save each other from calamity.

WILLIAM O. DOUGLAS

from STRANGE LANDS AND FRIENDLY PEOPLE

"MY HUT is poor and dirty but you may sit in the light of my eyes," said a goatherd who turned over his whole house to Justice Douglas, giving him bed, food, and privacy. A friendly traveler finds such good hospitality wherever he goes.

THE WELCOME which a Kurdish tribe gives a guest is not only hearty; it is a bloody affair as well. On the outskirts of the village a delegation of men hold a steer ready for the slaughter, and as the guest approaches, one of them stabs the animal in the throat. There is the last agonizing moment when the steer lets loose a bloody, gurgling bellow before it is dragged across the road, leaving a stream of blood in its wake. The guest then steps across the blood. The executioner saws vigorously on the neck of the beast until the head is severed. Then he heaves it to the side of the road and the khan or other ranking host turns to the guest, takes him by the hand, and says in a loud, ringing voice, "May that happen to the heads of all your enemies."

It is a robust, primitive, and genuine welcome. The ceremony is not the Asian equivalent of one of our stereotyped greetings. The sacrifice builds a bond of blood between guest and host. The new arrival is now a member of the tribe. He has special privileges, too. Every last man will give his life to defend him. Every man, woman and child will cater to his needs and show him every courtesy. We of the Western world have no acquaintance with that quality of hospitality. It is a pledge of friendship and fealty.

In origin it was an expression of gratitude that the guest had arrived safely and in good health. The best way of showing thanks was to kill something precious to the host. In ancient days when a Persian king came to a village or a tribe, the head man would go through the motions of killing a son, since an heir would be closest to his heart. And the villagers or tribesmen, playing their part, would rush in and prevent it. The king, understanding the play, would be deeply moved.

I usually managed to avoid the slaughter of the steer by having an interpreter rush forward with a request that the animal be released. There was no offense in that request. The welcome was still warm

Stairway procession, Persepolis.

and hearty; and a needless sacrifice was avoided. It was just as well there was no sacrifice at Zindasht. It would have been a messy as well as a bloody affair, for we arrived just about dark.

Amar Khan Sharifi stood on the outskirts of the village to greet us. With him stood his twelve sons—from forty-eight to eight years old. At a respectful distance behind him stood a group of villagers.

Amar Khan, over six feet tall, sparsely built, trim, with a head of close-cropped gray hair, stepped forward to greet me. He took my hand in both of his and held it for at least five minutes while we talked through my interpreter.

*   *   *

Western civilization owes much to Persia. The English-speaking community is especially indebted. Through Persian literature and trade a rich stream of words has entered our language—khaki, divan, hocus-pocus, shawl, julep, sash, awning, turquoise, taffeta, orange, lemon, peach, hazard, and hundreds of others. There are also many words that sound close: two—do, six—shesh, it—ist, daughter—dakhtar, no—na, brother—brader, mother—mader, father—pedar.

I have mentioned earlier the contribution of Persia to the arts and to medicine. Persia gave the world rug weaving; and it put immortal poetry on the lips of all men. The Persian cat should be added to the list—an animal bred for long hair which is useful in making brushes for artists. And Persia has probably done more to perfect the breeding of the Arabian horse than even the Arabs themselves.

Yet the finest gift, I think, that the Persians have shown the world is hospitality. It can be illustrated by a lunch with the Shah, a dinner with the Prime Minister, a garden party tendered by the Governor of Isfahan, or by the reception of Amar Khan Sharifi or Morteza Gholi Khan Samsam. But as I told the present Shah of Persia, Mohammed Reza Shah Pahlavi, the finest example I experienced was in the Bakhtiari mountains.

We were camped at Oregon and scheduled to climb Mount Kalar the morning of our last day. The aim of the trip was primarily to hunt the ibex and secondarily to do a bit of mountaineering. Kalar, over twelve thousand feet high, rises about five thousand feet above Oregon. Once the approaches are cleared, the mountain itself is a series of cliffs of Jurassic limestone with setbacks reminiscent of New York City skyscrapers. The higher ledges are streaked with snow beyond mid-summer. The climbing is mostly rock work, nothing daring or particularly hazardous, only wearing. The cliffs and slopes offer no shade; there's not a shrub or

a tree to be seen. The cliffs are warm to the touch from the hot Persian sun; there are practically no springs from top to bottom; one needs to dress lightly and carry a good supply of water with him.

I awoke that morning with a temperature of 101 degrees and a nauseating attack of dysentery. But since it was my last day in Bakhtiari country, I decided to climb Kalar anyway. We had planned to leave at 5 A.M. and finally managed it at 7. We had an hour's horseback ride to the base of Kalar, and took another hour hunting partridge in the thistle-filled ravine where we left the horses. These partridge—buff-colored and a bit larger than our Gambel's quail—have a low, fast, swooping flight. They are difficult to hit. But when they are flushed from thistles there is a split second when they are vulnerable. They must first rise vertically three or four feet before they can take off. It is that instant when the Bakhtiari like to shoot them. We had several from each covey; and a Bakhtiari would carefully slit the throat of each. Otherwise the meat would be unclean by Moslem standards.

By the time we had finished hunting partridge and started the ascent, the sun was burning with authority. It was to be a still, hot day.

I climbed about two thousand feet and then turned back. My canteen was empty, my tongue stuck to my mouth, my temples throbbed. I was sick and weak from fever and dysentery. So far as the hunt was concerned and apart from the item of pride, my turning back made no particular difference. This hunting party would never have bagged an ibex. I was accompanied by a dozen Bakhtiari. The climb for them was a lark; they were like school boys on a vacation. They ran up the rocks with the agility of the ibex, talking, laughing, shouting as they climbed. Any ibex could have heard them a mile away.

When I turned back, they continued the hunt. I cleared the ledges and returned to the base of Kalar where we had left the horses. I was three hours ahead of the time when the horses would return; the sun was relentless; and the fever had me badly shaken. In the distance a black Bedouin-like tent hugged the base of the mountain, and I headed for it.

These tents are made of goat wool. Women spin a thread about as coarse as a heavy string and weave the cloth into black strips about eighteen inches wide and twenty feet long. They then sew the strips together, making the cloth for the back and top of the tent. The other side and the two ends are usually open.

There was not a tree or shrub in sight; no shade but that of the tent. A small spring was a stone's throw away. A man, a young boy, three children, and two girls about fifteen and sixteen years old were by the tent. One girl was spinning wool into yarn; the other was milking the fifty sheep and goats that were patiently standing in line.

The man invited me in. He went to the back of the tent and unrolled a small but beautiful Persian rug and laid it in front of me, motioning for me to sit. He brought out a blanket and placed it under my head for a pillow. He took a large kettle of mast, poured some of it into a smaller pot, and mixed it with water from a goatskin. This mixture is known as dugh, a very healthy drink in this area. He scattered some brownish spice over the dugh and handed it to me. I drank deeply and then lay back to sleep.

Just before I went to sleep, I thought how gracious and genuine a Persian's hospitality can be. When I walked into the tent, it became mine. I was left to myself. The man, the girls, and the children went about their own business. No one stood gaping at me. This was my new home for the moment. I had complete privacy.

How long I slept I do not know. But when I awoke, I was fresh and renewed and I went my way after thanking the man and presenting a jackknife to the boy. The scene came back to me over and again as I passed through the drawing rooms of America, Europe, and Asia. There I met gracious hosts and hostesses—well-educated, charming, and warm-hearted—who showed me every courtesy and consideration. Yet somehow the hospitality of the little goatherd on Mount Kalar surpassed all the rest. He not only turned over his whole house to me, made me a bed, gave me nourishing food, and respected my privacy, but when I first asked if I might rest in his tent, he bowed graciously and said in musical words that still ring in my ears: "My hut is poor and dirty but you may sit in the light of my eyes."

*   *   *

Damascus is an oasis. It is surrounded by bleak and dreary foothills on the north and west and on the east by a barren wasteland that stretches five hundred miles to Baghdad. In between lies a lush, circular garden thirty miles wide. The oasis yields annually thousands of tons of apricots, wheat, barley, vegetables, and grapes and thousands of pounds of walnuts, hemp, apples, and other fruit. The surrounding country, though dry and barren and showing only camel thorn and licorice root in the summer, is a rash of colorful wild flowers and green grasses in the spring. Anemones, poppies, iris, and the purple-headed onopordons give streaks of color even to the desertic steppe on the east. But by July all the land surrounding the oasis is brown. A dry, stinging heat has seared and baked the ground,

sapping the strength from every bit of stubble that the Bedouins leave behind.

For centuries the Bedouins have roamed the desertic steppe to the east of Damascus with camels or sheep. Both the sheep men and the camel men are called Bedouins; but a Bedouin in the strict sense is a camel-breeding nomad and a member of one of a dozen tribes.

Nomadism is a necessity in this barren land. Wells or springs are few and far between. The grazing is so sparse that one must keep on the move. The winters are cold, the summers hot. One moves north to the hills in summer and south to valleys in the winter.

A Bedouin seldom runs caravans for the transportation of goods. He is a breeder of animals—principally camels, but sheep, goats, and horses as well—which he sells in the markets. To the Bedouin, manual labor—on farms or in town—has been an ignominy. To call him a worker or fellah was to insult him. In recent years, however, the pinch of circumstances has changed that attitude. It has driven many of the poorest Bedouins into work for hire.

The Bedouins in modern days are poor folks. The wealthiest sheikh these days probably has an income of no more than one hundred dollars a month; the poorest Bedouin has perhaps three dollars a month. He lives almost entirely on flour, rice, and dates. When grazing is good he will have milk and cheese from his goats and sheep. He will have a sack of wool and some butter to exchange on the market for coffee, olive oil, sugar, and perhaps tea.

Yet this man—poor and on the edge of starvation—has the attitude and philosophy of an aristocrat. By his standards there are two occupations fit for free men—hunting and warfare.

There is considerable game in the desertic steppe east of Damascus—gazelles (fleet animals weighing around forty pounds with legs as small as dogs'), hares, black partridge, sand grouse, and a small species of the famous bustard. The Bedouin hunts chiefly with hawks and greyhounds. But his main preoccupation has always been war and raiding. He was a mercenary who would hire out to any ruler. He might forsake one ruler for another who paid a higher fee, but if he did so he had no traitorous intent; it was like a man in this country shopping around for a better job.

The Bedouin liked it best when central authority was weak. Then he could make the raiding of adjoining tribes his profession. It was a sport in which there was honor and excitement. The Bedouin entered it with fanaticism. There was always the prospect of untold wealth in flocks of camels, goats, and sheep. There were long night marches across the desert and the attacks at dawn. There was the strategy of smaller raids —waiting until a herd was far from camp and then driving it off before an alarm could reach the owner; or stealthily entering a camp in dead of night and running off a few horses or camels.

If the venture was successful, the raiders became wealthy overnight. If they were apprehended and failed, the consequences were not apt to be serious. If they survived the fighting and were captured, the chances were that the intended victims would then tender them a dinner, give them quarters where they could rest, and supply them with food for their return journey across the hot desert. Such is the chivalry of raiding. Raiding persists to a degree to this day, though it is on the decline.

Formerly the Bedouins were the sole masters of the desert. They alone had riding camels that could melt into the desert and travel days without water. The Bedouins alone knew every acre of the desert: the water holes, the wadis, the places where men and herds could hide. A man on horseback could not follow them many miles into this waterless wasteland. Hence the Bedouins were in command of the vast desert area, and collected tribute from travelers and from those who lived along the edge of the steppe, promising safety of passage and immunity from raiding.

That monopoly of the Bedouins has been practically broken. Motorcars manned by high-powered rifles have put even raiding parties moving on fast camels within reach. The patrol cars have been particularly successful when manned by Bedouins, and Bedouins have been increasingly available for those jobs. The economics of the desert has made work for the army and the police very attractive.

But the bulk of the Bedouins are today as they were centuries ago. They are on the move—free men owing allegiance only to their own tribe. They move as silently as the dawn; when the sun rises their night encampment is empty with no trace of their departure.

At night one will see lights on the desert hundreds of miles from nowhere. The lights are from small fires built of camel chips, marking a Bedouin encampment. Here these camel men sit far into the night sipping their slightly bitter coffee from small cups. Around these fires plans for new raids are laid and the history of old ones retold. Much of the telling is in the recitation of poetry, for the Bedouins, though largely illiterate, have their poets and venerate them.

I have been among the Bedouins and learned something of their hospitality. Generosity may well be at its best among the desperately poor. In India I saw people on the edge of subsistence make such generous division of their meager food with a guest that they would go without for days. The same is true of the Bedouins. One of these nomads may own but one goat or sheep and be wholly dependent on it for milk and cheese. Yet for a guest—a casual guest who comes as a stranger—he will kill it and prepare a feast. This is a hearty hospitality—a hospitality with abandon. The Bedouin also has other extremes of character. He is a cruel and ruthless person when it comes to killing. If he has his enemy in his grasp, he can sit on the man's chest and cut his throat out as easily as a New Englander can shuck an oyster—and with the same unconcern.

One evening in late August I returned to Damascus from a visit to some Bedouin encampments in the desert. The smell of the camels was on these people, for there is little water for bathing in the desert. It was still in my nostrils as I found the black asphalt highway that runs to the edge of this wasteland. It was dusk when I reached the outskirts of town. Here are large fields of grapes, each patch being marked by platforms on stilts—platforms that hold tiny thatched houses. These are lookouts where watchers stay night and day when harvest is near to protect the crop against the Bedouins. As I passed, many farmers were climbing crude ladders to these platforms to start the night's vigil.

I drove through the city and north along the highway that leads over the Lebanon Mountains to Beirut. I was headed for a tea house on the Barada.

The rivers Barada (formerly called the Abana) and Pharpar are the life of Damascus. Damascus—founded by the grandson of Shem and by many thought to be the Garden of Eden—has had staying qualities that other cities lacked. Damascus was old when Rome was young. David captured Damascus; so did Alexander and Pompey. Wave after wave of the invaders swept over it and around it. They sacked and burned it and yet left it strangely untouched. Palmyra—two days' ride east of Damascus—was the home of Queen Zenobia. It was indeed a capital of splendor. Today it is a ghost. Baalbek—across the Anti-Lebanon Mountains —was built when Damascus was teeming with life. Damascus lives on, while Baalbek is lost in the mists of history.

The staying qualities of Damascus have come from its two rivers.

Long, long ago in the days of Elisha, Naaman was the King of Syria. Like the present-day rulers Naaman lived in Damascus. He was a leper who came to Elisha for a cure. Elisha said, "Go and wash in Jordan seven times, and thy flesh shall come again to thee, and thou shalt be clean." (II Kings 5:10.)

Naaman eventually followed that advice and was cured. But his initial reaction was one of anger. He said, "Are not Abana and Pharpar, rivers of Damascus, better than all the waters of Israel? may I not wash in them, and be clean?" (II Kings 5:12.)

The Barada boils out of the limestone of the Anti-Lebanon Mountains about fifty miles north and west of Damascus. Its water is clear and cold and carried by gravity flow through a system of canals into every house and garden of Damascus. In its lower reaches it is lined with cafes which hang on its edges under groves of willow and poplar. At one of these I stopped.

A cool wind swept down the valley. My table was at the water's edge. The babel of tongues from adjoining tables where a few men smoked water pipes was drowned in the roar of the river.

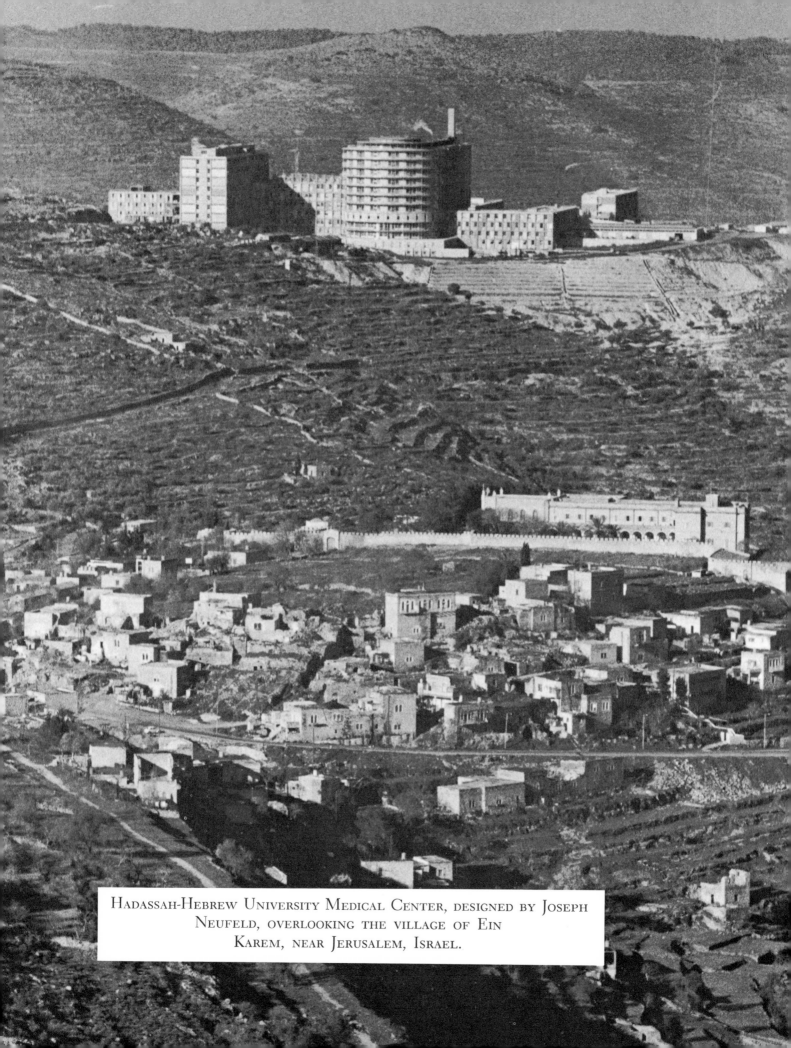

HADASSAH-HEBREW UNIVERSITY MEDICAL CENTER, DESIGNED BY JOSEPH
NEUFELD, OVERLOOKING THE VILLAGE OF EIN
KAREM, NEAR JERUSALEM, ISRAEL.

AFRICA

AFRICA

When you have made up your mind to go to West Africa the very best thing you can do is to get it unmade again and go to Scotland instead.

MARY KINGSLEY

LAWRENCE DURRELL

from BALTHAZAR

ALEXANDRIA and environs, at the end of an era, caught by a brilliant novelist.

OUTSIDE IN THE SQUARE with its palms nibbled by the sea wind, a light rain was falling. It was the tenth Zu-el-Higga, the first day of Courban Bairam, and fragments of the great procession were assembling in their coloured robes, holding the great silk banners and censers, insignia of the religion they honoured, and chanting passages from the litany: litany of the forgotten Nubian race which every year makes its great resurrection at the Mosque of Nebi Daniel. The crowd was brilliant, spotted with primary colours. The air rippled with tambourines, while here and there in the lags of silence which fell over the shouts and chanting, there came the sudden jabbering of the long drums as their hide was slowly stiffened at the hissing braziers. Horses moaned and the gonfalons bellied like sails in the rain-starred afternoon. A cart filled with the prostitutes of the Arab town in coloured robes went by with shrill screams and shouts, and the singing of painted young men to the gnash of cymbals and scribbling of mandolines: the whole as gorgeous as a tropical animal.

*   *   *

The two brothers now mounted their horses and started slowly along the network of embankments and causeways which led them over the lake with its panels of cultivation. Nessim always loved this ride for it evoked his real childhood—so much richer in variety and beauty than those few years spent in the house at Aboukir where Leila had moved for a while after their father's death. "All your new lift pumps should be here next month," he shouted, and Narouz chuck-led with pleasure; but with another part of his mind he allowed the soft black earthworks of the river with its precarious tracks separating the squares of cultivated soil to lead him steadily back to the remembered treasures of his childhood here. For this was really Egypt—a Copt's Egypt—while the white city, as if in some dusty spectrum, was filled with the troubling and alien images of lands foreign to it—the intimations of Greece, Syria, Tunis.

It was a fine day and shallow draught boats were coursing among the beanfields towards the river tributaries, with their long curved spines of mast, lateen rigs bent like bows in the freshets. Somewhere a boatman sang and kept time on a finger-drum, his voice mixing with the sighing of *sakkias* and the distant village bangings of wheelwrights and carpenters manufacturing disc-wheels for wagons or the shallow-bladed ploughs which worked the alluvial riverside holdings.

Brilliant kingfishers hunted the shallows like thunderbolts, their wings slurring, while here and there the small brown owls, having forgotten the night habits of their kind, flew between the banks, or nestled together in songless couples among the trees.

The fields had begun to spread away on either side of the little cavalcade now, green and scented with their rich crops of *bercim* and beanrows, though the road still obstinately followed along the banks of the river so that their reflections rode with them. Here and there were hamlets whose houses of unbaked mud wore flat roofs made brilliant now by stacks of Indian corn which yellowed them. They passed an occasional line of camels moving down towards a ferry, or a herd of great black *gamoose*—Egyptian buffalo—dipping their shiny noses in the rich ooze and filth of some backwater, flicking the flies from their papery skins with lead tails. Their great curved horns belonged to forgotten frescoes.

It was strange now how slowly life moved here, he reflected with pleasure as he moved towards the Hosnani property—women churning butter in goat-skins suspended from bamboo tripods or walking in single file down to the river with their pots. Men in robes of blue cotton at the waterwheels, singing, matrons swathed from crown to ankle in the light dusty black robes which custom demanded, blue-beaded against the evil eye. And then all the primeval courtesies of the road exchanged between passers-by to which Narouz responded in his plangent voice, sounding as if it belonged to the language as much as to the place. *"Nabarak Said!"* he cried cheerfully, or *"Said Embarak!"* as the wayfarers smiled and greeted them. "May your day be blessed," thought Nessim in remembered translation as he smiled and nodded, overcome at the splendour of these old-fashioned greetings one never heard except in the Arab quarter of the city; "may today be as blessed as yesterday."

He turned and said "Narouz" and his brother rode up beside him tenderly, saying "Have you seen my whip?" Laughing downwards again, his tooth showing through the rent in his lip. He carried a splendid hip-popotamus-hide whip, loosely coiled at his saddle-bow. "I found the perfect one—after three years. Sheik Bedawi sent it down from Assuan. Do you know?" He turned those brilliant blue eyes upwards for a moment to stare into the dark eyes of his brother with intense joy. "It is better than a pistol, at any rate a .99," he said, thrilled as a child. "I've been practicing hard with it—do you want to see?"

Without waiting for an answer he tucked his head down and rode forward at a trot to where some dozen chickens were scratching at the bare ground near a herdsman's cot. A frightened rooster running faster than the others took off under his horse's hooves: Nessim reined back to watch. Narouz' arm shot up, the long lash uncurled slowly on the air and then went rigid with a sudden dull welt of sound, a sullen thwack, and laughing, the rider dismounted to pick up the mutilated creature, still warm and palpitating, its wings half-severed from its body, its head smashed. He brought it back to Nessim in triumph, wiping his hand casually on his baggy trousers. "What do you think?" Nessim gripped and admired the great whip while his brother threw the dead fowl to his factor, still laughing himself, and so slowly remounted. They rode side by side now, as if the spell upon their communication were broken, and Nessim talked of the new machinery which had been ordered and heard of Narouz' battle against drought and sand-drift. In such neutral subjects they could lose themselves and be-

come natural. United most closely by such topics, they were like two blind people in love who can only express themselves through touch: the subject of their lands.

The holdings became richer now, planted out with tamarisk and carob, though here and there they passed the remains of properties abandoned by owners too poor or too lazy to contend with the deserts, which encircled the fertile strip on three sides. Old houses, fallen now into desuetude, abandoned and overgrown, stared out across the water with unframed windows and shattered doors. Their gates, half-smothered in bougainvillaea, opened rustily into gardens of wild and unkempt beauty where marble fountains and rotted statuary still testified to a glory since departed. On either side of them one could glimpse the well-wooded lands which formed the edge, the outer perimeter of the family estates—palm, acacia and sycamore which still offered the precarious purchase to life which without shade and water perished, reverted to the desert. Indeed, one was conscious of the desert here although one could not see it—melodramatically tasteless as a communion wafer.

Here an old island with a ruined palace; there tortuous paths and channels of running water where the slim bird-forms of river-craft moved about their task of loading *tibbin* (corn); they were nearing the village now. A bridge rose high upon mudbanks, crowned by a magnificent grove of palms, with a row of coloured boats waiting for the boom to lift. Here on the rise one glimpsed for a moment the blue magnetic haze of a desert horizon lying beyond this hoarded strip of plenty, of green plantations and water.

Round a corner they came upon a knot of villagers waiting for them who set up cries of "What honour to the village!" and "You bring blessings!" walking beside them as they rode smiling onwards. Some advanced on them, the notables, catching a hand to kiss, and some even kissing Nessim's stirrup-irons. So they passed through the village against its patch of emerald water and dominated by the graceful fig-shaped mina-ret, and the cluster of dazzling beehive domes which distinguished the Coptic church of their forefathers. From here, the road turned back again across the fields to the great house within its weather-stained outer walls, ruined and crumbling with damp in many places, and in others covered by such *graffiti* as the superstitious leave to charm the *afreet*—black talis-manic handprints, or the legend *"B'ism'illah ma'sha'l-lah"* (may God avert evil). It was for these pious villagers that its tenants had raised on the corners of the wall tiny wooden windmills in the shape of men with revolving arms, to scare the *afreet* away. This was the manor-house of Karm Abu Girg which belonged to them.

Emin, the chief steward, was waiting at the outer gate with the usual gruff greetings which custom demanded, surrounded by a group of shy boys to hold the horses and help their riders dismount.

The great folding doors of the courtyard with their pistol bolts and inscribed panels were set back so that they could walk directly into the courtyard against which the house itself was built, tilted upon two levels —the ceremonial first floor looking down sideways along the vaulted arches below—a courtyard with its granaries and reception-rooms, storehouses and stables. Nessim did not cross the threshold before examining once more the faded but still visible cartoons which decorated the wall at the right-hand side of it—and which depicted in a series of almost hieroglyphic signs the sacred journey he had made to bathe in the Jordan: a horse, a motorcar, a ship, an aeroplane, all crudely represented. He muttered a pious text, and the little group of servants smiled with satisfaction, understanding by this that his long residence in the city had not made him forget country ways. He never forgot to do this. It was like a man showing his passport. And Narouz too was grateful for the tact such a gesture showed—which not only endeared his brother to the dependants of the house, but also strengthened his own position with them as the ruling master of it.

*   *   *

Narouz always shunned Alexandria while he loved it passionately, with an exile's love; his hare-lip had made him timid to visit the centre, to encounter those he might know. He always hovered about its outskirts, not daring to go directly into the great lighted heart of it where his brother lived a life of devoted enterprise and *mondanité*. He came into it always humbly, on horseback, dressed as he was always dressed, to fulfill the transactions which concerned the property. It took a great effort to persuade him to put on a suit and visit it by car, though when absolutely necessary he had been known to do this also, but reluctantly. For the most part he preferred to do his work through Nessim; and of course the telephone guarded him from many such unwelcome journeys. Yet when his brother rang up one day and said that his agents had been unable to make the Magzub tell them what he knew about Justine's child, Narouz felt suddenly elated—as if fired by the consciousness that this task had now devolved on him. "Nessim," he said, "what is the month? Yes, *Misra*. Quite soon there will come the feast of *Sitna Mariam*, eh? I shall see if he is there and try to make him tell us something." Nessim pondered this offer for so long that Narouz thought the line had been cut and cried sharply, "Hallo— hallo!" Nessim answered at once. "Yes, yes. I am here. I am just thinking: you will be careful, won't you?"

Narouz chuckled hoarsely and promised that he would. But he was always stirred by the thought that perhaps he might be able to help his brother. Curiously, he thought not at all about Justine herself, or what such information might mean to her; she was simply an acquisition of Nessim's whom he liked, admired, loved deeply, indeed automatically, because of Nessim. It was his duty to do whatever was necessary to help Nessim help her. No more. No less.

So it was that with soft stride, the awkward jaunty step (rising and falling on his toes, swinging his arms), he walked across the brown dusk-beshadowed *meidan* outside the main railway station of Alexandria on the second day of *Sitna Mariam*. He had stabled his horse in the yard of a friend, a carpenter, not far from the place where the festivities of the saint were held. It was a hot rank summer night.

With the dusk that vast and threadbare expanse of empty ground always turned first gold and then brown —to brown cracked cardboard—and then lastly to violet as the lights began to prick the on-coming darkness, as the backcloth of the European city itself began to light up window by window, street by street, until the whole looked like a cobweb in which the frost has set a million glittering brilliants.

Camels somewhere snorted and gnarred, and the music and odour of human beings came across the night towards him, rich with the memories of the fairs he had visited with his parents as a child. In his red *tarbush* and work-stained clothes he knew he would not be singled out by the crowd as one different from themselves. It was characteristic too that, though the festival of *Sitna Mariam* celebrated a Christian Coptic saint, it was attended and enjoyed by all, not least the Moslem inhabitants of the town, for Alexandria is after all still Egypt: all the colours run together.

A whole encampment of booths, theatres, brothels and shops—a complete township—had sprung up in the darkness, fitfully lit by oil and paraffin stoves, by pressure lamps and braziers, by candle-light and strings of dazzling coloured electric bulbs. He walked lightly into the press of human beings, his nostrils drinking in the scent of aromatic foods and sweetmeats, of stale jasmine and sweat, and his ears the hum of voices which provided a background to those common sounds which always followed the great processions through the town, lingering on the way at every church for a recital of sacred texts, and coming gradually to the site of the festival.

To him all this scattered novelty—the riches of bear-dancers and acrobats, the fire-swallowers blowing six-foot plumes of flame from up-cast mouths—the dancers in rags and particoloured caps—everything that to the stranger would have been a delight was so to him only because it was utterly commonplace—so much a belonging part of his own life. Like the small child he once was he walked in the brilliance of the light, stopping here and there with smiling eyes to stare at some familiar feature of the fair. A conjurer dressed in tinsel drew from his sleeve endless many-coloured handkerchiefs, and from his mouth twenty small live chicks, crying all the time in the voice of the seabird: "*Galli-Galli-Galli-Galli Houp!*"; Manouli the monkey in a paper hat brilliantly rode round and round his stall on the back of a goat. Towering on either side of the thoroughfare rose the great booths with their sugar figurines brilliant with tinsel, depicting the loves and adventures of the creatures inhabiting the folk-lore of the Delta—heroes like Abu Zeid and Antar, lovers like Yunis and Aziza. He walked slowly, with an unpremeditated carelessness, stopping for a while to hear the storytellers, or to buy a lucky talisman from the famous blind preacher Hussein who stood like an oak tree, magnificent in the elf-light, reciting the ninety-nine holy names.

From the outer perimeter of darkness came the

EGYPTIAN GUIDES EAGER TO SHOW VISITORS AROUND THE PYRAMIDS.

crisp click of sportsmen at singlestick, dimly sounding against the horse rumble of the approaching procession with its sudden bursts of wild music—kettle-drums and timbrels like volleys of musketry—and the long belly-thrilling rolls of the camel-drums which

THE SPHINX, EGYPT.

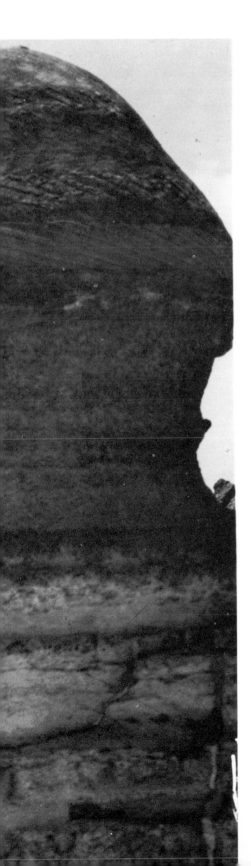

drowned and refreshed the quavering deep-throated flute-music. "They are coming. They are coming." A confused shouting rose and the children darted here and there like mice among the stalls. From the throat of a narrow alley, spilled like a widening circle of fire upon the darkness, burst a long tilting galley of human beings headed by the leaping acrobats and dwarfs of Alexandria, and followed at a dancing measure by the long grotesque cavalcade of gonfalons, rising and falling in a tide of mystical light, treading the peristaltic measures of the wild music—nibbled out everywhere by the tattling flutes and the pang of drums or the long shivering orgasm of tambourines struck by the dervishes in their habits as they moved towards the site of the festival. "All-ah All-ah" burst from every throat.

Narouz took a stick of sugar-cane from a stall and nibbled it as he watched the wave moving forward to engulf him. Here came the Rifiya dervishes, who could in their trances walk upon embers or drink molten glass or eat live scorpions—or dance the turning measure of the universe out, until reality ran down like an overwound spring and they fell gasping to the earth, dazed like birds. The banners and torches, the great openwork braziers full of burning wood, the great paper lanterns inscribed with texts, they made staggering loops and patterns of light upon the darkness of the Alexandrian night, rising and falling, and now the pitches were swollen with spectators, worrying at the procession like mastiffs, screaming and pulling; and still the flood poured on with its own wild music (perhaps the very music that the dying Antony in Cavafy's poem heard) until it engulfed the darkness of the great meidan, spreading around it the fitful contours of robes and faces and objects without context but whose colours sprang up and darkened the edges of the sky with colour. Human beings were setting fire to each other.

Somewhere in that black hinterland of smashed and tumbled masonry, of abandoned and disembowelled houses, was a small garden with a tomb in it marking the site which was the sum and meaning of this riot. And here, before a glimmering taper would be read a Christian prayer for a Christian saint, while all around rode the dark press and flood of Alexandria. The dozen faiths and religions shared a celebration which time had sanctified, which was made common to all and dedicated to a season and a landscape, completely obliterating its canon referents in lore and code. To a religious country all religions were one and while the faithful uttered prayers, for a chosen saint, the populace enjoyed the fair which had grown up around the celebration, a rocking carnival of light and music.

And through it all (sudden reminders of the city itself and the full-grown wants and powers of a great entrepôt) came the whistles of steam-engines from the dark goods-yards or a sniff of sound from the siren of a liner, negotiating the tortuous fairways of the harbour as it set off for India. The night accommodated them all—a prostitute singing in the harsh chipped accents of the land to the gulp and spank of a finger-drum, the cries of children on the swings and sweating roundabouts and goose-nests, the cock-shies and snake-charmers, the freaks (Zubeida the bearded woman and the calf with five legs), the great canvas theatre outside which the muscle-dancers stood, naked except for loin-cloths, to advertise their skill, and motionless, save for the incredible rippling of their bodies—the flickering and toiling of pectoral, abdominal and dorsal muscles, deceptive as summer lightning.

Narouz was rapt and looked about him with the air of a drunkard, revelling in it all, letting his footsteps follow the haphazard meanderings of this township of light. At the end of one long gallery, having laughingly shaken off the grasp of a dozen girls who plied their raucous trade in painted canvas booths among the stalls, he came to the brilliantly lighted circumcision booths of which the largest and most colourful was that of Abdul's master, Mahmoud Enayet Allah, splendid with lurid cartoons of the ceremony, painted and framed, and from whose lintel hung a great glass jar cloying with leeches. The doyen himself was there tonight, haranguing the crowd and promising free circumcision to any of the faithful too poor to pay the ordinary fee. His great voice rolled out and boomed,

while his two assistants stood at attention behind the ancient brass-bound shoe-black's chair with their razors at the alert. Inside the booth, two elderly men in dark suits sipped coffee with the air of philologists at a congress.

Business was slack. "Come along, come along, be purified, ye faithful," boomed the old man, his thumbs behind the lapels of his ancient frock-coat, the sweat pouring down his face under his red *tarbush*. A little to one side, rapt in the performance of his trade sat a cousin of Mahmoud, tattooing the breast of a magnificent-looking male prostitute whose oiled curls hung down his back and whose eyes and lips were heavily painted. A glass panel of great brilliance hung beside him, painted with a selection of designs from which his clients could choose—purely geometric for Moslems, or Texts, or the record of a vow, or simply beloved names. Touch by touch he filled in the pores of his subject's skin, like a master of needlecraft, smiling from time to time as if at a private joke, building up his *pointilliste* picture while the old *doyen* roared and boomed from the step above him "Come along, come along, ye faithful!"

PAUL BOWLES

from THEIR HEADS ARE GREEN
AND THEIR HANDS ARE BLUE

IN THE 1950's Americans discovered North Africa.

IT HAD TAKEN the truck fourteen hours to get from Kerzaz to Adrar and, except for the lunch stop in the oasis of El Aougherout, the old man had sat the whole time on the floor without moving, his legs tucked up beneath him, the hood of his burnoose pulled up over his turban to protect his face from the fine dust that sifted up through the floor. First-class passage on vehicles of the Compagnie Générale Trans-saharienne entitled the voyager to travel in the glassed-in compartment with the driver, and that was where I sat, occasionally turning to look through the smeared panes at the solitary figure sitting sedately in the midst of the tornado of dust behind. At lunch, when I had seen his face with its burning brown eyes and magnificent white beard, it had occurred to me that he looked like a handsome and very serious Santa Claus.

The dust grew worse during the afternoon, so that by sunset, when we finally pulled into Adrar, even the

driver and I were covered. I got out and shook myself, and the little old man clambered out of the back, cascades of dust spilling from his garments. Then he came around to the front of the truck to speak to the driver, who, being a good Moslem, wanted to get a shower and wash himself. Unfortunately he was a city Moslem as well as being a good one, so that he was impatient with the measured cadence of his countryman's speech and suddenly slammed the door, unaware that the old man's hand was in the way.

Calmly the old man opened the door with his other hand. The tip of his middle finger dangled by a bit of skin. He looked at it an instant, then quietly scooped up a handful of that ubiquitous dust, put the two parts of the finger together and poured the dust over it, saying softly, "Thanks be to Allah." With that, the expression on his face never having changed, he picked up his bundle and staff and walked away. I stood looking after him, full of wonder, and reflecting upon the difference between his behavior and what mine would have been under the same circumstances. To show no outward sign of pain is unusual enough, but to express no resentment against the person who has hurt you seems very strange, and to give thanks to God at such a moment is the strangest touch of all.

Clearly, examples of such stoical behavior are not met every day, or I should not have remembered this one; my experience since then, however, has shown me that it is not untypical, and it has remained with me and become a symbol of that which is admirable in the people of North Africa. "The world we see is unimportant and ephemeral as a dream," they say. "To take it seriously would be an absurdity. Let us think rather of the heavens that surround us." And the landscape is conducive to reflections upon the nature of the infinite. In other parts of Africa you are aware of the earth beneath your feet, of the vegetation and the animals; all power seems concentrated in the earth. In North Africa the earth becomes the less important part of the landscape because you find yourself constantly raising your eyes to look at the sky. In the arid landscape the sky is the final arbiter. When you have understood that, not intellectually but emotionally, you have also understood why it is that the great trinity of monotheistic religions—Judaism, Christianity and Islam—which removed the source of power from the earth itself to the spaces outside the earth—were evolved in desert regions. And of the three, Islam, perhaps because it is the most recently evolved, operates the most directly and with the greatest strength upon the daily actions of those who embrace it.

For a person born into a culture where religion has long ago become a thing quite separate from daily life, it is a startling experience to find himself suddenly in the midst of a culture where there is a minimum of discrepancy between dogma and natural behavior, and this is one of the great fascinations of being in North Africa.

*   *   *

North Africa is inhabited, like Malaya and Pakistan, by Moslems who are not Arabs. The *Encyclopaedia Britannica's* estimate of the percentage of Arab stock in the population of Morocco dates from two decades ago, but there has been no influx of Arabs since, so we can accept its figure of ten percent as being still valid. The remaining ninety percent of the people are Berbers, who anthropologically have nothing to do with the Arabs. They are not of Semitic origin, and were right where they are now long before the Arab conquerors ever suspected their existence.

Even after thirteen hundred years, the Berbers' conception of how to observe the Moslem religion is by no means identical with that of the descendants of the men who brought it to them. And the city Mos-

lems complain that they do not observe the fast of Ramadan properly, they neither veil nor segregate their women and, most objectionable of all, they have a passion for forming cults dedicated to the worship of local saints. In this their religious practices show a serious deviation from orthodoxy, inasmuch as during the *moussems*, the gigantic pilgrimages which are held periodically at the many shrines where these holy men are buried, men and women can be seen dancing *together*, working themselves into a prolonged frenzy. This is the height of immorality, the young puritans tell you. But it is not the extent, they add, of the Berbers' reprehensible behavior at these manifestations. Self-torture, the inducing of trances, ordeal by fire and the sword, and the eating of broken glass and scorpions are also not unusual on such occasions.

The traveler who has been present at one of these indescribable gatherings will never forget it, although if he dislikes the sight of blood and physical suffering he may try hard to put it out of his mind. To me these spectacles are filled with great beauty, because their obvious purpose is to prove the power of the spirit over the flesh. The sight of ten or twenty thousand people actively declaring their faith, demonstrating *en masse* the power of that faith, can scarcely be anything but inspiring. You lie in the fire, I gash my legs and arms with a knife, he pounds a sharpened bone into his thigh with a rock—then, together, covered with ashes and blood, we sing and dance in joyous praise of the saint and the god who make it possible for us to triumph over pain, and by extension, over death itself. For the participants exhaustion and ecstasy are inseparable.

This saint-worship, based on vestiges of an earlier religion, has long been frowned upon by the devout urban Moslems; as early as the mid-thirties restrictions were placed on its practice. For a time, public manifestations of it were effectively suppressed. There were several reasons why the educated Moslems objected to the brotherhoods. During the periods of the protectorates in Tunisia and Morocco, the colonial administrations did not hesitate to use them for their own political ends, to ensure more complete domination. Also, it has always been felt that visitors who happened to witness the members of a cult in action were given an unfortunate impression of cultural backwardness. Most important was the fact that the rituals were unorthodox and thus unacceptable to true Moslems. If you mentioned such cults as the Derqaoua, the Aissaoua, the Haddaoua, the Hamatcha, the Jilala or the Guennaoua to a city man, he cried, "They're all criminals! They should be put in jail!" without stopping to reflect that it would be difficult to incarcerate more than half the population of any country. I think one reason why the city folk are so violent in their denunciation of the cults is that most of them are only one generation removed from them themselves; knowing the official attitude toward such things, they feel a certain guilt at being even that much involved with them. Having been born into a family of adepts is not a circumstance which anyone can quickly forget. Each brotherhood has its own songs and drum rhythms, immediately recognizable as such by persons both within and outside the group. In early childhood rhythmical patterns and sequences of tones become a part of an adept's subconscious, and in later life it is not difficult to attain the trance state when one hears them again.

A variation on this phenomenon is the story of Farid. Not long ago he called by to see me. I made tea, and since there was a fire in the fireplace, I took some embers out and put them into a brazier. Over them I sprinkled some *mska*, a translucent yellow resin which makes a sweet, clean-smelling smoke. Moroccans appreciate pleasant odors; Farid is no exception. A little later, before the embers had cooled off, I added some *djaoui*, a compound resinous substance of uncertain ingredients.

CITY GATE, FEZ, MOROCCO.

Farid jumped up. "What have you put into the *mijmah?*" he cried.

As soon as I had pronounced the word djaoui, he ran into the next room and slammed the door. "Let air into the room!" he shouted. "I can't smell djaoui! It's very bad for me!"

When all trace of the scent released by the djaoui was gone from the room, I opened the door and Farid came back in, still looking fearful.

"What's the matter with you?" I asked him. "What makes you think a little djaoui could hurt you? I've smelled it a hundred times and it's never done me any harm."

He snorted. "You! Of course it couldn't hurt you. You're not a Jilali, but I am. I don't want to be, but I still am. Last year I hurt myself and had to go to the clinic, all because of djaoui."

He had been walking in a street of Emsallah and had stopped in front of a café to talk to a friend. Without warning he had collapsed on the sidewalk; when he came to, he was at home and a drum was being beaten over him. Then he recalled the smoke that had been issuing from the café, and knew what had happened.

Farid had passed his childhood in a mountain village where all the members of his family were practicing Jilala. His earliest memories were of being strapped to his mother's back while she, dancing with the others, attained a state of trance. The two indispensable exterior agents they always used to assure the desired alteration of consciousness were drums and djaoui. By the time the boy was four or five years old, he already had a built-in mechanism, an infallible guarantee of being able to reach the trance state very swiftly in the presence of the proper stimulus. When he moved to the city he ceased to be an adept and, in fact, abandoned all religious practice. The conditioned reflex remained, as might be expected, with the result that now as a man in his mid-twenties, although he is at liberty to accept or refuse the effect of the specific drum rhythms, he is entirely at the mercy of a pinch of burning djaoui.

His exposition of the therapeutic process by which he is "brought back" each time there is an accident involves a good many other details, such as the necessity for the presence of a member of the paternal side of his family who will agree to eat a piece of the offending djaoui, the pronouncing of certain key phrases, and the playing on the *bendir* the proper rhythms necessary to break the spell. But the indisputable fact remains that when Farid breathes in djaoui smoke, whether or not he is aware of doing so, straightway he loses consciousness.

One of my acquaintances, who has always been vo-

ciferous in his condemnation of the brotherhoods, eventually admitted to me that all the older members of his family were adherents of the Jilala cult, citing immediately afterward, as an example of their perniciousness, an experience of his grandmother some three years before. Like the rest of the family, she was brought up as a Jilala but had grown too old to take part in the observances, which nowadays are held secretly. (Prohibition, as usual, does not mean abolition, but merely being driven underground.) One evening the old lady was alone in the house, her children and grandchildren having all gone to the cinema, and since she had nothing else to do she went to bed. Somewhere nearby, on the outskirts of town, there was a meeting of Jilala going on. In her sleep she rose and, dressed just as she was, began to make her way toward the sounds. She was found next morning unconscious in a vegetable garden near the house where the meeting had taken place, having fallen into an ant colony and been badly bitten. The reason she fell, the family assured me, was that at a certain moment the drumming had stopped; if it had gone on she would have arrived. The drummers always continue until everyone present has been brought out of his trance.

"But they did not know she was coming," they said, "and so the next morning, after we had carried her home, we had to send for the drummers to bring her to her senses." The younger generation of French-educated Moslems is infuriated when this sort of story is told to foreigners. And that the latter are interested in such things upsets them even more. "Are all the people in your country Holy Rollers?" they demand. "Why don't you write about the civilized people here instead of the most backward?"

I suppose it is natural for them to want to see themselves presented to the outside world in the most "advanced" light possible. They find it perverse of a Westerner to be interested only in the dissimilarities between their culture and his. However, that's the way some of us Westerners are.

Not long ago I wrote on the character of the North Africa Moslem. An illiterate Moroccan friend wanted to know what was in it, and so, in a running translation into Moghrebi, I read him certain passages. His comment was terse: "That's shameful."

"Why?" I demanded.

"Because you've written about people just as they are."

"For us that's not shameful."

"For us it is. You've made us like animals. You've said that only a few of us can read or write."

"Isn't that true?"

"Of course not! We can all read and write, just like you. And we would, if only we'd had lessons."

I thought this interesting and told it to a Moslem lawyer, assuming it would amuse him. It did not. "He's quite right," he announced. "Truth is not what you perceive with your senses, but what you feel in your heart."

"But there is such a thing as objective truth!" I cried. "Or don't you attach importance to that?"

He smiled tolerantly. "Not in the way you do, for its own sake. That is statistical truth. We are interested in that, yes, but only as a means of getting to the real truth underneath. For us there is very little visible truth in the world these days." However specious this kind of talk may seem, it is still clear to me that the lawyer was voicing a feeling common to the great mass of city dwellers here, educated or not.

With an estimated adult illiteracy rate of eighty to ninety percent, perhaps the greatest need of all for North Africa is universal education. So far there has been a very small amount, and as we ourselves say, a little learning is a dangerous thing. The Europeans always have been guilty of massive neglect with regard to schools for Moslems in their North African possessions. In time, their shortsighted policy is likely to prove the heaviest handicap of all in the desperate attempt of the present rulers to keep the region within the Western sphere of influence. The task of educating

these people is not made easier by the fact that Moghrebi, the language of the majority, is purely a spoken tongue, and that for reading and writing they must resort to standard Arabic, which is as far from their idiom as Latin is from Italian. But slowly the transition is taking place. If you sit in a Moroccan café at the hour of a news broadcast, the boy fanning the fire will pause with the bellows in his hand, the card players lay down their cards, the talkers cease to argue as the announcer begins to speak, and an expression of ferocious intensity appears on every countenance. Certainly they are vitally interested in what is being said (even the women have taken up discussing politics lately), for they are aware of their own increasing importance in the world pattern, but the almost painful expressions are due to each man's effort to understand the words of standard Arabic as they come over the air. Afterward, there is often an argument as to exactly what the news contained.

"The British are at war with Yemen for being friendly to Gamal Abd el Nasser."

"You're crazy. He said Gamal Abd el Nasser is making war against Yemen because the British are there."

"No. He said Gamal Abd el Nasser *will* make war against Yemen if they let the British in."

"No, no! Against the *British* if they send guns to Yemen."

This state of affairs, if it does not keep all members of the populace accurately informed, at least has the advantage of increasing their familiarity with the language their children are learning at school.

There is a word which non-Moslems invariably use to describe Moslems in general: fanatical. As though the word could not be applied equally well to any group of people who care deeply about anything! Just now, the North African Moslems are passionately involved in proving to themselves that they are of the same stature as Europeans. The attainment of political independence is only one facet of their problem. The North African knows that when it comes to appreciating his culture, the average tourist cannot go much closer toward understanding it than a certain condescending curiosity. He realizes that, at best, to the European he is merely picturesque. Therefore, he reasons, to be taken seriously he must cease being picturesque. Traditional customs, clothing and behavior must be replaced by something unequivocally European. In this he is fanatical. It does not occur to him that what he is rejecting is authentic and valid, and that what he is taking on is meaningless imitation. And if it did occur to him, it would not matter in the least. This total indifference to cultural heritage appears to

be a necessary adjunct to the early stages of nationalism.

Hospitality in North Africa knows no limits. You are taken in and treated as a member of the family. If you don't enjoy yourself, it is not your host's fault, but rather the result of your own inadaptability, for every attempt is made to see that you are happy and comfortable. Some time ago I was the guest of two brothers who had an enormous house in the *medina* of Fez. So that I should feel truly at home, I was given an entire wing of the establishment, a tiled patio with a room on either side and a fountain in the center. There were great numbers of servants to bring me food and drink, and also to inquire, before my hosts came to call, whether I was disposed to receive them. When they came they often brought singers and musicians to entertain me. The only hitch was that they went to such lengths to treat me as one of them that they also assumed I was not interested in going out into the city. During the entire fortnight I spent with them I never once found my way out of the house, or even out of my own section of it, since all doors were kept locked and bolted, and only the guard, an old Sudanese slave, had the keys. For long hours I sat in the patio listening to the sounds of the city outside, sometimes hearing faint strains of music that I would have given anything really to hear, watching the square of deep-blue sky above my head slowly become a softer and lighter blue as twilight approached, waiting for the swallows that wheeled above the patio when the day was finally over and the muezzins began their calls to evening prayer, and merely existing in the hope that someone would come, something would happen before too many more hours had gone past. But as I say, if I was bored, that was my own fault and not theirs. They were doing everything they could to please me.

Just as in that twelfth-century fortress in Fez I had been provided with a small hand-wound phonograph and one record (Josephine Baker singing "J'ai deux amours," a song hit of that year), so all over North Africa you are confronted with a mélange of the very old and the most recent, with no hint of anything from the intervening centuries. It is one of the great charms of the place, the fact that your today carries with it no memories of yesterday or the day before; everything that is not medieval is completely new. The younger generation of French and Jews, born and raised in the cities of North Africa, for the most part have no contact with that which is ancient in their countries. A Moroccan girl whose family moved from Rabat to New York, upon being asked what she thought of her new home, replied: "Well, of course, coming from a

BASKET BAZAAR IN MOROCCO.

new country as I do, it's very hard to get used to all these old houses here in New York. I had no idea New York was so *old*." One is inclined to forget that the French began to settle in Morocco only at the time of World War I, and that the mushroom cities of Casablanca, Agadir and Tangier grew up in the 'thirties. Xauen, whose mountains are visible from the terrace of my apartment in Tangier, was entered by European troops for the first time in 1920. Even in southern Algeria, where one is likely to think of the French as having been stationed for a much longer time, there are war monuments bearing battle dates as recent as 1912. Throughout the whole first quarter of the century the North African frontier was continuously being pushed southward by means of warfare, and south of the Grand Atlas it was 1936 before "pacification" came to an end and European civilians were allowed, albeit on the strict terms laid down by the military, to look for the first time into the magic valleys of the Draa, the Dadès and the Todra.

Appearing unexpectedly in out-of-the-way regions of North Africa has never been without its difficulties. I remember making an impossible journey before the last world war in a produce truck over the Grand Atlas to Ouarzazat, full of excitement at the prospect of seeing the Casbah there with its strange painted towers, only to be forced to remain three days inside the shack that passed for a hotel, and then sent on another truck straight back to Marrakech, having seen nothing but Foreign Legionnaires, and having heard no music other than the bugle calls that issued every so often from the nearby camp. Another time I entered Tunisia on camelback from across the Great Eastern Erg. I had two camels and one hard-working camel driver, whose job it was to run all day long from one beast to the other and try, by whacking their hind legs, to keep them walking in something resembling a straight line. This was a much more difficult task than it sounds; although our course was generally due east, one of the animals had an inexplicable desire to walk southward, while the other possessed an equally mysterious urge to go north. The poor man passed his time screaming: "Hut! Aïda!" and trying to run both ways at once. His turban was continually coming unwound, and he had no time to attend to the scarf he was knitting, in spite of the fact that he kept the yarn and needles dangling around his neck, ready to work on at any moment.

We did finally cross the border and amble into Tunisia, where we were immediately apprehended by the police. The camel driver and his beasts were sent back to Algeria where they belonged, and I started on my painful way up through Tunisia, where the French authorities evidently had made a concerted decision to make my stay in the country as wretched as possible. In the oasis at Nefta, in the hotel at Tozeur, even in the mosque of Sidi Oqba at Kairouan, I was arrested and lugged off to the commissariat, carefully questioned and told that I need not imagine I could make a move of which they would not be fully aware.

The explanation was that in spite of my American passport they were convinced I was a German; in those days anybody wandering around *l'Afrique Mineure* (as one of the more erudite officers called this corner of the continent), if he did not satisfy the French idea of what a tourist should look like, was immediately suspect. Even the Moslems would look at me closely and say: "*Toi pas Français. Toi Allemand*," to which I never replied, for fear of having to pay the prices that would have been demanded if my true status had been revealed to them.

Algeria is a country where it is better to keep moving around than to stay long in one place. Its towns are not very interesting, but its landscapes are impressive. In the winter, traveling by train across the western steppes, you can go all day and see nothing but flat stretches of snow on all sides, unrelieved by trees in the foreground or by mountains in the distance. In the summer these same desolate lands are cruelly hot, and the wind swirls the dust into tall yellow pillars that move deliberately from one side of the empty horizon to the other. When you come upon a town in such regions, lying like the remains of a picnic lunch in the middle of an endless parking lot, you know it was the French who put it there. The Algerians prefer to live along the wild and beautiful seacoast, in the palm gardens of the south, atop the cliffs bordering the dry rivers, or on the crests of the high mountains in the center of the country. Up there above the slopes dotted with almond trees, the Berber villages sit astride the long spines of the lesser ranges. The men and women file down the zigzagging paths to cultivate the rich valleys below, here and there in full view of the snowfields where the French formerly had their skiing resorts. Far to the south lie the parallel chains of red sawtooth mountains which run northeast to southwest across the entire country and divide the plains from the desert.

No part of North Africa will again be the same sort of paradise for Europeans that it has been for them these last fifty years. The place has been thrown open to the twentieth century. With Europeanization and nationalism have come a consciousness of identity and the awareness of that identity's commercial possibilities. From now on the North Africans, like the Mexicans, will control and exploit their own charms, rather than being placed on exhibit for us by their managers, and the result will be a very different thing from what it has been in the past. Tourist land it still is, and doubtless will continue to be for a while; and it is on that basis only that we as residents or intending visitors are now obliged to consider it. We now come here as paying guests of the inhabitants themselves rather than of their exploiters. Travel here is certain not to be so easy or so comfortable as before, and prices are many times higher than they were, but at least we meet the people on terms of equality, which is a healthier situation.

If you live long enough in a place where the question of colonialism versus self-government is constantly being discussed, you are bound to find yourself having a very definite opinion on the subject. The difficulty is that some of your co-residents feel one way and some the other, but all feel strongly. Those in favor of colonialism argue that you can't "give" (quotes mine) an almost totally illiterate people political power and expect them to create a democracy, and that is doubtless true; but the point is that since they are inevitably going to take the power sooner or later, it is only reasonable to help them take it while they still have at least some measure of good will toward their erstwhile masters. The die-hard French attitude is summed up in a remark made to me by a friendly immigration officer at the Algiers airport. "Our great mistake," he said sadly, "was ever to allow these savages to learn to read and write." I said I supposed that was a logical thing to say if one expected to rule forever, which I knew, given the intelligence of the French, that they did not intend to try, since it was impossible. The official ceased looking sad and became much less friendly.

At a dinner in Marrakech during the French occupation, the Frenchman sitting beside me became engaged in an amicable discussion with a Moroccan across the table. "But look at the facts, *mon cher ami*. Before our arrival, there was constant warfare between the tribes. Since we came the population has doubled. Is that true or not?"

The Moroccan leaned forward. "We can take care of our own births and deaths," he said, smiling. "If we must be killed, just let other Moroccans attend to it. We really prefer that."

ANDRÉ GIDE

from TRAVELS IN THE CONGO

A GREAT MAN seems to carry his world with him when traveling (Tagore was another, like Gide), but he sees no less of the world around him for that.

End of December

EVEN IN the early morning the splendour—the intensity—of the light is dazzling. We are on the other side of hell. At Fort Archambault, on the marches of Islam, barbarism is behind one, and one enters into contact with another civilization, another culture. A still rudimentary culture, no doubt, but yet one that brings with it a fineness, a comprehension of nobility and hierarchy, a disinterested spirituality, and a feeling for what is immaterial.

In the regions we have just been through, there are nothing but down-trodden races, not so much vile in themselves perhaps as made vile by others, enslaved, without an aspiration but for the grossest material well-being. Here at last are to be found real homes; at last, individual possessions; at last, specializations.[1] The native town consists of rectangular enclosures, fenced round with palisades made of rushes (seccos).

Behind these are the Saras' huts, where they live in families. The rush mats are just high enough to allow a medium-sized man on horseback to see over them. As one rides by, one can look down upon the strangest privacies. This is the quintessence of the exotic. The beauty of the huts with their trellised roofs, edged by a sort of mosaic made with straw, is very great—like the work of insects. In these enclosures the few trees preserved from the annual burnings become very fine. The ground is of level white sand. There are quantities

[1] On re-reading these notes they seem to me greatly exaggerated; but when I wrote them, we had hardly shaken ourselves dry after a long soaking in the realms of limbo. And yet this impression of the nondifferentiation of the individual from the herd receives confirmation and explanation in the following words taken from a recent circular issued in Ubangui-Shari, forbidding the native to exploit any kind of plantation whatever for his own personal profit:

"Each native group is the sole owner of the plantations and cultures created by the *collective* labour of its members."

Fort Archambault

of little hanging granaries, so placed as to be out of reach of the goats, which make these minute settlements look like a Lilliputian village, built on piles. The climbing plants (kinds of hipomæa or flexible, broad-leaved cucurbitaceæ) enhance one's sensation of long-drawn-out hours, of slowness, of idleness, of sinking into a delicious dream. The atmosphere is one of peace, forgetfulness, happiness; the people here are smiling; yes, even the suffering, even the sick. (I remember an epileptic child in the first village of Bosoum; he had fallen into the fire and one whole side of his handsome face was frightfully burnt; the other side of his face smiled—an angelic smile.)

I have left off putting down dates. Days here go by all alike. We get up at dawn, and I hurry down to the Shari to see the sun rise. The air is cool. There are quantities of birds on the river shore—tame enough, for they have never been hunted or shot at; fishing eagles, carrion-crows, hawks, sparkling emerald-green bee-eaters, little purple-headed swallows, and quantities of small black and white birds like those we saw on the banks of the Congo; on the farther shore flocks of big wading birds. Then I come in for breakfast—porridge, tea, cheese or cold meat or eggs; read; pay visits; lunch with Marcel de Coppet; siesta; work; take tea with Coppet and look over his translation of Bennett's *Old Wives' Tale*; go out riding.

The way in which these people, who are so sensitive to rhythm, caricature and distort our bugle calls is very curious. They keep the notes, but change the rhythm to such an extent that they are unrecognizable.

. . . The sou here is worth eight blue beads. When a child buys a handful of ground-nuts, he gets four beads as change.

The two cook's boys we left at Bouca rejoined us here on the evening of 1 January.

The contact of Islam elevates and spiritualizes these peoples. The Christian religion, of which they only too often absorb nothing but the superstitions and the fear of hell, only too often turns them cowardly and sly. . . .[2]

Fort Archambault
Paid a visit to the two principal chiefs—Bézo and Belangar, Sara-Madjingayes by race. They have both sent their eldest sons to the school at Fort Lamy. The boys are just returning to Fort Archambault. The

curious thing is that an exchange has been effected; and when we said to Bézo: "And now you will have both your sons back again?" "No," he answered, "I shall take his and he will take mine."

"Why?"

He then explained to us that each of the two fathers is afraid of being weak and over-indulgent with his own son.[3]

The banks of the Shari, going down stream, are admirable. Took a long walk by myself (very imprudent, says Coppet). Islands; long sandy stretches; varieties of strange birds.

I am reading *Cinna* again with rapture, and learning the beginning of it by heart—re-learning it.

What a headlong and stupendous flight of our literature towards the abysses of artificiality!

It would be impossible to push abstraction, preciosity, inflation, anti-realism (not to say factitiousness) further than in Emilie's opening soliloquy. And I know no more admirable lines.

Impatients désirs d'une illustre vengeance
Dont la mort de mon père a formé la naissance,
Enfants impétueux de mon ressentiment,
Que ma douleur séduite embrasse aveuglément. . . .

This is the triumph of art over nature. Mallarmé's abstrusest sonnet is not more difficult of comprehension than the tangles of this sublime rigmarole would be, if the spectator were not prepared beforehand and prepossessed in its favour.

I re-read *Iphigénie* immediately after. What an extraordinary writer Corneille must have been to have made it possible to talk of Racine's "realism"!

Archambault, 10 January
Marcel de Coppet has been appointed acting Governor of Chad and must be at Fort Lamy within five days. We have settled to go with him. The weather has been very hot for the last three days—too hot. I have a little fever towards evening and rather bad nights. I am disturbed by the bats that come into my room, in spite of the mats I put in front of my window, and the newspapers I put over the doors.

As soon as I had finished reading *Iphigénie*, I began

---

[2] I take care not to generalize, and what I say is, in any case, only true of certain races.

[3] But perhaps, as an eminent anthropologist has pointed out to me, this is merely an example of the "maternal family." In certain tribes—the Sérèces, for instance (the region of Thies in Senegal)—fortune and situation are transmitted, not from father to son, but from uncle to nephew; the chief transmits his power to his sister's son.

it over again. Today I have finished it, with an ever-increasing wonder and admiration. I now think that this play is as perfect as any of the others and in nothing inferior to its sisters; but probably not one of them is as difficult to act. Not one of the parts can be left in the background or afford to be sacrificed. One might almost say there is no principal part, and that, turn and turn about, Iphigénie, Agamemnon, Clytemnestre, Achille, and Eriphile demand the actor's finest interpretation.

Agamemnon's character is admirably drawn by Racine. His shameful answer when Arcas says he is afraid that Achille may object to Agamemnon's using his name in a way that in fact amounts to forgery:

. . . *Achille était absent.*

And, even in the smallest details, his irresolution, his self-contraditions:

VA, dis-je, sauve-la de ma propre faiblesse.
Mais surtout NE VA POINT . . . etc.

And this vileness:

. . . *D'une mère en fureur épargne-moi les cris.*

17 January

Descent (I was going to say ascent) of the Shari, that strange river that turns its back upon the sea. A whole people assembled on the bank when we left Archambault.

The *d'Uzès* is flanked by four whale-boats. Marc and I occupy the starboard ones. We embarked at about three o'clock in roasting heat.

5 o'clock

Great strips of golden sand, of a burning purity, are pieced together at long intervals by stretches of prairie—the pastures of the hippopotamus and the buffalo.

18 January

The *d'Uzès* stopped not far from an extraordinary up-heaval of great granite boulders. This is the place where Bretonnet's mission succumbed. Although the sun was on the point of setting, I could not resist the desire to see these strange rocks (I thought at first they were made of sandstone) close to. I led my companions at a breakneck pace, first through sand and then through bog. I climbed one of the heights—but I was being waited for and the night was already falling.

19 January

This is a landscape "for lines," with little doum palm-trees and burnt brushwood—wonderful in its ferocity.

An antelope shot. Coppet killed three enormous ones.

The zebra-like markings of the crocodiles are very fine.

I have neither time nor inclination to note anything. Entirely absorbed by contemplation.

20 January

The landscape, without being exactly changed in appearance, is broadening out. It is tending towards a desert-like perfection and gradually becoming more and more denuded. There are still a great many trees, however, which are not palm-trees; sometimes when the height of the ground protects them from the periodical floods, they grow quite close to the river banks. They are trees with which I am unacquainted—like large mimosas or terebinth-trees.

Then little doum palm-trees, which have the bearing of dracænas, began to show themselves, and for some kilometres there was nothing else.

But it is in the fauna rather than in the flora of the country that its perpetual interest lies. There are moments when the sand-banks are all abloom with wading birds and snipe and ducks—quantities of birds so charming and so various that one cannot turn one's eyes away from the shores; and sometimes a great cayman half rouses himself at our passage and lets himself drop into the blue.

Then the distance between the shores widens; there is an invasion of azure. The landscape becomes spiritual. The waters of the river broaden like a plated sheet.

I shall have to throw away the box of beetles I was collecting for the museum. I had thought it would be a good plan to dry them in the sun; they have become so brittle that not a single one has kept its legs or antennæ complete.

We frequently stick in the mud; the crew then get down, and, with the water up to their waists, they push the boat along as if it were a motor-car. This process sometimes lasts an hour before we are dis-lodged. But the landscape itself is so vast, so slow, that one has no wish to go quickly.

An enormous crocodile came quite close up to us—two balls and a convulsive leaping in the river! We stopped the boat and went back to the place in a whale-boat. There was nothing to be found. Animals that are killed in this way sink immediately and come to the surface only a few hours later.

At twilight, when it was already nearly dark, we again saw the strange bird which I have already mentioned (before Bouca). It was flying over the sandy shore and a shot from Coppet brought it down. It fell into the river and Adoum fished it out. Two enormous *pennæ*, consisting merely of a bare central rib, start from under the wing almost perpendicularly to the other feathers.

They are about twice as long as the whole length of the bird, and at their extremities, at a paradoxical distance, are two biggish disks, which it seems the bird is able to move and raise independently of the action of its wings. Coppet, who gave me the bird for the museum, calls it the aeroplane bird and declares that some naturalists offer six thousand francs for it; not that it is extremely rare, but it comes out only at nightfall and its fantastic flight protects it.

Boingar

A small village. Numbers of weaving-looms being worked chiefly by children. Marc took a cinematograph of one of the children, who was still quite young and prodigiously skilful. The strip he was weaving was only a few centimetres wide and looked like a strip of bandage. These strips are joined together by their side edges to make a piece of stuff. (It takes as many as forty-eight to make a pair of trousers that reach up to the waist.) The loom is as simple as possible: two pedals cross the threads of the web; a comb, which is hung across the strip, drops on to the chain every time the shuttle has passed. The threads of the web are kept tight by a little flat basket which is placed on the ground a little way off and which is kept steady by being filled with pebbles. The child, as he works and as his strip of "gabak" grows longer, winds it up between his legs and pulls the basket towards him. He sings as he works and the throw of the shuttle accentuates the rhythm of his song.

Farther on, in a *secco* enclosure, there were seven looms placed side by side. No doubt the administration exacts a certain amount of "gabak" from the village. This work, we are told, is often made over to captives —the work that is considered honourable being the culture of crops and the raising of animals.

VICTORIA FALLS, SOUTHERN RHODESIA.

These woven stuffs, of which the materials are native and which are entirely unadulterated, are particularly beautiful. One can follow the process of fabrication from the beginning; there is no outside intervention whatever. There is some talk of reforming it. What for? If it were taken up a little by fashionable people, this "homespun" might be at a premium in the market.

A fishing eagle in the middle of the river—the captive of its too enormous prey—struggled anxiously towards the shore, using its wings as oars.

Fort Lamy. How ugly! How ill-favoured!

Except for its quays, which are fairly well laid out, and for its situation at the apex of the triangle made by the juncture of the Shari and the Logone, how poor it is, in comparison with Archambault! At the point where the river flows out of the town are two extraordinary towers—huge brick buildings of the same height, which one can see must have been terribly expensive to make, and of which no one knows the use.

The native town adjoins the French town and lies parallel to the river, widening out at each extremity, so that in reality it forms two towns, each equally sordid and dusty, with just enough of the Sahara about them to recall some of the South Algerian oases—but how infinitely less lovely! The houses are built of a rough clay and are ash-coloured; the clay is always mixed with sand and straw. The inhabitants all look timid and skulking.

We are told that this dismal town is becoming rapidly depopulated, owing to recurrent fever and emigration. The natives, who are not allowed to assemble for a tamtam, or even to go about their own villages after nightfall, quit out of sheer boredom. The whites are kept here by their functions, but are equally bored and long to escape.

JAMES MORRIS

from CITIES

STILL a land of inherited certainties, Ethiopia, too, is being swept by the winds of change.

A YOUNG LION vetted me in Addis Ababa one morning. He lay at ease in a compound outside the palace of the Emperor of Ethiopia, his paws neatly crossed, his tail straight behind him, and he looked me long, cold, detached and calculating in the eye. I would like to have known his views on the future of Addis, that ebony legend among capitals, but he did not encourage advances. Like the city itself, he looked back at me with an expression not exactly forbidding, and certainly not malevolent, but rather secretive or bemused, as though he had recently swallowed a dormouse, and was determined not to belch.

Addis Ababa, too, is in a digestive condition, and having some trouble with her juices, but she possesses nevertheless a certain leonine dignity. I cannot call her a handsome city. Her pattern is formless and straggled, her architecture ranges from the mud shack to the pseudo-Corbusier by way of a thousand baroque and Bauhaus aberrations. She is a city without much focus, her slums and her palaces intermingled; here the pony-tailed misses streaming out of the lycée, there the palsied beggars crawling on blistered knees through the market. She offers no shock of vicious contrast, for her separate elements are too intimately fused, but physically she is a faceless kind of place, a little blurred perhaps, a little splodgy.

She has travelled a long, long way from *Black Mischief*, still the Western world's standard handbook to her character. Among African cities today Addis Ababa is one of the cleanest, one of the least squalid, one of the calmest. This is partly politics, for she is the capital of a patriarchal autocracy not at all encouraging to effervescence and high jinks; but it is mostly geo-history. Addis Ababa compensates for what she is by where she is, and when. Around her the delightful Shoa highlands lie like a Wiltshire evocation, and groves of junipers, larches, figs and eucalyptus trees sidle into the heart of the city, like the magical forests that invest Kyoto. A glorious half-alpine climate gives a sparkle and a sting to this capital, keeps it free from sludge and stinks, fructifies its shanty slums and humours the wild polychromatic abstracts painted on the walls of its newest apartment blocks. The name Addis Ababa means "New Flower," because she was founded in the odour of hope towards the end of the last century; and to this day the city feels young and unexpectedly charming, graced alike by the superb manners and the green fingers of the Ethiopians.

Never was there a more handsome citizenry, since the days of the Assyrian bas-reliefs. I once paused to watch a merchant weighing millet in the market-place of this city. His wife sat loyally beside him, dressed in a long white gown and a string cap, and three or four labourers in ragged tunics hastened backwards and forwards with their sacks. The merchant sat on a kitchen chair as lordly as any Prester John, bowed gravely over his scales, and when he looked up at me I saw burning black eyes sunk deep between the cheek-bones, a nose chiselled like granite, a mouth at once haughty and infinitely delicate, grey hair curling Homerically around the temples, a thin face cold with authority, a look marvellously salted with dry and knowing humour. He smiled when he noticed me, the thin quiver of a smile, and as he did so he slammed the lock of his scales with a gesture terribly final, as though he had ordered the instant expulsion of the Jesuits, or had just beheaded his grandfather.

Addis Ababa is full of faces just as memorable: the resigned, distant, Biblical faces of the old men who loiter, leaning lightly on their crooked sticks, outside the iron-roofed shack of the district courts; the intelligent, wary faces of the young bloods home from Europe and America; the aloof, incurious faces of the Muslims washing their feet in the fountains of the mosque; the gentle, empty, haunting faces of the young prostitutes, in virginal white and vicarage embroidery, who wait outside their dim-lit boudoirs (sickly pink, blue, or conventionally red) along the pavements of Churchill Street. This is Africa with Semitic injections. These are not the coarse, laughing faces of Accra. Here there is something extra in the blood, something more restrained and lofty, something that suggests to me the black nobles of legend, or the Magus at the stable door.

For Addis Ababa has nobility; the nobility of a proud but gentle Christian faith, and of an immemorial self-respect. This is a city, like Bangkok, that has scarcely known the long humiliations of colonialism, and has not been obliged to wallow through the sad morass of recrimination, frustration and twisted emotion that belabours the emancipation of subject capitals. Amid all the thump and hubbub of the African renaissance, Addis Ababa stands alone as the capital of an ancient and truly African State. She thus retains a trace of feudal hauteur. There is a Minister of the Pen here, and a functionary called the Mouth of the King. Lions of Judah abound in gilded effigy, and from every hotel office, every restaurant wall, every barber's mantelpiece, there gazes the image of His Imperial Majesty, the Elect of God, Conquering Lion of the Tribe of Judah, splendidly ceremonial in Court dress, austerely military in khaki. This is a traditionalism rich and lovable, but flecked with pathos. It reminds me a little of Honolulu, a city still fragrant with the frail memories of the Hawaiian monarchs, who dressed themselves in the feathers of the o-o bird, and set great store by orbs and sceptres. There are not many kings left on the earth, and it is moving still to encounter one who claims direct descent from Solomon and the Queen of Sheba.

It cannot last, this lion's style. It is fretted, frayed and mocked already. Isolation bred the grandeur of the Ethiopians, but this is a capital no longer remote or mysterious. I can think of half a dozen capitals more difficult to reach, and several more backward and obscure. There is a daily air service nowadays to Europe, and the London Sunday papers get here on Monday. Addis has all the appurtenances of a modern city, from cold-jet dentistry to espresso coffee bars. Americans from Berkeley, Germans from Frankfurt, sometimes think this an insufferably primitive capital, with its beggars and lepers and bumbling bureaucracy, but to us old hands of Empire and Bandung, us habitual waiters in anterooms and addicts of enterovioform—to wanderers like us Addis Ababa is a haven of convenience. Mr. Waugh would scarcely recognize her now. Mr. Wilfred Thesiger would hastily saddle his camels for the wasteland. Mr. Graham Greene might begin to feel at home.

For the sleazier corrosions of progress are also beginning to show, and a little of the Pan-African fizz is bubbling around the inherited certainties. The patriarchal order is doomed, and even the Emperor himself, that grand old warrior-sage, is no longer sacrosanct. Addis Ababa seethes with foreigners, Swedes and Germans and Americans and Englishmen, connecting telephones, teaching woodwork, managing hotels, building roads, squabbling and intriguing and exhorting and complaining and making money and always, night and day, year after year, syllable by syllable, assuring this antique comity that its systems are wrong and its values misguided. Addis Ababa is not a passionate city, daubed with slogans and loud with demonstrations; but as this flood of alien energies pours in, as ever more young Ethiopians come home from Harvard, Bonn or Oxford, so we may expect the new hybrid culture of Africa to take root here, too, swamp the old gardens of Ethiopia with its jazzy proliferation, and reduce this still lofty metropolis to the level of our times.

But it has not happened yet. The Emperor still rules in Ethiopia, and this remains a capital of high-flown protocol. There were thirty-five other lions in the compound that morning, some young and cuddly, some majestically mature, and as I walked away I fancied the ruminative gaze of each one of them fastened steadily upon my person. They were very silent and absolutely still. It was like that moment of polite but faintly embarrassed hush when the ladies are leaving with a swish for the drawing-room, and the men are eyeing the port. Those animals did not really want me there at all, but they were cubs of the Conquering Lion, and they would not dream of showing it.

EVELYN WAUGH

from TOURIST IN AFRICA

"*M*R. WAUGH *would scarcely recognize her now,*" writes Mr. Morris of Addis. True, Mr. Waugh's East Africa has changed, but what part of the world has not?

FEBRUARY 6TH   A cool, fresh breeze down the Red Sea. For an Englishman the English make ideal travelling companions. I have been accosted twice only; once by a woman who took me for my brother, Alec, and again by a man who mysteriously claimed to have been at Cambridge with Ronald Knox.

The constant music, I suppose, caused genuine pleasure to 5 per cent of the passengers; pain to 1 per cent; a vague sense of well-being to 50 per cent; the rest do not notice it.

FEBRUARY 8TH   Anchored off Steamer Point, Aden, after luncheon. The ship stays until midnight. A bazaar is set up on a raft below the gangway. Launches ply to and from the quay.

Since I was last here Aden has grown green; not very green, but there are distinct patches of foliage where there was only dust. We originally occupied Berbera, in Somaliland across the straits, in order to have somewhere to grow cabbages and fruit for the garrison of Aden. Water has at last been struck and piped. The continuous trains of shabby camels no longer pad along the road from Crater Town. There are taps and water-closets now in the settlement. I saw only one camel, and that was a sleek riding animal from up-country, sitting beside its master at an Arab café feeding on a hamper of green vegetables.

Most of the passengers drove off to see the water tanks ascribed to King Solomon. In a thousand years' time will Central African guides show tourists the mighty ruin of the Kariba dam as one of the works of Solomon? I wish I could think so.

I took a taxi to Crater Town and walked its narrow streets for an hour looking for remembered landmarks and finding none. Not that there has been much modernization, but things have disappeared. I could find no trace of the "Padre Sahib's Bungalow" where I once spent a week. Nor of Mr. Besse's emporium. I was Mr. Besse's guest on several occasions in his rooms above his offices and warehouse. I also went with him on an appalling climb to the edge of the crater and across the burning volcanic debris to his shark-infested bathing beach on the far side of the little peninsula. He was an enchanting man. I described him in a book called *Remote People* as "Mr. Leblanc," and was told later that he greatly relished the portrait. I wish he had shown his gratification by leaving me something. He was a rich man then. His great fortune came later, and I was astounded ten years ago to read that he left 2,000,000 pounds to Oxford University, an institution which can never have caused him a moment's pleasure. I do not know what he was by race or religion. They named the college he founded St. Anthony's, but, when I enquired here, no one knew or had troubled to conjecture which of the twelve canonized Anthonies they were commemorating.

The smells of Crater Town are unchanged—spices, woodsmoke, coffee, incense, goats, delicious Arab and Indian kitchen smells, garlic and curry, sewage and hair oil. It is always a wonder to me that the English, who cheefully endure the reek of their own country— silage, spaniels, cabbages, diesel fumes, deodorizers, fish and chips, gaspers, ice cream—fight shy of "native" streets.

Wireless rang out everywhere, I suppose from Cairo. There were portraits of Nasser in many of the Arab shops.

Back to Steamer Point. Here there has settled all the tourist trade which used to flourish in Port Said, but in a sadly standardized form. Simon Arzt's in the 1920s was richly cosmopolitan. You could find most of the luxuries of Europe there. At Aden the shops are all kept by Indians and each has an identical stock of Japanese counterfeits—"American" fountain pens, "Swiss" watches, "French" scent, "German" binoculars. I searched for cigars but found none. There used to be two hotels at the extremes of the crescent. Their verandahs were haunted by touts and money-changers and shirt-tailors and each possessed a "mermaid"—a stuffed manatee, I think—which was kept in a chest and exhibited on payment. Now one of these hotels has gone and in its place has arisen a large, modern, air-conditioned building; no place for a mermaid. The other is its old shabby self.

I had a personal interest in the mermaids, because six years ago I suffered briefly from hallucinations in the course of which I imagined myself to be in communication with a girl in Aden. She complained of having nothing to do there. I went into some detail (which I omitted from the account I wrote of the experience) about the rather limited diversions of the settlement. Among them I mentioned the mermaid. "It's gone, Evelyn, it's gone," she said later, in tones of reproach as though I had maliciously sought to raise false hopes of pleasure, "it isn't here any more."

I was curious to discover whether in this particular as in all others my "voices" had been deceiving me. But here she spoke the plain truth. The first servant I addressed at the hotel looked blank and shrugged, supposing I was demanding some exotic drink. But a much older man came forward. "Mermaid finish," he said.

"How?"

"One man came finish mermaid."

"When?"

"Not so long."

The curse of Babel frustrated further enquiries. I should have liked to know how the mermaid was finished—bought, stolen, destroyed by a drunk?—and particularly when it disappeared—before or after or even during my conversations with my forlorn confidante?

*   *   *

FEBRUARY 16TH   Kilimanjaro was visible in the morning, a snowy camel's hump. Explorers of the last century wrote lyrically of this huge, odd, dead volcano that rises out of the plain. It looks less than its height, perhaps because of the high level of vegetation. From the hotel at Kibo parties set out from time to time to climb it. There are rest-huts for the nights and the tramp is made in three days. Ropes and axes are not needed. It is a heavy walk, not a feat of mountaineer-ing, but many strong men fail in the last lap, overcome by mountain sickness. The successive belts of vegetation are a joy to the botanist.

I spent the day with my driver, who was happy to be at home and proud to act as guide. At every turn we met friends and relations of his. I shall have more to say of the Chagga later, the most prosperous and intelligent of the native peoples of East Africa. The Germans gave them security against their war-like neighbours; Catholic and Lutheran missionaries and a revered Commissioner named Charles Douglas taught them the arts of peace; but before the white man appeared the Chagga had shown themselves an ingenious people, excavating deep caves for refuge from slave-traders and building a stone-walled canal which follows a valley contour and irrigates a village ten miles distant. Many streams from the snow-line fall in green-fringed cascades to be lost in the torrid plain below. It is a scene of theatrical charm. Save for its sturdy black inhabitants it might be in Polynesia. Then into this Arcadia there came strolling two elegant, arrogant old men, each dressed in a single cotton length, very tall, upright and slender. "Masai," said my driver, in the voice he had used to point out the game in the reserve, but with an unmistakable note of fear in it, as though he were warning me of something more dangerous than beautiful, for it is not fifty years since the Masai used to raid here and drive the Chagga literally underground, and the memory survives. These two men had come in from their lands beyond the mountain on a peaceful errand, carrying long wands instead of spears, to visit a doctor; but their shadows cast a brief gloom as they passed.

At lunchtime the other tourists from the *Rhodesia Castle* arrived at Kibo. They had been out at the watering-places in the reserve at dusk and dawn, had seen many animals and taken many photographs, and were well content with their experiences.

FEBRUARY 17TH   Back to Mombasa. That night I found a jolly, bearded doctor who was willing to go with me to the Star Bar. It was his first visit, and it was he who decided after a very few minutes that it was no place for us, after a girl from Zanzibar—who, he diagnosed, was intoxicated with hashish—had taken an unreasonable and demonstrative dislike to his benign appearance. I must admit I was enjoying it awfully.

NADINE GORDIMER

from A WORLD OF STRANGERS

A GOTHIC *landscape hostile with thorn—South Africa.*

AT EVENING, the low horizon of bush ran together as the light left it and seemed to sink over the edge of the world with the sun. And in the morning, it emerged again, a strangely even line of grayish trees and, afar, was present all day. When we walked up to it, where it bordered the great mealie lands, it separated and thinned into growths of various characters: flat-topped, spreading trees with mean and sparse foliage; waist- or shoulder-high bushes with short grass between them; low patches of briar; thickets of all three—trees, bush and briar—through which not even the dog could crawl. And all these things were fanged with thorns. Everything that grew in this stunted forest had its particular weapon of thorn. The trees had long white spikes, clean and surgical looking, like a doctor's instrument, giving off a powdery glitter in the sun. Some of the bushes had the same kind of thorn, but others had shorter, thicker ones, more like those of a rosebush, and some had thorns like fishhooks from which clothing, flesh or fur could not easily be released. The aloes with their thick fleshy leaves were spiked with red thorns. But worst and cruelest were the black, shiny quills, so sharp and smooth that they slid into your skin as quickly as a hypodermic needle, that covered the trailing briars, ankle-high. As you tore through them you heard them clawing at your boots, and no matter how careful you tried to be, every now and then one would stab into your ankle or calf. If it did not break off in your flesh as you pulled free, it would tear a bloody groove through the skin, as if reluctant to let you go without a taste of your blood. If it broke off, it would fester in your flesh, just beyond the grasp of fingernails or tweezers, until the inflammation it had set up around itself softened and swelled the skin enough for you to press it out.

Walking through this landscape, so thinly green, so hostile with thorn that the living growth seemed a thing of steel rather than sap, I thought of old religious pictures, with their wildernesses and their bleeding, attenuated saints. This was a Gothic landscape, where the formalized pattern of interwoven thorns that often borders such pictures was real; where one could imagine a martyrdom symbolized by the brutality of these clutching, inanimate yet live instruments of malice.

In some places, where the bush had been cleared but the ground had not been plowed for crops, fields of tall dead grass made a hissing noise as you pushed through it. Here and there, there was a break, and you would come upon a clearing where the low thorn briars spread over the earth, and no one, man or beast, could walk there. Bristling branches, which had no foliage to stir in the currents of the breeze and give them an air of life, maintained grim guard.

Grass like wood shavings, pinkish as if permanently touched with the light of sunset. Khaki weed, the growth of neglect and desolation, standing dead and high. The seed burs, round and sharp as porcupines, of some weed that had been cleared away, which crippled the dog the moment she set foot among them.

And more thorns—thorns in your hair and your hands, catching at your clothes, pulling you this way and that. And in silence. Silence on the fringes of which the soothing *sotto voce* of the doves, settling into the trees in some part of the bush which you never seemed to reach, was like the slowed heartbeat of the heat of the day. Now and then, the cheep, or the imagined cheep, of guinea fowl. Where, where, where?

And a shot, from one of the others. And silence.

Out of the bush, on the borders of the mealie acres, a shot sounded differently. There, it rang right around the sky, as if the sky were finite. It was like a message, beaten upon the four vast doors of the world, North, South, East, West.

We didn't get away early in the morning because when John Hamilton came to pick me up, not only did he still have some provisions to buy but it was found that I didn't have the right clothing for the trip. He raced me briskly around the town, in and out Army and Navy stores and various other shops, hustling me into long khaki pants that didn't fit me (shorts, he said, were the one thing you could not be comfortable in in the bushveld), making me stamp up and down in bright yellow veldschoen, buckling me into anklets. In between, he collected the last urgent items on his list—salami and tinned soup, eggs, bread, matches, cigars and lavatory paper. He did all this with the truant joy of a businessman on holiday among the buildings and streets where usually he is to be seen hurrying from appointment to office. And there *was* a certain pleasure in going about the city on a grimly busy Friday morning, fitting oneself out in clodhopper clothing from dark deep shops—whose existence behind gilded hotels and cinemas was unsuspected—stocked, it seemed, with props from an old Trader Horn film.

We met the rest of the party at someone's house, and after scenes of confusion amid guns and yapping dogs and harassed servants, the great mound of stuff that was to be taken along was packed into and on top of a car and a station wagon. Johannesburg dropped away and we were out on an open road where the winter morning lost its edge and the chromium rim of the car's window, on which I was resting my arm, warmed in the current of the sun. Past Pretoria, the winter was gone entirely; there was a fine, fragrant warmth, like the breath from a baker's shop.

I was in Hamilton's car with a man named Patterson who was some sort of senior official in Hamish Alexander's mining group. The car was one of those huge, blunt, swaying-motioned American ones that Johannesburg people like so much, and the three of us sat in front, with a space just big enough for John's setter bitch among the gear in the back. John and Patterson talked of the probable state of the birds, the height of the grass, and the possibility of persuading a farmer named Van Zyl to let them shoot over his land. It was happy, practical talk, the talk of good children occupied in a game, and it put me to sleep, reassuringly. I dozed and wakened, like a convalescent on a journey, looking out at the thin bush that marked no progress because in its sameness it did not seem to pass. Suddenly there was a railway siding with a grain silo, a butcher shop and a shoddy modern hotel. We got out of our great, overloaded barges of cars and had cold meat and pickles and beer in a dining room that had one blue, one green and one terra-cotta wall, and smelled deeply of a summer of insect repellent. One of the men from the other car, a stocky, fair chap with a jeering schoolboy's face, leaned his elbows on the table and said, in his grim South African voice, "We've got it taped, boy. Jist you wait, this time. It'll be the biggest bag you ever seen."

John was full of doubts, like a thoughtful general on the eve of a campaign. "The trouble is, with so much rain this summer, a lot of chicks must've got drowned. I don't think we'll find the big flocks we had last year, Hughie."

"There'll be plenty birds, don't you worry." He looked as if he'd know the reason why, if there were not. "We must get old Bester to get Van Zyl to let us go over to his dam, too. I'm telling you, it's lousy with duck."

Patterson said, in his amused Cambridge voice, "Blast, I didn't bring my waders."

"Is that so," John said, in the excited way of one confirming a rumor. "What's he got there, mallard, yellow-bill, or what?"

"Man, there's everything." Hughie was both shrewd and expansive, putting another head on his beer. "I know Willard—he's the brother-in-law of one of those big guys that run the duck shoots for Anglo-American, and he goes down with this guy to the farm next door; old man by the name of Geck, old German, owns it. There's geese too."

"Geese?"

"By God," said John, "have you ever tasted a spurwing goose? Two years ago, a shoot out Ermelo way, I got one."

"You can't compare geese with anything else. A turkey's got nothing on a young goose."

"We could go over there to old Van Zyl with a couple of bottles of whisky."

"Well, I don't know, waterfowl are damned tricky; once they've been shot over they're wild as hell."

"That time at Ermelo, up to the waist in freezing cold water . . ."

"I got my waders," Hughie said.

"I can see us all with frozen balls," Patterson murmured gracefully. It was from him that John had borrowed a gun for me. He said, "I hope you won't find that bloody thing too cumbersome. I wanted to give you my Purdie, but the ejector keeps jamming, and I wouldn't trust it. I had to give it over to the gunsmith." I told him I hadn't yet seen the gun he was lending me, and he explained that it was a Geyger, old as the hills, but still useful, and had belonged to his father. We discussed the personality of the gun; Patterson had the amused, objective, slightly Olympian manner of the ex-hero—as if he were not entirely there, but in some way remained still, like an actor on an empty stage, in the battle air from which, unlike most of his kind, he had not been shot down. I had met men like him before, in London, those men ten years or so older than myself who had survived their own glory; who, having looked their destiny in the face, did not expect that face anywhere and everywhere, as young men like myself whose war was the tail end of childhood expected it. I knew him slightly from the Alexanders'. He didn't actually talk much about his war, but you felt that in thirty years people would come simply to look at him, as, early in the century, you could still go and look at some old man who had fought in the Crimea.

The alert, anxious, feminine face of the dog was waiting for us at the window of John's car. The three

Africans who had been packed in along with the rest of the gear sat eating over paper packets in the station wagon and did not even look up when we came out of the hotel. Hughie Kidd and his companion, Eilertsen, drew a trail of dust around us and went ahead with a curt wave.

The talk of guns and birds went on, mile after mile, an assessment of known hazards, calculable satisfactions, action within the order of limits that will never change, handicaps that will remain fixed forever, for men cannot fly and birds cannot fire guns. It was all improbable: the elaborate instrument panel of the car before me, trembling with indicators and bright with knobs that didn't work, the talk that, with a few miles and a change of clothes, had slipped gear and gone, like a wandering mind, easily back to the old concept of man against nature, instead of man against man. Outside, the bush was endless. The car was a fat flea running through the pelt of a vast, dusty animal.

We came at last to great stretches of farmland, where the mealies stood in tattered armies, thousands strong, already stripped of their cobs of corn. Children waved from ugly little houses. From road to horizon, there was a stretch of black plowed earth, and the smell of it, rousing you like the smell of a river. Then, in a dead straight line, exactly where the plow had cut its last furrow, the bush began again, from road to horizon. We drove through farm gates and made a choice at ocher sand crossroads where the roads were as indistinguishable as those of a maze. A plump, pastel-colored bird—John said it was the lilac-breasted roller—sat at intervals on a telephone pole, looking overdressed, like a foolish woman, in that landscape that had dispensed with detail.

At three o'clock in the afternoon, we skirted a mound of mealie-chaff at which a few dirty sheep were nibbling, passed a house with a broken windmill, like a winged bird, behind it, roused a ferocious old yellow dog, and bumped off on a track through the mealies. After a short way, there were mealies on one side of us and bush on the other; we came to a shallow clearing where Hughie Kidd's car was already at rest. John backed up under a thin tree whose thorns screeched along the car's side, and with a flying open of doors and an immediate surge of voices and activity, camp was set up. John, Patterson and Hughie rushed about like boys who have come back to an old hideout; they appropriated their own low, shallow trees as hanging places for their things and shelter for their blankets, and allotted places to Eilertsen and me, to whom this clearing on the fringe of the bush was simply a piece of ground. Hughie chivvied everyone, shouting at the Africans, pummeling at and joking with his friends and with determined impatience; the idea was to get a shoot in that afternoon and not wait until morning.

When I had done my share of lugging things from the cars, I thought I had better have a look at the gun Patterson had brought for me, and I walked out with it twenty yards or so into the field of dry mealie stalks to get the feel of it. It was bigger than anything I'd used before, but well balanced. In my hand, in the sun, it had the peculiar weight that weapons have; even a stone, if you are going to throw it, feels heavy. At school, in cadet target practice, I had shown a cool eye and a steady hand—a minor distinction that my mother had found distressing. Hardly anyone can resist the opportunity to do the thing he happens to do well, and for a year or two, I had gone shooting whenever I had the opportunity, more because I wanted to show off a bit than out of any particular enthusiasm for the sport. On the other hand, I've never shared my family's sentimental horror of killing what is to be eaten; I've always felt that so long as you eat meat, you cannot shudder at the idea of a man bringing home for the pot a rabbit or a bird which he himself has killed. Among the people I knew in England, my somewhat freakish ability as a shot was regarded as a sort of trick, like being double-jointed or being able to wiggle one's ears, only in rather poorer taste, and I had lost interest in my small skill and hadn't used a gun for at least a year before I came to South Africa. But, like most things you don't care about, the small skill stayed with me whether I used it or not, and when I felt the gun on the muscle of my shoulder and I looked, like a chicken hypnotized by a chalk mark on the ground, along the shine of the barrel, I knew that I could still bring something down out of the sky.

EUROPE

COLOR PLATES

EUROPE

Happy the nations of the moral North.

Lord Byron

It is not that the British take their pleasures sadly but that they take pleasure in such tiny, tiny things.

Robert Benchley

I have seen much brighter faces at a funeral than in the Piazza of St. Mark's.

Aldous Huxley

If you're looking for someplace different, here in Portugal people go to the night spots to have a good cry. You will have to admit, that is pretty different.

Horace Sutton

REBECCA WEST

from Black Lamb and Grey Falcon

AN intellectual Englishwoman confronts the "raging polyglot intellectual curiosity" of the South Slavs.

"This is a very delightful place," said my husband the next morning. It was Easter Sunday, and the waiter had brought in on the breakfast-tray dyed Easter eggs as a present from the management, and we were realizing that the day before had been wholly pleasant. "Of course, Austria did a lot for the place," said an Englishman, a City friend of my husband's, who was staying in the hotel and had come to have breakfast. "I suppose so," said my husband, and then caught himself up. "No, what am I saying? It cannot be so, for this is not in the remotest degree like Austria. Austrians do sit in cafés for hours, and they talk incessantly, but they have not this raging polyglot intellectual curiosity, they have not this way of turning out universal literature on the floor as if it were a rag-bag, which indeed it is, and seeking for a fragment that is probably not there, but is probably part of an arcanum of literature that exists only in their own heads. In cultured Vienna homes they often give parties to hear the works of great writers read aloud: only a few months ago I spent an evening at the house of a Viennese banker, listening to the poems of Wildgans. But it would be impossible to read aloud to a party of Yugoslavs, unless one bound and gagged the guests beforehand."

There came into the room Constantine and Gregorievitch, who was still a little cold to us because of the company we had kept on the previous night. "What has Austria done for you?" asked my husband. "Nothing," said Constantine; "it has not the means. What can a country without history do for a people with a glorious history like the Serbs?" "I was talking of Croatia," said my husband. Gregorievitch said anxiously, as if he had been detecting himself looking in the mirror, "The answer stands." "But the Austrians have their history," objected my husband. "No," said Gregorievitch, "we are its history. We Serbs in general, we Croats in particular. The Habsburgs won their victories with Czechs, with Poles, and, above all, with Croats. Without us the Austrians would have no history, and if we had not stood between them and the Turks, Vienna would now be a Moslem city." The Englishman laughed, as if a tall story that knew its own height had been told. Gregorievitch looked at him as if he had blasphemed. "Is it a little thing that only yesterday it was decided that Europe should not

322

be Islamized?" he asked. "What does he mean?" asked the Englishman. "That the Turks beseiged Vienna in 1683 and were turned back," said my husband, "and that if they had not been turned back it is possible that they would have swept across all Europe." "Is that true?" asked the Englishman. "Yes," said my husband. "But it's not yesterday," said the Englishman. "To these people it is," said my husband, "and I think they are right. It's uncomfortably recent, the blow would have smashed the whole of our Western culture, and we shouldn't forget that such things happen." "But ask them," said the Englishman, "if Austria did not do a lot for them in the way of sanitary services." Gregorievitch looked greenly into the depths of the mirror as if wondering how he showed not signs of gaiety but signs of life under the contamination of these unfastidious English. "Your friend, who showed no emotion at the thought of the spires of Vienna being replaced by minarets, doubtless would expect us to forgive the Austrians for building oubliettes for our heroes so long as they built us chalets for our necessities. Are you sure," he said, speaking through his teeth, "that you really wish to go to hear mass at the village of Shestine? It is perhaps not the kind of expedition that the English find entertaining?"

We drove through a landscape I have often seen in Chinese pictures: wooded hills under snow looked like hedgehogs drenched in icing sugar. On a hill stood a little church, full to the doors, bright inside as a garden, glowing with scarlet and gold and blue and the unique, rough, warm white of homespun, and shaking with song. On the women's heads were red handkerchiefs printed with yellow leaves and peacocks' feathers, their jackets were solidly embroidered with flowers, and under their white skirts were thick red or white woollen stockings. Their men were just as splendid in sheepskin leather jackets with appliqué designs in dyed leathers, linen shirts with fronts embroidered in cross-stitch and fastened with buttons of Maria Theresa dollars or lumps of turquoise matrix, and homespun trousers gathered into elaborate boots. The splendour of these dresses was more impressive because it was not summer. The brocade of a rajah's costume or the silks of an Ascot crowd are within the confines of prudence, because the rajah is going to have a golden umbrella held over him and the Ascot crowd is not far from shelter, but these costumes were made for the winter in a land of unmetalled roads, where snow lay till it melted and mud might be knee-deep, and showed a gorgeous lavishness, for hours and days, and even years had been spent in the stuffs and skins and embroideries which were thus put at the mercy of the bad weather. There was lavishness also in the singing that poured out of these magnifi-

cently clad bodies, which indeed transformed the very service. Western church music is almost commonly petitioning and infantile, a sentiment cozening for remedy against sickness or misfortune, combined with a masochist enjoyment in the malady, but this singing spoke of health and fullness.

The men stood on the right of the church and the women on the left. This is the custom also in the Orthodox Church, and it is reasonable enough. At a ceremony which sets out to be the most intense of all contacts with reality, men and women, who see totally different aspects of reality, might as well stand apart. It is inappropriate for them to be mixed as in the unit of the family, where men and women attempt with such notorious difficulty to share their views of reality for social purposes. From this divided congregation came a flood of song which asked for absolutely nothing, which did not ape childhood, which did not pretend that sour is sweet and pain wholesome, but which simply adored. If there be a God who is fount of all goodness, this is the tribute that should logically be paid to Him; if there be only goodness, it is still a logical tribute. And again, the worship, like their costume, was made astonishing by their circumstances. These people, who had neither wealth nor security, nor ever had had them, stood before the Creator, and thought not what they might ask for but what they might give. To be among them was like seeing an orchard laden with apples or a field of ripe wheat, endowed with a human will and using it in accordance with its own richness.

This was not simply due to these people's faith. There are people who hold precisely the same faith whose worship produces an effect of poverty. When Heine said that Amiens Cathedral could have been built only in the past, because the men of that day had convictions, whereas we moderns have only opinions, and something more than opinions are needed for building a cathedral, he put into circulation a half-truth which has done a great deal of harm. It matters supremely what kind of men hold these convictions. This service was impressive because the congregation was composed of people with a unique sort of healthy intensity. At the end we went out and stood at the churchyard gate, and watched the men and women clumping down a lane to the village through the deep snow, with a zest that was the generalized form of the special passion they had exhibited in the church. I had not been wrong about what I had found among the Yugoslavs.

"Are they not beautiful, the costumes of Croatia?" asked Gregorievitch, his very spectacles beaming, his whole appearance made unfamiliar by joy. "Are they not lovely, the girls who wear them, and are not the

young men handsome? And they are very pious."
"Yes," I said, "I have never heard a mass sung more
fervently." "I do not mean that," he said irritably, "I
meant pious in their Croat patriotism." It appeared
that the inhabitants of Shestine wore these wonderful
clothes not from custom but from a positive and virile
choice. They would naturally wear ordinary Western
European clothes, as most other peasants round Za-
greb do, but they are conscious that the great patriot
Anton Starchevitch is buried in the graveyard of their
church, and they know that to him everything
Croatian was precious. We went and stood by his
tomb in the snow, while Gregorievitch, taller than
ever before though not erect, hung over its railings
like a weeping willow and told us how Starchevitch
had founded the Party of the Right, which defied both
Austria and Hungary and attempted to negotiate his
country back to the position of independence it had
enjoyed eight hundred years before. "It was Starchevitch's motto, 'Croatia only needs God and the
Croats,'" said Gregorievitch. "For thirty years when
the glamour and wealth and triumphant cruelty of
nineteenth-century Hungary might have tempted us
young Croats to forget our country, he made us understand that if we forgot the tradition of our race we
lost our souls as if by sin." We were conscious of the
second coat that lies about a snow-covered world,
the layer of silence; we smelt the wood-smoke from the
village below. "As a child I was taken to see him," said
Gregorievitch, his voice tense as if he were a Welsh
evangelist; "we all drew strength from him." Constantine, looking very plump and cosy, announced,
"His mother was a Serb." "But she had been received
at the time of her marriage into the True Church,"
said Gregorievitch, frowning.

We moved away, and as Constantine and I stepped
into the snowdrifts of the lane we passed three men,
dark as any Hindu, carrying drums and trumpets.
"Ohé! Here are the gipsies," said Constantine, and we
smiled at them, seeing pictures of some farm kitchen
crammed with people in dresses brighter than springtime, all preparing with huge laughter to eat mountains of lamb and pig and drink wells of wine. But
the men looked at us sullenly, and one said with
hatred, "Yes, we are gipsies." Both Constantine and I
were so startled that we stopped in the snow and
gaped at each other, and then walked on in silence.
In the eastern parts of Yugoslavia, in Serbia and in
Macedonia, the gipsies are proud of being gipsies,
and other people, which is to say the peasants, for
there are practically none other, honour them for their
qualities, for their power of making beautiful music
and dancing, which the peasant lacks, and envy them
for being exempt from the necessities of toil and order
which lie so heavily on the peasant; and this has always
been my natural attitude to those who can please as
I cannot. It was inconceivable to both Constantine
and myself that the gipsies should have thought we
held them in contempt or that we should have expressed contempt aloud if we had felt it.

The whole world was less delightful. The snow
seemed simply weather, the smell of the wood-smoke
gave no pleasure. "I tell you, Central Europe is too
near the Croats," said Constantine. "They are good
people, very good people, but they are possessed by the
West. In Germany and Austria they despise the gipsies.
They have several very good reasons. The art of the
gipsies commands no respect, for the capitalist system
has discredited popular art, and only exploits virtuosos.
If I go and play Liszt's scaramoucheries very fast,
thump-thump-thump and tweedle-tweedle-tweedle,
they will think more of it than the music those three
men play, though it is perfectly adapted to certain
occasions. Also the gipsies are poor, and the capitalist
system despises people who do not acquire goods. Also
the West is mad about cleanliness, and the gipsies
give dirt its rights, perhaps too liberally. We Serbs are
not bourgeois, so none of these reasons make us hate
the gipsies, and, believe me, our world is more
comfortable."

I looked back at the gipsies, who were now breasting
the hill, huddled under the harsh wind that combed
its crest. Life had become infinitely poorer since we
left church. The richness of the service had been
consonant with an order of society in which peasants
and gipsies were on an equal footing and there was
therefore no sense of deprivation and need; but here
was the threat of a world where everybody was needy,
since the moneyed people had no art and the people
with art had no money. Something alien and mur-
derous had intruded here into the Slav pattern, and
its virtue had gone out of it.

HENRY MILLER

from THE COLOSSUS OF MAROUSSI

*F*OOTLOOSE *in Greece with Henry Miller and his friend Lawrence Durrell.*

IT WAS ALMOST high noon when the boat pulled in at Corfu. Durrell was waiting at the dock with Spiro Americanus, his factotum. It was about an hour's drive to Kalami, the little village towards the north end of the island where Durrell had his home. Before sitting down to lunch we had a swim in front of the house. I hadn't been in the water for almost twenty years. Durrell and Nancy, his wife, were like a couple of dolphins; they practically lived in the water. We took a siesta after lunch and then we rowed to another little cove about a mile away where there was a tiny white shrine. Here we baptized ourselves anew in the raw. In the evening I was presented to Kyrios Karamenaios, the local gendarme, and to Nicola, the village schoolmaster. We immediately became firm friends. With Nicola I spoke a broken-down French; with Karamenaios a sort of cluck-cluck language made up largely of good will and a desire to understand one another.

About once a week we went to town in the caique. I never got to like the town of Corfu. It has a desultory air which by evening becomes a quiet, irritating sort of dementia. You are constantly sitting down drinking something you don't want to drink or else walking up and down aimlessly feeling desperately like a prisoner. Usually I treated myself to a shave and haircut whenever I went to town: I did it to while away the time and because it was so ridiculously cheap. It was the King's barber, I was informed, who attended me, and the whole job came to about three and a half cents, including the tip. Corfu is a typical place of exile. The Kaiser used to make his residence here before he lost his crown. I went through the palace once to see what it was like. All palaces strike me as dreary and lugubrious places, but the Kaiser's madhouse is about the worst piece of gimcrackery I have ever laid eyes on. It would make an excellent museum for Surrealistic art. At one end of the island, however, facing the abandoned palace, is the little spot called Kanoni, whence you look down upon the magical Toten Insel. In the evening Spiro sits here dreaming of his life in Rhode Island when the boot-legging traffic was in full swing. It is a spot which rightfully belongs to my friend Hans Reichel, the water-colourist. The associations are Homeric, I know, but for me it partakes more of Stuttgart than of ancient Greece. When the moon is out and there is no sound save the breathing of the earth it is exactly the atmosphere which Reichel creates when he sits in a petrified dream and becomes *limitrophe* to birds and snails and gargoyles, to smoky moons and sweating stones, or to the sorrow-laden music which is constantly playing in his heart even when he rears like a crazed kangaroo and begins smashing everything in sight with his prehensile tail. If he should ever read these lines and know that I thought of him while looking at the Toten Insel, know that I was never the enemy he imagined me to be, it would make me very happy. Perhaps it was on one of these very evenings when I sat at Kanoni with Spiro looking down upon this place of enchantment that Reichel, who had nothing but love for the French, was dragged from his lair in the Impasse Rouet and placed in a sordid concentration camp.

* * *

One day Theodore turned up—Dr Theodore Stephanides. He knew all about plants, flowers, trees, rocks, minerals, low forms of animal life, microbes, diseases, stars, planets, comets and so on. Theodore is the most learned man I have ever met, and a saint to boot. Theodore has also translated a number of Greek poems into English. It was in this way that I heard for the first time the name Seferis, which is George Seferiades' pen name. And then with a mixture of love, admiration and sly humour he pronounced for me the name Katsimbalis which, for some strange reason, immediately made an impression upon me. That evening Theodore gave us hallucinating descriptions of his life in the trenches with Katsimbalis on the Balkan front during the World War. The next day Durrell and I wrote an enthusiastic letter to Katsimbalis, who was in Athens, expressing the hope that we would all meet there shortly. *Katsimbalis . . .* we employed his name familiarly, as if we had known him all our lives. Soon thereafter Theodore left and then came the Countess X with Niki and a family of young acrobats. They came upon us unexpectedly in a little boat laden with marvellous victuals and bottles of rare wine from the Countess' estate. With this troupe of linguists, jugglers, acrobats and water nymphs things went whacky right from the start. Niki had Nile-green eyes and her hair seemed to be entwined with serpents. Between the first and second visits of this extraordinary troupe, who always came by water in a boat heavily laden with good things, the Durrells and myself went camping for a stretch on a sandy beach facing the sea. Here time was completely blotted out. Mornings we were awakened by a crazy shepherd who insisted on leading his flock of sheep over our prone bodies. On a cliff directly behind us a demented witch would suddenly appear to curse him out. Each morning it was a surprise; we would awake with groans and curses followed by peals of laughter. Then a quick plunge into the sea where we would watch the goats clambering up the precipitous slopes of the cliff: the scene was an almost faithful replica of the Rhodesian rock drawings which one can see at the Musée de l'Homme in Paris. Sometimes in high fettle we would clamber up after the goats, only to descend covered with cuts and bruises. A week passed in which we saw no one except the mayor of a mountain village some miles away who came to look us over. He came on a day when I was dozing alone in the shade of a huge rock. I knew about ten words of Greek and he knew about three words of English. We had a remarkable colloquy, considering the limitations of language. Seeing that he was half-cracked I felt at ease and, since the Durrells were not there to warn me against such antics, I began to do my own cracked song and dance for him, which was to imitate male and female movie stars, a Chinese mandarin, a bronco, a high diver and such like. He seemed to be vastly amused and for some reason was particularly interested in my Chinese performance. I began to talk Chinese to him, not knowing a word of the language, whereupon to my astonishment he answered me in Chinese, his own Chinese, which was just as good as mine. The next day he brought an interpreter with him for the express purpose of telling me a whopping lie, to wit, that some years ago a Chinese junk had been stranded on this very beach and that some four hundred Chinamen had put up on the beach until their boat was repaired. He said he liked the Chinese very much, that they were a fine people, and that their language was very musical, very intelligent. I asked did he mean *intelligible*, but no, he meant intelligent. The Greek language was intelligent too. And the German language. Then I told him I had been in China, which was another lie, and after describing that country I drifted to Africa and told him about the Pygmies with whom I had also lived for a while. He said they had some Pygmies in a neighbouring village. It went on like this from one lie to another for several hours, during which we consumed some wine and olives. Then someone produced a flute and we began to dance, a veritable St Vitus' dance which

went on interminably to finish in the sea where we bit one another like crabs and screamed and bellowed in all the tongues of the earth.

We broke up camp early one morning to return to Kalami. It was a strange sultry day and we had a two-hour climb ahead of us to reach the mountain village where Spiro awaited us with the car. There was first of all a stretch of sand to be traversed at a gallop, because even with sandals on the sand scorched one's feet. Then came a long trek through a dried-up river bed which, because of the boulders, was a test for even the stoutest ankles. Finally we came to the path that led up the mountain side, a sort of gully rather than path, which taxed even the mountain ponies on which we had loaded our things. As we climbed a weird melody greeted us from above. Like the heavy mist sweeping up from the sea, it enveloped us in its nostalgic folds and then as suddenly died away. When we had risen another few hundred feet we came upon a clearing in the midst of which was a huge vat filled with a poisonous liquid, an insecticide for the olive trees, which the young women were stirring as they sang. It was a song of death which blended singularly with the mist-laden landscape. Here and there, where the vapourish clouds had rolled apart to reveal a clump of trees or a bare, jagged fang-like snag of rocks, the reverberations of their haunting melody sang out like a choir of brass in an orchestra. Now and then a great blue area of sea rose out of the fog, not at the level of the earth but in some middle realm between heaven and earth, as though after a typhoon. The houses too, when their solidity burst through the mirage, seemed to be suspended in space. The whole atmosphere was ridden with a shuddering Biblical splendour punctuated with the tinkling bells of the ponies, the reverberations of the poison song, the faint boom of the surf far below and an undefinable mountain murmuring which was probably nothing more than the hammering of the temples in the high and sultry haze of an Ionian morning. We took spells of resting at the edge of the precipice, too fascinated by the spectacle to continue on through the pass into the clear, bright work-a-day world of the little mountain village beyond. In that operatic realm, where the Tao Teh King and the ancient Vedas fused dramatically in contrapuntal confusion, the taste of the light Greek cigarette was even more like straw. Here the palate itself became metaphysically attuned: the drama was of the airs, of the upper regions, of the eternal conflict between the soul and the spirit.

Then the pass, which I shall always think of as the *carrefour* of meaningless butcheries. Here the most frightful, vengeful massacres must have been per-

RUINS AT LINDOS, ISLAND OF RHODES.

petrated again and again throughout the endless bloody past of man. It is a trap devised by Nature herself for man's undoing. Greece is full of such death-traps. It is like a strong cosmic note which gives the diapason to the intoxicating light world wherein the heroic and mythological figures of the resplendent past threaten continually to dominate the consciousness. The ancient Greek was a murderer: he lived amidst brutal clarities which tormented and maddened the spirit. He was at war with every one, including himself. Out of this fiery anarchy came the lucid, healing metaphysical speculations which even to-day enthrall the world. Going through the pass, which demands a sort of swastika manoeuvring in order to debouch free and clear on the high plateau, I had the impression of wading through phantom seas of blood; the earth was not parched and convulsed in the usual Greek way, but bleached and twisted, as must have been the mangled, death-stilled limbs of the slain who were left to rot and give their blood, here in the merciless sun, to the roots of the wild olives which cling to the steep mountain slope with vulturous claws. In this mountain pass there must also have been moments of clear vision when men of distant races stood holding hands and looking into one another's eyes with sympathy and understanding. Here too men of the Pythagorean stripe must have stopped to meditate in silence and solitude, gaining fresh clarity, fresh vision, from the dust-strewn place of carnage. All Greece is diademed with such antinomian spots; it is perhaps the explanation for the fact that Greece has emancipated itself as a country, a nation, a people, in order to continue as the luminous *carrefour* of a changing humanity.

At Kalami the days rolled by like a song. Now and then I wrote a letter or tried to paint a water colour. There was plenty to read in the house, but I had no desire to look at a book. Durrell tried to get me to read Shakespeare's Sonnets and, after he had laid siege to me for about a week, I did read one, perhaps the most mysterious sonnet that Shakespeare ever wrote. (I believe it was "The Phoenix and the Turtle.") Soon thereafter I received a copy in the mail of *The Secret Doctrine* and this I fell on with a will. I also reread Nijinsky's Diary. I know I shall read it again and again. There are only a few books which I can read over and over—one is *Mysteries* and another is *The Eternal Husband*. Perhaps I should also add *Alice in Wonderland*. At any rate, it was far better to spend the evening talking and singing, or standing on the rocks at the edge of the water with a telescope studying the stars.

When the Countess again appeared on the scene she persuaded us to spend a few days on her estate in another part of the island. We had three wonderful days together and then in the middle of the night the Greek army was mobilized. War had not yet been declared, but the King's hasty return to Athens was interpreted by every one as an ominous sign. Every one who had the means seemed determined to follow the King's example. The town of Corfu was in a veritable panic. Durrell wanted to enlist in the Greek army for service on the Albanian frontier; Spiro, who was past the age limit, also wanted to offer his services. A few days passed this way in hysterical gesturings and then, quite as if it had been arranged by an impresario, we all found ourselves waiting for the boat to take us to Athens. The boat was to arrive at nine in the morning; we didn't get aboard her until four the next morning. By that time the quay was filled with an indescribable litter of baggage on which the feverish owners sat or sprawled themselves out, pretending to look unconcerned but actually quaking with fear. The most disgraceful scene ensued when the tenders finally hove to. As usual, the rich insisted on going aboard first. Having a first-class passage I found myself among the rich. I was thoroughly disgusted and half minded not to take the boat at all but return quietly to Durrell's house and let things take their course. Then, by some miraculous quirk, I discovered that we weren't to go aboard first, that we were to go last. All the fine luggage was being taken out of the tenders and thrown back on the quay. Bravo! My heart went up. The Countess, who had more luggage than any one, was the very last to go aboard. Later I discovered to my surprise that it was she who had arranged matters thus. It was the inefficiency that had annoyed her, not the question of class of privilege. She hadn't the least fear of the Italians apparently—what she minded was the disorder, the shameful scramble. It was four in the morning, as I say, with a bright moon gleaming on a swollen, angry sea, when we pushed off from the quay in the little caiques. I had never expected to leave Corfu under such conditions. I was a bit angry with myself for having consented to go to Athens. I was more concerned about the interruption of my blissful vacation than about the dangers of the impending war. It was still Summer and I had by no means had enough of sun and sea. I thought of the peasant women and the ragged children who would soon be without food, the look in their eyes as they waved goodbye to us. It seemed cowardly to be running away like this, leaving the weak and innocent to their doom. Money again. Those who have escape; those who have not are massacred. I found myself praying that the Italians would intercept us, that we would not get off scot free in this shameless way.

When I awoke and went up on deck the boat was

gliding through a narrow strait; on either side of us were low barren hills, soft, violet-studded hummocks of earth of such intimate human proportions as to make one weep with joy. The sun was almost at zenith and the glare was dazzlingly intense. I was in precisely that little Greek world whose frontiers I had described in my book a few months before leaving Paris. It was like awakening to find oneself alive in a dream. There was something phenomenal about the luminous immediacy of these two violet-coloured shores. We were gliding along in precisely the way that Rousseau *le douanier* had described it in his painting. It was more than a Greek atmosphere—it was poetic, and of no time or place actually known to man. The boat itself was the only link with reality. The boat was filled to the gunwales with lost souls desperately clinging to their few earthly possessions. Women in rags, their breasts bared, were vainly trying to nurse their howling brats; they sat on the deck floor in a mess of vomit and blood and the dream through which they were passing never brushed their eyelids. If we had been torpedoed then and there we would have passed like that, in vomit and blood and confusion, to the dark underworld. At that moment I rejoiced that I was free of possessions, free of all ties, free of fear and envy and malice. I could have passed quietly from one dream to another, owning nothing, regretting nothing, wishing nothing. I was never more certain that life and death are one and that neither can be enjoyed or embraced if the other be absent.

*   *   *

At Patras we decided to go ashore and take the train to Athens. The Hotel Cecil, which we stopped at, is the best hotel I've ever been in, and I've been in a good many. It cost about twenty-three cents a day for a room the likes of which could not be duplicated in America for less than five dollars. I hope everybody who is passing through Greece will stop off at the Hotel Cecil and see for himself. It is an event in one's life. . . . We breakfasted towards noon on the terrace of the solarium overlooking the sea. Here a terrible wrangle ensued between Durrell and his wife. I felt quite helpless and could only pity them both from the depths of my heart. It was really a private quarrel in which the war was used as a camouflage. The thought of war drives people frantic, makes them quite cuckoo, even when they are intelligent and far-seeing, as both Durrell and Nancy are. War has another bad effect—it makes young people feel guilty and conscience-stricken. In Corfu I had been studying the antics of a superbly healthy young Englishman, a lad of twenty or so, who had intended to be a Greek scholar. He was running around like a

chicken with its head off begging some one to put him in the front line where he could have himself blown to smithereens. Now Durrell was talking the same way, the only difference being that he was not so crazy to be killed as to be with the Greek forces in Albania—because he thought more of the Greeks than he did of his own countrymen. I said as little as possible because if I had attempted to dissuade him I would only have succeeded in abetting his suicidal impulse. I didn't want to see him killed; it seemed to me that the war could very well be fought to its fruitless end without the sacrifice of one destined to give so much to the world. He knew what I thought about war and I think in his heart he agrees with me, but being young, being serviceable, being English despite himself, he was in a quandary. It was a bad place in which to discuss a subject of this sort. The atmosphere was charged with memories of Byron. Sitting there, with Missolonghi so near, it was almost impossible to think sanely about war. The British Consul of Patras was far more clear-headed. After a brief talk with him I felt a renewed respect for the British Empire. I also reminded myself that war hadn't actually been declared yet. It had threatened to break out so often—possibly it wouldn't happen after all.

We had a good meal at the public square and towards the late afternoon we took the automotrice for Athens. During the course of a conversation with some fellow travellers a Greek returning from America hailed me in jovial fashion as a brother American and began a long, irritatingly stupid monologue about the glories of Chicago, which I doubt he had ever lived in more than a month. The gist of it was that he was eager to get back home—meaning *America;* he found his countrymen ignorant, dirty, backward, inefficient and so on and so forth. Durrell interrupted once to inquire what language the man was speaking—he had never heard a Greek speaking that kind of American. The men I had been talking with were eager to know what this strange countryman of theirs was so excited about. We had been talking in French until this Yahoo came along. I told them in French that the man was an ignoramus. At this the Greek asked me what language I was speaking and when I said French he answered—"I don't know those languages; American's good enough for me . . . I'm from Chicago." Though I showed him plainly that I wasn't interested in listening to his stories he insisted on telling me all about himself. He said he was now on his way to a little mountain village where his mother lived; he wanted to say good-bye to her before leaving. "Show you how ignorant these people are," he added, "I brought a bath tub for my mother all the way from Chicago; I set it up with my own hands too. Think they appreciated it? They laughed at me, said I was crazy. They don't want to keep themselves clean. Now in Chicago . . ." I apologized to my fellow passengers for the presence of this idiot; I explained to them that that's what America does to its adopted sons. At this they all laughed heartily, including the benighted Greek at my side who hadn't understood a word I had said, since it was in French I made the remark. To cap it all the dolt asked me where I had learned my English. When I told him I was born in America he replied that he had never heard any one speak English like me; he said it in a way to imply that the only decent English worth speaking was his own slaughter-house variety.

*   *   *

In Athens it was actually chilly enough to wear an overcoat when we arrived. Athens has a temperamental climate, like New York. It has plenty of dust, too, if you start walking towards the outskirts. Even in the heart of the city sometimes, where the most fashionable, ultra-modern apartment houses are to be seen, the street is nothing but a dirt road. One can walk to the edge of the city in a half hour. It is really an enormous city containing almost a million inhabitants; it has grown a hundred times over since Byron's day. The colour scheme is blue and white, as it is throughout Greece. Even the newspapers use blue ink, a bright sky-blue, which makes the papers seem innocent and juvenile. The Athenians practically devour the newspapers; they have a perpetual hunger for news. From the balcony of my room at the Grand Hotel I could look down on Constitution Square, which in the evening is black with people, thousands of them, seated at little tables loaded with drinks and ices, the waiters scurrying back and forth with trays to the cafés adjoining the square.

Here one evening on his way back to Amaroussion I met Katsimbalis. It was definitely a meeting. As far as encounters with men go I have only known two others to compare with it in my whole life—when I met Blaise Cendrars and when I met Lawrence Durrell. I didn't have very much to say that first evening; I listened spellbound, enchanted by every phrase he let drop. I saw that he was made for the monologue, like Cendrars, like Moricand the astrologer. I like the monologue even more than the duet, when it is good. It's like watching a man write a book expressly for you: he writes it, reads it aloud, acts it, revises it, savours it, enjoys it, enjoys your enjoyment of it, and then tears it up and throws it to the winds. It's a sublime performance, because while he's going through with it you are God for him—unless you happen to be an insensitive and impatient dolt. But in that case the kind of monologue I refer to never happens.

He was a curious mixture of things to me on that first occasion; he had the general physique of a bull, the tenacity of a vulture, the agility of a leopard, the tenderness of a lamb, and the coyness of a dove. He had a curious overgrown head which fascinated me and which, for some reason, I took to be singularly Athenian. His hands were rather small for his body, and overly delicate. He was a vital, powerful man, capable of brutal gestures and rough words, yet somehow conveying a sense of warmth which was soft and feminine. There was also a great element of the tragic in him which his adroit mimicry only enhanced. He was extremely sympathetic and at the same time ruthless as a boor. He seemed to be talking about himself all the time, but never egotistically. He talked about himself because he himself was the most interesting person he knew. I liked that quality very much—I have a little of it myself.

We met a few days later to have dinner together—he, his wife Aspasia and the Durrells. After dinner we were to meet some friends of his. From the time he met us he was bubbling over. He was always that way, even on bad days when he complained of headache or dizziness or any of the hundred and one ailments which pestered him. He was taking us to a *taverna* in Piraeus, he said, because he wanted us to enjoy Greek cooking in the Greek way. It was one of his favourite hang-outs in the old days. "I made a mistake to get married," he said—his wife listening and smiling indulgently—"I wasn't cut out for marriage—it's ruining me. I can't sleep. I can't smoke, I can't drink any more. . . . I'm finished." He was always talking about himself as of some one who was done for: it was a little motif which he wove into the monologue by way of warming up to a subject. Things which happened only yesterday fell into this same nostalgic done-for past. Sometimes, when he talked this way, he gave me the impression of being an enormous tortoise which had slipped out of its shell, a creature which was spending itself in a desperate struggle to get back into the shell which it had outgrown. In this struggle he always made himself look grotesque and ridiculous— he did it deliberately. He would laugh at himself, in the tragic way of the buffoon. We would all laugh, his wife too. No matter how sad or morbid or pathetic the story might be he would have us laughing continuously. He saw the humorous aspect of everything, which is the real test of the tragic sense.

The food . . . food was something he was passionate about. He had been enjoying good food since childhood and I guess he will go on enjoying it until he dies. His father had been a great gourmet and Katsimbalis, though perhaps lacking some of his father's sensual refinements and accomplishments, was following the family tradition. Between great carnivorous gulps of food he would pound his chest like a gorilla before washing it down with a hogshead of *rezina*. He had drunk a lot of *rezina* in his time: he said it was good for one, good for the kidneys, good for the liver, good for the lungs, good for the bowels and for the mind, good for everything. Everything he took into his system was good, whether it was poison or ambrosia. He didn't believe in moderation or good sense or anything that was inhibitory. He believed in going the whole hog and then taking your punishment. There were a lot of things he couldn't do any more—the war had bunged him up a bit. But despite the bad

arm, the dislocated knee, the damaged eye, the disorganized liver, the rheumatic twinges, the arthritic disturbances, the migraine, the dizziness and God knows what, what was left of the catastrophe was alive and flourishing like a smoking dung-heap. He could galvanize the dead with his talk. It was a sort of devouring process: when he described a place he ate into it, like a goat attacking a carpet. If he described a person he ate him alive from head to toe. If it were an event he would devour every detail, like an army of white ants descending upon a forest. He was everywhere at once, in his talk. He attacked from above and below, from the front, rear and flanks. If he couldn't dispose of a thing at once, for lack of a phrase

THE HARBOR AT MYKONOS, A BROWN-AND-WHITE AEGEAN ISLAND.

or an image, he would spike it temporarily and move on, coming back to it later and devouring it piecemeal. Or like a juggler, he would toss it in the air and, just when you thought he had forgotten it, that it would fall and break, he would deftly put an arm behind his back and catch it in his palm without even turning his eye. It wasn't just talk he handed out, but *language*—food and beast language. He always talked against a landscape, like the protagonist of a lost world. The Attic landscape was best of all for his purpose: it contains the necessary ingredients for the dramatic monologue. One has only to see the open air theatres buried in the hillsides to understand the importance of this setting. Even if his talk carried him to Paris, for example, to a place like the Faubourg Montmartre, he spiced and flavoured it with his Attic ingredients, with thyme, sage, tufa, asphodetl honey, red clay, blue roofs, acanthus trimmings, viole, light, hot rocks, dry winds, dust, *rezina*, arthritis and the electrical crackle that plays over the low hills like a swift serpent with a broken spine. He was a strange contradiction, even in his talk. With his snake-like tongue which struck like lightning, with fingers moving nervously, as though wandering over an imaginary spinet, with pounding, brutal gestures which somehow never smashed anything but simply raised a din, with all the boom of surf and the roar and sizzle and razzle-dazzle, if you suddenly observed him closely you got the impression that he was sitting there immobile, that only the round falcon's eye was alert, that he was a bird which had been hypnotized, or had hypnotized itself, and that his claws were fastened to the wrist of an invisible giant, a giant like the earth. All this flurry and din, all these kaleidoscopic prestidigitations of his, were only a sort of wizardry which he employed to conceal the fact that he was a prisoner —that was the impression he gave me when I studied him, when I could break the spell for a moment and observe him attentively. But to break the spell required a power and a magic almost equal to his own; it made one feel foolish and impotent, as one always does when one succeeds in destroying the power of illusion. Magic is never destroyed—the most we can do is to cut ourselves off, amputate the mysterious antennae which serve to connect us with forces beyond our power of understanding. Many a time as Katsimbalis talked, I caught that look on the face of a listener which told me that the invisible wires had been connected, that something was being communicated which was over and above language, over and above personality, something magical which we

WINDMILL AT MYKONOS.

recognize in dream and which makes the face of the sleeper relax and expand with a bloom such as we rarely see in waking life. Often when meditating on this quality of his I thought of his frequent allusions to the incomparable honey which is stored by the bees on the slopes of his beloved Hymettos. Over and over he would try to explain the reasons why this honey from Mount Hymettos was unique. Nobody can explain it satisfactorily. Nobody can explain anything which is unique. One can describe, worship and adore. And that is all I can do with Katsimbalis' talk.

*   *   *

It was later, after I had returned to Corfu and had had a good taste of solitude, that I appreciated the Katsimbalistic monologue even more. Lying nude in the sun on a ledge of rock by the sea I would often close my eyes and try to re-weave the pattern of his talks. It was then that I made the discovery that his talk created reverberations, that the echo took a long time to reach one's ears. I began to compare it with French talk in which I had been enveloped for so long. The latter seemed more like the play of light on an alabaster vase, something reflective, nimble, dancing, liquid, evanescent, whereas the other, the Katsimbalistic language, was opaque, cloudy, pregnant with

STREET TWISTING BETWEEN WHITEWASHED HOUSES ON MYKONOS.

MYKONOS CHURCH.

resonances which could be understood only long afterwards, when the reverberations announced the collision with thoughts, people, objects located in distant parts of the earth. The Frenchman puts walls about his talk, as he does about his garden: he puts limits about everything in order to feel at home. At bottom he lacks confidence in his fellow-man; he is sceptical because he doesn't believe in the innate goodness of human beings. He has become a realist because it is safe and practical. The Greek, on the other hand, is an adventurer: he is reckless and adaptable, he makes friends easily. The walls which you see in Greece, when they are not of Turkish or Venetian origin, go back to the Cyclopean age. Of my own experience I would say that there is no more direct, approachable, easy man to deal with than the Greek. He becomes a friend immediately: he goes out to you. With the Frenchman friendship is a long and laborious process: it may take a lifetime to make a friend of him. He is best in acquaintanceship, where there is little to risk and where there are no after-maths. The very word *ami* contains almost nothing of the flavour of friend, as we feel it in English. *C'est mon ami* can not be translated by "This is my friend."

There is no counterpart to this English phrase in the French language. It is a gap which has never been filled, like the word "home." These things affect conversation. One can converse all right, but it is difficult to have a heart-to-heart talk. All France, it has often been said, is a garden, and if you love France, as I do, it can be a very beautiful garden. For myself I found it healing and soothing to the spirit; I recovered from the shocks and bruises which I had received in my own country. But there comes a day, when you are well again and strong, when this atmosphere ceases to be nourishing. You long to break out and test your powers. Then the French spirit seems inadequate. You long to make friends, to create enemies, to look beyond walls and cultivated patches of earth. You want to cease thinking in terms of life insurance, sick benefits, old age pensions and so on.

After the succulent repast at the *taverna* in Piraeus, all of us a bit stinko from the *rezina*, we moved back to the big square in Athens. It was midnight or a little after and the square still crowded with people. Katsimbalis seemed to divine the spot where his friends were seated. We were introduced to his bosom comrades, George Seferiades and Captain Antoniou of the good ship *Acropolis*. They soon began plying me with questions about America and American writers. Like most educated Europeans they knew more about American literature than I ever will. Antoniou had been to America several times, had walked about the streets of New York, Boston, New Orleans, San Fran-

cisco and other ports. The thought of him walking about the streets of our big cities in bewilderment led me to broach the name of Sherwood Anderson, whom I always think of as the one American writer of our time who has walked the streets of our American cities as a genuine poet. Since they scarcely knew his name, and since the conversation was already veering towards more familiar ground, namely Edgar Allan Poe, a subject I am weary of listening to, I suddenly became obsessed with the idea of selling them Sherwood Anderson. I began a monologue myself for a change—about writers who walk the streets in America and are not recognized until they are ready for the grave. I was so enthusiastic about the subject that I actually identified myself with Sherwood Anderson. He would probably have been astounded had he heard of the exploits I was crediting him with. I've always had a particular weakness for the author of *Many Marriages*. In my worst days in America he was the man who comforted me, by his writings. It was only the other day that I met him for the first time. I found no discrepancy between the man and the writer. I saw in him the born story teller, the man who can make even the egg triumphant.

As I say, I went on talking about Sherwood Anderson like a blue streak. It was to Captain Antoniou that I chiefly addressed myself. I remember the look he gave me when I had finished, the look which said: "Sold. Wrap them up, I'll take the whole set." Many times since I've enjoyed the pleasure of rereading Sherwood Anderson through Antoniou's eyes. Antoniou is constantly sailing from one island to another, writing his poems as he walks about strange cities at night. Once, a few months later, I met him for a few minutes one evening in the strange port of Herakleion in Crete. He was still thinking about Sherwood Anderson, though his talk was of cargoes and weather reports and water supplies. Once out to sea I could picture him going up to his cabin and, taking a little book from the rack, bury himself in the mysterious night of a nameless Ohio town. The night always made me a little envious of him, envious of his peace and solitude at sea. I envied him the islands he was always stopping off at and the lonely walks through silent villages whose names mean nothing to us. To be a pilot was the first ambition I had ever voiced. I liked the idea of being alone in the little house above the deck, steering the ship over its perilous course. To be aware of the weather, to be in it, battling with it, meant everything to me. In Antoniou's countenance there were always traces of the weather. And in Sherwood Anderson's writing there are always traces of the weather. I like men who have the weather in their blood. . . .

We separated in the early hours of the morning. I went back to the hotel, opened the window and stood for a while on the balcony looking down on the square which was now deserted. I had made two more stalwart Greek friends and I was happy about it. I began to think of all the friends I had made in the short time that I was there. I thought of Spiro, the taxi-driver, and of Karemenaios, the gendarme. There was also Max, the refugee, living like a duke at the King George Hotel; he seemed to have nothing on his mind but how to make his friends happy with the drachmas which he couldn't take out of the country. There was also the proprietor of my hotel who, unlike any French hotel keeper I have ever met, used to say to me at intervals—"Do you need any money?" If I told him I was taking a little trip he would say: "Be sure to wire me if you need any money." Spiro was the same way. When we said good-bye at the dock the night of the general panic, his last words were—"Mr Henry, if you come back to Corfu I want you to stay with me. I don't want any money, Mr Henry—I want you to come and live with us as long as you like." Everywhere I went in Greece it was the same tune. Even at the prefecture, while waiting to have my papers put in order, the gendarme would send out for a coffee and cigarettes to put me at ease. I liked the way they begged too. They weren't shamefaced about it. They would hold you up openly and ask for money or cigarettes as if they were entitled to it. It's a good sign when people beg that way: it means that they know how to give. The French, for example, know neither how to give nor how to ask for favours—either way they feel uneasy. They make a virtue of not molesting you. It's the wall again. A Greek has no walls around him; he gives and takes without stint.

The English in Greece—a sorry lot, by the way—seem to have a poor opinion of the Greek character. The English are torpid, unimaginative, lacking in resiliency. They seem to think that the Greeks should be eternally grateful to them because they have a powerful fleet. The Englishman in Greece is a farce and an eye-sore: he isn't worth the dirt between a poor Greek's toes. For centuries the Greeks have had the cruellest enemy a people could have—the Turks. After centuries of enslavement they threw off the yoke and, had the big Powers not interfered, they would probably have driven the Turks into the ground and annihilated them. Today the two peoples, after an exchange of populations which is nothing if not extraordinary, are friends. They respect one another. And yet the English, who would have disappeared from the face of the earth had they been subjected to the same treatment, pretend to look down on the Greeks.

Everywhere you go in Greece the atmosphere is pregnant with heroic deeds. I am speaking of modern Greece, not ancient Greece. And the women, when you look into the history of this little country, were just as heroic as the men. In fact, I have even a greater respect for the Greek woman than for the Greek man. The Greek woman and the Greek Orthodox priest—they sustained the fighting spirit. For stubbornness, courage, recklessness, daring, there are no greater examples anywhere. No wonder Durrell wanted to fight with the Greeks. Who wouldn't prefer to fight beside a Bouboulina, for example, than with a gang of sickly, effeminate recruits from Oxford or Cambridge?

I made no English friends in Greece. I felt apologetic towards the Greeks whenever I was found in their company. The friends I made in Greece were Greek and I am proud of them, honoured that they consider me a friend. I hope that the few Englishmen I knew in Greece will realize, when they read these lines, what I thought of their behaviour. I hope they will consider me an enemy of their kind.

I'd rather talk about something more interesting—about Katsimbalis, for instance, about the visit to his home in Amaroussion one day towards twilight. Another marvellous day, another red letter day in my life! We had been asked to come early in order to watch the sunset. Stephanides had made a translation of some Greek poems—we were going to hear them in English. When we arrived Katsimbalis hadn't quite finished his nap. He was rather ashamed of being caught napping because he was always bragging about how little sleep he required. He came downstairs looking a bit foggy and pasty. He was talking as if to himself, making little futile gestures with his hands as if to get the damned spinet working. He was mumbling something about a word which he had remembered in his dream a few moments ago. He was always rummaging about in his brain for adequate English words and phrases to express some remarkable Greek image which he had just stumbled on in a book. Anyway, as I say, we had roused him from a sound sleep and he was moving about in a drugged way, muttering and gesturing like a man trying to shake off the cobwebs which still enveloped him. His talk began on the fringe of this dream which he had not wholly shaken clear of. To begin you begin anywhere, and since he had just been dreaming he talked dream. The dream was unimportant, forgotten in a moment, but the remembrance of the dream led him back to the word which had been bothering him, which he had been tracking down for days, so he said, and which was now becoming clearer as he himself became clearer, as the cobwebs fell away. The word, whatever it was, led to language and language led to honey and honey was good for one, as were other things, *rezina* for example, especially *rezina*, good for the lungs, good for the liver, good for anything that ailed you, especially too much of it, which one should not do, not take too much of it, but which he did anyway regardless of the doctor's orders, particularly if it were a good *rezina* such as the one we had the other night at the *taverna* in Piraeus. The young lamb was good too, had we noticed? He made the gesture of licking his fingers, wiped his mouth with the back of his hand, sniffed the air as though to breathe again the aromatic smoke from the oven. He paused a moment and looked about him, as if searching for something with which to wet his tongue before going into the monologue full tilt. Nobody said anything. Nobody dared to interrupt now just as he was getting into his stride. The poems were lying on the table; Seferiades was expected any moment and the captain with him. I could feel that he was growing a bit frantic inwardly, that he was making a rapid calculation to see if there were time enough to get it off his chest before his friends arrived. He was fluttering a bit, like a bird whose wing is caught. He kept on mumbling and muttering, just to keep the engine going until he had decided on his direction. And then somehow, without being aware of the transition, we were standing on the aerial verandah overlooking the low hills, on one of which there was a lone windmill, and Katsimbalis was in full flight, a spread eagle performance about the clear atmosphere and the blue-violet hues that descend with the twilight, about ascending and descending varieties of monotony, about individualistic herbs and trees, about exotic fruits and inland voyages, about thyme and honey and the sap of the arbutus which makes one drunk, about islanders and highlanders, about the men of the Peloponnesus, about the crazy Russian woman who got moonstruck one night and threw off her clothes, how she danced about in the moonlight without a stitch on while her lover ran to get a strait-jacket. As he talked I was taking in for the first time with my own eyes the true splendour of the Attic landscape, observing with a growing exhilaration that here and there over the bare brown sward, amidst anomalous and eccentric growths, men and women, single, solitary figures, were strolling about in the clear fading light, and for some reason they appeared to me as being very Greek, walking as no other people walk, making clear-cut patterns in their ethereal meandering, patterns such as I had seen earlier in the day on the vases in the museum. There are so many ways of walking about and the best, in my opinion, is the Greek way, because it is aimless, anarchic, thoroughly and discordantly human. And this walking about on the brown sward amidst the eccentric, inelegant trees, the thick foliage flying like hair stiff-brushed in the well of the distant mountains, blended strangely with the Katsimbalistic monologue which I heard, digested and silently communicated to the Asiatic loungers below who were fading softly now in the dimming light. . . . On the high verandah in Amaroussion, just as the light from the other worlds began to shed its brilliance, I caught the old and the new Greece in their soft translucence and thus they remain in my memory. I realized at that moment that there is no old or new, only Greece, a world conceived and created in perpetuity. The man who was talking had ceased to be of human size or proportion, but had become a Colossus whose silhouette swooned backwards and forwards with the deep droning rhythm of his drug-laden phrases. He went on and on, unhurried, unruffled, inexhaustible, inextinguishable, a voice that had taken form and shape and substance, a figure that had outgrown its human frame, a silhouette whose reverberations rumbled into the depths of the distant mountain sides.

HERBERT KUBLY

from EASTER IN SICILY

A PREMIER American authority on Italy casts an eye on the strange island at the toe of the boot.

BETWEEN EUROPE AND AFRICA in the Mediterranean lies the island on which Plato dreamed of establishing his republic.

When I set out on the series of journeys which have resulted in this book, an American businessman who has lived in Palermo for many years said, "You will be talking with Sicilians. Do not believe them. Remember that Sicilians do not comprehend truth as we do. Sicilian truth is a relative mixture of legend and fantasy."

Living at the crossroads of both time and space, the Sicilian is the most enigmatic of Europeans. The twenty-seven hundred years of his recorded history is a roll call of invaders—Phoenicians, Greeks, Romans, Carthaginians, Byzantines, Vandals, Saracens, Normans, Spaniards, Garibaldi's red-shirted thousand and the Nazis and Allies of World War II. His blood is the blood of many races, his culture the repository of many cultures. His religion is a Christianity which incorporated rather than displaced the ancient paganism of his ancestors. His homeland is an Eden from which he has been cast by the sinful greed of landlords. He lives in a world of his own, escaping the brute reality of his material life into one of fantasy and legend.

Legends arise from nature; the Sicilian creates his from the landscape about him. It is possible even for a northerner to believe in the birth of Aphrodite as he looks down to the sea from the exalted perch of Erïce; as he stands on the terrible cliffs of Enna, the abduction of Persephone is utterly comprehensible. From Aphrodite and Persephone to Mary the Virgin Mother, from Charlemagne and the Norman heroes of the Crusades to the twentieth-century Salvatore Giuliano, the Sicilian peoples his life with gods and lives with them on intimate terms.

Sicily is the Easter island not in the limited Christian sense—though Sicilians will tell you that Jesus' first earthly appearance after the Resurrection was in Sicily—but in the sense of a reawakening of life. From January to June, Sicily is the land of spring, a *campo dei fiori*, a field of flowers. These are the months Persephone lives on earth—in Sicily, of course. The months when she is underground with her abductor, Sicily is scorched with sorrow. Living close to the earth, a Sicilian is keenly aware of the Easter cycle of renewal: it makes him an optimistic and exuberant lover of life.

*   *   *

Sicilians say nature covers their island with wild flowers to celebrate Persephone, who was gathering them when Pluto abducted her. We drove through fields of daisies, anemones, marigolds, meadows of red poppies, valleys of iris bluer than the heavens, and rows of ripening orange groves. There were also flaming spikes which I didn't recognize and a tiny lilac blossom that looked like heather. It was the time of the spring harvest and the farmers were gathering peas, piling the green pods high on their gay donkey carts. Cart painters are Sicily's popular historians; they treat legend and fact with equal spontaneity. Sicily's history is long and tumultuous. The ancient tribes of Sicani and Siculi were conquered by, and in turn absorbed, Phoenicians, Greeks, Romans, Vandals, Byzantines, Saracens, Normans, and Spaniards. In addition to the blood of their conquerors, the Sicilians also absorbed

their legends. Venus rises from her shell, the Virgin is assumed into heaven. Charlemagne commissions his knights, and the cross-eyed Orlando duels with Saracens; Garibaldi unites Italy and Salvatore Giuliano is martyred by an assassin's bullet. It was all on the carts.

*   *   *

The Mediterraneo stood on a ledge between the sea and the town. From the terrace I could look out on my left to the sea seven hundred feet below, on my right to Mount Venus two thousand feet above. Across a piazza was a roofed shrine covering an old, armless Madonna. The piazza was a busy crossroads opening on one side to the town's public gardens, and on the other to one of the steep and dangerous footpaths going down to the seaside railroad station of Giardino.

Each morning was like watching the Creation. First there was light, rising like a coral flame to warm the world; then the sea lashing against the ancient grottoes and turning into a thousand shades of turquoise. The earth followed, with the graceful profile of Etna wearing a nimbus halo and a snow mantle of glowing cerise. Soon it was light enough to see the lemons, almonds, cedars, palms, red poppies, white arum lilies, amaryllis, hibiscus, and paper-crisp purple azalea, all growing in jungle profusion. Animals came next—slinking cats winding up their nocturnal missions and dogs sniffing across the piazza. The birds in the garden heralded the day, cocks crowed in the town, and fantailed white doves made love.

Finally man appeared on the piazza in all his curious variations. First the young blades of the town, in their pin-striped suits and camel's-hair coats, going wearily home from their night's assignations; then barefoot fishermen, returning with their catch in sacks on their backs. As the town awakened, the dairyman drove his goats to the piazza, where the animals bleated impatiently while he bowed for a morning prayer before the Madonna. Then he milked them into the pans and pails of the women of the neighborhood.

Women carried everything on their heads. On one a bundle of laundry bobbled like a fantastic headdress, on another a basket of greens. One wide old woman swayed like a camel as she balanced a crock on her head. She was old and lame and tackled each stair sideways, like a donkey, zigzagging up the whole long climb. The brown-skinned boy who sold jellyfish carried a basket of the nasty gray stuff in one hand and in the other a brass-chained scale to weigh it. Children were the last—wrestling little boys and girls who skipped rope and brought nosegays of daisies and violets to lay before the Madonna.

(continued on page 390)

KRONFELD © PAA

KRONFELD © PAA

KRONFELD © PAA

KRONFELD © PAA

(continued from page 337)

At eight o'clock the watchman unlocked the iron garden gates, and the children rushed in, followed by camera-laden tourists, Austrians in *Lederhosen*, Swiss in knit stockings, Swedes in embroidered blouses. New arrivals from the morning train trudged arduously up the path, stopping for breath by the Madonna. Nuns held hands as if they were children; priests, their sandaled feet covered with dust, recited breviaries. If it was Sunday, the caravan was long, with carefree Sicilian families, the father and older children carrying baskets of food and wine, and musical instruments, and the mother following with the little ones. When the morning caravan had arrived, I considered the day well born.

Many have called Taormina the most beautiful place in the world. I know none more beautiful. The youngest of Sicily's Greek colonies, it rose from the ashes of the oldest, called Naxos. Naxos was founded in the eighth century B.C. by Greek traders who landed their craft in a natural harbor and raised an altar to Apollo, laying the way for five centuries of Greek domination by Sicily. Only three years ago Taormina fishermen discovered at the bottom of the sea in the vicinity of ancient Naxos the remnants of a temple and a rich archaeological vein of vases and coins.

Dionysius destroyed Naxos; her survivors climbed to the ledge above the sea and founded Taormina, which flourished for three centuries as a Greek city. Today it is a village of less than five thousand citizens who live by serving tourists, mostly German, English, American, and Scandinavian. Northern visitors are drawn not only by its natural beauty but by its reputation for license. For this Taormina is largely indebted to the German baron with a camera who for forty years before his death in 1931 made and sold some four thousand nude photographs of the natives. These were the photographs which the Canadian had wanted for his anthropological alter ego. Taormina's greatest prosperity, however, came in the thirties, when Mussolini's luxury-loving Nazi admirers filled her hotels. During the war, Taormina held the historical spotlight for a brief moment when it was the headquarters for the German general staff.

The inevitable Allied bombings cost Taormina dearly in lives and property. Though the scars are evident—the destroyed San Domenico church probably never will be rebuilt—Taorminians, with their eyes on the tourist dollar, have worked hard to restore their town. But for some of the war's changes there is no restoration. Dwindling fortunes and higher taxes kept people away, and the expected postwar boom came slowly. What with fewer idle Americans and the English unable to export funds, there is no longer a distinguished foreign colony. Some of the villas are closed.

A few are rented on short-term leases to Americans, and more have been converted into *pensioni*. It is from the *pensione* dwellers that Taorminians maintain a moderate and steady prosperity. Their town is the cleanest in Sicily. A strong civic organization encourages the people to keep the streets scrubbed, as in a Dutch village. Begging is illegal. Prices are moderate and the tradespeople, most of whom speak enough English and German to do business, are congenial.

The place affects each man in his own way. For me Taormina was an extravagant theater with a never-ending polyglot drama—exaggerated, grotesque, bizarre, and tragic—played against a setting of wondrous beauty, with the incidental music supplied by Etna's *Götterdämmerung* rumblings and the sweet melodies of shepherds' pipes. The Reverend John Henry Newman, of the Church of England, who eventually became a famous cardinal of the Roman Church, looking down from the hilltop ruins of Taormina's Greek theater in 1833, said: "I felt for the first time in my life that I should be a better and more religious man if I lived there." Taormina's impact on modern visitors would have disturbed the Reverend Newman. A lady painter who left Oslo and a Norwegian husband to settle in Taormina said, "The moral landscape here is as different as the physical landscape. I found when I came here that the light was entirely different from the light in Norway. I needed different colors to paint. It's the same in matters of morality. One has to accept the different light, the different colors. It is useless to fight them. If you did not accept them, you could not live here."

In matters of sex, the lights and colors were certainly confused. Italy's double standard, her age-old battle between pagan and Christian morality, is nowhere more apparent than in this Sicilian village. Every young male fancies himself to be a satyr. Every young girl must remain a virgin. Although much of the everlasting boasting of the men is fantasy, one seldom sees unmarried native girls on the streets. Their virtue, an educated young Sicilian explained, "is something to be preserved, to be carried to the altar on a satin pillow." No matter how profligate he is, the young man demands virginity of the girl he marries. A sister's honor is protected at any cost. A young man who boasted constantly of his sexual exploits had a lovely sister whom I had seen stitching behind drawn curtains in the family's embroidery shop. When I asked him if I might meet her, he became hostile; soon word reached me from friends that he was threatening to beat me if I dared to look at her through the window again.

With tourists, young Taorminians are purposefully earnest. Their concept of hospitality toward ladies is not only bedding and boarding them, but also bedding with them. With the compulsive polarity of the fair for the dark, Calvinist guilt for Latin innocence, unattached women flock from northern winters to the southern sun. A young Sicilian said, "Brünnehilde comes to Dionysius for the phallic cure."

Some generous visitors are men, and for them the youths of Taormina make an easy adjustment. In a book called *Sicily, the New Winter Resort*, published in London in 1905, Douglas Sladen writes with curious Victorian innocence:

"Boys are a feature in Sicily. There are always dozens around a stranger. I think the best-looking boys that have come into my experience have been at Girgenti [Agrigento]. In the province of Messina [including Taormina] especially, you constantly meet boys as beautiful as Greek statues. At Modica you get a superb, aquiline type of men, but not beautiful youths."

Young Sicilian males are narcissists, and their sexuality is their godhead. They also feel a strong attachment to their mothers. Later they may lavish their affection on their children, the proud fruit of the phallus. Because childlessness is a disgrace, marriage is necessary. A wife is as essential to a man as a donkey to a farmer, but she is not necessarily an object of sentiment. An American girl with a camera was asked by a proud young Sicilian father to take photographs of his new twins, about to be released from the hospital. He arrived for the occasion resplendent in new suit and flashy necktie, ignored his wife, and posed with the babies as proudly, said the girl, "as if he'd done all the work." When he called for the pictures several days later, he made amorous overtures, explaining that "my wife is only the mother of my children."

Though "Swedish women" (Taorminians use the term loosely to cover all Scandinavian women, including Norwegians and Danes) and German girls are in abundance, English and Americans are popular—especially Americans, who usually have the most money. Since most women come for no more than a fortnight, little time is lost. The young men meet tourist busses in the town square and trains at the Giardino station, surveying prospects as the cars unload, introducing themselves in working English or German, carrying bags, arranging for hotels and taxis. In the village the young men frequent cafés, bars, and night clubs, walking usually in twos and threes up the Corso Umberto, from the Messina gate to the Catania gate, and down again. Some of the more enterprising take waiters' jobs in the hotels, working for as little as thirty-two cents a day, for the opportunity to make advantageous contacts. The most exotic operations are down by the sea. Like a chorus of young Apollos, they sport their browned bodies, chase one another in games, and strike up acquaintances with strangers. A few, pretending to be fishermen, own boats with which to beguile visitors to the jutting promontory of rock known as Isola Bella. The beach boys put a high price on themselves. An Englishwoman complained that her twenty-one-year-old fisherman cost her more money than it took to send her son, of the same age, to Oxford. With the money she was giving the fisherman, however, he was supporting a wife and two children.

When a holiday is over, the visitor is gaily escorted back to the station. Unless she has learned in the meantime the cynical ease with which the word *amore* flows from her swain's tongue, unless she has discovered that sentiment is a northern characteristic, she does not know that during the farewell kisses an eye over her shoulder is watching new arrivals stepping off the train. She finds out quickly enough, however, when she sees through a coach window her lover-unto-death returning to the village with another girl.

H. V. MORTON

from A TRAVELLER IN ROME

TO MOST VISITORS a lifetime seems too short to begin to survey and comprehend Roman history.

HAUNTED BY DAY, the Pincio and the Borghese Gardens are even more ghostly in the dark. Here is a part of Rome that has never been built upon since ancient times, the place where Lucullus had his fabulous palace and laid out gardens, and where he gave those feasts which have become even more famous in the long perspective of time than his victory over Mithradates.

The quickest way to a fortune in Roman times was to be governor of a province: and some of the most cultivated of Romans milked the Empire and returned, as Lucullus did, rich with the spoils of Asia, to settle down as millionaires and startle contemporaries by their extravagance. The Gardens of Lucullus stretched over the Pincian Hill, but the palace itself, with its porticoes, library, and a series of dining-halls, occupied the southern slopes, where the Spanish Steps are today. Plutarch says that once when Pompey was ill, his doctor ordered him a dish of thrushes—alas, still a Roman delicacy!—which could be found nowhere at that particular time of year except in the breeding pens of Lucullus on the Pincian Hill. Lucullus was the first to introduce cherries into Italy from Asia, and so to western Europe. Plutarch also tells the story of Cicero and Pompey, who, meeting Lucullus by chance in the Forum, decided to find out if the rumour were true that the famous epicure ate hardly anything when alone. As it was presumably near dinner time, and Lucullus was not giving a party, they asked if they might dine with him, and he, seeming rather confused, asked for a day's warning, to which they would not agree. Lucullus then sent a message to his steward, saying that he intended to dine in the Apollo Room; and when the three arrived they sat down to one of the stupendous feasts for which their host was famous. It appeared that each room had its own standard of expenditure, scale of entertainment and style of menu, and it was sufficient for the steward merely to know the name of the room in which his master would dine for him to put on the appropriate banquet.

But the ghost that comes stealing out of the shadows on the Pincian Hill is not that of Lucullus, securely resting beneath a mound of honeyed dormice and nightingales' tongues, but of the frightened Messalina, who was murdered in those same halls. This puzzling woman seized the Gardens some years after the death of Lucullus, when they belonged to her enemy, Valerius Asiaticus. Having hounded this wretched man to his death, she took possession of his property, and the gardens on the Pincian Hill became her favourite retreat. Here it was that she took refuge when at last her doting husband, the elderly Claudius, apparently the last man in Rome to hear of her escapades, was eventually roused against her. We shall never know whether Messalina was as bad as she had been portrayed. It is possible that a woman like Agrippina, her successor in the imperial palace, played a great part in her defamation. Messalina was only twenty-six at the time of her death, which seems an early age for her to have accomplished all the infamies attributed to her. However, the night poor Claudius was told that she was even worse than his former wives, Messalina, realizing that at last she had roused the unpredictable cruelty of a weak man, fled to the Gardens of Lucullus, hoping that the storm would blow over. So it

might have done had not Narcissus, the freedman, quickly despatched a tribune with a detachment of the guard with orders to execute the Empress. They found her on the Pincian Hill, seated on the floor of an apartment, weeping in her mother's arms: the mother who had remained in the background during the years of her prosperity and had now hastened to comfort her in her despair. As the garden gates were opened and the tramp of the approaching soldiers was heard, Lepida tried to persuade her daughter to leave the world like a Roman and to take her own life. The tribune and his guard entered the room. A dagger was handed to Messalina. She pointed it at her throat, then at her breast, but lacked the courage to press it in. The tribune then drew his sword and killed her at a blow.

Some time later the Emperor, noticing that she was not at the dinner table, asked where she was.

*   *   *

The Roman piazza, whose ancestor was the Forum and whose children are the squares of Europe, is capable of great variety. A piazza can be a junction, like the Piazza dell' Esedra and the Piazza Venezia; it can also be a backwater hardly more than a slightly wider street, like the Piazza dei Santi Apostoli, or the tiny Piazza Mattei, which nevertheless holds the most enchanting fountain in Rome—the Fountain of the Tortoises—or it can be a little local exchange where men are always discussing employment and suchlike things, as they do in the Piazza della Rotonda, opposite the Pantheon.

Those which linger in my memory are the Piazza di Spagna, with its ochre houses and its sweep of steps; the Piazza dell' Esedra with the gaunt pink ruins of the Baths of Diocletian in the background; the Piazza Colonna with its cafés and the surging Corso; the Piazza Barberini, with the Triton sitting so calmly in a traffic roundabout; and the Piazza del Popolo, in which you take your life in your hands whenever you leave the pavement. Neither the Piazza del Campidoglio nor that of St. Peter's comes within the normal category.

Of all the piazze in Rome the one which gave me the greatest pleasure was the Piazza Navona, near the Pantheon, in the old Campus Martius. It is a long, narrow piazza whose shape corresponds to that of the stadium of Domitian which once stood there, and I do not know of a more striking illustration of the process which has continued throughout Roman history of the transformation of the old into the new. The piazza still looks like a Roman racecourse. When a taxi rushes from a side street and encircles the piazza, it is repeating on the same ground the course of ancient chariots, and even the *spina* of the stadium is represented today by the three groups of statuesque fountains in the centre.

In the cellars of the houses are to be seen the well-preserved foundations of the seats and corridors of the stadium, and the most accessible are those beneath the church of St. Agnes. A priest took me down into an ancient Roman brothel, which is the strange shrine preserved in this church: it is the place where St. Agnes was flung naked, and where her hair covered her and she received a miraculous garment of light. The three or four rooms covered with frescoes, unfortunately now peeling from the walls with damp, clearly show the *fornix*, or arch, of the old stadium.

The chief features of the piazza are the uninhibited fountains by Bernini and his pupils. The Fountain of the Rivers is fascinating, and though I admired the vigorous figures, I thought there was a faint touch of absurdity about the Nile, with its shrouded head, for its source was then a mystery, the horse plunging out of the cavern, the lion slinking down to drink, and the heavy obelisk resting, apparently, on nothing: but I returned time after time to enjoy them and the splash of water which had come underground from the Trevi and was on its way, with typical Roman wastefulness where water is concerned, to the Tiber.

In the eyes of Pope Urban VIII Bernini could do no wrong. At that time there were two other artists in the same happy situation: Velazquez in Spain, who was steadily painting the ever more upward mustachios of Philip IV, and Van Dyck in London, whose studio at Blackfriars was so frequently visited by Charles I. Though Bernini in his long life of over eighty years served eight Popes and filled Rome with his exuberant genius, no one gave him greater admiration and encouragement than Urban VIII, and he, of course, knew only Bernini's earlier works, the Barberini Palace, the Triton, and the baldacchino in St. Peter's. It is recorded that after his election Urban VIII summoned Bernini and said: "It is your great good luck to see Barberini pope; but we are even luckier that Bernini lives at the time of our pontificate." The Pope loved to watch the artist at work, and someone entering Bernini's studio one day was astonished to see the Pontiff quietly holding a mirror while Bernini made a self-portrait.

After Urban's death Bernini's hasty Neapolitan tongue, and his rivals, brought him into disfavour with Innocent X, whose sister-in-law, the avaricious Donna Olimpia Pamphili, tried to wear the tiara. The only thing to do was to make friends with that terrifying woman. The house in which he succeeded in doing so, and in which she lived, occupies a corner of the piazza, a dark and solemn building, the Palazzo Pam-phili. Prevented by disfavour from erecting the obelisk and designing the fountains in the piazza, Bernini was persuaded to design and make a model in silver, which Donna Olimpia placed skilfully in a room through which the Pope would pass one evening. Innocent was fascinated by the model and would consider no other artist's designs.

Innocent X was seventy-two at the time of his election, a gentle and compassionate man, but completely dominated by his widowed sister-in-law. The Vatican grew shrill with feminine disputes from which the poor Pope tried to hide himself, and the Pamphili Palace became the place where most decisions were made. As Innocent X lay dying, in the only shirt he possessed, and covered with a torn blanket, his sister-in-law slipped into the room and drew from beneath the bed two boxes of money which the Pope had managed to keep concealed from her. Innocent died alone, deserted by his enriched family. When asked to provide for his burial, Donna Olimpia said she was a poor widow and could not afford to do so. The body was taken to St. Peter's and placed in a room where the masons kept their tools: a workman, out of pity, lit a candle beside it, and, as the place was full of rats, someone was paid to watch for two or three nights. Eventually a compassionate canon, whom Innocent had once dismissed, spent five crowns on the Pope's funeral. It is difficult to believe this sad story as you look at the portrait of Innocent X by Velazquez in the Palazzo Doria, or at his memorial in the church of St. Agnes, erected a hundred years later.

The portrait was painted in 1649, when Velazquez was in Rome buying antique statues for Philip IV of Spain. Many believe it to be one of the three or four best portraits ever painted, and Joshua Reynolds considered it the finest portrait in Rome. I have often stood before it in the long corridor of the Doria palace, full of Louis XIV gilt settees and tables, and wondered if Innocent X may not have been rather a Jekyll and Hyde. As Velazquez saw him, this Pope was not a man to be bullied and pilfered by any woman; he looks shrewd and implacable, and not an attractive personality. Yet in the same palace is Bernini's bust, and here we see a kind and gentle dreamer, a man who would seek peace and give away his last farthing to avoid a scene. Which is the real Innocent X? Bernini knew him better than Velazquez, yet one must remember that Bernini had every reason to flatter the Pope, whereas Velazquez had none. I doubt whether two great artists have ever interpreted a man so differently, and it is a pity that most visitors to the Palazzo Doria leave after having seen the portrait and do not look for the bust.

During the pontificate of Innocent X there began

in the Piazza Navona those curious water festivals which lasted until 1867. On Sundays during the great heat of July and August the pipes carrying away the fountain water were closed, and the fountains were allowed to overflow until the square was deep in water. Parties were given in the houses round about, bands were engaged to play, and the aristocracy in their gilded coaches drove slowly through the water. Among those who enjoyed this festival were the Old Pretender and Maria Clementina, who were known in Rome as James III and Queen Clementina of England. On one occasion in 1727 someone, happening to glance up at a balcony, saw Bonnie Prince Charlie, then a child of seven, excitedly throwing coins into the water for the street urchins. At the first stroke of the Ave Maria bell the coaches would disappear and the square was drained.

The Piazza Navona has known every kind of public entertainment: in Roman times there were chariot racing and athletic sports; in the Middle Ages there were tournaments and bullfights; and in the eighteenth century there was the Festa di Agosto. Today its annual excitement is the Befana, a corruption of the word Epiphany, which is held in January. The Romans visualize Befana as an elderly fairy, a gruff old woman like a female Santa Claus, who gives toys, especially noisy ones such as trumpets and drums, to children. Like most public festivals, it is not, I am told, what it used to be; still, for a few days every year the piazza is bright with coloured balloons and eager, excited children.

Whenever I visited the Piazza Navona, I would contemplate the fountains and eat an ice in the *Gelateria* where the best ices in Rome are to be found, and would then look into the Palazzo Braschi, at the corner near the Pamphili Palace. This is now the Museum of Rome and is full of interesting things, particularly old pictures of the city and the Papal Court. There are also casts from the Cosmati tombs of Edward the Confessor and Henry III from Westminster Abbey. On the ground floor are coaches of the railway train made in Paris for Pius IX in 1858. The guardian will tell you that "Pio Nono" was the first Holy Father to trust himself to this form of locomotion, and he proudly opens the doors so that you may enter the train. The coaches are quite fantastic, the art of the eighteenth century applied to steam locomotion. They consist of a saloon, a throne room, and a chapel. Doors of mirror glass admit to a papal couch upholstered in red satin. Most visitors are so dazzled by the rococo splendours that they are blind to the irony: that the first papal railway coach should belong to the first "Prisoner of the Vatican."

In a picture gallery upstairs I found a portrait of a black and white cat. This lordly and imposing creature prowled the marble halls of some seventeenth century palace and is here seen enthroned upon a tasselled cushion, wearing a broad collar to which bells are attached. Pinned to a curtain behind the cat is a little poem which says that a great and beautiful lady once kissed the cat and bade him keep his heart and mouth pure, and to remember her kiss. No one knows who the lady was. Let us hope she was not the countess in the old Roman story who, after her widowhood, doted on a cat and had a chicken cooked every day for him. One day she left home for a friend's villa in the Campagna, and during her absence the servants decided to eat the chicken themselves and place the bones in the usual place. The countess was surprised, when she returned, to notice that the cat did not run to welcome her, but sat looking the other way, deeply offended.

"What's the matter with the cat? Hasn't he had his chicken?" asked the countess.

"Yes, Signora Contessa," answered the servants, "see, the bones are on the floor where he always leaves them."

The countess could not deny this, and shortly after went up to bed. The cat followed, for he slept on her bed. That night the cat suffocated and killed the countess.

Romans explain this story by saying that a cat is intelligent, but selfish and cruel. He reasoned that if his mistress had not gone out and left him to the mercy of the servants, he would not have been so badly treated. Therefore she was to blame and must die. Dogs are faithful, say the Romans, and cats are traitors. I am sure, however, that there is no need to say that the loyalty of English and Siamese cats has never been questioned! Perhaps every country gets the cats it deserves.

Before leaving the Braschi Palace I paused in the gateway to remember an undemocratic scene that occurred during the pontificate of Pius VI. The usual excitable Roman mob, trying to blame Napoleon's preparations to invade Italy on the Pope, attacked the palace of his nephew, the Duke of Braschi-Onesti, and called for his blood. Suddenly the gates were flung open and the Duke stood there, holding a dog-whip in each hand. Footmen appeared with baskets of gold which they cast into the crowd. While the yelling ceased and the crowd began to scramble for the coins, the Duke strolled about hitting right and left with his whips. Having demonstrated how to deal with a Roman mob, he walked back to the palace and the gates were shut.

*   *   *

At the back of the Palazzo Braschi is the battered

fragments of a marble group which once represented Menelaus supporting Patroclus, and has been known for centuries as Pasquino. During the Renaissance witty and sometimes libellous puns and comments would be found attached to this statue, and were answered by the statue of Marforio, who reclines so plumply on the Capitol. Some popes resented these pasquinades—so called from a tailor named Pasquino who was believed to be the orginator—and rewards were offered to those who had composed them. The bait was rarely taken, but on one occasion a guileless punster went to claim the reward, but was unable to carry it away, for both his hands were cut off. Journalism was a dangerous occupation in Renaissance Rome.

A typical pasquinade was one which commented on the great number of English visitors who crowded the Sistine Chapel so that Romans could not find room there. It began with a question from Pasquino.

"Where are you going brother, with your black dress and sword?"

In the morning the reply was found on Marforio.

"I am going to the Sistine Chapel to hear the Miserere."

Pasquino then remarked,

"You will go in vain. The Swiss Guard will turn you out, and the Pope's *camerieri* will send you about your business."

Marforio retorted,

"There is no danger, brother: I am certain to get in: *I turned heretic yesterday.*"

A road runs from the Pasquino statue across the Piazza Navona and by a side street into the Piazza S. Eustachio, where Marion Crawford remembered one of the old taverns of Rome, the *Falcon*. It was famous in winter for boar's head served with a sweet sauce

JAPANESE TOURISTS IN ROME.

and pine nuts, and for baked porcupine and other dishes now as extinct as the *Falcon* itself: but the *Orso*, one of Rome's mediaeval inns, in which Dante is said to have stayed, still exists beside the Tiber. It is now a fashionable restaurant where waiters in evening dress pass beneath Gothic chandeliers and the barman knows that bourbon has nothing to do with the French monarchy.

A few steps more and you are in the busy little piazza in front of the Pantheon. You leave its light and noise and enter a hushed and windowless circle of masonry, and you look up instinctively to see where the light is coming from. In the centre of the coffered roof is a circle of sky, and at noon the sun thrusts a shaft of golden light into this inverted bowl, which travels slowly up the walls so that those on duty in the church must always know what time of day it is by this odd sundial. Nearly everyone who has visited the Pantheon mentions the strange effect of the clouds moving across this circle of sky, though I never saw this. One day, however, happening to be passing during a sudden shower of rain, I went inside and saw a funnel of grey raindrops glistening and hurrying down, a silvery moving cobweb against the gloom of the building. The water is carried away into a channel made by Agrippa, which drained this part of the Campus Martius. J. H. Middleton said that in his time water was sometimes pushed backwards during floods and sprang up in the centre of the floor with the effect of a fountain. The sight of snow in the Pantheon must be even stranger, and perhaps this may have suggested to the poetic imagination of the Middle Ages the custom of showering down white rose-petals at Pentecost, while the Pope officiated, as a symbol of the descent of the Holy Spirit.

Like Smollett and President de Brosses, I was at first disappointed by the Pantheon, but after two or three visits I realized that it is the greatest of the architectural relics which have remained to us from ancient Rome. Imagine the dome of St. Peter's on ground level: the Pantheon is slightly larger. It was cast in concrete on one piece, and I wonder whether our age of steel and concrete could reproduce such a work. We see the building now stripped of its glories: the veneers of precious marbles which once covered its walls have gone, and also the gilt tiles from the roof. As the Romans did not use gold leaf, but pure gold laid on in plates, the Pantheon must have looked like a golden mountain. What the Goths left of this splendour was taken in 663 by the Emperor Constans to adorn Constantinople, but he was slain at Syracuse on the way home and the tiles of the Pantheon were lost. The ceiling of the noble porch was so rich in bronze that Urban VIII was able to cast eighty guns

ROME'S TREVI FOUNTAIN AT NIGHT.

from it, which he mounted on the bastions of S. Angelo, but the story that he also had enough for Bernini's great baldacchino with the twisted columns in St. Peter's is not correct. Perhaps a few thousand pounds of the Pantheon bronze went into it, but most of the metal came from Venice.

While I was in the Pantheon one day, I noticed a woman enter with a bunch of carnations, which, after encircling the building and pausing at the tombs of kings and artists, she left at the tomb of Raphael. The great master, whose working life was only about sixteen years, died from fever at the age of thirty-seven and was followed to his grave by the whole of Rome. His unfinished *Transfiguration* was carried in the procession like a banner.

Raphael's love for a baker's daughter sends thousands of visitors every year to the Barberini Palace to look at the supposed portrait of *La Fornarina*. When Raphael was dying, the poor girl was driven weeping from her lover's death bed, for the messengers bearing the Pope's last blessing refused to enter until she had left; and she had the mortification of knowing that

Raphael himself had asked to be buried near the remains of his fiancée, Maria Bibbiena.

When Goethe was in Rome a skull said to be that of Raphael was in the Academy of St. Luke. The poet was greatly impressed by it and said that the noble bone structure was that "wherein a beautiful soul might freely dwell": but the beautiful soul was certainly not that of Raphael. On September 14, 1833, a strange and macabre scene was witnessed in the Pantheon when a committee of churchmen and artists opened the tomb of Raphael. There they found the skull and bones of the artist, lying in a deposit of Tiber mud. They were on view in a glass case for some days and were finally reburied.

The bronze doors of the Pantheon, which somehow escaped the despoiler, were once covered with plates of beaten gold. You may spend days in the Forum trying to imagine what Rome was like in the days of its imperial greatness, but the Pantheon remains the only visible evidence, and is the only mighty building with roof and doors intact which has survived the storms and perils of eighteen centuries.

AUBREY MENEN

from ROME FOR OURSELVES

TO MOST ROMANS life seems too short to bother with much history.

THE WIND, I remember, had failed. It is called the *ponente*, and it determines the mood of Romans more than anything else—more than love, more than money, more than the news of the day, which few Romans think about unless it is scandalous. The *ponente* blows in the evening. It is a light wind and it comes trickling into the narrow streets of Old Rome like a refreshing drink. The sun sets, the lights go on, and everybody save the bedridden and the people in gaol go out for a walk. You walk along the streets, you walk in the piazzas, you walk under the trees in the Pincian Gardens. You do not sit in cafés, unless you are imitating foreigners or are with elderly women. Coffee costs money and sitting still, for a Roman when out of his house, is a tremendous effort. He prefers to be on the move, to go from place to place, preferably without any purpose at all.

His mind, like the professor's, will be on girls, whom he will eye from head to foot. I do not know for sure what Roman women think about when they are strolling because I am too shy to ask, but I should imagine

that, if they are girls, they reciprocate, and if they are married women I suppose they worry about the girls their husbands are looking at. I would, I know. In the early evening in Rome, unfaithfulness is in the air. There is a play of eyes, of glances, a slight turning of pretty heads that must be very disturbing to a mother of a family. For others, it is a delight.

A delight, that is, to be enjoyed only when the wind blows. When it doesn't, the game is off. The air grows heavy, one's step is less jaunty, the streets seem narrower than ever. The Roman men still eye the girls— I have seen them do it from doorways even in a cloudburst—but the girls look fierce and gaze straight ahead. At such times, I usually take my evening walk by the Tiber. On the evening that I am describing, I walked further along the banks than I had ever done before. I walked, as I thought, right out of Rome. The road ended abruptly at the gates of a gas-works. I turned off left and immediately I was lost. The neighbourhood was shabby, ill-lit and profoundly depressing, even, I fancied, when the *ponente* blew. I walked more quickly. I got more lost. But ahead of me I saw brilliant lights, surprisingly high in the sky. I made for them. In a few moments I came out of the slums into the Piazza of the Navigators. It is named after the Italian seamen, who discovered much of the New World. When I looked around me, I was almost as astonished as they.

The Piazza of the Navigators is a vast hemicycle of new buildings, perhaps a third of a mile across. The buildings are massive and run up to eleven stories. The centre building is crowned with a gigantic electric sign, the light that I saw in the sky. At the foot of these buildings runs an arcade, dazzling with more electric signs and brilliantly-lit shop windows. From the open side of the hemicycle runs a wide road, with many carriage-ways, that leads, after several miles, straight to the sea. On this evening, one side of it seemed a river of rubies, because it was filled with swiftly moving automobiles, while the other side ran with gold from their headlamps.

I had never seen it before. I told myself it could not be Rome. But I looked about me and there were Romans in the arcade, walking to and fro, doing nothing, eyeing the girls. And there was a breeze. It was not the *ponente*. It came, I suppose, up the wide road from the sea.

As the professor had foreseen, I found it beautiful. It was brash, but I was enchanted with the lights, the size, the spaciousness. I felt alive. I wondered if I had felt so alive in Rome since I came there. In the middle of the piazza that honoured the great discoverers, I had made a discovery myself. I thought this called for a drink in celebration, and I made for one of the bars. As I approached its chrome, glass and neon front my joy was completed. From out of the doorway came the thump and bounce of music from a loudspeaker, and it was playing the song that the errand-boy whistled under my window every morning.

I went in. The bar was shiningly clean. A tall pillar in the centre ran up to its high ceiling. On the sides of the pillar were ceramic reliefs, brightly coloured, making fun of the more portentous episodes of Roman history.

I examined the ceramics and decided that the Roman dignitaries in togas were perfect portraits of the Romans as I had discovered them to be. I went to the bar and ordered my drink. The bar-tender was polite enough to serve me, although, as I remembered, I should have bought a ticket at the cash-desk first. But I had almost never gone into such places. They disturbed, I had thought, my sense of history, so I had used restaurants.

Then I saw that the music was coming from a juke-box. I drank off my drink to give me courage and for the first time in my life I put a coin in one of these much-criticised machines.

I found that it was all very pretty. There are knobs,

dials, twinkling lights, like some inaccessibly expensive toy that one saw as a child going Christmas-shopping. I found there was even a pane of glass to press my nose against.

But I am letting my memory run away with me. I did not, in fact, put my first coin in a juke-box with my own hands. I was much too stupid to follow all the instructions. A young boy next to me very kindly did the thing for me. He then asked me, with an apprehensive look, what tune I would like.

"That one that's just finished playing."

He beamed. I was delighted that my taste had been approved. Machinery turned, arms wove complicated patterns, and from a golden and silver grid worthy to be a screen in a Roman Emperor's palace, came my errand-boy's song.

The record, to my surprise, was in English. The voice was innocent, the sentiments most worldly.

"Bernardine," said the gold and silver grid, "Bernardine! Your separate parts are not unknown, but the way you assemble them's all your own." *

I laughed. Some ten Romans, men, boys, girls, standing round about me laughed too. When the record was finished, it occurred to me that it was most unlikely that any of them would have understood a single line of the song. The tune elated them, as it had elated me each morning when it woke me in Old Rome.

The boy at the knobs looked up at me, his dark eyes dancing. He had the round face and flopping curls that marked the Roman boy even in the times of the Renaissance.

"Enjoying yourself?"

"Very much. What's your name?"

"Nino."

"How old are you?"

"Thirteen."

"You look like a Roman. Are you?"

"Roman of Romans. My father is, too, and so's my grandfather."

He spoke proudly, as he should. Three generations of Romans is nowadays a long span to be able to boast of.

"Do you go to school?"

"No. I work in a filling-station."

"What are you going to be when you grow up?"

"A Teddy-boy."

He used the English phrase, to the delight of his listeners.

"Where did you hear that phrase, Nino?"

"We all use it here," said one of the listeners.

"But Nino, a Teddy-boy is a delinquent."

---

* Copyright by Johnny Mercer.

"Yes, I know."

"And you want to be a delinquent?"

"I'll have to be. My father says I'm going to grow up to be one, and he says I mustn't ever say he's wrong about anything."

"What are you going to do when you're a Teddy-boy?"

He brushed back the hair from his forehead. His black eyes grew intense with anticipated joys.

"Run around in gangs."

"Doing what?"

"Wearing blujins. My father won't let me wear blujins yet."

Blue jeans (the word is pronounced with neat Italian vowels) are slowly making their way in Rome. Boys wearing them are frowned upon by their elders.

"What crimes are you going to commit?"

His eyes sparkled.

"Play flippers."

Every Roman is unshakably convinced that Americans call pinball games "flippers." Playing at pin-tables is considered by the older generation a vice so terrible that they have succeeded in having them prohibited by the police. Clandestine clubs in cellars have sprung up where adolescents furtively tread the primrose path: for joy, not money, since the boys do not bet.

"You like American things?"

He frowned. "American?"

"Yes. Blue jeans are American. So are pin . . . I mean flippers. That rock 'n' roll record you have just put on is an American tune."

He looked away. He gave a quick little yawn, a sign among Roman boys that one is talking nonsense to them. I realised then that, to him, since he had never known Rome without them, such things were Roman.

It was eleven o'clock. The barman told us it was time to go.

Outside the Piazza of the Navigators was still bustling with life. The great red sign still blazed. The cars were even thicker upon the road.

"I'm glad I lost my way," I said to Nino.

"Would you like to come again? I can show you the new houses. They're *belle . . . belle . . . belle . . . belle!*"

"All right! When?"

"Sometime. When you're this way again. Good-night."

I found a taxi. I drove into Old Rome. I stopped the taxi near my house, for I felt I wanted to stretch my legs before I went to bed. I walked a little, then I turned into the vast courtyard of the Borghese Palace. Fountains were playing. Great statues of Roman god-

desses stood on plinths, buxom, broad-beamed and serene.

I stood in front of one of them, as I had done a hundred times before, admiring them. But the tune of *Bernardine* was running in my head. I hummed it. I thought of the words. Suddenly the goddess seemed very funny. I sang her a snatch of *Bernardine*. "Your separate parts are not unknown, but the way you assemble them's all your own," I told her.

The policeman on guard moved towards me. He recognised me.

"Have you had a happy evening, sir?"

"Very, very happy, Officer."

"A reception?"

"No. I've been seeing Rome."

"They say, sir," he remarked, sagely, "that there's always something you haven't seen in Rome, even if you live here a hundred years."

"There certainly is, Officer," I said. "There certainly is."

I subsequently found that there is, in fact, something new to see in Rome every week. It is one of the fastest-growing cities in Europe. In 1939 it had a population of a million. Now it has two and a half. The Romans, though, like all Italians, they are not averse to begetting children, could not have produced this stupendous expansion by their own efforts. Other Italians have flocked to Rome from every corner of Italy, and the stream shows no sign of stopping. It has been calculated that, in all the city of Rome, only two hundred thousand people can, like Nino, really call themselves Romans.

I did not see Nino again until the Feast of St Peter and St Paul. On that day a gigantic fisherman's net is hung over the entrance of St Peter's. The Pope comes in wearing his tiara, but Romans stay away until he is gone. Then they take over the church. They come in thousands with their children. The children used to be held up to kiss the bronze toe of the statue of St Peter, but fewer and fewer do this now. New Rome has found a new game. The children are taken round the basilica and introduced to all the marble animals on the tombs of the pontiffs. They pat a lion's rump, they stroke a griffin's head. Does that, I wonder, happen in any other sacred place in the world?

Since I had never had the privilege as a child, I stroked and patted, too, when suddenly I saw Nino in the crowd. I waved. I shouted (you can, in St Peter's, on such days). He waved back and after a little pushing and elbowing, we met.

Nino gave a slight wave of his hand in the air. That is the fashion among the younger Romans. But he introduced me to the man who stood near to him.

It was his father and he shook my hand in the stately manner of older Rome.

Nino's father was a broad-shouldered man, with his son's round face and lively eyes. The roughness of his hand in mine, the power of his shoulders told me that he was a manual labourer. Nothing else did. The Roman poise, Roman courtesy, Roman charm belong to all its citizens. Every class is well-mannered except, perhaps, the highest, which sometimes has no manners at all.

"My son said you wanted to see the new apartment blocks."

"Yes. He said they were beautiful."

Nino's father smiled with pleasure. He threw out his chest.

"They are. I built them myself."

A fussy verger making way for a priest in vestments through the crowd separated us for a while. Nino's father, who was tall, talked over the head of the priest.

"Why don't you come down and see it with me? Yes? Good! Today. Six o'clock." He gave me an address. It was in Garbatella, one of the most notorious slums of Rome.

I arrived on time. Garbatella is known throughout Rome as the haunt of thieves and loose women. It was a sordid network of streets lined with houses from which the plaster had in part fallen off. My taxi twisted and turned for a while, then pulled up outside a ruinous house with an iron fence round it. Some of the fence lay in a tangle on the ground. Outside this fence stood Nino, his father and another man. Their suits were worn, but neat and pressed. Plainly they were poor, yet they managed, as all Romans do, to look elegant.

The third man was introduced as Nino's uncle. He was in his thirties, and he was the most elegant of the three. I saw at once from his glance that he thought I was slumming from curiosity and he disliked me for it. He suggested that instead of going into the house, we went to the wine-shop.

The wine-shop was of the sort that is fast disappearing. It was low-ceilinged, it had wooden tables and benches and it served only the cheapest wine. But it was good wine. Even had it not been, the manners of Nino and his father were so graceful that it would have seemed so. Even the uncle lost a little of his suspicion after the first glass and warmed to me.

The wine drunk, Nino said:

"Now you must come home and meet my mother. My uncle doesn't want you to, because we're very poor and we all live in two rooms. At least, three, because I sleep in the hall. Still, you've got to come because Mother wants to see you."

The hallway was about ten feet square. Nino's bed stood vertically against the wall. The other two rooms were each about twelve feet square. In one of them lived Nino, his mother, his father and three children, one two years old, another five and another three. In the next room lived Nino's uncle and his young wife and their first baby.

Nino's mother greeted me cheerfully, her youngest child on her arm.

"I thought you'd like to see the worst," she said. "You couldn't get more crowded than this, could you? But we get along."

The rooms had almost no furniture save the beds. We stood in Nino's hall and talked. Then I noticed, on a shelf, a record-player and a small pile of records.

"That's Nino's" said his mother. "He bought it out of his money. He hangs over it for hours. We call it his girl-friend."

"It's busted," said Nino. "But you can listen to the needle. It plays quite loud, especially when everything's quiet and they've all gone to bed."

He picked up a disc, absently. He looked at the broken record-player. He stood quite still for a moment and his eyes grew dark and wide. None of us spoke.

He tossed back his head, laughed, and said:

"I bought it off another boy. What a swindler! But we are all crooks in Garbatella."

Everybody laughed. The uncle seized the moment to ease me out of the door. Nino's mother made her youngest say *ciao* and wave good-bye. We set out to see the new world round the corner.

On the way I said to Nino, "I'll get you a record of that tune we played on the juke-box."

"The one you liked? *Bernardine?* Thanks, but I've got it. It's one of my favourites, too."

I thought of Johnny Mercer's sophisticated words and music coming through the needle of the player at midnight, in Garbatella, and Nino listening, dreaming. I thought of all it must have meant to him in that cramped room. I wished that I did not write books for people to read, but songs for them to sing.

Nino's uncle was explaining something to me earnestly. I brought my attention back to him. They were bricklayers, he was telling me. They were very poor, but it wasn't always like that. When the new building started, bricklayers came in from all over Italy. The pay was good, when you got it. But there were many months, especially in winter, when nobody would hire you.

"Here we are," said Nino's father. "Now, what do you think of *that?*"

We stood on a slight rise. To our left, a quarter of a mile away, ran the brown walls of ancient Rome. In front of us, stretching away to the right, was a whole new city. It was made of great blocks of apartments, each block bright with balconies painted in different colours. We walked on further, entered the new city and passed down its wide new roads. The buildings had fine entrances, some lined with the beautiful marbles of Italy. The balconies were hung with flowering plants. Broad windows with coloured blinds let in the sun and air. People sat out on the terraces under the awnings, watching the sunset.

"Ten years ago all this was waste-land," said Nino's father. "Just over there, where that building is, with the broad blue bands of tile round it, exactly where that is today was a sort of hollow. It was filled with hovels in which people lived. They were even worse off than we were. Now look at it."

Augustus, who boasted that he had found Rome brick and left it marble, could not have been more proud of his new Rome than Nino's father was of this.

"And over there," said Nino's uncle, "where you see they're building, is going to be a block for working-people like us. We've got our name down. We'll be in next year."

"If only," said Nino, with the dark distrust of thirteen years, "you and Father make enough money to pay the deposit."

"God willing," said Nino's father, "we shall."

I suppose a housing settlement of great concrete buildings does not come within the province of beautiful things. But to me, standing there and remembering Garbatella, it seemed more beautiful than the palaces that line my street. I thought so then. I have just got up from my desk and looked out of the window at Prince Ruspoli's palace and Prince Borghese's palace, and I think so still.

But on the day that I first saw new Rome—or a single part of it, for there are a dozen of these new Romes ringing the old city—there was one thing wrong with it. There were hardly any residents. There were a few people on the balconies and terraces. They were mostly elderly. It was plain that all the apartments were inhabited, but nobody came in or out of the marble entrances and the brand-new streets were deserted.

I asked Nino's father about it.

"Well," he said, "today's a national holiday, you see."

"I know," I said, "but wouldn't that mean that more people than usual would be at home?"

"Twenty years ago," said Nino's father, "you *had* to stay at home on a holiday, otherwise Mama or Grandmama would be offended. Now nobody does, unless they're ill."

Nino looked down a road wistfully. He pointed to the west.

"They've all gone to Ostia," he said. "I was going

too, but we hadn't any money in the house, as it happened, so we went to church."

"They're about due back now," said Nino's uncle, once more embarrassed. "Let's stroll about for a while and watch."

We strolled. We went into a bar. I returned the hospitality that had been offered to me, and we watched. Ostia is the nearest seaside to the city, and about seven o'clock the return from the beaches began. It is an astonishing sight.

The roads slowly fill with hundreds upon hundreds of small family cars, mostly all alike. Packed into each are families of six or seven, bronzed, in beach dress, and inebriated with hours under the Mediterranean sun. They wave, they shout, they sing the latest songs. The cars stop at their houses and they tumble out, clatter up the marble staircases, pour into their apartments, fling open the balcony doors and come out on to the terraces to snatch the last pleasures of the day.

"And over there," said Nino's father, "is the Cristoforo Colombo."

The Cristoforo Colombo is a wide arterial road with six lanes of traffic that runs from the Piazza of the Navigators straight to the sea. It is the Tiber of modern Rome. The Tiber has lost its romance for the contemporary Roman. He barely mentions it, and then only in connection with traffic jams and suicides by drowning. But the six concrete ribbons of the Cristoforo Colombo have won his affection and engaged his pride.

The lanes on the far side of the dividing strip were filled with returning cars. The one that led to the sea was empty. A fast car making an evening trip to Ostia shot past us.

"Wow-aah!" said Nino, imitating its noise. He gazed after it, his eyes gleaming. "If only I could go in a car like that."

The very next week he did, because I took him. In the months that followed I hired every sort of car. I took Nino to Ostia, I took his father, his uncle, his mother, Nino's friends and my own. I no longer walked along the Tiber when the *ponente* failed. I rang the garage. Within fifteen minutes I was at the gates of Rome. In eighteen minutes more I saw the sea. Two more minutes and I was at Ostia. Rome has become a city by the sea.

Old Ostia is a stretch of ruins that nobody I know goes to see. I pass it, usually at ninety miles an hour. New Ostia is a rabble of concrete buildings. Architecturally, it is a disaster. No Roman cares. Old Rome has the finest architecture in the world, and it is precisely that from which he wants to get away. New Ostia is ugly, vulgar and alive.

But, in any case, you do not stay there. You bathe,

you eat sea-food, clamber back into the car and spin further along the coast. There are great pine woods that once belonged to kings. I have been shown their delights by Nino and his friends. I have hunted wild asparagus and taken it to a restaurant, had it cooked and eaten it with melted butter. I have picked the prickly red fruit they call a sea-cherry and tasted its strange blend of the sweetness of fruit and the bitterness of the sea. I have hunted rabbits, watched the sky flat on my back under a pine-tree. I have startled lovers. For young Romans, the pine woods are more part of the city than the Forum, in which most of them have never set foot.

I have even been to the rocky promontory called San Felice Circeo: it is known as the Capri of Rome, but it is not, thank heaven, like Capri at all, except for the shape of its mountain. Everybody runs away from Rome, but some refined and expensive people find Ostia too coarse. They go to a hotel by the sea in San Felice where they can sunbathe, water-ski, and in the evenings dance, secure that nobody will be in the hotel but their own sort. I explored this hotel a little. It is well-appointed: and I was charmed to find that the refined Roman dances to the music of a juke-box. It was just an ordinary juke-box. Nobody had thought of adapting the mechanism to make it four times as expensive. Rich and poor alike pay fifty lire for a tune.

The Cristoforo Colombo and the regular exodus has changed the whole Roman way of life. The road, and others like it, were completed just at the time when Italian engineers had applied their resourcefulness to methods invented by Henry Ford, and produced vehicles which even the ordinary Italian could afford to buy. They produced the tiny automobile which is called the Mouse (the *topolino*), they produced the family car that costs little to run, and above all they produced the motor-scooter which almost everybody in regular employment can afford.

Motoring immediately became a passion. The Roman, as I have said, does not like to sit still. Here was a means of keeping on the go beyond his dreams. He has even found a way of looking at the girls while he drives. He drives slowly beside her (the only time he will drive slowly in the course of his trip), makes a Roman remark, and speeds off before she can slap his face. As an example, for those whom it may interest, I may quote a friend of mine, who selects women who are plentifully endowed and remarks, in the politest of voices: "Young lady, tell me, does all that belong to you?"

The modern Romans are having a great deal of fun. But they periodically empty Rome. The result is that Rome is the one capital city in Europe or America with only the vestiges of a theatre. There are very few

of them. They are open intermittently and they have been left to the intellectuals, who have succeeded in driving out even the customers who, not yet having bought a motor-car, still kept up the habit of theatre-going. The cinemas are so badly hit that in the summer most of them close down completely, while on a fine day in winter (and Rome has many) they are barely a third full. The opera, which used to depend on the well-heeled middle-class, is now resigned to living off the foreigner. The third night at an opera is the cheapest. The modest Roman music-lover used to fill the theatre. It is now the modest tourist. The music-lovers are all by the sea, or driving in the country, loving music by means of transistor radios.

Perhaps the greatest change that Henry Ford and modern road-making machinery has brought about is in the social life of Rome. The capital has been, for centuries, the seat of the greatest families of Italy. They had their own way of living, which largely consisted in impressing the rest of the Romans that they had an aristocratic disdain for money. But the great families were great landowners, and land, especially near the old limits of the city, has grown to be immensely valuable. The princes and princesses have dropped their well-bred disdain for cash (since there is so much to be made) and are rapidly turning themselves into landlords and landladies. I do not know what the Roman nobility talked about before the change. But I am told that it was the latest fashion from Paris, the latest shows in London, horses, hunting, marriage and adultery. They also had a continuous flow of private witticisms which were quite unamusing except to themselves. From my experience among them in Rome today, their conversation consists in the rental values of seaside villas, how to raise buildings by a storey to accommodate more people and what so-and-so said to such-a-one about where the new arterial road was really going to be built.

I recall inviting a Countess to a dinner-party. She once was one of the best conversationalists I have known. She came straight from her lawyers. She was dressed for dinner, but she clutched a large file of documents. No sooner had she sat down than she opened the file and began talking of a vexing lawsuit about one of her houses that she rents. She talked about it till we went to the restaurant where we were to eat. I noticed that her file had disappeared. I wondered, for a moment, where it had gone, because we had walked straight from the taxi to the table. When we rose to go I found that she had been sitting on it.

I think the upper stratum of Roman society will adapt itself to the new middle-class Rome of outings to the sea, small cars and suburbs. Indeed, I know it will. There is a restaurant to which I sometimes take visitors. It is a place where the gilded youth of Rome gathers in the evening. A short while ago an Italian who had returned home after many years in South America asked the guitarist to play some of the old Italian songs. The guitarist obliged with a heartbreaking song about somebody's Mama. The returned Italian sang it, in a sweet tenor. The young men all took out their handkerchiefs, buried their faces in them and heaved their shoulders as though they were moved to uncontrollable tears. The Roman is an excellent clown when he chooses: he is proud of the fact. The song died away. The returned Italian fell silent. The guitarist struck up another song which the young men greeted by cheering. It was not *Bernardine*, but it was an excellent Italian imitation of it.

Rome was not built in a day, but the bigger part of it was built in the last twenty years. New Rome is not in the guide-books. All that side of Roman life has no interest for the new Roman at all. Thousands of them do not come to the centre of the city for months on end. New Rome is building its own suburban life, a more vigorous, more happy, more healthy way of living than Rome has known for centuries.

For the visitor who comes to the city to see only its ancient monuments, I know that new Rome is an intrusion and a disappointment. But he should see it: he will gain a better comprehension of why the men who built the older city built as they did. It should be remembered that the romantically beautiful Spanish Steps were a piece of development. They were put up

to replace a patch of wasteland surrounded by hovels that had persisted through the centuries. The Piazza del Popolo was deliberately designed to make a grand finale to one of the roads that lead into Rome, precisely as the architects of today have designed the Piazza of the Navigators. The Imperial Forums, whose vast ruins are still noble, replaced the slums of a place called, in classical times, the Suburra. The sweeping colonnades of Bernini before St Peter's were a piece of town-planning that was intended to liberate the basilica from a warren of nondescript buildings, two of which remained down to the days of my boyhood. In the very heart of the city, under the Capitoline Hill, are the ruins of a Roman apartment house, a relic of another time when the population of Rome was bounding upwards. The Via Giulia, the street in Rome most evocative of the past, was in fact a piece of planned urban development initiated by a pope who detested the crooked streets and airless buildings of the city which he ruled. Some part of Rome has always been new.

As for Old Rome, there is talk of banning traffic from it and making it a sort of historical reservation. If they do, my apartment will be very quiet, which is a good thing for a writer. As for me, I shall move: probably to Ostia.

I shall, in a word, do as the Romans do: for Rome, to them, is not old at all, but young.

ALDOUS HUXLEY

from ALONG THE ROAD

THE Palio in Siena, seen by a man who comforts himself with the hope that the vice of traveling may be of some profit.

OUR ROOMS WERE in a tower. From the windows one looked across the brown tiled roofs to where, on its hill, stood the cathedral. A hundred feet below was the street, a narrow canyon between high walls, perennially sunless; the voices of the passers-by came up, reverberating, as out of a chasm. Down there they walked always in shadow; but in our tower we were the last to lose the sunlight. On the hot days it was cooler, no doubt, down in the street; but we at least had the winds. The waves of the air broke against our tower and flowed past it on either side. And at evening, when only the belfries and the domes and the highest roofs were still flushed by the declining sun, our win-

dows were level with the flight of the swifts and swallows. Sunset after sunset all through the long summer, they wheeled and darted round our tower. There was always a swarm of them intricately manœuvring just outside the window. They swerved this way and that, they dipped and rose, they checked their headlong flight with a flutter of their long pointed wings and turned about within their own length. Compact, smooth and tapering, they seemed the incarnation of airy speed. And their thin, sharp, arrowy cry was speed made audible. I have sat at my window watching them tracing their intricate arabesques until I grew dizzy; till their shrill crying sounded as though from withing my ears and their flying seemed a motion, incessant, swift and bewilderingly multitudinous, behind my eyes. And all the while the sun declined, the shadows climbed higher up the houses and towers, and the light with which they were tipped became more rosy. And at last the shadow had climbed to the very top and the city lay in a grey and violet twilight beneath the pale sky.

One evening, towards the end of June, as I was sitting at the window looking at the wheeling birds, I heard through the crying of the swifts the sound of a drum. I looked down into the shadowy street, but could see nothing. Rub-a-dub, dub, dub, dub—the sound grew louder and louder, and suddenly there appeared round the corner where our street bent out of sight, three personages out of a Pinturicchio fresco. They were dressed in liveries of green and yellow— yellow doublets slashed and tagged with green, particoloured hose and shoes, with feathered caps of the same colours. Their leader played the drum. The two who followed carried green and yellow banners. Immediately below our tower the street opens out a little into a tiny piazza. In this clear space the three Pinturicchio figures came to a halt and the crowd of little boys and loafers who followed at their heels grouped themselves round to watch. The drummer quickened his beat and the two banner-bearers stepped forward into the middle of the little square. They stood there for a moment quite still, the right foot a little in advance of the other, the left fist on the hip and the lowered banners drooping from the right. Then, together, they lifted the banners and began to wave them round their heads. In the wind of their motion the flags opened out. They were the same size and both of them green and yellow, but the colours were arranged in a different pattern on each. And what patterns! Nothing more "modern" was ever seen. They might have been designed by Picasso for the Russian Ballet. Had they been by Picasso, the graver critics would have called them futuristic, the sprightlier (I must apologize for both these expressions) jazz. But the flags were not Picasso's; they were designed some four hundred years ago by the nameless genius who dressed the Sienese for their yearly pageant. This being the case, the critics can only take off their hats. The flags are classical, they are High Art; there is nothing more to be said.

SIENA'S GREAT MEDIEVAL PIAZZA DEL CAMPO, SITE OF THE PALIO, WITH THE HORIZONTAL-STRIPED TOWER OF THE CATHEDRAL RISING BEHIND.

The drum beat on. The bannermen waved their flags, so artfully that the whole expanse of patterned stuff was always unfurled and tremulously stretched along the air. They passed the flags from one hand to the other, behind their backs, under a lifted leg. Then, at last, drawing themselves together to make a supreme effort, they tossed their banners into the air. High they rose, turning slowly, over and over, hung for an instant at the height of their trajectory, then dropped back, the weighted stave foremost, towards their throwers, who caught them as they fell. A final wave, then the drum returned to its march rhythm, the bannermen shouldered their flags, and followed by the anachronistic children and idlers from the twentieth century, Pinturicchio's three young bravos swaggered off up the dark street out of sight and at length, the drum taps coming faintlier and ever faintlier, out of hearing.

Every evening after that, while the swallows were in full cry and flight about the tower, we heard the beating of the drum. Every evening, in the little piazza below us, a fragment of Pinturicchio came to life. Sometimes it was our friends in green and yellow who returned to wave their flags beneath our windows. Sometimes it was men from the other *contrade* or districts of the town, in blue and white, red and white, black, white and orange, white, green and red, yellow and scarlet. Their bright pied doublets and particoloured hose shone out from among the drabs and funereal blacks of the twentieth-century crowd that surrounded them. Their spread flags waved in the street below, like the painted wings of enormous butterflies. The drummer quickened his beat, and to the accompaniment of a long-drawn rattle, the banners leapt up, furled and fluttering, into the air.

To the stranger who has never seen a Palio these little dress rehearsals are richly promising and exciting. Charmed by these present hints, he looks forward eagerly to what the day itself holds in store. Even the Sienese are excited. The pageant, however familiar, does not pall on them. And all the gambler in them, and all the local patriot looks forward to the result of the race. Those last days of June before the first Palio, that middle week of August before the second, are days of growing excitement and tension in Siena. One enjoys the Palio the more for having lived through them.

Even the mayor and corporation are infected by the pervading excitement. They are so far carried away that, in the last days of June, they send a small army of men down in the great square before the Palazzo Comunale to eradicate every blade of grass or tuft of moss that can be found growing in the crannies between the flagstones. It amounts almost to a national

characteristic, this hatred of growing things among the works of men. I have often, in old Italian towns, seen workmen laboriously weeding the less frequented streets and squares. The Colosseum, mantled till thirty or forty years ago with a romantic, Piranesian growth of shrubs, grasses and flowers, was officially weeded with such extraordinary energy that its ruinousness was sensibly increased. More stones were brought down in those few months of weeding than had fallen of their own accord in the previous thousand years. But the Italians were pleased; which is, after all, the chief thing that matters. Their hatred of weeds is fostered by their national pride; a great country, and one which specially piques itself on being modern, cannot allow weeds to grow even among its ruins. I entirely understand and sympathise with the Italian point of view. If Mr. Ruskin and his disciples had talked about my house and me as they talked about Italy and the Italians, I too should pique myself on being up-to-date; I should put in bathrooms, central heating and a lift, I should have all the moss scratched off the walls, I should lay cork lino on the marble floors. Indeed, I think that I should probably, in my irritation, pull down the whole house and build a new one. Considering the provocation they have received, it seems to me that the Italians have been remarkably moderate in the matter of weeding, destroying and rebuilding. Their moderation is due in part, no doubt, to their comparative poverty. Their ancestors built with such prodigious solidity that it would cost as much to pull down one of their old houses as to build a new one. Imagine, for example, demolishing the Palazzo Strozzi in Florence. It would be about as easy to demolish the Matterhorn. In Rome, which is predominantly a baroque, seventeenth-century city, the houses are made of flimsier stuff. Consequently, modernisation progresses there much more rapidly than in most other Italian towns. In wealthier England very little antiquity has been permitted to stand. Thus, most of the great country houses of England were rebuilt during the eighteenth century. If Italy had preserved her independence and her prosperity during the seventeenth, eighteenth and nineteenth centuries, there would probably be very much less mediæval or Renaissance work now surviving than is actually the case. Money is lacking to modernize completely. Weeding has the merit of being cheap and, at the same time, richly symbolic. When you say of a town that the grass grows in its streets, you mean that it is utterly dead. Conversely, if there is no grass in its streets, it must be alive. No doubt the mayor and corporation of Siena did not put the argument quite so explicitly. But that the argument was put somehow, obscurely and below the surface of the mind, I do not doubt. The weeding was symbolic of modernity.

With the weeders came other workmen who built up round the curving flanks of the great piazza a series of wooden stands, six tiers high, for the spectators. The piazza which is shaped, whether by accident or design I do not know, like an ancient theatre, became for the time being indeed a theatre. Between the seats and the central area of the place, a track was railed off and the slippery flags covered parsimoniously with sand. Expectation rose higher than ever.

And at last the day came. The swallows and swifts wove their arabesques as usual in the bright golden light above the town. But their shrill crying was utterly inaudible, through the deep, continuous, formless murmur of the crowd that thronged the streets and the great piazza. Under its canopy of stone the great bell of the Mangia tower swung incessantly backwards and forwards; it too seemed dumb. The talking, the laughter, the shouting of forty thousand people rose up from the piazza in a column of solid sound, impenetrable to any ordinary noise.

It was after six. We took our places in one of the stands opposite the Palazzo Comunale. Our side of the piazza was already in the shade; but the sun still shone on the palace and its tall slender tower, making their rosy brickwork glow as though by inward fire. An immense concourse of people filled the square and all the tiers of seats round it. There were people in every window, even on the roofs. At the Derby, on boat-race days, at Wembley I have seen larger crowds; but never, I think, so many people confined within so small a space.

The sound of a gunshot broke through the noise of voices; and at the signal a company of mounted carabiniers rode into the piazza, driving the loungers who still thronged the track before them. They were in full dress uniform, black and red, with silver trimmings; cocked hats on their heads and swords in their hands. On their handsome little horses, they looked like a squadron of smart Napoleonic cavalry. The idlers retreated before them, squeezing their way through every convenient opening in the rails into the central area, which was soon densely packed. The track was cleared at a walk and, cleared, was rounded again at the trot, dashingly, in the best Carle Vernet style. The carabiniers got their applause and retired. The crowd waited expectantly. For a moment there was almost a silence. The bell on the tower ceased to be dumb. Some one in the crowd let loose a couple of balloons. They mounted perpendicularly into the still air, a red sphere and a purple. They passed out of the shadow into the sunlight; and the red became a ruby, the purple a glowing amethyst. When they had risen above the level of the roofs, a little breeze caught

them and carried them away, still mounting all the time, over our heads, out of sight.

There was another gunshot and Vernet was exchanged for Pinturicchio. The noise of the crowd grew louder as they appeared, the bell swung, but gave no sound, and across the square the trumpets of the procession were all but inaudible. Slowly they marched round, the representatives of all the seventeen *contrade* of the city. Besides its drummer and its two bannermen, each *contrada* had a man-at-arms on horseback, three or four halbardiers and young pages and, if it happened to be one of the ten competing in the race, a jockey, all of them wearing the Pinturicchian livery in its own particular colours. Their progress was slow; for at every fifty paces they stopped, to allow the bannermen to give an exhibition of their skill with the flags. They must have taken the best part of an hour to get round. But the time seemed only too short. The Palio is a spectacle of which one does not grow tired. I have seen it three times now and was as much delighted on the last occasion as on the first.

English tourists are often sceptical about the Palio. They remember those terrible "pageants" which were all the rage some fifteen years ago in their own country, and they imagine that the Palio will turn out to be something of the same sort. But let me reassure them; it is not. There is no poetry by Louis Napoleon Parker at Siena. There are no choruses of young ladies voicing high moral sentiments in low voices. There are no flabby actor-managers imperfectly disguised as Hengist and Horsa, no crowd of gesticulating supernumeraries dressed in the worst of taste and the cheapest of bunting. Nor finally does one often meet at Siena with that almost invariable accompaniment of the English pageant—rain. No, the Palio is just a show; having no "meaning" in particular, but by the mere fact of being traditional and still alive, signifying infinitely more than the dead-born English affairs for all their Parkerian blank verse and their dramatic re-evocation. For these pages and men-at-arms and bannermen come straight out of the Pinturicchian past. Their clothes are those designed for their ancestors, copied faithfully, once in a generation, in the same colours and the same rich materials. They walk, not in cotton or flannelette, but in silks and furs and velvets. And the colours were matched, the clothes originally cut by men whose taste was the faultless taste of the early Renaissance. To be sure there are costumiers with as good a taste in these days. But it was not Paquin, not Lanvin or Poiret who dressed the actors of the English pageants; it was professional wig-makers and lady amateurs. I have already spoken of the beauty of the flags—the bold, fantastic, "modern" design of them. Everything else at the Palio

is in keeping with the flags, daring, brilliant and yet always right, always irreproachably refined. The one false note is always the *Palio* itself—the painted banner which is given to the *contrada* whose horse wins the race. This banner is specially painted every year for the occasion. Look at it, where it comes along, proudly exposed on the great mediæval war chariot which closes the procession—look at it, or preferably don't look at it. It is a typical property from the wardrobe of an English pageant committee. It is a lady amateur's masterpiece. Shuddering, one averts the eyes.

Preceded by a line of *quattrocento* pages carrying festoons of laurel leaves and escorted by a company of mounted knights, the war chariot rolled slowly and ponderously past, bearing aloft the unworthy trophy. And by now the trumpets at the head of the procession sounded, almost inaudibly for us, from the further side of the piazza. And at last the whole procession had made its round and was lined up in close order in front of the Palazzo Comunale. Over the heads of the spectators standing in the central area, we could see all the thirty-four banners waving and waving in a last concerted display and at last, together, all leaping high into the air, hesitating at the top of their leap, falling back, out of sight. There was a burst of applause. The pageant was over. Another gunshot. And in the midst of more applause, the racehorses were ridden to the starting place.

The course is three times round the piazza, whose shape, as I have said, is something like that of an ancient theatre. Consequently, there are two sharp turns, where the ends of the semicircle meet the straight diameter. One of these, owing to the irregularity of the plan, is sharper than the other. The outside wall of the track is padded with mattresses at this point, to prevent impetuous jockeys who take the corner too fast from dashing themselves to pieces. The jockeys ride bareback; the horses run on a thin layer of sand spread over the flagstones of the piazza. The Palio is probably the most dangerous flat-race in the world. And it is made the more dangerous by the excessive patriotism of the rival *contrade*. For the winner of the race, as he reins in his horse after passing the post, is set upon by the supporters of the other *contrade* (who all think that *their* horse should have won), with so real and earnest a fury that the carabiniers must always intervene to protect man and beast from lynching. Our places were at a point some two or three hundred yards beyond the post, so that we had an excellent view of the battle waged round the winning horse, as he slackened speed. Scarcely was the post passed when the crowd broke its ranks and rushed out into the course. Still cantering, the horse came up the track. A gang of young men ran in pursuit, waving sticks and shouting. And with them, their Napoleonic coat tails streaming in the wind of their own speed, their cocked hats bobbing, and brandishing their swords in their white-gloved hands, ran the rescuing carabiniers. There was a brief struggle round the now stationary horse, the young men were repulsed, and surrounded by cocked hats, followed by a crowd of supporters from its native *contrada*, the beast was led off in triumph. We climbed down from our places. The piazza was now entirely shaded. It was only on the upper part of the tower and the battlements of the great Palazzo that the sun still shone. Rosily against the pale blue sky, they glowed. The swifts still turned and turned overhead in the light. It is said that at evening and at dawn these light-loving birds mount on their strong wings into the sky to bid a last farewell or earliest good-morrow to the sinking or the rising sun. While we lie sleeping or have resigned ourselves to darkness the swifts are looking down from their watchtower in the height of heaven over the edge of the turning planet towards the light. Was it a fable, I wondered, looking up at the wheeling birds? Or was it true? Meanwhile, some one was swearing at me for not looking where I was going. I postponed the speculation.

SEAN O'FAOLAIN

from A Summer in Italy

AN Irishman who loves Rome questions and probes for the secret of Florence.

Whistler, often impatient and always immodest, said of Rome, in irreverence and ignorance: "This is a stucco city. Ruins don't count. I'm quit-ting," and left after three days. If that sort of disappointment and disgruntlement has been an almost universal first experience in Florence and Rome, and I could quote a dozen examples offhand from Hawthorne to Zola, it is largely because we expect Florence and Rome to give up their stories at a glance, as if the

The Palio circles in front of Siena's Town
Hall, the Palazzo Pubblico.

age of each were not a hundred times overlaid by a lava through whose cracks it slowly steals, one might say is lured. Nobody can read Rome without footnotes. Florence is not an open book. Its otherness or strangeness and its human appeal are neither superficial nor immediate.

So, in spite of the promise of that skyline, I have to admit that the face of Florence was at first sight far from attractive. It is a heavy, dusky masculine face. It has what the Spaniards call bullishness. Why it was so popular all through the nineteenth century I do not understand even yet. The last thing anybody could call it is pretty. It has immense human interest. It contains countless beautiful things. It has many picturesque corners and views. It has many natural charms. These could not have sufficed to give it its fame. It was certainly not its climate which attracted so many foreign residents and visitors. Some physician has said that he could not understand how anybody dies there in the summer or lives there in the winter; though, in practice, it is in summer that the residents leave it for the sea or the hills. Why ailing Elizabeth Barrett Browning chose to live in Florence and, unlike Landor, not on the heights but down on the flat of the city, is something that I cannot explain; for the heights are lovely. Probably the popularity of Florence developed accidentally. One traveller came and loved it; then another, and another in his tracks until the habit grew. Why is it that most Italians in Dublin have come from one small region outside Rome? Why do Venetians gravitate to the north of France and Tuscans to the south?

One of the first things that struck me here—it seems a rather childish remark—was that there is a great deal of stone. The windows are set far apart and seem, thereby, smaller than they are. My second impression was that the streets are oppressively narrow. So, it is true, are the streets of Genoa; but Genoa has the sea. True also that many of the Roman streets are dark; but Rome has those seven hills which lift us above the tiles, and more open spaces. The streets of Venice can be stifling; but Venice has her vast lagoons. And in those dusky, narrow Florentine streets the buildings are of a cyclopean ponderousness which, for a while, overshadows their grace of form and the detail of their decoration. They are as forbidding as an attractive but over-sized woman. Everybody's first impression of the famous palaces, with their rough-hewn ground-floor façades and thick-barred windows, the Palazzo Riccardi, or the Pitti Palace, has been one of awe. Not until we have lounged often and idly about the Bobboli Gardens and mentally placed the immense palace in its magnificent setting of walks and avenues, its thickets of sweet bay, of cypress, laurel,

privet, quince, poplars, oleanders and stone-pines; become familiar with its fountain, pool and lofty belvedere, its statues of gods and goddesses, heroes and hermaphrodites set in shadowy niches; not until one has come to long for its several views, such as that from the belvedere north to San Miniato, or from the corner by the balustrade back between the smoking cypresses at the rose-stalk of the Palazzo Vecchio, which is one of the deservedly best-known "little views" in Florence, or down the terraces at the gleam in the Vasca dell' Isotta, all of it a vital contrast of dark foliage and blue sky; not until familiarity and association have made us accustomed to the forceful character of all Florentine architecture, in its setting, do we come to enjoy its fascinating mixture of Roman order, mediaeval strength and Renaissance ambition whose final satisfaction is a sense of magnificence and muscularity like the *David* of Michelangelo.

This weighty duskiness was always in the character of this city, but in its hey-day there would have been more variety and higgledy-piggledy, less anatomy, less classic line and far more colour. The citizens then carried brilliance on their backs, even as they lavished the green-veined marbles of Genoa on their churches as if in thirst for some relief from the ubiquitous brown stone. One may at first be almost shocked by the gaudiness of the Duomo and the Campanile. How oppressive the two would be if they were masses of northern Gothic devouring the sun! And is not much of the joy of San Miniato, set against dark foliage, the satisfaction of this same unconscious thirst for colour. Ruskin wisely warns travellers in Italy, approaching Venice for the first time, to expect coloured architecture, so novel to us in the North; he might have warned us, too, to expect the delight and force of this Florentine contrast. Besides, the *pietra d'Istria* of Venice is much more kind to the eye than this grey stone of Monte Ceneri, flatteringly called *pietra serena*, which is the dominant tone of Florence. It may once have been *sereno*, clear or bluish; it has aged forbiddingly.

Our century does not counter duskiness with colour. It lets in light. A good comparison of the results of our method greets the traveller to Florence immediately he arrives, if he comes by train, in the spaciousness and clean openness of the modern railway station, opposite the brilliance of Santa Maria Novella. Each building is admirable in its way; both are products of Renaissance man; the emphasis being now on science rather than on poetry; though Ruskin would have gasped to hear anybody say a good word for a railway station.

*   *   *

This duskiness of Florence puzzles me. Did the

THE BELOVED PONTE VECCHIO, THE ONLY BRIDGE IN
FLORENCE NOT DESTROYED IN THE SECOND WORLD WAR.

Renaissance Florentine not feel our thirst for light? To see the Baptistery ceiling properly one has to have the electric light switched on. The interior of Or San Michele is cavernous. Gozzoli must have painted the frescoes of the Palazzo Riccardi chapel by lamplight, for it originally had no window at all. Over and over again one is well advised to accept the guide-book's ominous advice—"morning (or evening) light best."

Quattrocento man could certainly not be called "light-conscious." He never paints direct sunlight. He virtually ignores shadow. His paintings glow; but with colour. Faces and bodies are moulded; but not by the effects of sun. Never—I think it is safe to be so positive—does one come before Tintoretto on a picture in which light recognisably streams from its source, from any source, as in, say, Vermeer's "The Artist in the Studio," in which the light pours from the left through a window hidden behind a dark curtain in the foreground. Never do we come on a landscape like Corot's "The Road from Sèvres," with its translucent shadows thrown across the road and its sunlight pouring from behind a screen of trees. Botticelli's "Pallas and the Centaur" is an exquisite example of this fifteenth-century Florentine treatment of light. A few frail shadows, cast by the near-zenith, point the artificial rocks, and the hairy part of the Centaur's body seems to darken the ground beneath his hoofs. Everything else, the face of Pallas, her hands, breasts and thighs, and even her toes are visible thanks to an all-enveloping calm diffusion as of early dawn, an ambient, universal lucidity sieved from nowhere and distributed everywhere like the air itself, so that every detail is seen as by the magical luminosity of its own colour, independently of the sun. Light in our strong modern sense does not exist in these pictures.

Tintoretto threw the bridge across from sun to

shadow. . . . Caravaggio, who was contemporaneous with the elderly Tintoretto, took this naturalism of light and shade to the limit.

"How sad!" Ruskin might have said, expounding the triumphant "infinity," as he called it, or the "idealism" which the old unnaturalism managed to achieve. But, then, Ruskin does not explain why it was that those homes are sometimes so poorly lighted, those churches often so obscure that we cannot properly see their triumphs. He must have frequently seen, as every traveller still may see, an obliging sacristan ingeniously lighting a picture in a dim church by means of mirrors; standing one mirror against a bench in the church and running out into the bright campo with another to direct the sun inwards on the first mirror, and so on to the face of a picture otherwise lost in the dusk. Colour the quattrocento loved; light, as such, it did not see. Ruskin loathed and reviled classical architecture, and suspected everything painted after 1508, but it was, ultimately, classical architecture not Gothic architecture which let the sun into the study. I can only remember one modern building which Ruskin praises wholeheartedly: the little church of Saint Margaret's, a stone's throw from Broadcasting House in London, and it is as dark as a coal-hole.

The precision of that date 1508 is amusingly characteristic of Ruskin. In Raphael's twenty-fifth year, he records, he began to decorate the Vatican for Julius II. "In the first chamber he decorated he placed a picture of the kingdom of Theology presided over by Christ. On the sidewall of that same chamber he placed a picture of the kingdom of poetry presided over by Apollo. And from that spot and from that hour the intellect and the art of Italy date their degradation."

He was inordinately fond of these years of doom. Speaking of the rebuilding of the Ducal Palace in Venice, begun in 1423, he says: "The first hammer-stroke upon the old palace of Ziani was the first act of the period properly called the Renaissance. It was the knell of the architecture of Venice—and of Venice herself" (*Stones of Venice*, Vol. II). Earlier he was more precise. Unless he gave the hour he could not have been more so. "I date the commencement of the Fall of Venice from the death of Carlo Zeno, 8th May, 1418." But he does add that the *visible* commencement began five years later with the death of Doge Mocenigo (*Stones of Venice*, Vol. I). One does not have to be a Marxist to think it more likely that the "Fall of Venice" began in 1497, when Vasco de Gama rounded the Cape of Good Hope and Venice ceased to control the overland trade route to India. In fairness to him we must remember that he excepted certain achievements from this general Fall.

He had to. Tintoretto and Veronese take us to the brink of the seventeenth century, and he pronounced Tintoretto's "Paradise," in Venice, "the most wonderful piece of pure, manly, and masterly oil-painting in the world."

*   *   *

There is one other all too obvious reason why Florence does not immediately please. One may expect to see an old city: one finds a modern one. When Ruskin was writing *Modern Painters* in the 1840's modernity was already overlaying much of the old Florence. In his second volume, which appeared in 1846, he was already listing the ravages which he characteristically attributed to the moral decay of the century. "There is not a monument throughout the cities of Europe that speaks of old years and mighty people but is being swept away to build cafés and gaming-houses." One can hardly accept so patent an exaggeration; we may in sympathy let it pass, for he had and we have much to regret. Here in Florence he saw a whole street being wiped out, the Via dei Calzaioli ("The Street of the Stocking-Makers"), once a cobbled street of towers and casements, where Bronzino lived, and Donatello and Michelozzo worked, and where stands the lovely church of Or San Michele (if one could only see it), a church once so revered that anybody who made too much noise in the street could be fined sharply, and if he did not pay he was ducked in the Arno. The street was destroyed and rebuilt in the French style at public cost. "It consists now," he remarked, and it is still true, "almost exclusively of shops of bijouterie and parfumerie." And he goes on to record, in legitimate wrath, that the old refectory of Santa Croce had been turned into a carpet factory, so that he had to stand on a loom to see the frescoes; even as he speaks in horror of seeing Gentile da Fabriano's "Adoration of the Magi" lying supine under the rain in a cart, until he protested, whereupon somebody threw an old piece of matting over it and wheeled it away *per essere pulito*, a cleaning process he interprets bitterly having seen the "divine distant landscape" of a Perugino painted over in French ultramarine with a common house-brush.

Yet did not the golden age itself carry Cimabue's Madonna in procession through the streets in every weather, with immense respect, but scarcely with immense prudence? And how much of Renaissance Florence, and indeed of all Italy, grew on the bones of the Middle Ages? God knows what the seventeenth century did to the sixteenth! When we find that decrees had to be passed in Florence in the seventeenth century to prevent works of art from being taken out of it we can form an opinion on what made them necessary. Botticelli was neglected completely for four

FLORENCE'S PIAZZA DELLA SIGNORIA IS AN OPEN-AIR MUSEUM.

hundred years after his death. His "Pallas and the Centaur" was first discovered under the dust in an attic of the Uffizzi in the late nineteenth century by Walter Spence, and it was Rossetti who mainly restored to his name its rightful fame.

Every age has changed and meddled with its inheritance, sometimes impairing it, sometimes enriching it. The architectural history of the Piazza San Marco is a wholly successful mosaic of the endeavours of many generations. Santa Maria del Fiore, begun in 1296, was not finished, in its present form, until 1887. When we stand on the Capitol to-day, silenced by its countless memories, we are excited rather than depressed by the knowledge that it has undergone change after change from the days of Romulus to the seventeenth century. The Venetians were working on the mosaics of San Marco in Ruskin's day; destroying them in his opinion—though he was probably right in that, even though, if he had lived in the sixteenth century, and had his way, he would have likewise damned almost everything "new."

It is right that people should argue about changes and innovations; but are not many changes disliked rather because all change is felt as a betrayal than because every change is for the worse? People are never done complaining about what has been done to Rome. "No other city," Mr. Raymond Mortimer wrote in 1946, "has been so deliberately spoiled by its rulers." Is this true? I agree that the approach to Saint Peter's is at present monstrous. We can only hope that some day it will be enlarged further and laid out in gardens, with tall poplars or cypresses spearing up against the great façade. But the main question is, Was it ever a good approach; and what is the meaning of the word "spoiled" if it was not? I disagree with him about the Via del Impero, which I find spacious and noble. I regret with him, but think it a futile regret, the withdrawal of country greenness from what were once the city's outskirts; for this, surely, was not deliberate and it has been going on for hundreds of years. Seventy years ago Mr. Augustus Hare felt that Rome was already ruined. "Fifty years of United Italy," he wrote (it was one of his milder outbursts), "have done more for the destruction of the artistic beauty of Rome than all the invasions of the Goths and Vandals." Ruskin was cursing change sixty years before that and, if Keats had lived on into Ruskin's day he would probably have sighed for the perfection of the Rome of 1820; so small, a country town, with goats lying in the streets and cows being milked below the Spanish steps. Ruskin adored Saint Mark's. Countless buildings were ravished to create it. He adored the Middle Ages, which, for a thousand years, used ancient Rome as a quarry, or a foundation, or a rubbish-heap, and forgot the very name of the Forum. And so back and back to the days of Juvenal's savage regrets for a still older and better Rome.

Cities are not museums. Bruges is like a lovely stuffed bird. Cities must not only be seen to be believed, but felt as growing, living things. The only people who can demur at this will be those who see buildings pictorially. To know buildings we must get their physical impact, their movement under light and shadow, the livingness of their surroundings, the to-and-fro of people, their noise, dust, heat, smells, grime, all the finger-marks of time and use. Purely visual Rome or visual Florence is a disparate collection of post cards. Florence in stone is what you touch, you living and the stone living and the people living behind the stone; and for all this we have to take the rough with the smooth, permanence enlivened, even when insulted, by mutability. Architecture is dead. Buildings have blood in them. It is as impossible to study cities out of books as it is to study men, and neither can be ordered to stop growing. If Florence and Rome are the Herculaneum and Pompeii of the centuries the modern dust we blow away to reveal their beauty is also part of their age. Modernity is part and parcel of their continuum, for Florence and Rome were always modern. I agree that the act of imagination which reaches backward, to pause at some part of the perpetual flux, can be incited by a perfectly preserved ruin, but I think it is helped far more by a perfectly managed café—provided it has been created in an unbroken tradition with the living past. It is only when the continuum is arrested that the past dies. Then we really do get the most horrible sort of modernity, that is another age, another race cut off from its roots. If we really want modernity in that horrible sense let us preserve the past. If we want to avoid it we must accept endless growth and endless alteration.

*   *   *

This may be the secret of Florence. It may have always been the most popular Italian city with foreigners not because of its past, but because it opens its doors, its somewhat austere doors, slowly at first, but in the end wide and welcoming, both to the past and to the present. Venice, by contrast, is more generous with its treasures of the past—being so little changed in outward appearance, so outwardly like what it always was—but, as for its continuing or present life it is, like the Venetians themselves, secretive, aloof and remote. It is the one drawback of Venice that it is so exactly what you expect it to be—lagoons, gondoliers in ribboned hats, deserted islands, winding lanes, songs under the moon on the Adriatic, lost ramos, all the trappings of romance—that you find yourself living not in a mortal city, but in a fairyland. In the end I found myself looking there madly for a dentist's brass plate.

Guide-books do us a certain disservice by romancing about the mere paraphernalia of strangeness. Writers on Florence often begin on such a top note of lyricism that you wonder where on earth they will end. They start with talk of the City of Flowers and would be pained if one reproached them afterwards that the characteristic smell of Florence is horse-dung, its characteristic noise motor-cycles and its characteristic sight money-changers. Browning is a better guide than any guide-book. After all when he lived in No. 9, off the Piazza San Felice, and entered

> Under the doorway where the black begins
> With the first stone slab of the staircase cold,

stumbling on the step as he still read his square old yellow book, he had not only stepped across several centuries to the Past but found the way thither in the Piazza San Lorenzo market, all tumbled and jumbled with its realism of

> . . . fire-irons, tribes of tongs, shovels in sheaves
> Skeleton bedsteads, wardrobe drawers agape,
> Rows of tall, slim brass lamps with dangling gear
> And worse, cast clothes a-sweetening in the sun . . .

Trappings seem romantic only when they are gone or when somebody (like Browning) has made them seem so. We could so easily become sentimental about Carabiniere in red facings and cocked hats, horse buses, Austrian bands, bottled spring-water from the Mugello, warming-pans, gentlemen carrying shoulder-shawls in the Pitti, Spagnolette Avana, Vienna bread, Miss Penrose's school for young ladies in the Villa Lalletta, the English Club, soldi, scudi, "The Florence Herald"— a list I compile out of an old Baedeker—if we did not remember that to the man who bought that Baedeker when it was new these things were as normal as motor-cycles and money-changers to-day.

MARY McCARTHY

from VENICE OBSERVED

MONTAIGNE found Venice as expensive as Paris. So it still is, and, like Paris, unique, valuable beyond price.

No stones are so trite as those of Venice, that is, precisely, so well worn. It has been part museum, part amusement park, living off the entrance fees of tourists, ever since the early eighteenth century, when its former sources of revenue ran dry. The carnival that lasted half a year was not just a spontaneous expression of Venetian license; it was a calculated tourist attraction. Francesco Guardi's early "views" were the postcards of that period. In the Venetian preserve, a thick bitter-sweet marmalade, tourism itself became a spicy ingredient, suited to the foreign taste; legends of dead tourists now are boiled up daily by gondoliers and guides. Byron's desk, Gautier's palace, Ruskin's boarding house, the room where Browning died, Barbara Hutton's plate-glass window—these memorabilia replace the Bucintoro or Paolo Sarpi's statue as objects of interest. The Venetian crafts have become sideshows—glass-blowing, bead-stringing, lace-making; you watch the product made, like pink spun sugar at a circus, and bring a sample home, as a souvenir. Venetian manufactures today lay no claim to beauty or elegance, only to being "Venetian."

And there is no use pretending that the tourist Venice is not the real Venice, which is possible with other cities—Rome or Florence or Naples. The tourist Venice *is* Venice: the gondolas, the sunsets, the changing light, Florian's, Quadri's, Torcello, Harry's Bar, Murano, Burano, the pigeons, the glass beads, the vaporetto. Venice is a folding picture-post-card of itself. And though it is true (as is sometimes said, sententiously) that nearly two hundred thousand people live their ordinary working lives in Venice, they too exist in it as tourists or guides. Nearly every Venetian is an art-appreciator, a connoisseur of Venice, ready to talk of Tintoretto or to show you, at his own suggestion, the spiral staircase (said to challenge the void), to demonstrate the Venetian dialect or identify the sound of the Marangona, the bell of the Campanile, when it rings out at midnight.

A count shows the Tiepolo on the ceiling of his wife's bedroom; a dentist shows his sitting-room, which was formerly a ridotto. Everything has been catalogued, with a pride that is more in the knowledge than in the thing itself. "A fake," genially says a gentleman, pointing to his Tintoretto. "Réjane's," says a house-owner, pointing to the broken-down bed in the apartment she wants to let. The vanity of displaying knowledge can outweigh commercial motives or the vanity of ownership. "Eighteenth century?" you say hopefully to an antique-dealer, as you look at a set of china. "No, nineteenth," he answers with firmness, losing the sale. In my apartment, I wish everything to be Venetian, but "No," says the landlady, as I ask about a cabinet: "Florentine." We stare at a big enthroned Madonna in the bedroom—very bad. She would like me to think it a Bellini and she measures the possibility against the art knowledge she estimates me to possess. "*School* of Giovanni Bellini," she announces, nonchalantly, extricating herself from the dilemma.

A Venetian nobleman has made a study of plants peculiar to Venice and shows slides on a projector. He has a library of thirty thousand volumes, mainly devoted to Venetian history. In the public libraries, in the wintertime the same set of loungers pores over Venetian archives or illustrated books on Venetian art; they move from the Correr library, when it closes, to the heatless Marciana, where they sit huddled in their overcoats, and finally to the Querini-Stampaglia, which stays open until late at night.

The Venetians catalogue everything, including themselves. "These grapes are brown," I complain to the young vegetable-dealer in Santa Maria Formosa. "What is wrong with that? *I* am brown," he replies. "I am the housemaid of the painter Vedova," says a maid, answering the telephone. "I am a Jew," begins a cross-eyed stranger who is next in line in a bakeshop. "Would you care to see the synagogue?"

Almost any Venetian, even a child, will abandon whatever he is doing in order to show you something. They do not merely give directions; they lead, or in some cases follow, to make sure you are still on the right way. Their great fear is that you will miss an artistic or "typical" sight. A sacristan, who has already been tipped, will not let you leave until you have seen the last Palma Giovane. The "pope" of the Chiesa dei Greci calls up to his housekeeper to throw his black hat out the window and settles it firmly on his broad brow so that he can lead us personally to the Archaeological Museum in the Piazza San Marco; he is afraid that, if he does not see to it, we shall miss the Greek statuary there.

This is Venetian courtesy. Foreigners who have lived here a long time dismiss it with the observation: "They have nothing else to do." But idleness here is alert, on the *qui vive* for the opportunity of sightseeing; nothing delights a born Venetian so much as a free gondola ride. When the funeral gondola, a great black-and-gold ornate hearse, draws up beside a fondamenta, it is an occasion for aesthetic pleasure. My

neighbourhood was especially favoured in this way, because across the campo was the Old Men's Home. Everyone has noticed the Venetian taste in shopdisplays, which extends down to the poorest bargeman, who cuts his watermelons in half and shows them, pale pink, with green rims against the green side-canal, in which a pink palace with oleanders is reflected. *Che bello, che magnifico, che luce, che colore!*—they are all *professori delle Belle Arti*. And throughout the Veneto, in the old Venetian possessions, this internal tourism, this expertise, is rife. In Bassano, at the Civic Museum, I took the Mayor for the local art-critic until he interrupted his discourse on the jewel-tones ("like Murano glass") in the Bassani pastorals to look at his watch and cry out: "My citizens are calling me." Nearby, in a Palladian villa, a Venetian lady suspired, *"Ah, bellissima,"* on being shown a hearthstool in the shape of a life-size stuffed leather pig. Harry's Bar has a drink called a Tiziano, made of grapefruit juice and champagne and coloured pink with grenadine or bitters. "You ought to have a Tintoretto," someone remonstrated, and the proprietor regretted that he had not yet invented that drink, but he had a Bellini and a Giorgione.

When the Venetians stroll out in the evening, they do not avoid the Piazza San Marco, where the tourists are, as the Romans do with Doney's on the Via Veneto. The Venetians go to look at the tourists, and the tourists look back at them. It is all for the ear and eye, this city, but primarily for the eye. Built on water, it is an endless succession of reflections and echoes, a mirroring. Contrary to popular belief, there are no back canals where a tourist will not meet himself, with a camera, in the person of the other tourist crossing the little bridge. And no word can be spoken in this city that is not an echo of something said before. *"Mais c'est aussi cher que Paris!"* exclaims a Frenchman in a restaurant, unaware that he repeats Montaigne. The complaint against foreigners, voiced by a foreigner, chimes querulously through the ages, in unison with the medieval monk who found St. Mark's Square filled with "Turks, Libyans, Parthians, and other monsters of the sea." Today it is the Germans we complain of, and no doubt they complain of the Americans, in the same words.

Nothing can be said here (including this statement) *that has not been said before.* One often hears the Piazza described as an open-air drawing room; the observation goes back to Napoleon, who called it "the best drawing-room in Europe." A friend likens the ornamental coping of St Mark's to sea foam, but Ruskin thought of this first: ". . . at last, as if in ecstasy, the crests of the arches break into a marbly foam, and toss themselves far into the blue sky in flashes and wreaths of sculptured spray . . ." Another friend observes that the gondolas are like hearses; I was struck by the novelty of the fancy until I found it, two days later, in Shelley: "that funereal bark." Now I find it everywhere. A young man, boarding the vaporetto, sighs that "Venice is so urban," a remark which at least *sounds* original and doubtless did when Proust spoke of the "always urban impression" made by Venice in the midst of the sea. And the worst of it is that nearly all these clichés are true. It is true, for example, that St Mark's at night looks like a painted stage flat; this is a fact which everybody notices and which everybody thinks he has discovered for himself. I blush to remember the sound of my own voice, clear in its own conceit, enunciating this proposition in the Piazza, nine years ago.

"I envy you, writing about Venice," says the newcomer. "I pity you," says the old hand. One thing is certain. Sophistication, that modern kind of sophistication that begs to differ, to be paradoxical, to invert, is not a possible attitude in Venice. In time, this becomes the beauty of the place. One gives up the struggle and submits to a classic experience. One accepts the fact that what one is about to feel or say has not only been said before by Goethe or Musset but is on the tip of the tongue of the tourist from Iowa who is alighting in the Piazzetta with his wife in her fur-piece and jewelled pin. Those Others, the existential enemy, are here identical with oneself. After a time in Venice, one comes to look with pity on the efforts of the newcomer to disassociate himself from the crowd. He has found a "little" church—has he?—quite off the beaten track, a real gem, with inlaid coloured marbles on a soft dove grey, like a jewel box. He means Santa Maria dei Miracoli. As you name it, his face falls. It is so well known, then? Or has he the notion of counting the lions that look down from the window ledges of the palazzi. They remind him of cats. Has anybody ever noticed how many cats there are in Venice or compared them to the lions? On my table two books lie open with chapters on the Cats of Venice. My face had fallen too when I came upon them in the house of an old bookseller, for I too had dared think that I had hold of an original perception.

The cat = the lion. Venice is a kind of pun on itself, which is another way of saying that it is a mirror held up to its own shimmering image—the central conceit on which it has evolved. The Grand Canal is in the shape of a fish (or an eel, if you wish to be more literal); on the Piazzetta, St Theodore rides the crocodile (or the fish, if you prefer). Dolphins and scallop shells carry out the theme in decoration. It becomes frozen in the state ceremonial; the Doge weds the Adriatic in a mock, i.e., a punning, marriage. The lion enters the state myth in the company of the Evangelist and begets litter on litter of lions—all allusions, half jesting, half literary, to the original one: the great War Lion of the Arsenal gate whose Book ("Peace be with you") is ominously closed, the graduated lions from Greece below him, in front of the Arsenal, like the three bears in the story, the King of Beasts with uplifted tail in *trompe-l'œil* on the Scuola di San Marco, the red, roaring lions on the left of St Mark's who play hobbyhorse for children every day, the lion of Chioggia, which Venetians say is only a cat, the doggy lion of the Porta della Carta being honored by the Doge Foscari . . . From St Mark's Square, they spread out, in varying shapes and sizes, whiskered or clean-shaven, through Venice and her ancient territories, as far as Nauplia in the Peloponnesus. But St Mark's lion is winged, i.e., a monster, and this produces a whole crop of monsters, basilisks and dragons, with their attendant saints and slayers, all dear to Venetian artists. St Jerome, thanks to his tame lion, becomes a favourite saint of the Venetians.

The twinning continues. The great pink church of the Frari is echoed on the other side of the city by the great pink church of the Dominicans, the other preaching order. And in St Mark's shelter, near the Pietra del Bando, four small identical brothers, called the Moors, in porphyry embrace two and two, like orphans. The famous Venetian *trompe-l'œil*, marble simulating brocade or flat simulating round, is itself a sort of twinning or unending duplication, as with a repeating decimal.

Venice is a game (see how many lions you can count; E. V. Lucas found 75 on the Porta della Carta alone), a fantasy, a fable, a city of Methuselahs, in which mortality has almost been vanquished. Titian, according to the old writers, was carried off by the plague in his hundredth year. How many Venetian painters can you count who, like him, passed three score and ten before they were gathered to their fathers? Jacopo Bellini (70 years), Gentile Bellini (78), Giovanni Bellini (86), Lorenzo Lotto (76), Tintoretto (76), Palma Il Giovane (84), Tiepolo (80), G. D. Tiepolo (77), Pietro Longhi (83), Alessandro Longhi (80), Piazzetta (71), Canaletto (71), Guardi (81). And among the sculptors and architects, Pietro Lombardo (65), Sansovino (93), Alessandro Vittoria (83), Palladio (72), Longhena (84). This makes Venice, the nourisher of old men, appear as a dream, the Fountain of Youth which Ponce de Leon sought in the New World. It brings us back to the rationalist criticism of Venice, as a myth that ought to be exploded.

"Those Pantaloons," a French ambassador called the Venetian statesmen in the early seventeenth century, when the astuteness of their diplomacy was supposed to be the wonder of Europe. The capacity to arouse contempt and disgust in the onlooker was a natural concomitant, not only of Venice's prestige, but of the whole fairy tale she wove about herself; her Council of Ten, her mysterious three Inquisitors, her dungeons, her punishments, "swift, silent, and sure." Today, we smile a little at the fairy tale of Venetian history, at the doge under his golden umbrella, as we smile at the nuns entertaining their admirers in Guardi's picture in the Ca' Rezzonico, at the gaming tables and the masks; it is the same smile we give to the all-woman regatta, to the graduated lions, to Carpaccio's man-eating dragon. If we shiver as we pass through the Leads or as we slip our hand into the Bocca del Leone, it is a histrionic shiver, partly self-induced, like the screams that ring out from the little cars in an amusement-park tunnel as they shoot past the waxworks. For us, Venetian history is a curio; those hale old doges and warriors seem to us a strange breed of sea-animal who left behind them the pink, convoluted shell they grew to protect them, which is Venice.

The old historians took a different line and tended to view Venice as an allegory in which vice and reckless greed (or undemocratic government) met their just reward. They held up Venice as a cautionary example to other nations. But we cannot feel this moral indignation or this solemn awe before the Venetian spectacle. In Ravenna or Mantua, we can sense the gloom of history steal over us like a real shadow. These cities are truly sad, and they compel belief in the crimes and tragedies that were enacted in them. Venice remains a child's pageant, minute and ingenious, brightened with touches of humorous "local colour," as in the pageant pictures of Gentile Bellini and Carpaccio. Or, with Tintoretto and Veronese, it swells into a bepearled myth. The sumptuous Apotheoses of the rooms of the Doge's Palace, the blues and golds and nacreous flesh tones, discredit the reality of the Turkish disasters that were befalling the Republic at the time they were painted, just as Giorgione's idylls discredit the reality of the League of Cambrai. With the eighteenth-century painters, the pneumatic goddess is deflated. The pictures of Canaletto and Guardi and Longhi take us back again into playland, with toy boats (the gondolas) and dominos and masks and lacy shawls, while the pictures of Tiepolo with their chalky tones take us to a circus, in which everyone is a clown or a trapeze artist, in white theatrical make-up and theatrical costuming. Napoleon was at the gates, but it is hard to believe it. It was hard for the Venetians, at the time. For them, their "liberation" from the oligarchy was simply another pageant, another procession, with allegorical figures in costume before the old stage flat of St Mark's, which was hung with garlands and draperies. At the opera that night,

BELVEDERE CASTLE, VIENNA.

the fall of the Republic was celebrated by a ballet danced by the workers of the Arsenal; the patricians were there, in silks and laces and brocades, gold and silver lamés, diamonds and pearls, and, in honour of the occasion, gondoliers were admitted free.

Everything that happens in Venice has this inherent improbability, of which the gondola, floating, insubstantial, at once romantic and haunting, charming and absurd, is the symbol. "Why don't they put outboard motors on them?" an American wondered, looking on the practical side. But a dream is only practical in unexpected ways; that is, it is *resourceful*, like the Venetians. "It is another world," people say, noting chiefly the absence of the automobile. And it *is* another world, a palpable fiction, in which the unexpected occurs with regularity; that is why it hovers on the brink of humour.

A prominent nobleman this autumn, rushing to the sickbed of a friend, slipped getting into his motorboat and fell into the Grand Canal. All Venice laughed. But if the count had had his misadventure in Padua, on *terra ferma*, if he had fallen getting out of his car, everyone would have condoled with him. Traffic lights are not funny, but it is funny to have one in Venice over a canal-intersection. The same with the Venetian fire brigade. The things of *this* world reveal their essential absurdity when they are put in the Venetian context. In the unreal realm of the canals, as in a Swiftian Lilliput, the real world, with its contrivances, appears as a vast folly.

ST. STEPHEN'S CATHEDRAL, VIENNA.

V. S. PRITCHETT

from The Spanish Temper

"THEY are noble people," and their country is a place apart, seemingly unrelated to the rest of Europe.

AND SO CASTILE stretches towards its backbone, the Guadarrama and the Gredos mountains. There will be miles where the soil looks like stripes of red lead or ochre, distances of sulphur and tin, the sharp colours of incineration, as if great areas of the kingdom had been raked out of a furnace. As the train climbs to Santa Teresa's Ávila, there will be miles of wilderness where granite is piled up among the oaks or the short pines, and one sees the red fan of the partridge as it flies and the hunter standing with his horn and his gun. One feels lonely and free in the vast space of Castile, and the few roads suggest long, monotonous journeys. The eye picks up the green of the rare acacias or poplars which mark the metalled roads. On some mule track we mark the figure of some peasant riding away on a mule: miles between that figure and ourselves—who is he? What is the solitary insect thinking? What peasant with skin incised by wind and sun? We become absorbed, in these dawdling hours, in the task of overtaking a man who would greet one openly, talk in a pure, almost Biblical tongue, and who will speak his business straight out and expect to hear all yours.

"Good day. I am going to Santa X with this corn. I am from that village. There I have my family, my so many brothers, my so many sisters. Where do you come from? What country, what village? Where is England? Is that in France? Are you married? How many children have you? If you have, good; if you have not, bad. God has not granted them. What is your employment? How much do you earn? In your country"—the final deciding question—"is there plenty to eat?" And after that—some string of proverbs, a page of Don Quixote, a page of Sancho Panza. And then that lordly Spanish sentence of farewell and one's impression that one has been talking as a nobleman to a nobleman—as the Aragonese say, "We are as noble as the King but not as rich."

The egalitarianism of the Spaniards is not like the citizenship of the French, nor the anonymity of the English or American democracy, where we seek the lowest common denominator and try to hide our distinctions. The Spanish live in castes, but not in classes, and their equality—the only real equality I have met anywhere in the world—is in their sense of nobility or, rather, in the sense of the absolute quality of the person. One will hear this sentence spoken of people living in the lowest wretchedness: "They are noble people." These words are not especially a compliment, nor do they convey resignation, pity, or regret; they are meant, almost conventionally, to describe the normal condition of man.

If we were to travel with this man on the mule or donkey, we would not see his village until we were right upon it. It is some ruinous, dusty place, the colour of the soil it stands in, and most houses will be of a single storey. Only the fortress wall of its church will stand out, plainly buttressed high above the hut roofs of the village and built to last till the end of the world. It is the spire, the belfry, or the dome of the church that one sees first in the plain, rising inch by inch like a spear or a helmet, and it will give to the mind a lasting sense of a bare, military country, frugal and hard. In the wars of reconquest against the Moors, some of the churches—and cathedrals like Ávila— were built as forts, and of that time it has been said that the Spaniards did not know which they wanted most —the Kingdom of God or their own land. The centre of the village is a square of tottering stone arcades; the mule carts or the occasional lorry stand there. The inn, if there is one, will not be a hotel, nor even a *fonda*—the Arab word—but perhaps a *posada*: a place one can ride into with mule or donkey, where one can stable an animal and lie down oneself on a sack of straw, the other side of the stall. There are grand *posadas* like the Posada de la Sangre of Cervantes, which still exists in Toledo, places of heavily beamed roofs, and of courtyards upon which one may look down from the interior galleries; if the village is small enough there may only be a *venta* or tavern for the sale of wine and aguardiente. But there will be a ewer of water in the corner of the stone floor with a tin dipper in it, and that is what, in this dusty country, you make for. The water is cold and beautiful. Everyone praises its purity, and the man or woman staring at you with that prolonged and total Spanish stare will tell you soberly that this particular water is famous throughout the world as the best water on earth.

At nine o'clock at night they will ask you what you want to eat.

HOUSE IN DEYÁ, MAJORCA, SPAIN.

"What have you got?"

"Whatever the señor wishes."

And a Dutch auction begins. Meat, alas there isn't any; chicken, they regret; it comes down in the end to garlic soup and how many "pairs of eggs" can you eat, with a chunk of garlic sausage thrown in? They have "wonderful wine, the finest for miles"—but it turns out to be thin, vinegarish, and watered. The oil is rancid, but the stick fire blazes, the smoke fills the room, and there is war in your stomach that night unless you are used to the crude Spanish fry and to garlic as strong as acetylene. The food might turn out better than this of course; there might be bacalao, if you can eat dry salted cod; there might be pork off the black pigs; and resinous wine, scraping the top off your tongue, with flavour of the pine cask. They might

catch and kill that screeching chicken in the yard or give you goat cheese and the close white bread which has come in again after the years of war and starvation. But good or bad, full or meagre, the meal will not be squalid or sluttish. There will be a piety and honourableness about it, no scrambling round the trough. The woman's hard voice will command the room and one will break one's bread with the dignity of a lean person who speaks of other things. "We give what we have"—not the "you eat the official portion which you're given or go without" of our sour democracies. They still—even after the Civil War, in which so much of Spanish custom died—turn to their neighbour before they eat and say: "Would you like this?" and even lift the plate.

"Please enjoy it yourself," is the reply.

Being so noble, they could (they convey) do without food altogether; or like the penniless starving lord in the picaresque tale of Lazarillo de Tormes, send in the starving servant to say: "Thank you, we have eaten already." Sober, frugal, austere is the Castilian living in these small towns that look like heaps of broken pottery in the plain.

* * *

Twenty-five years ago Madrid was a flat Spanish city hardly visible on its cliff above the river Manzanares except as a low line of heavy red roofs. Only the large façade of the Royal Palace disclosed the existence of a city as one approached it. Now skyscrapers and tall white blocks of flats like upended sugar cubes break the horizon and give the city an American appearance from the distance. Large white suburbs have sprung around it, and, like Barcelona, the capital has doubled its population in a generation. Although it is despised by foreigners, who find little of old Spain in it, for Madrid was built in the seventeenth century at the orders of the King, it is an agreeable modern city in the spring and the autumn. Its harsh, wet or snowy, winter climate is hard to bear, and the heat in July and August is intolerable. At this season all who can afford to do so get out of the capital to the mountains or to the north; those who stay resign themselves to very little sleep because of the heat, and the population sits up half the night in the streets.

The Talgo arrives at the right hour—the time of the *paseo*, when the cafés are packed and the streets are crowded with people in the sacred evening promenade of Spanish life. They have gone to the main streets in the centre of the city, which has become a hive. In some towns at this hour one is drawn by a sustained, dry roar of voices which sounds like the roar of a football match, a bullfight, or a political meeting; but, making one's way towards it, through streets that are strange because they are empty, one arrives at the Plaza Mayor, or some street where the traffic has been barred, to find most of the population has gathered there by custom, to talk and walk endlessly round and round. The Spaniards have little social life in their houses—though a little social life imitated from Europe does go on among the better off or the very Europeanized; tea parties and cocktail parties are occasionally given by such people—the majority of Spaniards treat the street as their place of entertainment.

At this hour the women appear and display themselves as if they had walked into a drawing-room. External display is important to Spaniards; they will spend more on their persons than on their houses, in which they easily dispense with the mania for furnishing and interior decoration which possesses northerners, and not entirely because the general standard of wealth is much lower. But in the street they dress well. Any Spanish crowd, even in the poor districts, is the best-dressed crowd in Europe, but they are rarely elegant or fashionable. They have simply a firm conservative sense of what is fitting, not of what attracts extravagant attention. Only in their jewelry do the Spanish women display extravagance.

There is no chic and there is no sophistication in Spain, not even in Madrid, except when it has obviously been imitated from Paris or brought in and Frenchified by South Americans; one is always struck by the conservative temperament of the people, their love of the purely formal, and even by a national provinciality. They have always kept to their own ways, have always sustained their own genre, and they withdraw, with a sort of disapproving or even positive scorn, from the contagion of other manners. In this they are resolute rather than complacent, egotistic rather than hostile—perhaps a little snobbish. In their preoccupation with what is "suitable" they resemble the English.

One finds a seat in a café and orders a glass of their iced beer and watches the crowd. One is deafened by their voices and the violent noise of the traffic. In England the general standard of looks is low; one is struck only by the large number of very individual faces which suggest that the English are characters out of Cruikshank's drawings. In France the standard of looks is not much higher than in England; at any rate in the north of France it is not. The Spaniard level is high; indeed, a certain regularity of feature, boldness of nose, and brilliance of eye appear to have been standardized. The amount of Jewish blood is, one would think, high. This is not as fantastic a generalization as it may sound: the Jewish population, open or hidden, was enormous in Spain, and the exodus cannot have excluded its deep racial infiltration altogether. There is a classical Spanish type, grave, dark, sallow, a little heavy sometimes; and there is the small, monkeyish type, quick, melancholy, mischievous. The crowd falls into those natural divisions which may be broken by an occasional woman of great beauty or a figure of grotesque ugliness. Only the old, bent, and ill carry themselves badly. Round shoulders are rarely seen. The dry, electric air of the city enlivens these walkers. One has the impression of great natural vitality, undistracted by northern nerves.

Many travellers have noticed what has seemed to them an almost racial difference between Spanish men and women. (The difference is really social: the life

OLD OLIVE TREE, MAJORCA.

of the Spanish male is likely to be more anxious, less fulfilled than the life of the Spanish female. He is encumbered, as the woman is not exclusively, by the condition of Spain, the frustration of the will.) The women of Madrid, as they go by in their twos and threes, and so rarely with a man, have a militant, formal, prim appearance. Sociable and talkative—for all Spaniards love talking for its own sake—they are trained to a double role: they display themselves, they have great personal pride; yet never for one moment do they allow their eyes to meet the eyes of a man as they walk the street. The decorum is complete and is distinctly Victorian.

The Spanish language is decisive and quick, packed with turns of phrase. What is called "gracia," a gay shrewdness in repartee rather than wit, is always sought. To a foreign ear, the language sounds granular and rapid, rather harsh and unmusical, and this gives a male assertiveness and roughness to the voices of the women. As they walk by, carrying themselves so well,

MADRID'S PLAZA MAYOR.

they are rather a collected, rather severe female race. For all this dominant appearance—and they clearly dominate the men by having their role in life firmly marked out and mixed with the male role very little socially—they have the reputation of being homely, innocent, and sensual. They are passionate lovers of children: there is marriage and eight children in their eyes. Yet in the past ten or fifteen years Spain has gone through revolutionary changes, and Spanish girls are experiencing a belated and relative emancipation. One unexpected effect of the Civil War, although it ended with the victory of reactionary forces in religion and politics, is this emancipation of women. In the twenties and thirties, it is true that in educated families there was considerable freedom for women, especially for those who went to the Free or International schools. They could go about a good deal on

their own, they took up intellectual careers, they travelled; most revolutionary, they read what they wanted and did not accept the censorship of the priests. (This is far from saying these girls were non-Catholics; they were deeply Catholic, but Spanish notions of what is suitable for girls to read are simple and severe. Spanish literature is barred to them—if they are obedient.) In the reaction that has followed under Franco, it is the fashion to despise the educated generation socially. It is not done to be educated; yet, paradoxically, the young girls now growing up have far more freedom of movement and go to university courses. Some cynical people think that this passion for socially despised education is a scheme for getting out of the house.

Display, a certain extravagance of state, is—by the continual paradox of Spanish life—loved by this frugal and sober people. The question has been gone into thoroughly by Galdós, the Spanish Balzac, as he is called, and moralist historian of the late nineteenth and early twentieth century. The moral basis of life in Madrid has been thoroughly described by this moralist who soaked himself in the life of all classes, and in spite of the social changes he is still a valuable guide. Societies do not change as fast as they like to think they do from generation to generation. Galdós went into the question of social state and display in his novel called *La de Bringas* and it is concerned with a family that spends everything on social position. In the golden age when the treasure was brought back from the Indies, in the time of Goya, when the *majà* and the *majo* wore their fantastic clothes, in the gorgeous uniforms of the various police forces which the Spaniard cannot do without, one can trace the phases of the Spanish extravagance.

HORACE SUTTON

from SUTTON'S PLACES

WHERE else on earth is life so sweet as in the provinces of France?

THE VALLEY OF THE DORDOGNE, alias the Périgord, is a scenic enclave in southern France where the principal occupations are eating and watching the old stones get older. All this, as you can imagine, is a wonderful relief from radio commercials, radioactivity, and the irradiation of junior senators. The old stones can hardly do anything but get older, and as long as the pâté and truffles hold out, life can be beautiful.

The cardinal blooper to be committed in the Périgord—after all, I'd better tell you right off—is to bring up the pâté de foie gras as manufactured in the city of Strasbourg. Soap! Kirkman's laundry bars in terrines, that's what! If you're going to eat pâté, eat the real stuff, pâté du Périgord, with black truffles. Now there are many ways of finding a truffle, as any gentleman of the Périgord can tell you. Périgord is to truffles as Pennsylvania is to coal, and for that matter coal and truffles look alike, except that you eat truffles, especially if you are from the Périgord. Since the truffle is a subterranean fungus, it must be uprooted; and in this valley the job is done by trained pigs, sometimes by dogs, and also by bees. The pigs are persuaded to go agrunting along the ground until they whiff a truffle. They dig the black morsel out of the earth with a nudge of their snout, but before they can swallow it, a nimble truffle-gatherer whisks it away. This makes for frustrated pigs and well-garnished pâté de foie gras. About the same process is carried on with dogs, but the bee routine I find hard to take. In certain seasons of the year the truffle-searchers just beat the ground, and wherever the bees rise, chances are there will be a black nugget underneath. At least that's what a fairly impeachable source told me.

Black fungus shows up not only in the local pâté, but also in omelette aux truffes, an inescapable dish in these parts. The goose is put to other uses here (they do everything but race them), particularly in the manufacture of confit d'oie, which is goose wing redolent of garlic—not much garlic, mind you, just enough to make your eyes tear. All this gets washed down with a white, dry and smoky wine called Château Panisseau and another called Château Bonnecoste. The ultimate adventure is a round of spirits made from the essence of walnuts, there being practically nothing from which a thirsty man cannot fabricate alcohol. It comes in a crock and is called La Vieille Noix, or the Old Nuts.

Before this becomes merely a voyage along the alimentary canal, I would hasten to say that between meals in the Périgord there is a string of fascinating, unspoiled things to see. You will almost certainly need a car, either picking one up in Limoges or else stopping off en route to Spain. The most striking attraction are the caves of Lascaux at Montignac, which were only discovered in 1940 by a group of boys looking for their lost dog. Besides the dog the boys also found a cavern covered with prehistoric paintings so sharp and well preserved as to make skeptics doubt their authenticity. Horses, bison, reindeer, oxen, and one strange man adorn the walls, all of them having been drawn at least fifteen thousand years ago, and perhaps twice as long ago as that. The grotto entrance is in a pine woods and is open daily except from twelve until two—for the "renouvellement de l'atmosphère" and also, I would judge, for the renouvellement of caretaker's eating habits as well.

You've seen the best grotto after you've done Lascaux, but the capital of France's prehistory is nearby at Les Eyzies, and you shouldn't miss it. The town

THE MATTERHORN, CHALETS, AND ALPINE FLOWERS—SWITZERLAND.

leans against high limestone cliffs, and with such natural abutments at hand, the villagers were merely required to build three walls on their houses, using the natural rock for the fourth. You can achieve a fair idea of how it was to live like a caveman at the Cro-Magnon Hotel, which has three walls built by man, one by glaciers, and charges about two dollars and fifty cents a day for a single room with private bath, and about six dollars for the same premises including three meals.

La Roque-Gageac is a one-street village absolutely pasted against the side of a cliff, with the lovely Dordogne River flowing past the façades in a great sweeping curve. The view is magnificent, the peace is hypnotizing; perhaps the Romans found it that way, too, for they built strange shelters high among the cliffs and relics of them still stand. A great château commands the road at the entrance to the village, but the greatest threat to security in town nowadays is the river, which occasionally swells its banks and creeps up the cliffside. Villagers have been soaked so often by the Dordogne that all shops have since been installed on the second floor, and Main Street is as dead as a Colorado town twenty years after the lode ran out.

To see all the valley of the Dordogne laid out in front of you, just like Cinerama, you drive a few miles down to Domme and take the high road up to the lookout. There in the mist is La Roque-Gageac, gray and smoky against its hillside, with the back road from Domme leading up to it in a white, chalky line. The green plain is rolled out flat, and the river wanders through it, making a great, open U. Poplar trees, long and slender as a couturier's mannequin, run the river bank, bursts of white plum blossoms lie on the valley floor like wind-blown popcorn, and the morimeaux wheel and wing and are happy about the springtime.

Rocamadour is a fantastic site, a rocky cliff face jutting up from a deep valley trough, with houses, hotels, and a church stuck on every available promontory right up to the top. You stop your car on the single street just under the hotel where you plan to stay, and they drop a basket on a rope to pull your baggage up to the heights with a winch. There is hardly a hotel or a room or a rock without a fabulous view.

It is a legend that Zacchaeus, who climbed a sycamore tree at Jericho to watch Christ pass, came to Gaul and built an oratory on the highest point of the rock. His name became Amadour, and long after he died, pilgrims came to see his bones, among them Henry II of England, Louis IX and Louis XI of France. Pilgrims still come, doing the stairs on their knees; and tourists come, too, from Easter until fall, gasping at the views and wondering about the strange sword stuck into a crevice in the rocks high up over a chapel door. The sword used to be just eight feet off the ground and the legend was that girls who touched it would be married in a year. So the girls got ladders and climbed up to touch the hilt, while the boys stood below enjoying the view. The curé thought this constituted indecent exposure and had the sword placed up out of reach, and so the legend is gone and so is the boys' favorite panorama.

Working back toward Limoges is the village of Collonge, known as Collonge La Rouge, because now the earth is red and the rocks are red and so are all the buildings. There is no pavement in Collonge La Rouge, the chickens squawk along in the street, and a blacksmith in those startled-blue coveralls the French like to wear bangs his anvil. Overhead are strange red arches that span the alleys and red towers rising against the brilliant blue sky, and everywhere the quiet except for the chickens and the anvil.

I could hardly think of a better way to leave the Périgord than on a full stomach. That can be accomplished with infinite pleasure at the town of Brive, which has one of those multistarred inns over which the gourmets do nip-ups and the guidebook people pull out the bold-face type. This one is called the Hotel de la Truffe Noire, or the Black Truffle Hotel, and it is being operated by a gentleman both ample and affable named André Dupart, half of the Paris restaurant team of Yvonne and André which drew such ravenous royalty as the Duke of Windsor, the Aga Khan, Churchill, Harriman, and who knows all. The Paris place is sold now, but the famous regulars have been journeying down to Brive for jambonneau truffé, foie gras truffé, omelette aux truffes, truit truffe noire, volaille bresse truffe noire, probably followed by l'Alka Seltzer truffe noire. I know people who wouldn't travel to Weehawken for a truffle, but these gourmets are strange coves indeed. With them one man's fungus may be another man's delight.

M. F. K. FISHER

from MAP OF ANOTHER TOWN

AFTER decades of subtle relationships with French landladies the writer knows "that now I can live almost anywhere, with almost anyone, and be the better for it."

SOMETIMES AT MADAME LANES' I would be hard put to it not to ask to be excused from the table in a silent pet, when she would ask me blandly if I objected to some delicious dish which she had ordered to please one of the other boarders.

"I know you Americans don't care what you eat," she would state, and it was not until I knew her better that I could hear the friendliness in her teasing. "It always amazes me about how little you notice flavor and seasoning. You seem to have no definite tastes . . . only prejudices." And so on.

Then she would detail the gastronomical requirements of her other more demanding and therefore more sensitive and worldly boarders: the Swiss must have cream sauces with their meat; the Swedes would not tolerate garlic, olive oil or even tomatoes; the English wanted mustard always with meat; the Corsicans loathed cream sauce as well as mustard, but could not subsist without garlic, olive oil and tomatoes. Furthermore, Frenchmen from different regions must eat their native dishes and follow their set table-habits. All this was in exciting and glamorous contrast to the sterile monotony of American tastes: we apparently cared nothing at all for the niceties of palate.

And so on.

And so on.

No, I would rage silently. No, we crude Yanks are too polite, too well taught, to demand Boston baked beans or tamales from a French hostess. And I would smile politely, and curse the forthright boarders from Stockholm and Ajaccio, and enjoy what was set before me, for it was good.

Gradually I stopped my secret flashes of exasperation at the table, and knew with an increasing awareness that there were indeed many areas of perception where I would always remain innocent, at least more so than a person of an older wearier race could be. It became a strangely satisfying thing to know, on the other hand, that there were so many things I could and did appreciate, for which people like Madame would never credit me. It helped me to live alone from them, which I had to do anyway.

My outward blandness with Madame Lanes became increasingly sweetened with a real affection and an understanding of her veiled mockery, but occasionally in Aix I decided swiftly to wipe out this or that sneering person from my life and thoughts. It was as satisfying as discarding a rotten apricot from a bowl of fresh fruit, or lopping off a dead branch from a healthy tree. I had no personal feeling about either them or my ruthlessness; I did not care if they found me, the quiet perhaps colorless woman, unperceptive and oafish. I did care that I was thought to be so because I was an American . . . and when this was made plain in an ill-bred or stupid way, I simply eliminated the culprit.

Once, for instance, I was introduced through friends in Dijon to a very important and in some ways charming older woman. She gave me valuable advice about finding a good family for my children to stay with . . . things like that. Finally she asked me to have lunch with her and a few people who might be interested in helping me with my French, which,

CHÂTEAU OF CHAMBORD, FRANCE.

she assured me smoothly, was already past any real need for improvement.

The apartment above the Place des Prêcheurs was beautiful, one of the long airy waxed places that seem to exist only in old French towns, from Paris to Bordeaux to Strasbourg to Marseille. Tall windows looking into the green boughs, curtains drifting over the polished floors, books everywhere, noble armoires lined with padded Provençal cottons: it was a harmonious simplicity, where only man was vile.

My hostess was a short hearty woman, married late in years to a much older man, a retired colonel who mumbled distantly as he came into the drawing room, where a tiny fire burned in the marble hearth and the windows shook a little now and then from the great organ in the Church of the Madeleine next door, playing for a noon Mass.

There was a fire in the dining room too, made like the other one of the five-inch twigs I was soon to grow used to as the only heat in my room at Madame Lanes'.

There were three other guests, two near-mute assistant teachers from the Lycée who might possibly consent to exchange conversation with me once a week, and a red-headed tall thin Englishwoman with a deliberately throbbing bass voice and department store tweeds, who spoke nothing but schoolgirl French to me and often passed me later on the Cours without nodding, pretending not to see me.

At the table I sat next to the Colonel, who ate steadily. He was very senile, and unbelievably obscene in a quiet way which he knew nobody but I could hear. Now and then he would glance slyly at me through his crumbs and driblets, and murmur an invitation straight from the walls of Pompeii, and then chuckle as he popped a whole chestnut tart into his sagging mouth.

Gradually I came to believe, almost frantically, that my hostess had hated my old friends in Dijon since her first college days with them, and that now she was avenging herself, on me, for their greater worth, their brilliance, their strength and bounty. I was her victim. It shook me. She shook me. I could feel my inner head flapping back and forth on its neck like a rag doll's as she battered me with her merry little chuckles, her understanding glances.

"Tell me, dear lady," she would shriek down the table at me with a comradely twinkle, "tell me . . . explain to *all* of us, how one can dare to call herself a writer on gastronomy in the United States, where, from everything we hear, gastronomy does not yet exist? Explain to us, dear self-styled Gastronomer, to us poor people of this older world . . ." and so on.

And so on.

The other guests smiled or snorted genteelly, according to their natures, except for the Colonel, who stuffed more sweets into his toothless face. It seemed the longest meal I had ever endured, and its rich tedious courses bit like acid inside me, metamorphosed by anger and ennui.

"And now, dear lady," my hostess would sing out gaily, "now that we have eaten this little French luncheon, so simple but so typical of our national *cuisine*, tell us just how you managed to invent such profitable fiction about one of the sciences, when even Brillat-Savarin could not! We await your dictum!"

They would lean forward obediently at her signal, the two girls stunned with food and fear, the Englishwoman rigid with snobbish inferiority. The Colonel would belch and finger his fly under his spotted napkin. I would stiffen my mask and steady my voice behind it, firm in my ruthless decision: I would never speak anything but a civil good day to this person again.

The next day I sent her a huge box, shaped like a coffin woven of reeds and twigs, filled with the most beautiful flowers I could find in Aix, fresh from the gardens of Nice. It was my private funeral piece for her.

*   *   *

I have lived with several families in France. More often than not while I was with them I fretted and even raged at the strictures of sharing my meals and my emotions and my most personal physical functions with people almost as strange to me as spiders or nesting egrets. In retrospect I understand that they shaped such strength as may be in me as surely as ever did my inherited genes and my environmental mores. Of course they had these to build on, for I did not meet my first landlady until I was in my early twenties.

She was a born Dijonnaise who lived down the street from the University because she liked to rent rooms to students, not because the house she rented was beautiful or otherwise desirable to them. She *liked* students. She liked to feed them and talk with them and play Chopin for them and occasionally sleep with ones who pleased her enough. She did all this with ferocious amusement. She was a kind of explosion in what had been until my first meeting with her a safe insular well-bred existence.

From then on I was aware.

She has been followed by decades of less robust but equally subtle relationships with French landladies.

A STREET IN MONTMARTRE.

ARC DE TRIOMPHE WITH TRICOLOR, PARIS.

Now I know that I can live almost anywhere, with almost anyone, and be the better for it. This is a great comfort in contemplating the probabilities of the future. . . .

First impressions are perhaps not as important as they are said to be, but they are good preparation for what may happen later, and I know that every landlady I ever met was part of preparing me for Madame Lanes, of Aix.

My mother would understand and accept my feeling that this old lady had almost as much to do with my development as did she, and would not ask for any explanation. It is at once an overt admission that I matured very slowly and a proof that people can grow at any stage in their lives. My mother would be pleased that I could still grow.

I was nearing fifty when I first met Madame Lanes, and well past it when last I saw her. It is improbable that I shall be with her again, for she is old and seven thousand miles away, but I feel serene and sure that if that happened I would be the better for it, and stronger to surmount the admiration, exasperation, impatience, ridicule, and frustration that she has always fermented in me.

A FOUNTAIN IN THE PLACE DE LA CONCORDE, WITH PART
OF THE EIFFEL TOWER IN THE DISTANCE.

STATUE OF LIBERTY, SMALLER SCALE, ON THE SEINE.

THE PALACE OF VERSAILLES.

NIRAD C. CHAUDHURI

from A Passage to England

"IT SEEMED as if I had given deep offence to a large number of my patriotic fellow-Indians by an indiscreet enthusiasm," writes Mr. Chaudhuri of the first reactions to his comments on England. "I was even called pro-British. . . ."

LONDON IS BIG AND COMPLEX, and most visitors get lost in it, not only physically but also intellectually. Even the Londoner does, for he very often speaks only of particular features of London, and shrinks from summing it all up. He says that London has never been planned or even built, it has grown. He would even be proud to add that it does not possess any obvious beauty of appearance, it has not acquired any form that can be easily captured by the eye, being more or less inchoate; one has to live in London to sense its personality; a man might spend a lifetime in it making daily discoveries, and yet his discoveries would not end; so you have to accept London in parts.

This is so obviously true that most foreign visitors just ignore the formlessness of London, or, if they are clever, air a kind of cynicism over its untidiness. I had heard so much of it from my countrymen who had been to England that when I actually saw London I was quite surprised to find that it was much more tidy and orderly than I had thought it would be. I oriented myself very easily there with the help of the axis furnished by the continuation of Bayswater Road into Oxford Street, and of Oxford Street into Holborn.

The cynical vein was really started by English literary men. Byron wrote:

> A mighty mass of brick, and smoke, and shipping,
>   Dirty and dusty, but as wide as eye
> Could reach . . . a wilderness of steeples peeping
>   On tiptoe through their sea-coal canopy;
> A huge, dun cupola, like a foolscap crown
> On a fool's head—and there is London Town.

That was written not long after Canaletto had painted the Thames in London. What would Byron have thought today?

Less gifted people try to get round the overpowering vastness and variety of London by sampling it. I also did, to begin with. I looked for its beauty spots.

Although it is not usual, or fashionable either, to speak of the beauty of London, I would repeat that it has its beauty spots, St James's Park, for instance. I thought it was the most charming city park I had seen, and I do not go back on that opinion even after seeing the Tuileries Gardens and the Luxembourg. From the suspension bridge I saw a view which took my breath away. In a book of photographs by Helmut Gernsheim I had seen that view, but I was never quite convinced of its faithfulness. There seemed to have been some photographic manipulation to secure the effect.

But the photograph was absolutely realistic, as I discovered from the bridge. There was the same view before me, the same transparent mist, the same domes and cupolas, and the same toning down of the architectural masses. With the exception of the Banqueting Hall, Whitehall itself is stodgy. Indeed so successful was it in giving a consistent and thoroughgoing impression of heaviness that I had some difficulty in finding its famous architectural masterpiece. I overlooked it completely, going down from Trafalgar Square towards Westminster, and, feeling very ashamed, walked up again, noting every building until I came upon it. But from the bridge in the park Whitehall looked transformed. It became capable of suggesting not only the château of Chambord, from which the architect is said to have copied the skyline, but even the Kremlin. It looked so dreamy, aerial, and exotic that it was not difficult to imagine that Ivan the Terrible, or his latterday successor, Stalin the Terrible, was ruling from it.

There are innumerable other beauty spots to be seen in London. I also tried a second method of sampling it—looking at its historical monuments and scattered gems of architecture. Both the Norman and the Gothic style can be admired in London in detail, if not as complete wholes in their proper setting, as in the cathedral towns. Henry VII's Chapel is one of the most beautiful Gothic interiors I have seen, though it might not produce the same mood of spiritual elevation as the naves at Winchester and Chartres. I was glad to escape into it from the Abbey itself, which to my thinking was sadly spoilt by the white marble funereal sculpture. I would have denied every son of Britain, however great, that kind of honour and homage to save the Abbey from this vandalism.

As regards classical architecture, London has St Paul's. After seeing both Paris and Rome, I would not concede that anything in these two cities surpasses St Paul's for massive beauty and symmetry. It is the supreme manifestation of English classicism in architecture, rivalling the great achievements of classicism in literature, and putting to shame its tawdry expression in sculpture.

I also tried to see London in the way I did Paris. I stood on Westminster Bridge, wondering if it had a clearly felt façade. Certainly, there was a very impressive river front from the Houses of Parliament to St Paul's. It took form, but only a form that suggested power, and not architectural harmony. The other bank crystallized into nothing, in spite of County Hall, Lambeth Palace, and what was then the latest addition, the Royal Festival Hall. I also contemplated the river. Most definitely it was not part of the architectonic of London. It was a waterway, attractive at a few points, ugly at some, and plain for the greater part. But at certain times and in certain lights it can become transfigured. I saw this once, and I shall never forget the scene.

As a sort of overture, I saw the Thames from the huge foyer of the Festival Hall. A kind of Diwali, the Hindu light festival, seemed to be on, and then, as I walked back to my hotel, I saw the whole north bank from Waterloo Bridge. It was very quiet, and a keen breeze was blowing, making the atmosphere crisp and clean. Before me was Somerset House, softly floodlit, and standing out as it never does in the day. The dome of St Paul's was also illuminated, and so were the towers of the Houses of Parliament. For once the river and the city had become one. I had just heard the Second Symphony of Beethoven, for me the first live performance of a work which on records had been familiar for something like twenty-five years. Its lovely slow movement has never ceased to be a wonder to me. Tovey has written about it that "to many a musical child, or child in musical matters, this movement has brought about the first awakening to a sense of beauty in music." This was literally true of the child in Western music that I was in my early thirties. The themes were still in my ear, and they supplied a musical accompaniment to the luminous vision on which my eyes were resting.

Yet I am perfectly sure that not one of these ways is the right one to see London qua London, not only of our days but also of the eighteenth century, the London of which Dr Johnson said that to be tired of it was to be tired of life. In order to feel how true this dictum is and to understand the meaning of London as a centre of human life in our times, one must see it as a whole. It is curious that the great Londoner should also be the man to point that out.

"Sir," he said, "if you wish to have a just notion of the magnitude of this city, you must not be satisfied with seeing its great streets and squares, but survey the innumerable little lanes and courts. It is not in the showy evolutions of buildings, but in the multiplicity of the human habitations which are crowded together, that the wonderful immensity of London consists."

I discovered that soon enough. After being able to find my way about in central London or rather the West End during the first few days of my stay, I acquired a wholly false confidence, and thought that I had mastered the city. A very disconcerting experience was to follow. On the fourth day after my arrival I was going to Canterbury by car, and when it passed by the Elephant and Castle I sat up, expecting to see the built-up areas thinning out and the famous English countryside making its appearance. But as we sped on, the unending blocks of buildings became more and more solid, and I was not sure that I had left London behind even when we had passed through Bromley. I am not familiar with the topography of Greater London, and I cannot say whether I was not going along one of those ribbons which are the tentacles by means of which London clutches the countryside, but even the main bulk of Greater London was crushing enough.

My experience was similar when I motored out to the north. On that side, however, I saw an additional belt. I passed along a vista of detached buildings, which were remarkably alike, and stood in immensely long rows like uniformed soldiers on parade. Red roofs, pink or cream walls, white windows, porches, little garden plots, following one another in endless succession, looked like a string of beads held together by the unbroken road and pavement. My English companion identified the houses sometimes as mid-Victorian, sometimes as late Victorian, sometimes as Edwardian, and did not seem to be wholly happy about them. I thought that this must be the famous Suburbia, on remembering which the intellectuals and aesthetes shudder and grow grey with fear. I did not, however, see much harm in the houses, for I was used to the suburbs of Calcutta and Delhi. None the less, I learned that beyond the London of history, and of my previous knowledge, there was another London, of whose immensity and mass, gravitation and power, I was totally unaware.

Parade grounds, Whitehall, London.

London's St. James's Park.

This impression becomes stronger, almost night-marish, if one goes out of London by train from one or other of the main stations. I did so from Paddington, Euston, Liverpool Street, Charing Cross, and Waterloo. I shall never forget those journeys. The train seemed to cut through the living but grey and grimy flesh of the city, exposing backyards, clothes-lines, peeled-off plaster, kitchens, bathrooms and coal-heaps, in its desperate anxiety to break out into the countryside, where it was more at home and could breathe more freely. I had seen something like this in Calcutta, but was wholly unprepared for the scale on which it was exhibited in London.

Once I saw a very unexpected and bizarre spectacle behind this townscape. Suddenly, there appeared above the untidy tiers of brickwork a forest of derricks and cranes, suggesting water and a crowded port. At the time I could not make out what exactly that meant, but later I found out that I was passing south of the Pool.

It was in these comings and goings that I formed a truer idea of the structure and function of London than I could have done by merely seeing its sights. But it was an idea which was opposed to that which might have been arrived at by reading its history—that London might be loose and straggling because it had expanded from the nucleus furnished by the City or Westminster, swallowing up village after village in its haphazard growth. On the other hand, whatever loose spaciousness is to be found in it, lies at its core—the Royal Parks, the gay West End, and the City, silent and deserted at night. If one had to estimate the difference between Pitt and Addington today from Canning's famous quip, "Pitt is to Addington, as London is to Paddington," none would be likely to be felt.

After seeing London I have discovered at least one of the reasons for which my countrymen prefer to travel in it by the Underground. It is not simply that they want to go about quickly and without physical effort, or to reduce the sense of distance; they must also wish, subconsciously at all events, to escape the incessant and oppressive bombardment of the spirit by the brickwork of outer London. Astronomers say that the earth grows denser from layer to layer towards the centre; here it is a case of the clanging nickel and iron being in the thick crust.

I am sure that if I had had to live continuously in London, I should have been crushed. Even as it was I felt overpowered, although I spent half the time in the country. The exhaustion did not come merely from the lack of spaciousness. I did not feel what I felt in parts of London in the narrow Rue du Bac of Paris, or in the Corso in Rome, or even in the labyrinthine quarters around the Piazza Navona or Palazzo Farnese there. The oppressive sensation came not only from the houses, but also from the apparent quality of the life lived in these parts. I did not get it in Brook Street. Anyhow, the feeling remained so strong that after my return, when I sent one of my sons to London for his education, I tried to secure accommodation for him near Hyde Park, and finally felt very happy to have him fixed up north of Hampstead Heath, not very far from Ken Wood.

But I cannot allow my personal inclinations and lack of robustness to influence my opinion about the proper method of understanding London, which must be seen in its total functioning, rather than in its history and architecture. Very soon I became aware that there was a Greater London of the spirit as there was one of administration. That London gave a sensation of throbbing power and vitality, in spite of wearing a thoroughly workaday look. This is felt very strongly in the outlying parts, Hammersmith or Camberwell, especially on a Saturday afternoon.

London must be regarded as the base of a new mode of human existence, and that is what it has been in the last hundred years or so, and is today. It is a town which has broken out of the old classification of human habitations as rural and urban. It is no longer a historic city, although it has a long history. London is neither Westminster Abbey, nor the Tower, nor Lincoln's Inn Fields, nor St Bartholomew-the-Great, not St Paul's, nor Chelsea, nor even nineteenth-century Whitehall. Also, it is not of the Roman times, nor of the Middle Ages, nor of the Renaissance, nor of the Augustan Age, although it has monuments from every epoch. In spite of being overwhelmingly Victorian in appearance, it does not belong to the Victorian age as Paris belongs in some measure to the age of Baron Haussmann. It has absorbed all its past, near and distant, in its present.

* * *

When I spoke about the power and modernity of London an American friend smiled. I am familiar with that smile. It lights up the faces of our very modern young ladies when one speaks of the modernity of their mothers, who were born around 1900. The sleek, streamlined and facile modernity of these girls is not to be compared with the modernity of the mothers, which was vital, weighty, struggling, and uneven. But while the previous generations have begotten, the new generations remain barren, however full they may be living for and by themselves.

WELLINGTON MEMORIAL, HYDE PARK CORNER, LONDON.

London's modernity is old-fashioned, but it is still living and creative. It is old but it has not ceased to grow. I am sure that even now it has not taken its final shape, and it is not possible to foresee what it will ultimately be. To me the greatest wonder about London is that it is historical and young at the same time, illustrating the process of evolution of the modern city besides being one of its most notable products. I may be a man of the past, unable to accept the wholeness of London, but I am not so narrow as to underestimate its stupendous role and overlook its gigantic presence.

HORACE SUTTON

from SUTTON'S PLACES

A MIDSUMMER rail tour of the thawed-out frozen North, or a look at Lapland from the lap of luxury.

THINGS HAVE IMPROVED considerably up here since the days when Amundsen, Nansen, Peary, and other hearties stood on the back runners of a dog sled and hollered, "Mush!" For the better part of a week we have been exploring the northlands from the observation car of a fabulous Swedish train, hollering such lusty phrases of the Arctic as "Steward!" or sometimes just "Beer!"

A staff of seventeen is on hand to wait on forty-

PICADILLY CIRCUS.

TRAFALGAR SQUARE FOUNTAIN, LONDON.

eight passengers; hot water flows unfailingly at any hour from the tap in each compartment; there is a special car equipped with showers, a hair dryer, and an iron; we have a telephone, movies on rainy days, and each morning the hostess rustles the explorers by wafting ethereal poems over the loud-speakers, followed by soft matinal music. Ah, where are the sourdoughs of yesteryear?

This painless scheme for traipsing across the tundra is the invention of the Swedish State Railways, which each summer operates a series of Sunlit Nights Land Cruises to the Scandinavian highlands. Garden-club secretaries, the bridge-and-bonbon brigade, ladies who remember Lincoln, and other hardy types can plough across the Arctic on cushioned rails, taking side excursions by upholstered bus each day, sleeping in a downy berth each night, frequently at a quiet siding. Newspapers are whisked up from Stockholm daily, a bar

maintains the proper percentage of alcohol in the blood, and a minimum of meals are served on the train. Eight days and eight nights of this kind of high living in the low latitudes costs between two hundred and fifty and three hundred dollars depending upon the accommodation you choose.

The excursion gathers steam the first night out of Stockholm when the explorer's express rolls into Rättvik in Dalecarlia, a Swedish province where the houses are painted a vivid red and trimmed in stark white, and the village folk sometimes go to church in longboats dressed in native costumes whether tourists are on hand or not. For our pleasure the Dalecarlians put on a picnic at a *fäbod*, which is a farm cottage in the mountains where cowherds are kept for summer grazing. A trio of fiddlers met us at the foot of the hill on the morning we arrived and took us up to the picnic grounds Dalecarlian-style, march-

PUNTING ON THE CAM, NEAR THE BRIDGE OF KINGS,
CAMBRIDGE, ENGLAND.

English country house and acres.

STONEHENGE, ENGLAND.

ing to a Swedish jig. A bellow on a long birchbark horn normally used to call in the cattle summoned the tourists with equal effect, and all hands, save the squeamish, sat down to dabble gingerly in long milk, a sourish sort of cream that some of the more irreverent were unkind enough to liken to milk of magnesia. Those thus disturbed could sprinkle cinnamon, nutmeg, sugar, and ginger on top, or turn to the thin wafer pancakes rolled with a filling of sour milk and newly turned butter. For dessert there was a dish of cloudberries, a northland specialty resembling a brown raspberry and served with whipped cream. Scandinavia would be in an awful fix if there was ever a blight on cows.

In the afternoon one could return to the train for a nap, put on a bathing suit for a swim in Lake Siljan, which lay alongside the tracks, or walk back to the club car and call New York. As the summer night came to Dalecarlia the sun hardly bothered to set. A troupe of fourteen dancers, the men looking modish in chamois plus-fours embossed with flower vines, the girls in peasant rig, appeared on the lawn of the Hotel Persborg and danced under the birch trees with the lake as a backdrop. Then the dancers, the fiddlers, and the whole hotel marched us to the station and we rolled on toward the Arctic.

Now we were in the province of Jämtland, and the lumber floated in big corrals on the river. We rode

Canal-side street in Amsterdam.

Fishermen in Volendam, Netherlands.

the basket lift four thousand six hundred and fifty-five feet up Mount Åreskutan, where the international ski championships were to be an event of winter, and looked down into the magnificence of the Åre Valley. On a Sunday afternoon the train rolled into Östersund on Lake Storsjon, and we rode out to the tiny Frösö Church on an island and sat in silence while an organ played the music of Peterson-Berger, who was strange and famous and lived nearby.

On the fourth day out of Stockholm, the Sunlit Nights Land Cruise crossed the Arctic Circle and pulled into the tiny station called Polcirkeln. The explorers got a speech and a certificate from King Boreas, who in more serious hours is the assistant station manager at Kiruna. The king was glad to see us, and well he might have been, for we were en-richening the area not only with our money but with our blood. The blood was for the mosquitoes, who smacked their lips over the prospect of all those rich American corpuscles and did gleeful barrel rolls in the heavens as they zoomed down to supper. A preparation called Djungel Olja makes you smell like rotten eggs to a mosquito, but we applied it in heavy doses so the stingers couldn't get a footing even if they could stand the odor. It wasn't necessary to venture into the northern djungels to find the mosquitoes, for people standing on the railway station were brushing the young vampires away with switches cut from birch trees. It's an old north-country custom. That night at Björkliden, on an equal latitude with the middle of Greenland or the top of Alaska, the sun didn't bother to set at all. We hiked up to the Fjället Mountain Hotel, an establishment which maintains a rack for mosquito switches outside its front door, and signed up for golf on its course, which I have come to reflect on fondly as Buzzing Bunkers. At midnight we teed off, driving the ball and the mosquitoes, with a Lapp in full regalia for a caddy. By full regalia I mean a blue tunic caught with a great leather belt, blue knickers trimmed with red, and a hat with an immense pompon. At any rate, it was enough to scare the mosquitoes away, for they never raised a Lappish welt on his skin, which was unvarnished with oil of the jungles.

The greens proved to be really browns, and the Lapp proved hardly a caddy, since he merely carried the bag, distributed new balls, and remained happily

TIVOLI GARDENS, COPENHAGEN.

GEIRANGER FJORD, NORWAY.

oblivious of where the old ones landed. If for nothing else than the sheer novelty of it, the links at Björkliden proved one of the rare places in the world where a man could in good conscience waltz home at two in the morning and tell the wife he had come straight from the golf course.

Lapps who follow more natural pursuits than caddying for Americans who play golf in the midnight sun are more difficult to find, for up here there are few roads and the sole connecting link between many communities is the Swedish State Railways. Up at the edge of the Norwegian border we left the train for a day and, decked out in knee-high boots, followed a guide into the world of Lapland. Except for Russia, the Swedish mountain regions form the largest wilderness in Europe, and civilization fell away abruptly behind the depot at Vassijaure. We emerged within minutes into a land of midsummer snowfields, rolling marshes, and four-thousand-foot peaks dappled with snow. It was a four-mile walk to the first lake, which lay banked with snow and spotted with icebergs. An outboard motorboat took us across, but then we had to portage the motor across two more lakes until, ten miles from the depot, we found a Lapp camp. It had taken us three hours to get there, but all we found was a bronzed Lapp woman and a five-year-old boy, with widespread Asiatic eyes and an elfin look, dressed in a red Lapp suit and a black hat that looked like a chauffeur's. Everybody else had crossed over the next mountain into Norway, following the reindeer herd. There was a pile of clean reindeer horns and a house that looked rather like a mud-and-stone igloo with a wooden door. Our hostess, who had been wearing her Lapp cap and an old print dress, disappeared for some minutes and returned done up in her red and blue Lapp costume, carrying a chunk of dried meat under her arm. We sat at the table and drank Lapp coffee with lump sugar and pulled on pieces of dried reindeer, which in all ways resembles dark red leather.

On the way back home we found another Lapp tent along the lake filled with a family of five children in bright orange and blue and red costumes. We braved the family dogs that looked like Spitzes and acted like wolves, and sat on reindeer skins which covered a carpet of birch branches. An iron pot simmered over an open fire in the middle of the tent floor, the smoke curling out of the roof. We got no coffee, probably because the lady of the place was too busy turning out a red and blue belt on a sewing machine that rested on the birch branches near the portable radio.

We found our train back at its siding some hours later. People were sitting in the bar drinking beer, reading the Paris *Herald Tribune*, listening to the loud-speaker which was dispensing the "Grand Canyon Suite" piped from a tape recorder in the club car. On the lawn by the station an old Lapp woman was selling slippers of reindeer hide and brushing away clouds of mosquitoes, which should have had more sense since she had skin like a T-34 tank and the slippers smelled worse than a man swabbed in Djungel Olja. The program called for dinner that night in a nearby resort hotel, then a trip up a mountain to look at the midnight sun. The next day we were to look at Narvik, and after that we would shoot the rapids at Kiruna in a long boat. It was enough to make any man fresh from the tundra long for nightfall. Unfortunately, the sun wasn't scheduled to set for another three weeks.

REINDEER IN NORTHERN SWEDEN.

TRUMAN CAPOTE

from THE MUSES ARE HEARD

A VISIT to Leningrad with the cast of Porgy and Bess.

THE FIRST SITTING, fifty strong, marched into the dining car and took their places at linen-covered tables, each seating four, that ran down either side of the aisle. The tables were set with white crockery and smoothly worn silver. The diner itself seemed as old as the silver, and the smell of cooking, a half-century's worth, hung in the air like a visible steam. Savchenko was absent, but Miss Lydia and the three young men from the Ministry played host at different tables. The young men kept gazing round, as though silently calling to each other from separate islands of exile and misery.

Miss Lydia shared a table with Lyons, Miss Ryan and myself. One sensed that for this middle-aged woman, who said that her ordinary life was translating articles and living in a room in Moscow, the unique experience, the one that brought such a flush to her cheeks, was not that she was talking to foreigners, but that she was sitting in a dining car riding on a train. Something about the silver and the clean cloth and a little basket of puckered apples, like those the Chinese man had sold, made her fuss with her ivory rose and tuck up the straying ends of her hair. "Ah, we eat!" she said, her eyes shifting toward a quartet of chunky waitresses who came waddling down the aisle with trayloads of the first course.

Those whose palates had been anticipating iced caviar and chilled carafes of vodka were a bit chagrined to see, set before them, yogurt accompanied by bottles of raspberry soda. Miss Thigpen, seated behind me, was the sole voice expressing enthusiasm: "I just could kiss them! More proteins than a steak and only half the calories." But across the aisle, Mrs. Gershwin warned Miss Putnam not to ruin her appetite by eating it. "Don't, darling, I'm sure the cavy will come along next." The next course, however, consisted of stiff noodles lying like sunken logs in a watery broth. The entree that followed featured breaded veal cutlets, boiled potatoes, and peas that rattled on the plate like gunshot; to wash this down, there were further provisions of raspberry soda. Miss Putnam said to Mrs. Gershwin, "It's not *my* stomach I'm worried about. It's Twerp's," and Mrs. Gershwin, sawing at her cutlet, said, "Do you suppose they could be saving the

cavy for dessert? You know, with little pancakes?"

Miss Lydia's cheeks bulged, her eyes popped, her jaws pumped like pistons, a trickle of sweat ran down her neck. "Eat, eat," she urged, "it's good, yes?" Miss Ryan told her it was wonderful, and Miss Lydia, swabbing her plate with a quarter loaf of black bread, nodded vehemently: "You will not obtain better in Moscow itself."

* * *

St. Isaac's Square is hemmed on one side by a canal stemming from the Neva, a river that in winter threads through the city like a frozen Seine, and on the other by St. Isaac's Cathedral, which is now an antireligious museum. We walked toward the canal. The sky was sunless grey, and there was snow in the air, buoyant motes, playthings that seethed and floated like the toy flakes inside a crystal. It was noon, but there was no modern traffic on the square except for a car or two and a bus with its headlights burning. Now and then, though, horse-drawn sleds slithered across the snowy pavement. Along the embankments of the Neva, men on skis silently passed, and mothers aired their babies, dragging them in small sleds. Everywhere, like darting blackbirds, black-furred school children ice-skated on the sidewalks. Two of these children stopped to inspect us. They were twins, girls of nine or ten, and they wore grey rabbit coats and blue velvet bonnets. They had divided a pair of skates between them, but by holding hands and pushing together, they managed very well on one skate apiece. They looked at us with pretty brown puzzled eyes, as though wondering what made us different: Our clothes? Miss Ryan's lipstick? The soft waves in her loose blond hair? Most foreigners in Russia soon become accustomed to this: the slight frown of the passer-by who is disturbed by something about you that he can't at once put his finger on, and who stops, stares, keeps glancing back, even quite often feels compelled to follow you. The twins followed us onto a footbridge that crossed the Neva, and watched while we paused to look at the view.

The canal, no more than a snow ditch, was a sporting ground for children whose laughing shrillness combined with a ringing of bells, both sounds carrying on the strong, shivery winds that blow from the Bay of Finland. Skeleton trees, sheathed in ice, glittered against the austere fronts of palaces that lined the embankments and stretched to the distant Nevsky Prospekt. Leningrad, presently a city of four million, the Soviet Union's second largest and northernmost metropolis, was built to the taste of the Czars, and Czarist taste ran to French and Italian architecture, which accounts not only for the style but also for the coloring of the palaces along the Neva and in other old quarters. Parisian blacks and greys predominate, but suddenly, here and there the hot Italian palette intervenes: a palace of bitter green, of brilliant ochre, pale blue, orange. A few of the palaces have been converted into apartments, most are used for offices. Peter the Great, who is given high marks by the current regime because he introduced the sciences to Russia, would probably approve the myriad television aerials that have settled like a swarm of metal insects on the roofs of his once Imperial city.

We crossed the bridge and wandered through opened iron gates into the deserted courtyard of a blue palace. It was the beginning of a labyrinth, an arctic Casbah where one courtyard led into another via arcades and tunnels and across narrow streets snow-hushed and silent except for sleigh horses stamping their hooves, a drifting sound of bells, an occasional giggle from the twins, still trailing behind us.

The cold was like an anesthetic; gradually, I felt numb enough to undergo major surgery. But Miss Ryan refused to turn back. She said, "This is St. Petersburg, for God's sake. We're not just walking anywhere. I want to see as much as I can. And I'd better. From now on, you know where *I'll* be? Locked in a room typing a lot of nonsense for the Breens." But I saw that she couldn't last much longer, her face was drunkard-red, a frostbite spot whitened the tip of her nose. Minutes later, feeling its first sting, she was ready to seek the Astoria.

The trouble was, we were lost. It amused the twins greatly to see us rotating round the same streets and courtyards. They screeched and hugged each other with laughter when we came on an old man chopping wood and begged him for directions by swinging our arms like compass needles and shouting, *Astoria! Astoria!* The woodchopper didn't understand; he put down his axe and accompanied us to a street corner, where we were required to repeat our pantomine for three swarthy friends of his, none of whom got the point, but nevertheless beckoned us up another street. On the way, out of curiosity, we were joined by a gangly boy carrying a violin case, and a woman who must have been a butcher, for over her coat she was wearing an apron splattered with blood. The Russians babbled and argued; we decided they were taking us to a police station, and neither of us cared, as long as

it was heated. By now, the moisture in my nose had frozen, my eyes were unfocused with cold. Still, I could see well enough to know that abruptly we were back at the Neva Canal footbridge. I wanted to grab Miss Ryan's hand and run. But she felt our entourage had been so faithful they deserved to see the mystery solved. From woodchopper to violinist, the procession, led by the twins who skated ahead like pied pipers, convoyed us across the square and straight to the Astoria's entrance. While they surrounded one of the Intourist limousines that stay parked in front of the hotel, and began to question its chauffeur about us, we rushed inside, collapsed on a bench and sucked the warm air like divers who have been too long underwater.

*   *   *

It's a stone's throw from the Astoria to the semi-Gothic mass of St. Isaac's Cathedral. I left the hotel at exactly three-thirty, the time Orlov had said he would meet me. But on stepping out the door, I found myself confronting a pair of ski glasses. There was an Intourist Ziv parked at the curb, and the man was sitting in the front seat talking to a chauffeur. For a moment I thought of returning to the hotel; it seemed the sensible course if Orlov was concerned that his rendezvous be off the record. But I decided to stroll past the car and see what happened; as I went by, nerves and an unreliable sense of etiquette prompted me to nod at the man. He yawned and averted his face. I didn't look back until I'd crossed the square and was in the shadows of St. Isaac's. By then, the car was gone. I walked slowly around the cathedral, pretending to admire the architecture, though there was no reason to pretend anything, for the sidewalks were deserted. Still, I felt conspicuous, and not quite lawful. Night swept the sky like the black crows that wheeled and cawed overhead. On the third lap around, I began to suspect Orlov had changed his mind. I tried to forget the cold by counting my steps, and had ticked off two hundred and sixteen when, turning a corner, I came on a scene that made the flow of numbers stop like the hands of a dropped watch.

It was this: four men in black had a fifth man backed against the cathedral wall. They were pounding him with their fists, pushing him forward and hitting him with the full weight of their bodies, like football players practicing on a dummy. A woman, respectably dressed and carrying a pocketbook tucked under her arm, stood on the sidelines as though she were casually waiting while some men friends finished a business conversation. Except for the cawing of crows, it was like an episode from a silent film; no one made a sound, and as the four attackers relinquished the man, leaving him spread-eagled on the snow, they glanced at me indifferently, joined the woman and walked off without a word between them. I went over to the man. He was fat, too heavy for me to lift, and the drink on his breath would have killed scorpions. He was not bleeding and he was not unconscious, but he wanted to speak and couldn't; he gazed up at me like a deaf-mute attempting to communicate with his eyes.

A headlighted car pulled alongside the curb. The strip of black and white checks bordering its frame identified it as a taxi. The rear door opened, and Stefan Orlov called my name. Leaning in the door, I tried to explain what had happened and ask him to help the man, but he was impatient, he didn't want to listen, he kept saying, "Get in," and, "Will you please get in"; and at last, with a fury that shocked me, "You're an idiot!" he said, yanking me onto the seat. As the taxi swung in a U-turn, its headlights exposed the man sprawled on the sidewalk, his lifted hands plowing the air, like the claws of an insect cruelly tumbled on its back.

"I'm sorry," said Orlov, regaining a civil voice that also managed to sound sincerely remorseful. "But other peoples's quarrels. They are not so much interesting, you understand. Now, enjoy yourself. We are going to the Eastern." He commented on Miss Ryan's absence and regretted "deeply" that she'd been unable to accept his invitation. "The Eastern is where you want to take a girl like Nancy. Very good food. Music. A bit of Oriental atmosphere." After the clandestine nature of our meeting, it struck me as curious that we were now proceeding anywhere as gay and public as he described; and I said so. He was hurt. "I have no fears, but I'm not an idiot either. The Astoria is a sensitive place. You understand? It's a nuisance to go there. Why shouldn't I see you if I like?" he said, asking himself the question. "You are a singer, I'm interested in music." He was under the impression that both Miss Ryan and myself were singers in the cast of *Porgy and Bess*. When I corrected him, and told him I was a writer, he seemed upset. He had lighted a cigarette, and his lips, pursed to blow out the match, tautened. "Are you a correspondent?" he asked, letting the flame burn. I said no, not what he meant by a correspondent. He blew on the match. "Because I hate correspondents," he said, rather warningly, as though I'd best not be lying to him. "They're filthy. And Americans, it's too bad to say, are the worst. The filthiest." Now that he knew I was a writer, I thought perhaps he saw the situation in a different, less harmless perspective, and so suggested that if the taxi would take me within walking distance of the Astoria, we could amicably part company then and there. He

interpreted this as a protest to his opinion of American correspondents. "Please, you misunderstand. I admire so much the American *people*," he said, and told me that the years he'd spent in Washington "were of a happiness I never forget. The Russians who lived in New York were always very snobbish about the Russians who had to live in Washington; they said, 'Oh, my dear, Washington is so *boring* and provincial.'" He laughed at his grande-dame imitation. "But for me, I liked it there. The hot streets in the summer. Bourbon whiskey. I liked so much my flat. I open my windows and pour myself a bourbon," he said, as though reliving these actions. "I sit in my underwear and drink the bourbon and play the Vic loudly as I like. There is a girl I know. Two girls. One of them always comes by."

The so-called Eastern is a restaurant attached to the Hotel Europa, just off the Nevsky Prospekt. Unless a few desiccated potted-palms connote the Orient, I am at a loss to explain Orlov's contention that the place had a slant-eyed atmosphere. The atmosphere, if any, was a discouraging one of yellow-walled drabness and sparsely occupied tables. Orlov was self-conscious, he picked at his tie and smoothed his dark hair. While we crossed an empty dance floor, an ensemble, four musicians as spidery as the palms they stood among, were scratching out a waltz. We climbed a flight of stairs that led to a balcony where there were discreet dining booths. "I'm sure you think the Astoria is more elegant," he said, as we were seated. "But that is for foreigners and large snobs. Here is for smaller snobs. I am *very* small snob."

It worried me that he probably couldn't afford the Eastern at all. His overcoat featured a luxurious sable collar and he had a hat of gleaming sealskin. Still his suit was a poor, thin plaid and the laundered freshness of his white shirt somehow made more apparent its frayed cuffs and collar. But he gave sumptuous instructions to the waiter, who brought us a 400-gram carafe of vodka and a huge helping of caviar heaped in silver ice-cream dishes, toast and slices of lemon on the side. With a passing thought for Mrs. Gershwin, I dispatched every soft, unsalted, grey, pearly bead of it, and Orlov, marveling at the speed of my accomplishment, asked if I would like another serving. I said no, I couldn't possibly, but he saw that I could, and sent the waiter for more.

Meanwhile, he proposed toasts in honor of Miss Ryan. "To Nancy," he said, draining his glass, then, with a refill, "To Nancy. She is a beautiful girl"; and, again pouring, "That beautiful Nancy. Beautiful girl. Beautiful."

The succession of fast-gulped vodka flushed his pale, almost handsome face. He told me he could drink "a fool's fill" and not get drunk, but a gradual dimming of intelligence in his fine blue eyes belied the boast. He wanted to know if I thought Miss Ryan was partial to him. "Because," he said, leaning forward in an attitude of excessive confidence, "she is a beautiful girl, and I like her." I said yes, I gathered he considered her highly. "But you think I'm an idiot? Because I'm nearly forty and I'm married five years?" He spread his hand on the table to show me a plain gold wedding ring. "I would never do harm to my marriage," he said piously. "We have two babies, little girls." He described his wife as "not beautiful, but my principal friend," and told me that, aside from the children, the mutual interests they shared made the marriage "a serious composition." Among professional classes in Russia, it can be observed that persons seldom make alliances with anyone outside their own field of work. Doctors marry doctors; lawyers, lawyers. The Orlovs, it seemed, were both mathematicians who taught at the same Leningrad school. Music and the theatre formed their main pleasures; they had taken turns, he said, waiting in line to buy tickets for the *Porgy and Bess* first-night, but in the end they had been allowed just one ticket. "Now my wife pretends she doesn't want to go. That is so I can go." The previous year they had bought a television set as a New Year's present to each other, but now they regretted having spent the money on something "so boring and childish." He expressed himself with equal harshness on the subject of Soviet films. His wife, however, was fond of going to the *kino*, but he himself would only be enthusiastic if ever again they showed American pictures. ("I should like to know. What has happened to that beautiful girl, Joan Bennett? And the other one, Ingrid Bergman? And George Raft? What a wonderful actor! Is he still alive?") Apart from this disagreement on the merits of movie going, his wife's tastes coincided with his at every point; they even, he said, enjoyed the same sport, "boating," and for several years had been saving to buy a small sailboat, which they intended docking at a fishing village near Leningrad where each summer they spent two months' vacation. "That is what I live for—guiding a boat through the poetry of our white nights. You must come back when the white nights are here. They are a true reward for nine months' dark."

The vodka was exhausted, and Orlov, after calling for a replenishment, grumbled that I wasn't keeping pace with him. He said it "disgusted" him to watch me "just tasting," and demanded that I "drink like a decent fellow or leave the table." I was surprised how easy it was to empty a glass in one swallow, how pleasant, and it appeared not to affect me except for a tickling warmth and a feeling that my critical faculties

were receding. I began to think that after all Orlov was right, the restaurant did have an Oriental atmosphere, a Moorish coziness, and the music of the orchestra, scraping like cicadas among the palms, seemed to acquire a beguiling, nostalgic lilt.

Orlov, at the stage of repeating himself, said, "I'm a good man and I have a good wife," three times before he could reach the next sentence, which was, "But I have strong muscles." He flexed his arms. "I'm passionate. A lusty dancer. On hot nights, with the window open, and the Vic playing loud as we like . . . and the Vic playing loud as we like. One of them always comes by. And we dance like that. With the window open on hot nights. That's all I want. To dance with Nancy. Beautiful. A beautiful girl. You understand? Just to dance. Just to . . . Where is she?" His hand swept the table. Silverware clattered on the floor. "Why isn't Nancy here? Why won't she sing for us?" With his head tilted back he sang, "Missouri woman on the Mississippi with her apron strings Missouri woman drags her diamond rings by her apron strings down the bad Missouri on the Mississippi blues . . ." His voice grew louder, he lapsed into Russian, a hollering still obscurely associated with the tune of "St. Louis Blues." I looked at my watch. To my astonishment it was nine o'clock. We'd been sitting in the Eastern almost five hours, which meant I couldn't be as sober as I reckoned. The realization and the proof of it struck simultaneously, like a pair of assassins who had been lying in wait. The tables seemed to slide, the lights swing, as though the restaurant were a ship riding a rough sea. At my request, insistence, Orlov asked for the check, but he went on singing while he counted out his rubles, sang his way down the stairs and waltzed by himself across the dance floor, ignoring the orchestra for his own accompaniment, "Missouri woman you're a bad Missouri woman on the Mississippi blues . . ."

In front of the Eastern there was a vendor selling rubber animals. Orlov bought a rabbit and handed it to me. "Tell Nancy from Stefan." Then he pulled me along a street that led away from the Nevsky Prospekt. As mud lanes replaced pavement it became clear that our destination was not the Astoria. For this was no neighborhood of palaces. Instead it was as though I were walking again through the slums of New Orleans, a district of dirt streets and broken fences, sagging wooden houses. We passed an abandoned church where wind wailed round the domes like a widow at the grave. Not far from the church, sidewalks resumed, and, with them, the city's imperial façade. Orlov headed toward the lighted windows of a café. The cold walk had quietened, somewhat sobered him. At the door, he said, "Here it is better. A workingman's place."

It was as if one had fallen into a bear pit. The body heat and beery breath and damp-fur smell of a hundred growling, quarreling, pawing customers filled the bright-lighted café. Ten and twelve men huddled around each of the room's half-dozen tables.

The only women present were three look-alike waitresses, brawny girls, wide as they were tall, and with faces round and flat as plates. In addition to waiting, they did duty as bouncers. Calmly, expertly, with an odd absence of rancor and less effort than it takes to yawn, they could throw a punch that knocked the stuffings out of men double their size. Lord help the man who fought back. Then all three girls would converge on him, beat him to his knees, literally wipe the floor with him as they dragged his carcass to the door and pitched it into the night. Some men, would-be customers decidedly persona non grata, never got into the café, for as soon as any of these undesirables appeared at the door the ladies of the establishment formed a flying, flailing wedge to drive him out again. Yet they could be courteous. At least they smiled at Orlov, impressed, I think, by his sable collar and expensive hat. One of them showed us to a table where she told two men, young jut-jawed bruisers wearing leather coats, to get up and give us their chairs. One was willing, the other argued. She settled his objections by snatching his hair and twisting his ear.

For the most part, only upper-strata restaurants are licensed to sell vodka, and since the café was not in that category, Orlov ordered Russian cognac, a brackish liquid that came in large tea glasses overflowing their brim. With the blitheness of a man blowing foam off a beer, he emptied a third of his glass and asked if the café "pleased" me, or did I think it "rough." I answered yes, and yes. "Rough, but not hooligan," he differentiated. "On the waterfront, yes, that is hooligan. But here is just ordinary. A workingman's place. No snobs." We had eight companions at the table and they took an interest in me, picked at me like magpies, plucked a cigarette lighter out of my hand, a scarf from around my neck, objects they passed from one to the next, glaring at them, grinning over them, and showing, even the youngest, rows of rotted teeth, wrinkles for which age could not account. The man nearest was jealous and wanted all my attention. It was impossible to guess how old he was, anywhere from forty to seventy. He had an eye missing and this circumstance enabled him to do a trick, which he kept forcing me to watch. It was meant to be a parody of Christ on the Cross. Taking a swallow of beer he would stretch his arms and droop his head. In a moment a trickle of beer came crying out the gaping redness of his hollow eye socket. His friends at the table thought it was an uproarious stunt.

Another favorite of the café was a boy who roamed around with a guitar. If you bought him a drink he'd sing you a song. He played one for Orlov, who translated it to me, saying it was the kind of song "we" like. It was the lament of a sailor longing for the village of his youth and a lost love called Nina. "The green of the sea is the green of her eyes." The boy sang well, with plaintive flamenco waverings in his voice. I sensed, though, that he was not concentrating on the lyrics. His thoughts and his gaze too were directed toward me. His white face had a sadness that seemed to be painted on, like a clown's. But it was his eyes that bothered me. Then I knew why. It was because they reminded me of the expression, the deaf-mute pleadings, in the eyes of the man left lying on the cathedral sidewalk. When he stopped playing, Orlov told him to sing another song. Instead the boy tried to speak to me.

"I . . . you . . . mother . . . man." He knew about ten words of English and he struggled to pronounce them. I asked Orlov to interpret, and as they talked together in Russian it was as though the boy were singing again. While his voice wove some sorrowful prose melody, his fingers tinkered with the strings of the guitar. Tears sprang to his eyes, and he rubbed them away with the flat of his palm, leaving grimy smudges like a child. I asked Orlov what he was saying. "It's not so much interesting. I'm not interested in politics." It seemed inconceivable the boy was talking politics, and when I persisted, Orlov was annoyed. "It's nothing. A nuisance. He wants you to help him."

Help was a word the boy understood. "Help," he said, nodding vigorously. "Help."

"Isn't he a nuisance?" said Orlov. "He says his father was English and his mother Polish, and because of this he says he's very badly treated in our country. He wants you to write the British Ambassador. Something like that. He wants to go to England."

"English man," said the boy, pointing at himself proudly. "Help." I didn't see how I could, and as he looked at me despair began to shade the hopeful shine of his wet eyes. "Help," he repeated reproachfully. "Help. Help."

Orlov gave him a coin and told him the name of a song he wanted to hear. It was a comedy song with unending choruses, and though the boy drudged through it listlessly, even the waitresses laughed and roared out the key lines, which everybody seemed to know. The one-eyed man, angry that there should be such laughter for anything except his trick, climbed on his chair and stood like a scarecrow Jesus, beer oozing from the empty socket and dribbling down his cheek. At five minutes to midnight, closing time, the waitresses began to switch the lights on and off, warningly. But the customers kept the song going, clung to these last minutes, as though they loathed to trade the café's camaraderie for cold streets, the fierce lonely journeys homeward. Orlov said he'd walk me to St. Isaac's Square. But first, a final toast. He proposed, "To a long life and a merry one. Is that what they say?" Yes, I told him, that's what they say.

The boy with the guitar blocked our path to the door. Exiting customers were still warbling his song; you could hear their voices echoing down the street. And in the café the waitresses were shooing out the last die-hards, darkening the lights in earnest. "Help," said the boy, gently catching hold of my sleeve. "Help," he said, his eyes full on me, as a waitress, at Orlov's request, pushed him aside to let us by. "Help, help," he called after me, a door between us now, and the words a muted sound fading into nothing like the night-falling snow.

"I think he's a crazy person," said Orlov.

EPILOGUE

Tourism and politics have laid waste everywhere.
EVELYN WAUGH

S. J. PERELMAN

from WESTWARD HA!

PERELMAN's first travel book ends with this chapter, "Home Is the Hunted," which records the joy most travelers feel at the end of a long trip, encompassed by the familiar comforts of home. Wild horses couldn't drag them away again; they wouldn't cross the street to see another ruin, another museum, another exotic landscape. The feeling passes, as it did for Perelman, who was soon off on another tour, this time with the wife and kiddies, writing The Swiss Family Perelman.

SILHOUETTED against the afterglow of the fiery red sun which had vanished a moment before over the Mid-Atlantic horizon, the chief officer of the *Queen Mary* paced the bridge, frowning into the gathering darkness. From the deck beneath his feet came the even, measured throb of the ship's pulse as she cleft the trackless deep, driving ever onward toward the shores of the New World. It had been a halcyon day; wind and water were favoring the voyage, passengers and crew alike were in a frame of high good humor, and all indications pointed to a smooth, uneventful run to Ambrose Channel sixty hours distant. And yet this vigilant watcher of the skies, on whose shoulders rested the responsibility for the leviathan and her cargo of four thousand souls, was oppressed by a vague disquiet. A feeling of remissness, as of some major obligation neglected, gnawed his conscience. Again and again he grappled with it, seeking to ferret out its source, but try as he would, the reason eluded him. At last, with a sigh of frustration, he threw open the door of the chartroom, entered, and addressed the young officer hunched over a set of calipers.

"Look here, ffoulis," he said abruptly, "a feeling of remissness, as of some major obligation neglected, has been gnawing my conscience. Can you give me any clue to this vague disquiet?"

"Why, yes, sir," said ffoulis, whose business it was to know everything, "perhaps it concerns that colorful pair of birds in Cabin 541 which their cognomens are Hirschfeld and Perelman and which they have for the last eight months been running the gamut of exotic climes from the frozen barrens of Manchuria to the sun-baked delta of the Nile."

"By Jove—of course!" exploded his senior. "Wonderful chaps—salt of the earth! I meant to have a drink with them, but I was too busy out there having my conscience gnawed. Tell me: has any stone been left unturned to provide for their animal comfort whilst aboard this here microcosm?"

"No, indeed, sir," said the other, "their fastidious palates have been tickled with our choicest viands, their tongues loosened with our rarest vintages, and their ears regaled with our most lilting dance harmonies."

"In short," nodded the chief, "they have been living

like pigs in clover."

"I don't know about the clover part," admitted ffoulis, "but believe me, chief—"

"That will do, ffoulis," the chief interrupted sternly. "Where are these two arresting personalities at this instant?"

"Where they usually are," said the young man, "in the Pompeian bar getting fractured on Manhattans."

"Then we need not addle our pates anent them," said the chief, picking up the calipers and unfurling a map. "Come, let us put the chart before the course." And he fell to work with a will.

Actually, the junior's surmise as to our whereabouts was mistaken; at the moment we were seated in the ship's lounge in a state of dreamy absorption, listening to a string ensemble sawing Cécile Chaminade in half and wondering why we felt like a couple of characters in *Outward Bound*. For there was a definitely eerie quality about the vast salon with its glaring candelabra, its ghostly creak of woodwork, and its half-dozen cardiac cases slumbering in the overstuffed furniture. The stewards flitted soundlessly over the thick carpets, and frequently, when they passed between us and the light, a faint ectoplasmic glow seemed to outline their forms. Any minute you expected a grave but kindly messenger, impersonated by Edward Everett Horton or Claude Rains, to materialize to the muted sound of bells and beckon you into the hereafter.

The same sense of unreality, of other-worldliness, had in fact obsessed us ever since embarking on the *Mary* two days before at Southampton. Lost in her sheer magnitude, submerged in the endless swarms of passengers circulating through her myriad smoking rooms, restaurants, shopping galleries, verandas, and foyers, we found ourselves assuming an anonymous, wraithlike aspect. Our conversation was pitched in whispers and our normal gait slowed to a shuffle; we reported obediently at meals, queued up at the merest tinkle of a gong, salaamed in the most servile fashion to anyone wearing a wisp of gold braid. From the labels on our luggage and the occasional whiff of salt air that penetrated our porthole, we were dimly aware that we were at sea, but every artful device of modern hotel management had been employed to insulate us. Our cabin, a luxurious affair in brown and beige, was a marvel of compression, elevators inlaid in semi-precious stones whisked us from keel to topmast, and a host of barbers, tailors, masseurs, trainers, couriers, and assorted lackeys trembled at our whim. It was hemispheric travel on its loftiest level, and, to a couple of peasants like Hirschfeld and myself, unaccustomed to such splendors, a wholly spectral experience. It was made even more so by the appearance at our

table of a brace of citizens, Cozine by name, bizarre enough to unhinge the strongest reason. Wallace Cozine was a sallow, rumpled individual in tweeds and a pale red beard who modestly confessed at our only luncheon together that he was perhaps the world's foremost surrealist photographer. He and his wife, a gaunt, cavernous-eyed creature laden with quantities of abstract costume jewelry, had been visiting Paris the previous month in behalf of a small advance-guard magazine called *Umlaut!*, and there was no phase of French culture, politics, or cuisine they were not equipped to discuss in exhaustive detail and with absolute authority. It was obvious from the start that they had conceived a very low opinion of our taste, and they could not comprehend how we had passed through France without meeting the people who were doing the really challenging things.

"Who did you see there?" demanded Cozine. "Did you see Hans Raffia?"

"Who's that?" asked Hirschfeld.

"You mean to tell me you never heard of Hans Raffia?" hooted Cozine. "Why, the man's ceramics have practically revolutionized the whole conception of modern art!"

"We—er—we didn't get to look at much crockery," I faltered.

"Anybody who calls ceramics crockery is a boob, a barbarian, and a Yahoo," announced Cozine in a voice audible across the dining room. We accepted the classification with submissive smiles and pretended to be engrossed in our chicken patties. After a pause, his wife resumed the inquisition.

"What about Stanislaus Farkas?" she probed. "Did you see his show of non-objective horseshoes at the Galérie Frugl?"

"We . . . got there right after it closed," said Hirschfeld lamely. "The director was just putting up the shutters—"

"Aha," murmured Cozine cynically, "and I don't suppose you saw Serge Smetana's invisible ballet either."

"How could we if it was invisible?" I protested. "I mean—"

"*Nothing's* invisible unless you close your mind to it," snapped Cozine, "but of course you couldn't have seen Smetana—he didn't give any recitals at the American Express Company." By the conclusion of the meal, they had so effectively demolished our self-esteem that we slunk off to the stateroom and thereafter had our food sent in on a tray. A day or two later, an envelope containing a picture postcard of the Eiffel Tower was slipped surreptitiously under the door. "Thought you'd like this," the note with it read.

"Maybe it'll convince *somebody* you were in Paris, even if we don't think so." There was no clue to the sender, but the left-hand corner of the envelope bore the crisp legend "Umlaut! A Lance to Puncture Hypocrisy and Sham."

On the fourth morning, a new air of energy and purposefulness animated the ship; the bulletin boards bloomed with landing instructions, batteries of fountain pens scratched away at customs declarations, mountains of trunks choked the promenade decks. Caught up in the universal hysteria of homecoming, we pelted through the shops buying last-minute gifts that duplicated ones we already had and feverishly sent off dramatic cablegrams announcing our advent to families long oppressed by the fact. Then, loins girded, we attacked the job of winnowing from our baggage the exotic chaff the experts had insisted we take on the tour. Out through the porthole went the glass beads, red cloth, and Mother Hubbards we had planned to trade to savage tribes. After them went the maps of Tasmania, the Swahili dictionaries, the collapsible drinking cups, the Primus stoves, the underwater goggles, and the medical kit comprising every malaria specific, dysentery remedy, antivenin, vitamin, ointment, lotion, plaster, poultice, and powder known to hypochondria. Our knottiest problem was what to do with the score of empty leatherette folders which had contained our travelers' checks. We finally presented them to our cabin steward in lieu of a tip and the poor fellow's emotion as he realized the extent of our generosity was pitiful. He just stood there and fumbled for words, many of which I am sure were familiar to us, but we thought it kinder to leave him to his own salvation and tiptoed out.

The arrival of the *Queen Mary* in New York, far from being the noisy, vivid pageant we expected, was as fleeting and elusive as an episode in a Kafka novel. Stealthily, almost as if fate begrudged us the satisfaction of seeing the harbor and the skyline, we were wafted from the open sea one evening to a North River pier the following dawn. The whole process was a grotesque mixture of the ephemeral and the banal; we descended the gangplank with no more illusion of having spanned the Atlantic than as though we had commuted from Weehawken. It was only when our consorts and the fledglings streamed toward us from behind the barrier that our bewilderment abated. To say it disappeared entirely would be untrue; at one point in the resulting scrimmage, I discovered myself bussing a willowy showgirl under the impression that she was Hirschfeld's infant daughter, at another I was dandling a peppery old gentleman on my knee and quizzing him about his progress at

school. At last, however, we managed to unsnarl our respective kinfolk, and after a breathless résumé of the fire, flood, and famine that had occurred in our absence, plunged into the ordeal of the customs examination.

Three quarters of an hour afterward, a fetching tableau might have presented itself to anyone sufficiently curious to invade the section bearing my initial. Knee-deep in a mound of shawls, brocades, bracelets, necklaces, purses, fans, and bric-a-brac resembling the contents of a thrift shop, three nonplused inspectors were attempting to calculate the duty I owed. My wife and I, our faces drawn, sat on the sidelines tonelessly discussing some practical solution to the dilemma—flight, a rubber check, a fifth mortgage on our home, selling the children. Under the circumstances, the last seemed the most feasible, inasmuch as they were loading the antique pistols I had bought them with percussion caps and discharging them into our eardrums. I am still not sure how I ever got off the hook, except that a few weeks afterward Hirschfeld showed me an I.O.U. with my name signed in a shaky scrawl. It was, needless to say, a blatant forgery and beneath contempt, but rather than see my friend victimized by some unscrupulous rascal, I shouldered the responsibility and settled with him for ten cents on the dollar.

Speeding across town from the pier to the family flat, I was dismayed to find hardly any civic recognition of our return; no bunting decked the buildings, almost no crowds clustered about the cab showering it with confetti and cheering hoarsely, and a minimum of brass bands lined the sidewalk before my residence. The sole member of the welcoming committee, a beery doorman chewing a half-dead cigar stump, eyed me with restrained enthusiasm as I sprang from the taxi. "Oh, *you're* back, are you?" he commented sourly. "Well, won't be long before I'll be carrying you upstairs four o'clock in the morning."

A similarly fervent salutation greeted me on entering our front door. The woolly little puppy I remembered cuddling in my arms, now grown to mastiff proportions, took one rapid sniff and zestfully sank his fangs into my ankle. By stroking him gently on the head with a length of chain, though, I won his confidence, and, dusting glass and shredded wallpaper from my shoulders, groped my way into the nest. Nothing was changed; the veneer on our installment furniture curled as crazily as ever and a disgruntled maid (not the one I recalled, but another equally morose) was stuffing herself with caviar and watering the whisky. Subsequently I observed her comparing me furtively with my photograph on the piano and shaking her head. "Don't try and tell *me* that's the same man," I overheard her declaring to the broom. Whoever I was, she obviously thought me worthy of respect, because from then on she seldom ventured into my presence without a bread-knife concealed under her apron.

For the next week I filled a dubious role in the family unit, a cross between that of Santa Claus and a second-story worker. I was never certain, when I came through a doorway, whether my relatives would overwhelm me with caresses or recoil as from a phantom. Conditioned to the idea that I was mousing around in Asia or Africa, my proximity unnerved them. Even inanimate objects seemed to resent my presence; my clothes-closets were jammed with bicycles, vacuum-cleaners, moth-proof bags, and corresponding household impedimenta that resisted any effort to dislodge them. The telephone rang constantly with what I supposed would be joyful greetings from friends but invariably proved to be the children's playmates and credit managers. Neither of the latter appeared to be enthralled by my adventures, and I finally decided that if they preferred to live in abysmal ignorance of the true state of the world, I personally had done my utmost by them.

No trip of the scope of ours, naturally, would have been complete without a motion-picture record, and Hirschfeld, an ardent cameraman, had exposed over four thousand feet of sixteen-millimeter film on the journey. On a brisk autumn evening in November, a select audience of two or three dozen friends crowded into my living room to witness the results. The party buzzed with anticipation; it was generally admitted that by all existing standards, this bade fair to be the outstanding travel picture of the decade. And in many respects it was. Though the greater part of it was upside down, backward, and out of focus, it had moments of breathtaking beauty—the traffic on Wilshire Boulevard in Los Angeles, the traffic on Hornby Road in Bombay, and the traffic in Leicester Square in London. In between were illimitable miles of shoreline in Siam and countless shots of monkeys picking fleas out of each other, interspersed here and there with gaudy sunsets. Unluckily for my commentary, I swallowed a poisoned highball half-way through it and confused many of the locales, a mischance that led to protracted bickering between the projectionist and myself. The audience tactfully muffled our squabble by yawning as loudly as it could, and everybody agreed that you would have to get up pretty early in the morning to find a more piquant film. Most of them were willing to try, nevertheless, and, since it was already way past nine o'clock, hurriedly took their leave. To show what degree of wanderlust the travelogue inspired, not a single one of those who saw it on that occasion was available for a second showing. They had all left town within forty-eight hours, and I can only assume they must have set forth immediately for the romantic places we had visited.

One year from the day on which our project to circle the globe had been hatched, Hirschfeld and I sat in a chophouse off Broadway and solemnly clinked glasses. Our pilgrimage was over. Behind us lay the twenty-five thousand miles of desert, sea, and jungle we had traversed; we had trod a perilous course through wars, revolutions, uprisings, and insurrections; we had undergone greater extremes of heat and cold, seen more underprivileged people, and eaten worse food than either of us had dreamed existed. And now, looking at the whole thing in retrospect, we saw with incredulity that we had come through our adventure absolutely unscathed. In our faces was none of that rich harvest of serenity and wisdom, that fund of mellow philosophy to lighten the daily burden, and that broad tolerance for human frailty guaranteed to shine forth from the countenance of the returned traveler. If anything, we were more crabbed, pettifogging, and ornery than before we had set off.

"Yes, sir," murmured Hirschfeld, leaning back in the booth with a sigh, "it's been a glorious year—and do you know what I'd say if anyone offered me a million dollars to go through it again?" The words had hardly left his lips when a portly, well-to-do individual in a black Homburg, pince-nez, white piping on his vest, and gold-headed cane, strode up to the table.

"Have I the honor of addressing Mr. Hirschfeld?" he inquired.

"You have," returned Hirschfeld steadily.

"Capital," said the stranger, spreading his coattails. "Then we need not waste time in idle formalities. I have been delegated by a group of powerful men whose identity I may not reveal to ask you to go around the world. Realizing, of course, that you have other commitments, we are prepared to offer you this trifling emolument." He withdrew his wallet and extended a certified check for a million dollars. Hirschfeld arose, took the check, and carefully tore it into a dozen tiny pieces.

"That, sir, is my answer," he said, flinging them in the astounded emissary's face. He turned toward me, proffering his arm. "Shall we stroll?" he suggested. "The air has a rather pleasant tang this afternoon, don't you think?" And with a courtly bow to our would-be benefactor, we brushed past him into the eddying mass of humanity in Times Square.